The Appraisal of Real Estate

THE APPRAISAL OF REAL ESTATE

Tenth Edition

Appraisal Institute
875 North Michigan Avenue
Chicago, Illinois 60611-1980

Acknowledgments
Vice President of Publications: Christopher Bettin
Manager, Book Development: Michael R. Milgrim, PhD
Editor: Stephanie Shea-Joyce
Design & Production Manager: Mary Jo Krysinski

For Educational Purposes Only
The opinions and statements set forth herein reflect the viewpoint of the Appraisal Institute at the time of publication but do not necessarily reflect the viewpoint of each individual member. While a great deal of care has been taken to provide accurate and current information, neither the Appraisal Institute nor its editors and staff assume responsibility for the accuracy of the data contained herein. Further, the general principles and conclusions presented in this text are subject to local, state and federal laws and regulations, court cases and any revisions of the same. This publication is sold for educational purposes with the understanding that the publisher is not engaged in rendering legal, accounting or any other professional service.

Nondiscrimination Policy
The Appraisal Institute advocates equal opportunity and nondiscrimination in the appraisal profession and conducts its activities without regard to race, color, sex, religion, national origin, or handicap status.

Printed in the United States of America
97 96 95 94 93   7 6 5 4 3

The photos appearing in this text were supplied by H. Armstrong Roberts, Inc. and HISTORICAL PICTURES/STOCK MONTAGE

Library of Congress Cataloging-in-Publication Data
The Appraisal of real estate. — 10th ed.
          p.   cm.
     Includes bibliographical references and index.
     ISBN 0-922154-04-X
     1. Real property—Valuation.   2. Personal property—Valuation.
I. Appraisal Institute (U.S.)
HD1387.A663   1992
333.33'2—dc20
                                                            92-8824
                                                            CIP

TABLE OF CONTENTS

FOREWORD

Real estate appraisal is a highly dynamic profession even in the most ordinary of times. Market conditions are always in flux, and real estate investors and underwriters must periodically reexamine their expectations. The theory and practice of appraisal continue to evolve in response to the changing concerns and behaviors of market participants. The technology available to appraisers expands as computerized applications and databases are developed. If change typifies the appraisal field in normal periods, the late 1980s and early 1990s have witnessed an extraordinary volume of events affecting the appraisal profession. The entire working environment of appraisers has recently been altered by the impact of new legislation and regulation. In today's unpredictable economy, it is absolutely essential for appraisers to keep up with current developments and to incorporate the latest concepts into their work.

To meet the needs of both seasoned practitioners and students entering the field, *The Appraisal of Real Estate* has been extensively revised and updated to address current concerns. I am especially pleased, therefore, to introduce the tenth edition to appraisal professionals of the 1990s. The tenth edition provides state-of-the-art analysis and discussion of the appraisal process and the three approaches to value. New topics covered include state licensing and certification, legislation affecting appraisers, professional liability, review appraisal, environmental hazards, recent monetary policy, and ongoing events in the thrift industry. Of the wealth of data collected for the 1990 census, the GIS database and TIGER files are specifically highlighted for their usefulness to real estate research. Market analysis, which has become increasingly important within the appraisal field, has received expanded coverage. Where relevant, the tenth edition also reflects the provisions and usage in the Standards of Professional Appraisal Practice of the Appraisal Institute.

The Appraisal Institute would like to especially acknowledge the dedicated work of Howard C. Gelbtuch, MAI, Chair of the Publications Committee, and Paula O. Thoreen, MAI, Chair of the Textbook and Dictionary Revision Committee. Both of these individuals guided the extensive decision-making process required to ensure that the content of the tenth edition is useful and current. I would also like to thank the many developers and reviewers for their contributions to the project: Charles B. Akerson, MAI; Norman R. Benedict, MAI; Robert C. Cantwell IV, MAI; David Cavanaugh; David W. Childers, MAI; William Lowell Christensen, MAI, SRA; Carlton W. Cole, MAI; Winfield L. Cooper, SRA; Max J. Derbes, Jr., MAI; John D. Dorchester, Jr., MAI; J.D. Eaton, MAI; Alfred J. Ferrara, MAI, SRA; Clifford F. Fisher, Jr., MAI; Jeffrey D. Fisher, PhD; Kenneth G. Foltz, MAI; Robert L. Foreman, MAI; W. West Foster, MAI; Kathryn Mason Gearheard, MAI; James E. Gibbons, MAI; Richard E. Hanton, MAI; Frank E. Harrison, MAI, SRA; Stephen J. Hobbs, SRPA, SRA; David J. Lau, MAI; Mark L. Levine, MAI, PhD; A. Scruggs Love, Jr., MAI, SRA; Kenneth M. Lusht, SRPA, PhD; Richard Marchitelli, MAI; James J. Mason, MAI; C. David Matthews, MAI, SRA; J. Virginia Messick, MAI; Bill Mundy, MAI, PhD; Terrell R. Oetzel, MAI; Robert L. Parson, MAI; David A. Pearson, MAI; Joseph Rabianski, PhD; Charles W. Rex III, MAI; Anthony Reynolds, MAI; Judith Reynolds, MAI; Thomas L. Roberts, MAI; Felice A. Rocca, MAI; Alan M. Schmook, MAI, SRA; Lee B. Smith, MAI; Richard C. Sorenson, MAI; Richard L. Stallings, MAI, SRA; Lloyd Stebbins, PE;

Gary P. Taylor, MAI; Roger E. Tegenkamp, MAI, SRA; J. Donald Turner, SRPA, SRA; John R. Underwood, Jr., MAI, SRA; James D. Vernor, MAI, PhD; and Ted R. Whitmer, MAI.

Patricia J. Marshall, MAI
1992 President
Appraisal Institute

THE APPRAISAL OF REAL ESTATE

Tenth Edition

Chapter 1

REAL PROPERTY AND
ITS APPRAISAL

*U*nder all is the land. This statement implies more than a physical reality. Land is the surface of the earth and the source of all minerals, vegetable matter, and animals. It is the foundation for the social and economic activities of people as well as a commodity and source of wealth.

Because land is essential to life and society, it is the subject of various disciplines, including geography, law, sociology, and economics. Each of these disciplines employs a somewhat different concept of real estate. Geography focuses on describing the physical elements of land and the distribution and activities of the people who use it. In law the ownership of land is considered. Sociology focuses on the dual nature of land: as a resource to be shared by all people and a commodity to be owned, traded, and used by individuals. In economics, land is regarded as one of the four agents of production, along with labor, capital, and coordination. Land represents all the natural elements of a nation's wealth.

Land value is an economic concept. A common understanding of the attributes of land is shared by geographers, lawyers, sociologists, and economists.

1. Each parcel of land is unique in its location and composition.
2. Land is physically immobile.
3. Land is durable.
4. The supply of land is finite.
5. Land is useful to people.

Real estate appraisers also recognize these attributes of land. They are concerned with the concepts of land used in other disciplines because these concepts provide the basic perceptions on which real estate value rests. In real estate appraisal the emphasis is on real estate markets, which result from the actions of people who respond to, and often are directed or limited by, all the important attributes of land delineated in other disciplines.

CONCEPTS OF LAND

Geographic

An understanding of land begins by recognizing its diverse physical characteristics and how these characteristics combine in a particular area. Developing a sense of land includes an awareness of how physical characteristics influence the use of land.

Land is affected by a number of processes. Ongoing physical and chemical processes modify the land's surface, biological processes affect the distribution of life forms, and socioeconomic processes direct human habitation and activity on the land. Together, these processes influence the characteristics of land and, therefore, land use.

Land may be used for many purposes, including agriculture, commerce, industry, habitation, and recreation. Land-use decisions are influenced by climate, topography, and the distribution of natural resources, population centers, and industry. Land use is also affected by economic conditions, population pressures, technological practices, and cultural influences. The influence of each of these factors varies depending on the geographic area.

Geographic considerations are particularly significant to appraisers. The importance of land's physical characteristics—e.g., climate, geology, soils, water, and vegetation—is obvious, but the distribution of people, facilities, and services and the movement of goods and people are equally important. The geographic concept of land, which emphasizes matters such as resources and resource bases, the location of industry, and actual and potential markets, provides much of the background knowledge required in real estate appraisal.

Legal

The cultural, political, governmental, and economic attitudes of a society are reflected in its laws. The legal profession does not focus on the physical characteristics of land, but on the rights and obligations associated with various interests in land. Under the law the right of individuals to own and use land for material gain is maintained, while the right of all people to use the land is protected. In other words, the law recognizes the possible conflict between private ownership and public use.

"Whose is the land, his it is, to the sky and the depths." This ancient maxim is the basis of the following legal definition:

> Land includes not only the ground, or soil, but everything that is attached to the earth, whether by course of nature, as are trees and herbage, or by the hand of man, as are houses and other buildings. It includes not only the surface of the earth, but everything under it and over it. Thus, in legal theory, a tract of land consists not only of the portion on the surface of the earth, but is an inverted pyramid having its tip, or apex, at the center of the earth, extending outward through the surface of the earth at the boundary lines of the tract, and continuing on upward to the heavens.[1]

This definition may seem to suggest that land ownership includes complete possession of land from the center of the earth to the ends of the universe. In practice, however, ownership is limited. For example, the U.S. Congress has declared that the federal government has complete and exclusive sovereignty over the nation's airspace and that every citizen has "a public right to freedom of transit in air commerce through the navigable air space of the United States."[2] Because land ownership can be limited, ownership rights are the subject of law, and the value of these rights is the subject of real estate appraisal.

The laws that govern the use and development of land in the United States give the landowner the greatest possible freedom to decide how to use the land. The owner's rights are restricted only if they unreasonably harm the rights of others. The definition of reasonable use has been argued in many court cases.

Legal matters of particular concern to appraisers include easements, access regulations, use restrictions, and the recording and conveyance of titles. Real estate appraising involves the valuation of real property rights, which are defined by local and state law. Appraisers must be familiar with local and state law because jurisdiction over land is vested primarily at local and state levels.

---

1. Robert Kratovil and Raymond J. Werner, *Real Estate Law*, 8th ed. (Englewood Cliffs, N.J.: Prentice-Hall, Inc., 1983), 6.
2. The Air Commerce Act of 1926 (formerly 49 USC 171 *et seq.*); the Civil Aeronautics Act of 1938 (formerly 49 USC 401 *et seq.*); and the Federal Aviation Act of 1958 (see 49 USC 401).

Social

As the physical characteristics and legal limitations of land increasingly affect its use, society has become concerned with how land is used and how rights are distributed. The supply of land is fixed, so increased demand for land exerts pressure for land to be used more intensively. Conflicts often arise between groups with different views on proper land use. Some people believe that land is a resource to be shared by all. They want to preserve the land's scenic beauty and important ecological functions. Others view land primarily as a marketable commodity; they believe that society is best served by private, unrestricted ownership. Because land is both a resource and a commodity, there are no clear-cut solutions to this conflict.[3]

Both points of view have legal support. As a resource, land is protected for the good of society. As a marketable commodity, the ownership, use, and disposal of land are regulated so that individual rights are not violated.

In 1876 the U.S. Supreme Court established government's right to regulate "the manner in which [a citizen] shall own his own property when such regulation becomes necessary for the public good." The court quoted the words of England's Lord Chief Justice Hale: "When private property is 'affected with a public interest,' it ceases to be *juris privati* only."[4] Throughout American history, land ownership has been recognized as fundamental. John Adams wrote, "If the multitude is possessed of real estate, the multitude will take care of the liberty, virtue, and interest of the multitude in all acts of government."[5]

In the public interest, society may impose building restrictions, zoning and building ordinances, development and subdivision regulations, and environmental controls. Environmental controls include provisions to protect the air and water from wastes, dirt, chemicals, and excessive noise. To preserve land in its natural state, there are regulations that protect wetlands, beaches, and navigable waters. Real estate appraisers must be familiar with the regulations and restrictions that apply to the use of a property and understand the way in which these regulations are enforced.

Economic

Land is a physical substance with inherent ownership rights that can be legally limited for the good of society. Land is also a major source of wealth which, in economic terms, is measured in money or exchange value. Land and its products have economic value only when they are converted into goods or services that are useful, desirable, and paid for by consumers. The economic concept of land as a source of wealth and an object of value is central to appraisal theory.

The economic concept of land reflects a long history of thought on the sources and bases of value, which is referred to as *value theory*.[6] Value theory contributes to the definitions of value used in appraisal reports and appraisal liter-

3. Richard N. L. Andrews, *Land in America* (Lexington, Mass.: D.C. Heath and Company, 1979), ix.
4. 94 U.S. 113 (1896). Quoted in "Land as a Commodity 'Affected with a Public Interest'" by Richard F. Babcock and Duane A. Feurer in Richard N. L. Andrews' *Land in America* (Lexington, Mass: D.C. Heath and Company, 1979), 110.
5. Ibid, 31.
6. Paul F. Wendt, *Real Estate Appraisal: Review and Outlook* (Athens: University of Georgia Press, 1974), 17.

ature, and it is an important part of the philosophy on which professional appraisal practice is founded. The development of value theory and its relationship to other systems of thought, which form the ideological basis for real estate appraisal, are discussed in Chapter 2.

THE DISCIPLINE OF APPRAISAL

Geographic, legal, social, and economic considerations all relate to the real estate appraiser's concept of land. Land, legally defined to include everything attached to the land, constitutes real estate. Appraisers study the value of physical real estate and its accompanying ownership rights, recognizing that real estate exists within the context of our society as a whole. Because the potential uses of land are influenced by geographic, legal, social, and economic factors, these considerations form the background against which appraisal activities are conducted.

REAL ESTATE, REAL PROPERTY, AND PERSONAL PROPERTY

To begin the study of real estate appraisal, an important distinction must be made between the terms *real estate* and *real property*. Although these concepts are different, some state laws treat them as synonymous.

Real estate is the physical land and appurtenances affixed to the land, e.g., structures. Real estate is immobile and tangible. The legal definition of real estate includes land and all things that are a natural part of land (e.g., trees, minerals) as well as all things that are attached to it by people (e.g., buildings, site improvements). All permanent building attachments (e.g., plumbing, electrical wiring, heating systems) as well as built-in items (e.g., cabinets, elevators) are usually considered part of the real estate. Real estate includes all attachments, both below and above the ground.

Real property includes all interests, benefits, and rights inherent in the ownership of physical real estate. A right or interest in real estate is also referred to as an *estate*. Specifically, *an estate in land is the degree, nature, or extent of interest that a person has in it.*

Interests vary, so real property is said to include a "bundle of rights" that are inherent in the ownership of real estate. Ownership rights include the right to use real estate, to sell it, to lease it, to enter it, to give it away, or to choose to exercise all or none of these rights. The bundle of rights is often compared to a bundle of sticks, with each stick representing a distinct and separate right or interest. Private enjoyment of these rights is guaranteed by the U.S. Constitution subject to certain limitations and restrictions, which are discussed below.

It is possible to own all or only some of the rights in a parcel of real estate. The extent of ownership determines the kind of interest, or estate, that is held. A person who owns all the property rights is said to have *fee simple title. A fee simple estate implies absolute ownership unencumbered by any other interest or estate.* Partial interests in real estate are created by selling, leasing, or otherwise limiting the bundle of rights in a fee simple estate. Partial estates include leased fee and leasehold estates.

A leased fee estate is an ownership interest held by a landlord with the right of use and occupancy conveyed by lease to others; the rights of the lessor (the leased fee owner) and the leased fee are specified by contract terms contained within the lease. In the appraisal of income-producing property, the leased fee estate is the most frequently valued property interest. An appraisal assignment may call for the appraisal of a fee simple estate or a partial interest such as a *leasehold estate, which is held by a lessee (the tenant and renter) and conveys the right of use and occupancy for a stated term under certain conditions.* (A detailed discussion of the valuation of partial interests is presented in Chapter 6.)

All estates in real property are subject to, and limited by, the four powers of government: taxation, eminent domain, police power, and escheat.

Taxation is the right of government to raise revenue through assessments on valuable goods, products, and rights. Because the U.S. Constitution effectively precludes the federal government from taxing real property directly, the right of taxation is reserved for state and local governments.

Eminent domain is the right of government to take private property for public use upon the payment of just compensation. This right can be exercised by an entity acting under governmental authority such as a housing authority or public utility. *Condemnation is the act or process of enforcing the right of eminent domain.*

Police power is the right of government under which property is regulated to protect public safety, health, morals, and general welfare. Zoning ordinances, use restrictions, building codes, air and land traffic regulations, access rights, and health regulations are based on police power.

Escheat is the right of government that gives the state titular ownership of a property when its owner dies without a will or any ascertainable heirs. The government also controls *overflight, the air space over a property through which aircraft may pass so long as the property's occupants suffer no inconvenience beyond established standards.*

In addition to government restrictions on property, private legal agreements may also impose limitations. One type of agreement is a restriction inserted in a

ARTICLE V.

Provisions concerning Prosecution, Trial and Punishment—Private Property Not to Be Taken for Public Use, Without Compensation.

No person shall be held to answer for a capital or other infamous crime unless on a presentment or indictment of a Grand Jury, except in cases arising in the land or naval forces, or in the militia, when in actual service, in time of war or public danger; nor shall any person be subject for the same offense to be twice put in jeopardy of life or limb; nor shall be compelled in any criminal case to be a witness against himself, nor be deprived of life, liberty, or property, without due process of law; nor shall private property be taken for public use without just compensation.

The Fifth Amendment to the U.S. Constitution requires the payment of just compensation whenever private property is taken for public use.

deed. Private restrictions can limit the use or manner of development and even the manner in which ownership can be conveyed. The purchaser of a property may be obligated to use the property subject to a private restriction such as an easement, right-of-way, or party-wall agreement.

The individual rights in the bundle of rights can be sold, leased, transferred, or otherwise disposed of separately, subject to government limitations and private restrictions. Owners of certain parcels of land have a number of options. For example, one property owner could sell or lease the mineral rights to his property and retain the rights to use the surface area. Another owner could lease the property's surface rights to one party and the subsurface rights to another. Owners can also sell or lease the air rights to a property for construction or avigation (i.e., air traffic control). Thus, certain rights can be severed from the ownership of a property and be sold, leased, or given to others.

Appraisers must not only understand the distinction between real estate and real property, but they must also differentiate between *real estate* and *personal property*. *Personal property includes movable items of property that are not permanently affixed to, or part of, the real estate.* Personal property is not endowed with the rights of real property ownership. Examples of personal property are furniture and furnishings such as refrigerators and freestanding shelves that are not built into the structure. Under specific lease terms, items such as bookshelves and venetian blinds may be installed in a leased property by the tenant and remain personal property to be removed at the termination of the lease.

Although personal property generally consists of tangible items, called *chattels personal*, an intangible personal property right, called *chattels real*, may be created by a lease.[7]

It is sometimes difficult to determine whether an item should be considered personal property or real estate. Often, the courts must resolve such a conflict. *A fixture is an article that was once personal property, but has since been installed or attached to the land or building in a rather permanent manner; it is regarded in law as part of the real estate.* Therefore, a fixture is endowed with the rights of real property ownership and is part of the real estate. Indeed, the components of all real estate improvements were once personal property. When attached to the land, they become real estate.

Although fixtures are real estate, trade fixtures are not. *A trade fixture, also called a chattel fixture, is an article that is owned and attached to a rented space or building by a tenant and used in conducting a business.* Thus, trade fixtures are not real estate endowed with the rights of real property ownership; they are personal property regardless of how they are affixed.

Some examples of trade fixtures are restaurant booths and bars, gasoline station pumps and storage tanks, and the body building equipment in a health club. In industrial real estate, the term can be used to refer to fixed building equipment installed for human comfort (e.g., plumbing, lighting, heating, air-conditioning) and to industrial equipment (e.g., air hoses, water pipelines, craneways, bus

---

7. Historically, ownership rights to real estate for a fixed number of years, such as a tenant's interest, were considered personal property. These rights were called *chattels real*, to distinguish them from movable personal objects, or *chattels personal*. Today, it is more common to refer to a lessee's interest as an interest in, or right to, real estate.

Trade fixtures are personal property.

ducts). A trade fixture is to be removed by the tenant when the lease expires unless this right has been surrendered in the lease.

To decide whether an item is a trade fixture, and therefore personal property, or part of the real estate, courts use the following criteria.

1. The manner in which the item is affixed. Generally, an item is considered personal property if it can be removed without serious injury to the real estate or to itself. There are exceptions to this rule.

2. The character of the item and its adaptation to the real estate. Items that are specifically constructed for use in a particular building or installed to carry out the purpose for which the building was erected are generally considered permanent parts of the building.

3. The intention of the party who attached the item. Frequently, the terms of the lease reveal whether the item is permanent or to be removed at some future time.[8]

Appraisers must know whether an item is personal property or a fixture to decide if it will be included in the property value indication. If an item is classified as a fixture, and therefore part of the real estate, its contribution to value is included in the value estimate. It may not be possible, however, to exclude personal property from a value estimate. Because the distinction between fixtures and personal property is not always obvious, appraisers should know how courts in their jurisdictions define these items. Personal property that is related to real estate and is to be included in an appraisal should be identified and described in the appraisal.

---

8. Kratovil and Werner, 18-23.

APPRAISAL PRACTICE

In our complex society, professional real estate appraisers perform a variety of functions and services. They estimate several types of defined value and may advise clients and participate in decisions about real estate.

Appraisers perform analyses and render opinions or conclusions relating to the nature, quality, value, or utility of specified interests in, or aspects of, identified real estate. *Appraisal is defined as the act or process of estimating value.*[9] Real estate appraisal involves selective research into appropriate market areas; the assemblage of pertinent data; the use of appropriate analytical techniques; and the application of knowledge, experience, and professional judgment to develop an appropriate solution to an appraisal problem.

The nature of the real estate problem indicates whether the task is an appraisal (valuation) or a consulting assignment (analysis or evaluation). The value estimated may be market value, insurable value, investment value, or some other properly defined value of an identified interest or interests in a specific parcel or parcels of real estate as of a given date. Valuation assignments may produce market value estimates of fee simple estates, leasehold estates, preservation easements, and many other interests. *Consulting is the act or process of providing information, analysis of real estate data, and recommendations or conclusions on diversified problems in real estate other than estimating value.*[10] Consulting assignments include land utilization studies, supply and demand studies, economic feasibility studies, highest and best use analyses, and marketability or investment considerations that relate to proposed or existing developments.

In an appraisal assignment, the appraiser provides the client with an estimate of real property value which reflects all pertinent market evidence. In a consulting assignment, current market activity and evidence are studied to form a conclusion which may not lead to a specific value indication. In both types of assignments, conclusions are derived from appropriate data analysis performed in conformance with accepted standards of professional practice.

The application of appraisal procedures and the report that communicates the appraiser's conclusions are guided by the nature of the assignment. To avoid misunderstandings, it is important that the client and the appraiser determine whether the assignment is an appraisal or a consulting assignment.

A third type of assignment that appraisers perform is *appraisal review*, which refers to *the act or procedure of critically studying a report prepared by another appraiser.*[11]

PURPOSE AND USE OF AN APPRAISAL

The purpose of an appraisal is the stated reason for an appraisal assignment, i.e., to estimate a defined value of any real property interest, or to conduct an evaluation study pertaining to real property decisions.[12] The purpose of an appraisal is established by the client. It points to the information that the client needs to an-

---

9. The Appraisal Foundation, *Uniform Standards of Professional Appraisal Practice* "Definitions" and Appraisal Institute, *Supplemental Standards of Professional Appraisal Practice* "Definitions Problems."
10. Ibid.
11. Ibid.
12. Specific definitions of the terms *appraisal* and *appraisal assignment* are cited in the Code of Professional Ethics and Standards of Professional Appraisal Practice of the Appraisal Institute. Members and affiliates of the Appraisal Institute should be familiar with these definitions.

swer specific questions pertaining to real property. If the client's questions are understood, the purpose of the appraisal can be clearly and fully stated in terms of the information requested.

When an estimate of value is required in an appraisal, the type of value sought must be defined at the outset. The defined value may be market value, insurable value, going-concern value, assessed value, use value, or investment value. Distinctions among these terms are discussed in Chapter 2.

The purpose of a valuation appraisal establishes the foundation for the final value conclusion, which does not change to accommodate the use of the appraisal. The structure of an appraisal report may be adapted to the intended use of the valuation estimate, but the valuation estimate itself will not change. For example, the valuation of a single-family property might be reported on a form for use in a purchase or sale, on a form for mortgage financing, in a letter report for rehabilitation decisions, or in a narrative report for use in litigation. Whatever the circumstances, the dollar figure or figures associated with the defined value will be the same.

The use of an appraisal is the manner in which a client employs the information contained in the appraisal report. The use of an appraisal is determined by the client's needs. For example, a client may want to know the market value of a residence to avoid paying too much for it or accepting too little for it in a sale. Corporate clients may need to ascertain the rent levels or demographic trends in an area to help determine the advisability of relocating there. Insurance companies and private citizens may wish to know the insurable value of buildings, and a developer may need to know the supply and demand factors at work in a community before constructing an apartment complex.

An appraisal provides a basis for a decision concerning real property, so the use of an appraisal depends on the decision the client wishes to make. In defining the appraisal problem, the appraiser should develop an understanding of the client's requirements that is acceptable to both parties and consistent with accepted standards of professional practice.

An appraisal may be requested in a number of situations. The following list does not reflect all possible uses for appraisals, but it does indicate a broad sampling of professional appraisal activities.

Transfer of ownership

- To help prospective buyers set offering prices
- To help prospective sellers determine acceptable selling prices
- To establish a basis for real property exchanges
- To establish a basis for reorganizing or merging the ownership of multiple properties
- To determine the terms of a sale price for a proposed transaction

Appraisers may be called on by the courts to present expert testimony. (H. Armstrong Roberts, Inc.)

Financing and credit
- To estimate the value of the security offered for a proposed mortgage loan
- To provide an investor with a sound basis for deciding whether to purchase real estate mortgages, bonds, or other types of securities
- To establish a basis for a decision to insure or underwrite a loan on real property

Just compensation in condemnation proceedings
- To estimate the market value of a property as a whole—i.e., before the taking
- To estimate the market value of the remainder after the taking
- To estimate the damages to the property

Tax matters
- To estimate assessed value
- To separate assets into depreciable (or capital recapture) items such as buildings, and nondepreciable items such as land, and to estimate applicable depreciation (or capital recapture) rates
- To determine gift or inheritance taxes

Investment counseling and decision making
- To set rental schedules and lease provisions
- To determine the feasibility of a construction or renovation program
- To help corporations or third parties purchase homes for transferred employees
- To serve the needs of insurers, adjusters, and policyholders
- To facilitate corporate mergers, the issuance of stock, or the revision of book value
- To estimate liquidation value for forced sale or auction proceedings

- To counsel clients by considering their investment goals, alternatives, resources, and constraints, and the timing of their activities
- To advise zoning boards, courts, and planners, among others, on the probable effects of proposed actions
- To arbitrate between adversaries
- To determine supply and demand trends in a market
- To ascertain the status of real estate markets

LICENSING AND CERTIFICATION

Appraisers who perform assignments for federally regulated agencies often must be licensed or certified by the state in which the assignment property is located. State licensing and certification of appraisers has become increasingly important because of two recent developments:

1. Issuance of Circular A-129 by the Office of Management and Budget (OMB) in 1988, which mandates the use of state certified or licensed appraisers by federal agencies under the OMB's jurisdiction. This circular became effective July 1, 1991.
2. Passage of the Financial Institutions Reform, Recovery and Enforcement Act (FIR-REA), Title XI, in 1989. This act is a modified version of an earlier bill introduced in Congress by Representative Doug Barnard to bring the appraisal industry under federal regulation.[13]

Most states have enacted or are in the process of enacting regulatory legislation to establish a state licensing and certification system. This system will help ensure that appraisers meet training and experience qualifications and perform appraisals in compliance with accepted professional standards.

APPRAISERS' LIABILITY

As the appraisal industry strives for greater professionalism, the scope of appraiser responsibility and potential liability grows. Appraisers may be held liable for negligence, misrepresentation, fraud, breach of contract, or noncompliance with the standards imposed by both government agencies and the Appraisal Institute. Appraisers are advised to take measures to safeguard themselves from unintentional or involuntary malpractice. Ensuring competency through continuing education, the use of checklists and backup reviews, and strict adherence to the Standards of Professional Appraisal Practice can help reduce an appraiser's exposure to civil action.[14] Professional liability insurance is available but an appraiser is advised to review all policy exclusions and retroactive dates.

Litigation over contested value estimates may result from rapid changes in market conditions, the presence of contaminated materials on properties subject to appraisal, enforcement of environmental and preservation easements, and changes in legal and regulatory guidelines. The proliferation of legal proceedings

---

13. For further information on licensing and certification, see the chart titled "Federal Legislation Affecting the Appraisal Profession" in Appendix A.
14. For more information on appraiser liability, see *Real Estate Appraisers' Liability* by Mark Lee Levine (New York: Clark Boardman Callaghan, 1991).

suggests that litigation will continue to increase in the appraisal field as it has in other professions.

SUMMARY

Land is the subject of a variety of disciplines. The uniqueness, fixity, durability, finiteness, and usefulness of land are acknowledged in the fields of geography, law, sociology, and economics. Geography is concerned with the physical characteristics, demographic patterns, and economic uses of land, while the legal profession is concerned with land ownership. In sociology the competition between private and public interests over the use and distribution of land is considered, and in economics land is regarded as an agent of production and a source of wealth.

The distinction between *real estate* and *real property* is fundamental to appraisal. Real estate includes the physical land and all appurtenances affixed to the land. Real property includes all the interests, benefits, and rights inherent in the ownership of physical real estate.

Ownership rights can be held, leased, sold, transferred, or otherwise disposed of as a whole or in parts. The ownership of real property rights unencumbered by any other interest is known as a *fee simple estate*. An ownership interest held by a landlord with the right of use and occupancy conveyed to a tenant by a lease is a *leased fee estate*. The right of use and occupancy held by a tenant is known as a *leasehold estate*. All real property is subject to the four powers of government: taxation, eminent domain, police power, and escheat.

The distinction between *personal property* and *real estate* is very important to appraisers. Personal property includes movable items of property that are not permanently affixed to, or part of, the real estate. Fixtures are considered real estate, but trade fixtures are personal property.

Appraisers perform analyses and render opinions or conclusions relating to the nature, quality, value, or utility of specified interests in, or aspects of, identified real estate. *Appraisal is the act or process of estimating value.* The value estimate derived may be market value, insurable value, investment value, or another properly defined value of an identified interest or interests in a specific parcel or parcels of real estate as of a given date. Appraisal and consulting are two different kinds of assignments; the distinction between them is derived from the nature of the real estate problem. *Consulting is the act or process of providing information, analysis of real estate data, and recommendations or conclusions on diversified problems in real estate other than estimating value.* A third type of assignment that appraisers perform is *review appraisal, the act or procedure of critically studying a report prepared by another appraiser.*

The *purpose of an appraisal* is based on the client's needs for information about the defined value of a real property interest. The *use of an appraisal* is the manner in which the client employs this information. The appraisal conclusion is communicated in accordance with the purpose of the appraisal, but the value estimate is not adjusted to accommodate the use of the appraisal. Appraisals are needed in situations involving the transfer of ownership, financing, estimates of just compensation in condemnation proceedings, tax settlements, the determination of rent and leasing provisions, insurance matters, feasibility and marketability considerations, investment decision making, zoning, and community planning.

Many federally regulated agencies require that state licensed or state certified appraisers perform their assignments. Regulatory legislation is being enacted by the states to establish state licensing and certification systems. In light of the increasingly litigious environment in which they work, appraisers should adhere to the Standards of Professional Appraisal Practice and take other precautions to reduce their exposure to civil action.

Chapter 2

THE NATURE OF VALUE

*T*he concept of value pervades every segment of the real estate industry. Value considerations are of central importance in a broad and diverse range of real estate activities. The term *value* is often used imprecisely in common speech, but in economics it has a specific meaning which distinguishes it from the related concepts of price, market, and cost.

DISTINCTIONS AMONG PRICE, MARKET, COST, AND VALUE

Appraisers make careful distinctions among the terms *price, market, cost,* and *value.* The term *price* usually refers to a sale or transaction price and applies to an exchange; a price is an accomplished fact. *A price represents the amount a particular purchaser agrees to pay and a particular seller agrees to accept under the circumstances surrounding their transaction.*

Generally the circumstances of a transaction reflect conditions within one or several markets. *A market is a set of arrangements in which buyers and sellers are brought together through the price mechanism.* A market may be defined in terms of geography, products or product features, the number of available buyers and sellers, or some other arrangement of circumstance.

A real estate market is the interaction of individuals who exchange real property rights for other assets, such as money. Specific real estate markets are defined on the basis of property type, location, income-producing potential, typical investor characteristics, typical tenant characteristics, or other attributes recognized by those participating in the exchange of real property. The market for new, single-family residences selling for $100,000 and the market for older apartment buildings located near the central business district and available for renovation are examples of specific real estate markets.

The term *cost* is used by appraisers in relation to production, not exchange; cost may be either an accomplished fact or a current estimate. Appraisers distinguish among several types of costs: direct costs, indirect costs, construction costs, and development costs.

Direct costs are expenditures for the labor and materials necessary to construct a new improvement. Direct costs are also called *hard costs.* A contractor's overhead and profit are generally considered direct costs.

Indirect costs incurred in construction refer to expenditures for items other than labor and materials. Indirect costs include administrative costs; expenses incurred by the owner for professional fees, financing, taxes, and interest and insurance during construction; and lease-up costs, which are the net expenses of operating the project until it reaches a stable occupancy level. Indirect costs are sometimes referred to as *soft costs.*

Construction cost, or contractor's bid price, normally includes the direct costs of labor and materials plus the contractor's indirect costs.

Development cost is the cost to create a property, including the land, and bring it to an efficient operating state, as distinguished from the cost to construct the improvements. Development cost includes the profit to the developer or entrepreneur who brings the project into being.

These real estate-related expenditures are directly linked to the price of goods and services in competitive markets. For example, the costs of roofing materials, masonry, architectural plans, and rented scaffolding are determined by the interaction of supply and demand in specific areas and are subject to the influence of social, economic, governmental, and environmental forces.

Price, market, and cost relationships also incorporate concepts of value. Value can have many meanings in real estate appraisal; the applicable definition depends on the context and usage.[1] In the marketplace, value is commonly perceived as the *anticipation of benefits to be obtained in the future.* Because value exists at a given moment, an appraisal reflects value at a particular point in time. *Value as of a given time represents the monetary worth of property, goods, or services to buyers and sellers.* To avoid confusion, appraisers do not use the word *value* alone; instead they refer to "market value," "use value," "investment value," "assessed value," or other specific kinds of value. Market value is the focus of most real property appraisal assignments and its estimation is the purpose of most appraisals.

MARKET VALUE, USE VALUE, AND OTHER VALUES
Market Value

The concept of market value is of paramount importance to business and real estate communities. Vast sums of debt and equity capital are committed annually to real estate investments and mortgage loans, which are based on market value estimations. Real estate taxation, litigation, and legislation also reflect an ongoing, active concern with market value issues. In virtually every aspect of the real estate industry and its regulation at local, state, and federal levels, market value considerations are of vital importance and essential to economic stability.

The definition of market value used by appraisers and the clients they serve must be clearly understood and communicated. However, in real estate appraisal, definitions of market value can and do represent different beliefs and assumptions about the marketplace and the nature of value. Market value is inherently a simple concept—it is an objective value created by the collective patterns of the market—but the definition of market value is controversial. Debate on the subject continues and often centers on rather fine distinctions.

Current definitions of market value reflect different schools of thought on five key points.

1. All cash and terms equivalent to cash versus noncash-equivalent financing terms
2. Specified property rights versus the real estate
3. Price versus the highest price
4. Most probable price versus the highest price
5. Equilibrium value versus market value

One school subscribes to the belief that market value is best measured in terms of all cash. This opinion originated in the first half of the twentieth century when economic conditions were remarkably stable. During this period mortgage rates remained nearly level, real estate prices rose slowly, and the fee simple interest was the subject of most appraisals. Because of these static conditions, financing terms were not of great importance and market value in appraisals most frequently implied all-cash transactions.

---

1. See Halbert C. Smith, "Value Concepts as a Source of Disparity Among Appraisals," *The Appraisal Journal* (April 1977).

A second school of thought emerged in the latter part of the twentieth century when changes in real estate markets and financing created increasingly complex real property interests. Today long-term, fixed-rate loans are increasingly supplemented or replaced with more complicated financing instruments. Many clients now request estimates of the market value of a property subject to leases, easements, or mortgages. Therefore, real estate analysts have focused their attention on the interrelationships of debt and equity interests and fee simple, leased fee, and leasehold interests.

Financing terms, which may or may not be equivalent to cash, affect value. Value affected by financing or leases can be market value, because it is created by the activity of the collective market. However, the sale price of a comparable property that sold with atypical financing terms must be adjusted to reflect typical market terms before it can be used to derive a value indication for the subject property. This adjustment produces a *cash equivalent price.*

A market value appraisal is always a valuation of specified rights in the subject property, not the physical real estate. The specified property rights can be the fee simple estate, the estate subject to a lease or mortgage, or some other interest in the real estate.

General dictionaries define market value as "a price at which both buyers and sellers are willing to do business" and "what a property can be sold for on the open market."[2] Professional appraisers recognize, however, that in general commerce the amount of this price depends on custom, encumbrances, and conditions; in legal use, price may depend on regulations, statutes, or an appellate court decision. These differences are not necessarily inadvertent.

Although there is considerable logic and simplicity in the concept of market value as the most probable selling price, this definition does not exclude duress. If duress is present, it will be reflected in a transaction price and this price may not be market value.

The concept of market value as the highest price under a set of specific conditions, as opposed to market value as a central tendency under the same conditions, is also controversial. For a market to exist, there must be enough buyers, sellers, and product to provide competition; out of this competition a central tendency and a highest tendency will develop. The notion of the highest price was originally rooted in the idea that market value should be the highest possible price represented by the central tendency; it was not thought to be the highest possible price obtainable. However, any definition that includes the word *highest* may be subject to misinterpretation.

Equilibrium value is the price that would be available in the market if supply and demand were in balance. When the forces of supply and demand are out of equilibrium, market value can and does differ significantly from market value in a more balanced situation. During the Depression, for example, values fell dramatically, and many people believed or wanted to believe that property had intrinsic value although it was not then obtainable in the market. When the market is extremely active, prices rise above the level some people believe to be normal or intrinsic. In all cases, however, market value is the price that is available in the

2. *Webster's Ninth New Collegiate Dictionary* (Springfield, Mass.: Merriam-Webster Inc., 1983) and *Random House Dictionary of the English Language,* unabr. ed. (New York: Random House, 1967).

market. Intrinsic value is regarded by some practitioners and theorists as meaningless in relation to market value.

Despite differing opinions on individual aspects of the market value definition, it is generally agreed that market value results from collective value judgments rather than isolated judgments. A market value estimate must be based on objective observation of the collective actions of the market. Because the standard measure of these activities is cash, the increments or diminutions in market value caused by financing and other terms are measured against an all-cash value.

The following definition from *The Dictionary of Real Estate Appraisal*, second edition, incorporates the concepts that are most widely accepted, such as willing, able, and knowledgeable buyers and sellers who act prudently, and gives the appraiser a choice among three bases: all cash, terms equivalent to cash, or other precisely revealed terms. It also requires increments or diminutions from the all-cash market value to be quantified in terms of cash.

> The most probable price, as of a specified date, in cash, or in terms equivalent to cash, or in other precisely revealed terms, for which the specified property rights should sell after reasonable exposure in a competitive market under all conditions requisite to fair sale, with the buyer and seller each acting prudently, knowledgeably, and for self-interest, and assuming that neither is under undue duress.

Some appraisers cite this definition verbatim in their appraisal reports and state separately that the value is stated in cash, in terms equivalent to cash, or in other terms. Other appraisers simply change one phrase in the value definition— i.e., they may substitute "in cash," with "in terms arithmetically equivalent to cash" or "in terms precisely revealed below" as appropriate.

The Standards of Professional Appraisal Practice of the Appraisal Institute require that the following items directly related to the market value definition be included in every appraisal report.

1. Identification of the specific property rights to be appraised.
2. Statement of the effective date of the value opinion.
3. Specification as to whether cash, terms equivalent to cash, or other precisely described financing terms are assumed as the basis of the appraisal.
4. If the appraisal is conditioned upon financing or other terms, specification of whether the financing or terms are at, below, or above market interest rates and/ or contain unusual conditions or incentives. The terms of above- or below-market interest rates and/or other special incentives must be clearly set forth; their contribution to, or negative influence on, value must be described and estimated; and the market data supporting the valuation estimate must be described and explained.

Although this definition includes noncash-equivalent financing terms within the scope of the market value of appraised property rights, these rights are valued in relation to cash. Increments or diminutions in market value attributable to financing terms are measured against an all-cash standard, and the dollar amount of variance from the cash standard must be reported.

The following definition of market value is used by many federal financial institutions including the Resolution Trust Corporation (RTC), which was established under the Financial Institutions Reform, Recovery and Enforcement Act of 1989 (FIRREA) to dispose of the assets of insolvent thrift institutions.

> the most probable price which a property should bring in a competitive and open market under all conditions requisite to a fair sale, the buyer and seller each acting prudently and knowledgeably, and assuming the price is not affected by undue stimulus. Implicit in this definition is the consummation of a sale as of a specified date and the passing of title from seller to buyer under conditions whereby:
> (1) Buyer and seller are typically motivated;
> (2) Both parties are well informed or well advised, and acting in what they consider their own best interests;
> (3) A reasonable time is allowed for exposure in the open market;
> (4) Payment is made in terms of cash in U.S. dollars or in terms of financial arrangements comparable thereto; and
> (5) The price represents the normal consideration for the property sold unaffected by special or creative financing or sales concessions granted by anyone associated with the sale.[3]

This definition is compatible with the definition of market value in *The Dictionary of Real Estate Appraisal*. The FIRREA definition requires that the effect of any special or creative financing or sales concessions on property value be determined and that the value estimate reflect cash-equivalent terms. Special financing or sales concessions often characterize transactions in depressed markets to which the FIRREA definition applies. This definition, therefore, addresses select categories of appraisal assignments in a real estate market characterized by unique circumstances. The Standards of Professional Appraisal Practice caution appraisers to seek the exact legal definition of market value in the jurisdiction in which they perform their services. Market value definitions can be found in a variety of sources, including appraisal texts, real estate dictionaries, and court decisions. One of the best known definitions came out of a decision from the Supreme Court of California, known as the Heilbron case. This definition has been widely employed in appraisal literature.

> The highest price estimated in terms of money which the land would bring if exposed for sale in the open market, with reasonable time allowed in which to find a purchaser, buying with knowledge of all of the uses and purposes to which it is adapted and for which it was capable of being used. [*Sacramento Southern R.R. Co. v. Heilbron* 156 Cal. 408, 104 p. 979 (1909).]

In litigation matters appraisers must use the exact definition of market value that applies in the jurisdiction in which the services are being performed. Moreover, government and regulatory agencies redefine or reinterpret market value from time to time so individuals performing appraisal services for these agencies or institutions under their control are cautioned to use the applicable definition. (See Appendix A for a summary of federal legislation affecting appraisers.)

---

3. *Federal Register*, vol. 55, no. 163, August 22, 1990, pages 34228 and 34229; also quoted in the introduction to the Standards of Professional Appraisal Practice of the Appraisal Institute.

Two recent definitions have been put forth in attempt to capture the essence of the market value concept. The first is

> The price in cash and/or other identified terms for which the specified real property interest is expected to sell in the real estate marketplace under all conditions requisite to a fair sale.[4]

This definition does not include any reference to a specified date. The second definition is

> The value or distribution of values inferrred by a competent observer from sufficient patterns of clearly understood, correctly reported, representative, and uncompelled transactions found in an adequate market which is either identical or sufficiently congruent to the market in which the property will be traded.[5]

This definition does not refer to the date of value or to property rights, but assumes that these are understood.

Use Value

The realities of current real estate and mortgage practices not only place new emphasis on market value, but also require more frequent consideration of other kinds of value. One of these, use value, is a concept based on the productivity of an economic good. *Use value is the value a specific property has for a specific use.* Use value focuses on the value the real estate contributes to the enterprise of which it is a part, without regard to the property's highest and best use or the monetary amount that might be realized upon its sale. Use value may vary depending on the management of the property and external conditions such as changes in the business. For example, a manufacturing plant designed around a particular assembly process may have one use value before a major change in assembly technology and another use value afterward.

Real property may have a use value *and* a market value. An older factory that is still used by the original firm may have considerable use value to that firm, but only a nominal market value for another use.

Use value appraisal assignments may be performed to value assets, including real property, for mergers, acquisitions, or security issues. This type of assignment is particularly common in appraising industrial real estate when the existing business enterprises include real property.

Court decisions and specific statutes may also create the need for use value appraisals. For instance, many states require agricultural use appraisals of farmland for property tax purposes rather than value estimates based on highest and best use.

When appraising a type of property that is not commonly exchanged or rented, it may be difficult to determine whether an estimate of market value or use value is appropriate. Such properties, called *limited-market properties*, can cause special problems for appraisers. *A limited-market property is a property that has relatively few potential buyers at a particular time.* A property may be a limited-market property because of unique design features or changing market

4. See Peter F. Korpacz and Richard Marchitelli, "Market Value: A Contemporary Perspective," *The Appraisal Journal* (October 1984) and "Market Value: Contemporary Applications," *The Appraisal Journal* (July 1985).
5. Jared Shlaes, "The Market in Market Value," *The Appraisal Journal* (October 1984).

conditions. Large manufacturing plants, railroad siding properties, and research and development properties are examples of limited-market properties that typically appeal to relatively few potential purchasers.

Many limited-market properties include structures with unique designs, special construction materials, or layouts that restrict their utility to the use for which they were originally built. These properties usually have limited conversion potential and, consequently, are often called *special-purpose* or *special-design properties*. Examples of such properties include houses of worship, museums, schools, public buildings, and clubhouses.

Limited-market properties may be appraised for market value based on their current use or the most likely alternative use. Due to the relatively small market and the lengthy market exposure needed to sell such properties, there may be little evidence to support a market value estimate based on their current use. There is generally a continuum between market properties and limited-market properties. If a market exists for a limited-market property, the appraiser must search diligently for whatever evidence of market value is available.

If a property's current use is so specialized that there is no demonstrable market for it, but the use is viable and likely to continue, the appraiser may render an estimate of use value. Such an estimate should not be confused with a market value estimate. If no market can be demonstrated or if data are not available, the appraiser cannot estimate a market value and should state so in his or her report. However, it is sometimes necessary to estimate market value in these situations for legal purposes. In these cases, the appraiser must comply with the legal requirement, relying on his or her judgment rather than direct market evidence.

Investment Value

While use value focuses on the specific use of a property, investment value represents the value of a specific investment to a particular investor. As used in appraisal assignments, *investment value is the value of an investment to a particular investor based on his or her investment requirements*. In contrast to market value, investment value is value to an individual, not value in the marketplace.

Investment value reflects the subjective relationship between a particular investor and a given investment. It differs in concept from market value, although investment value and market value indications may be similar. When measured in dollars, investment value is the price an investor would pay for an investment in light of its perceived capacity to satisfy his or her desires, needs, or investment goals. To estimate investment value, specific investment criteria must be known. Criteria to evaluate a real estate investment are not necessarily set down by the individual investor; they may be established by an expert on real estate and its value, that is, an appraiser.

An investment value appraisal may be sought by the potential purchaser of an existing investment or income-producing property or by the developer of a new property.

Going-Concern Value

Going-concern value is the value of a proven property operation. It includes the incremental value associated with the business concern, which is distinct from the value of the real estate only. Going-concern value includes an intangible enhancement of the value of an operating business enterprise which is produced by the assemblage of the land, building, labor, equipment, and marketing operation. This process creates an economically viable business that is expected to continue. Going-concern value refers to the total value of a property, including both real property and intangible personal property attributed to business value.

Going-concern appraisals are commonly conducted for hotels and motels, restaurants, bowling alleys, industrial enterprises, retail stores, shopping centers, and similar properties. For these types of property, the physical real estate assets are integral parts of an ongoing business. It may be difficult to separate the market value of the land and the building from the total value of the business, but such a division of realty and nonrealty components of value is not impossible and is, in fact, often required by federal regulations.

Insurable Value

Insurable value is based on the replacement and/or reproduction cost of physical items that are subject to loss from hazards. *Insurable value is that portion of the value of an asset or asset group that is acknowledged or recognized under the provisions of an applicable loss insurance policy.* This value is often controlled by state law and varies from state to state.

Assessed Value

Assessed value applies in ad valorem taxation and refers to the value of a property according to the tax rolls. Assessed value may not conform to market value, but it is usually calculated in relation to a market value base.

FACTORS OF VALUE

Value is extrinsic to the commodity, good, or service to which it is ascribed; it is created in the minds of the individuals who constitute a market. The relationships that create value are complex, and values change when the factors that influence value change. Typically, four interdependent economic factors create value: utility, scarcity, desire, and effective purchasing power. All four factors must be present for a property to have value.

Utility

Utility is the ability of a product to satisfy a human want, need, or desire. All properties must have utility to tenants, owner-investors, or owner-occupants. Residential properties satisfy the need for shelter; the useful benefits of these properties are called *amenities*. Usually the value of amenities is related to their desirability and utility to the owner-occupant, but this value can be converted into income in the form of rent. The benefits derived from income-producing properties can usually be measured in cash flow. The influence of utility on value depends on the characteristics of the property. Size utility, design utility, location utility, and other specific forms of utility can significantly influence property value.

The benefits of real property ownership are derived from the bundle of rights that an owner possesses. Restrictions on ownership rights may inhibit the flow of benefits and, therefore, lower the property's value. Similarly, a property can only achieve its highest value if it can legally perform its most useful function. Environmental regulations, zoning regulations, deed restrictions, and other limitations on the rights of ownership can enhance or detract from a property's utility and value.

Scarcity

Scarcity is the present or anticipated supply of an item relative to the demand for it. In general, if demand is constant, the scarcity of a commodity makes it more valuable. Land, for example, is still generally abundant, but useful, desirable land is relatively scarce and, therefore, has greater value. No object, including real property, can have value unless scarcity is coupled with utility. Air, which has a high level of utility, has no definable economic value because it is abundant.

Desire

Desire is a purchaser's wish for an item to satisfy human needs (e.g., shelter, clothing, food, companionship) or individual wants beyond essential life support needs. Desire, along with utility and scarcity, is considered in relation to purchasing power.

Effective Purchasing Power

Effective purchasing power is the ability of an individual or group to participate in a market—that is, to acquire goods and services with cash or its equivalent. A valid estimate of the value of a property includes an accurate assessment of the market's ability to pay for the property.

SUPPLY AND DEMAND

The complex interaction of the four factors that create value is reflected in the basic economic principle of supply and demand. The utility of a commodity, its scarcity or abundance, the intensity of the human desire to acquire it, and the effective power to purchase it all affect the supply of and demand for the commodity in any given situation.

Demand for a commodity is created by its utility and affected by its scarcity. Demand is also influenced by desire and the forces that create and stimulate desire. Although human longing for things may be unlimited, desire is restrained by effective purchasing power. Thus, the inability to buy expensive things affects demand.

Similarly, the supply of a commodity is influenced by its utility and limited by its scarcity. The availability of a commodity is affected by its desirability. Land is a limited commodity, and the land in an area that is suitable for a specific use will be in especially short supply if the perceived need for it is great. Sluggish purchasing power keeps the pressure on supply in check. If purchasing power expands, the supply of a relatively fixed commodity will dwindle and create a market-driven demand to increase the supply.

THE HISTORY OF VALUE THEORY

The development of modern value theory began in the eighteenth and nineteenth centuries when economic thinkers of the classical school first identified the four agents of production—labor, capital, coordination, and land—and examined the relationships between the basic factors that create value and supply and demand. Classical theory was largely based on the contributions of the Physiocrats, whose ideas were put forth in reaction to the mercantilist doctrines that dominated earlier economic thought.

Mercantilism focused on wealth as a means of enhancing a nation's power. National wealth was equated with an influx of bullion into the national treasury. Mercantilists sought to maintain a favorable balance of trade by selling goods to accumulate gold, the chief medium of exchange. Between the fifteenth and eighteenth centuries, economic activity in western Europe was associated with overseas exploration, colonization, and commerce. Mercantilist doctrine promoted strong, central economic controls to maintain monopolies in foreign trade and ensure the economic dependency of colonies.

Physiocratic thinkers of the mid-eighteenth century objected to the commercial and national emphasis of mercantilism. They stressed other considerations in formulating a theory of value. Agricultural productivity, not gold, was identified as the source of wealth, and land was cited as the fundamental productive agent. The Physiocrats also identified the importance of factors such as utility and scarcity in determining value.[6]

The Classical School

The classical school expanded and refined the tenets of Physiocratic thought, formulating a value theory that attributed value to the cost of production. The Scottish economic thinker, Adam Smith (1721-1790), suggested that capital, in addition to land and labor, or productivity, constituted a primary agent of production. Smith acknowledged the role of coordination in production, but did not study its function as a primary agent. He believed that value was created when the agents of production were brought together to produce a useful item.

In *The Wealth of Nations* (1776), the first systematic treatment of economics, Adam Smith considered value as an objective phenomenon. By virtue of its existence, an item was assumed to possess utility. Scarcity also imparted exchange value to goods. The "natural price" of an object generally reflected how much the item cost to produce. In contemporary appraisal practice, the classical cost of production theory of value has influenced the cost approach.

Later economic thinkers who are regarded as members of the classical school offered theoretical refinements on the cost of production theory of value, but none contested its basic premises. David Ricardo (1772-1823) developed a theory of rent based on the concept of marginal land and the law of diminishing returns.

---

6. François Quesnay (1694-1774) and Anne Robert Turgot (1727-1781) put forth an individualistic, agrarian-based concept of economic behavior without centralized state control. They popularized the phrase *laissez-faire*, "to let people do as they choose," which underscores their individualistic approach. Quesnay's concept of economic rent introduced the role of competition in determining price and influencing profits. Turgot suggested that "subjective elements," not competition, more directly determined value. Turgot referred to these elements as "the ability to satisfy a want, the ease with which a commodity could be obtained, its scarcity, and other considerations." See Eric Roll, *A History of Economic Thought*, 3rd ed. (Englewood Cliffs, N.J.: Prentice-Hall, Inc., 1964), 134.

Classical economists associated rent with land residual and the law of diminishing returns. (HISTORICAL PICTURES/STOCK MONTAGE)

Land residual returns were referred to as *rent*. Ricardo's theory has contributed significantly to the concept of highest and best use and the land residual technique used in the income capitalization approach to value. Thomas Malthus (1776-1834) elaborated on Ricardo's theory of rent and, in the process, identified value in use, value in exchange (price), and intrinsic value. Although his contribution represents a departure from the cost of production theory of value, it did not alter prevailing economic thought.

Jean Baptiste Say (1767-1832) rejected the relationship between labor and value, concentrating instead on utility as the determinant of value. Say focused on the role of the entrepreneur as an agent of production providing management and coordination. John Stuart Mill (1806-1873) reworked Adam Smith's ideas in *The Principles of Political Economy* (1848), which became the leading economic text of its time. Mill defined the relationship between interest and value in use, which he referred to as "capital value"; the role of risk in determining interest; and the inequities of "unearned increments" accruing to land.[7] Confident in his analysis of the cost of production theory, John Stuart Mill asserted, "Happily, nothing in the laws of value remains for the present or any future writer to clear up; the theory of the subject is complete."

---

7. For further discussion of value theory, see James H. Burton, *Evolution of the Income Approach* (Chicago: American Institute of Real Estate Appraisers, 1982).

Adam Smith   John Stuart Mill

(HISTORICAL PICTURES/STOCK MONTAGE)

Challenges to the Classical Theory

In the second half of the nineteenth century, two serious challenges to classical value theory were put forward. One was the labor theory of value, an extreme position zealously espoused by Karl Marx (1818-1883). Marx claimed that all value is the direct result of labor and that increased wages to labor would lower capitalistic profits. Marx envisioned an inevitable struggle between the social classes which would eventually result in a violent political upheaval.

The other challenge was presented by the marginal utility, or Austrian, school, which was critical of both the classical and Marxian theories. The central concept of marginal utility links value to the utility of, and demand for, the marginal, or additional, unit of an item. Thus, if one more unit than is needed or demanded appears in a given market, the market becomes diluted and the cost of production becomes irrelevant. Value is regarded as a function of demand, with utility as its fundamental precept.

William Stanley Jevons (1835-1882), a founder of modern statistics and a principal proponent of marginal utility, wrote "Labor once spent has no influence on the future value of any article: it is gone and lost forever." Eugen von Boehm-Bawerk (1835-1882), another member of the Austrian school, defined value as "that significance a good acquires in the contribution of utility toward the well-being of an individual."[8] Marginal utility is the theoretical basis for the concept of contribution.

The Neoclassical Synthesis

These formidable challenges to the classical theory of value inspired economists to reconsider the problem. In the late nineteenth and early twentieth centuries, the neoclassical school successfully merged the supply-cost considerations of the clas-

8. W. Stanley Jevons, *The Theory of Political Economy*, 5th ed. (New York: Augustus M. Kelley, 1965), 164; Burton, 17.

sicists with the demand-price theory of marginal utility. Alfred Marshall (1842-1924) is credited with this synthesis, which forms the basis for contemporary value theory.[9]

Marshall compared supply and demand to the blades of a pair of scissors, because neither concept could ever be separated from the determination of value. He stressed the importance of time in working out an adjustment between the two principles. Marshall maintained that market forces tend toward an equilibrium where prices and production costs meet. Utility-demand considerations operate in the limited span of a given market. In the short term, supply is relatively fixed and value is a function of demand. Cost-supply considerations, however, extend over a broader period, during which production flows and patterns are subject to change. Marshall believed that a perfect economic market would eventually result and that price, cost, and value would all be equal.[10]

Marshall was the first major economist to consider the techniques of valuation, specifically the valuation of real estate. In this regard his writings, and the writings of those who built upon his work, are important sources on the distinction between value theory and valuation theory, the method of estimating, measuring, or predicting a defined value. (The development of valuation theory and the three approaches applied in the valuation process are discussed in Chapter 4.)

SUMMARY

Because the concept of value is central to appraisal, clear distinctions must be drawn among the related terms *price, market, cost,* and *value*. A *price* represents the amount a particular purchaser agrees to pay and a particular seller agrees to accept under the circumstances surrounding a transaction. A *market* is a set of arrangements in which buyers and sellers are brought together through the price mechanism. Real estate markets involve the exchange of property rights for other assets, such as money. *Cost* applies to production rather than exchange, and can be divided into direct, or hard, costs and indirect, or soft, costs as well as construction and development costs. *Value* represents the monetary worth of property, goods, or services to buyers and sellers.

Although *market value* is a simple concept, different beliefs and assumptions about the marketplace and the nature of value render any definition controversial. Most market value definitions share common elements. The following definition incorporates the concepts that are most widely accepted:

> the most probable price, as of a specified date, in cash, or in terms equivalent to cash, or in other precisely revealed terms, for which the specified property rights should sell after reasonable exposure in a competitive market under all conditions requisite to fair sale, with the buyer and seller each acting prudently, knowledgeably, and for self-interest, and assuming that neither is under undue duress.

9. In 1890 Marshall published *Principles of Economics*, which succeeded Mill's *Principles of Political Economy* as the authoritative text on economic thought. In this book Marshall advocated a dynamic theory of value to explain real world events. See Alfred Marshall, *Principles of Economics*, 8th ed. (London: Macmillan and Company, 1920) Reprint. (Philadelphia: Porcupine Press, 1982), 288-290, 664-669.
10. See Robert L. Heilbroner, *The Worldly Philosophers*, rev. ed. (New York: Simon and Schuster, 1964), 178-179, and Paul F. Wendt, *Real Estate Appraisal: Review and Outlook* (Athens: University of Georgia Press, 1974), 18-19.

The Appraisal Institute's Standards of Professional Appraisal Practice require that an estimate of market value 1) include a statement that specifies whether the financing terms are at, below, or above market interest rates and whether unusual conditions or incentives are present; and 2) quantify their contribution to, or negative influence on, value. Because other market value definitions are used by federal financial institutions or have been upheld in the courts, appraisers should seek the definition appropriate to the specific assignment or jurisdiction.

Other types of value are also considered in real estate: use value, investment value, going-concern value, insurable value, and assessed value. *Use value* focuses on the real estate's contributory value to the enterprise of which it is a part, without regard to the property's highest and best use. (Limited-market properties may be appraised for market value based on their current use or most likely alternative use.) *Investment value* is the value of an investment to a particular investor, based on his or her investment requirements. *Going-concern value* is the value created by a proven property operation in which the physical real estate assets are an integral part of an ongoing business. *Insurable value* is the portion of value that is covered by casualty insurance. *Assessed value* refers to the property's value according to the tax rolls.

Four interdependent factors create value: utility, scarcity, desire, and effective purchasing power. The interaction of these four factors affects the balance of supply and demand. Various schools of economic thought have contributed to the development of modern value theory. The classical school represented by Adam Smith departed from mercantilist theory by attributing value to the cost of production. The labor theory of value, set forth by Karl Marx, and the opposing concept of marginal utility, which linked value to demand, both challenged the classical theory of value. The neoclassical economics of Alfred Marshall combined classical supply-cost considerations with the demand-price theory of the marginal utility school.

Chapter 3

FOUNDATIONS OF APPRAISAL

$\mathcal{T}$he characteristics of land and real property, which are the focus of appraisal activity, reflect our society's attitudes and beliefs. Because real estate has value, the possession and successful management of real estate create opportunities for individuals to achieve economic goals that are generally perceived to be desirable by society. Financial stability, freedom from excessive restrictions, and high returns on investments are a few of the goals that can be achieved by participating in real estate markets.[1]

In determining their level of participation in the market, individuals consider their wants and needs as well as the choices available to them at different times. These choices represent the variety of market characteristics and help support a free market economy in which both individual and collective decisions contribute to the nation's economic success.

Similarly, the production of the goods, services, and income that comprise the consumable portion of our economy depends on the combined effects of several essential economic ingredients. These ingredients are the agents of production: labor, capital, coordination, and land. The combination of human effort, tangible wealth, production systems, and natural resources allows a society to pursue its economic goals.

The human actions that collectively shape the operation of the market reflect the pursuit of economic goals. To analyze the many dynamic and interactive factors that influence people's attitudes and beliefs about value, the fundamental concepts of anticipation and change must be addressed.

ANTICIPATION

Anticipation is the perception that value is created by the expectation of benefits to be derived in the future. In the real estate market, the current value of a property is usually not based on its historical prices or the cost of its creation; rather, value is based on market participants' perceptions of the future benefits of acquisition.

The value of owner-occupied property is based primarily on the expected future advantages, amenities, and pleasures of ownership and occupancy. The value of income-producing real estate is based on the income it will produce in the future. Therefore, real property appraisers must be aware of local, regional, and national real estate trends that affect the perceptions of buyers and sellers and their anticipations of the future. Historical data on a property or a market are relevant only insofar as they help interpret current market anticipations.

CHANGE

Change is the result of the cause and effect relationship among the forces that influence real property value. Although change is inevitable and continuous, the process may be gradual and not easily discernible. In active markets, change may occur rapidly; new properties may be put up for sale and others may be sold on a daily basis. Abrupt changes may be precipitated by plant closings, tax law revisions, or the start of new construction. The pervasiveness of change is evident in

---

1. Constance Perin, *Everything in Its Place; Social Order and Land Use in America* (Princeton, N.J.: Princeton University Press, 1977).

the dynamic real estate market, where the social, economic, governmental, and environmental forces that affect real estate are in constant transition. Changes in these forces influence the demand for and supply of realty and, therefore, individual property values. Appraisers attempt to identify any current or anticipated changes in the market that could affect current property values. However, change is inevitable, so appraisal value estimates are valid only for the date specified in the appraisal report.

The inevitability of change is also evident in the physical, functional, and economic impairments observed in buildings as they age. These impairments create *depreciation, defined as a loss in property value from any cause.* Depreciation may be seen as the difference between the cost to reproduce or replace a property and its present value. In general, losses in property value are caused by deterioration or obsolescence. Because deterioration and obsolescence begin the moment a building or improvement is completed, the different types of deterioration and obsolescence found in a property have unique implications in appraisal. (A detailed discussion of deterioration and obsolescence is presented in Chapter 16.)

The appraisal principles of supply and demand, substitution, balance, and externalities, which are founded in general economics, can be applied to the unique physical and legal characteristics of a particular parcel of real property. When these principles are in proper accord, they indicate highest and best use, a concept of great significance in real property appraisal.

SUPPLY AND DEMAND

In economic theory, the principle of supply and demand states that the price of a commodity, good, or service varies directly, but not necessarily proportionately, with demand, and inversely, but not necessarily proportionately, with supply. In a real estate context, the appraisal principle of supply and demand states that the price of real property varies directly, but not necessarily proportionately, with demand, and inversely, but not necessarily proportionately, with supply. Thus, increasing the supply of an item or decreasing the demand for an item tends to reduce the price obtainable in the market; the opposite is also true. The relationship between supply and demand may not be directly proportional, but the interaction of these forces is fundamental to economic theory. The interaction of suppliers and demanders, or sellers and buyers, constitutes a market.

Usually property values vary inversely with changes in supply. If properties for a particular use become more abundant than they were in the past, their value declines; by contrast, if properties become more scarce, their value increases. The supply of and demand for commodities always tend toward equilibrium. At this theoretical point, market value, price, and cost are equal.

In real estate, supply is the amount of a type of real estate available for sale or lease at various prices in a given market at a given period of time. Typically, more of an item will be supplied at a higher price and less at a lower price. Therefore, the supply of an item at a particular price, at a particular time, and in a particular place indicates that item's relative *scarcity*, which is a basic factor of value.

The supply of real estate is a function of the four agents of production, including the amount of capital needed to put a parcel of land to a given use rela-

Figure 3.1 Proportionate Shifts in Supply and Demand

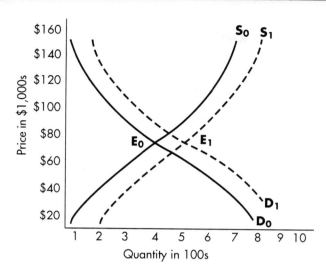

Proportionate shifts in supply and demand occur when the rate of increase in the demand for a type of property is the same as the rate of increase in the supply of the property. The equilibrium price remains at the same level, but the number of properties sold at the equilibrium price increases. In Figure 3.1 the increase in supply from S_0 to S_1 and the increase in demand from D_0 to D_1 were proportionate. The equilibrium price of $80,000 ($E_1$) remained the same, but the number of properties sold at the equilibrium price increased from 400 to 500. If supply and demand had decreased at a proportionate rate, the equilibrium price would remain the same, but the number of properties sold would decrease.

tive to the current price of existing properties providing that use. For example, as the price of houses increases, builders may find it profitable to build on land that was previously considered too expensive for residential development. The supply of new properties in a particular market generally increases when demand increases, driving property prices up, or when the prices of the agents of production decline. Increases in the productivity of labor or the efficiency of technology (capital goods) contribute to reducing development costs. A building boom set in motion by rising expectations of profit on the part of developers may result in an oversupply of properties.

Because real property is both a physical commodity and a service, the supply of real estate refers to the amount of service, or the usability of the space, as well as the quantity of physical space. Consequently, those involved in real estate are primarily concerned with the supply of land suitable for a specific use, not the total number of acres available. The supply of real estate incorporates both the quality and quantity of service space provided. Proper comparisons can be made only between properties that are similar both qualitatively and quantitatively. The quality of space may affect property value even more than its quantity. Quality is

Figure 3.2 Disproportionate Shifts in Supply and Demand

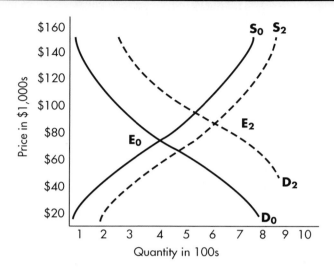

Disproportionate shifts in supply and demand occur when the rate of increase in the demand for a type of property is different from the rate of increase in the supply of the property. Disproportionate shifts in supply and demand produce changes in both the equilibrium price and the number of properties sold at that price. In Figure 3.2 the increase in demand from D_0 to D_2 outpaced the increase in supply from S_0 to S_2. The equilibrium price (E_2) rose from $80,000 to $90,000 for the 200 additional properties (400 to 600) sold at the equilibrium price. If supply and demand had decreased at disproportionate rates, both the equilibrium price and the number of properties sold at that price would decline.

a function of the tangible attributes of a property, such as its size, shape, and condition, and its intangible attributes or amenities. The supply of a specific property type may be inventoried to reflect existing improvements on the resale market and new construction entering the market for the first time.

Generally the quantity of space supplied for a given use is slow to adjust to changes in price levels. The length of time needed to build new structures, the large amount of capital required, and government regulations often hamper a supplier's ability to meet changes in the market. The quality of service space, however, can change more rapidly because suppliers can convert nonproductive space to alternative uses, defer maintenance, and partition existing space into smaller units.

Demand is the desire and ability to purchase or lease goods and services. In real estate, demand is the amount of a type of real estate desired for purchase or rent at various prices in a given market for a given period of time. Typically less of an item will be demanded at a higher price, and more will be demanded at a lower price. Property values tend to vary directly with shifts in demand; prices tend to increase if demand increases and other factors remain constant. Usually

Figure 3.3 Unilateral Shift in Demand

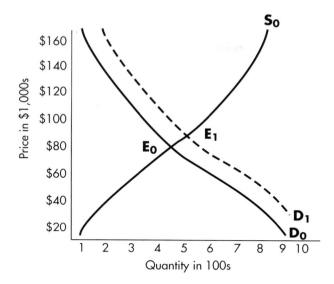

A shift in equilibrium price may also result from unilateral changes in either the supply of or demand for a type of property. In Figure 3.3 demand for a stable supply (S_0) of properties had increased from D_0 to D_1. The equilibrium price rose from \$80,000 (E_0) to \$90,000 (E_1).

the relationship between demand and price is not fixed. This changing relationship is described as the *elasticity of demand.*

Because the supply of real property for a specific use is difficult to adjust, especially in a short time, values are most affected by current demand. Demand, like supply, can be characterized in terms of both quantity and quality. For example, demand in a residential market may be defined by the number of households in the market area and the household income as well as the size and characteristics of the households and the specific housing preferences. Demand that is supported by purchasing power results in effective demand, which is the type of demand considered by the market. Residential demand generally increases in the long term as the number of households in the market area and their household incomes increase. Residential demand is further strengthened in the short term by declining mortgage interest rates.[2]

---

2. In the disinflationary environment of the 1980s, however, financial assets were more attractive investments than tangible assets. Home prices lagged behind inflation and home ownership rates fell. Home ownership is likely to continue to decline during the 1990s as a result of further disinflation and the falling rate of household formation. Other factors, however, may work to stabilize or even increase home prices. These positive factors include 1) demographics with baby boomers entering the high-productivity, high-earning stage of their lives, and 2) the special attributes of residential real estate. The demand for housing usually increases as real income rises, and owner-occupied properties are among the few assets still treated as tax shelters. See Leonard Sahling, "Rent or Buy: A Market Analysis," in *Real Estate Economics Special Report* (June 1990) published by Merrill Lynch.

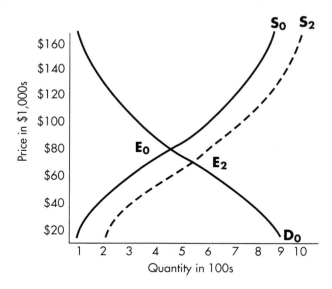

Figure 3.4 Unilateral Shift in Supply

In Figure 3.4 the supply of properties increased from S_0 to S_2, while demand (D_0) remained stationary. The equilibrium price fell from $80,000 ($E_0$) to $70,000 ($E_2$).

Typically there is a direct, but not proportional, relationship between demand and price. If demand increases and supply remains constant, prices tend to increase; if demand falls, prices tend to fall. Appraisers must interpret market behavior to ascertain the existing relationship between the supply of, and the demand for, the type of property being appraised.

COMPETITION

The concept of competition is related to the principle of supply and demand. *Competition between buyers or tenants represents the interactive efforts of two or more potential purchasers or tenants to make a sale or secure a lease. Between sellers or landlords, competition represents the interactive efforts of two or more potential sellers or landlords to effect a sale or lease.* Competition is fundamental to the dynamics of supply and demand in a free enterprise, profit-maximizing, economic system.

Because competition causes continual shifts in the levels of commodities that are available, it affects the levels of demand for these commodities. Buyers and sellers of real property operate in a competitive market setting; in essence, each property competes with all other properties that are suitable for the same use. For example, a profitable motel faces competition from newer motels nearby; existing residential subdivisions compete with new subdivisions; and downtown retail properties compete with suburban shopping centers.

Over time, competitive market forces tend to reduce unusually high, or excess, profits. Profit encourages competition, but excess profits tend to breed ruinous competition. For example, the first retail store to open in a new and expanding area generates more profit than is considered typical for that type of enterprise. If owners of similar retail enterprises then gravitate to the area to compete for the surplus profits, eventually there may not be enough business to support all the retailers. A few stores may earn normal profits, but others will fail. The effects of competition and market trends on profit levels are especially important to appraisers making income projections in the income approach to value.

SUBSTITUTION

The principle of substitution states that when several similar or commensurate commodities, goods, or services are available, the one with the lowest price attracts the greatest demand and widest distribution. This principle assumes rational, prudent market behavior with no undue cost due to delay. According to the principle of substitution, a buyer will not pay more for one property than for another that is equally desirable.

Property values tend to be set by the cost of acquiring an equally desirable substitute property. The principle of substitution recognizes that buyers and sellers of real property have options, i.e., other properties are available for similar uses. The substitution of one property for another may be considered in terms of use, structural design, or earnings. The cost of acquisition may be the cost to purchase a similar site and construct a building of equivalent utility, assuming no undue cost due to delay; this is the basis of the cost approach. On the other hand, the cost of acquisition may be the price of acquiring an existing property of equal utility, again assuming no undue cost due to delay; this is the basis of the sales comparison approach.

The principle of substitution is equally applicable to properties such as houses that are purchased for their amenity-producing attributes and properties purchased for their income-producing capabilities. Residential properties may be purchased for their excellence of design, quality of workmanship, or superior construction materials. In regard to income-producing property, substitution refers to alternative investment properties that produce equivalent investment returns with equivalent risk. The limits of property prices, rents, and rates tend to be set by the prevailing prices, rents, and rates of equally desirable substitutes. The principle of substitution is fundamental to all three traditional approaches to value—cost, sales comparison, and income capitalization.

OPPORTUNITY COST

Opportunity cost is the cost of options forgone or opportunities not chosen. An investor who selects one type of investment forgoes the opportunity to invest in other types of available investments. A well-informed investor will select an investment that seems likely to provide the highest rate of return at the lowest level of risk. The illiquidity the investor endures over the term of the investment poses a potential opportunity cost if alternative investments at comparable levels of risk outperform the investment chosen.

The concept of opportunity cost is related to the principle of substitution. Opportunity cost is particularly significant in estimating the rates of return necessary to attract capital. By analyzing and comparing the prospective rates of return offered by alternative investment opportunities, an appraiser can estimate the required rate of return indicated by the market for the property being appraised. Interviews with investors regarding their yield expectations and assumptions about inflation and market growth may provide support for current estimates of property yield rates. Furthermore, actual investor projections for properties recently acquired lend credence to estimates of property yield estimates.

BALANCE

The principle of balance holds that real property value is created and sustained when contrasting, opposing, or interacting elements are in a state of equilibrium. This principle applies to relationships among various property components as well as the relationship between the costs of production and the property's productivity. Labor, capital, coordination, and land are the agents of production, but for most real estate the critical combination is the land and the improvements. The point of economic balance is achieved when the combination of land and improvements is optimal—i.e., when no marginal benefit or utility is achieved by adding another unit of capital. *The law of increasing returns* holds that larger amounts of the agents of production produce greater net income up to a certain point. At this point, *the point of decreasing returns*, the maximum value is developed. Any additional expenditures will not produce a return commensurate with the additional investment, according to *the law of decreasing returns*. This concept is also known as the *principle of diminishing marginal productivity* or *law of diminishing returns*.

The fertilization of farmland provides a simple example. Applying fertilizer to the land increases crop yield only up to a point, beyond which the cost of the fertilizer will exceed the price of the additional crop yield. The optimum amount of fertilization is achieved when the value of the increment in yield resulting from the last unit of fertilizer equals the additional expenditure on fertilizer. This is the point of balance.

An example specific to real estate provides further illustration. Consider a developer determining how many bedrooms to include in a single-family house being developed for sale on the residential market. If the typical single-family house in this particular residential market has three bedrooms, including a fourth bedroom may invoke the law of decreasing returns. Constructing a fourth bedroom will not be economically feasible if its cost exceeds the value added to the property.

The principle of balance also applies to the relationship between a property and its environment. Balance affirms that a proper economic mix of various types and locations of land uses in an area creates and sustains value.

The principle of balance and the related concepts of contribution, surplus productivity, and conformity are interdependent and crucial in estimating highest and best use and market value. These concepts form the theoretical foundation for estimating all forms of depreciation in the cost approach, making adjustments in the sales comparison approach, and calculating expected earnings in the income capitalization approach.

CONTRIBUTION

When appraisers apply the principle of balance to component property parts, they study the concept of contribution. *The concept of contribution states that the value of a particular component is measured in terms of its contribution to the value of the whole property, or as the amount that its absence would detract from the value of the whole.* The cost of an item does not necessarily equal its value. A swimming pool that costs $10,000 to install does not necessarily cause the value of a residential property to increase by $10,000. Rather, the pool's dollar contribution to value is measured in terms of how valuable its benefit or utility is in the market. Its contribution to value may be lower or higher than its cost. Thus, in some cases, a property's market value may not increase even though the real estate has undergone alteration, modification, or rehabilitation.

The existing improvements may not reflect a proper balance for the total property. Especially in areas of rapid transition, a property's present use may underutilize of the land. Nevertheless, an existing, less optimal use, called an *interim use*, will continue until it is economically feasible for a developer to absorb the costs of converting the property by razing or rehabilitating the existing improvements.

SURPLUS PRODUCTIVITY

Surplus productivity is the net income that remains after the costs of various agents of production have been paid. The classical economists identified the surplus with land rent, suggesting that it tended to fix land value. Traditionally, the concept of surplus productivity has provided the basis for the residual concept of land returns and residual valuation techniques. Some twentieth-century economists argue that surplus productivity should be ascribed to coordination—i.e., the entrepreneurship required to combine the other agents of production in a complete real estate product.

CONFORMITY

Conformity is the appraisal principle that holds that real property value is created and sustained when the characteristics of a property conform to the demands of its market. The styles and uses of the properties in an area may conform for several reasons, including economic pressures; the shared preferences of owners for certain types of structures, amenities, and services; and the enforcement of uniform standards by means of zoning. Through local zoning ordinances, the government encourages conformity by restricting land use. Standards of conformity are set by the market and are therefore subject to change. Zoning codes, however, tend to establish conformity in basic property characteristics, including size, style, and design. A particular market also sets standards of conformity, especially in terms of price. Usually, the value of an overimproved property will decline, or regress, toward the value level of surrounding, conforming properties; the value of an underimproved property may increase, or progress, toward the prevailing market standard.

EXTERNALITIES

The principle of externalities states that economies outside a property have a positive effect on its value while diseconomies outside a property have a negative effect on its value. When external economies affect a great number of people, the product or service is often provided by government. Bridges, highways, police and fire protection, and other essential services can be provided more cheaply through common purchase by the government than through separate acquisition by individuals. External diseconomies result when the costs of inconveniences are imposed on other people by an individual or a firm. A person who violates environmental law by dumping hazardous waste, for example, imposes the cleanup costs on others.

Real estate is affected by externalities more than any other economic good, service, or commodity. Because it is physically immobile, real estate is subject to many types of external influences. Externalities may refer to the use of properties located near the subject property or to the physical attributes of these properties. Externalites may also establish the economic conditions that affect the market in which the subject property competes. For example, an increase in the purchasing power of the households that constitute the trade area for a retail facility will likely affect the sales (income-producing) potential of the property.

External influences may be international or national in origin or they may emanate from the region, community, or neighborhood. Externalities may be as broad as international currency and gold prices or as narrow as a neighbor's standard of property maintenance. The appraiser should observe and analyze how external influences affect the parcel of real estate being appraised.

At the international and national levels, trade policy, manufacturing efficiency, interest rates, and socioeconomic priorities can greatly affect real estate values. For example, a combination of these influences caused some U.S. real estate values to stagnate or fall in the early 1980s. Foreign imports depressed some U.S. industries, and old plants and equipment tended to make U.S. manufacturing operations less efficient than their foreign counterparts. High interest rates depressed home buying and industrial expansion. Competition for credit stiffened as borrowers who wanted to buy a home had to compete for capital with government and industry.

At the regional level, real estate values in the early 1980s fared better in some areas than in others. In general the population migration to the Sunbelt tended to enhance values there at the expense of older regions in the north, where values tended to stabilize or decline. Industrial areas with manufacturing operations that were susceptible to foreign competition suffered more than areas less reliant on such industries. By the mid-1980s the decline in oil prices brought about a recession in the oil-producing regions of the Sunbelt. In addition, the great volume of construction activity over the previous decade resulted in an oversupply of office buildings. Simultaneously, the northern Rustbelt experienced moderate economic recovery. The decline in construction in this section of the country during the early 1980s coupled with pent-up demand led to higher real estate prices and a construction boom. With many markets overbuilt by the late 1980s, a nationwide slowdown in new development occurred.

At the community and neighborhood levels, property values are affected by local laws, local government policies and administration, property taxes, economic growth, and social attitudes. Different property value trends are frequently noted among communities in the same region and among neighborhoods in the same community. Appraisers should be familiar with external events at all levels and be able to assess their impact on individual property values.

FORCES THAT INFLUENCE REAL PROPERTY VALUES

The value of real property reflects and is influenced by the interaction of basic forces that motivate human activity. These forces are divided into four major categories: *social* trends, *economic* circumstances, *governmental* controls and regulations, and *environmental* conditions. The forces are dynamic; they exert pressure on human activities and are in turn affected by these activities. The interaction of all the forces influences the value of every parcel of real estate in the market.

To estimate value an appraiser interprets how the market views a particular property; the scope of investigation is not limited to static, current conditions. Rather, the appraiser analyzes trends in the forces that influence value to determine the direction, speed, duration, strength, and limits of these trends.

Social Forces

Social forces are exerted primarily through population characteristics. The demographic composition of the population reveals the potential, basic demand for real estate services; therefore, proper analysis and interpretation of demographic trends are imperative in real estate appraisal. Real property values are affected not only by population changes and characteristics, but also by the entire spectrum of human activity. The total population, the rate of family formation and dissolution, and age distributions strongly influence real property values.

Economic Forces

Economic forces are also significant to real property value. Appraisers analyze the fundamental relationships between current and anticipated supply and demand and the economic ability of the population to satisfy its wants, needs, and demands through its purchasing power. Many specific market characteristics are considered in the analysis of economic forces—e.g., employment, wage levels, industrial expansion, the economic base of the region and the community, price levels, and the cost and availability of mortgage credit. Most of these are considered demand-side economic characteristics. Supply-side economic characteristics include the stock of available vacant and improved properties, new development under construction or in the planning stage, occupancy rates, the rental and price patterns of existing properties, and construction costs. Other economic trends and considerations may be studied as the appraiser's analysis focuses on successively smaller geographic areas.

Governmental Forces

Governmental, political, and legal actions at all levels have a great impact on property values. The legal climate at a particular time or in a particular place may overshadow the natural market forces of supply and demand. The government provides many necessary facilities and services that affect land use patterns. Therefore, appraisers must diligently identify and examine the potential value influences of

- Public services such as fire and police protection, utilities, refuse collection, and transportation networks
- Local zoning, building codes, and health codes, especially those that obstruct or support land use
- National, state, and local fiscal policies
- Special legislation that influences general property values (e.g., rent control laws, statutory redemption laws, restrictions on forms of ownership such as those imposed by condominiums and timeshare arrangements, homestead exemption laws, environmental legislation regulating new developments, and legislation affecting the types of loans, loan terms, and investment powers of mortgage lending institutions)

Environmental Forces

Both natural and man-made environmental forces influence real property values. Environmental forces that may be analyzed for real estate appraisal purposes include climatic conditions such as snowfall, rainfall, temperature, and humidity; topography and soil; toxic contaminants such as asbestos, radon, or PCBs; natural barriers to future development such as rivers, mountains, lakes, and oceans; primary transportation systems, including federal and state highway systems, railroads, airports, and navigable waterways; and the nature and desirability of the immediate area surrounding a property. (The treatment of hazardous substances in real estate appraisal is discussed in Chapters 8 and 9.)

The environmental forces that affect a specific real property value may be best understood in relation to the property's location. *Location is the time-distance relationships, or linkages, between a property or neighborhood and all possible origins and destinations of residents coming to or going from the property or neighborhood.* Time and distance are measures of relative access. To analyze locational forces, the linkages between the property and important points or places outside the property are identified, and the distance and time required to cover those distances by the most commonly used types of transportation are measured. Depending on the area and the property type, the appraiser may investigate the property's access to public transportation, schools, stores, service establishments, parks, recreation and cultural facilities, places of worship, sources of employment, product markets, suppliers of production needs, and processors of raw materials.

An understanding of all value-influencing forces is fundamental to the appraisal of real property. Although the four forces are discussed separately here, they work together to affect property values. These forces provide the background against which appraisers view every parcel of real property. (Value influences are discussed in detail in Chapters 7 and 8.)

HIGHEST AND BEST USE

By identifying and interpreting the market forces that affect a specific property in a local and regional context, the appraiser determines the property's highest and best use. Highest and best use is a fundamental concept in real estate appraisal because it focuses market analysis on the subject property and allows the appraiser to consider the property's optimum use in light of market conditions on a specific date.

Highest and best use reflects a basic assumption about real estate market behavior—that the price a buyer will pay for a property is based on his or her conclusions about the most profitable use of the site or property. Therefore, sites and improved properties tend to be put to their highest and best uses. However, the determination of a property's highest and best use set forth in an appraisal may or may not conform with the existing use. The determination of highest and best use must be based on careful consideration of prevailing market conditions, trends affecting market participation and change, and the existing use of the subject property.

Highest and best use may be defined as

the reasonably probable and legal use of vacant land or improved property, which is physically possible, appropriately supported, financially feasible, and that results in the highest value.

Because the use of land can be limited by the presence of improvements, highest and best use is determined separately for the land or site as though vacant and available to be put to its highest and best use and for the property as improved.

The first determination reflects the fact that land value is derived from potential land use. Land has limited value unless there is a present or anticipated use for it; the amount of value depends on the nature of the land's anticipated use, according to the concept of surplus productivity. *Among all reasonable, alternative uses, the use that yields the highest present land value, after payments are made for labor, capital, and coordination, is generally regarded as the highest and best use of the land as though vacant.* In other words, the highest and best use of land as though vacant is the use that brings the highest return to the land after the three other agents of production have been compensated.

To determine the highest and best use of the land as though vacant, the appraiser assumes that the parcel of land in question has no improvements. Even a site with a large building on it can be made vacant by demolishing the building. The question to be answered is: If the land were vacant, what improvement will create the most value?

The second determination refers to the optimum use that could be made of the property and all existing structures. *Analysis of the highest and the best use of a property as improved implies that the existing improvement should be renovated or retained as is so long as it continues to contribute to the total market value of the property, or until the return from a new improvement would more than offset the cost of demolishing the existing building and constructing a new one.* For example, a large, old house could continue to be used as a single-family residence, or it could be converted into apartments or offices. The decision depends on the rents or prices that could be charged for the existing property under the alternative uses and how these amounts compare with the costs of conversion. Although the existing improvement does not represent the highest and best use of the site as though vacant, it should not necessarily be demolished. Demolition is indicated when the land as though vacant has more value than the parcel as presently improved.

Determining the highest and best use of land as though vacant is useful for land or site valuation; determining the highest and best use of an improved property facilitates a decision as to whether the use should continue or the improvements should be demolished.

The relationship between the supply of, and demand for, land adaptable to a particular use is significant in determining highest and best use. A site or improved property may be placed under an interim use until demand is sufficient to support its highest and best use. If a more profitable use must be delayed due to insufficient present demand, the interim use will continue until the value of the land as though vacant, minus the cost of demolishing the existing improvements, exceeds the total value of the improved property at its current use.

When properties are devoted to temporary, interim uses, the concept of consistent use must be addressed. *Consistent use is the concept that land cannot be valued on the basis of one use while the improvements are valued on the basis of another.* Improvements must contribute to the land value to have any value themselves. Improvements that do not represent the land's highest and best use, but do have substantial remaining physical lives, may have an interim use of temporary value or they may have no value at all. In fact, the improvements could even have negative value if substantial costs would be incurred for their removal. (Highest and best use is discussed in detail in Chapter 12.)

REAL ESTATE MARKETS

Appraisers consider value in the context of real estate markets, so delineating real estate markets and submarkets is an essential part of appraisal. In valuation assignments, particularly in estimations of market value, an appraiser's understanding of the market for a specific property provides the criteria with which to research, select, and interpret the comparability of other properties. To arrive at an estimate of market value, the appraiser must identify and analyze the market or markets that influence the subject property.

Evaluation studies in which a value estimate is not necessarily required are often conducted to determine and interpret the characteristics of markets for investors and developers. For example, a feasibility study may focus on the profitability of a specific real estate undertaking in terms of the criteria of the specific market. To provide credible evaluation conclusions, real estate appraisers must thoroughly understand the real estate market or markets that are relevant to the assignment.

Buyers and sellers of real estate interact in different areas for different reasons and different types of property. Thus, real estate markets are divided into categories based on the differences among property types and their appeal to different market participants. The markets for various categories of real estate are further divided into submarkets, which correspond to the preferences of buyers and sellers. Differentiating real estate markets facilitates their study.

All real estate markets are influenced by the attitudes, motivations, and inter-actions of buyers and sellers of real property, which in turn are subject to many social, economic, governmental, and environmental influences. Real estate markets may be studied in terms of their geographic, competitive, and supply-and-demand characteristics, which relate to overall real estate market conditions.

The identification and interpretation of real estate markets is an analytical process. Appraisers analyze the utility and scarcity of property, as well as the de-sire and effective purchasing power of those who seek to acquire property rights, to answer questions about real estate markets and submarkets.

Characteristics of Real Estate Markets

Real estate markets do not possess the same economic characteristics as the more efficient markets for other goods and services. The efficiency of a market is based on assumptions about the behavior of buyers and sellers and the characteristics of the products traded.

The goods or services in an efficient market are essentially homogeneous items that can be readily substituted for one another. In contrast, each parcel of real estate is unique and its location is fixed. No two parcels of real estate are physically identical. Although some parcels may be economically similar and could be substituted for one another, they differ geographically. The inherent features of real estate preclude its diverse markets from being highly efficient.

In an efficient market there is a large number of buyers and sellers who create a competitive, free market, and none of these participants has a large enough share of the market to have a direct and measurable influence on price. In real estate markets, only a few buyers and sellers may act at one time, within one price range, and at one location for any type of property. The high relative value of real estate requires great purchasing power, so real estate markets are very sensi-tive to changes in wage levels, the stability of income, and the number of individ-uals employed. Construction costs, housing costs, and rent levels are all affected by market participants' ability to pay.

In an efficient market, prices are relatively uniform, stable, and low. They are often the primary consideration in purchase or sale decisions because quality tends to be uniform at a set price. In real estate markets, prices are relatively high and very few purchasers have enough money to pay for property in cash. There-fore, the types of financing offered, the amount of mortgage money available, interest rates, down payment requirements, and typical loan duration affect the decision to purchase real estate. If a property cannot be financed favorably, it usually will not be bought. Investors are less likely to buy income-producing prop-erty if the debt service exceeds a certain percentage of cash flow. The debt cover-age ratio, the ratio of net operating income to annual debt service, becomes the likely focus of their analysis.

An efficient market is self-regulating. There are very few government restric-tions on open and free competition. Real estate markets, on the other hand, are not self-regulating. Federal, state, county, and local regulations govern the owner-ship and transfer of real estate; contract and deed restrictions further regulate the sale and purchase of property. A deed restriction, for example, may require that houses in a subdivision contain at least 2,000 square feet of area.

Supply and demand are never far out of balance in an efficient market because the market tends to move toward balance through the effects of competition. Although the supply of, and demand for, real estate also tend toward equilibrium, this point is theoretical and seldom achieved. The supply of real estate suitable for a specific use is slow to adjust to market demand, unlike the supply of less durable commodities. Furthermore, shifts in demand may occur while new real estate units are being constructed, so an oversupply, rather than market equilibrium, may result.

Units of real estate that are comparable in size and quality tend to sell at comparable prices; if supply and demand are in relative balance, real estate prices tend to be stable. But if the demand for real estate increases suddenly, an additional supply cannot be provided quickly. Similarly, if demand declines suddenly, the excess supply cannot be quickly removed from the market.

In real estate markets, supply and demand *are* considered causal factors and price is the result of their interaction. Price changes usually are preceded by changes in market activity. Often, supply or demand may shift suddenly in a period of no activity or increased activity.

Buyers and sellers in an efficient market are knowledgeable and fully informed about market conditions, the behavior of others, past market activity, product quality, and product substitutability. Any information needed on bids, offers, and sales is readily available. Buyers and sellers of real estate may not be well informed. Most people do not buy and sell real estate frequently, so they are not very familiar with the procedure or knowledgeable about how to judge a property. Information on bids, offers, and sales of a particular property or similar properties may not be readily available to buyers and sellers since some states prohibit disclosure of such information.

Buyers and sellers in an efficient market are brought together by an organized market mechanism, such as the New York Stock Exchange, and it is relatively easy for sellers to enter into the market in response to market demand. In real estate markets, however, demand may be volatile due to sudden shifts in population. A sudden influx of population in an area may result in high prices because it will take months or years to construct new buildings and increase development to meet the demand. A sudden out-migration due to unfavorable economic conditions can result in an oversupply and lower prices.

Finally, in an efficient market, goods are readily consumed, quickly supplied, and easily transported. Real estate is a durable product and, as an investment, it may be relatively unmarketable and illiquid. Real estate is not usually sold quickly because its sale involves large sums of money and the appropriate financing may not always be readily secured. The supply of real estate is relatively inflexible and, because property is fixed in location, the supply cannot be adjusted quickly on a national or regional level.

Real estate markets are not efficient and, due to imperfections such as a lack of product standardization and the time required to produce a new supply, it is difficult to predict their behavior accurately. Recognizing that real estate markets do not operate like the markets for other commodities, appraisers must analyze the significant aspects of market activity that make markets inefficient. Therefore, real estate market analysis focuses on the motivations, attitudes, and interaction of market participants as they respond to the particular characteristics of real estate and to external influences that affect its value. This focus underscores the importance of objective real estate appraisal in a free market economy and the responsibility of appraisers to the communities they serve.

Types of Real Estate Markets

Different real estate markets are created by the needs, desires, motivations, locations, and ages of market participants and the types, locations, designs, and zoning restrictions of property.

Five real estate markets can be identified to correspond to five broad categories of property.

1. Residential (single-family homes and duplexes; multitenanted apartment buildings)
2. Commercial (office buildings, retail centers, hotels and motels)
3. Industrial (manufacturing plants, warehouses, research and development buildings)
4. Agricultural (cropland, orchards, pastureland, timberland)
5. Special-purpose (properties with unique design or construction which restricts their utility to the use for which they were built—e.g., schools, public buildings, airports, convention facilities, amusement/theme parks, golf courses)

Each market for a particular type of property can be subdivided into smaller, more specialized, markets called *submarkets*. Submarkets for urban, suburban, and rural residential property can be further divided in terms of the purchasers' preference for high-, medium-, or low-priced properties. Multitenanted apartment buildings, which are income-producing residential properties, and offices, stores, loft buildings, parking garages, motels, hotels, and shopping centers, which are commercial properties, typically appeal to different groups of investors. Industrial properties include factories, warehouses, and mining operations. The market for agricultural properties can be divided into markets for pastureland, timberland, cropland, orchards, and ranchlands. Special-purpose properties include parks, cemeteries, houses of worship, clubs, golf courses, historic or recreational government properties, and public utilities.

The process of identifying and analyzing submarkets within a larger market is called market segmentation.[3] Segmentation usually applies to consumers, differentiating the potential users of a subject property from the general population by their characteristics. *Disaggregation* is a related term that applies to the property. Disaggregation differentiates the subject property from other properties by creating subclassifications with differing product characteristics.[3] These terms are discussed in more detail in a subsequent section of this chapter.

A submarket can be created by changes in the demand side of the market; for example, a certain type of property may be in demand by a particular group. Families looking for homes and companies in need of warehouses may be considered real estate markets. The properties within these large markets are heterogeneous because residences and warehouses can be large or small, old or new, well

3. Neil Carn, Joseph Rabianski, Ronald Racster, and Maury Seldin, *Real Estate Market Analysis* (Englewood Cliffs, N.J.: Prentice-Hall, 1988).

designed or poorly designed. A market is divided into a number of smaller, more homogeneous submarkets by recognizing the different product preferences of buyers and sellers. These preferences may include building size and design, price range, and property location.

Real estate appraisers identify and study market segments by considering locational, demographic, socioeconomic, psychological, and product-related characteristics. They may use survey research techniques to discover, quantify, analyze, and form conclusions about the composition of particular submarkets.

MARKET ANALYSIS

Market analysis is the identification and study of the market for a particular economic good or service. The market analysis component of an appraisal must specifically relate market conditions to the property under investigation. It must show how the interaction of supply and demand affects the value of the subject property. Appraisers use market analysis to determine whether there is appropriate market support for an existing property under a specified use or evidence that there will be market support for a proposed use of a site at some time in the foreseeable future. If current market conditions do not indicate adequate demand for a proposed development, market analysis may identify the point in time when adequate demand for the project will likely emerge. Thus, market analysis informs the appraiser as to the timing of a proposed improvement and the amount of demand in a particular period of time.

Market analysis forms the basis for determining the *highest and best use* of a property. An existing or proposed improvement under a specified use may be considered in terms of the criteria of financial feasibility and maximum productivity only after an appropriate level of market support has been demonstrated to exist for that use. In-depth market analyses go much further in specifying the character of that support. Such studies may determine key marketing strategies for an existing or proposed property, address the design characteristics of a proposed development, or provide estimates of the share of the market the property is likely to capture and its probable absorption rate.

To measure the market support for a specified property use, the analyst must identify the relationship between demand and competitive supply in the subject real estate market—both now and in the future. This relationship indicates the degree of *equilibrium* or *disequilibrium* that characterizes the present market and the conditions likely to characterize the market over the forecast period.

The market value of a property is largely a function of its competitive position in its market. Familiarity with the characteristics and attributes of the subject property will enhance the appraiser's ability to identify competitive properties (supply) and to understand the comparative advantages and disadvantages that the subject offers potential buyers or renters (demand). With an understanding of economic conditions, their effect on real estate markets, and the momentum of these markets, an appraiser can better appreciate the externalities affecting the property. In its broadest sense, therefore, market analysis provides vital information needed to apply the three approaches to value.

Market analysis provides an appraiser with information about current building costs and market conditions for use in the cost approach. This information enables the appraiser to make more accurate estimates of the profit an entrepreneur will expect and any economic advantage or obsolescence the property may have suffered since its construction.

In the sales comparison approach, market analysis helps the appraiser identify competitive properties and determine their exact degree comparability with the subject. With a thorough understanding of current market conditions gained through market analysis, the appraiser is able to adjust the sale prices of comparable properties for changes in market conditions that may have occurred since the sales were transacted.

In the market analysis process an appraiser also collects data on vacancy and absorption rates, current and anticipated rates of return, and the competitive position of the subject property in its specific market. In the income capitalization approach, this information is used to determine the anticipated lease-up or sell-out rate for the subject, the share of the market that the subject is likely to capture, the future income stream it is likely to enjoy, and an appropriate discount rate to apply to this income stream projection.

The principles of market analysis seem simple, but the techniques and procedures applied by market analysts can be extremely sophisticated. Market studies can be developed into elaborate analyses. The levels of market analysis that can be performed reflect a spectrum of increasingly complicated methods and procedures.[4]

Estimates of demand are formulated differently depending on the level of analysis. In some cases, demand may be simply inferred from current market conditions or rates of change used to develop projections. Because of shortcomings in this simple approach, caution is advised. To perform an in-depth analysis of forecast (fundamental) demand, on the other hand, the analyst must gather and segment extensive data and apply sound judgment to project data. An analyst refines a forecast (fundamental) demand estimate by considering the perceptions of market participants and assessing the likelihood that current trends will continue.

TWO APPROACHES

There is no universally accepted set of steps or procedures to be applied in market analysis because each assignment depends on the specific needs of the client and these needs vary. Moreover, appraisers do not agree on the best way for the market analysis component of an appraisal to be integrated with the determination of highest and best use. It is possible, however, to identify two schools of market analysts. (See Figure 3.5.) Many practitioners proceed from the general economy to the specific property; other practitioners begin with the specific property and then consider the general economy. It is important to note that regardless of the procedure employed, each approach considers a full complement of factors.

Appraisers approaching real estate market analysis as market researchers generally tend to emphasize the need to begin the analysis with an economic overview of the community in which the subject property is located. Their first concern is the local or regional economic base, its linkages to the national and even global

4. For a comprehensive discussion of the various levels of market analysis, see Stephen F. Fanning and Jody Winslow "Guidelines for Defining the Scope of Market Analysis in Appraisals," *The Appraisal Journal* (October 1988), 466-476.

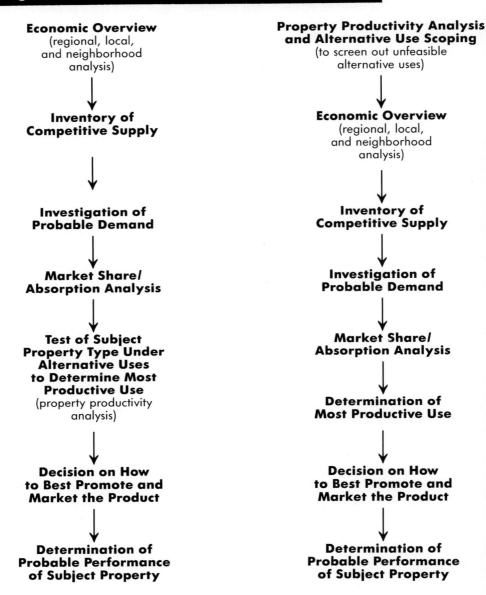

Figure 3.5 Two Approaches to Market Analysis

Economic Overview
(regional, local,
and neighborhood
analysis)

↓

**Inventory of
Competitive Supply**

↓

**Investigation of
Probable Demand**

↓

**Market Share/
Absorption Analysis**

↓

**Test of Subject
Property Type Under
Alternative Uses
to Determine Most
Productive Use**
(property productivity
analysis)

↓

**Decision on How
to Best Promote and
Market the Product**

↓

**Determination of
Probable Performance
of Subject Property**

**Property Productivity Analysis
and Alternative Use Scoping**
(to screen out unfeasible
alternative uses)

↓

Economic Overview
(regional, local,
and neighborhood
analysis)

↓

**Inventory of
Competitive Supply**

↓

**Investigation of
Probable Demand**

↓

**Market Share/
Absorption Analysis**

↓

**Determination of
Most Productive Use**

↓

**Decision on How
to Best Promote and
Market the Product**

↓

**Determination of
Probable Performance
of Subject Property**

economy, and the broad dynamics of supply and demand which determine prices and absorption rates in real estate markets. Depending on the type of study required, critical items in this economic overview can include population, employment, income, major industries, principal retail centers, areawide housing, and overall urban growth trends.

Analysts of this first school examine market-specific data. Population, employment, and income data serve as indicators of *area demand*; data on the amount of space currently available from occupancy or vacancy rates and space under construction or proposed for development provide a measure of competitive supply. Comparing demand and competitive supply identifies the extent of present and prospective equilibrium or disequilibrium in the market.

After supply and demand analysis, these market analysts study the probable alternative uses of the property and estimate the values associated with these uses. They consider the physical, legal or regulatory, and locational attributes of the subject property and ultimately arrive at a conclusion regarding its highest and best use.

A second school of practitioners contend that demand and supply are both embodied in the real estate product.[5] They believe that the best way to begin market analysis is to examine the characteristics or attributes that contribute to the productivity of the subject property and determine the subject's competitive position in its specific market. These analysts believe that understanding the physical, legal or regulatory, and locational attributes of a property is essential to identifying the market participants likely to purchase or rent the property and those likely to sell or lease it. Potential buyers or tenants and sellers or landlords represent the forces of demand and supply that create the dynamics of the subject market.

Adherents of this second school argue that a property productivity analysis focusing on the characteristics and attributes of the subject property facilitates identification of competitive properties and, thus, definition of the subject market. After property productivity analysis is completed, these appraisers investigate the economic base and analyze demand and competitive supply in the delineated market area. Market-specific data are examined to arrive at estimates of current and future demand and an inventory of available and projected supply. The extent of market equilibrium or disequilibrium is determined, and future market conditions are forecast. To develop a complete understanding of the market for which a forecast is being made, the analyst studies critical variables such as the rate of employment growth, changes in population and household size, income levels, and retail sales.

Next these analysts consider the feasibility of the most probable alternative uses of the property in terms of present and prospective market support. Financial analysis is then performed to determine which of the feasible uses is most productive and thereby qualifies as the highest and best use of the property.

Whichever approach the appraiser chooses to follow, the purpose of the market analysis should at all times guide the appraiser's efforts. Fundamentally, the purpose of market analysis is to establish whether appropriate market support exists for a property under a specified use or there is evidence of market support for a proposed use at some time in the foreseeable future. Market analysis focuses on understanding the effect of the local economy on market conditions, specifically the conditions that characterize the market in which the subject property competes.

. These practitioners subscribe to the writings of Richard U. Ratcliffe and James A. Graaskamp.

Fundamental Concepts

Market Definition

At the outset of the market analysis process, the appraiser must clearly identify the real estate product and the real estate market in which the subject competes. These two functions may be considered complementary. Analyzing the characteristics and attributes of the real estate product helps the appraiser identify competitive properties. Defining the real estate market for the subject property clearly enhances the appraiser's understanding of how externalities affect the subject.

Market analysis breaks down a specific real estate market into submarkets or market segments. It also disaggregates the real estate product from other types of properties.

To understand the process of market segmentation, it is useful to reexamine the definition of a real estate market. *A real estate market is a group of individuals or firms that are in contact with one another for the purpose of conducting real estate transactions.* Market participants may be buyers, sellers, renters, lessors, lessees, mortgagors, mortgagees, developers, builders, managers, owners, investors, or brokers. Each market participant does not have to be in contact with every other participant; a person or firm is part of the market if that person or firm is in contact with another subset of market participants. The actions of market participants are prompted by their expectations about the use or uses of a property and the benefits it will afford its users. Market segmentation, therefore, must differentiate the most probable users of a property from the general population by their consumer characteristics.

A real estate market is made up of market participants engaged in real estate transactions. The activity of these individuals focuses on a real estate product and the service it provides. Product disaggregation, therefore, differentiates the subject property and competitive properties from other types of properties on the basis of their attributes or characteristics.

To delineate a specific real estate market, an appraiser investigates the following factors:

1. *Property type* (e.g., single-family residential, retail shopping center, office building).
2. *Property features* such as occupancy, customer base, quality of construction, and design and amenities.
   a. *Occupancy*—single-tenant or multitenant (residential, apartment, office, retail)
   b. *Customer base*—the most probable users (Data on population, employment, income, and activity patterns are analyzed. For residential markets, data are broken down according to the profile of the likely property owner or tenant; for commercial markets, data are segmented according to the likely users of the space. For retail markets, the clientele that the prospective tenants will draw represents the customer base; for office markets the customer base reflects the space needs of prospective companies leasing office units.)
   c. *Quality of construction* (class of building)
   d. *Design and amenity features*

3. *Market area*—defined geographically or locationally (A market area may be local, regional, national, or international in scope. It may be urban or suburban; it may correspond to a district or neighborhood of a city. Retail and residential market areas are often delineated by specific time-distance relationships.)
4. *Available substitute properties*—i.e., equally desirable properties competing with the subject in its market area.
5. *Complementary properties*—i.e., some other property or property type that is complementary to the subject. (The users of the subject property need to have access to complementary properties, which are also referred to as *support facilities*.)

Thus a market segment is delineated by identifying the market participants likely to be involved in transactions focused on the subject real estate and the type of real estate product and service it provides. The market segment includes both the subject property and competitive and complementary properties. Thus, market analysis combines market segmentation and product disaggregation.

Demand

Demand reflects the needs, material desires, purchasing power, and preferences of consumers. Demand analysis identifies the potential users of a subject property—the buyers, renters, or clientele it will attract. For each particular type of property, demand analysis focuses on the end product or service that the real estate provides. Thus, a demand analysis for retail space would attempt to determine the demand for retail services generated by potential customers in the market area. A demand analysis for office space would attempt to identify businesses in the area that occupy office space and their space or staffing needs.

Demand analyses for residential and retail markets specifically investigate the households in the subject's market area. (A *household* is defined as a number of related or unrelated people who live in one housing unit; thus a single individual may constitute a household.) In addition to the number of households in the market area, these analyses focus on the disposable income or effective purchasing power of these households and the ages, gender, preferences, and behavioral patterns of household members. The following factors are important in demand analysis for a residential market:

- Population of the market area—size and number of households, rate of increase or decrease in household formation, composition, and age distribution
- Income and wages
- Employment types and unemployment rate
- Household breakdown reflecting owner and renter percentages
- Financial considerations such as savings levels and lending requirements (e.g., interest rates on mortgages, points charged, loan-to-value ratios)
- Land use patterns and directions of city growth and development
- Factors affecting the physical appeal of the neighborhood, e.g., geography and geology (climate, topography, drainage, bedrock, and natural or man-made barriers)
- Local tax structure and administration

- Availability of support facilities and community services (cultural institutions, educational facilities and the quality of schools, health and medical facilities, fire and police protection)

The following factors are important in demand analysis for a retail market:

- Population of trade area(s)—size and number of households, rate of increase or decrease in household formation, composition and age distribution of households
- Per capita and household income (mean and median)
- Percentage of household income spent on retail purchases and percentage of disposable income (effective purchasing power) spent on various retail categories
- Rate of sales retention in the trade area
- Required volume of sales for a retail facility to operate profitably and existing sales volume per square foot
- Retail vacancy rate in the market
- Percentage of retail purchases captured from outside the trade area
- Land use patterns and directions of city growth and development
- Accessibility (transportation facilities and highway systems) and cost of transportation
- Factors affecting the appeal of the retail center (image, quality of goods, and tenant reputation)

The following factors are important in demand analysis for an office market:

- Area employers who use office space; current and estimated future staffing needs
- Average square foot areas of office space required by an office worker (Requirements vary according to the category of work, the rank of the office worker, and whether the office is located in the suburbs or CBD)
- Vacancy rate for the specific class of office building
- Move-up or fall-out demand for Class A and Class B buildings in an active or declining market
- Land use patterns and directions of city growth and development
- Accessibility (transportation facilities and highway systems) and cost of transportation
- Factors affecting the appeal of the office building (quality of construction, management, and tenancy) and availability of support facilities (shops, restaurants, recreational centers)

Demand for housing and most retail space is projected on the basis of growth rates in population, income, and employment levels.[6] A few pointers can be especially useful in understanding demand projections.[7]

---

6. See Chapter 7 for a discussion of the data used to estimate the demand for and competitive supply of a specific property type or use.
7. Dowell Myers, "Housing Market Research: A Time for a Change," *Urban Land* (October 1988), 16-19.

Households Based on Robust Economy

(Numbers in thousands)

Age of householder	1990	1995	2000
All households	95,724	103,235	110,689
Under 25 years	5,569	5,710	6,379
25-34 years	22,212	21,428	19,996
35-54 years	34,902	41,063	45,923
55 years and over	33,041	35,034	38,391

Households Based on Moderately Growing Economy

(Numbers in thousands)

Age of householder	1990	1995	2000
All households	93,437	98,848	103,835
Under 25 years	5,313	5,238	5,616
25-34 years	21,472	20,142	18,237
35-54 years	34,269	39,707	43,665
55 years and over	32,383	33,761	36,317

Demand for residential and commercial properties is projected on the basis of household formation rates.

U.S. Department of Commerce, *Current Population Reports: Population Estimates and Projections*, Series P-25, No. 986, May 1986, "Projections of the Number of Households and Families: 1986 to 2000."

First, the rate of household formation varies significantly with income and age (cohort) groups in the existing population; this rate is even more sensitive to migration. Estimating the number of households in an area by dividing the total population by the average household size may result in considerable error. The rate of household formation is much higher for people between the ages of 25 and 34 and those between 35 and 64 than for people between the ages of 15 and 24. However, precise data may be difficult to obtain.

Second, household size is not a constant. Over the past decade average household size has declined significantly. Between 1980 and 1990 household size fell from 2.76 to 2.63.[8]

Third, while average or median income is generally projected in current (inflationary) dollars, real income in the United States calculated in constant dollars did not grow between 1973 and 1990. Income projections based on current dollars will thus reflect future, inflated dollars.

8. *The Statistical Abstract of the United States: 1990*, 10th ed., U.S. Department of Commerce, Bureau of the Census (Washington, D.C.: U.S. Government Printing Office, 45), Table 55.

Finally, population projections for small areas are published by public agencies and market research firms, but such projections can be misleading. Therefore, the appraiser should also consult projections for the overall metropolitan area. The availability of land and the adequacy of the infrastructure in the subject area will help determine what share of the overall projected growth will go to that area.

Competitive Supply

Supply refers to the availability of the real estate product. To analyze supply the appraiser must compile an inventory of properties competitive with the subject. Competitive properties include the stock of existing units, the units under construction that will enter the market, and projects in planning. Care must be exercised in developing and analyzing data on proposed or announced projects as not all may be constructed. The appraiser must also determine the number of units lost to demolition, and the number added or removed through conversion. Data may be gathered from field inspection, building permits (issued and acted upon), plat maps, surveys of competitive sites, and interviews with developers and city planners.

To analyze the supply of competing properties, the following factors must be studied:

- Quantity and quality of available competition (standing stock)
- Volume of new construction (competitive and complementary)—projects in planning and under construction
- Availability and price of vacant land
- Costs of construction and development
- Currently offered properties (old and new)
- Owner occupancy versus tenant occupancy
- Causes and number of vacancies
- Conversions to alternative uses
- Special economic conditions and circumstances
- Availability of construction loans and financing
- Impact of building codes, zoning ordinances, and other regulations on construction volume and cost

Market Equilibrium

Over the short term the supply of real estate is relatively fixed and price is responsive to demand. If demand is unusually high, prices and rents will start to rise before new construction can begin. The completion and lease-up of a building may lag considerably behind the shift in demand. Thus disequilibrium generally characterizes markets over the short term.

Theoretically, the supply of and demand for real estate move toward equilibrium over the long term. However, this point is seldom achieved. In some markets such as those characterized by a very specialized economy, supply responds slowly to changing market conditions. Even when an excess of supply becomes apparent, projects currently under construction generally have to be completed. More stock will continue to be added to the existing surplus causing greater disequilibrium. A decline in demand may also occur while new real estate units are being constructed, further exacerbating the oversupply.

Analysts and market participants describe the activity of real estate markets in a variety of ways. An *active market* is a market characterized by growing demand, a corresponding lag in supply, and an increase in prices. An active market is also referred to as a *seller's market* because the sellers of available properties can obtain higher prices. A *depressed market* is a market in which a drop in demand is accompanied by a relative oversupply and a decline in prices. A depressed market is also referred to as a *buyer's market* because buyers have the advantage.

Other terms applied to markets are subject to interpretation. For example, markets are sometimes characterized as "strong" or "weak." Strong markets may reflect either high demand and increasing price levels or a large volume of transactions. Weak or soft, markets may be identified by low demand and declining price levels. Other loosely defined terms include "broad" and "narrow" markets, "loose" and "tight" markets, and "balanced" and "unbalanced" markets.[9]

All markets cannot be described with simple characterizations. In some situations supply and demand do not act as expected. Supply may fail to respond to increasing demand because the rate of demolition exceeds the rate of new construction. In this case prices will continue to rise. Or supply may outpace rising demand because of a glut of existing properties on the market, and prices will decline.

The activity of the real estate market is cyclical. Like the business cycle, the real estate cycle is characterized by successive periods of expansion, peak, contraction, and trough. The real estate cycle is not, however, synchronized with the business cycle. Real estate activity responds to two sets of stimuli, one of which operates over the long term and the other over the short term.

The long-term, or *secular,* cycle is a function of changes in the characteristics of the existing population and of its income. If the local economy is able to provide stable employment and generate new jobs, the present population will remain in the area and others will migrate there seeking employment. The specific types of employment offered by the local economy determine the levels of disposable income in the community.

The short-term cycle is largely a function of the availability of credit. Interest rates serve as indicators of short-term cycles. Real estate activity, measured in the number of housing starts and home sales, is extremely sensitive to fluctuations in the interest rate. Therefore, the real estate industry generally takes the lead in upturns and downturns in the business cycle. Vacancy and absorption rates may be considered indicators of short-term cycles, although in especially depressed markets low rates may persist for many years. Industrial relocation and labor migration at high levels may also create short-term cycles.

Short-term indicators typically reflect only the immediate future. Interest rates are very volatile, and vacancy and absorption rates can rarely be forecast with any accuracy beyond two or three years. In developing a market forecast, an appraiser should identify long-term trends. Indicators of long-term trends include the economic base and planned infrastructure. These factors, among others, determine the future growth potential of the community.

---

9. Carn et al, 76-77 and 81-82.

Sample Procedures for Conducting Market Analysis

A market analysis is performed to estimate the demand for a specific category of real estate (e.g., residential units, retail space, office space) and the extent of market support for the subject property. Market analysis may be undertaken to examine an existing property under a specified use or a proposed use of a property that presently is vacant or under another use. In either case the objective of the market analysis is to demonstrate whether adequate market support exists for the given property use. The market analysis procedure is the same for existing properties and proposed properties.

For existing properties, the analyst can study the sales or income history of the property and infer its future performance and market capture on the assumption that the property can maintain or improve its present level of performance. To perform market analysis for a proposed property, which is frequently required to evaluate project feasibility, the analyst has to determine whether the project will achieve a competitive level of performance. Demand for a proposed property generally must be forecast. The capture potential of a proposed property requires extensive analysis.

The procedures presented below reflect a conventional approach to market analysis, beginning with an economic overview and market identification rather than property productivity analysis.

Housing Demand

To forecast housing demand for proposed units in a single-family subdivision over a given period (i.e., typically five years), an appraiser may follow the steps described below.[10]

1. *Preliminary economic overview.* Analyze the community's economic base by surveying the industries and businesses that generate employment and income, as well as the rate of population growth and levels of income, both of which are functions of employment. Study economic activity as reflected in retail sales and investigate the local real estate market by surveying the level of sales, the level of construction activity, and interest, mortgage, and absorption rates.

2. *Market and property identification.* Analyze the characteristics of likely buyers to whom the specified housing units would appeal. Develop a consumer profile describing income (i.e., ability to afford the housing), household size, age, and preferences. The market area of potential buyers may be defined in terms of time-distance relationships (the commuting time to employment centers), social or political boundaries (school districts, voting precincts), man-made or natural boundaries (major thoroughfares, physical barriers) and the location of competitive housing. Perform a preliminary analysis of the legal, physical, and locational attributes of the subject units and units in competitive subdivisions.

---

10. Procedures for estimating housing, retail space, and office space demand are discussed in J.R. Kimball and Barbara S. Bloomberg, "The Demographics of Subdivision Analysis," *The Appraisal Journal* (October 1986) and J.R. Kimball, "Office Space Demand Analysis," *The Appraisal Journal* (October 1987). The focus of the market analysis will determine the sequence of steps in the study. For example, rather than specifying the housing unit, retail facility, or office building to be developed, a client may want to know the best type of unit, facility, or building to develop. In this case, the analyst must investigate supply and demand before the property can be identified.

3. *Demand analysis.* Determine the size of the current and projected population within the defined market area. Determine the current and projected number of households keeping in mind that household size varies with the age of the head of the household. Segment the number of current and projected households into those headed by owners and those headed by renters. There may be an overlapping category of renters who can afford to buy. Divide the number of owner-headed households according to their income levels to determine the percentage of households that are or will be able to meet the mortgage payments required by local lending practices and interest rates and other housing expenses such as maintenance, insurance, and taxes. Adjust the number of owner-headed households that are or will be able to afford the housing by the vacancy rate in the market to determine the existing and anticipated demand for the subject property.

4. *Competitive supply analysis.* Inventory existing competitive properties, properties under construction, planned properties for which building permits have been obtained, and proposed properties. Refine the inventory by checking the total number of building permits issued against those actually put to use in recent years. Tally the inventory of existing and anticipated competitive supply for the projection period. Rate the subject and its competition for specific amenities and attributes that give housing units a competitive advantage or disadvantage.

5. *Equilibrium analysis.* Compare existing and potential demand with current and anticipated competitive supply to determine whether demand for additional units or square footage of housing (marginal demand) exists or when it may develop. Analyze the competitive rating to forecast the likely capture rate for the subject.

Retail Space Demand

To forecast the demand for an existing or proposed community shopping center at a specific site over a given period (i.e., five or 10 years), an appraiser might follow these steps:

1. *Preliminary economic overview.* Analyze the community's economic base by surveying the industries and businesses that generate employment and income as well as the rate of population growth and levels of income, both of which are functions of employment. Study economic activity as reflected in retail sales and the local real estate market by surveying the level of retail sales, the level of construction activity, and interest, mortgage, and absorption rates.

2. *Market and property identification.* Define the trade area for the facility using techniques such as gravitational models and customer spotting, or by adjusting preliminary trade area boundaries for the specific geographic, demographic, and economic characteristics of the community. Perform a preliminary analysis of the legal, physical, and locational attributes of the subject center and competitive centers in or near its trade area.

3. *Demand analysis.* Identify the amount of supportable leasable retail space in the trade area using projected demographic and income data. An estimate of supportable leasable retail space may be obtained by multiplying the number of households in the trade area by the median household income. To this figure apply the following percentages: the percentage of household income spent on retail purchases, the percentage of retail purchases made at a facility such as the subject, and the percentage of sales retention in the trade area. Then divide this estimate

of total potential retail sales by an estimate of the sales per square foot required for the facility to operate profitably. Adjust the resulting figure for the normal vacancy rate in the market to obtain an estimate of the supportable leasable retail space in the trade area. This estimate may be further adjusted to account for retail income from outside the trade area and leakage of retail income to other areas.

4. *Competitive supply analysis.* Determine the amount of existing retail space currently leased or vacant, and space under construction or in planning in or near the defined trade area. Refine the inventory by checking the total number of building permits issued against those actually put to use in recent years. Rate the subject and its competition for specific amenities and attributes that give a community shopping center a competitive advantage or disadvantage.

5. *Equilibrium analysis.* Compare the estimate of supportable leasable space with the existing and anticipated retail space. The difference between the two will be the estimate of additional space needed, or marginal demand. Sales per square foot in individual retail stores may also indicate the performance level of an existing shopping center and whether there is opportunity for additional development. These data may be used to check the reasonableness of the marginal demand estimate. If there is a current surplus of retail space, the forecast of market conditions may identify when in the future the available retail space will have been absorbed and demand for additional retail space (marginal demand) will begin to come on line. Analyze the competitive rating to obtain the likely market capture rate for the subject. A cost of occupancy analysis allows rents to be fixed. For example, a ratio of occupancy costs to sales equal to or less than 15%-20% may be compatible with the anticipated rent levels.

Office Space Demand

To forecast the demand for existing or additional office space in a particular node or district over a given period, an appraiser analyzes the relationship between supply and demand in the overall market area and the district's actual and potential share of the existing and projected demand. The time when a proposed building will reach stabilized occupancy can be forecast in this way. Demand for office space in the overall market area is estimated with the following steps:

1. *Preliminary economic overview.* Analyze the community's economic base by surveying the industries and businesses that generate employment and income as well as the rate of population growth and levels of income, both of which are functions of employment. Study economic activity as reflected in retail sales and investigate the local real estate market by surveying the level of real estate sales, the level of construction activity, and interest, mortgage, and absorption rates.

2. *Market and property identification.* Segment the market of property users according to the type of tenants leasing office units currently or in the future, their space or staffing needs, and the clientele they draw. For example, law firms may seek space in prestigious, centrally located buildings, while businesses providing other types of services may prefer suburban offices with ample parking facilities and reasonable rents. The market area for an office building is generally diffused over a broad metropolitan area. Competitive office space is disaggregated on the basis of the class of building, tenancy, and location. A preliminary analysis of the subject and competitive buildings includes comparison of the nodes or clusters of

office buildings within the metropolitan area as well as competitive buildings within the subject node. Determining the share of overall demand that a district will capture is discussed below.

3. *Demand analysis.* Project employment for the overall market area. Based on job projections provided by forecasting agencies such as municipal departments and econometric services, develop estimates of the number of office workers projected in each economic and occupational sector. Consider historical employment growth rates to check the reasonableness of these projections.[11] Convert the number of office occupants into the annual demand for office space. The average space required for an office worker ranges from 175 to 200 square feet.[12] In soft markets with high vacancy rates, businesses often lease extra space and employees may occupy more area. The total number of office workers is multiplied by the average space required per worker. If steady growth is anticipated, this space estimate is divided by the number of years over which growth in the work force is projected.

4. *Competitive supply analysis.* Inventory currently leased and vacant competitive space as well as competitive space under construction or in planning. The competitive supply inventory may also be affected by demolitions, renovations, and the adaptation of space now under other uses. Refine the inventory by checking the total number of building permits issued against those actually put to use in recent years. Rate the subject and the competition within the subject's node for specific amenities and attributes that give the office space a competitive advantage or disadvantage.

5. *Equilibrium analysis.* Compare the existing and projected demand for office space with the total supply of current and anticipated competitive office space. If projected demand exceeds total available competitive supply, subtract total available competitive supply from the projected demand to arrive at the unsatisfied demand for office space. Refine the marginal demand forecast by checking the accuracy of the demand projection against historic demand pattern. For Class A or Class B buildings, potential move-up or fall-out demand should be considered, i.e., a tenant who moves up from Class B to Class A space in a down market with rents in decline, or a tenant who falls out from Class A to Class B space in an active market with rents on the increase. In an in-depth analysis, also consider space subject to pre-leasing as well as space that will become vacant upon the expiration of tenant leases. If demand is anticipated to grow at a steady rate, total supply may be divided by projected annual demand to determine the absorption period. At the end of the absorption period, additional space will be required. This point in time represents a "window" for development. Analyze the competitive rating to forecast likely subject capture.

---

11. An alternative method for calculating the number of office space occupants in each economic and occupational sector in past years involves establishing the ratio between the number of office workers and the number of total workers in each sector. Approximately two-thirds of all office workers occupy space in freestanding office buildings—i.e., buildings entirely occupied by office workers. Thus, each ratio is multiplied by 0.67. With these adjusted ratios, the number of office workers in each sector can be determined and the total number of office workers in all sectors can be calculated. See Ian Alexander, *Office Location and Public Policy* (New York: Chancer Press, 1979.)

12. Average area requirements are estimated by the Building Owners and Managers Association (BOMA). Market analysts should consult BOMA estimates directly because the square foot area required per employee varies widely with community size and the type of employment in the community. Other national and local sources may also vary from BOMA estimates.

To determine a particular node or district's share of the overall demand projection, development patterns in the district must be analyzed. Until recently suburban office construction outpaced construction in central business districts. Not all suburbs shared equally in this growth. Development patterns in areas (analogs) that closely resemble the subject district should be compared. Key demographic features such as total population and educational and income levels are believed to be closely correlated with the ability of a suburban area to support an office building.

The appraiser may develop a ratio by dividing the amount of existing office space in the district by the amount of office space in the overall market area. Such a ratio only reflects the district's "fair share" of the market, however, and may not provide an accurate forecast. Market preferences must also be considered in determining the ratio. The projected demand for office space in the overall market area may be multiplied by this ratio.

Projected demand is compared with current and anticipated supply, and the accuracy of demand projections is checked against historic patterns. These are the same procedures used to analyze demand and absorption in the overall market area.

To forecast when a proposed building will reach stabilized occupancy, the appraiser can estimate the construction period and an absorption rate based on pre-leasing requirements, if any, and the historic performance of competitive buildings. Historic performance is interpreted and used to forecast expectations, but it must be considered in its proper context. Performance may have been especially high during periods of rapid growth and unusually low during periods of stagnation. Detailed data on occupancy may describe not only nodal and district patterns, but also absorption rates for different building types (e.g., low-, mid-, and high-rise) or different building classes (e.g., Class A, Class B, Class C) and different occupants (e.g., anchor tenants or nonanchor tenants, corporate management, research and development departments, professional services).

SUMMARY

A number of important principles support society's understanding of value. These principles provide the rationale for market behavior and, therefore, help explain changes in property value. The principle of *anticipation* is the perception that value is created by the expectation of future benefits. The principle of *change* holds that the social, economic, government, and environmental forces affecting value are in continuous flux. The physical deterioration and functional and economic obsolescence of property are other manifestations of the inevitability of change.

The principle of *supply and demand* holds that the price of real property varies directly, but not necessarily proportionately, with demand, and inversely, but not necessarily proportionately, with supply. Theoretically, the supply of and demand for commodities tend toward equilibrium where market value, price, and cost are equal. Supply and demand both have qualitative and quantitative dimensions.

Competition between buyers or tenants refers to the interactive efforts of two or more potential purchasers or tenants to secure a purchase or a lease; competition between sellers or landlords refers to their interactive efforts to effectuate a sale or lease. Competition is fundamental to the operation of supply and demand.

The principle of *substitution* affirms that when several similar or commensurate commodities, goods, or services are available, the one with the lowest price will attract the greatest demand and the widest distribution. *Opportunity cost*, a related concept, is the cost of options forgone or opportunities not chosen.

The principle of *balance* holds that real property value is created and sustained when contrasting, opposing, or interacting elements are in a state of equilibrium. These elements may include the physical components of the property (i.e., land and improvements), the costs of production or development, and the relationship between the property and its environment. The *laws of increasing and decreasing returns* govern how balance is established. The concepts of *contribution, surplus productivity,* and *conformity* are related to the principle of balance. Because real estate is physically immobile, its value is subject to the positive and negative effects of *externalities,* economies or diseconomies that exist outside a property and may be local, regional, national, or international.

Four basic forces interact to influence the value of real property: social trends (population characteristics), economic circumstances (demand-side and supply-side economic indicators), government controls and regulations (public services, zoning and building codes, tax policies, and specific real estate laws), and environmental conditions (climate, topography, soil, natural barriers to development, the availability of transportation systems and the suitability of the *location* in terms of linkages, and the accessibility of the location).

The concept of *highest and best use* is predicated on the assumption that buyers and sellers set prices for properties based on their conclusions about the most profitable use of the site or property. Highest and best use is the reasonable and probable use that supports the highest present value of the vacant land or improved property as of the date of the appraisal; the use must be legally permissible, physically possible, financially feasible, and result in the highest estimate of land value. Highest and best use is determined separately for the land or site as though vacant and available for the anticipated use and for the property as improved. The related concept of *consistent use* states that the land and improvements must be valued on the basis of the same use.

Real estate markets and submarkets are delineated based on differences among property types and the preferences of buyers and sellers. Real estate markets do not possess the same economic characteristics as markets for many other goods and services. Real estate markets are not efficient because real estate is not a homogeneous, readily substitutable item. Few buyers and sellers are involved in a real estate market at any given time in a particular price range or location. Real estate prices are fairly high, so most transactions involve financing. Because many government regulations apply to real estate, the market cannot be self-regulating. The real estate market is slow to reach supply-demand equilibrium. Market participants are not always well informed, and shifts in the demand for real estate can be volatile. Real estate is an immobile, durable product, and its supply is relatively stable.

Appraisers study the behavior of market participants, both buyers and sellers, to identify patterns and trends. There are five general real estate markets: residential (single-family and multitenanted apartments), commercial, industrial, agricultural, and special-purpose. *Market segmentation* is the process by which submarkets within a larger market are identified and analyzed.

Market analysis is the identification and study of a pertinent market for an economic good or service. Market analysis in an appraisal must specifically relate market conditions to the property under investigation. It must show how the interaction of supply and demand affects the value of the subject property. Market analysis determines the level of current and anticipated market support for existing properties under specified uses and future properties under proposed uses. Market analysis provides the basis for determining the highest and best use of a property as well as information used in applying the three approaches to value.

Market analysis covers a spectrum of increasingly complicated methods and procedures. In-depth studies may specify the nature of market support for an existing or proposed use as specifying design and amenity features, marketing strategies, and probable capture and absorption rates. Market analysis may be approached either through the general economy with economic base analysis or through the specific property with productivity analysis. Both approaches consider a full complement of factors in determining the effect of the local economy on market conditions, specifically those that characterize the market in which the subject property competes.

Many interested concepts are fundamental to market analysis. *Market definition* considers property type, property features (occupancy, consumer base, construction quality, design and amenities), market area (local, regional, national, or international), the availability of substitute properties, and the presence of complementary properties. *Market segmentation* identifies submarkets within a larger market by focusing on the potential users of a property. *Disaggregation* differentiates the subject and competitive properties from other groups of properties on the basis of their attributes or characteristics.

Demand reflects the needs, desires, purchasing power, and preferences of consumers. Demand indicators vary for residential, retail, and office markets. Demand projections rely on the household formation rate, average household size, average or median income, and employment levels. Projections for small areas should be compared with those for the overall metropolitan area.

Competitive supply refers to the availability of the real estate product, or the inventory of properties competitive with the subject (existing stock, units under construction, and projects in planning). The number of units lost to demolition and the number removed through conversion must also be considered.

Market equilibrium is a point toward which the supply of and demand for real estate theoretically gravitate over the long term. However, because of lags between demand and supply, markets are rarely at equilibrium. Furthermore, supply and demand do not always act as expected. Real estate activity is subject to the effects of *long-term* (secular) cycles and *short-term cycles*. The former are a function of long-term indicators such as existing and projected population employment and income. The latter are triggered by changes in the availability of credit (reflected in interest rates) and industrial relocation or in-migration (reflected in vacancy and absorption rates).

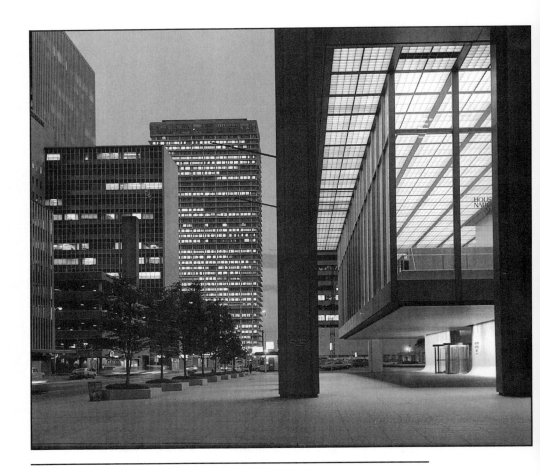

Chapter 4

THE VALUATION PROCESS

$\mathcal{T}$he concepts that are fundamental to appraisal thought serve as the basis for all the actions appraisers perform in addressing their clients' needs. These actions constitute *the valuation process, a systematic procedure employed to provide the answer to a client's question about real property value.* The valuation process is both a model and a mirror of appraisal activity and, as such, it reflects many attitudes, beliefs, techniques, and methods that relate to questions of value.

The theory of valuation, as distinct from the theory of value, began to take form in the late nineteenth century. Alfred Marshall (1842-1924), the British economist who formulated the neoclassical theory of value as a synthesis of earlier theories, anticipated and developed many of the concepts employed in contemporary appraisal practice. These concepts include the determination of site value through capitalization of income, the impact of depreciation on buildings and land, and the influence of different building types and land uses on site value.

Alfred Marshall
(HISTORICAL PICTURES/
STOCK MONTAGE)

Marshall is also credited with identifying the three traditional approaches to value: market (sales) comparison, replacement cost, and capitalization of income. Irving Fisher (1867-1947), an influential American economist associated with the neoclassical school, fully developed the income theory of value, which is the basis for the income capitalization approach used by modern appraisers.[1]

MODERN APPRAISAL THEORY

The writings of Marshall, Fisher, and other economists of the late nineteenth and early twentieth centuries were read by scholars and business professionals interested in economic thought. At the same time, the field of real estate appraisal was emerging and a few practitioners were gaining experience estimating market value

---

1. Paul F. Wendt, *Real Estate Appraisal: Review and Outlook* (Athens: University of Georgia Press, 1974), 18-19.

and other kinds of value for properties of various types. In the 1920s and 1930s, several events helped to establish appraisal as a young, but viable, real estate function.

One motivating force was the introduction of land economics as an academic discipline. Land economics developed from the interrelationship of several disciplines and attracted scholars and students who contributed significantly to real estate and appraisal literature over the next 40 years. This influential group included Richard T. Ely (1854-1943), the founder of land economics as an academic subject, Frederick Morrison Babcock (b. 1898), Ernest McKinley Fisher (1893-1981), and Arthur J. Mertzke (1890-1970). Each of these men participated in research and publication programs that advanced real estate education.

Ely, Babcock, and Fisher contributed to the Land Economics Series published by the National Association of Real Estate Boards, the predecessor of the National Association of Realtors®. The Land Economics Series was the first major publication effort designed to provide real estate professionals with current technical information. The first texts in this series were Fisher's *Principles of Real Estate* (1923), Ely and Moorehouse's *Elements of Land Economics* (1924), and Babcock's *The Appraisal of Real Estate* (1924).[2]

Another significant event in appraisal history was the publication of *Real Estate Appraising* by Arthur J. Mertzke in 1927. In this book Mertzke used Alfred Marshall's ideas to produce a tangible link between value theory and valuation theory. In the words of one scholar, "Mertzke translated the economic theory of the equivalence between long-run costs, normal value, and capitalized-income values (under specifically assumed conditions of perfect competition and economic equilibrium) into a working appraisal theory."[3]

Mertzke helped establish a clear emphasis on the three approaches to value and explained the use of capitalization rates as indexes of security.

The preeminence of the three approaches to value in the appraisal process was underscored in publications by K. Lee Hyder (1888-1947), Harry Grant Atkinson (1890-1979), and George L. Schmutz (1893-1958).[4] Each of these works set forth systematic procedures for applying the sales comparison, cost, and income capitalization approaches under appropriate conditions to answer clients' questions about value. Schmutz presented this process in diagram form, suggesting a model in which appraisal activity leads to a conclusion of value. Later, this model was incorporated into *The Appraisal of Real Estate*, first published by the American Institute of Real Estate Appraisers in 1951.

In the years following these early works, appraisal theory continued to evolve. Today education requirements have become stringent and appraisers make use of many analytical methods and techniques. Applying these methods and techniques to an expanding database presents new challenges and raises questions as to how applicable the valuation model is to actual appraisal assignments, how well it

---

2. See A. M. Weimer, "A Note on the Early History of Land Economics," *AREUEA Journal* (Fall 1984) and Pearl Janet Davies, *Real Estate in American History* (Washington, D.C.: Public Affairs Press, 1958), 126, 154, 161.
3. Wendt, 218.
4. K. Lee Hyder, "The Appraisal Process," *The Appraisal Journal* (January 1936); Harry Grant Atkinson, "The Process of Appraising Single-Family Homes," *The Appraisal Journal* (April 1936); and George L. Schmutz, *The Appraisal Process* (North Hollywood, Calif.: the author, 1941).

analyzes the forces that affect value, and how accurately it interprets the actions and motivations of market participants.

THE VALUATION PROCESS

The valuation process begins when an appraiser identifies the appraisal problem and ends when he or she reports a conclusion to the client.

Each real property is unique and many different types of value can be estimated for a single property. The most common appraisal assignment is performed to estimate market value; the valuation process contains all the steps appropriate to this type of assignment. The model also provides the framework for estimating any other defined value. Furthermore, evaluation assignments often call for value estimates which are derived through application of the valuation process.

The valuation process is accomplished through specific steps; the number of steps followed depends on the nature of the appraisal assignment and the data available. The model indicates a pattern that can be used in any appraisal assignment to perform market research and data analysis, to apply appraisal techniques, and to integrate the results of these activities into an estimate of defined value.

Research begins after the appraisal problem has been defined. The analysis of data relevant to the problem starts with an investigation of trends observed at all market levels—international, national, regional, community, and neighborhood. This examination will help the appraiser understand the interrelationships among the principles, forces, and factors that affect real property value in the specific area. It also provides raw data from which to extract quantitative information and other evidence of market trends such as positive or negative percentage changes in property value over a number of years, the population movement into an area, and the number of employment opportunities available and their effect on the purchasing power of potential property users. These data can be analyzed and employed to estimate a defined value.

Traditionally, appraisal techniques are the specific procedures within the three approaches that are applied to derive indications of real property value. Other procedures such as the use of inferential statistics and economic models also contribute to appraisals. One or more approaches to value may be used depending on their applicability to the particular appraisal assignment.

In assignments to estimate market value, the ultimate goal of the valuation process is a well-supported value conclusion that reflects all the factors that influence the market value of the property being appraised. To achieve this goal, an appraiser studies a property from three different viewpoints, which correspond to the three traditional approaches to value.

1. The current cost of reproducing or replacing the improvements, minus the loss in value from depreciation, plus site value—the cost approach
2. The value indicated by recent sales of comparable properties in the market—the sales comparison approach
3. The value of a property's earning power based on the capitalization of its income—the income capitalization approach

The three approaches are interrelated; each requires the gathering and analysis of cost, sales, and income data that pertain to the property being appraised. Each approach is outlined briefly in this chapter and discussed in detail in the subsequent chapters.

From the approaches applied, the appraiser derives separate indications of value for the property being appraised. One or more of the approaches may not be applicable to a specific assignment or may be less reliable due to the nature of the property, the needs of the client, or the data available.

To complete the valuation process, the appraiser integrates the information drawn from market research and data analysis and from the application of approaches to form a value conclusion. This conclusion may be presented as a single point estimate of value or as a range within which the value may fall. An effective integration of all the elements in the process depends on the appraiser's skill, experience, and judgment.

The valuation process is depicted in Figure 4.1.

DEFINITION OF THE APPRAISAL PROBLEM

The first step in the valuation process is development of a clear statement of the appraisal problem. This sets the limits of the appraisal and eliminates any ambiguity about the nature of the assignment. The statement of the problem should include:

- Identification of the real estate
- Identification of the property rights to be valued
- Use of the appraisal
- Definition of value
- Date of the value estimate
- Description of the scope of the appraisal
- Other limiting conditions

Identification of the Real Estate

A property is first identified by a street address, a location, or some other descriptive data that enable it to be located. A complete legal description specifying the exact location and boundaries of the property is provided later. Examples of property identification follow.

Reference:	The Kennedy Building, commercial offices
Street address:	2600 South Zephyr Denver, Colorado
Legal Description:	Lots 7–10, inclusive, Block 3 of Sterns Addition, Fifth Filing, City and County of Denver, Colorado

If the property is identified with a legal description, the description should be accurate. Legal descriptions of real estate are usually derived from land surveys and preserved in public records in accordance with local or state law. Appraisers should be familiar with the specific system or systems used to describe land in

Figure 4.1 The Valuation Process

Definition of the Problem

Identification of real estate	Identification of property rights to be valued	Use of appraisal	Definition of value	Date of value estimate	Description of scope of appraisal	Other limiting conditions

Preliminary Analysis and Data Selection and Collection

General (Region, city and neighborhood)	**Specific** (Subject and comparables)	**Competitive Supply and Demand** (The subject market)
Social Economic Governmental Environmental	Site and improvements Cost and depreciation Income/expense and capitalization rate History of ownership and use of property	Inventory of competitive properties Sales and listings Vacancies and offerings Absorption rates Demand studies

Highest and Best Use Analysis

Land as though vacant
Property as improved

Specified in terms of
use, time, and market participants

Land Value Estimate

Application of the Three Approaches

Cost	Sales comparison	Income capitalization

Reconciliation of Value Indications and Final Value Estimate

Report of Defined Value

various areas and be sure that the legal description is reasonable. Systems of land description include the metes and bounds system, the rectangular or government survey system, and the lot and block system (or plat map system). (These systems are described in Chapter 9.)

Identification of the Property Rights to Be Valued

The valuation of real property includes both the physical real estate and the rights that one or more individuals or legal entities may hold or contemplate holding in the ownership or use of the land and improvements. An appraiser may estimate the value of a fee simple estate or of partial interests created by the severance or division of ownership rights. Special attention must be given to any limitations on ownership rights such as easements, encroachments, liens, or leases. Financing must also be considered because fee simple estates, leasehold estates, and leased fee estates can all be mortgaged. The specific rights to be valued and the probable or actual financing involved must be ascertained at the start of the assignment because the complexity of these rights and terms will determine the procedures, skills, and time required to complete the assignment.

The fee simple estate in property is often valued before partial interests are considered. However, the dollar value of the fee simple estate is not necessarily equal to the sum of the values of all partial interests; the value of a partial interest may differ from the value of its contribution to the whole. For instance, a 50% interest in a property in which the owner does not have majority control may have significantly less value than 50% of the fee simple value; this lower value could be a direct result of dividing the fee simple estate. To estimate the market value of a partial interest in real property, direct market evidence of market attitudes toward the particular aspects of that partial interest is usually sought.

Use of the Appraisal

The use of an appraisal is the manner in which a client employs the information contained in an appraisal report. The client may specify the use of the appraisal when requesting it; if not, the appraiser may have to solicit this information, guiding the client to ensure a clear understanding of the question. Because an appraisal provides the basis for a decision regarding real property, the nature of the decision affects the character of the assignment and the appraisal report. A value estimate may be needed to determine the:

- Price at which to buy or sell
- Amount of a loan
- Basis for taxation
- Terms of a lease
- Value of real property assets in financial statements
- Basis for just compensation in eminent domain proceedings

To avoid wasted effort, the appraiser and the client must reach a mutual understanding concerning the use and ownership of the appraisal report and its conclusions.

Definition of Value

The purpose of the valuation process is to estimate the value of a real property interest, so the specific type of value and the interests involved must be clearly identified. The statement of purpose in the final report of defined value specifies the stated reason for the valuation assignment, i.e., to estimate a defined value of a real property interest. Types of appraised value include market value, use value, going-concern value, investment value, assessed value, and insurable value.

A written statement of the defined value to be estimated must be included in every appraisal report. This precise statement establishes the question to be answered for the client, the appraiser, and all readers of the report. It explains the data selected for consideration and the methods employed to analyze the data, thus supporting the logic and validity of the final value estimate. The statement also specifies whether the value estimate is reported in terms of cash, terms equivalent to cash, or other precisely revealed terms.

Date of the Value Estimate

The date of a value estimate must be specified because the forces that influence real property value are constantly changing. Although conditions observed at the time of the appraisal may persist for a considerable time after that date, an estimate of value is considered valid only for the exact date specified. Market value is generally seen as a reflection of market participants' perceptions of future economic conditions, and these perceptions are based on market evidence at a specific point in time. Value influences reflect economic conditions at a particular time, and sudden changes in business and real estate markets can dramatically influence value.

Most appraisals call for current value estimates but, in some cases, a valuation as of a date in the past is required. Retrospective appraisals may be required for inheritance tax (date of death), insurance claims (date of casualty), income tax (date of acquisition), law suits (date of loss), and other purposes. It is sometimes necessary to estimate a property's value as of March 1, 1913, the date when the federal income tax system was established, to calculate the capital gain on a property owned since that date. In condemnation proceedings appraisers may estimate property value as of the date of filing the declaration or petition to condemn, the date of trial, or another date stipulated by the parties involved or by the court. Historical market data are often available, so market value can be estimated in retrospect.

Appraisals as of a future date, or prospective appraisals, may be required to estimate the value of property interests in proposed developments or value at the end of a cash flow projection. The anticipation of future benefits is involved whenever an appraiser estimates the present value of a projected income stream or reversion. Prospective value estimates for proposed developments are frequently required as of the time the development is to be completed and when the development is projected to achieve stabilized occupancy. Appraisers may be employed to derive opinions of prospective values, which owners, buyers, investors, and lenders can use to make real estate-related decisions.

Description of the Scope of the Appraisal

The scope of the appraisal refers to the extent of the process in which data are collected, confirmed, and reported. The scope is described to protect third parties whose reliance on an appraisal report may be affected by this information. An appraiser determines the extent of the work and of the report based on the significance of the appraisal problem. The appraiser is responsible for describing the scope of the appraisal in the report.

Other Limiting Conditions

The identification of the real estate and the property rights to be appraised, the date of the value estimate, the use of the appraisal, and the definition of value are limiting conditions that govern the appraisal. Typically other limiting conditions are also applicable. Statements of limiting conditions are included in a report for the appraiser's protection and to inform and protect the client and other users of the report. For example, an appraisal report may state that the valuation of sub-surface oil, gas, or mineral rights is not part of the appraisal. Another limiting condition might establish that the appraiser is not required to provide court or hearing testimony or to attend court proceedings unless arrangements are made a reasonable time in advance. Other limiting conditions might specify that no engineering survey was made or that, except as specifically stated, property data were taken from sources considered to be reliable. (For further examples, see the discussion of assumptions and limiting conditions in Chapter 24.)

PRELIMINARY ANALYSIS AND DATA SELECTION AND COLLECTION

After defining the problem, the appraiser is ready to perform a preliminary analysis to determine the character and scope of the assignment and the amount of work that will be required to gather the necessary data. The preliminary analysis and work plan depend on the assignment and the type of property being valued. For example, much more information will be required in the valuation of a large apartment building than in the valuation of a single-family residence.

To complete an assignment quickly and efficiently, each step in the valuation process must be planned and scheduled. Time and personnel requirements will vary with the amount and complexity of the work. Some assignments may be completed in a few days; for more complex appraisal problems, weeks or months may be spent gathering, analyzing, and applying all pertinent data.

Some assignments can be performed by a single appraiser; others may require the assistance of other staff members or appraisal specialists. Sometimes the assistance of specialists in other fields is needed. For example, in valuing a rural property the appraiser's findings may be augmented by the professional opinion of a soil engineer. Recognizing when work can or must be delegated improves efficiency and ensures accuracy.

A planned work schedule is helpful, particularly in performing large, complicated assignments. A clear and precise understanding of individual responsibilities can help expedite an assignment. Because the appraiser bears the ultimate responsibility for the work, he or she must see the assignment as a whole as well as a collection of numerous procedures and details. With a comprehensive view, the appraiser can recognize the type and volume of work to be done and schedule and delegate it properly.

The appraiser's work plan usually includes an outline of the proposed appraisal report. The major parts of the report are delineated and the data and procedures involved in each section are noted. By means of this outline, data can be assembled intelligently and the appropriate amount of time can be allocated to each step in the valuation process.

Three types of data are gathered for appraisals: general, specific, and competitive supply and demand data. General data consist of information about trends in the social, economic, governmental, and environmental forces that affect property value. *A trend is a series of related changes brought about by a chain of causes and effects.* Trends such as population shifts, declining office building occupancy rates, or increased housing starts in an area are identified by analyzing general data. General data can contribute significantly to an appraiser's understanding of the marketplace.

Specific data relate to the property being appraised and to comparable properties. These data include legal, physical, locational, cost, and income and expense information about the properties and the details of comparable sales. Financial arrangements that could affect selling prices are also considered. The history of ownership and use of the property should be searched to establish whether toxic waste or hazardous materials may be present on the property.

Competitive supply and demand data relate to the competitive position of the property in its future market. Supply data include inventories of existing and proposed competitive properties, vacancy rates, and absorption rates. Demand data include population, income, employment, and survey data pertaining to potential property users. From these data an estimate of future demand for the present use or prospective uses of the property is developed.

The amount and type of data collected for an appraisal depend on the approaches used to estimate value. These approaches, in turn, relate directly to the appraisal problem. In a given valuation assignment, more than one approach to value is usually appropriate and necessary to determine a value indication. However, the problem or problems to be addressed may require that one approach be given greater emphasis in making a final value estimate. In conducting a particular assignment, the appraiser's judgment and experience and the quantity and quality of data available for analysis may determine which approach or approaches are used.

Meaningful data are collected for a purpose. All value influences, pertinent facts, and conclusions about trends should be clearly indicated in the report and related specifically to the property being appraised. Because the data selected form the basis for the appraiser's judgments, a thorough explanation of the significance of the data reported ensures that the reader will understand these judgments.

HIGHEST AND BEST USE ANALYSIS

Analysis of the highest and best use of the land as though vacant and of the property as improved is essential in the valuation process. Through highest and best use analysis, the appraiser interprets the market forces that influence the subject property and identifies the use upon which the final value estimate is based. (Highest and best use analysis is discussed in detail in Chapter 12.)

Analyzing the highest and best use of the land as though vacant serves two functions. First, it helps the appraiser identify comparable properties. The property being appraised is always compared with similar properties that have been sold recently in the market. Each comparable property's highest and best use of the land as though vacant should be similar to that of the subject property. Potentially comparable properties that do not have similar highest and best uses are usually eliminated from further analysis.

The second reason to analyze the property's highest and best use as though vacant is to identify the use that would produce maximum income to the land after property income is allocated to the improvements. In the cost approach and some income capitalization techniques, a separate land value estimate is required. Estimating the land's highest and best use as though vacant is a necessary part of deriving a land value estimate.

There are also two reasons to analyze the highest and best use of the property as improved. The first is to help identify comparable properties. Each improved property should have the same or a similar highest and best use as the improved subject property.

The second reason to analyze the highest and best use of the property as improved is to decide whether the improvements should be demolished, renovated, or retained in their present condition. They should be retained as long as they have some value and the return from the property as improved exceeds the return that would be realized by a new use, after deducting the costs of demolishing the old improvement and constructing a new one. Identification of the existing property's most profitable use is crucial to this determination.

The highest and best use conclusion should specify the optimal use, the time or date that the property will be put to this use or achieve stabilized occupancy, and the market participants whose involvement in the property is a function of this use—e.g., an owner-user of the property, an equity investor in the property, or a debt investor in the property.

LAND VALUE ESTIMATE

Land value is directly related to highest and best use. The relationship between highest and best use and land value may indicate whether an existing use is the highest and best use of the land.

Land value may be a major component of total property value. Appraisers often estimate land value separately, even when valuing properties with extensive building improvements. Land value may change at a different rate than building value. Improvements are almost always subject to depreciation after the effects of inflation are removed. For many appraisals, a separate estimate of land value is required.

Although a total property value estimate may be derived in the sales comparison or income capitalization approaches without separating land and improvement values, it may be necessary to estimate land value separately to isolate the value the land contributes to the total property. In the cost approach the value of the land must be estimated and stated separately.

In the valuation process land value estimation is a separate step, which may be accomplished applying six different techniques. The most reliable way to estimate land value is by sales comparison. When few sales are available, however, or when the value indications produced through sales comparison need additional support, other procedures may be used to value land. Six procedures can be used to obtain land value indications—sales comparison, allocation, extraction, subdivision development, land residual technique, and ground rent capitalization.

1. *Sales comparison.* Sales of similar, vacant parcels are analyzed, compared, and adjusted to provide a value indication for the land being appraised.

2. *Allocation.* Sales of improved properties are analyzed and the prices paid are allocated between the land and the improvements. Allocation can be used in two ways: to establish a typical ratio of land value to total value, which may be applicable to the property being appraised, or to isolate the value contribution of either the land or the building from the sale for use in comparison analysis.

3. *Extraction.* Land value is estimated by subtracting the estimated value of the improvements from the known sale price of the property. This procedure is frequently used when the value of the improvements is relatively low or easily estimated.

4. *Subdivision development.* The total value of undeveloped land is estimated as if the land were subdivided, developed, and sold. Development costs, incentive costs, and carrying charges are subtracted from the estimated proceeds of sale, and the net income projection is discounted over the estimated period required for market absorption of the developed sites.

5. *Land residual technique.* The land is assumed to be improved to its highest and best use. All expenses of operation and the return attributable to the other agents of production are deducted, and the net income imputed to the land is capitalized to derive an estimate of land value. An alternative land residual technique is applied by valuing the land and improvements and deducting the cost of the improvements and any entrepreneurial profit. The remainder is the residual land value.

6. *Ground rent capitalization.* This procedure is used when land rents and capitalization rates are readily available such as in well-developed areas. Net ground rent, the net amount paid for the right to use and occupy the land, is estimated and divided by a land capitalization rate. Either actual or estimated rents can be capitalized using rates that can be supported in the market. This procedure may be seen as an extension of direct sales comparison but, where applicable, it provides a specific unit of comparison.

APPLICATION OF THE THREE APPROACHES

The valuation process is applied to develop a well-supported estimate of a defined value based on consideration of all pertinent general and specific data. Appraisers estimate property value with specific appraisal procedures which reflect three distinct methods of data analysis—cost, sales comparison, and income capitalization. One or more of these approaches are used in all estimations of value; the approaches employed depend on the type of property, the use of the appraisal, and the quality and quantity of data available for analysis.

All three approaches are applicable to many appraisal problems, but one or more of the approaches may have greater significance in a specific assignment. For example, the cost approach may be inappropriate in valuing properties with older improvements that suffer substantial accrued depreciation due to physical deterioration, functional obsolescence, and external obsolescence, which are difficult to estimate. The sales comparison approach cannot be applied to very specialized properties such as garbage disposal plants because comparable data may not be available. The income capitalization approach is rarely used to value owner-occupied residential interests, although it may be used with market support. Income capitalization can be particularly unreliable in the market for commercial or industrial property where owner-occupants outbid investors. Wherever possible, appraisers should apply at least two approaches. The alternative value indications derived can serve as useful checks on one another.

Cost Approach

The cost approach is based on the understanding that market participants relate value to cost. In the cost approach the value of a property is derived by adding the estimated value of the land to the current cost of constructing a reproduction or replacement for the improvements and then subtracting the amount of depreciation (i.e., deterioration and obsolescence) in the structures from all causes. Profit for coordination by the entrepreneur is included in the value indication. This approach is particularly useful in valuing new or nearly new improvements and properties that are not frequently exchanged in the market. Cost approach techniques can also be employed to derive information needed in the sales comparison and income capitalization approaches to value.

The current costs to construct the improvements can be obtained from cost estimators, cost estimating publications, builders, and contractors. Depreciation is measured through market research and the application of specific valuation procedures. Land value is estimated separately in the cost approach.

Sales Comparison Approach

The sales comparison approach is most useful when a number of similar properties have recently been sold or are currently for sale in the subject property market. Using this approach, an appraiser produces a value indication by comparing a subject property with similar properties, called *comparable sales.* The sale prices of the properties that are judged to be most comparable tend to indicate a range in which the value indication for the subject property will fall.

An appraiser estimates the degree of similarity or difference between the subject property and the comparable sales by considering various elements of comparison.

- Real property rights conveyed
- Financing terms
- Conditions of sale
- Market conditions
- Location
- Physical characteristics
- Economic characteristics
- Use
- Nonrealty components of value

Dollar or percentage adjustments are then applied to the sale price of each comparable property with consideration for the real property interest involved. Adjustments are made to the sale prices of the comparables because the prices of these properties are known, while the value of the subject property is not. Through this comparative procedure, the appraiser estimates the value defined in the problem identification as of a specific date.

Data such as income multipliers and income rates may also be extracted through sales comparison analysis. In the sales comparison approach, appraisers consider these data, but do not regard them as elements of comparison. These data are applied in the income capitalization approach.

Income Capitalization Approach

In the income capitalization approach, the present value of the future benefits of property ownership is measured. A property's income streams and its resale value upon reversion may be capitalized into a present, lump-sum value. Two basic formulas are used in this approach.

$$\frac{\text{Income}}{\text{Rate}} = \text{Value}$$

$$\text{Income} \times \text{Factor} = \text{Value}$$

where

$$\text{Factor} = \frac{1}{\text{Rate}}$$

Like the cost and sales comparison approaches, the income capitalization approach requires extensive market research. Research and data analysis for this approach are conducted against a background of supply and demand relationships, which provide information about trends and market anticipation.

An investor in an apartment building, for example, anticipates an acceptable return *on* the investment as well as a return *of* the invested funds. The level of return needed to attract investment capital is a function of the risk inherent in the property. Moreover, the level of return required by investors fluctuates with changes in money markets and the returns offered by alternative investments. Appraisers must be alert to the changes in investor requirements indicated by the current market for comparable investment properties and by changes in the more volatile money markets which may suggest future trends.

The specific data that an appraiser investigates for this approach might include the property's gross income expectancy, the expected reduction in gross income caused by vacancy and collection loss, the anticipated annual operating expenses, the pattern and duration of the property's income stream, and the anticipated resale value or the value of other real property interest reversions. After income and expenses are estimated, the income stream or streams are capitalized by applying an appropriate rate or factor, or converted into present value through discounting. In discounted cash flow analysis, the quantity, variability, timing, and duration of a set of periodic incomes and the quantity and timing of the reversion are specified and discounted to a present value at a specified yield rate. The rates used for capitalization or discounting are derived from acceptable rates of return for similar properties.

RECONCILIATION OF VALUE INDICATIONS

The final analytical step in the valuation process is the reconciliation of the value indications into a single dollar figure or a range into which the value will most likely fall. The nature of reconciliation depends on the appraisal problem, the approaches that have been used, and the reliability of the value indications derived.

When all three approaches have been used, the appraiser examines the three, separate indications. The relative dependability and applicability of each approach are considered in reconciling the value indications into a final estimate of defined value. In the reconciliation section of the report, the appraiser can explain variations among the indications derived with the different approaches and account for any inconsistencies between the value conclusions and methods with which they were derived.

REPORT OF DEFINED VALUE

The final estimate of defined value, which is the goal of the valuation process, may be reported as a single figure or as a range of values. The assignment is not complete until the conclusion is stated in a report and presented to the client. A narrative appraisal report includes all the data considered and analyzed, the methods applied, and the reasoning that led to the final value estimate. A concise valuation analysis allows the reader to understand the problem and the factual data presented and to follow the reasoning behind the appraiser's conclusion of value.

The value estimate is the appraiser's opinion and reflects the experience and judgment that he or she applied to the study of the assembled data. The appraisal report is the tangible expression of the appraiser's work. In preparing a narrative report, the appraiser should pay particular attention to writing style, organization, presentation, and overall appearance. The conclusions of an appraisal may also be communicated to the client in an oral report, a letter report, or a form report. Chapter 24 describes the requirements that apply to appraisal reports and the circumstances under which they are submitted.

SUMMARY

The *valuation process* is a systematic procedure employed to provide the answer to a client's question about real property value. It is a model of appraisal activity, reflecting an understanding of value and the methods used in value estimation.

The theory of valuation took form in the late nineteenth century. Alfred Marshall identified the three approaches to value used by contemporary appraisers, and Irving Fisher formulated the theory on which the income capitalization approach is based. Throughout the twentieth century, appraisal theory has continued to evolve and adapt to the needs of market participants.

The first step in the valuation process is the *definition of the appraisal problem*, which includes identification of the real estate and property rights to be valued, specification of the use of the appraisal, definition of the value sought, specification of the date of the value estimate, description of the scope of the appraisal, and identification of other limiting conditions.

Property identification can be accomplished with a street address, a location, or a legal description. The *property rights* are identified by the form of ownership (individual, partnership, or corporation) limitations on ownership rights such as easements , the financial interests (mortgage or equity), and the legal estate (fee simple, leased fee, or leasehold).

The *use of the appraisal* is decided by the client and affects the character of the assignment. An appraisal may be used to estimate a price at which to buy or sell, to set the amount of a loan, to prepare tax returns, to fix rent, to estimate real property assets for financial statements, or to determine just compensation in eminent domain proceedings.

The *definition of value* in most appraisals is market value, but use value, going-concern value, investment value, assessed value, or insurable value may also be sought.

Specifying the date of the *value estimate* indicates the point in time when the value estimate is relevant. The value estimated may be a current value, a prospective value, or an historical value estimated for inheritance tax, income tax, insurance claims, law suits, or capital gains.

The *scope of the appraisal*, or the extent of the process in which data are collected, confirmed and reported, depends on the significance of the appraisal problem. A statement of *other limiting conditions* identifies specific qualifications of the appraisal that were not cited previously.

Once the appraisal problem is defined, other steps in the valuation process may be carried out. The *preliminary analysis* is an overview of the character and scope of the assignment. In the *selection and collection of data*, the appraiser gathers general data on value influences and *trends*; specific data pertaining to the property's financing, cost, income and expenses, and legal, physical, and locational features; and competitive supply and demand data that describe the position of the property in its future market.

Highest and best use analysis of the *land as though vacant* helps the appraiser identify comparable properties and derive an estimate of land value. Highest and best use analysis of the *property as improved* is used to identify comparable properties and to determine whether the existing improvements should be retained, renovated, or demolished.

A *land value estimate* is required when the land's contribution to total property value is sought or when improvements are valued separately, as they are in the cost approach. There are six procedures for estimating land value: sales comparison, allocation, extraction, subdivision development, the land residual technique, and ground rent capitalization.

Three approaches can be applied to the analysis of data to derive a well-supported value conclusion. Although the approaches are interrelated, the property type and use will determine which approach or approaches are most appropriate.

The *cost approach* is effective in valuing new improvements and properties that are not frequently exchanged in the market. In this approach a separate land value estimate is added to an estimate of the current cost to construct a reproduction or replacement of the improvements. Entrepreneurial profit is also added. From this total, estimated depreciation and obsolescence from all causes is subtracted.

The *sales comparison approach* is useful when data concerning recently sold or currently offered properties similar to the subject property are available. These comparable data are adjusted to reflect the differences between the comparable properties and the subject property.

The *income capitalization approach* is used to appraise income-producing properties. The present value of the future benefits of property ownership is measured, and the property's anticipated income stream and resale value, or reversion, are capitalized into a present value. There are two basic capitalization formulas: *income/rate = value* and *income × factor = value* (where factor = 1/rate). In discounted cash flow analysis, periodic income and the reversion may also be converted into present value by application of a specified discount rate.

Reconciliation of the value indications derived from the approaches used may provide a single value indication or a range of most probable values. In this process the reliability of the value indications and the applicability of the approaches are explained. Reconciliation also provides an opportunity to resolve variations and inconsistencies among the value indications and the methods with which they were derived.

The *report of defined value* provides the client with a summary of the data analyzed, the methods used, and the reasoning that led to the value estimate. The appraisal report should be carefully written, well organized, and clearly presented.

Chapter 5

MONEY MARKETS AND CAPITAL MARKETS

$\mathcal{M}$oney is the medium of exchange commonly employed in selling and purchasing goods and services. The parties to a business transaction agree on the value of the good or service and this value is expressed in terms of money. Each nation has a monetary system with hard currency of gold, silver, or copper, paper currency, or a combination of the two. The relative values of national currencies are established through trading and international banking agreements. In fact, prevailing free trade practices and instantaneous wire fund transfers have made the exchange of currencies a global market operation influencing worldwide monetary conditions. Real estate is priced in terms of money and real estate investments are money, so the value of money influences real estate prices. Therefore, it is imperative that appraisers understand domestic and global monetary trends.

The term *money* is difficult to define and various definitions are used by economists. Some believe that money is "currency in the hands of the public plus demand deposits at commercial banks." *Demand deposits* are funds that can be withdrawn at any time such as money in checking accounts. Others say that money is "currency plus demand and time deposits at commercial banks." *Time deposits* are funds that can be withdrawn only after proper notification such as money in certificates of deposit. Money has also been defined as "currency plus demand and time deposits plus the liabilities of nonbank financial intermediaries."[1] Economists such as Samuelson and Nordhaus as well as Federal Reserve statisticians disaggregate the money supply further into five components."[2]

Most of the money in circulation is in checking accounts. Whether the money supply is defined in terms of currency, account balances, or both, its value is influenced by its availability. The value of money is a global, rather than simply domestic, consideration. Important relationships are well established, but subject to variable exchange ratios between national currencies and the rapid movement of free-flowing funds.

MONEY SUPPLY AND DEMAND

Supply and demand relationships set the cost, or price, of money. When money becomes plentiful, the price declines; as it becomes scarce, the price rises. The price of money is expressed as an interest rate—i.e., the cost to borrow funds. Interest rates are particularly important in the real estate industry because most investments are created by combining debt and equity funds. When the demand

---

1. Howard R. Vane and John L. Thompson, *Monetarism—Theory, Evidence and Policy* (New York: Halsted Press, 1979), 49.
2. *Transaction money* (M_1) consists of money used to buy and sell things. It includes money in circulation—i.e., coins and paper currency (fiat money), demand deposits, and interest-paying checking accounts. *Broad money* (M_2), which is also called *asset money* or *near-money*, includes M_1 plus savings accounts, small deposits of less than $100,000 (e.g., money market accounts), and overnight repurchase agreements and Eurodollars. *Additional near-monies* (M_3) consist of M_2 plus savings accounts or institutional time deposits of more than $100,000 (money market funds), term repurchase agreements, and term Eurodollars.

Two *money-type assets* which may be added to M_3 are *liquid assets* (L), which include M_3 plus short-term U.S. Treasury securities, savings bonds, bankers' acceptances, and commercial paper and *total credit* (D), which includes L plus all debt of the domestic, nonfinancial sectors (e.g., mortgages, bonds, and similar instuments). See Paul A. Samuelson and William D. Nordhaus, *Economics*, 13th ed. (New York: McGraw-Hill, 1989), 227-230 and *Statistical Abstract of the United States, 1990,* U.S. Department of Commerce, Bureau of the Census, Washington, D.C.: U.S. Government Printing Office, Table No. 832, "Money Stock and Liquid Assets."

for money is high and its supply is low, capital costs, or interest rates, increase. These higher interest rates affect real property values.

There is a difference between money and other commodities on the supply side of the pricing formula. The demand for money is a product of the operation of economic forces. The supply of money available for lending is a function of the level of savings, which reflect personal, corporate, and governmental accumulation, both domestic and foreign.

Economics determines the amount of savings, but the quantity of U.S. currency is subject to regulation by the Federal Reserve (the Fed). The Fed has the power to regulate general interest rate levels, which strongly influence the discount rates and overall capitalization rates used in real estate valuation. In foreign countries, various central banks perform the same functions as the Fed, and they generally have the same powers. Because monetary operations are global, the availability of funds must be considered on a worldwide basis. This has been especially true in recent years as the United States has become a net importer of capital, which has to be sought on terms and conditions established not by the Fed, but by international trading and exchange rates.

Trading Money Instruments

A money market represents the interaction of buyers and sellers who trade short-term money instruments. Short-term money instruments with maturities of less than one year include federal funds, Treasury bills, Treasury notes, and other government securities; repurchase agreements and reverse repurchase agreements; certificates of deposit; commercial paper; bankers' acceptances; municipal notes; and Eurodollars. Although it is called a "market," the money market is not formally organized like the New York Stock Exchange. Rather, it is an over-the-counter operation which employs sophisticated communications and computer systems to provide traders with accurate, readily available information on national and international transactions. Because the Federal Reserve regulates the money supply, it influences daily trading activity in the money market and the cost (i.e., interest rates) of money market funds. The money market, in turn, greatly affects the real estate industry because its short-term financing vehicles are needed to fund real estate construction and development. This is one of many ways in which the availability and cost of money regulates the volume and pace of the real estate industry.

A capital market reflects the interaction of buyers and sellers trading long- or intermediate-term money instruments. Long- and intermediate-term instruments usually mature in more than one year and include bonds or debentures, stocks, mortgages, and deeds of trust. Although stocks are capital market items, they are equity investments with no fixed maturities. The distinction between money markets and capital markets is not sharply defined because both involve trading in funds for varying terms and both are sources of capital for all economic activities, including real estate.

In money markets and capital markets, there are observable relationships between various instruments that stem from differing interest rates, maturities, and investment risks. Normally an individual who invests in a long-term instrument is believed to assume greater risk than one who invests in a short-term instrument. Therefore, the long-term investor is compensated with higher yields. In other words, long-term instruments usually offer higher yields than short-term instru-

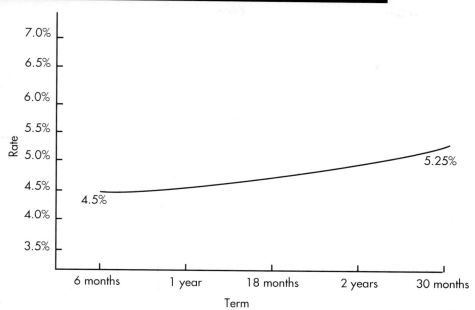

Figure 5.1 Normal Yield Curve: Low Inflation Period—Certificates of Deposit

ments. This situation is graphically portrayed in what has come to be known as the normal yield curve. (See Figure 5.1.)

The relationship can be reversed. In periods of high inflation, investors are reluctant to take long-term positions. They fear that escalating interest rates will

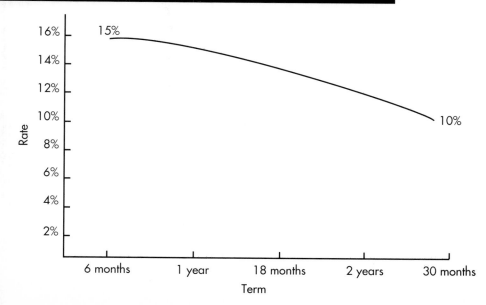

Figure 5.2 Inverse Yield Curve: High Inflation Period—Certificates of Deposit

erode their capital, so they try to keep their money in short-term instruments. The Federal Reserve, however, wants to combat inflation, so it causes interest rates to rise. This action is intended to be temporary, lasting just long enough to dampen investors' inflationary expectations. Consequently, in inflationary times short-term yields may be greater than long-term yields, and the yield curve is said to be inverse. (See Figure 5.2.)

Fractional Reserve Banking

When a commercial bank makes a loan to a business or an individual, it credits the checking account of that business or person with the amount loaned. In a sense banks manufacture money through this loan process because they create money by monetizing debt. Commercial banks effectively fund a large volume of loans by entering the money market. They raise the required cash by selling their paper— e.g., certificates of deposit—to a broad group of investors. Of course, the money-creating activities of banks are restricted because the Federal Reserve requires that they maintain reserves equal to specified percentages of their deposits. If a bank has a 20% reserve requirement, each dollar of its reserves can support four dollars of deposits, which can be created by extending four dollars in loans and crediting them to the borrowers' accounts. This arrangement is called *fractional reserve banking* and it is used by central banking systems throughout the world.

FEDERAL RESERVE SYSTEM

In 1913 the U.S. Congress passed the Federal Reserve Act which created the Federal Reserve System, a central bank to manage money and credit and promote orderly growth of the economy. The framers of the act studied central banking in other countries and attempted to create a balanced banking system that was neither politically nor privately controlled. The Federal Reserve System is independent of Congress and the president; this independence distinguishes it from central banks in most other countries, which are government entities. Although the Fed is independent, it functions within the general structure of the U.S. government. Thus, the system operates in accordance with national economic policies, but has the power to exercise independent judgment.

The Fed is composed of 12 regional banks, which serve the 12 Federal Reserve regional districts, and a number of member banks, which include all nationally chartered commercial banks and many state-chartered banks. (See Figure 5.3.) The Fed is directed by a seven-member board of governors, who are appointed by the president and confirmed by the U.S. Senate for 14-year terms. Members of the Federal Reserve Board cannot be dismissed during their term of service. The geographic distribution and occupations of board members are considered in their selection. Only one member from each region can serve at a time, so the regions have equal representation on the board. To avoid conflicts of interest, bank officers, directors, and stockholders cannot serve on the Federal Reserve Board.

Credit Regulation

Reserve requirements, discount rates, and the Federal Open Market Committee are the three principal credit-regulation devices that the Fed uses to accomplish the

Figure 5.3 Federal Reserve System

Federal Open Market Committee 7 governors, 5 federal reserve bank presidents	**Board of Governors** 7 governors appointed by the President and confirmed by the Senate	**Federal Advisory Council** 12 members, 1 from each federal reserve bank

12 Federal Reserve Banks
9 directors on each board: member banks elect 6 (3 from banking and 3 from commerce agriculture, or industry) and Board of Governors appoints 3

6,200 Member Banks
(represents 85% of U.S. banking activity)

duties assigned to it by Congress. These duties include promoting the orderly growth of the U.S. economy and acting as a lender of last resort. In periods of economic crisis, the Fed supplies financial markets with necessary liquidity. For example, when the stock market crashed in October of 1987, the central bank immediately announced that, as a lender of last resort, it would supply necessary funds. The Federal Reserve regulates money and credit, which are the lifeblood of the real estate industry. Therefore, appraisers should be familiar with the Fed's day-to-day activities as they affect the supply of money and interest rates. Because of the global nature of financial markets, the prevalence of instantaneous communications, and the securitization of realty interests, the monetary activities of the central bank can have an immediate impact on real estate markets.

Reserve Requirements

Within statutory limits, the Federal Reserve Board can fix the amount of reserves that member banks must maintain. One requirement of membership in the system is that member banks cannot make all their deposit liabilities available for business loans; they must agree to keep part frozen in reserve accounts at Federal Reserve banks. The Federal Reserve changes the amount of its reserve requirements from time to time and these changes expand or contract the volume of money and credit available within the banking system. If the Fed wants to restrict the money supply, it increases deposit reserve obligations; if it wants to increase the supply, it lowers the obligations. In recent years, demand deposits (i.e., checking accounts) have been subject to a reserve requirement of approximately 12%, and time funds (i.e., savings accounts) have been subject to a reserve requirement between 3% and 8%.

Federal Discount Rate

The discount rate is another major, credit-regulation tool. Banks in the Federal Reserve System can borrow from the Fed and obtain funds for their customers even in periods of great demand. To get these loans, member banks agree to pay the Federal Reserve interest at its established discount rate. The borrowing privilege of member banks is not unrestricted, however. The Fed denies loan requests when it believes that borrowing is not in the best interests of the national or regional economy. When credit is refused, it is said that "the discount window is closed."

The borrowing privilege is a vehicle for expanding the monetary supply; its curtailment limits or contracts credit. When the discount rate is low, banks are encouraged to borrow and the amount of money available to the economy expands. When the discount rate is high, member banks are reluctant to borrow and credit is generally restricted. Thus, the federal discount rate helps determine *the prime rate, the interest rate that a commercial bank charges for short-term loans to borrowers with high credit ratings.* The federal discount rate is generally about two percentage points below the prime rate.

Federal Open Market Committee

The Fed's third credit-regulation tool is the Federal Open Market Committee (FOMC). The FOMC is probably the most extensively used and most potent of the Federal Reserve's credit-regulating devices. The committee is composed of the Federal Reserve Board of Governors, the president of the New York Federal Reserve Bank, and four district reserve bank presidents who serve for one-year terms on a rotating basis. The FOMC buys and sells U.S. government securities in the open market, thereby exerting a powerful influence on the supply of money and the interest rate. In fact, through its daily operations, the FOMC maintains short-term money rates at selected target levels. When the committee buys securities, money is infused into the banking system in an amount that can equal five to eight times the purchase amount.

The FOMC buys securities from bond dealers with Federal Reserve checks, which the dealers deposit in their accounts in the commercial banking system. These payments increase balances in member banks' reserve accounts, often creating free reserves which permit greater loan activity at these banks. In turn, the money supply is increased by expanding checking account balances. Fractional reserve requirements determine the monetary leverage obtained by banks when the Federal Open Market Committee buys securities. If, for example, banks have a reserve requirement of 12% on demand deposits, the amount of money infused into the economy when the FOMC purchases securities may be 8.33 times (100/12) the amount to be kept on deposit. Thus, by purchasing securities the FOMC stimulates economic growth and expansion. When the FOMC sells securities, it causes funds to be removed from member banks' reserve accounts, which reduces the supply of money and credit. Thus, economic growth is discouraged.

Usually, the FOMC meets once a month to set monetary policy strategies. The minutes of these meetings are kept secret for 30 days and then published. Before the minutes become public, money dealers watch the actions of the committee to infer its current policy. Financial market participants may be guided by the opinions of experts, called Fed *watchers*, who often correctly interpret and predict Fed policy by analyzing the committee's activities. Real estate investors and appraisers, whose success may depend on interpreting and forecasting financial markets, may profit from the extensive information provided by Fed watchers.

FISCAL POLICY

While the Fed determines monetary policy, the Department of the Treasury manages the government's financial activities. The Congress and the President shape fiscal policy through decisions involving the federal budget, expenditures, and revenues. The Treasury Department implements these policy directives. Essentially, the U.S. Treasury raises funds and pays bills. It is authorized to generate currency, collect taxes, and borrow money. Expenditures for national projects and activities are made pursuant to congressional appropriations.

When income matches or exceeds spending, the federal budget is balanced. When the outflow of funds exceeds collections, a federal deficit results. Spending that is not covered by tax funds produces deficits, which are financed by the sale of public debt instruments such as government bonds, bills, and notes issued by the Treasury. When deficits are monetized by selling large amounts of debt, the Fed is tacitly expected, though not mandated, to cooperate by supplying the banking system with sufficient reserves to accommodate the debt sales program and still leave enough credit for the private sector.

In theory expenditures should expand the economy, increasing government tax collections and eventually producing an operating surplus that will reduce government debt. In practice, however, spending has grown much faster than revenues. In the late 1970s and early 1980s, government deficits materially contributed to severe inflation. Throughout this time, the Fed supplied whatever money was needed to fund the federal deficit. Financial dealings are based on forecasts of the future, and perceptions are often more consequential than realities. Thus, financial institutions became concerned that excessive borrowing by the Treasury might use up credit supplies, short-changing private sector needs and crowding out smaller borrowers. These economic developments were damaging to the real estate industry, which was threatened by the loss of long-term mortgage capital due to the volatility of money markets and capital markets.

Inflation slowed and the economy recovered in the mid-1980s, which helped to stabilize the real estate industry, but the federal deficit continues to grow. Large amounts of this debt are monetized by foreign investment, which can be expected to continue, if interest rates remain high enough to ensure profitability in light of the devaluation of the dollar. The consensus in financial circles is that the growth of the federal deficit may produce a resurgence of inflation.

In 1989 and 1990 a long-running conflict between the fiscal policy of the Treasury Department and the monetary policy of the Fed came to a head. Controversy arose over the exchange value of the U.S. dollar with respect to foreign currencies, particularly the Japanese yen and German mark. In the years following 1985, the United States consistently ran trade deficits, importing more goods and services from foreign countries than it exported. At the same time, the size of the budget deficit was growing astronomically, and the United States found it necessary to borrow foreign funds, becoming a net importer of capital. The trade deficit added to the existing strain on U.S. finances.

The Treasury Department concluded that a cheaper dollar would be a remedy for the trade deficit making U.S. goods and services more price-competitive in world markets. Such a policy was expected to stimulate exports in the manufacturing sector. To lower the value of the dollar, the Treasury Department conducted a two-pronged campaign: "jawboning," or talking down the dollar's value, and directing the Fed to conduct large-scale sales of dollars in world money markets. This strategy met with appreciable success. However, the Fed voiced opposition to the policy, contending that it was inflationary. Cheaper dollars did not discourage imports, but made them more expensive, triggering price escalations. The Fed viewed any cheapening of our currency as inflationary and was obliged to oppose it. The tug-of-war between the two positions has continued. Much of the debate has taken place behind the scenes and off the record, but each side has had occasion to defend its policy with unusual candor.

MONEY MARKET INSTRUMENTS

The prices of financial instruments, which are established in a free and active money market, determine their investment yields. These yields consist of the instruments' face, or stated, interest rates plus any price discounts earned, or minus any price premiums paid. The price of money is properly called an *interest rate* because when a borrowing instrument is created, it carries that day's market interest level for the maturity involved.

If a six-month-term instrument is sold when it is three months old, and prevailing interest rates are higher than when the instrument was created, the buyer will not be satisfied with the face, or coupon, rate. To make a deal, the seller will have to discount the paper; the investment yield to the buyer will then be the face rate plus amortization of the discount. If lower interest rates prevail at the time of sale, the buyer cannot purchase at the coupon rate, because the seller will demand a premium. The yield to the buyer will then be the face rate minus amortization of the premium paid. These conditions are reflected in the real estate market where buyers price property to provide good prospects for what they believe will be competitively attractive yields on the equity invested.

Money markets, which deal in instruments with maturities of one year or less, are especially important to real estate development activities. Construction loans are short-term mortgages with variable interest rates that are tied to market indexes. For example, borrowing costs in the market might be two to four percentage points above the floating *prime rate*, which is the short-term loan rate that commercial banks offer to favored customers. It is not unusual for building loan rates to be adjusted monthly with a floor, or minimum, rate, but no cap, or upper limit. When the demand for short-term money is intense and supply is limited, market interest rates escalate and construction funds become extremely expensive. The high real estate project costs that result can destroy economic feasibility and cause project failures and bankruptcies.

The anticipated cost and availability of short-term funds is a key consideration for developers, and their perceptions cause real estate activity to expand or contract. Appraisers must factor projected construction loan costs, which constitute a large portion of so-called *soft costs*, into their cost approach valuations. This is particularly important when appraising projects that will require more than one year to complete.

In money markets, various instruments and arrangements are offered and sold by the federal government, banks, corporations, and local governments. Important instruments include federal funds, Treasury bills, Treasury notes, other government securities, repurchase and reverse repurchase agreements, certificates of deposit, commercial paper, bankers' acceptances, municipal notes, and Eurodollars.

Federal Funds

When member banks experience intense loan demand, their reserve account balances may fall below the Federal Reserve System's requirements. To increase their reserves, these banks can borrow at the Fed's discount window or from other banks that have experienced slack demand and have excess reserves to loan for a short term. The funds borrowed or loaned from bank to bank are called *federal funds* because they are used to meet Federal Reserve requirements. To obtain federal funds, banks may deal directly with one another or they may employ brokers to arrange the transactions.

The federal funds rate is influenced by any or all of the Federal Reserve's credit-regulation devices as well as supply and demand relationships between banks. It is a key rate and its movements generate sympathetic trends in other money market and capital market costs. The rates for various instruments in these markets differ largely because of differences in their investment qualities and maturities. The federal funds rate is of particular interest to Fed watchers because it is the only money cost that is directly manipulated by the Federal Reserve System. It is clear that money and capital markets follow and react to variations in the federal funds rate.

Treasury Bills

A Treasury bill is a short-term, direct debt obligation of the U.S. government, usually with a maturity of three months, six months, or one year. Treasury bills are issued in denominations of $10,000, $15,000, $100,000, $500,000, and $1 million. These instruments do not bear a coupon interest rate; they are sold at a discount, which provides investor earnings. The yield on a Treasury bill is calculated for a 360-day year, but maturities are based on a 52-week year.

Treasury bills are backed by the full faith and credit of the U.S. government and are sold at frequent auctions. In preparing bids, purchasers study recent levels and movements in the federal funds rate to determine the direction of monetary policy. This plainly demonstrates the close relationship between these money rates.

Treasury bills greatly influence real estate activity. In the early 1980s, banks and savings and loan associations received regulatory permission to sell government-backed, six-month savings certificates at yields equal to or 25 basis points above the six-month Treasury bill yield established at the most recent auction. The arrangement was introduced to help these institutions attract savings funds, which they would channel into home mortgage loans. If the thrift industry could not compete for savings funds, mortgage fund shortages were expected to occur. The thrift industry was later deregulated and the program was eliminated, but Treasury bill rates are still the principal guide for short-maturity loan costs, particularly in the construction and development sectors of the real estate industry.

Other Government Securities

U.S. Treasury notes, which have longer maturities than most money market instruments, are traded in money and capital markets. They are backed by the full faith and credit of the U.S. government and are issued in maturities of one to 10 years. Many notes are issued for two to four years. Treasury notes are issued in denominations of $1,000, $5,000, $10,000, $100,000, and $1 million. They bear interest and carry a face rate.

After Treasury notes are issued, they are traded freely and priced to reflect current market yields. In these transactions, the remaining maturities are frequently short and the rates indicated fit typical patterns for similar money market investments.

Because of their long maturities, the earning rates on Treasury notes influence the rate levels of real estate "bridge" mortgages. Bridge mortgages are real estate loans that property owners or developers might obtain for two- to four-year periods while they are waiting for more favorable, longer-term financing or converting rental properties to condominium or cooperative ownership.

Other important securities are created and sold by government-sponsored agencies such as the Federal National Mortgage Corporation, the Federal Farm Credit System, the Federal Home Loan Bank, the Federal Land Bank, and the UN-affiliated World Bank. These instruments are supported by borrowing lines from the U.S. Treasury. They are freely and actively traded over the counter and offer yields slightly higher than those offered by direct Treasury obligations.

Repurchase Agreements and Reverse Repurchase Agreements

Repurchase agreements and reverse repurchase agreements are short-term financing arrangements made by securities dealers, banks, and the Federal Reserve System in which a person who needs funds for a short period uses his or her portfolio of money market investments as collateral and sells an interest in the portfolio with the obligation to repurchase it, with interest, at a specified future time. These agreements provide borrowers with needed liquidity and lenders with securities as collateral. Individuals and businesses with excess short-term cash invest in repurchase agreements. The time of repurchase may be one day or up to several months in the future.

The Fed has used these agreements to fine-tune money markets to achieve selected interest rate levels and smooth out seasonal distortions in the supply of and demand for money. By arranging a purchase from a securities dealer who is obligated to repurchase in a few days, the Fed temporarily creates additional bank reserves because the dealer deposits the transaction proceeds in a commercial bank. A reverse repurchase agreement is created when the Fed sells securities to dealers who must sell them back with interest. In this way the Fed temporarily withdraws reserves from the banking system because the dealer will pay with a check drawn on a commercial bank account.

Repurchase agreements enable corporations to lend excess cash for short periods. This is especially important because these businesses cannot engage in Federal Reserve funds trading, which is usually reserved for banking organizations. The interest rates applied in repurchase agreements are determined by prevailing supply and demand conditions in short-term money markets. They are also influenced by the quality of the collateral, which is usually excellent.

Certificates of Deposit

Certificates of deposit (CDs) are financial instruments that represent time deposits with banking organizations. Certificates of deposit may be issued for terms of one month, three months, six months, one year, or up to seven years. Most large certificates of $100,000 or more are for one- or three-month terms. A CD is a contract between a bank or savings and loan institution and a depositor in which the institution agrees to pay negotiated rates of interest and the depositor agrees to maintain the deposit for a fixed period of time. A CD is backed only by the credit of the issuing bank, which is usually supported by FDIC insurance. Many CDs are negotiable and can be traded.

Although the interest rate on a CD is negotiated, the Federal Reserve imposed constraints on CD rates for many years through its Regulation Q. In the early 1980s, however, deregulation legislation relaxed or removed these limitations, and Congress established the Depository Institutions Deregulation Committee to assure equality among all financial institutions.

Commercial Paper

Commercial paper is a corporation's promissory notes to borrow short-term funds for current operations. By trading commercial paper, organizations with excess cash can lend to those in need of money. This money market sector is well organized, and transaction data on prices and interest rates are widely and quickly disseminated by computer. Dealers specializing in commercial paper "make markets" and are able to consummate deals quickly and efficiently. Because commercial paper is backed solely by the credit of the corporations issuing it, only the largest, soundest companies can use it effectively. Due to the vagaries of money supply and demand conditions, commercial paper rates are frequently lower than bank loan costs; hence, large corporations benefit from the ability to use commercial paper.

In the real estate industry, commercial paper is used to raise short-term construction funds. For example, a real estate investment trust (REIT) might issue commercial paper to raise the money to fund construction loans. For the REIT, the key consideration is that interest rates on the commercial paper be sufficiently below construction mortgage rates to give the trust enough earnings to handle expenses and provide a satisfactory profit. Commercial paper is exempt from federal securities registration regulations provided 1) it is for a short term, 2) the funds are for current operations, and 3) there is an unequivocal takeout commitment for the loan. When these requirements are met, the Securities and Exchange Commission will issue "no action" letters.

Bankers' Acceptances

A bankers' acceptance is a bank's obligation or promise to pay. The main difference between commercial paper and bankers' acceptances is that commercial paper is backed by the corporation's credit only, while the corporation and the bank both stand behind bankers' acceptances. Thus, the latter carries less risk, which often causes yields on bankers' acceptances to be less than yields on commercial paper.

Bankers' acceptances are short-term, noninterest-bearing notes that are sold at discount and redeemed at par, or the face amount, like Treasury bills. Most bankers' acceptances are created in the course of foreign trade, so large banks with foreign departments participate in this market. These instruments are not directly related to real estate operations, but they reflect trends in short-term interest rates for investments of varying quality.

Municipal Notes

Municipal notes are short-term obligations of local governments such as villages, cities, and counties that are used to finance current operations until satisfactory long-term funds are obtained. Because municipal notes are exempt from federal and state taxation, they are favored by many investors. This tax advantage has caused the interest rates on these notes to be relatively low. The earning rates on municipal notes may indicate real estate investor's requirements for after-tax yields. Although real estate investments are generally for longer terms, studying the rates on municipal notes does provide some insight into investment strategies.

Eurodollars

Eurodollars are dollars deposited outside the United States. This monetary element has grown enormously since World War II. The growth of Eurodollars has been aided by the fact that U.S. trading deficits are paid in dollars, world oil bills are settled in dollars, and an increasing number of multinational business operations are using and requiring dollars. Banks and businesses that require short- and intermediate-term financing have profited from borrowing this type of capital.

While the REIT industry expanded, many trusts secured Eurodollar loans to fund mortgage lending operations. Eurobond and debenture issues with five- to seven-year maturities have been employed, but maturities of one to six months are more common. When supply and demand conditions generate favorable interest levels, Eurodollar loans can provide bridge financing for real estate ventures.

Yield Levels

Appraisers consult published daily financial market reports to study money market activity for indications of changing monetary values. These reports provide information on various debt and equity instruments and their yield rates. Since this information represents the market's discounting of economic futures, it is a portrayal of the state of the economy and can be expected to affect real estate industry operations. Figure 5.4 is a sample report from the *New York Times* daily financial section. It shows the yield levels evidenced in the day's trading. Other financial publications also provide this type of information.

Figure 5.4

Key Rates

In percent

	Yesterday	Previous Day	Year Ago
PRIME RATE	**6.50**	6.50	9.50
DISCOUNT RATE	**3.50**	3.50	6.50
FEDERAL FUNDS*	**4.75**	4.50	6.68
3-MO. TREAS. BILLS	**3.73**	3.78	6.05
6-MO. TREAS. BILLS	**3.81**	3.84	6.17
7-YR. TREAS. NOTES	**6.73**	6.69	8.07
30-YR. TREAS. BONDS	**7.62**	7.59	8.39
TELEPHONE BONDS	**8.80**	8.74	9.60
MUNICIPAL BONDS**	**6.66**	6.65	7.52

*Estimated daily average, source Telerate
**Municipal Bond Index, The Bond Buyer
Salomon Brothers and Telerate for Treasury's bell-
wether bonds, notes and bills

Reprinted from *The New York Times*, Key
Rates, January 23, 1992.

Figure 5.5

Active Bond Issues

WEDNESDAY, JANUARY 22, 1992

Issues	Moody's Rating	Current Bid&Asked	Chng	Yield
UTILITY BONDS				
SoCen8½s29	Aaa	101⅛-101¾	...	8.40
SoCalEd9½s20	Aa2	107⅞-109	...	8.75
CORPORATE BONDS				
Amoco 8⅝s16	Aaa	104½-105⅝	...	8.20
ATT7s01	A1	97-98⅜	...	7.43
FordC9½s00	Aa2	107⅛-107⅞	...	8.37
INTERMEDIATE NOTES				
Anhr8¾s99	A1	110⅛-110⅞	...	7.18
Bowater9s09	A3	107⅞-108⅞	...	8.17
Citicorp9s99	A2	94¾-95¼	...	9.95
duPont9.15s00	Aa2	111-111¾	...	7.47
GMAC9⅜s00	Aa3	106⅜-107	...	8.37
PhiMorris9¼s00	A3	109½-110⅛	...	7.77
INTERNATIONAL ISSUES				
Hydro QueB8½s29	Aa3	101⅛-101¾	...	8.40
World Bank 9¼s17	Aaa	114⅞-115½	...	7.90

Source: First Boston Corp.

Reprinted from *The New York Times*, Active
Bond Issues, January 22, 1992.

CAPITAL MARKET INSTRUMENTS

Traditional capital market operations are described in this section, but readers
must keep in mind that the conditions influencing the use of long-term, fixed- or
variable-rate instruments may change over time. Appraisers and market analysts
must keep abreast of shifts in monetary policy that invariably effect market
changes and interpret how they may influence the financing arrangements discussed below.

Bonds

*A bond is a capital market instrument with a fixed interest rate issued for a term
of one year or more.* The U.S. government, business corporations, states, and
municipalities, among others, issue bonds to raise long-term capital for operations
and development. Earnings from government-issued bonds are not free from federal taxation, but they are often exempt from local taxes. Generally, the short-
term funding discussed earlier is used for project development, and long-term
arrangements are made when the real estate project is completed.

Bonds are usually sold with a par value of $1,000; thus, if the issue carries an
interest rate of 12%, each bond will earn $120 per year. The buyer will receive
this earnings rate and, at maturity in 20 or 30 years, will be repaid the $1,000
principal.

The bond market is closely related to real estate investment activities. Real
estate is normally bought with a combination of equity capital and medium- to
long-term debt funds, called *mortgage money*. Most real estate deals are structured with a substantial amount of mortgage money and a smaller amount of
equity, or venture, funds. Institutions with long-term capital to invest usually sur-

vey bond markets, then examine mortgage opportunities, and finally make investment decisions to secure the best earnings for the risk involved.

Correlating bond market yields and mortgage capital costs can be intriguing. Until the 1970s and early 1980s when high inflation caused money market volatility, there was a close correlation between good-quality mortgages and AA-rated utilities bonds. The unstable financial conditions of this period reduced the availability of long-term, fixed-interest capital and created a need for new method of real estate investment analysis. Today, mortgage-equity combinations may involve debt funds with variable interest rates, and property feasibility studies must account for expected rate changes. Appraisers must be cognizant of expert opinion about interest rate forecasts for the projected investment term and apply this knowledge in making their judgments.

The municipal bond yields observed in daily trading reflect investors' after-tax earnings requirements for a wide range of risk ratings. A popular proxy for these bonds is the Bond Buyers Index, which is published in the financial press. Figure 5.5 is extracted from "Active Bond Issues," a regular feature in the *New York Times*, which contains information on maturities, risk ratings, and daily price changes. The quoted yields are calculated from indicated prices and interest rates, assuming full payment at maturity. Some bonds are traded on organized exchanges such as the New York Stock Exchange, but many others are traded over the counter.

Stocks

A stock is an ownership share in a company or corporation. A stock corporation is a common legal entity in which investors provide organizational capital by subscribing to shares that represent ownership and a right to all proprietary benefits. These shares are subject to the prior claims of operating expenses and debt service on capital raised by selling bonds, debentures, and other money market instruments. Shareholder benefits consist of any cash or stock dividends declared, augmented by share price appreciation or diminished by price depreciation.

Marketing mechanisms in the form of stock exchanges—e.g., the New York Stock Exchange (NYSE) and the American Stock Exchange (AMEX)—were established to give business ventures ready access to capital sources and to provide a flexible, easy means for trading shares. Through continuous refinement of exchange operations, orderly market conditions have been established and share values, declared dividends, and other important financial data are published on a regular basis.

Mortgages

A mortgage is a legal instrument for pledging a described property interest as collateral or security for the repayment of a loan under certain terms and conditions. A mortgage constitutes a lien on the interest pledged. Mortgage loans supply most of the capital employed in real estate investments. A borrower gives a lender a lien on real estate as assurance that the loan will be repaid. If the borrower fails to make payment, the lender can foreclose the lien and acquire the real estate, thereby offsetting the loss.

Traditionally mortgage loans were made for long terms of 20 to 30 years and carried fixed interest rates. A level-payment mortgage, which requires that the same dollar amount of payment be made each period for the entire loan term, is a popular contract. The payments are calculated to pay interest at a certain rate and amortize the loan fully over its term so that less of each successive payment is required for interest and more is available for debt reduction. Other payment arrangements and schedules are also used. The parties to a mortgage are usually free to contract in any fashion they desire, subject only to limitations of usury and public policy.

A borrower may pledge a real property interest to more than one lender, thereby creating several liens; in such cases, the time sequence or order of the liens is important. The first loan contract executed and recorded is the first mortgage, which has priority over all subsequent transactions. Second and third mortgages are sometimes referred to as *junior liens*; because they involve more lending risk than first mortgages, higher rates of interest are charged for second and third mortgages.

Mortgages can be categorized based on how they are protected against the risk of default; the three major categories are guaranteed, insured, and conventional. Veterans Administration (VA) home mortgages are the most notable example of guaranteed mortgages, but other state and national government agencies also provide guarantees. Federal Housing Administration (FHA) mortgages are the most extensively used insured mortgages, but other government bodies and private insurance companies offer loan insurance as well. Conventional mortgages are neither insured nor guaranteed. Although regulations vary from state to state, in most states institutional lenders are limited to a 75% to 80% conventional loan-to-value ratio. Private mortgage insurance (PMI), however, is available for conventional loans with higher loan-to-value ratios.

Mortgage terms and interest rates are set by contractual agreement between the lender and the borrower, and are traditionally subject to usury limitations set by the states and other public policy restrictions. Because loan procedures may change too slowly to keep pace with rapidly changing money markets, the practice of paying points has emerged. Points are a percentage of the total loan amount that the lender is paid up front to enhance the loan yield and make it competitive with current capital market rates.

The effects of competition for capital are clearly evident in mortgage markets. In the early 1980s, yields soared and changes were so frequent that investors preferred to acquire short-term, liquid investments, which offered generous rates and maximum flexibility. In a volatile climate, investors resist long-term positions and fixed-rate instruments because they provide little protection against inflation. In response to erratic conditions, contracts such as variable-rate mortgages, adjustable-rate mortgages, renegotiable rate mortgages, and rollover mortgages were created. These mortgage instruments provide for periodic adjustment of interest rates to keep yields competitive with those available in capital markets. Although these contracts may cover long periods, the payment requirements change at frequent intervals so real estate owners cannot budget for fixed debt service. An owner managing a property subject to a variable-rate mortgage may feel impelled to arrange leasing programs that permit rapid rental adjustments to offset increases in mortgage payments caused by money market fluctuations.

Deeds of Trust

A mortgage is a contract between a borrower and a lender, but a deed of trust involves a third party as well. *A deed of trust is defined as a legal instrument similar to a mortgage that, when executed and delivered, conveys or transfers property title to a trustee.* In such an arrangement, a borrower conveys or transfers property to a trustee for the benefit of a lender. A deed of trust states the trustee's name and the lender's name. The borrower conveys title to the trustee, but retains the right to use and occupy the property. In many states where deeds of trust are used, they are recorded in the county and given to the lender or trustee for safekeeping until the loan is paid off.

Deeds of trust are used to eliminate the need for foreclosure proceedings against a defaulting debtor. A *trust agreement* accompanies the deed and sets forth the terms of the security and instructions to the trustee. If the buyer defaults, a public sale by the trustee in accordance with state law provides funds to compensate the trustee and repay the debt with interest. In some states, deeds of trust are used in place of mortgage contracts.

Nonmoney Credit Instruments

Land contracts, frequently called *installment sale contracts* or *contracts for deed*, are instruments that provide for the future delivery of a property deed to a buyer after certain conditions are met. A seller finances the sale of a property by permitting the buyer to pay for it over a period of time, but the title is delivered only after all payments are made. In the event of default, the buyer normally forfeits all payments made and the seller may also elect to hold the buyer to his or her contract. Because such contracts are sometimes not recorded, a buyer usually ensures that the agreement contains provisions to protect against any liens or encumbrances that may be filed against the property before title passes.

The purchase-money mortgage (PMM) is a common real estate financing device that typically resembles a junior lien. With this instrument, a buyer can finance all or much of a property's cost by arranging for the seller to accept a purchase-money mortgage as part of the purchase price. The contract specifies the required interest rate, the amortization payments, and a date for final and full repayment. To facilitate a transaction, a seller may take a purchase-money mortgage so that the buyer does not have to obtain funds from other sources. The buyer takes title immediately and becomes the property owner. If the buyer defaults on a payment or some other requirement, the seller may foreclose. When used for land acquisition, a purchase-money mortgage should contain release clauses that specify the principal payments that must be made to release parts of the property from the lien of the mortgage. Other procedural matters such as the order in which lots may be released are normally set forth as well.

RATE RELATIONSHIPS

Observing daily trading activity over a period of time may reveal relationships among the earning rates of various instruments traded in money and capital markets. For example, there may be a relatively constant spread of 50 basis points between the yields on three-month and six-month Treasury bills. However, market volatility can cause the spread between these yields to increase or decrease at times. Similarly, the spread between three-month and six-month commercial paper may widen to 70 basis points and remain steady at that level for several months. These observations are significant because they reveal how the length of an instrument's maturity influences its yield.

The federal funds rate is a foundational rate. In money and capital markets, fluctuations in this rate are closely followed and produce sympathetic reactions in prices and yields. Another key investment yield is reflected in the weekly auction of Treasury bills. Because these instruments represent top credit quality and short maturity, their yields establish a base from which market participants measure all short-term money costs, including real estate construction loan rates. Money market and capital market rate relationships are created by prime investment considerations, which include borrowers' credit, loan maturity, monetary supply and demand conditions, and existing and anticipated inflation rates. All of these factors are important in rating the risk of various investments.

With an understanding of rate relationships, appraisers can correlate real estate investment risk with the risks associated with actively traded capital market instruments, and thereby select market-driven and market-supported discount and capitalization rates. The financial press contains a plethora of pricing and yield information to facilitate this process.

Figure 5.6 Key Rate Trends 1988 to 1991

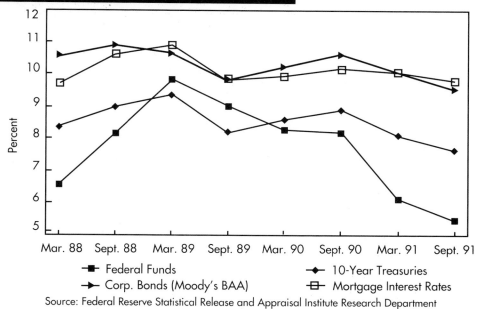

Source: Federal Reserve Statistical Release and Appraisal Institute Research Department

Key rates serve as indicators signaling the general direction of economic activity.

Pattern of Rates

Traditionally, long-term financial instruments have provided the most generous yields. In the early 1980s, however, financial market trading reflected an inverse yield curve, and short-term rates exceeded longer-term investment returns. This was caused by the prevailing high rate of inflation, which made long-term investments unattractive and drove available capital into short-term maturities. Mortgage money was naturally in short supply. The steep debt service requirements created by high interest rates drained business earnings and reduced equity returns. Consequently, many real estate ventures at that time were not economically feasible. When money costs declined, many projects that were previously infeasible became practical and profitable.

CYCLES, TRENDS, AND INFLATION

Money and capital market conditions are cyclical. As the economy expands, competition for capital intensifies, the costs of goods and services increase, and inflation escalates. Then the Fed tightens money and credit until the economy slows down. The demand for funds subsides, interest rates decline, and economic conditions become stable enough for businesses to expand. When the frequency of the economic cycle accelerates and its range increases, business and money conditions change drastically and rapidly. This creates an unattractive economic environment for long-term investments.

Inflation is often described as price escalations throughout the economy; when goods and services become increasingly expensive, inflation accelerates. Inflation occurs when the general level of prices rises. The *inflation* rate is the rate of change in the price level such as is reflected in the consumer price index, or CPI. Inflation can be measured with the following formula:[3]

$$\text{Rate of inflation (year t)} = \frac{\text{price level (year t)} - \text{price level (year t} - 1)}{\text{price level (year t} - 1)} \times 100$$

Inflation is also described as the proliferation of monetary units—i.e., a currency expansion. When monetary units proliferate with no apparent growth in underlying wealth, the value of each unit declines; more units are required in exchange for goods and services, and price levels rise.

The effect of inflation on real estate can be seen in the single-family residential market. In the late 1970s, the supply of money in the United States expanded sharply; simultaneously, the median prices of new and used dwelling units escalated drastically, and these prices were accepted and supported by healthy demand.

The economic importance of inflation also can be seen in the concept of "real" interest rates. Nominal interest rates, like those reported daily in the financial press, are said to be composites of the "real" cost of funds, or real interest rate, and the premiums that investors demand to protect their currency value from being eroded by inflation. Thus, the nominal rate equals the real interest rate plus an inflation premium. Economists suggest that the real interest rate has remained steady at 3% to 4%. Therefore, if the capital market shows a nominal rate of 11% for 10-year U.S. Treasury notes, the real interest rate concept would indicate an inflation premium of 7%.

---

3. Paul A. Samuelson and William D. Nordhaus, *Economics*, 13th ed. (New York: McGraw-Hill, 1989), 306.

11% (nominal rate) = 4% (real interest rate) + 7% (inflation premium)

This example demonstrates how investors' perceptions of inflation can affect prices in market trading and change the interest rates on instruments of different maturities.

Traditional real estate investment practices involve the use of two types of capital—debt and equity—and a typical venture is structured with a substantial mortgage amount and a smaller equity contribution. Before 1970 the largest suppliers of mortgage funds were thrift institutions such as savings banks and savings and loan associations and life insurance companies. However, the high interest rates of the 1970s and early 1980s had a negative effect on these organizations' mortgage positions. Their portfolio yields became inadequate, their liquidity diminished, and their mortgages were being repaid with funds that were cheaper than those originally loaned. High interest rates increased yields on competing investments, leading depositors to withdraw funds to take advantage of alternative opportunities. Traditional mortgage lenders were, therefore, unable to offer as many loans. The term *disintermediation* was coined to describe these inflation-generated conditions.

Business and Real Estate Cycles

Obviously money market and capital market activities and trends affect the real estate industry. In the years following World War II (1946-1966), distinct patterns emerged in real estate and general business cycles. As business prospered, the demand for capital intensified, inflation accelerated, and an oversupply of goods and services was produced. Then Federal Reserve monetary policy and other economic controls were used to slow the pace of the economy and a recession ensued.

When Congress wanted to revive the economy, the industry invariably selected to provide economic stimulation was real estate, particularly home building. Programs were developed to provide abundant, moderately priced mortgage money. These programs usually involved loan insurance or guarantees to induce capital managers to participate. Because there was a substantial demand for housing, the programs were well received and residential development expanded, increasing employment in all economic sectors. Manufacturers of hardware, supplies (e.g., heating, plumbing, and electrical), paints, furniture, equipment, and other goods saw business improve. The economy finally revived, then inflation started to accelerate, and the cycle was repeated. When loan insurance and guarantee programs supplied inexpensive long-term capital, real estate prospered and the general economy expanded.

SOURCES OF CAPITAL FOR REAL ESTATE

The different aspirations of equity and debt investors are revealed in their market actions. The debt investor participates in bonds or mortgages, usually pursuing conservative paths in search of certain income and the repayment of principal. This type of investor expects a priority claim on investment earnings and often looks for security in the form of a lien on the assets involved. While a debt investor is relatively passive, an equity investor is active. An equity investor is more willing to assume risk, so the funds used for equity investment are known as *venture capital*.

Inflation tends to change traditional investor attitudes. Institutions that normally restrict their real estate positions to debt in the form of mortgages become dismayed when they realize that the rates of return they bargained for, and once deemed adequate, are woefully low. They also realize that the expensive money they loaned will be repaid with cheap, inflated dollars. In the early 1980s, these conditions impelled institutional investors to alter their investment policies and seek real estate equity positions, which they believed to be reasonable hedges against inflation. In those years, many financial authorities thought that long-term, fixed-rate debt capital would become a thing of the past. The economic and monetary changes of the late 1980s, however, suggest a return to more traditional investor attitudes and policies.

Equity

Equity investors realize that their earnings are subordinate to a project's operating expenses and debt service requirements. Equity income earnings are called dividends, but they are only one part of the total return that the investor anticipates. Investors also expect that the value of their original investment will increase, although there is a risk that it will remain stable or decline.

Trusts

Trust entities are used extensively to amass equity funds for real estate investment. *A trust is a temporary, conditional, or permanent fiduciary relationship in which the legal title to, and control of, property are placed in the hands of a trustee for the benefit of another person.*

One frequently employed trust is the Massachusetts business trust, in which holders of shares of beneficial interest have no personal liability for the trust's actions. Usually, this protection is achieved by using a corporate business structure. This type of trust also allows shareholders to avoid the double income taxation incurred by corporations. A corporate entity is taxed on its earnings, and from its after-tax net income it distributes dividends to shareholders, who are then personally taxed on that income. The earnings on a Massachusetts business trust, however, are passed through to beneficial shareholders; no income tax is paid by the trust and only a single tax is paid by the shareholders. Investors have found these income and tax pass-through arrangements very attractive.

Real estate investment trusts (REITs) have been successful in pooling the funds of small investors to acquire real estate investment positions that could not be handled by these people individually. REITS offer shareholders freedom from personal liability, the benefit of expert management, and readily transferred shares. To qualify for a tax pass-through, a REIT must pay dividends of at least 90% of its net income. With complicated income-measuring practices, trusts have attempted to pay almost all net income and, therefore, have been precluded from establishing reserves for possible losses.

Partnerships

A partnership is a common vehicle for pooling real estate equity funds. *A partnership is a business arrangement in which two or more persons jointly own a busi-*

ness and share in its profits and losses. There are two kinds of partnerships—general and limited.

A general partnership is an ownership arrangement in which all partners share in investment gains and losses and each is fully responsible for all liabilities. A general partner has complete liability for the acts of the other partners and is responsible for debts incurred by them. This is one major disadvantage of this type of business arrangement. General partners may legally participate in the active management of the business. The most attractive feature of a general partnership in a real estate investment is the ability to pass the tax-shelter benefits of depreciation, interest, and real estate taxes through to partners. In recent years new tax legislation has substantially changed the scope of these benefits.

A limited partnership is an ownership arrangement consisting of general and limited partners; general partners manage the business and assume full liability for partnership debt, while limited partners are passive and liable only to the extent of their own capital contributions. Limited partnerships are popular because they permit an uneven distribution of tax-shelter benefits. Although limited partners' financial liability is restricted to their capital contributions, they may receive tax benefits in excess of that amount.

Syndications

Another popular arrangement for raising real estate equity capital is a syndication. *A syndication is a private or public partnership that pools funds for the acquisition and development of real estate projects or other business ventures.* Private syndications are limited to small groups of investors and are relatively free from government regulation. Public syndications involve large groups of investors and generally operate in more than one state, so they are subject to Security Exchange Commission (SEC) registration regulations. Drawing from large groups of investors, public syndications can amass great amounts of equity funds by combining the contributions of individuals who do not have the resources to handle a venture alone.

Often a syndication is organized or promoted by a general partner, who has full financial liability for the partnership's activities. The other syndicate investors are limited partners. To attract investors, syndication agreements may provide for an unequal distribution of investment benefits, allocating the major share of tax-shelter benefits to purchasers of syndicate shares, not the general partner.

Joint Ventures

A joint venture is a combination of two or more entities that join to undertake a specific project. Although a joint venture often takes the form of a general or limited partnership, it differs from a partnership in that it is intended to be temporary and project-specific. The parties may later embark on other ventures, but each venture is the subject of a separate contractual agreement. General and limited partnership arrangements are popular in real estate joint ventures because they permit uneven distribution of tax-shelter benefits. Tenancy in common is a form of joint ownership that is usually employed in small property holdings.

A joint-venture arrangement is frequently used in large real estate projects. One party, usually a financial institution, supplies most of the required capital and the other party provides construction or management expertise. Life insurance companies and pension trusts have joined with entrepreneurial building organizations in joint ventures to develop large offices, shopping malls, and other major real estate projects. If the financial partner wants the restricted liability of a limited partner, it must be willing to forego active project management. Home or condominium builders may participate in joint ventures with the service corporations of savings and loan associations. Combinations such as these have produced a substantial amount of much-needed housing.

Pension Funds

Private and government-operated pension funds comprise a huge and rapidly growing source of investment capital. Usually, the pension contributions of employers and employees are placed with a trustee, who is obliged to invest and reinvest the money prudently, accumulate funds, and pay designated plan benefits to retirees. The trustee may be a government body, a trust company, an insurance company, or an individual. In performing these duties, an individual trustee may employ the trust departments of commercial banks, insurance companies, and other financial institutions.

U.S. pension funds totaled approximately $2.58 trillion in 1988 and they are expected to increase steadily through the next decade. A capital source of such huge proportions cannot fail to have a major impact on the general economy and the real estate industry. Pension trusts are the only group that can feasibly consider some long-term investments because their funds are collected and their pension benefits are paid out over an extended period of time.

Traditionally, pension funds have been involved primarily in securities investments such as stocks and bonds. The development of pass-through securities by the Government National Mortgage Association (Ginnie Mae), however, has made it easier for pension funds to invest in mortgages, and they have made sizable investments. Pension trusts have also shown a willingness to invest in real estate equities by purchasing or participating in the real estate investments created by life insurance companies and commercial banks. Banks and life insurance companies acquire high-quality real estate equities, pool the investments in separate accounts, and supply the necessary portfolio management for a fee. Pension trusts commit funds to these accounts and share in all earnings, which consist of both income returns and sales profits.

Life Insurance Companies

Through normal insurance sales and operations, life insurance companies accumulate large amounts of funds which they place in diverse investments. Insurance companies are substantial mortgage lenders, and they make many real estate equity investments for their own accounts and as managers of separate accounts. Their investment officers regard equities as attractive earning situations that offer growth potential and reasonable protection against the capital erosion caused by inflation.

International Equity Capital

The investment activities of foreign individuals, countries, financial institutions, and pension funds also provide equity capital for the real estate industry. These off-shore capital sources have become increasingly important to U.S. real estate. Foreign investors often take a long-term investment view, bidding up prices, accepting relatively low initial cash flow returns, and looking to future income and value growth to supply a major part of their anticipated total equity return. Often foreign investors do not hesitate to make 100% equity acquisitions when the properties involved are attractive and have exciting growth potential. Many of these investors will undoubtedly mortgage their properties later, when monetary conditions improve and lower interest rates permit positive leveraging.

International capital comes from a variety of sources, including individual and institutional investors in Japan, the oil-rich nations of the Middle East, and financial institutions and individuals in Western Europe. Although foreign investors have supplied needed equity capital to realty ventures in this country, they still represent only a very small fraction of total U.S. real estate investment.

Debt

Because mortgage money is so important in real estate, investors, appraisers, and counselors must be familiar with the sources and costs of debt capital.

Savings and Loan Associations

Savings and loan associations, along with mutual savings banks, life insurance companies, credit unions, and others, are financial intermediaries. They receive savings deposits, lend them at interest, and distribute dividends to depositors after paying operating expenses and establishing appropriate reserves. When short-term interest rates are high, savers tend to withdraw funds and reinvest them in higher-yielding, short-term money market instruments and funds. Because savings and loan associations are financial intermediaries, high interest rates reduce the availability of mortgage funds and increase their cost.

Savings and loan associations promote thrift, pool savings, and invest funds in home mortgages. Such thrift institutions may be state or federally chartered. Until 1989 federal savings and loan associations were supervised by the Federal Home Loan Bank Board (FHLBB), which was created in 1932 to provide credit to thrift and home financing institutions and to alleviate liquidity problems in the savings and loan industry by assuring a constant flow of funds. The Financial Institutions Reform, Recovery and Enforcement Act of 1989 (FIRREA), the savings and loan bailout legislation, created the Office of Thrift Supervision (OTS) under the direction of the Treasury Department. In addition to taking over the functions of the defunct FHLBB, the OTS had been authorized to examine and supervise all federal and state savings and loans (and all savings and loans holding companies) and to establish strict uniform accounting standards for thrift institutions similar to those established for commercial banks. FIRREA also set up the Resolution Trust Corporation (RTC), which is charged with disposing of the assets of insolvent thrift institutions. The Federal Deposit Insurance Corporation (FDIC) has assumed all the assets of the now defunct Federal Savings and Loan Insurance Corporation (FSLIC). (See Appendix A for a summary of federal legislation affecting appraisers.)

The origins of the savings and loan crisis can be traced back to the escalating inflation of the late 1970s and early 1980s, which underscored the mismatch between the assets and the liabilities of the savings and loan industry. The assets of savings and loan institutions were overwhelmingly fixed-rate, long-term mortgages, while their liabilities were made up of demand deposits and other accounts with short-term maturities. During the years of high inflation, savings and loan institutions were seriously affected by disintermediation as depositors withdrew funds to invest in higher-earning competitive investments.

The deregulatory legislation passed in the early 1980s to make savings and loan institutions more competitive phased out controls on interest rates, allowing the thrifts to pay more competitive rates. However, the effect was that the savings and loans had to pay more for the money deposited with them than their earnings rate allowed. Earnings were held down by their portfolios of fixed-rate, long-term mortgages. To liquidate such assets, the institutions resorted to selling at substantial price discounts. The thrifts then gained legislative approval to get into new, purportedly high-earning lines of business such as equities, development loans, and so-called "junk bonds."

The collapse of real estate markets, starting in the Southwest, and the junk bond debacle wiped out the net worth of many thrift institutions. Legislation to rescue the thrifts took an inordinately long time to set up. With the inexorable laws of compound interest, the problem has grown to exponential proportions, and the cost of the savings and loan bailout is now large enough to pose a serious threat to the health of the general economy.

Commercial Banks

Commercial banks are privately owned institutions that offer a variety of financial services to businesses and individuals. They may be state or federally chartered. Commercial banks are managed by boards of directors, who are selected by stockholders but are subject to regulation by state agencies and the Federal Deposit Insurance Corporation (FDIC). The FDIC is an independent agency that insures individual deposits in all state and federally chartered banks in the Federal Reserve System.

In keeping with their role as short-term lenders, commercial banks have traditionally supplied construction and development loans. They usually require construction borrowers to obtain commitments from long-term, permanent lenders, obliging them to take out a loan when the project is completed. Large commercial banks make a limited number of permanent mortgage loans, usually on commercial and industrial properties. In small communities, commercial banks are also expected to supply their customers with home loans.

One important real estate credit function of commercial banks is warehousing mortgages for mortgage bankers and other financial institutions. The banks provide mortgage bankers with short-term loans secured by their mortgage inventories. This arrangement gives mortgage bankers the liquidity to continue their lending operations while they try to sell the accumulated mortgages to a permanent lender.

Life Insurance Companies

Life insurance companies, which supply a large amount of real estate mortgage credit, are of two principal types—mutual and stock. Mutual life insurance companies are owned by policyholders, who share in net earnings by receiving dividends that can be used to reduce their premium expenses. The profits of stock life insurance companies belong to shareholders, who may or may not be policyholders.

Life insurance companies have always invested heavily in real estate. Their activities include both mortgage lending and property ownership. Life insurance companies usually acquire real estate positions that are long term and relate well to their regular business, in which policy premiums are collected over extended periods. The recent development and popularity of "universal" life insurance has deprived companies of much long-term investment capital. In this insurance arrangement, the policyholder, not the company, directs the investment of policy reserves.

The mortgage investments of life insurance companies cover the full range of realty types—e.g., residences, apartments, offices, shopping malls, hotels, and industrial properties. Because many companies have great financial resources, they have been important in mortgaging large income-producing properties. Large companies prefer loans on offices and shopping malls; they have less interest in rental apartments.

Life insurance companies may acquire full ownership of real estate for their own investment accounts or for the separate investment accounts that they manage for pension trusts. Although real estate ownership may amount to only 3% to 5% of a company's assets, a large dollar investment is involved because major life companies may have billions of dollars in assets.

Mutual Savings Banks

Mutual savings banks are located in many states and are regulated by the FDIC and various state banking departments. They are very similar to mutual savings and loan associations, promoting thrift and investing substantial amounts of savings in real estate mortgages. Generally they have broader investment powers than savings and loan associations. With deregulation in the early 1980s, mutual savings banks began to expand the scope of their activities, which now almost match those of commercial banks. Mutual savings banks have grown substantially and continue to change rapidly; they now control assets of more than $100 billion.

Savings banks are important mortgage lenders on local and national levels. When the FHA became dominant in home mortgage lending, savings banks participated extensively in FHA programs. Like savings and loan associations, mutual savings banks have supplied large amounts of mortgage funds for the one- to four-family residential real estate market. Savings banks have reasonably broad investment powers, but they usually concentrate on mortgages, which may account for 65% to 75% of a bank's assets. They also invest in government bonds, corporate bonds, and, to a lesser degree, real estate and stock equity investments.

Thrift institutions have been in the unfortunate position of borrowing short and lending long—i.e., their deposits are of the demand type, but they are invested in long-term mortgages. When unusually large amounts of funds are withdrawn, liquidity is threatened and banks must borrow at high costs to meet their obligations. An earnings squeeze resulted from deregulation of the interest rates that might be paid on savings. When interest rate ceilings were lifted, banks and savings and loan associations had to pay high, competitive dividend rates to keep the funds they previously received and invested in low-yield, fixed-rate mortgages. This situation has eroded many institutions' net worth and limited their lending. For the real estate industry, this has meant less available mortgage money and greater money costs. When interest rates escalate, fewer aspiring home purchasers qualify as acceptable credit risks because debt service would consume too much of their disposable income. These conditions depress home building and sales.

Junior Mortgage Originators

Real estate investments are structured not only with first mortgages, but also with second, third, and fourth mortgages. Junior mortgages can be used to raise substantial amounts of mortgage funds and to achieve various investment goals, such as creating additional leverage and facilitating sales in money markets that are not conducive to refinancing first mortgages. In most jurisdictions, loans must be legally recorded to establish their priority. The first lien recorded takes priority over any that are subsequently filed. When a mortgagor defaults, junior lien holders must keep the senior positions financially current or they run the risk of being cut off by foreclosure of the prior liens. Obviously, junior mortgages involve greater risk than senior liens, and therefore command higher interest rates.

Legal regulations usually preclude banks, savings and loan associations, and life insurance companies from making large junior mortgage loans. However, various regulatory "leeway" or "basket" clauses allow institutions to make junior mortgage loans in amounts that do not exceed 3% or 4% of institutional assets. Other private lenders such as REITs, financing companies, and factoring organizations provide secondary financing as a regular line of business. They offer expensive secondary financing in the form of junior mortgages or subordinated land sale-leasebacks, but they are not supervised to the same degree that banks and life insurance companies are.

Secondary Mortgage Market

Government and monetary authorities often see housing activity as the most effective way to deal with a general economic slump. Government and private organizations stimulate home building through the secondary mortgage market. In this market mortgagees sell packages of mortgages at prices consistent with existing money market rates. Selling mortgages frees up capital, creates liquidity, and permits mortgagees to lend when they might otherwise lack funds. The three agencies discussed below are the principal operators in the secondary mortgage market.

Federal National Mortgage Association (FNMA). A major influence on the secondary mortgage market is exerted by the Federal National Mortgage Association (Fannie Mae). Fannie Mae's principal purpose is to help the housing industry by purchasing mortgages from primary mortgage markets, thus increasing the liquidity of primary lenders. The agency issues long-term debentures and short-term discount notes to raise most of its funds. Two important Fannie Mae programs are the over-the-counter program, in which the association posts the prices it will pay for the immediate delivery of mortgages, and the free market system commitment auction, in which separate but simultaneous auctions are held for FHA, VA, and conventional mortgages.

Federal Home Loan Mortgage Corporation (FHLMC). The Federal Home Loan Mortgage Corporation (Freddie Mac) was created in 1970 to increase the availability of mortgage funds and to provide greater flexibility for mortgage investors. Until 1989, the organization was directed by the Federal Home Loan Bank Board. Since then the regulatory functions of the defunct FHLBB have been assumed by the Office of Thrift Supervision (OTS). Freddie Mac facilitates the expansion and distribution of capital for mortgage purposes by conducting both purchase and sales programs.

In its purchase programs, Freddie Mac buys single-family and condominium mortgages from approved financial institutions. This allows the banking or mortgage banking organization that sells the mortgages to remain liquid in times of credit stringency and continue making mortgage funds available for housing. Although Fannie Mae programs include insured and guaranteed mortgages, the corporation's main interest is in conventional mortgage fields. Both whole mortgages and participations are purchased by Freddie Mac.

In its sales programs, Freddie Mac sells its mortgage inventories, acquiring funds from organizations that have excess capital. Through its purchases, the agency supplies these funds to other organizations that have shortages. Because its operations are conducted nationally, Freddie Mac generates mortgage capital availability throughout the United States.

Government National Mortgage Association (GNMA).
Another agency that influences the secondary mortgage market is the Government National Mortgage Association (Ginnie Mae). Its operations have made much mortgage capital available to housing markets. Fannie Mae is a private corporation, but Ginnie Mae is a government organization that gets financial support from the U.S. Treasury. Ginnie Mae provides special assistance in mortgage programs for loans that could not be handled without extraordinary support. It also manages and liquidates certain mortgages acquired by the government. Its most important role in the secondary market, however, is in the Mortgage-Backed Security Program.

Ginnie Mae is authorized to guarantee the timely payment of principal and interest on long-term securities that are backed by pools of insured or guaranteed mortgages. The most popular security is a pass-through arrangement in which mortgage payments are passed on to the holder of the security. In this program mortgage originators pool their loans in groups of $1 million or more, issue covering securities, and obtain a Ginnie Mae guarantee. Through the program investors who do not have the capacity to originate mortgages can become involved in home finance markets. Because of their excellent investment attributes, Ginnie Mae securities are traded extensively. Money and capital market investors regard the investment yields indicated by the agency as the current return on top-quality liquid paper.

The recent emergence of collateralized mortgage obligations (CMOs) as a major investment banking instrument was prompted by Ginnie Mae guarantee arrangements. CMOs are bonds issued and sold in the capital markets. They are attractive to investors because the debt involved is usually collateralized by Ginnie Mae certificates covering pools of residential mortgages. Because of Ginnie Mae's participation, these bonds receive an AAA, highest-quality risk rating and can be sold at attractively low interest rates. As CMOs have proliferated, they have involved collateral other than Ginnie Mae certificates, including Fannie Mae, Freddie Mac, and even conventional institutional mortgages. This vehicle has been a huge source of liquidity for the mortgage industry and has monetized the mortgage element in real estate investment.

A new variation in the CMO field is the real estate mortgage investment conduit (REMIC) option, which transforms the CMO from a pure debt (bond) vehicle into an equity-type investment. In a REMIC arrangement, the certificate represents a proportionate share of ownership in a pool of mortgages. The issuing organization, often an investment bank, avoids adding debt to its balance sheet by using the REMIC. The investor in a REMIC enjoys the benefit of a tax pass-through similar to that of a REIT, and thereby avoids the double taxation incurred by investors in corporations. The issuing entity is not taxed. The holders bear the sole burden of taxes on earnings.

CMOs of all types have brought enormous amounts of capital into the mortgage field. Through this type of securitization, pension trusts and other conservatively managed investment funds have assumed large positions in the real estate field, assured by the AA or AAA risk ratings granted CMOs by a major rating organization.

Private sector transactions. Although most secondary mortgage market activity has been generated by the Fannie Mae, the Ginnie Mae, and the Freddie Mac, the private sector has also played a role. Banks and insurance companies with mortgage-originating capability often sell loan portfolios, or participations, to private or institutional investors. Some REITs have purchased mortgages from institutions, thereby supplying the sellers with the liquidity needed to continue their lending programs.

The development and growth of private mortgage insurance programs have facilitated private secondary mortgage activity. In the residential market, private programs have successfully insured mortgage loan increments that exceed legal ratios. This has encouraged private secondary market operations that could not have occurred otherwise.

Debt and Equity Relationships

In money markets and capital markets, when the risks associated with different investments are comparable, funds flow to the investment that offers the best prospective yield. Risks are related to rewards; if capital is to be attracted, competitive yields must be offered. Debt and equity investments have different characteristics and appeal to different investors. A survey of these investment attributes is presented here to clarify the distinction between a real estate venture's mortgage and equity components.

Equity yield is cash flow or dividend income that is augmented by growth or diminished by depreciation. This is true whether the investment is an equity interest in real estate or a common stock. From 1955 to 1975, most real estate appraisers and analysts based their opinions about competitively attractive equity yields on real estate market data. Throughout this period, capital was generally available at modest, stable costs.

After 1975 an inflation-induced recession slowed real estate investment activity, reducing the availability of market data that could be analyzed for appraisal purposes. The information that was gathered was difficult to interpret because rapid, intense monetary changes quickly impaired its market relevance. If, for example, the general interest rate changes 10 times in one year, it is difficult to attach much importance to a capitalization rate that has been extracted from a sale transaction completed just six months ago. The adjustments required are too large to be reliable.

In an unstable economic climate, appraisers are well advised to search money markets and capital markets for data to support the conclusions they have developed from real estate data. There are hundreds of thousands of transactions each day in financial markets and billions of dollars are involved. These transactions reflect the discounting of economic futures by well-informed investors and provide useful insights for investment analysts.

The general, but unsteady, decline in interest rates since late 1983 has restored some reliability to real estate market data in equity yield analysis, but financial market data are of paramount significance. Every real estate investment depends on one commodity—money. The most persuasive indicators of competitive yield levels are found in money markets where billions of dollars of capital are traded daily, traders are sophisticated and well informed, and investments are often professionally rated for risk.

The largest equity market is the trading of common stocks. Transactions are reported daily, and share prices and current dividend rates are revealed. Most major newspapers carry full details on stock market operations, and financial publications offer abundant information about corporate earnings and general conditions in commercial and industrial enterprises. These data provide the basis for risk rating the securities issued by businesses. In the field of debt investments (bonds and debentures), the rating task is often performed by professionals such as Standard & Poor's and Moody's; their opinions are widely published and respected by the financial community.[4] Other information is furnished by the securities analysts of major banking institutions, brokerage companies, and the investment banking industry. Their opinions are readily available to the investors. Financial analysts generally follow groups of companies, examining their business affairs in detail and forecasting their prospects for earnings and growth.

Analysts' reports and financial publications do not reveal prospective stock yields, but they do provide information from which investment indexes can be drawn. Because value is the present worth of future income and reversion combined, a key element of value is anticipated appreciation or depreciation. In the stock market, securities analysts are the best sources of the in-depth information on which the investment community bases its growth or depreciation forecasts. In this regard a securities analyst functions like a real estate appraiser, who arrives at an estimate of value by discounting market-supported income and reversion forecasts.

The second, larger component in real estate investment is the debt capital segment, or mortgage funds. Again, capital markets offer abundant information on investor yield requirements for a great variety of debt instruments with different maturities and risk ratings. In the bond and debenture markets, there are hundreds of thousands of daily transactions involving billions of dollars. Each transaction represents one investor's discounting of perceived future economic conditions. The entire volume of transactions presents an excellent picture of well-informed expectations of debt capital performance.

There are differences in the investment yields produced by debt and equity instruments. With a debt instrument, the original lender is entitled to interest at a

---

Standard and Poor's Corporation and Moody's Investor Services, Inc., publish a variety of data on the performance of stocks and bonds. For a listing of these publications, see the bibliography.

specified rate, either fixed or variable, and full payment of the loan amount at maturity. The arrangement may call for periodic payments of interest only and full repayment of the principal at maturity, as in the case of bonds, or it may require periodic payments that combine interest and debt reduction, as in most mortgage loans.

If the original lender sells the investment during its contractual term, a different yield will be realized. If money market conditions are tight and interest rates are higher than when the loan was originated, the lender must sell the position at a discount. If money is freer and rates are lower, the lender may be able to sell at a premium. The purchaser collects the amount of interest specified in the original contract, but the earnings rate relates to a new investment basis. When the loan is repaid at maturity, the purchaser receives the full face amount, plus any discount involved in the acquisition, or minus any premium paid. The instrument's investment yield comprises the interest collected, plus any gain or minus any loss realized at loan maturity, and repayment.

It can be seen that the investment yield on a debt instrument is largely a contractual matter. Income earnings are defined in the instrument as a fixed or variable percentage of the debt's face amount paid at specified times over the term of the loan. The reversion is limited to the original face amount of debt, which may be more or less than the amount paid by the final holder of the instrument.

An equity investment has none of the contractual certainty or specificity of a debt position. The income or dividend earnings are simply the amount of a venture's income, if any, after operating expenses and debt service are paid. This cash flow can be positive or negative, depending on whether there is an excess or deficiency of income after all expenses. The reversion is simply the venture's market value at the end of the investment holding period—i.e., a future value. When entering into an investment, an investor considers the forecast dividend earnings and reversion in relation to the acquisition price; this relationship reflects the prospective equity yield. Upon termination of the investment, the dividends and reversion realized are related to the original amount of the investment to reflect the historic equity yield.

SUMMARY

Because the price of real estate is expressed in terms of money, appraisers must understand how the value of money influences prices. Supply and demand relationships determine the value of money. When supply is abundant, the interest rate, which is the cost of borrowing money, is low. When the supply is limited, the interest rate rises. The demand for money is the product of the operation of natural economic forces, but the supply of U.S currency is regulated by the *Federal Reserve System* (the Fed). Because trading and the exchange of currency is a global operation, the availability of funds must also be considered on a worldwide basis.

A major source of capital for real estate is the *money market*, the interaction of buyers and sellers who trade short-term money instruments. The Fed exerts a dominant influence on money market activity. Interest rates on short-term money market instruments affect the amount and cost of financing available for construction and development. A second source of capital for real estate is the *capital market*, the interaction of buyers and sellers who trade long- and intermediate-term money instruments with maturities of more than one year. The distinction between the money market and the capital market, however, is not sharp.

Banks "create" money by monetizing debt. The amounts that banks may lend is limited by the *fractional reserve requirements* of the Fed. To restrict the money supply, the Fed raises reserve deposit obligations; to increase the supply, it lowers the obligations. The Fed also controls the supply of credit by regulating the *federal discount rate*, which is the interest rate that banks pay on the funds they borrow. In turn, the federal discount rate helps determine the *prime rate*. The buying and selling of U.S. government securities by the *Federal Open Market Committee* is a third way in which the Fed influences interest rates and the supply of credit. The purchase of these securities with Federal Reserve checks increases the reserve accounts of member banks, thereby expanding the available supply of credit. The sale of government securities removes funds from these reserve accounts and reduces the supply of credit.

Through its fiscal policy, the Department of the Treasury raises revenues to cover federal expenditures. Spending has grown faster than revenues, producing inflation and a federal deficit that must be monetized by the Fed. This deficit consumes credit that would otherwise be available to the private sector. The trade deficit, which has grown since 1985, has also added to the burden on U.S. finances.

Short-term money market instruments include *federal funds, Treasury bills, Treasury notes, repurchase agreements and reverse repurchase agreements, certificates of deposit, commercial paper, bankers' acceptances, municipal notes, and Eurodollars.* If a money market instrument is sold before it matures, its investment yield consists of the face, or stated, interest rate and a discount or premium determined by the rates prevailing at the time of sale. Treasury bills have no stated interest rate, so the yield consists of the discount at which the issue was purchased. Yield levels are reliable economic indicators and exert an important influence on real estate activity.

Long- and intermediate-term capital market instruments include *bonds, stocks, mortgages,* and *deeds of trust.* The bond market is closely related to real estate activities because bonds and mortgages compete for the same investment capital. A mortgage is a legal instrument by which a described property interest is pledged for the repayment of a loan under certain terms and conditions. Mortgage loans supply most of the capital used in real estate investments.

The relationships among the earning rates of instruments actively traded in money and capital markets and the yield on real estate investments are functions of the risk rating of investments. The rates on federal funds and Treasury bills are key indicators of short-term yields. Although long-term instruments have generally provided the highest yields, in the early 1980s severe inflation produced an inverse yield curve and short-term rates exceeded longer-term returns.

Capital and money markets respond to the business cycle. *Inflation,* characterized by price escalation and currency expansion, accelerated in the late 1970s. Thrift institutions, the major suppliers of mortgage capital, suffered because loans were being repaid with funds that were cheaper than those originally loaned. *Disintermediation,* the transfer of money from low interest-bearing accounts to higher interest-bearing accounts, destabilized the flow of mortgage funds.

The capital invested in the real estate industry may be divided into debt and equity positions. Debt investment has prior claim to the earnings of an enterprise and is often secured by a lien on the assets involved. Debt investors receive fixed or variable interest on the money invested in bonds or mortgages and the principal is repaid at maturity. Equity investment is known as *venture capital* because it involves greater risk. Equity earnings are subordinate to operating expenses and debt service, but equity investors are compensated with dividends and possible appreciation in the value of their investments.

Vehicles for assembling real estate equity funds include *trusts, partnerships* (general and limited), *syndications, joint ventures, pension funds, life insurance companies,* and *international equity capital.* Sources of real estate debt investment are savings and loan associations, commercial banks, life insurance companies, mutual savings banks, junior mortgage originators, and the secondary mortgage market.

The different characteristics of debt and equity investments appeal to different kinds of investors. The trading of common stocks represents the largest equity market and provides data for analyzing the competitiveness and risk of real estate equity investments. Transactions in the bond and debenture markets reflect investors' perceptions of future economic conditions and the anticipated performance of debt capital investment in real estate.

Chapter 6

FEE SIMPLE AND PARTIAL INTERESTS

*A*ccording to the bundle of rights theory, complete real property ownership, or title in fee, consists of a group of distinct rights. Each of these rights can be separated from the bundle and conveyed by the fee owner to other parties in perpetuity or for a limited time period. When a right is separated from the bundle and transferred or mortgaged, a partial, or fractional, property interest is created.[1]

Appraisers must understand partial interests to define appraisal problems. At the start of any appraisal assignment, the property rights to be valued must be clearly identified. Valuations of partial interests are often required because many forms of real estate ownership and lease agreements involve less than the complete bundle of rights. Evaluations of partial interests are also needed in real estate decision-making.

Property interests may be examined from many perspectives because the ownership, legal, economic, and financial aspects of real estate overlap.

The ownership of property interests can be divided in various ways. For example, several parties may have undivided partial ownership rights in a specific property through joint tenancies, tenancies in common, or tenancies by the entirety. A land trust is a vehicle for partial property interests in which a group of property owners continues to operate and manage a property, but the legal title is conveyed to a trustee. Other legal arrangements and title-holding entities that divide property rights among groups of owners include corporations, partnerships, cooperative corporations, condominiums, and interval ownerships or timeshares. In these arrangements property rights or interests are divided among several parties, and an appropriate legal entity is chosen to hold the property title.

Separate economic and legal interests derived from the bundle of rights are involved in many kinds of income-producing properties, and each of these interests is distinct in its form and content. Leased fee, leasehold, and subleasehold estates are created when leases are conveyed in accordance with established legal procedures.

The leasing of real estate is one practical and familiar application of the bundle of rights theory. An owner of a complete bundle of rights (the lessor) may convey to a tenant (the lessee) rights to use and occupy a property for a fixed period of time. In return, the tenant agrees to pay periodic rent.

The U.S. Constitution establishes the right of freedom of contract, which allows for flexibility in lease arrangements. A variety of lease contract clauses and provisions have been developed and used, and many have been tested and interpreted by the courts. The flexibility of leasing arrangements has resulted in leasing practices that are responsive to changing economic and financial conditions.

In valuing the economic and legal interests created by leases, appraisers must consider the following factors: the relationship between contract rent and market rent, the length of the lease, and the credit (risk) rating of the tenant. These factors may strongly influence the selection of discount rates. If, for example, the tenant has a low credit rating, an appraiser may not give much consideration to the lease arrangement. If the same lease is assumed by a tenant that is a major business entity with an AAA credit rating, the appraiser would give significant weight to the lease terms. The outlook for future income is much clearer in this

---

1. For an historical view of how real property interests relate to U.S. law, see C. Reinold Noyes, *The Institution of Property* (London: Longmans, Green and Company, 1936).

case, and the value of the leased fee may exceed the market value of the property unencumbered by the lease.

Complex interrelationships may create a variety of situations. For example, a below-market contract rent to be paid by a tenant with a poor credit rating may be more certain than an above-market contract rent to be paid by a tenant with a good credit rating.

The financial aspects of property interests have a major impact on real estate investment practices. The analysis of mortgage and equity components is of particular importance. Mortgage funds are secured debt positions, while equity investments are venture capital. Mortgage and equity components may be subdivided into fee simple, leased fee, and leasehold interests. They may also be broken down according to the proportions of land and building in the overall property. Other possible financial arrangements include senior and subordinated debt, sale-leaseback financing, and equity syndications.

The ownership, legal, economic, and financial perspectives from which lease interests and other fractional property interests can be described illustrate the complexity and usefulness of the bundle of rights. A thorough understanding of the property rights to be valued in an appraisal assignment is needed not only to define the problem, but also to produce an appropriate solution.

TYPES OF PROPERTY INTERESTS

Fee Simple Estates

Possession of a title in fee establishes the interest in property known as the fee simple estate—i.e., *absolute ownership unencumbered by any other interest or estate, subject only to the limitations imposed by the governmental powers of taxation, eminent domain, police power, and escheat.*

Owners in fee simple may choose to improve or not to improve their property. They may also retain ownership or transfer property title by selling the property or giving it away. When a fee owner dies, the property passes to his or her heirs or to others named in the will. This creates *an estate, a right or interest in property.* Inherited property interests are frequently the subject of valuation assignments.

Life Estates

A life estate is defined as the total rights of use, occupancy, and control, limited to the lifetime of a designated party. The designated party is known as the *life tenant* and is obligated to maintain the property in good condition and pay all applicable taxes. Life estates can be created by wills or deeds of conveyance. For example, a fee owner may leave a will that gives land to his widow for her remaining lifetime and, at her death, the land is passed on to their children. Thus, the widow acquires a life estate and functions as a life tenant. A living fee owner may deed his property to a family member and, by the terms of the conveyance, retain a life estate for himself. This practice eliminates the expense of probating the will after the owner dies.

To estimate the probable duration of the income from a life estate, an appraiser must rely on life expectancy statistics from actuarial studies. Once the net operating income from the estate and its duration are established, an appropriate discount rate can be selected and applied.

Lease Interests

Lease interests result when the bundle of rights is divided by a lease. The lessor and the lessee each obtain interests, which are stipulated in contract form and are subject to contract law. The divided interests resulting from a lease represent two distinct, but related, estates of property—the leased fee estate and the leasehold estate. The leaseholder, or tenant, receives the right to use the real estate for specific purposes over a defined period of time.

The leased fee estate is the lessor's, or landlord's, estate. *A leased fee estate is an ownership interest held by a landlord with the right of use and occupancy conveyed by lease to others; the rights of lessor (the leased fee owner) and leased fee are specified by contract terms contained within the lease.* Although the specific details of leases vary, a leased fee generally provides the lessor with rent to be paid by the lessee under stipulated terms; the right of repossession at the termination of the lease; default provisions; and the rights to sell, mortgage, or bequeath the property during the lease period. When a lease is legally delivered, the lessor must surrender possession of the property to the tenant for the lease period and abide by the lease provisions.

The leasehold estate is the lessee's, or tenant's, estate. *A leasehold estate is the right to use and occupy real estate for a stated term under the conditions conveyed in the lease.* When a lease is transmitted, a tenant usually acquires the rights to possess the property for the lease period, to sublease the property if desired, and occasionally to improve the property under the restrictions specified in the lease. In return, the tenant is obligated to pay rent, surrender possession of the property at the termination of the lease, remove any improvements the lessee has modified or constructed if specified, and abide by the lease provisions.

LEASES

Lease Terms

A lease is both a contract and a conveyance. It is a conveyance by which the landlord gives the tenant the right to occupy the property for the term specified in the lease. It imposes a contractual obligation on the tenant to pay rent to the landlord, and it may contain other promises and agreements between the landlord and the tenant. The legal interest held by the tenant is the leasehold estate. Leases may stipulate the use and occupancy of structures or parts of structures. Ground leases specifically grant the right to use and occupy land.

Leases that cover a period of one year or more must be set down in writing. In some states leases for shorter periods may be verbal. A lease should clearly describe the rented property, specifying the geographic location, street address, and condition of the premises. The signatures of the lessor and the lessee effectively establish the legal power of a lease. The tenant's possession generally provides notice that the rights of the leasehold estate are being exercised. Long-term leases are usually recorded.

Most leases contain clauses pertaining to the duration of tenancy, rent, security deposit, insurance, payment of public utilities, right of entry, assignment and subleasing, maintenance and repair, fixtures, taxes, eminent domain, default, and renewal options. Other contractual clauses may address purchase options, rent escalations, alterations, and use restrictions. Many types of leases (e.g., ground leases) contain provisions for leasehold mortgaging provided the arrangement is economically sound, the term of the lease is not too short, and leasehold mortgaging is not forbidden by the lease.

Lease clauses can influence property value. Therefore, it is imperative that appraisers read and understand all leases that affect the property interests being appraised. In some instances it may be advisable or necessary for an appraiser to consult an attorney for assistance in interpreting lease provisions. By leasing real estate a lessor receives some advantages, including the receipt of a certain income or annuity, favorable income tax considerations, and the benefit of tenant-built improvements, unless these are reserved as the personal property of the tenant. These advantages can, and frequently do, enhance property value and provide the owner with a hedge against inflation. The potential advantages for a lessee include a minimum equity investment in property, an alternative to costly financing, favorable tax considerations, and reduced management responsibility.

Tenancy

When the bundle of rights is divided into property interests, tenancy is created. In real estate *tenancy* has two meanings: 1) *the holding of property by any form of title, and* 2) *the right to use and occupy property as conveyed in a lease.* The first definition usually refers to co-ownership of real estate; the second definition concerns the nature of the relationship between a landlord and a tenant.

Co-ownership may be described as joint tenancy, tenancy by the entirety, or tenancy in common. *Joint tenancy is joint ownership by two or more persons with right of survivorship.* Under this arrangement each party has an identical interest and right of possession. *Tenancy by the entirety is an estate held by a husband and wife in which neither has a disposable interest in the property during the lifetime of the other, except through joint action.* It has the same survivorship provision as a joint tenancy, but tenancy by the entirety applies only to spouses. *Tenancy in common is an estate held by two or more persons, each of whom has an undivided interest.* In this estate the undivided interest may or may not be equally shared by the holders and there is no right of survivorship.

The valuation of undivided partial interests poses a problem for appraisers. Because no party can exercise complete control, the interest of each party is usually not worth as much as the corresponding fraction of the property's market value. Minority interests have limited market appeal, so the appraiser must decide how to derive an appropriate value. Because either party can bring legal action to divide the property, which is known as *partition*, the cost of this proceeding is one measure of value diminution. However, a sale in partition is a forced sale, which does not reflect free market action. Due to the lack of pertinent market transactions, valuations of co-ownerships are often somewhat subjective.

The length of the relationship between a landlord and a tenant varies and is periodic in nature. *Tenancy from period to period* and *tenancy for years* are two legally recognized ways to describe this relationship. In tenancy from period to period, the leasehold interest owner pays rent periodically and each payment renews the interest for an additional period. The ultimate length of the leasehold interest is not stated. In a tenancy for years, the beginning and end of the estate are clearly specified. If the tenant does not default, the estate continues until it expires on the specified termination date.

Rental Payments

There are two basic kinds of leases, which are distinguished by who is financially responsible for property expenses. Gross leases and net leases delineate different responsibilities. *A gross lease is a lease in which the landlord receives stipulated rent and is obligated to pay all or most of the operating expenses and real estate taxes. A net lease is a lease in which the tenant pays all property charges in addition to the stipulated rent.* Typical property charges include real estate taxes, insurance premiums, assessments, and the costs of maintenance and structural repairs. In net lease arrangements the tenant assumes the risk that taxes may increase or the building may be destroyed. If the building is destroyed, the tenant may be obligated to rebuild the building and continue paying rent during its construction. The exact definitions of these two types of leases vary in different parts of the United States. Thus, the appraiser must understand the precise legal definition used in the local area.

The level and schedule of rental payments can also vary. *A flat rental, or level payment, lease has a specified level of rent that continues throughout the lease term.* In contrast, the payments required by a step-up or step-down lease change at specific points in time. *A step-up or step-down lease provides for a certain rent for an initial period, followed by an increase or decrease in rent over stated periods.* Other types of leases may stipulate that adjustments be made, although not necessarily at specified intervals. *An index lease provides for periodic rent adjustments based on the change in an economic index.* The Consumer Price Index (CPI) is frequently used to set rent levels in long-term leases. *A revaluation lease provides for rent adjustments at periodic intervals based on a revaluation of the real estate.* Rent payments can be annual, semi-annual, quarterly, monthly, weekly, or even daily. They may be required at the beginning of the specified rental period or at the end. An *escalator lease* may require the lessor to pay expenses for the first year of the lease and the lessee to pay any increase in expenses as additional rent over the subsequent years of the lease.

Lease terms shape the quantity and quality of the future benefits likely to flow to the interests created by the contract. The lease agreement provides that the lessor will receive specified rent or services during the term of the lease and a reversion of the tenant's rights of use and occupancy when the lease expires. The contract gives the tenant exclusive rights of use and occupancy during the lease term, subject to rent or service obligations. Other divisions of rights are common. For example, an original tenant may sublet a property and both the leased fee and leasehold positions may be mortgaged. (Analysis of income and expenses and the procedures for valuing leased fee and leasehold estates are discussed in Chapters 18, 19, and 20.)

A lease sets rental terms and presumably indicates the gross income to the leased fee. As mentioned previously, appraisers estimating the market value of leased fee interests must always consider the following factors: the relationship between contract rent (the actual rental income specified in the lease) and market rent (the rental income the property would most likely command currently in the open market), the length of the lease, and the credit (risk) rating of the tenant.

SPECIALIZED LEASE INTERESTS

Leasehold Position

The most important obligation associated with the rights to use and occupy a leasehold interest is the payment of rent. *Contract rent is the actual rental income specified in a lease.* Rent is commonly paid by the tenant or tenants to the lessor according to a specified schedule. A leasehold interest usually has value when contract rent is less than market rent. If the lessee has a rent advantage, the leasehold interest has positive value. This, in turn, may affect the value of the leased fee. A leased fee encumbered with a fixed rent that is below market rates may be worth less than the unencumbered fee estate. *Market rent is the rental income that a property would most probably command in the open market.* Only in an ideally negotiated lease would contract rent equal market rent. When contract rent exceeds market levels, the leasehold may have negative value.

Subleasehold Position

Normally a tenant is free to sublease all or part of a property, but many leases require that the lessor's consent be obtained. *A sublease is an agreement in which the lessee in a prior lease conveys the right of use and occupancy of the property to another. An assignment is a written transfer of the rights of use and occupancy of the property to be held by another legal entity or to be used for the benefit of creditors.* Leases usually provide that the lessor's consent "will not unreasonably be withheld." Over the years, court decisions have established that subleasing should not be subject to undue constraint. To deny permission lessors usually must show that the security of their position would be impaired.

In a sublease, the original lessee is "sandwiched" between a lessor and a sublessee. The original lessee's interest has value when the contract rent is less than the rent collected from the sublessee. Subleasing does not release the lessee from any of the obligations to the lessor as defined in the lease agreement.

The discount rates used in valuing different lease interests will vary because the rates selected must reflect the risks involved. Generally, a lessor's interest, the leased fee, entails less risk than a lessee's interest, the leasehold. The lessee, in turn, assumes less risk than the sublessee, whose position is exposed to the greatest risk.

A lease contract may contain a provision that explicitly forbids subletting. Without either the right to sublet or a term that is long enough to be marketable, a leasehold position cannot be conveyed and, therefore, has no market value. Furthermore, the value of the leased fee would likely be diminished. However, the leasehold position would have a use value to the lessee. However, the valuation of leaseholds under contractual provisions that prohibit subletting may be required for a variety of reasons (e.g., in cases involving condemnation and estate taxes).

Mortgaged Lease Interests

Leasehold mortgaging is a type of mortgage-equity financing in which a lessee, or tenant, agrees to subordinate the leasehold interest to a mortgage covering the leasehold. Such a mortgage is often obtained by a lessee developer, with the lessor's consent, to build improvements on the property. The problem is that if the tenant defaults on the terms of lease, he or she is subject to eviction. It is important to remember that, in this situation, it is the lessee, not the lessor, who is subordinating the leasehold to a mortgage. The rights of the leasehold mortgagee would be forfeit in an eviction of the tenant. The leasehold mortgagee may be protected by a "nondisturbance" clause in the lease or by a subordination of the lease to the leasehold mortgage. A "nondisturbance" clause gives the mortgagee the right to cure any default(s) by the lessee upon appropriate notice. In a lease subordination arrangement, the leasehold mortgagee can foreclose on the leasehold interest subject to the lease.

A leasehold mortgagee who finances building improvements should be certain that the rent required in the ground lease is not higher than a competitively attractive yield on the land value. The mortgagee should make sure that the lease terms include the right to cure any lessee default. If compelled to foreclose, the leasehold mortgagee can then take possession of the leasehold interest and the improvements, subject to the terms of the lease, and is only obliged to pay the rent required in the lease.

In current investment practice, investors seek maximum financing for favorable leveraging and the best tax shelter. Leases, the mortgaging of lease interests, and subordinations provide the necessary tools. For major investment projects, a more complex set of arrangements may be worked out. For example, a property may be divided into a leased fee and a leasehold interest. The mortgage on the leased fee is arranged and a leasehold mortgage is set up to construct improvements. By using different legal entities, one party can hold both the fee position and the leasehold position. In such a situation, expert legal advice is needed to ensure that the documentation supports the separation of the interests and does not effect a merger.

In appraising a leasehold estate subject to a mortgage, the appraiser should investigate whether the rent provisions of the ground lease are tied to the CPI, whether the debt service on the fee mortgage is variable, and whether the debt service on the leasehold mortgage includes an equity kicker or participation benefits. The appraiser must be aware of these provisions to appraise the property appropriately.

OTHER FRACTIONAL INTERESTS

The bundle of rights includes interests other than those created by leases for the use and occupancy of the physical real estate. Property ownership may also be divided by vertical interests, easements, and transferable development rights (TDRs), each of which can be considered separately in sales, leases, mortgages, and other realty transactions.

Vertical Interests

One important dimension of real property ownership concerns the distinction between subsurface and air rights.[2] *A subsurface right is the right to the use and profits of the underground portion of a designated property.* The term usually refers to the right to extract minerals from below the earth's surface and to construct tunnels for railroads, motor vehicles, and public utilities. *Air rights are the property rights associated with the use, control, and regulation of air space over a parcel of real estate.* Both of these fractional interests represent portions of a fee simple estate, but each embodies the idea of land as a three-dimensional entity.

The vertical division of real property is based on the legal conception of land as a volume of space with boundless height and depth.[3] This concept is significant because technological developments continue to expand our ability to use the earth's subsurface and atmosphere. In urban areas in particular, engineering advances have dramatically affected land use and, therefore, highest and best use considerations. The development of steel-framed building construction, the passenger elevator, deep tunnel excavation techniques, and communications technology are some examples of technological changes that have helped shape our urban landscape.

Changes in land use also reflect the forces and factors affecting value. As the density of building in urban areas increases, fewer sites are available for new construction and land values escalate. This trend has produced a growing interest in developing air rights. As early as 1902, the air rights associated with highly valued land along the New York Central Railroad in New York City were beginning to be developed. Park Avenue is one outstanding example of real estate development built on the acquisition of air rights. Many other examples of development established on air rights can be found in urban areas around the world.

When a large building is to be constructed in a space to which air rights apply, the base of the site is visualized as a platform constructed at some level (e.g., 30 or 40 feet) above the present surface. In the case of Park Avenue development, however, the platform is actually located below grade, just above the railroad tunnel. The platform must be supported by columns, which normally rest on a caisson foundation built underground. In this manner, a number of discrete, interrelated "lots" are created; the air, column, and caisson lots associated with different portions of the three-dimensional space comprise the land or site in question. Figure 6.1 illustrates a division of vertical space.

Air rights can be transferred in various ways. Often the air rights to one property are shifted to another within the same building zone under legal planning regulations. The transfer of air rights allows developers to adjust the density of land use without putting adverse pressure on owners, neighborhoods, or districts. This practice underscores the importance of local zoning authorities, which regulate building heights, building functions, setbacks, and other variables involved in the development of air rights.

---

2. Rights to surface areas may be divided by horizontal subdivision, *the division of a tract of land into smaller parcels for sale or lease.* A horizontal subdivision, however, is not a partial interest. Usually a large tract held in fee simple is divided into a number of smaller units, which are also held in fee simple. Rights-of-way over surface areas may be conveyed by easements, which are discussed later in this chapter.
3. B. Harrison Frankel, "Three-Dimensional Real Property Law: The Truth About 'Air Rights,'" *Real Estate Law Journal* (Spring 1984).

Figure 6.1 Three-Dimensional Division of Space for Air or Tunnel Rights

As an example, these divisions may be identified as air rights above air lot level; column lots between air lot level and ground (1-20); caisson lots below ground level (1-20); tunnel rights between ground level and subsurface (E)

Figure 6.2 The Merchandise Mart in Chicago

(H. Armstrong Roberts, Inc.)

Air rights can be sold in fee, with the seller retaining one or more easements for a specialized use such as the operation of a railroad. Air rights may also be subdivided; in this case the owner of the fee sells or leases only the land and air that are to be occupied by a particular improvement.

Air rights were subdivided to construct The Merchandise Mart in Chicago, which is shown in Figure 6.2. The structure was built between 1928 and 1931 in air space above The Chicago and Northwestern Railroad. The owners of the Mart, which is one of the world's largest mercantile buildings, actually possess 458 caisson lots extending 100 feet below ground, 458 column lots, a small surface parcel that houses building equipment, and the air lot 23 feet above Chicago's city datum level, where the building is constructed. The Merchandise Mart typifies the traditional development of air rights over existing railroad track; other developments may be more creatively designed.

Easements

Easements represent another division of property ownership. *An easement is an interest in real property that conveys use, but not ownership, of a portion of an owner's property.* Easements frequently permit a specific portion of a property to be used for access to an adjoining property or as a public right-of-way. Although surface easements are the most common, subterranean and overhead easements are used for public utilities, subways, and bridges.

Clearly, a property that acquires an easement is the beneficiary of additional rights; one that is subject to an easement is burdened. Easement rights can be conveyed in perpetuity or for a limited time period. An easement can be created by a contract between private parties or by adverse possession in accordance with state law. It can also be arranged by states, municipalities, or public utilities through the exercise of eminent domain. In these cases, a valuation is needed to estimate the price the easement beneficiary should pay to the burdened party.

An easement that affords ingress and egress to an otherwise landlocked parcel increases its value. Easement rights to a development's recreational facilities normally enhance the value of plots that have this advantage. The value of an easement is usually estimated as some part of the amount of value it adds to the property it benefits; the burdened property's loss in value can also be used to indicate the value of an easement. The value of an easement reflects the basic economic concept of contribution. No one should pay more for an easement than the amount of value gained by the property it benefits. The holder of an easement realizes a gain by paying less than the added value.

When an easement is acquired by a public utility company—e.g., for overhead power lines, valuation becomes more complicated. In all cases, however, an easement is a partial interest that is held by another party and burdens the real property estate. It is created by a deed and has measurable value.

Conservation easements, which restrict the future use of property to conservation or wildlife habitat, and are usually owned by a county, a state, or the federal government. Open space easements set land aside for nonbuilding uses and may encumber land in three ownership categories: private open space adjacent to dwellings owned by individual residents, public open space owned by the government, and common open space owned by a community association and set aside for the use of residents.

Preservation easements are used to protect certain historic properties by prohibiting physical changes to the property and, in many cases, limiting the uses to which the property can be put. Usually the owner must maintain the condition of the property at the time the easement is donated or immediately after a proposed restoration. Under federal law, a preservation easement can be deeded to a qualified nonprofit organization or government agency. In such instances, the property owner donates the easement and receives an income tax reduction that can be equal to, but not more than, the market value of the real property rights donated.

The economic theory on which the valuation of preservation easements is based is generally the same as that which governs eminent domain appraising, although the acquirer of a preservation easement receives rather than takes rights. Each easement document contains specific controls and restrictions that must be carefully analyzed to determine how it affects the encumbered property. The effect of historic district controls or individual landmark designations should be related to the subject property and to the provisions of the easement.

Transferable Development Rights

Transferable development rights (TDRs) emerged in the real estate industry during the 1970s. *A transferable development right is a development right that cannot be used by the landowner, but can be sold to landowners in another location.* Some TDRs are used to preserve property uses for agricultural production, open space, or historic buildings. In this arrangement a preservation district and a development district are identified. Landowners in the preservation district are assigned development rights, which they cannot use to develop their own land, but can sell to landowners in the development district. These landowners can use these transferred rights to build at higher densities than zoning laws in the development district would normally permit.

Appraisers can value TDRs with ordinary sales comparison techniques if there are sufficient transactions to constitute a market. When the market is inadequate, appraisers may use the income capitalization approach. In such cases the economic concept of contribution provides a foundation, and the value added to a property through the acquisition of a TDR is adjusted for the administrative, legal, and other costs incurred. Some, though not all, of the property's net value increase can be attributed to the TDR; no one is likely to undertake such a complicated procedure without the prospect of a reasonable profit.

SPECIALIZED FRACTIONAL OWNERSHIP

Condominium Ownership

A condominium is a form of fee ownership of separate units or portions of multiunit buildings that provides for formal filing and recording of a divided interest in real property. A condominium unit is a separate ownership, and title is held by an individual owner. The unit may be separately leased, sold, or mortgaged. A condominium owner also has title to a partial interest in the total project, whether it is a residential or commercial property. The owner possesses a three-dimensional space within the outer walls, roof or ceiling, and floors and, along with other owners, has an undivided interest in common areas—e.g., the land, the public portions of the building, the foundation, the outer walls, and the spaces provided for parking and recreation. The owners of units in a condominium project usually form an association to manage commonly held real estate in accordance with adopted bylaws. The expenses of management and maintenance are divided pro rata among the owners, who pay a monthly fee.

To value individual condominium units, appraisers generally use the sales comparison approach. Recent sales of units of comparable size, location, and quality are the best indicators of value. To value entire condominium projects, whether they are newly constructed buildings or conversions, appraisers usually apply the income capitalization approach using discounted cash flow analysis. The amount and timing of all capital outlays, expected monetary receipts, and returns are estimated, and these amounts are discounted at a rate consistent with competitive investment yields. The estimates of future sellout prices and the timing of sales are key elements in the valuation.

Cooperative Ownership

In certain areas the cooperative ownership of apartments is popular. *Cooperative ownership is a form of ownership in which each owner of stock in a cooperative apartment building or housing corporation receives a proprietary lease on a specific apartment and is obligated to pay a rental which represents the proportionate share of operating expenses and debt service on the underlying mortgage, which is paid by the corporation.*

A co-op is established when a stock corporation is organized to issue an authorized number of shares at a specified par value. The corporation takes title to an apartment building and prices the various apartments. The price per unit determines the number of shares that an apartment occupant must purchase to acquire a proprietary lease. The lease obligates the occupant to pay a monthly maintenance fee, which may be adjusted at times by the corporation's board of directors. The fee covers the expenses of management, operations, and maintenance of public areas. Because the shareholders can vote their shares in electing directors, they have some control over property conditions.

Recently, a new method for financing cooperatives has emerged in some areas. In the past cooperative corporations arranged mortgages on entire apartment properties. Cooperative shareholders had to fund their purchases with 100% equity or borrow the money from commercial banks on short-term, personal notes. Now, however, a cooperative corporation can arrange a mortgage on the total property, and individual apartment shareholders can mortgage their stock for up to 75% of its value. These new mortgage arrangements have made cooperative apartment properties much more marketable.

If the market for cooperative apartments is active, appraisers can value apartment units by the sales comparison approach. However, appraisers must remember that prices are influenced by the amount and terms of the mortgage financing that the corporation has placed on the building. In recent years co-op mortgages have ranged from 25% to 50% of total value, with the balance financed by individual apartment shareholders as pure equity or with cooperative apartment mortgages. Often corporate bylaws impose limitations on the property's marketability, which can affect the validity of comparable sales data.

Timesharing

Fractional interests created by timesharing have been marketed extensively in recent years. *Timesharing involves the sale of either limited ownership interests in, or rights to use and occupy, residential apartments or hotel rooms.*

There are two forms of timesharing. It is imperative that the appraiser distinguish between them when appraising timeshare projects or analyzing timeshare comparables. The first form is known as fee timesharing. The fee timeshare purchaser receives a deed that conveys title to a unit for a specific part of a year, thereby limiting the ownership interest. The purchaser has the right to sell, lease, or bequeath this real property interest. The interest can be mortgaged, and title can be recorded. The second form of timesharing is nonfee timesharing, which does not convey a legal title in the property. Typically a purchaser receives only the right to use a timeshare unit and related premises.

There are subcategories for both types of timesharing. The two types of fee timesharing are timeshare ownership and interval ownership. In timeshare ownership, purchasers receive a deed to an undivided interest in a particular unit as tenants in common. Each purchaser agrees to use the unit only during the time period stipulated in his or her deed. In interval ownership, the owner receives a terminable fee in the form of a tenancy for years (the specified time period), which may last for the duration of the project. At the end of the tenancy for years, interval owners as tenants in common are conveyed a vested remainder.

They then have the option of selling the property and dividing the proceeds, or continuing as tenants in common and renewing the interval estate.

Timeshare owners and interval owners pay operating expenses, including a proportionate share of taxes, insurance, and other costs, and a fee for common area maintenance (CAM) and management. In many projects, 50 one-week intervals are created; the remaining two weeks of each year are reserved for maintenance and major repairs.

The three types of nonfee timesharing are known as the leasehold interest, vacation license, and the club membership. The leasehold interest type of timesharing is essentially a prepaid lease arrangement. The vacation license involves the transfer of a license from the developer to the purchaser, giving the latter the right to use a given type of unit for specified time periods over the life of the vacation license contract. In the club membership format of ownership, timeshare patrons purchase membership for a specified number of years in a club which owns, leases, or operates the timeshare property. The purchaser receives the right to use a type of unit for a specified period during each year of membership.

The partial interests created by timesharing are valued through sales comparison. The appraiser begins by identifying the rights to be valued. The portion of the property allocated for use by the shareholder must also be established as well as any personal property included. In appraising existing timeshare properties, resales of comparables generally provide reliable indications of value. In valuing new timeshare projects, appraisers must consider 1) the time required for sellout, 2) seasonal variations that affect sales, 3) all direct and indirect costs required to create a facility that will command the prices anticipated, and most important, 4) competition in the market.

LEGAL ENTITIES AFFECTING OWNERSHIP
Stock Corporations

One common form of partial ownership is a stock corporation. A stock corporation may be organized to hold title to a single asset, such as a parcel of real property, or it may have a portfolio of investments. Corporate ownership is divided into partial interests by selling shares to an investment group. Any specific stock holding represents a percentage of total corporate ownership, which is derived from the ratio between the number of shares owned by a particular interest and the total number of shares issued by the corporation. The percentage is an ownership share in the corporation, and its book value is usually found by multiplying the corporate net worth by the ownership percentage.

The market value of a share of stock in a corporation that has a parcel of real estate as its sole asset may be higher or lower than its book value. *Book value is defined as the capital amount at which property is shown on the account books.* Book value usually equals the original cost of the asset after subtracting reserves for depreciation and adding allocations for capital recapture. Book value and market value are usually not the same, so the values of the pro rata shares of ownership associated with each differ.

Fractional corporate interests—i.e., shares of stock—typically sell for less than their pro rata value because a minority interest does not have the ability to control the investment. In a closely held corporation such as a real estate venture, additional discounts are required to reflect illiquidity because the market for shares is often limited.

Because stock market values often represent a discount from actual corporate net worth, the accounting profession and the Securities and Exchange Commission allow publicly owned real estate corporations to show both the book values and the current market values of assets on their annual financial statements. This practice, which is sometimes referred to as *current value accounting*, frequently reveals that present market values greatly exceed book values (i.e., cost less accumulated depreciation). Therefore, a corporation may have greater net worth than is indicated by book figures. Publicly owned real estate corporations employ professional appraisers to estimate the current market values used in these reports.

The International Assets Valuation Standards Committee (TIAVSC) was formed in 1980 to establish worldwide standards for the valuation of fixed assets in financial statements. Under international accounting standards, fixed assets are divided into tangible assets, intangible assets, and financial assets. Many in the accounting and financial communities believe that evaluations of the current and historical performance of businesses should be made with reference to the current value of their assets. In the United States, historical costs are commonly used to report the value of fixed assets.

Land Trusts

Trusts are sometimes used as legal vehicles for partial ownership interests in real property. *A land trust is often a legal vehicle for partial ownership interests in real property in which independently owned properties are conveyed to a trustee. Land trusts may be used to effect a profitable assemblage or in some cases to facilitate the assigning of property as collateral for a loan.* The trustee holds legal title in the property for a specified time and performs only the functions outlined in the trust agreement. The trustee may or may not actively manage the property or collect rent; when not performed by the trustee, these duties remain the responsibility of the beneficiaries, who are the original owners. One important legal aspect of a trust arrangement is that a judgment against a beneficiary is not a lien against the real estate.

To value a beneficiary's partial interest, an appraiser must first estimate the market value of the total property. The appraiser then adjusts the estimate to account for any effect on value that may result from the trust indenture provisions, which identify the rights and obligations of beneficiaries. The beneficiary's minority position will call for significant downward adjustment.

General and Limited Partnerships

Partnerships are used extensively in real estate acquisition because they pool funds for property ownership and operation. In a general partnership, all partners share in business gains and each is fully responsible for all liabilities. To value a partner's partial interest, an appraiser estimates the market value of the partnership's total real property assets and adjusts the estimate to reflect the partner's percentage of ownership. Other adjustments are made in light of the terms of the partnership agreement, which define the partners' rights and liabilities in sales and liquidations. The partners' ability or inability to control business operations (i.e., to decide when to sell, to select property managers, and to approve or disapprove prospective leases) has a major effect on the value of a general partnership. Another important aspect of a partnership is that it automatically terminates when a general partner dies. Because the provisions of partnership contracts shape and limit ownership benefits, they also influence the value of the partial interests involved.

Limited partnerships have both general partners and limited partners. The general partners manage the business and assume full liability for partnership obligations. The liability of each limited partner, however, is restricted to his or her capital contributions.

The investment value of limited partnership interests or syndicate shares often includes income tax shelter benefits. It is not unusual for such an investment to offer small income returns, at least in the early years, when the value of the investment is perceived to lie largely in the income tax benefits of building depreciation, mortgage interest, and other tax shelters. These tax deductions may offset the investor's income from other passive sources of income that are subject to certain limitations and restrictions. The resulting tax deferrals are seen as earnings of the partnership interest, even though the dollars involved do not flow from partnership property.

Frequently tax law changes alter the value of various tax shelter benefits. Early property disposition or foreclosure can damage these benefits due to tax law recapture provisions. These considerations should be weighed in rating the risk of partnership investments. The Tax Reform Act of 1986 significantly reduced the income-sheltering benefits offered by real estate.

Equity Syndications

Equity syndication is another popular financial division of property interests. *A syndication is a private or public partnership that pools funds for the acquisition and development of real estate projects.* Syndications, which may be referred to as partnerships, are established when an individual or group purchases interests in real estate for the purpose of transferring them to a limited partnership. The limited partnership interests are then sold to investors.

Such arrangements appear simple, but they may be very complex because syndications frequently purchase more than real estate, and the value of the interests in real estate and the aggregate value of the limited partnership interests differ in quality as well as quantity. Syndications create property interests, which are grouped as securities. Their value depends not only on the underlying real estate, but also on the additional, or more limited, rights created by contracts and other nonrealty considerations. Accordingly, any valuation of syndicated property other than market valuation of fee simple rights involves valuing more than real estate.

Real estate interests and the interests of the limited partnership differ in value because many non-real estate items or conditions are involved. In addition to the real estate interests conveyed, most sales of limited partnership interests by a syndicator include other items such as management services, the ability to invest in a major property that an investor might not be able to invest in alone, and the potential for improved liquidity. Potential capital appreciation and eligibility for tax benefits, which are not limited to syndications, also influence investors and may affect market value. These factors and conditions are difficult to isolate, so analyses of comparable sales may be difficult.

Decreased inflation, the prosecution of individuals who abuse tax shelters, and the failure of financial institutions have brought some mortgage and syndication practices into question. Appraisers must exercise great care in determining the exact nature of the interests to be valued in any assignment involving partnerships. The market values of syndication interests should not be presented as though they represent the assembled ownership of real estate assets.[4]

SUMMARY

Property rights include ownership, legal estate, economic benefits, and financial components. Ownership may be held by an individual, a partnership, or a corporation, and undivided ownership rights may belong to two or more parties in tenancies. Legal estate refers to the disposition of the rights to property use and occupancy. Economic benefits describe the income generated from rent or a percentage of profits. The financial components of a property consist of the equity and mortgage funds that secure it. The equity and mortgage interests in property may be further divided into *leased fee* and *leasehold interests* or into land and building components.

A *fee simple estate* represents absolute ownership of property unencumbered by any other interest or estate and subject only to the powers of government. Ownership of a fee simple estate can be retained, sold, bestowed, or bequeathed. A *life estate* is created by a will or deed of conveyance, which assigns life tenancy and provides for the property to be bequeathed when the life tenant dies.

Lease interests result when property rights are separated by legal contracts. The rights of the *lessor*, the leased fee owner or landlord, generally include the right to collect rent for the lease period; to repossess the property when the lease expires or the tenant defaults; and to dispose of the property through a sale, mortgage, or bequest during the lease period. The *lessee*, the leaseholder or tenant, has the right to use and occupy the property for the lease period and may have the right to sublease it and improve it. In return, the lessee is obligated by contract to pay rent, to surrender possession when the lease ends and to abide by the lease conditions, which also bind the lessor. Other lease provisions may address required security deposits; payments for utilities, maintenance and repair; rent escalations; and renewal or purchase options.

Tenancy is the right to use and occupy property as conveyed by a lease. The length of the leasing period may be renewed periodically or it may be clearly specified. Tenancy can also refer to a variety of arrangements involving property ownership by two or more persons—e.g., *joint tenancy, tenancy by entirety,* and *tenancy in common*. The valuation of co-ownerships involving undivided partial interests may be especially difficult because no one party can exercise complete control.

Leases may be *gross* or *net leases*, depending on whether the landlord or the tenant pays the operating expenses and taxes for the property. Lease provisions

---

4. Guide Note 1 to the Appraisal Institute's Standards of Professional Appraisal Practice addresses the valuation of real estate interests intended for syndication and the valuation of real estate partnership interests.

may call for level payments (flat rental), step-up or step-down payments, or payments that are periodically adjusted to reflect an economic index, an increase in expenses, or a revaluation of the property.

The market value of a leased fee interest depends on how *contract rent* relates to *market rent* and often on the credit rating of the tenant. A leasehold interest may acquire value if the lease allows for subletting or assignment and the term is long enough to be marketable. *Subleasehold* and *sandwich leasehold positions* are created through subleasing and assignment. *Leasehold mortgaging* is often arranged for lessee developers who, with the lessor's consent, subordinate their leasehold interest to any mortgage covering the cost of the improvements they build on the property.

Partial interests also include vertical interests, easements, transferable development rights (TDRs), and interests resulting from specialized fractional ownership. Vertical interests refer to *subsurface rights* (e.g., for mining or the construction of transportation tunnels) and *air rights* for the use, control, and regulation of air space. *Easements* generally permit use of a portion of a property for access (e.g., for public utility lines, subways, or bridges). Preservation easements, which are deeded by donors to nonprofit organizations or government agencies in return for tax write-offs, prohibit certain physical changes to historic properties.

Fractional ownership arrangements include condominiums, cooperatives, and timesharing. *Condominium* owners hold title to individual units and have an undivided interest in common areas. They share management and maintenance expenses on a pro rata basis. In *cooperatives*, tenant proprietors, or stockholders, pay a proportionate share of operating expenses and debt service on a mortgage that is held by the cooperative. *Timesharing* involves the sale of either limited ownership interests in, or rights to use and occupy, residential apartments or hotel rooms for a specified period of time.

Stock corporations, land trusts, general and limited partnerships, and equity syndications are legal entities that create partial ownership interests. Corporate shareholders own stock, but the market value of this stock is generally different from its *book value. Land trusts,* which are formed to effect a profitable land assemblage or to assign a property as loan collateral, convey legal title to a trustee, while property management and rent collection are retained by the beneficiaries.

Partnerships are classified as general or limited depending on the partners liability for possible losses. *Equity syndications* are partnerships set up to pool funds for the acquisition and development of real estate projects. Syndications are created by contracts and provide more benefits than real estate ventures.

Chapter 7

DATA COLLECTION AND ANALYSIS

$\mathcal{T}$he identification of property interests, and other investigations that define the appraisal problem, provide direction for the collection of useful data. Appraisers need patience, judgment, and research skills to direct the preliminary steps of data collection and analysis and to gather and manage information. In real estate appraisal the quality and quantity of information available for analysis are as important as the methods and techniques used to process the data and complete the assignment. Therefore, the ability to distinguish between different kinds of data, to research reliable data sources, and to manage information efficiently is essential to appraisal practice.

GENERAL DATA

General data include information on the social, economic, governmental, and environmental forces that affect property value. This information is part of the accumulated knowledge which appraisers bring to their assignments. All general data are ultimately understood in terms of how they affect the economic climate in which real property transactions occur. In analyzing general data, appraisers observe the operation of appraisal principles by studying the interaction of the four forces that affect property values in an area. Although the four forces provide convenient categories for examining general data, it is their interaction that creates trends and ultimately influences property value.

Economic Trends

The related series of events that comprise a trend are studied and used as historical evidence to support forecasts. Forecasting is an art that employs scientific processes to identify or quantify future events or conditions. Forecasts are developed by analyzing statistical data, examining the perceptions and behavior of market participants, and scrutinizing all assumptions upon which the forecast rests. The application of critical judgment is fundamental to forecasting. In making forecasts appraisers try to discern and consider all pertinent factors affecting future conditions. Appraisers cannot predict the future, but they are able to develop probable forecasts by observing past and current market trends and examining perceptions of market participants. To forecast market conditions, appraisers scrutinize the likelihood that current trends will continue and that the events anticipated by market players will occur.

Appraisers must recognize and understand the economic trends that affect the value of real property. It is not enough to know that economic changes have occurred; the probable direction, extent, and impact of these changes must also be studied to identify and forecast trends.

The particular trends considered by an appraiser vary with the appraisal problem and the type of real estate being appraised. To estimate the market value of a shopping center with the income capitalization approach to value, for example, the base rent and overage rent under a percentage lease must be forecast.[1] The shopping center's total potential gross income depends on trends in the number of households in the trade area, the income of these households, and their

---

1. See Chapter 6 for the definition of a *percentage lease* and Chapter 19 for definitions of *base rent* and *overage rent*.

typical expenditures on the goods and services supplied by the center; the availability of alternative shopping facilities also must be considered.

International Economic Trends

In the world economy the economic well-being of one nation may directly and indirectly affect many other nations. There is much foreign investment in U.S. real estate partly because land prices are relatively low and the stability of the U.S. government gives foreign investors some measure of protection. Thus, inflation and political instability in other countries influence the demand for, and value of, real estate in the United States.

The greater the intensity and duration of an economic trend, the wider its influence. Changes in basic national and international economic indicators such as the balance of foreign trade, rates of foreign exchange, commodity price levels, wage levels, interest rates, industrial production levels, and the volume of retail sales all merit consideration.

National and Regional Economic Trends

The state of the national economy is basic to any real estate appraisal. National economic conditions are indicated by the gross national product, national income, the balance of payments to other nations, price level indexes, interest rates, aggregate employment and unemployment statistics, the number of housing starts and building permits issued, the dollar volume of construction, and other general data. A time series of economic indicators, which describes and measures changes or movements over a period of time, may reveal fluctuations in a longer-term trend and help put current statistics in perspective.

Federal programs and tax policies can affect the value of real estate. The need for financial institutions to compete for loanable funds with one another and with money market mutual funds has increased lending rates and resulted in an adjustment of demand in the market. The 1981 Economic Recovery Tax Act permitted accelerated cost recovery for buildings held for the production of income or for use in one's trade or business. The Tax Reform Act of 1986, however, has reinstated the straight-line depreciation system. Investment tax credits for the rehabilitation of older, nonresidential real estate and for historic preservation projects enhance the profitability of investment property and, ultimately, affect its value.

The national economy also reflects the economic condition of the various geographic regions in the United States. A region's economic health depends on the status of its economic activity. This activity, in turn, encompasses economic activities in individual areas and communities within the region's geographical boundaries. Minor disruptions in the economic growth of one community, however, may not appreciably affect the region if the regional and national economies are strong.

The extent to which an appraiser is concerned with the national or regional economy and the economy of the city or neighborhood depends on the size and type of property being appraised. For example, a large regional shopping center that serves a trade area of 500,000 people and an automobile assembly plant that employs 5,000 workers are more sensitive to the general state of the economy than are medical-dental office buildings or retail service operations in suburban residential areas.

Local Economic Trends

The analysis of a local economy often focuses on trends in population, employment, and income. Population change, net household formation, the diversity of the economic base of the community, the level and stability of employment, wage rates, and household or family income all indicate the economic strength of a community.

The conditions and potential of the local economy are relevant to most appraisal assignments. The value of real estate in a community is influenced by the demand for its use. The demand for various types of real estate, including vacant land, depends on the population of the market that the real estate serves, the effective purchasing power of this population, and their desire to own real estate. Demand may change for various types of real estate and between real estate and nonrealty investment sources.

Employment and economic base analysis. The population and income in a region or a community depend on the employment that constitutes the economic base of the area. *The economic base is the economic activity of a community that enables it to attract income from outside its borders.* The ability to attract income gives a community an advantage over other communities and makes it relatively more successful in providing products or services.[2] The advantage of a community may be due to its proximity to commodity markets, the presence of natural resources, the availability of a trained work force, the climate, or a government decree that establishes the community as a county seat or state capital. As a result of this advantage, most of the community's work force may be engaged in specialized activities such as the production of durable goods or assembly and distribution.

The nature of employment in a community or region can affect population growth, the level and stability of income, the willingness of the population to spend disposable income, and the risk associated with investments in the area. These characteristics affect the demand for, and value of, all types of real estate. A community that has a diversified economic base with various types of employment is more attractive to investors than a single-industry town. The stability offered by a diversified local economy can reduce the risk of a real estate investment and increase property values.

City origins and growth patterns. Appraisers recognize that growth and change in an urban community can affect neighborhoods, districts, and other areas differently. An appraiser must be aware of the factors that contribute to urban growth patterns to analyze the neighborhood or district where the subject property is located and to determine how the area affects the quantity, quality, and duration of the property's future income stream or the amenities that create value.

The structure of urban land uses in a community usually reflects the origin of the settlement to some extent; this is known as the *siting factor*. Some U.S. cities were established at transportation centers such as seaports, river crossings, or the

---

2. For further discussion of economic base analysis and the significance of demographic change, see Anthony Downs, "Characteristics of Various Economic Studies," and Jerome Dasso, "Economic Base Analysis for the Appraiser," in *Readings in Market Research for Real Estate* (Chicago: American Institute of Real Estate Appraisers, 1985). See also Morton J. Schussheim, "The Impact of Demographic Change on Housing and Community Development," *The Appraisal Journal* (July 1984).

intersection of trade routes. Other cities were founded near power sources useful to manufacturing, and still others were located for defensive, commercial, or political reasons. As the national standard of living improved, climate and other natural advantages became siting factors responsible for the development of retirement areas, recreational resorts, and other specialized communities. From its initial site, a community grows outward in a pattern dictated by the nature and availability of developable land, the evolution of technology, and the government's ability and willingness to provide essential public services.[3]

Communities that have a scarcity of land, such as San Francisco and New York, experience an increase in the density of land use. Development corridors channel new construction to usable land. New technology, building materials, and construction methods make it possible to construct high-rise buildings in cities without bedrock and those subject to earth tremors.

Transportation improvements and the proliferation of automobiles have also shaped modern cities. Improved transportation allows urban settlements to grow in size serve larger markets. At the same time, the pattern of city growth is influenced by the local transportation network. Growth usually radiates from the central business district along major transportation routes; great dispersion is created by major freeway systems.

Local Market Considerations

To understand how national and even international economic demographic trends influence property value, an appraiser studies how the region and community where the subject property is located may respond to these trends. The appraiser should examine the economic structure of the region and the community, the comparative advantages that each possesses, and the attitudes of local government and residents toward growth and change. For example, the increasing number of elderly households in the nation is less significant to property values in Minnesota than to values in Sunbelt states, which attract more of these residents. A community with a no-growth policy may have substantially different local demographics and economic potential than one that does not discourage growth.

Regional economics have an influence on local market conditions, but local markets do not necessarily parallel regional markets. Macroeconomic studies, which are concerned with broad areas such as cities and regions, are important to an understanding of real estate and real estate trends. These studies should not be confused with microeconomic studies, which appraisers perform to evaluate the factors influencing the market value of a particular real estate parcel. For example, regional trends may suggest an expected increase in population, but the local data available to the appraiser indicate that the particular area will not benefit from this trend. While both studies are important, local trends are more likely to influence property values directly.

---

3. Various conceptual models of urban growth are used to describe land use patterns. These "social ecology" models include the concentric zone theory, the sector (wedge) theory, the multiple nuclei theory, and the radial (axial) corridor theory. For a more complete discussion of urban growth patterns, see W. B. Martin, "How to Predict Urban Growth Patterns," *The Appraisal Journal* (April 1984).

Demographics

The population and its geographic distribution are basic determinants of the need for real estate. Households must have shelter, and the production and distribution of goods and services require plants, stores, hotels, hospitals, warehouses, and offices. An appraiser should be aware of the potential for change in the aggregate population and in the demographic attributes of the population that constitutes the market for the subject property. Population growth is affected by birth rates, death rates, and migration. In turn, these determinants of aggregate population reflect the rate of household formation, the age distribution of households, the state of medical technology, the standard of living, social mores, and the regulations imposed on immigration.

Aggregate population growth is distributed among regions in response to changing economic opportunities. In the past people migrated from the South to the North and the Northeast, and from rural areas to urban areas. During the economic boom in the Sunbelt of the 1970s, the movement was reversed and people migrated from North to South. Recent economic recovery in the northern part of the country has diminished southward migration. The migration from urban to suburban areas has slowed due to transportation costs and the expense of providing municipal services and utilities to these outlying areas. As a result, the demand for housing in older, close-in neighborhoods is increasing in some cities.

Real estate improvements are provided in response to the demand generated by a population with effective purchasing power. *A household—i.e., persons who occupy a group of rooms or a single room that constitutes one housing unit—* imposes a basic demand for housing units. With income and a desire for property ownership, households transform their needs into effective demand. In analyzing a local housing market, a knowledge of trends in the formation of households and household characteristics is crucial. The age, size, income, and other characteristics of households must be considered to determine the demand for housing.

The demand for commercial and industrial real estate is created by a population's demand for the goods and services to be produced or distributed at these sites. An appraiser must be aware of changes in the characteristics and distribution of the population that consumes the goods and services, as well as changes in the work force that produces them. A changing population coupled with technological advances can rapidly alter the demand for the services provided by property, which can affect property value.

Government Regulations and Social Attitudes

General data include information about social attitudes and the government regulations and activities that reflect these attitudes. In response to social attitudes, the government establishes land use regulations and provides public services such as transportation systems and municipal utilities. Appraisers accumulate information on zoning, master plans, environmental impacts, transportation systems, local annexation policies, and other regulations that reveal governmental and social attitudes toward real estate.

Local zoning ordinances regulate land use and the density of development. In some areas retroactive zoning is employed to remove nonconforming uses gradually, giving owners time to alter property use. Zoning also can be used to preserve the architectural character of an area. With varying degrees of success, communities regulate zoning to halt or slow growth. To coordinate new development, they may expand capital improvement programs and construct sewage treatment facilities, fire stations, streets, and public recreational facilities. Zoning may also be used to enforce a community's master plan, which is usually based on economic growth projections and is sometimes modified for political reasons. The appraiser should be aware of the assumptions on which the master plan is based and of the potential for revision.

Environmental concerns have prompted increased regulation of land development at state and local levels. Zoning ordinances and building codes have long imposed additional costs on developers. To preserve the quality of the environment, developers are required to consider the impact of large developments on the ecology of a particular area and on the larger environmental system. They may be required to improve public roads, construct sewage treatment facilities, preserve natural terrain, or take other actions to conform to the recommendations of local, regional, or state planning agencies. These regulations can add significantly to the time required to complete a development and, therefore, increase its final cost. The value of subdivision land is obviously influenced by environmental regulations, which can affect the amount of time required to develop and sell the sites.

The creation or modification of a transportation system is a government action based on an analysis of the direct and indirect impact of the system on users and nonusers. An improvement in the transportation system can affect the accessibility of a site and, thus, its value. Improved transportation routes often cause new areas to be developed, which affects the value of other sites that must compete with the increased supply. To a great extent, the suburbanization of an urban population results from improvements in highways, commuter railroads, and bus routes.

The movement of commercial and retail enterprises between downtown areas and the suburbs has changed real estate markets and placed new emphasis on zoning systems, the administration of local government, and public expenditures. The highway system has opened certain regions to development and has increased their comparative advantage by decreasing the cost of transporting products to markets.

A municipality's willingness to annex and provide public services to outlying areas can affect the direction and amount of development. Conversely, sewer moratoriums have been used effectively to control local growth. This type of restriction can increase the value of developments that are already in place if demand is pressing on a limited supply.

To estimate value properly, the appraiser should understand the government regulations and actions that affect the subject property. The comparable properties selected for analysis should be similar to the subject property in terms of zoning, accessibility, and other characteristics.

Purchasing Power

Households obtain personal income from wages and salaries, yields on savings and other investments, profits from businesses, and private and government pensions. Many American households receive a significant proportion of their personal income in the form of government transfer payments such as social security, unemployment compensation, and farm subsidies. *Disposable income, the personal income that remains after deducting income taxes and all other payments to the government,* is either spent or saved. The amount of disposable income spent on goods and services indirectly determines the demand for properties such as shopping centers, industrial plants, office buildings, and warehouses.

Price Levels

Price-level changes influence the quantity of goods and services that can be purchased. Nominal prices that have been adjusted for changes in the price level are called "real" prices. The sale prices, rents, operating expenses, construction costs, and interest rates used to estimate market value are typically expressed in nominal dollars, unadjusted for price-level changes; the appraiser's final value estimate is also reported in nominal dollars.

Investments vary in their ability to retain real or constant value in inflationary periods. Owners of income-producing real estate often attempt to keep the real value of their property constant by including escalator clauses in leases. These clauses allow rents to be adjusted according to an inflation index so that the tenant pays for increases in operating expenses.

Many lenders are unwilling to accept the risk of changing price levels and look for protection against that portion of inflation that may not be fully covered in the mortgage interest rate. Many institutions making loans on income-producing property continue to ask for equity participation in the property's income and for a mortgage interest rate that includes a premium for anticipated inflation. Other lenders may use a floating rate tied to the prime rate or some other economic indicator. These loan provisions affect the net operating income and before-tax cash flows of properties and, therefore, the value indications derived using the income capitalization approach.

Building Fluctuations

Housing starts and the construction of commercial and industrial properties fluctuate in response to business cycles, wars, and the cost and availability of financing. These fluctuations follow the long-term trend of new construction, which has been moving upward. Short-term fluctuations result in temporary misallocations of supply, which can depress rents and prices.

The standing stock of housing units at any point in time consists of all units occupied by households as well as those that are vacant. The stock is continually altered by the construction or conversion of units in response to developers' perceptions of the demand for new housing and by the need to replace existing units.

Six months to two years may pass between the time the developer decides to supply units and the time they enter the market. During this period, changing conditions may reduce demand, and the units coming on the market may remain unrented and unsold, thus increasing vacancy rates. Developers may continue to produce additional units for some time, even in the face of rising vacancies. Once these excess units are produced, they remain on the market and can depress rents or prices until demand increases to remove the surplus. When the market tightens, the supply of units lags behind the increase in demand, resulting in abnormally low vacancy rates and upward pressure on rents and prices. Ultimately, supply materializes as developers respond to increased demand.

Fluctuations in the local supply of and demand for real estate are influenced by regional and national conditions. Therefore, an appraiser looks for regional and national trends that may indicate a positive or negative change in property values at the local level. Although all regions may not experience the same slump in construction, tight monetary policy affects the cost and availability of mortgage credit and exerts a moderating influence on supply, even in a rapidly growing region.

Commercial real estate is affected by business conditions and the cost and availability of financing. Because business firms pass their high financing costs on to consumers, residential construction may be restricted. If the demand for the goods and services produced or supplied by a business remains strong, the firm can raise prices and continue to expand even when credit is tight and interest rates are high.

The appraiser must recognize that a property's value as of a specific date may rise or fall due to a fluctuation in building activity. Because market value is influenced by the balance of supply and demand at the time of the appraisal, the appraiser should make certain that the client understands the economic conditions that affect the subject property's value at a specific time.

Building Costs

The cost of reproducing a building tends to follow the general price levels established over a long period, but these price levels vary from time to time and from place to place. Building costs generally decline in times of deflation and increase in periods of inflation. These costs are affected by material and labor costs, construction technology, architect and legal fees, financing costs, building codes, and public regulations such as zoning ordinances, environmental requirements, and subdivision regulations.

The cost of construction can alter the quantity and character of demand and, therefore, the relative prices of property in real estate submarkets. The high cost of new buildings increases the demand for, and prices of, existing structures. When the cost of new structures increases, rehabilitation of existing buildings may become economically feasible. High building costs increase prices in single-family residential submarkets, which can increase the demand for rental units and their prices. The size and quality of the dwelling units demanded decrease when building costs increase more rapidly than purchasing power.

Taxes

Real estate taxes are based on the assessed value of real property, hence the term *ad valorem* (according to value) taxes. The assessed value of property is normally based on, but not necessarily equivalent to, its market value. If, for example, the tax rate is $60 per $1,000 of valuation, the assessed value is equal to market value, and the taxes are based on 50% of assessed value, then the annual real estate tax equals 3% of assessed value.

$$\frac{\$60}{\$1,000} \times 50\% = 3\%$$

If assessed value is not consistent with market value, the formula is modified to reflect the inconsistency.

In jurisdictions where ad valorem real estate tax assessments have an established or implied relationship to market value, appraisal services may be required to resolve tax appeals. In some communities, the trend in real estate taxes is an important consideration. In cities where public expenditures for schools and municipal services have increased, this heavy tax burden can affect real estate values adversely. Under these circumstances, new construction may be discouraged. There may be several tax districts in a metropolitan area, each with a different policy. A system of ad valorem taxation in an area facilitates analysis of how taxes affect value.

Although income taxes are not usually treated as an expense in appraisal calculations, they can influence property value. Currently homeowners can deduct mortgage interest and property taxes when they itemize deductions in computing their taxable income. This tax benefit influences the overall price level of single-family residences and condominiums. Between 1981 and 1986 owners had the ability to recover costs by using accelerated depreciation in calculating the taxable income of investment property. This benefit influenced the market's perception of the value of these property types.

Different levels of sales taxes and earnings taxes can also affect the relative desirability of properties. Although these taxes may be uniform within a state, properties in different states often compete with one another. For example, for several years Vermont imposed relatively low taxes and attracted many more new residents and industries than surrounding New England states. This increased demand probably enhanced property values in Vermont relative to values in surrounding states.

Financing

Because the cost and availability of financing help to determine the demand for, and supply of, real estate, financing affects real estate values. The cost of financing includes the rate of interest on the mortgage instrument, deed of trust, or installment contract, as well as any points, discounts, equity participations, or other charges that the lender requires to increase the effective yield on the loan. The availability of financing depends on nonprice determinants that affect the borrower's ability to obtain financing, including the loan-to-value ratio, the housing expense-to-income ratio required for loans on single-family homes, and the debt coverage and breakeven ratios required for loans on income-producing properties. The cost and availability of financing typically have an inverse relationship; high interest rates and other costs usually are accompanied by a decrease in the availability of credit.

The cost and availability of credit for real estate financing influence both the quantity and quality of the real estate demanded and supplied. When interest rates are high and mortgage funds are limited, households that would have been in the home ownership market find that their incomes cannot support the required expenses. Purchases are delayed and smaller homes with fewer amenities are bought. The cost of land development financing and construction financing is reflected in the higher prices asked for single-family homes, which result in a further reduction in the quantity demanded.

The rental market is affected by the demand pressure of households that continue to rent and by the high cost of supplying new units, which results in part from financing costs. Occupancy rates and rents rise. Businesses try to pass on their higher occupancy costs to customers by increasing the prices of products or services. If they cannot fully recover the increased occupancy cost, the quantity of commercial and individual space demanded is reduced.

Sources of General Data

The general data needed to appraise real property are available from a wide variety of sources. A substantial amount of information is compiled and disseminated by federal, state, and local agencies; trade associations and private business enterprises may also provide data.

The largest body of national, regional, and city data comes from the federal government. The *Economic Report of the President,* published by the Council of Economic Advisors, includes data and analysis of housing starts and financing. *Economic Indicators* is a monthly publication prepared by the Council of Economic Advisors for the Joint Economic Committee. The *Federal Reserve Bulletin* and *Historical Chart Book*, which are published by the Federal Reserve Board, contain information on the gross national product, national income, mortgage markets, interest rates, and other financial statistics; installment credit; sources of funds; business activity; the labor force, employment, and industrial production; housing and construction; and international finance. The National Office of Vital Statistics compiles and disseminates statistics on birth and death rates.

The U.S. Department of Commerce, Bureau of the Census, publishes the *Census of Population*, the *Census of Housing*, the *Census of Manufacturers*, the *Census of Agriculture*, the *Annual Housing Survey*, and the *Statistical Abstract of the United States*, as well as various series on current population, population estimates, and population projections; consumer income; and housing completions, housing permits, and other housing statistics. These publications provide detailed information on population and housing characteristics for the nation, states, counties, metropolitan statistical areas (MSAs), municipalities, census tracts, and blocks in metropolitan areas. Interim reports on selected population, income, and housing data are also published by the Bureau of the Census.

The U.S. Department of Commerce, Bureau of Economic Analysis, publishes the *Survey of Current Business*. This is a source for data on the Consumer Price Index, the wholesale price index, mortgage debt, and the value of new construction. The U.S. Department of Housing and Urban Development issues reports on FHA building starts, financing, and housing programs administered by the department. It also disseminates FHA vacancy surveys for selected metropolitan areas. The U.S. Department of Labor, Bureau of Labor Statistics, publishes the *Monthly Labor Review*, which contains the Consumer Price Index, wholesale prices, and monthly and annual employment and earnings figures.

At state and local levels, departments of development, local and regional planning agencies, and regional or metropolitan transportation authorities can provide appraisers with data on population, households, employment, master plans, present and future utility, and transportation systems. Often they also publish directories of manufacturers that list, by county, the names of firms, their products, and their employment figures.

A state's Bureau of Employment Service can provide county data on employment, unemployment, and wage rates. Chambers of commerce offer a variety of information on local population, households, employment, and industry, which they often obtain from other secondary sources such as the census.

Trade associations can also be very useful sources. The National Association of Realtors® compiles information on existing home sales for the nation as a whole and for individual regions. The national association and its affiliates put out many publications with data useful to appraisers. The National Association of Homebuilders disseminates information on new housing starts as well as prices, construction costs, and financing. *Sales and Marketing Management Magazine, Survey of Buying Power* contains information on households, income distribution, and retail sales by county and for selected cities.

Other meaningful data can be gathered from private sources such as banks, utility companies, university research centers, private advisory firms, multiple listing services, and cost services such as E. H. Boeckh and Marshall Valuation Service. These sources offer a variety of information on bank debt, department store sales, employment indicators, land prices, corporate business indicators, mortgage money costs, wage rates, construction costs, deeds, mortgage recordings, and the installation of utility meters.

In recent years many databases have been developed for access by small computers. These databases cover a broad range of topics and offer many options for appraisers performing general or specialized research. The information available is virtually unlimited and includes topics such as current and historical news; industry analyses and reports; corporate earnings and analyses; local, regional, and national Yellow Page listings; publication indexes and articles; and much more.

General data are an integral part of an appraiser's office files. By cataloging and cross-indexing data obtained from various sources, an appraiser has quick access to important information. General data such as multiple listing information and census data can be stored and accessed by computer. Many local and regional planning and development agencies computerize information on housing inventory and vacancies, demolitions and conversions, commercial construction, household incomes, new land use by zoning classification, population and demographics, and housing forecasts by geographic area.

Recent developments in computer software and hardware have resulted in low-cost, high-performance databasing combinations for appraisers. Hundreds of individual programs are now used with desktop systems in appraisal offices. Some databases are contained in a single computer, while others are shared by several computers or terminals through local or telecommunication networks. Improvements in telecommunication programs and facilities, word processing, and electronic spreadsheets have facilitated appraisal analysis and report writing, as well as the use of database information.[4]

SPECIFIC DATA

Specific data include details about the property being appraised, comparable sales and rental properties, and relevant local market characteristics. In appraisals these data are used to determine highest and best use and to make the specific comparisons and analyses required to estimate market value. The specific data about a subject property provided in land and building descriptions help the appraiser select comparable specific data pertaining to sales, rentals, construction costs, and local market characteristics.

In analyzing general data, national, regional, and local trends in value are emphasized; in an analysis of specific data, the characteristics of the subject property and comparable properties are studied. From relevant comparable sales, an appraiser extracts specific sale prices, rental terms, income and expense figures, rates of return on investment, construction costs, the expected economic life of improvements, and rates of depreciation. These figures are used in calculations that lead to an indication of value for the subject property.

An appraiser needs specific data to apply each of the three approaches to value. The appraiser uses the data to derive adjustments for value-influencing property characteristics, to isolate meaningful units of comparison, to analyze capitalization rates, and to measure accrued depreciation. By extracting relevant data from the large quantity of data available, an appraiser develops a sense of the market. This perception is an essential component of appraisal judgment, which is applied in the valuation process and in the final reconciliation of value indications. The validity of a final estimate of market value depends to a great extent on how well it can be supported by market data.

Specific data are analyzed through comparison. In each approach to value, certain items of information must be extracted from market data to make comparisons. Specific data are analyzed to determine if these information items are present and if they can be used to make reliable comparisons with the subject property. If, for example, the subject property is an apartment building of three-bedroom units, the appraiser may be able to use data from sales of similar apartment buildings to make adjustments for the time of sale, the location, and physical property characteristics. The appraiser may also need to analyze data on competitive properties that have not sold recently to obtain information on the rental rates and expenses for apartment buildings in the area.

The appraiser's analysis of the highest and best use of the land as though vacant and the property as improved determines what comparable specific data are collected and analyzed. The nature and amount of research needed for a specific assignment depend on the property type and the purpose of the appraisal. The appraiser should gather all available data that may be pertinent to the assign

---

4. For further information on databasing and information processing, see Mary J. Dum, "Using an Electronic Spreadsheet in the Appraisal Office," *The Appraisal Journal* (July 1982); John D. Dorchester, Jr., "The Next Era in Appraisal: Opportunity vs. Obsolescence," *The Appraisal Journal* (January 1985); and Mark I. Roth, "Computer Connection," *The Appraisal Journal* (April 1985). Timely information can be found in *The Quarterly Byte*, a computer newsletter published by the Appraisal Institute.

ment, organize the data, and perform a preliminary analysis before applying any analytical techniques.

Investigation of Market Transactions

A detailed description and classification of the characteristics and components of a property are assembled in land and building analyses. With these analyses the appraiser selects and analyzes the data used in the cost, sales comparison, and income capitalization approaches. The data used for comparison in the three approaches should be derived from properties that are similar to the appraised property. To use sales as a valid basis for further analysis, the appraiser inventories the relevant characteristics and components of the properties selected as comparables.

To select comparable sale properties, an appraiser examines public records, published sources, office files, and information from buyers, sellers, and other knowledgeable persons. Interviews with property owners may reveal relevant sales that have not been recorded. Realtors®, salespeople, developers, and other appraisers are also good sources of sales and rental data. The selection of comparables is directed to some extent by the availability and scope of the data. Investigation of an active market usually reveals an adequate and representative number of transactions within a restricted area and time period.

The geographic area from which comparable sales can be selected depends on the property type. In valuing certain types of retail property, only properties with main street frontage may be pertinent. For many large industrial properties and most investment properties, the entire community should be studied; for larger properties, the national market may be relevant. For a residential appraisal, adequate data may occasionally be found within a block of the subject property. Even in these cases, however, the appraiser should consider the broader market to place the subject property and the comparables in a general market context.

In selecting market data for analysis, an appraiser focuses on transactions pertinent to the subject property's specific market. In general, comparable properties are those that compete with the property being appraised or have a demonstrable effect on prices or other relevant components of the market in question. With computer analysis, a large number of properties can be studied in the course of a single assignment, which may generate a deeper understanding of each property's contribution to, and influence on, a given market.

Appraisers seek data that will facilitate accurate comparisons, but because every real estate parcel is unique, absolute comparability is impossible. The comparability of properties varies, and the appraiser may find it necessary to place less confidence on a given comparable. Nevertheless, the appraiser may still want to consider this comparable for its evidence of, and effect on, the marketplace.

Appraisers have a special responsibility to consider carefully the comparability of all data used in a valuation assignment. They must fully understand the concept of comparability and should avoid comparing properties with different highest and best uses, limiting their search for comparables, or selecting inappropriate factors for comparison.

The first determinant of useful data is their degree of comparability. A second determinant is the quantity of information available, and a third, but equally important, factor is the authenticity and reliability of the data. An appraiser must not assume that all data pertinent to an assignment are completely reliable. Sales figures, costs, and other information subject to misrepresentation should be scrutinized for authenticity.

When comparable sales data in the subject property's immediate area are limited, the appraiser may need to extend the data search to adjacent neighborhoods and similar communities. When the selection of data is limited to an unacceptably narrow sample of current market activity, the appraiser may decide to use sales that are less current or to interview brokers, buyers, sellers, owners, and tenants of similar properties in the area to obtain evidence of potential market activity such as listings of offers to sell and purchase. With proper adjustment, these sales and listings may also be used as comparables.

An appraiser gathers broad information about a market from its pattern of sales. Important market data can be revealed by many significant characteristics including

- Number of sales
- Period of time covered by the sales
- Availability of property for sale
- Rate of absorption
- Rate of turnover (i.e., volume of sales and level of activity)
- Characteristics and motivations of buyers and sellers
- Terms and conditions of sale
- Use of property before and after its sale

While analyzing data to select comparable sales, an appraiser begins to form certain conclusions about the general market, the subject property, and the possible relationships between the data and the subject property. The appraiser ascertains market strengths and weaknesses; the probable supply of, demand for, and marketability of properties similar to the property being appraised; and the variations and characteristics that are likely to have the greatest impact on the value of properties in the market. Thus, an appraiser analyzes data against a background of information about the particular area and the specific type of property.

The information needed to apply the cost and income capitalization approaches must often be obtained from market sources other than sales. This information may also be used to refine adjustments made in the sales comparison approach. In the investigation of general and neighborhood data, an appraiser learns about trends in construction costs, lease terms, typical expenses, and vacancy rates. Examining trends in the market where the subject property is located provides additional specific data that can be used to derive value indications and successfully complete evaluation assignments.

Sources of Specific Data

Like sources of general data, sources of specific data are diverse. In addition to the data obtained from public records and published sources, personal contact with developers, builders, Realtors®, financial and legal specialists, property managers, local planners, and other real estate professionals can provide useful information. Thus, practicing appraisers need communication skills as well as analytical techniques to research sales, improvement costs, and income and expense data thoroughly and complete appraisal assignments.

Sources of sales data include public records; published news; Realtors®, appraisers, managers, and bankers; multiple listing books; listings and offers; and other local sources.

Public records. An appraiser searches public records for a copy of the property deed. The deed provides important information about the property and the sales transaction, including the full names of the parties involved and the transaction date. A legal description of the property, the property rights included in the transaction, and any outstanding liens on the title are shown.

Occasionally, the names of the parties may suggest that unusual motivations were involved in the sale. For example, a sale from John Smith to Mary Smith Jones may be a transfer from a father to a daughter; a sale from John Smith, William Jones, and Harold Long to the SJL Corporation may not be an arm's-length transaction arrived at by unrelated parties under no duress.

In some states the law requires that the consideration paid upon transfer of title be shown on the deed. However, this consideration does not always reflect the actual sale price. To reduce transfer taxes, some purchasers (e.g., buyers of motels or apartments) deduct the estimated value of personal property from the true consideration paid. Because these personal property values are sometimes inflated, the recorded consideration for the real property may be less than the true consideration. In one deed the indicated consideration may be overstated to obtain a higher loan than is warranted; in another, the consideration may be understated to justify a low property tax assessment. Although some states require that the true and actual consideration be listed on the deed, other states allow the consideration to be reported as "$10 and other valuable consideration."

The local tax assessor's records may include property cards for the subject property and comparables properties, with land and building sketches, area measurements, sale prices, and other information. In some locations legal or private publishing services issue information about revenue stamps and other facts pertaining to current transfers.

Published news. Most city newspapers feature real estate news. Although some of the news may be incomplete or inaccurate, an appraiser can use it to confirm details because the names of the negotiating brokers and the parties to a transaction are usually published.

Realtors®, appraisers, managers, and bankers. These professionals can often provide information about real estate transactions and suggest valuable leads. Individual sources may be definitive, but if the information obtained from real estate professionals is third-party data, the appraiser should look for separate verification.

Multiple listing books. Books of multiple listings are published in many communities. These books enumerate the properties listed for sale during the calendar year or a fiscal quarter and cite their listing prices. They contain fairly complete information about properties, including photographs, descriptions, and brokers' names. However, details about a property's square footage, basement area, or exact age may be inaccurate or excluded. In certain areas, multiple listing books can be purchased. Multiple listing services sometimes publish the sale prices of properties that have been sold.

Listings and offers. Whenever possible an appraiser should gather information on listings of properties offered for sale. An appraiser can request that his or her name be added to the mailing lists of banks, brokers, and others who offer properties for sale. Classified ads of properties offered for sale list asking prices and suggest the strength or weakness of the local market for a particular type of property or the sales activity in a particular area. Information on offers to purchase may also be obtained from brokers or managers. Listings are generally higher than actual transaction prices; offers are generally somewhat lower.

Improvement Cost Data

Useful construction cost data may be obtained from many sources. Contractors and suppliers of construction materials can provide cost information about recently constructed buildings that are similar to the subject property. Cost estimators may also be consulted for information on the costs involved in constructing building improvements. Appraisers should be aware that published cost estimates may or may not include indirect costs such as loan interest during construction.

In an active market cost information can be obtained by interviewing local property owners who have recently added building or land improvements similar to those found on the subject property. If work contracts and accounting records of recently improved properties are available, they can provide significant details.

Cost estimates are made by assembling, cataloging, and analyzing data on actual building costs. Detailed costs should be divided into general categories such as residential construction or commercial building costs; separate figures should be provided for special finishes or equipment. Costs for individual structural components should also be researched and kept on file.

Several cost-estimating services publish cost manuals that break down costs into square-foot and cubic-foot measures. Unit costs for building types usually start with a building of a certain size (i.e., a base area or volume) which serves as a benchmark. Then additions or deductions are made to account for the actual number of square feet or cubic feet in the subject property. Data provided by cost-estimating services can be used to confirm estimates developed from local cost data.

Cost manuals are updated periodically by including cost index tables that reflect changes in the cost of construction over a period of years. Cost indexes convert a known cost as of a past date into a current cost estimate. However, there is a practical limitation in applying this procedure because, as the time span increases, the reliability of the current cost indication tends to decrease. Sometimes cost index tables can be used to adjust costs for different geographic areas.

The use of cost index tables can pose problems because it may be difficult to ascertain which components are included in the reported original cost. Furthermore, capital expenditures for improvements added after original construction must be considered, and added improvements may affect the estimates of cost and accrued depreciation.

Some appraisers rely almost entirely on published cost manuals; others maintain files of specific cost comparables that are similar to their files of sale comparables. These files may be based on information furnished by contract-reporting services. Contract-reporting services may give building areas or a general building description, the low bids, and the contract award. The appraiser can then obtain any missing information, such as the breakdown of office and warehouse space, and classify the building type for filing purposes. When cost comparable files are carefully developed and managed, they can supply authentic square-foot costs on buildings of all types for use in appraisal assignments.

Income and Expense Data

To derive pertinent income and expense data, an appraiser investigates comparable sales and rentals of competitive income-producing properties in the same market. For investment properties, current and recent incomes are reviewed and vacancy and collection losses and typical operating expenses are studied. Finally, data on the mortgage terms, or debt service, should be examined and refined by the appraiser to make forecasts of future incomes and expenses.

Published information on property values for several consecutive years can suggest the rate of appreciation or depreciation applicable to various property types. Interviews with owners and tenants in the area can provide lease and expense data. Lenders may be contacted for information on available terms of financing.

An appraiser tries to obtain all income and expense data from the income properties used as comparables. These data should be tabulated in a reconstructed operating statement and filed by property type. (See Chapter 19 for a suggested format for reconstructed operating statements.)

Like expense data, rental information is difficult to obtain. Therefore, appraisers should take every opportunity to add rents to their rental databases. Long-term leases are usually on public record. A separate county index that cites the parties to recorded leases and the volume and page numbers of recorded leases may also be available. Sometimes this information is listed with deeds and mortgages, but it is usually coded for easy identification. In certain cities, abstracts of recorded leases are printed by private publishing services. Classified ads may also provide rental information. Many appraisers periodically check advertised rentals and recorded rental information by property type or area. It is convenient to file rental data under the same classifications used for sales data.

Income and expense comparables should be filed chronologically and by property type so they can be retrieved easily and used to estimate the expenses for a similar type of property. Income and expense figures should be converted into units of comparison for analysis. For example, income may be reported in terms of rent per apartment unit, per room, per hospital bed, or per square foot. Income is usually stated in terms of dollars per unit or units over a specified time period. Expenses for insurance, taxes, painting, decorating, and other maintenance charges can be expressed in the same units of comparison used for income, or they can be expressed as a percentage of the effective gross rent. The unit of comparison selected must be used consistently throughout the analysis.

Rental property data may show vacancy rates and operating expenses as a percentage of the effective gross income. These data are essential in valuing income-producing property. The age and type of construction and any utilities provided by the owner should be specified.

Capitalization Rates

Capitalization rates are another essential type of market data. They are rates or multipliers (e.g., a gross rent multiplier for a single-family property) that are extracted from market data. When net operating income and sale price information are available, an overall rate (R_O) can be calculated; if mortgage information is also available, the equity capitalization rate (R_E) can be calculated. Whenever possible, an appraiser should calculate these rates from available data and consider their meaning in the analysis. In making comparisons capitalization rates are analyzed in light of the similarity between the comparable sale's characteristics and the characteristics of the subject property. (The derivation of capitalization rates is discussed in detail in Chapters 20 and 21.)

The overall and equity capitalization rates derived from sales can also be used as bases for deriving other capitalization rates. If possible, overall property rates and equity yield rates should be extracted from market evidence. It is important that these rate indications be considered when adequate market information is available.

COMPETITIVE SUPPLY AND DEMAND DATA

The valuation process requires that a property be appraised within the context of its market. Of particular significance to the analysis are the supply of competitive properties, the future demand for the appraised property, and its highest and best use. After inspecting the subject property and gathering property-specific data, the appraiser inventories the supply of properties that constitute the major competition for the property in its defined market.

Required Analysis

Competitive Supply Inventory

The supply inventory includes all competitive properties: rental units, properties that have been sold, properties being offered for sale, and properties that will come on the market at some future time. The appraiser must recognize that the subject property will always compete in a future market. Thus the appraiser's investigation must cover not only existing competition, but also prospective projects that will compete with the subject.

Demand Study

Along with the supply inventory of major competitive properties, the appraiser analyzes the prospective demand for the subject property. The appraiser cannot assume the current use is necessarily the use for which the most demand will exist in the future. Even in the most stable markets, subtle shifts in the market appeal or utility of a category of properties can put some properties at a competitive disadvantage and benefit others. Even in volatile markets characterized by rapid change due to factors such as accelerating growth, precipitous decline, or an upturn in proposed construction, appraisers need to quantify demand in some manner.

The specific techniques applied to study market demand can be highly sophisticated and may fall outside the scope of normal appraisal practice. In these cases the appraiser might use data compiled by special market research firms to supplement the appraisal. Appraisers should, however, develop an understanding of market research techniques and to acquire the skills needed to conduct basic demand studies.

Vacancy Rates and Offerings

One approach to understanding local demand is to study the vacancy rates and offerings of competitive properties. A large number of vacancies may indicate an oversupply in relation to current demand. Very few vacancies and offering prices that are higher than recent sale prices or rental rates may indicate an increase in unsatisfied demand. Study of vacancies and offerings supports the appraiser's absorption projection and forecast of prospective demand for the appraised property.

The inventory of competitive properties extends beyond the analysis of comparable sales and rentals. The use and occupancy of competitive properties that have not recently been sold or are subject to long-term leases can indicate the overall health of the local market. It is also important that the appraiser recognize potential demographic and economic shifts that may affect future competition for the appraised property.

The appraiser should research and report listings and offerings of pertinent competitive properties. Appraisers are justifiably reluctant to base an appraised value on listings. Listings do not meet the normal appraisal criteria for comparable sales data, which specify completed, arm's-length transactions. Nevertheless, listings may be construed as collateral evidence of market activity.

Listings and offerings provide a useful indicator of the values anticipated by sellers and buyers as well as the prospective turnover of competitive properties. Listings are usually set at a level that will excite market interest and therefore may be employed to test market activity. They are relevant market phenomena which the appraiser should consider in analyzing competitive supply and demand. The appraiser may find that tabulating information about competitive properties in a market data grid is useful for comparing the market position of the subject property to that of the competition.

Sources of Competitive Supply and Demand Data

A competitive supply inventory is compiled using several methods. An appraiser often conducts a field inspection to inventory competitive properties in the subject neighborhood and competitive neighborhoods. The appraiser also interviews owners, managers, and brokers of competitive properties in the locality as well as developers and city planners. Field inspection and interviews are especially useful because investors rely heavily on local competitive supply and demand analyses. The examination of building permits (both issued and acted upon), plat maps, and surveys of competitive sites provides insight into prospective supply. Data on available space, and vacancy, absorption, and turnover rates in specific property markets can be obtained from reports issued by real estate research firms.

Demand can be estimated using demographic data (population and vital statistics) and economic data (employment and income statistics) for the market area. The Census Bureau (Department of Commerce) and Bureau of Labor Statistics compile statistical data which are available in published form and on computer tape. Other private and public sources provide past data and projections based on small area populations. Appraisers who rely on projections prepared by market research firms should have a clear understanding of the methodology used to make the projection, otherwise the data may represent little more than a blind data set. To test the reasonableness of small area projections, comparisons should be made between the demographic data and the supply data for the specified market. Supply data may include building permits and market sales or absorption rates kept by public agencies such as building inspection, city planning, and public works departments.

Personal observation is also useful in estimating local demand. For example, the planned closing of an army base should be considered in analyzing the future demand for adjacent commercial properties such as dry cleaners, motels, bars, and restaurants. An appraiser who had observed development near highway interchanges will be able to anticipate that a proposed freeway interchange will generate future demand for shops, service stations, and motels catering to the needs of motorists and tourists.

The Topographically Integrated Geographic Encoding and Reforming (TIGER) file established by the 1990 census is of special relevance to appraisals of sites being considered for development. The TIGER file is a Geographical Information System (GIS) for assembling data about microlevel locations. These data include information on traffic analysis zones (TAZ), acreage available for development, and zone densities. The spatial analysis format integrates a spreadsheet model with geographic information. The software for this system is competitively priced and readily available for use with microcomputers.[5]

ORGANIZATION AND ARRAY OF DATA

Understanding the content and sources of general and specific appraisal data facilitates their analysis in valuation and evaluation assignments. Before undertaking any analysis, however, an appraiser must organize all the specific data accumulated in the investigation. A market data grid is a carefully constructed spreadsheet that provides a tabular representation of market data organized into useful, measurable categories. If the information to be analyzed is very complex, the appraiser may need to design several market data grids to isolate and study specific data.

On the initial grid, the appraiser lists each characteristic of the subject and comparable properties that has been isolated. The market data grid should include the total sale price of each comparable property and the date of each sale, which can be expressed in relation to the subject property's date of valuation

---

5. See Lynn Bodin Wombold, "Tracking Population Change" and Michael L. Robbins, "Forecasting Retail Sales with Geographical Information Systems: A Preliminary Methodology" in *Forecasting: Market Determinants Affecting Cash Flows and Reversions*, Research Report 4 (Chicago: American Institute of Real Estate Appraisers, 1989). See also Bruce R. Weber, "Application of Geographic Information Systems to Real Estate Market Analysis and Appraisal," *The Appraisal Journal* (January 1990).

(e.g., one month ago, 16 months ago). The grid also includes information about the property rights conveyed, the financial arrangements of the sale, and any unusual motivations of the buyer or seller that may have resulted in a negotiating advantage such as a desire to liquidate a property for inheritance tax or a desire to acquire a particular property for expansion. Because financial arrangements and unusual motivations can significantly influence a property's sale price, they must be carefully examined.

The grid may also contain other market data that are significant to the appraisal assignment. Such data might include reproduction costs for building and land improvements; development costs; the amount of accrued depreciation; the indicated economic life of improvements similar to those on the subject property; income data such as market rent estimates, gross income, net operating income, and pre-tax cash flow or equity dividend; rates of return; the percentage of land value appreciation evident in the area; and the average value of the commodities or services provided by properties similar to the subject.

The initial market data grid can include all characteristics of the subject and comparable properties, sales transactions, and pertinent market data from other sources. An appraiser may choose to use one grid for comparable sales data and other grids for information derived from other sources. By using several grids the appraiser can isolate various aspects of individual sales and the total market that may be significant to the valuation problem. Isolating these specifics provides an early indication of the information the appraiser will be able to derive from the collected data and identifies variations among properties that may be significant to their value.

In examining the initial market data grid, the appraiser may find that certain data are not pertinent and will not be useful in applying the approaches to value. Additional data may be required and the appraiser may need to create other grids to include more information or to isolate the data required for specific approaches. Appraisers should see data analysis as a developing process and the grid as a tool that facilitates this process and the derivation of valid indications of property value.

Figures 7.1 and 7.2 show sample grids for the organization and array of market data. Figure 7.1 is a comparable sales data grid that can be used in analyzing data in the sales comparison approach to value. (Further discussion and examples of the use of market data grids for comparing and adjusting data are provided in Chapter 14.) Figure 7.2 shows how the basic market data grid can be used to organize and array data on rental properties, which may be helpful in deriving and applying market rent estimates in the income capitalization approach to value.

Units of Comparison

Units of comparison are used in analyzing data in all three approaches to value. In the sales comparison approach, the sale price may be divided by the unit of comparison. In the cost approach, the total cost of construction and total accrued depreciation are divided by the unit of comparison. In the income capitalization approach, the income and expense items and the net operating income may be divided by the chosen unit of comparison. Several different units of comparison may be used in each approach, depending on the information needed and the

Figure 7.1 Market Data Grid

Element	Subject	Sale 1	Sale 2	Sale 3	Sale 4	Sale 5
Sale price	?					
Property rights conveyed						
Financing						
Conditions of sale (motivation)						
Date of sale (market conditions)						
Location						
Gross building area (GBA)						
Rentable area						
Land area						
Lease expiration dates						
Rent concessions						
Escalation						
Market rent						
Potential gross income (PGI)						
Effective gross income (EGI)						
Net operating income (NOI)						
Income multiplier						
Overall cap rate (R_O)						
Equity cap rate (R_E)						
Property yield rate (Y_O)						
Equity yield rate (Y_E)						

focus of the analysis. However, the unit of comparison selected must be consistently applied to the subject property and all comparable sales properties in each analysis.

Typically, different units of comparison are used with different property types. Comparisons can be made on the basis of the price, cost, income, or expenses per unit, depending on the approach in which the comparable property is being analyzed. The following list shows common property types and the typical units of comparison used in their appraisal.

Single-family residences

- Entire property
- Gross living area
- Number of rooms

Figure 7.2 Organization and Array of Market Data for Rental Properties

Element	Subject	Sale 1	Sale 2	Sale 3	Sale 4	Sale 5
Sale price	?	$600,000	$920,000	$850,000	$990,000	$920,000
Property rights conveyed	Leased fee	Leased fee	Leased fee	Leased fee	Leased fee	Leased fee
Amount seller received	?	$600,000	see[a]	$850,000	see[b]	$920,000
Cash equivalent price	?	$600,000	$800,000	$850,000	$900,000	$920,000
Unit of comparison (number of sq. ft.)	400,000	200,000	320,000	430,000	380,000	480,000
Dollars per sq. ft. of GBA	?	$3.00	$2.50	$1.98	$2.37	$1.92
Conditions of sale (motivation)[c]	?	Arm's-length	Arm's-length	+10%	Arm's-length	Arm's-length
Date (market conditions)[d]	?	Current	+6%	Current	+2%	Current
Location[e]	Corner lot	Similar	+5%	Similar	+5%	Similar
Size[f]	Small lot	–5%	–2%	Similar	Similar	+2%
Other physical characteristics[g]	High ground	Similar	Similar	Similar	+5%	Similar
Zoning[h]	C-3	Similar	Similar	–10%	Similar	+15%
Contract rent[i]	Same as market rent	Similar	Similar	+30%	Similar	Similar
Dollars per sq. ft. of GBA after addition of percentage adjustments	?	$2.85	$2.72	$2.57	$2.65	$2.25
Rent per sq. ft. of GBA	?	$0.30	N/A	$0.18	$0.24	N/A
Gross income multiplier (GIM)	?	10.0	N/A	11.0	9.9	N/A
% of NOI to GI	?	81%	N/A	89.5%	80.4%	N/A
Overall capitalization rate (R_O)	?	8.10%	N/A	8.14%	8.12%	N/A
Mortgage capitalization rate (R_M)	?	9.2%	9.4%	10.5%	10.1%	9.6%
Equity capitalization rate (R_E)	?	7.4%	7.3%	7.6%	7.5%	7.4%

a. In Sale 2 the seller received $120,000 in cash and a note for $800,000 (including any interest) payable in 18 months; the cash equivalent value of the note is $680,000.

b. In Sale 4 the seller received $200,000 in cash and a note for $790,000, with a 20-year amortization schedule, quarterly payments including 8.5% interest, a seven-year call provision, and a balloon arrangement.

c. In Sale 3 the seller had to dispose of the property to settle an estate.

d. Considering the rate of inflation and the popularity of the neighborhood, a 2% increase is indicated for a one-year-old sale and a 6% increase is indicated for a two-year-old sale.

e. Sales 2 and 4 are not corner lots; the subject and the other sales are.

f. Within this range of sizes, small plots are worth more per square foot than large plots due to greater demand.

g. Sale 4 includes one-half acre of floodplain land.

h. Sale 3 includes two acres of land with R-5 zoning; the subject and the other sales are all zoned C-3. Sale 5 includes a nonexclusive vehicle right-of-way for the use of the subject property.

i. Sale 3 is leased at a rent that is 8.5% below market rent and there are three years remaining in the lease term.

- Potential or effective gross rent multiplier

Vacant land

- Entire property
- Square footage
- Front footage
- Potential subdivided lot
- Building units per acre

Agricultural properties

- Acreage
- Animal unit (AU)—for pastureland
- Hundred weight (cwt), tons, or bushel per acre—for farmland
- Thousand board feet (MBF)—for timberland

Apartments

- Square footage of livable area
- Number of apartments
- Number of rooms
- Potential or effective gross income multiplier

Warehouses

- Square footage of gross building area
- Ceiling height
- Cubic footage
- Loading dock or door
- Potential or effective gross income multiplier

Factories

- Square footage of gross building area
- Ceiling height
- Cubic footage
- Machine unit
- Potential or effective gross income multiplier

Offices

- Square footage of net rentable/net leasable area
- Number of offices
- Number of rooms
- Number of desks
- Potential or effective gross income multiplier

Hospitals

- Square footage
- Number of beds

Theaters
- Square footage
- Number of seats

The fundamental features of data analysis in the cost, sales comparison, and income capitalization approaches are described in the following section.

DATA ANALYSIS
Cost Approach

To apply the cost approach, appraisers often use sales data and cost and depreciation information derived from the market. Both types of information may contribute significantly to the cost approach, and each may serve as a check on the other. An analysis of sales data can supplement cost and depreciation data obtained from other sources. Sales analysis can provide direct indications of accrued depreciation, profit margin, and the value contribution of buildings or land improvements. The cost of an improvement recently added to a sale property may indicate current construction costs.

To develop cost estimates from data obtained through observation and interviews, the appraiser must ascertain precisely what the reported expenditure represents in relation to the total actual cost of property changes. If entrepreneurial profit is evident, it should be included in the appraisal estimate. Quoted costs for improvements may not reflect the owner's related risk, labor and equipment costs, financial charges, the costs of land preparation, engineering costs, or other indirect expenses. The appraiser must also recognize that cost estimates for the reproduction or replacement of improvements as of the appraisal date, which are developed in data analysis, may not reflect any profit that the current owner realized due to a change in the property. Of course, final cost estimates should include this profit if it is evident in the market.

Sales Comparison Approach

In the sales comparison approach to value, an appraiser analyzes data gathered primarily from comparable sales. The purpose of this analysis is to identify differences between the subject property and the comparable sale properties so that the value of these differences can be measured. The analysis of sales data reveals which features the market perceives to be valuable. It also suggests mathematical computations that can be applied to the known values of the comparables to arrive at indications of whole or per-unit value of the subject property.

The first step in data analysis is the selection of one or more appropriate units of comparison. In appraising single-family residential property, adjustments are typically made to the total property sale price; therefore, the basic unit of comparison is the total property. The total property unit is seldom used in appraising nonresidential properties because their sizes vary significantly.

After the appropriate unit of comparison is chosen, the appraiser reviews the data to determine which characteristics of the properties and which sales transactions should be used in the sales comparison approach. The dates of the sales indicate which properties will provide the best initial indication of change in value over time. Ideally this indication is derived from a recorded sale and subsequent resale of a property that was not substantially changed between the sales.

Further data analysis will suggest where the appraiser should begin to solve for the values contributed by individual property characteristics. Because properties usually have many components, the appraiser starts by finding a single component for which a value can be derived. For example, if the market data grid shows that two properties vary only in that one is fully landscaped and the other is not, the appraiser can estimate the contributory value of the landscaping by comparing the two sales. Then another market variable can be isolated from other sales with a second calculation. (Further discussion of paired data set analysis can be found in Chapter 17.)

The analysis of sales is progressive. An appraiser isolates and solves for one variable at a time, comparing known indications against unknown characteristics. This analytical process gives the appraiser an indication of the data that will be most useful in applying the sales comparison approach and suggests the pattern of calculations that will be needed to derive a value indication. Moreover, a careful review of market data may reveal that additional data are needed to substantiate the value indication reached through the sales comparison approach, or that more weight should be attributed to the value indications derived through the cost and income capitalization approaches.

Income Capitalization Approach

Comparable sales data, comparable rental data, and income and expense statements provide a variety of information for use in the income capitalization approach. Much of the data needed for this approach is derived from interviews with individuals who are familiar with the subject property or comparable sale and rental properties. An appraiser may also interview owners and managers of similar properties for information on typical rents, lease terms, vacancy rates, management fees, and other operating expenses.

If an appraiser is valuing an apartment in an area where there is a relative scarcity of apartment sales or other property data, the appraiser may study apartments located elsewhere to suggest income and expense trends and indicate the various relationships between income and value. If sufficient comparability exists, these data can provide support for the analysis.

When the data available provide adequate information on the income, expenses, and mortgage terms associated with each sale, the appraiser can derive an estimate of the net operating income (*NOI*) and pre-tax cash flow, or equity dividend, of each sale property. The overall capitalization rate and equity capitalization rate reflected in each sale can then be calculated.

This calculation is meaningful only if the appraiser uses the same income and expense categories to derive net operating incomes from comparable sales and to project the net operating income of the subject property. If, for example, an allowance for replacement is made in the expense statement for one comparable property and not in the others, the overall capitalization rate derived for that property will not be comparable to the rates derived for other properties.

By analyzing the market-derived overall capitalization rate and equity capitalization rate indicated by each comparable sale, the appraiser can develop an appro priate rate or rates to use in deriving a value indication for the subject property using direct capitalization techniques. When adequate comparable sale and rental data are available, it is often possible to calculate both an overall capitalization rate and an equity capitalization rate for the subject property. Although yield capitalization may produce a more detailed analysis, market-derived rates should be analyzed and explained in market value appraisals. If the results obtained with direct and yield capitalization methods differ, the appraiser must find market support for his or her conclusions and explain them in light of the market. (Yield capitalization techniques are discussed in Chapter 21.)

SUMMARY

Data collection and analysis are vital to an appraisal as the methods and procedures employed to estimate value. The information used by appraisers consists of general data on social, economic, governmental, and environmental forces; specific data on the property being appraised, comparable sales and rental properties, and local market characteristics; and market data on competitive supply and demand.

An appraiser studies general data to understand the interaction of value influences and to forecast economic trends. General data include economic indicators pertaining to the balance of trade, the gross national product, production levels, wage levels, the volume of retail sales, the prime interest rate, the CPI, and the unemployment rate; government activities relating to planning, the provision of public utilities, municipal services, and transportation systems; tax policies; and regulations on zoning, subdivision development, and environmental safeguards. General data reflect economic conditions at the international, national, regional, and local level.

The *economic base* of a community is the economic activity that enables it to attract income from outside its borders. It determines local population growth and the disposable income available for consumption or investment, which in turn affect household formation and purchasing power. To consider the impact of macroeconomic influences on microeconomic conditions, the appraiser examines how inflationary expectations relate to local price levels and construction costs, how the current phase of the business cycle relates to area building starts, how income and real estate taxes relate to local property values, and how monetary policy and capital availability relate to local financing rates.

Sources of general data include government publications sponsored by the Council of Economic Advisors; the Federal Reserve Board; the Department of Commerce, Bureau of the Census and Bureau of Economic Analysis; and the Department of Labor, Bureau of Labor Statistics. General data can also be obtained from state and local governments, chambers of commerce, trade associations, research institutions, multiple listing services, and databases.

An appraiser uses specific data to apply the three approaches to value and to ensure that the final conclusion reflects the market. Specific data on comparable properties identify value-influencing property characteristics, units of comparison, sale prices and rents, operating expenses, capitalization rates, construction costs, the anticipated economic life of the improvements, and accrued depreciation. The focus of data collection and analysis is defined by the appraiser's determination of the highest and best use of the property. Specific data are evaluated on their comparability, availability, and reliability.

Specific data provide basic information about market transactions—e.g., the number of sales, sale dates, the availability of properties for sale, absorption rates, the volume of sales or turnover rate, the motivation of buyers and sellers, the terms and conditions of sales, prior and subsequent use of comparable properties, and other significant factors affecting the market. This information can indicate the strength or weakness of the market, which is embodied in the relationship between supply and demand, and the marketability of the subject property.

Sources of specific sales data include public records, newspapers, real estate professionals, multiple listing services, and published property listings and offers. An appraiser may obtain specific cost data from contractors, suppliers of building materials, or cost-estimating manuals. To value investment properties, appraisers study data on property income, operating expenses, vacancy and collection losses, and mortgage terms or debt service. These data are available from public sources, such as recorded leases and advertised rentals, and private sources such as owners and tenants. When relevant data are available, overall capitalization rates and equity capitalization rates can be derived.

The supply of existing and prospective properties that are competitive with the subject property are inventoried and the current and future demand are studied to determine the level of market support for the appraised property and its highest and best use. Listings and offerings can provide indications of the values anticipated by buyers and sellers as well as prospective market activity.

Sources of data on competitive supply include inventories compiled through field inspection; interviews with owners, managers, brokers, developers, and city planners; and examination of building permits, plat maps, and surveys of competitive sites. Market research firms issue reports on available space and vacancy, absorption, and turnover rates. Demand studies are based on the demographic and economic data compiled by the Census Bureau and the Bureau of Labor. Small area projections are available from real estate research firms. The reasonableness of these projections should be checked against supply data for the specified market area such as building permits, market sales, or absorption rates. Developments affecting the local economy should also be studied. Geographical Information Systems integrate demand-specific data with geographic information.

The organization and array of specific data are shown on a market data grid, which is a spreadsheet for tabular representation. Developing such a grid helps the appraiser isolate the different characteristics of the subject and comparable properties and interpret the effect of these differences on value. The same units of comparison should be used to describe the property characteristics of the subject and comparable properties. The analysis of specific data indicates which information will be most useful and whether additional data will be required for substantiation.

In a cost analysis, the appraiser precisely delineates all expenditures that contribute to the total reproduction or replacement cost of the improvements. Estimates of accrued depreciation, any entrepreneurial profit, and the contribution of the improvement to the property should be supported with market evidence.

In a sales comparison analysis, the appraiser isolates the factors that are responsible for variations between the values of the subject property and comparable properties. The appraiser begins by determining the prices of the comparables and their dates of sale, which are used to account for market conditions. Then information on the property rights and financial arrangements involved and the conditions of sale are reviewed to clarify the motivations of the buyers and the sellers. The data will also indicate other differences in the characteristics of the subject and comparable properties.

In an income capitalization analysis, capitalization rates must be derived from the market. The data on income, operating expenses, vacancy and collection losses, and mortgage terms gathered reflect the experiences of comparable properties. Income and expense categories should be analyzed consistently.

Chapter 8

NEIGHBORHOODS AND DISTRICTS

$\mathcal{S}$ocial, economic, governmental, and environmental forces influence property values in the vicinity of a subject property which, in turn, directly affect the value of the subject property itself. Therefore, the boundaries of the area of influence must be delineated to conduct a thorough analysis. The area of influence is the area within which the forces affect all surrounding properties in the same way they affect the property being appraised. Although physical boundaries may be drawn, the significant boundaries are those that fix the limits of influences on property values. By coincidence, these limits may be physically observable.

The area of influence is commonly called a neighborhood. *A neighborhood is a group of complementary land uses.* A residential neighborhood, for example, may contain single-family homes and commercial properties that provide services for local residents. A clear distinction can be drawn between a neighborhood and a district. *A district is a type of neighborhood that is characterized by homogeneous land use.* Districts are commonly composed of apartments or commercial, industrial, or agricultural properties.

To identify neighborhood or district boundaries, an appraiser examines the subject property's surroundings. The investigation begins with the subject property and proceeds outward, identifying all relevant actual and potential influences on the property's value that can be attributed to its location. The appraiser extends the geographic search far enough to encompass all influences that the market perceives as affecting the value of the subject property. At the physical point where no factors influencing the value of the subject and surrounding properties are found, the boundaries for analysis are set. The appraiser's conclusions regarding the impact of the neighborhood or district on the subject property's value are significant only if area boundaries have been properly delineated.

Neighborhood or district analysis provides a framework, or context, in which property value is estimated. It identifies the area of analysis and establishes the potential limits within which the appraiser searches for data to be used in applying the three approaches to value. Realistic boundaries allow the appraiser to identify comparable properties in the same neighborhood or district; the sale prices of these properties usually require little or no adjustment for location.

Neighborhood or district analysis helps the appraiser determine the stability of an area and may indicate future land uses and value trends.

CHARACTERISTICS OF NEIGHBORHOODS AND DISTRICTS

A neighborhood exhibits a greater degree of uniformity than a larger area. Obviously, no group of inhabitants, buildings, or business enterprises can possess identical features or attributes, but a neighborhood is perceived to be relatively uniform. The relative uniformity of a neighborhood is reflected in many ways. Many shared features may be reflected in a neighborhood, including similar building types and styles, population characteristics, economic profiles of occupants, and zoning regulations that affect land use. The variables that suggest similarity are not limited to physical characteristics. The social, economic, and governmental forces operating within a neighborhood contribute as much to its definition as the physical environment. The diverse and varied nature of neighborhoods reflects this fact. Similarity may also be indicated by the dominant land use, rent and occupancy levels, the credit strength of occupants, and the ages of buildings.

NEIGHBORHOOD AND DISTRICT BOUNDARIES

Neighborhood and district boundaries identify the physical area that influences the value of a subject property. These boundaries may coincide with observable changes in prevailing land use or occupant characteristics. Physical features such as the type of structures, street patterns, terrain, vegetation, and lot sizes tend to identify land use districts. Transportation arteries (highways, major streets, and railroads), bodies of water (rivers, lakes, and streams), and changing elevation (hills, mountains, cliffs, and valleys) can also be significant boundaries.

The neighborhood of a house in a single-family subdivision usually ends where land uses change to commercial, apartment, or industrial use. However, another house in the same subdivision that is nearer to these different land uses may be influenced by them; the neighborhood of this house may not end at the same point.

In defining a district, variations in the relevant characteristics of properties may indicate that more limited boundaries should be established. For example, consider an urban area where many high-rise apartment buildings are constructed along a natural lakeshore and separated from other land uses by major transportation arteries. In this type of district, there may be great variation in apartments, prices, sizes, views, parking availability, proximity to public transportation, and building ages. These variations suggest limited district boundaries which must be identified to reveal market and submarket characteristics.

The properties closest to a subject property tend to exert the greatest influence on its value. Any property, even a commercial one, that is on the fringe of a residential area and near attractive, well-maintained, desirable properties tends to have a higher value than it would if it were located near less attractive, poorly maintained, undesirable properties.

Legal, political, and economic organizations collect data for standardized or statistically defined areas, so information about income and educational levels may be available for cities, counties, tax districts, census tracts, or special enumeration districts. Although these data may be relevant, they rarely conform to the area boundaries identified for property valuation. If secondary data are used to help identify neighborhood boundaries, the appraiser should verify and supplement the data with primary research.

To identify neighborhood and district boundaries, an appraiser follows several steps.

Step 1. Examine the area's physical characteristics. The appraiser should drive or walk around the area to develop a sense of place, noting the degree of similarity in land uses, types of structures, architectural styles, and maintenance and upkeep. Using a map of the area, the appraiser can identify points where these characteristics change and note any physical barriers—e.g., major streets, hills, rivers, railroads—that coincide with these points.

Step 2. Draw preliminary boundaries on a map. The appraiser draws lines on the map to connect the points that indicate where physical characteristics change. The physical barriers that coincide with or are near these points are identified.

Step 3. Test preliminary boundaries against demographic data. The appraiser then obtains accurate data on the ages, occupations, incomes, and educational levels of neighborhood residents.[1] The information generally available for census tracts, zip code regions, and counties must be segmented to represent pertinent subareas and neighborhoods. Reliable data may also be available from local chambers of commerce, universities, and research organizations.

In unusual cases an appraiser might consider sampling area residents to identify relevant characteristics. Appraisers may also interview neighborhood occupants, business people, brokers, and community representatives for their perceptions of how far the neighborhood extends. Through experience an appraiser learns to observe changes and understand how neighborhoods are perceived.

CHANGE

In neighborhood and district analysis, an appraiser recognizes the propensity for change and tries to determine how a particular neighborhood may be changing. Appraisers usually consider trends in historic growth and neighborhood composition when analyzing patterns of change. When values in a neighborhood are increasing, the appraiser must determine whether the subject property's value can be expected to exceed, equal, or lag behind the neighborhood trend. Similarly, if neighborhood values are stable or declining, the appraiser analyzes the value of the subject property relative to these trends.

Evidence of Change

Neighborhood change is often indicated by variations within the neighborhood. New uses may indicate potential increases or decreases in a neighborhood's property values. For example, a neighborhood in which some homes are well maintained and others are not may be undergoing either decline or revitalization. The introduction of different uses, such as rooming houses or offices, into a single-family residential neighborhood also indicates potential change.

Distinct change in land use with arterial and natural boundaries
(H. Armstrong Roberts, Inc.)

Every 10 years the Bureau of the Census, U.S. Department of Commerce, collects data on population ⸯd housing characteristics, employment, and earnings.

Changes in one neighborhood are usually influenced by changes in other neighborhoods and in the larger area of influence. In any relatively stable city, the rapid growth of one neighborhood or district may adversely affect a competing neighborhood or district. A city may grow until its center is not accessible from its more remote districts. In such instances new, competing business centers may be established to serve the needs of outlying areas.

Suburban business centers may have an adverse effect on a city's central business district. Newer residential areas may affect older areas. The added supply of new homes may induce residents to shift from old homes to new ones and place older homes on the market. This increase in supply may affect the market values of all homes in the area. If the location of a neighborhood makes it attractive for conversion to a more intensive use, the existing improvements may be extensively remodeled or torn down to make way for redevelopment.

Growth causes changes in the utility of both vacant and improved parcels of real estate. Utility may increase or decrease, and changes in value may result. No neighborhood or district is static; although it usually proceeds slowly, change is constant and inevitable.

Neighborhood and District Life Cycle

Because neighborhoods and districts are perceived, organized, constructed, and used by human beings, each has a dynamic quality of its own. Appraisers describe this quality as the life cycle of a neighborhood or district. The complementary land uses that comprise neighborhoods and the homogeneous land uses that comprise districts typically evolve through four stages.

1. *Growth—a period during which the neighborhood gains public favor and acceptance*
2. *Stability—a period of equilibrium without marked gains or losses*
3. *Decline—a period of diminishing demand*
4. *Revitalization—a period of renewal, modernization, and increasing demand*

Although these stages describe the life cycle of neighborhoods and districts in a general way, they should not be used as specific guides to market trends. No set number of years is assigned to any stage in the cycle. Many neighborhoods and districts remain stable for a very long time; decline is not necessarily imminent in all older areas. Unless decline is caused by a specific external influence—e.g., the construction of a new highway that changes traffic patterns—it may proceed at a barely perceptible rate and can be interrupted by a change in use or a revival of demand. There is no set life expectancy for a neighborhood or district, and the life cycle is not an inexorable process. At any point in the cycle, a major change can interrupt the order of the stages. For example, strong negative influence can cause a neighborhood that is in a stage of growth to decline precipitously rather than stabilize.

After a period of decline, a neighborhood may undergo a transition to other land uses or its life cycle may begin again due to revitalization. Neighborhood revitalization often results from organized rebuilding or restoration undertaken to preserve architecturally by significant structures. It may also be caused by a natural rekindling of demand. The rebirth of an older, inner-city neighborhood, for example, may simply be due to changing preferences and life styles, with no planned renewal program.

Gentrification and Displacement

One relatively recent neighborhood phenomenon is *gentrification, in which middle- and upper-income people purchase neighborhood properties and renovate or rehabilitate them.* The residents displaced by this process are often lower-income individuals, who moved into these older, urban neighborhoods when middle- and upper-income groups left or began to find the neighborhoods unappealing and unattractive. Often two or more low-income households would occupy what was formerly a single-family residence. Such neighborhoods often became blighted.

Neighborhood renovation
(H. Armstrong Roberts, Inc.)

Gentrification, which reverses the process of decline, appears to be the result of a preponderance of small families and single people who choose to live in urban areas.

ANALYSIS OF VALUE INFLUENCES IN NEIGHBORHOODS

The forces that influence value, which are manifested in the similar characteristics of properties in a neighborhood, are important in neighborhood analysis. These similar characteristics identify influences that have affected value trends in the past and may affect values in the future. The forces that influence value in districts are important in district analysis. The discussion that follows focuses on neighborhoods, but generally applies to districts as well.

Social Considerations

A neighborhood's character may be revealed by examining the reasons why occupants live or work in the area. Occupants are attracted to a location for its status, physical environment, services, affordability, and convenience.

In performing a neighborhood analysis, an appraiser identifies relevant social characteristics and influences. To identify and describe these characteristics, the appraiser must be aware that the characteristics that have the greatest influence on property values in a neighborhood tend to overlap. The overall desirability of the subject neighborhood in relation to other, competing neighborhoods is, of course, reflected in their respective price levels.

In neighborhood analysis, relevant social characteristics include

- Population density, which is particularly important in central business districts and high-rise residential neighborhoods
- Occupant skill levels or employment categories, which are particularly important in industrial or high-technology districts
- Occupant age levels, which are particularly important in residential neighborhoods
- Occupant employment status, including types of unemployment (temporary, seasonal, or chronic)
- Extent or absence of crime
- Extent or absence of litter
- Quality and availability of educational, medical, social, recreational, cultural, and commercial services
- Presence or absence of community or neighborhood organizations such as improvement associations, block clubs, and crime watch groups

It is difficult, if not impossible, to identify the social preferences of the many individuals who comprise a given market and to measure how these preferences affect property value. Therefore, an appraiser should not place too much reliance on social influences in arriving at a value conclusion. From an appraiser's viewpoint, the social characteristics of a residential neighborhood are significant only when they are considered by the buying public and can be objectively and accurately analyzed. Although race, religion, and national origin are social characteristics, they have no direct relationship to real estate values. Professional appraisers know that they must perform unbiased neighborhood analyses.

Economic Considerations

Economic considerations relate to the financial capacity of neighborhood occupants and their ability to rent or own property, to maintain it in an attractive and desirable condition, and to renovate or rehabilitate it when needed. The physical characteristics of the area and of individual properties may indicate the relative financial strength of area occupants and how this strength is reflected in neighborhood development and upkeep. Ownership and rental data can also provide clues to residents' financial capability. The income levels revealed by recent census information, newspaper surveys, and private studies may indicate the prices at which occupants can afford to rent or purchase property. Vacancy statistics compiled by newspapers, the U.S. Postal Service, and other fact-finding agencies combined with other information on the number of properties for rent or sale found in classified newspaper ads help an appraiser estimate the strength of demand and the extent of supply.

The presence of vacant lots or acreage suitable for development in an area may suggest future construction activity or indicate a lack of demand. Current construction creates trends that affect the value of existing improvements. A careful study of these trends can help an appraiser predict the future desirability of an area. Block-by-block information helps identify the direction of growth. A neighborhood may be developing, static, declining, or in a period of revitalization. A trend may be a local phenomenon or it may affect the entire community. A change in the economic base on which a community depends (e.g., the addition or loss of a major employer) is frequently reflected in the rate of population growth or decline. Ownership demand tends to remain strong and rental occupancy levels are high when the population is growing; demand weakens and occupancy levels decrease when the population is declining.

To analyze a neighborhood's economic characteristics, an appraiser expands the analysis to include economic trends over a three- to five-year period. Then the appraiser decides which economic variables significantly contribute to value differences among neighborhoods and compares the current economic characteristics of competing neighborhoods.

The economic characteristics that an appraiser may consider include

Occupant income levels

Extent of occupant ownership

Property rent levels

Property value levels

Vacancy rates for various types of property

Amount of development and construction

Effective ages of properties

Changes in property use

Governmental Considerations

Governmental considerations relate to the laws, regulations, and taxes that impinge on neighborhood properties and the administration and enforcement of these constraints. Some buyers are interested in neighborhoods that are subject to effective zoning laws, building codes, and housing and sanitary codes. The property tax burden associated with the benefits provided and the relative taxes and benefits provided by other neighborhoods are also considered. The enforcement of applicable codes, regulations, and restrictions should be equitable and effective. An appraiser gathers data about the governmental characteristics of the neighborhood and compares them with the characteristics of other, competing neighborhoods.

Tax burdens in different neighborhoods can vary significantly and variations in taxes are a significant basis for comparison. Sometimes the level of special assessments in a location can become so heavy that the marketability of property is seriously affected. The benefits resulting from these assessments may not enhance the sale prices that can be obtained for properties in proportion to their cost; nevertheless, the cost must be offset. As a rule, properties that are subject to special assessments can be expected to bring lower sale prices than comparable properties that are not subject to these taxes. For example, consider two identical properties located in the same block on different streets that are each worth $75,000 free of encumbrances. If one is subject to a special assessment lien of $3,000, its market value subject to the lien may be $72,000, even though an uninformed buyer might not discount for the lien.

Divergent tax rates may also affect market value. Local taxes may favor or penalize certain property types. Therefore, an appraiser should examine the local structure of assessed values and tax rates to compare the tax burdens created by various forms of taxes and ascertain their apparent effect on the values of different types of real estate.

Counties or cities may have the authority to impose optional taxes such as sales and earnings taxes on residents. When the sales and local earnings taxes applicable to competing communities vary, the relative desirability of the communities may be affected. Variations in optional taxes often have a more pronounced influence on the marketability and value of commercial and industrial property than real estate taxes do.

Most communities have detailed zoning ordinances, which are designed to implement a comprehensive plan. Zoning laws typically identify zones or districts where certain land uses are permitted and others are prohibited. The broadest zoning categories are residential (often indicated by R), commercial (indicated by C), and industrial (indicated by I). These categories are divided into subcategories, such as R1a for detached, single-family residences constructed on lots of a specified minimum size, shape, and frontage. Smaller lots may be allowed in areas zoned R1b, R2 zoning may allow duplexes, and R3 zoning might permit low-density apartments. The zoning code for a moderate-sized city may consist of several hundred pages which identify and explain the various zones. An appraiser should examine the zoning requirements for the neighborhood in question and attempt to assess their adequacy and enforcement provisions.

Private restrictions on land use may be established by private owners through provisions in deeds or plat recordings. These restrictions may specify lot and building sizes in a subdivision, permitted architectural styles, and property uses. Condominium bylaws also restrict property use. The appraiser should make certain that private restrictions do not limit property uses inordinately. In the absence of zoning, the appraiser should determine if private restrictions are adequate to protect long-term property values.

The governmental characteristics to be considered in neighborhood analysis include

- Tax burden relative to services provided, compared with other neighborhoods in the community
- Special assessments
- Zoning, building, and housing codes
- Quality of fire and police protection, schools, and other governmental services

Environmental Considerations

Environmental considerations consist of any natural or man-made features that are contained in or affect the neighborhood and its geographic location. Important environmental considerations include building size, type, density, and mainte nance; topographical features; open space; nuisances and hazards emanating from nearby facilities such as shopping centers, factories, and schools; the adequacy of public utilities such as street lights, sewers, and electricity; the existence and up-keep of vacant lots; general maintenance; street patterns, width, and maintenance; and the attractiveness and safety of routes into and out of the neighborhood.

Certain buildings may be overimprovements or underimprovements due to their excessive or deficient cost, quality, or size relative to their sites and sur-rounding properties. For example, a six-bedroom, four-bathroom house in an area of three-bedroom, one-bath houses might be an overimprovement, or it may sig-nal a trend toward larger homes in the area. Overimprovements may be worth less than their cost new, particularly in middle- and lower-income neighborhoods.

Topographical features can have positive or negative effects on neighborhood property values. The presence of a lake, river, bay, or hill in or near a neighbor-hood may give the area a scenic advantage. Conversely, the presence of a wetland may preclude development unless costly mitigation procedures are feasible. A hill may mean little in a mountainous area, but in a predominantly flat area an ele-vated or wooded section can enhance property value. A river subject to severe flooding may cause the value of homes along its banks to decline due to the risk of such a hazard. Sometimes a river, lake, or park serves as a buffer between a residential district and commercial or industrial enterprises. Land features may give a neighborhood protection against wind, fog, or flood, or they may expose it to damage.

The presence of asbestos or PCBs in buildings and environmental liabilities incurred due to past contamination may reduce property values. In certain areas, radon, a colorless, odorless gas linked to lung cancer, may limit the value of buildings. The U.S. Environmental Protection Agency has published interim guidelines for the design of buildings in radon-affected areas. Excessive traffic, odors, smoke, dust, or noise from commercial or manufacturing enterprises can limit a residential neighborhood's desirability.

Gas, electricity, water, telephone service, and storm and sanitary sewers are essential to meet the accepted standard of living in municipal areas. A deficiency in any of these services tends to decrease property values in a neighborhood. The availability of utilities also affects the direction and timing of neighborhood growth or development.

A neighborhood's environmental characteristics cannot be judged on an abso-lute scale; rather, they must be compared with the characteristics of other, com-peting neighborhoods. An appraiser asks: Do the terrain, vegetation, street patterns, structural density, property maintenance, public utilities, and other at-tributes of this neighborhood make it more or less desirable than other neighbor-hoods? What is the relative desirability of the neighborhood's location?

Location

Location represents the time-distance relationships, or linkages, between a prop-erty or neighborhood and all other possible origins and destinations of people going to or coming from the property or neighborhood. Time and distance are measures of relative access. Usually all the properties in a neighborhood have the same or very similar locational relationships with common origins and destinations.

To analyze the impact of neighborhood location, an appraiser must identify important linkages and measure their time-distances by the most commonly used types of transportation. The most suitable type of transportation usually depends on the preferences and needs of neighborhood occupants. It is not enough to note that transportation exists; the type of service provided and how it addresses the needs of neighborhood occupants must be considered.

Linkages should be judged in terms of how well they serve the typical users of real estate in the neighborhood. For example, in analyzing a single-family residential neighborhood, an appraiser considers where typical occupants need to go. If adequate facilities are not available for necessary linkages, the neighborhood will not be regarded as favorably as competing neighborhoods that have better linkages. For single-family residential neighborhoods, linkages with schools, grocery stores, and employment centers are usually the most important; linkages with recreational facilities, houses of worship, restaurants, and retail stores are less important. When current zoning does not restrict changes from the present land use, or when a change in the predominant land use is evident, the appraiser may need to examine linkages in terms of both the current land use and the anticipated predominant land use in the neighborhood.

Public transportation is important because some people do not own automobiles and others prefer not to use them often. Thus, residential properties in remote areas with unreliable or infrequent public transportation may command lower rentals and prices than properties that are more conveniently located or have better service. The distance to public transportation is considered in relation to the people who will use it.

A study of neighborhood transportation facilities must consider the territory through which users must pass. Most people would rather avoid poorly lighted streets and rundown areas. Generally, the closer a property is to good public transportation, the wider its market.

The market's perception of the desirability of different neighborhoods can be studied by analyzing comparable sales. The dollar and percentage differences among the sale prices of similar properties in different locations can provide the basis for this analysis.

Some important environmental characteristics to be considered in neighborhood analysis are

- Land use patterns
- Lot size and shape
- Terrain and vegetation
- Environmental liabilities
- Street patterns and width
- Density of structures and amount of open space
- Property maintenance and upkeep
- Availability and quality of utilities
- Nuisances and hazards (e.g., odors, noises, litter, vibrations, fog, smoke, and smog)

- Access to public transportation and type of system (e.g., bus, rail)
- Access to schools and quality of schools
- Access to stores and service establishments
- Access to parks and recreational facilities
- Access to houses of worship
- Access to workplaces

ENVIRONMENTAL LIABILITIES

In recent years the federal government has issued more than 70,000 pages of environmental laws and regulations. State and local governments have also adopted thousands of pages of environmental legislation. This vast network of regulations has defined natural and man-made conditions that constitute environmental liabilities affecting property valuation. Natural conditions include wetlands, aquifer replenishment areas, and habitats for endangered or threatened species. Man-made conditions may involve the presence of underground storage tanks, asbestos, PCBs, or other hazardous materials. The existence of one or more of these conditions can reduce the value of a property to only a fraction of its potential value.

The role and responsibility of the appraiser in detecting or measuring environmental substances affecting a property is addressed in Guide Note 8 to the Standards of Professional Appraisal Practice. The guide note takes its direction from the Competency Provision of the Uniform Standards of Professional Appraisal Practice which requires that the appraiser either 1) have the knowledge and experience necessary to complete a specific appraisal assignment competently or 2) disclose his or her lack of knowledge or experience to the client and take all steps necessary or appropriate to complete the assignment competently.

The typical appraiser may not have the knowledge or experience needed to detect the presence of hazardous substances or to measure the quantities of such material. Like buyers and sellers in the open market, the appraiser must often rely on the advice of others in matters that require special expertise. Although a professional appraiser could become an expert in another field, appraisers are not required or expected to be experts in the detection or measurement of hazardous substances. Even if there is no reason to believe that a property is affected by hazardous substances, it is recommended that the appraiser include a standard disclaimer or statement of limiting conditions pertaining to hazardous substances in the appraisal report. Such statements clarify the normal limits of the appraisal, disclose the appraiser's lack of expertise with regard to hazardous substances, and disclaim responsibility for matters beyond the appraiser's experience.

Comprehensive Environmental Response, Compensation, and Liability Act of 1980 (CERCLA)

The most far-reaching federal environmental law is the Comprehensive Environmental Response, Compensation, and Liability Act of 1980 (CERCLA), commonly known as Superfund. The act was created by Congress to serve as a mechanism to accelerate the cleanup of contaminated sites without long and costly legal entanglements. Under CERCLA the adjudication of liability is strict, joint, several, and retroactive.

Strict liability refers to the assigning of liability without regard to intentional fault or proof of negligence. *Joint and several liability* means that if several persons or entities have contributed hazardous waste to a site, each (several) and any (joint) is liable for the cost of assessing the damage, cleaning it up, and restoring the environment to an uncontaminated condition. Since many of the contamination issues that CERCLA addresses occurred in the past, the legislation is, by definition, *retroactive*.

The parties held liable include the generators, transporters, and disposers of hazardous waste materials. Through the legislation's retroactive provisions, the previous owner or operator of a property may be subject to CERCLA liability. The legal language is intentionally broad enough to apply to temporary owners, lessees, lessors, trustees, and even stockholders. The law empowers the U.S. Environmental Protection Agency to find sources to pay for waste cleanup by holding the perpetrators liable for the "deep pocket" costs. If no demonstrably liable party can be found, the federal government will use Superfund monies to clean up severely contaminated sites.

Congress attempted to remedy certain inequities in the CERCLA legislation by passing the Superfund Amendments and Reauthorization Act (SARA) in 1986. SARA addressed the matter of the so-called "innocent" purchaser. One of the few exemptions from charges of liability under CERCLA was the action or omission of a third party who could demonstrate no contractual relationship to the defendant. (Contractual relationships may include land contracts, deeds, or instruments transferring title or possession.) SARA extended this exemption to cover third parties who acquired real property after the disposal or placement of hazardous substances provided that these parties, at the time of the acquisition, "did not know and had no reason to know that any hazardous substance was disposed of on, in, or at the facility." SARA further specifies that "all appropriate inquiry into the previous ownership and uses of the property" must have been undertaken to establish that the defendant had no reason to know of the presence of hazardous substances. SARA also recognizes the exemption of defendants who acquire property by inheritance and government entities that acquire property through involuntary transfer or the exercise of eminent domain. (See Appendix A for a summary of environmental legislation affecting appraisers.)

Transactional Audits

Because the potential liability for a contaminated site is so far-reaching, some buyers, sellers, and lending institutions have routinely begun to commission *environmental property assessments* (EPRAs), sometimes called *transactional audits*, before executing a sale or a loan agreement. Most environmental audits required for real estate transactions are conducted by environmental consultants who are trained to investigate a broad range of environmental issues. Any specialized investigations are performed in phases. Phase one focuses on evidence of potential contamination; phase two confirms the existence of the contamination; and phase three describes the extent of the contamination. The enviromental consultant may then recommend a remedial course of action accomplish the actual cleanup.

A phase one environmental audit is most commonly associated with real estate transactions. Typically it includes a site visit; a review of aerial photographs; a review of the records of local, state, and federal environmental agencies; and a review of the pertinent regulatory legislation. During the site visit, the investigator interviews occupants of the subject and neighboring properties and looks for signs of contamination, such as a stained ground surface, defoliation, noxious odors, areas of inconsistent height or depth, uneven pavement, or the presence of drums and other debris.

An environmental audit cannot guarantee that a property is totally free of hazardous substances. An investigation does provide limited legal protection for the innocent purchaser, however, and a reasonable margin of assurance that contamination from asbestos, PCBs, or other hazardous substances is unlikely. To guarantee that a property is completely devoid of contaminants, every building component would have to be examined for asbestos and every cubic foot of soil and groundwater to the earth's core would have to be tested. The question of "how clean is clean?" continues to be debated in the courts.

Although the environmental liabilities associated with industrial plants are well known, many of the same liabilities may be present in commercial, residential and agricultural properties. One cannot assume that green, rural properties that appear clean are actually free of environmental liabilities.

In the 1940s and 1950s farmers commonly used cattle vats, trenches filled with fuel oil through which cattle were paraded to rid them of mites and small insects. The fuel oil was often treated with DDT and other pesticides. When this practice fell into disuse, the trenches were simply filled in. Farms often have aging underground storage tanks that held gasoline used to fuel farm vehicles. Farmland may also be contaminated by the accumulation of fertilizers and pesticides. Old railroad beds can also constitute an environmental hazard because railroad ties were commonly soaked in creosote-filled trenches dug on site whenever tracks were laid. Nor are timberlands free of contaminants. Old turpentine stills are often found in areas where forests were once harvested.

OBJECTIVITY IN NEIGHBORHOOD ANALYSIS

All amenities and detrimental conditions revealed in neighborhood or district analysis should be described specifically and impartially in the appraisal report. A general reference to "pride of ownership" in a report is too vague and subjective to indicate any actual effect on property value. Such references ascribe motives and attitudes to people, which should be avoided. Rather than generalities, the appraiser should record specific, impartial observations made during a personal inspection of the neighborhood. Descriptive phrases such as "many broken windows," "tall weeds present," "no litter present," and "well-kept lawns" convey direct, value-influencing information.

Appraisers' conclusions regarding neighborhood conditions and their effects on property values are considered by buyers, sellers, brokers, lenders, courts, arbiters, public officials, and other decision makers and advisers. Appraisers are often asked to provide specific evidence of neighborhood conditions and trends and to explain their findings in written reports.

DISTRICTS

The unique characteristics of districts require that special factors be considered in their analysis. The specific value influences affecting apartment districts, commercial districts, industrial districts, agricultural districts, and other types of districts are frequently not the same as the influences affecting single-family residential neighborhoods. One important factor that affects land value in all districts is the availability of public utilities, including sanitary and storm sewers and municipal or well water. Prevailing levels of real estate and personal property taxes also influence the desirability of districts and may be reflected in real estate values. Of course, the four forces that influence all real estate value affect districts.

Apartment Districts

In large cities an apartment district usually covers an extensive area; in smaller cities the district may be dispersed or limited in size. Apartment design may be multistory, garden, row, or townhouse; units may be rented or privately owned as cooperatives and condominiums.

Although apartment districts differ from single-family residential areas, they are subject to many similar influences. Therefore, an appraiser can identify the characteristics and amenities that affect an apartment district in a manner similar

High-rise apartment district (H. Armstrong Roberts, Inc.)

to that applied to a single-family residential neighborhood, but with a change of emphasis. In an apartment district, desirability and value may be influenced by

Access to workplaces

Transportation service

Access to shopping centers and cultural facilities

Schools

Neighborhood reputation

Residential atmosphere, neighborhood appearance, and protection against unwanted commercial and industrial intrusion

Proximity to parks, lakes, rivers, or other natural features

Supply of vacant apartment sites that are likely to be developed and could make present accommodations more desirable or less desirable

Parking for tenants and guests

Structures that concentrate radon

Economic and social status of tenants

Use of underground storage tanks for fuel oil to run central heating systems

Presence of friable asbestos insulation

Use of transformers containing PCBs

Maintenance standards

Vacancy and tenant turnover rate

These characteristics and other pertinent data form the basis for an appraiser's study of rental housing. In some cities, statistics on the supply of apartments, vacancy rates, and rent levels are available. When statistics are not available, the appraiser must gather data through research.

Commercial Districts

A commercial district is a group of offices or stores that influences the use and value of the commercial property being appraised. Commercial districts may include the enterprises along a local business street or freeway service road, a development adjacent to a traffic intersection, a regional or neighborhood shopping center, and a downtown central business district (CBD).

To analyze a commercial district, an appraiser identifies its trade area—i.e., the area the businesses serve. A commercial district and its property values are affected by factors that influence the values of surrounding properties. Therefore, the type and character of nearby land uses affect a commercial district.

For example, trends in population growth, suburbanization, and the use of private automobiles have made shopping centers important sources of commercial activity. Until the mid-1970s, inexpensive energy encouraged outward urban expansion. Large regional shopping centers and smaller community centers began to replace central business districts. Commercial businesses located in shopping centers often benefited from their association with complementary establishments, but businesses in downtown areas and strip developments did not fare so well. Commercial activity in many downtown areas has declined, but in some cases this has led to revitalization of CBDs.

During the late 1970s and early 1980s, increased energy costs dampened outward development in some cities. Most of the new shopping centers constructed in this period were in smaller cities. The CBDs of some cities have been revitalized and development has been encouraged by the general decline in interest rates since 1983. To analyze a commercial districts's trade area, an appraiser focuses on the quantity and quality of the purchasing power of the population likely to use the shopping area. An appraiser also considers other elements, including

- Significant locational considerations such as the time-distance from potential customers, access, highway medians, and traffic signals
- Economic trends in the buying power of the residential neighborhood served
- Physical characteristics such as visibility, attractiveness, quality of construction, and property condition
- Direction of observable growth
- Use of underground storage tanks
- Character and location of existing or anticipated competition
- Presence of friable asbestos insulation
- Retailers' inventory, investments, leasehold improvements, and enterprise
- Use of electrical devices containing PCBs
- Availability of land for expansion and customer parking
- Structures that concentrate radon
- Pedestrian or vehicular traffic count
- 100% location or anchors and core groupings

When analyzing a group of local retail enterprises that are not located in a shopping center, an appraiser also examines the zoning policies that govern the supply of competing sites, the reasons for vacancy and business failure, and the level of rents compared with current rent levels in new buildings.

Central Business Districts
A central business district (CBD) is the core, or downtown area, of a city where the major retail, financial, governmental, professional, recreational, and service activities of the community are concentrated. CBDs have not experienced the same pattern of growth and development as other commercial areas. Business surveys conducted by the U.S. Department of Commerce show that CBDs have lost commercial establishments and have experienced smaller sales increases than other commercial districts.[2]

Appraisers should be aware of the general trend for CBDs, but they should also recognize that many of them are undergoing revitalization. Transportation facilities in most cities are oriented to the CBD. Through downtown development associations, many merchants have attempted to revitalize CBDs with improved public transportation, larger parking areas, better access, and coordinated sales promotion programs.

The diverse operations located in CBDs usually reflect several types of land use—e.g., retail stores, offices, financial institutions, and entertainment facilities.

---

2. *Survey of Current Business* (Washington, D.C.: U.S. Department of Commerce). *Business Statistics* is a biennial supplement to this monthly publication.

Retail clothing stores serve office employees and other retail establishments tend to locate where large numbers of people work, shop, and live. Financial institutions are often found in areas with other financial institutions. Major entertainment and cultural facilities are usually established in or near CBDs to serve the greatest number of residents and out-of-town visitors. Different parts of the CBD attract different uses, and the enterprises within the same general use category may be diverse. For example, office buildings in different parts of a CBD may house a wide variety of business and professional firms.

Appraisers should recognize that shifting functions within CBDs can lead to changes in land use and potential increases in real estate values. For example, a shift from commercial use to office and entertainment uses may attract more restaurants, art galleries, and specialty shops to a downtown area.

To assess the viability of a CBD, an appraiser must consider the sales potential of various commercial products and services and determine whether establishments in the CBD can attract a share of the market. To evaluate the viability of a particular location within a CBD, the appraiser considers which use—e.g., office, hotel, retail, or entertainment—is most appropriate to the subject property's location. Appraisers must also recognize the possible presence of environmental hazards such as radon, asbestos, underground storage tanks, and long-term contamination in CBDs.

Regional Shopping Centers

A regional shopping center provides a variety of general merchandise, apparel, furniture, home furnishings, services, and recreational facilities built around one or more full department stores of at least 100,000 square feet each. Regional shopping centers contain a greater variety and number of the same type of stores found in neighborhood centers. A regional center may also have banks, service establishments, medical and business offices, and theaters.

A regional shopping center's trade area may include several neighborhood centers. Although neighborhood centers compete with a regional center for certain segments of economic support, neighborhood centers serve their immediate areas and may be seen as supplementing, rather than competing with, the major shopping services provided by a regional center.

The largest shopping centers are the superregional centers, which generally serve large metropolitan areas. *A superregional shopping center provides an extensive variety of general merchandise, apparel, furniture, home furnishings, services, and recreational facilities built around at least three major department stores of at least 100,000 square feet each.* The gross leasable area of a superregional center may exceed 1,000,000 square feet.

In addition to major department stores and other businesses found in regional centers, superregional centers contain specialty shops, arcades, and restaurants. Because a superregional center offers an exceptionally wide variety of retail goods and services, its trade area is extensive. Trade areas are also extended by major transportation arteries and linkages, so the trade areas for some superregional centers transcend state boundaries.

The siting of a superregional shopping center is a complex task, which includes consideration of existing regional shopping centers, demographic trends, and transportation corridors. The land costs for superregional centers are high, and a center can significantly affect the value of surrounding properties by creating a demand for uses that complement the uses found within the center.

Like superregional shopping centers, regional centers generate substantial value for the land they occupy and significantly influence the values of surrounding sites and tracts. Generally, regional centers increase the value of adjacent or nearby land because they create a demand for satellite stores, office buildings, and other commercial uses. These centers may also stimulate demand for new single-family or multifamily residential development.

Environmental liabilities in regional shopping centers may include radon, asbestos, PCBs, underground storage tanks, and long-term contamination.

Community Shopping Centers

A community shopping center is a center of between 100,000 and 300,000 square feet that usually contains one junior department store, a variety store or discount department store, a supermarket, and specialty shops. Community shopping centers may also offer professional and financial services and recreational facilities. A community shopping center is part of the community or area it serves.

A community center's customers usually come from an area that is 10 to 20 minutes away by car. The viability of such a center depends on the sales potential for the various products and services it offers. The market allocates this potential among the various competing establishments in the service area. Sales potential may be estimated from surveys of consumer buying patterns, which are conducted by the U.S. Department of Commerce, and from information gathered by universities, private companies, and trade organizations. Historical patterns and changes in the number and types of competing establishments may also be studied to determine the market share of a particular center.

Community shopping centers are subject to the same environmental liabilities as regional shopping centers.

Neighborhood Shopping Centers

A neighborhood shopping center is the smallest type of shopping center, with a gross leasable area of between 30,000 and 100,000 square feet. Neighborhood shopping centers provide for the sale of convenience goods (e.g., food, drugs, and sundries) and personal services (e.g., laundry, dry cleaning, shoe repair, and hair styling) to satisfy the daily needs of those residing in the immediate neighborhood. Neighborhood shopping centers must offer easy access and adequate parking and they must be situated in good locations, on or near public transportation routes. Potential environmental liabilities must be investigated.

Office Districts

Office districts consist of groups of office buildings, which can range in size from small structures to large, multistory buildings. They may contain offices primarily for members of one profession, such as doctors or lawyers, or offices that serve a variety of tenants. The offices may be executive suites of multinational corporations or back offices for small service companies.

Office districts include planned office parks and strip developments on or near major traffic arteries. Office parks are popular with some industrial users because they offer good locations, easy access, attractive surroundings, and utility

Office park
(H. Armstrong Roberts, Inc.)

without the congestion and high rents of the CBD. Office parks are increasingly providing facilities for service industries as well.

Office districts can contain environmental hazards such as asbestos insulation or electrical devices containing PCBs as well as underground storage tanks and potential radon seepage.

Industrial Districts

Land and building values in an industrial district are influenced by the nature of the district, the labor supply, transportation facilities, the economics of bringing in raw material and distributing finished products, the political climate, the availability of utilities and energy, and the effect of environmental controls. To arrive at an informed conclusion about the value of an industrial property, the appraiser must obtain pertinent data on these influences.

Industrial districts range from those that contain heavy industry such as steel plants, foundries, and chemical companies, to those that house assembly and other "clean" operations. In most urban areas, heavy industry and light industry districts are established by zoning ordinances, which may limit uses and place controls on air pollution, noise levels, and outdoor operations. In older manufacturing or warehouse districts, obsolete, multistory, elevator buildings are typical and parking and expansion areas are limited. Newer manufacturing districts and industrial parks usually consist of one-story buildings. Each industrial district has a value pattern which reflects the market's reaction to its location and the characteristics of its sites and improvements.

Availability of labor. A district is desirable to industry only if it has an adequate and suitable work force, so an appraiser must ascertain whether there is an acceptable labor supply. The characteristics and pay levels of the labor force are important, as is the recent history of local labor-management relations.

Industrial district
(H. Armstrong Roberts, Inc.)

Because industry depends on a labor supply, many industrial districts are located near residential communities. Workers may be attracted to a particular plant by special inducements such as a company cafeteria, other employee facilities, or social activities; a plant's parklike appearance may be an advantage.

Availability of materials. Manufacturing operations need a convenient, economical source of raw or semifinished materials, and facilities to distribute manufactured products conveniently and inexpensively. The desirability of a district or site depends greatly on its access to raw materials.

Distribution facilities. The size, weight, and nature of commodities and the distance to their destination determine how they are shipped—by air, rail, truck, or water. Access to major highways, adequate ingress and egress, and onsite parking and maneuvering areas are crucial considerations for most manufacturing and warehouse operations.

The environmental liabilities incurred by industrial properties are considerably more complex than those that affect other property types. Industrial properties may contain underground storage tanks for a broad range of chemicals. The use of asbestos and PCB equipment may be more widespread. Long-term contamination tends to be more severe and cleanup costs can be very high.

Agricultural Districts

Agricultural districts vary in size from a portion of a township to several counties. Most important value influences relate to individual properties rather than an entire agricultural district because farms may be far apart. Nevertheless, the physical features of an agricultural district are usually representative of the individual farms and contribute to their desirability. To define an agricultural district, an appraiser considers soil types, the crops grown, typical land use, the average size of the farming operations in the district, and whether the operations are run by owners or tenants.

Farm district
(H. Armstrong Roberts, Inc.)

Grain farm districts are usually characterized by soil types and topography that are conducive to growing and harvesting crops such as corn and wheat. Orchards and groves make up another type of district in which the soil type and climate combine to create a distinct economy. Areas that cannot produce cash crops may be adapted to growing certain grasses. Generally, grasslands are used for livestock production and their boundaries are determined by altitude and climate.

Dairies are found where the soil is suited for growing pasture grasses and hay. These areas are served by highways that lead to marketing centers where farm products are sold. Like an urban neighborhood, the farm community depends on government services such as roads and schools, the availability of utilities, and proximity to cultural institutions, markets, and shopping centers.

Environmental liabilities for agricultural properties may include cattle vats, turpentine stills, fertilizers, pesticides, asbestos, underground storage tanks, and railroad tie dipping vats.

Specialty Neighborhoods and Districts

Some areas that contain specialized activities qualify as neighborhoods or districts. An area can be regarded as a district or a neighborhood if it has common functions or land uses. Although similar procedures are used to analyze all neighborhoods and districts, the specific characteristics that contribute to the desirability and value of an area vary according to its function.

Medical Districts

A district may be composed entirely of hospitals, health care facilities, and physicians' offices. A medical district may include one or more hospitals with related facilities such as parking lots and patient services buildings, a number of physicians' offices, and several pharmacies. Medical districts can be found in densely populated urban areas and in spacious, parklike settings.

The desirability and value of a property such as a doctors' office building depend on its age and proximity to hospitals and other medical offices. The quality of professional personnel and the availability of modern equipment are also important considerations.

Hospital buildings may contain hazardous substances such as asbestos or PCBs. The disposal of medical waste and potentially infectious materials has become highly controversial. Many hospitals incinerate their waste, while others have it shipped offshore.

Research and Development Parks

Research and development parks may contain the research and development departments of large drug, chemical, or computer companies, or they may cater to firms that specialize in research activities. Research firms are usually small and specialize in identifying and developing new products, which are sold to other firms. Occasionally a small research firm will create, develop, and market a new product with considerable success, but then the nature of the firm must shift from research to marketing. Research and development parks are often sponsored and promoted by universities. Proximity to a university can provide a research operation with a convenient source of technical expertise and qualified employees. Universities may sponsor a park to sell excess land, provide employment for students and faculty, and raise an area's level of economic activity.

High Technology Parks

Firms engaged in high technology activities often locate near one another or in parks where technical expertise may be available from a nearby university or research park. Electronics and computer firms have dominated high technology parks, but firms involved with space equipment, drugs, cosmetics, and aviation may also have offices in these areas.

Education Districts

Local schools, colleges, and universities may constitute a district if they have several buildings or facilities and are considered an integral part of the surrounding residential neighborhood. Educational districts may contribute economically as well as socially and culturally to the surrounding community. Colleges and universities often attract students from far away who bring income to the community and thus contribute to its economic base. In some towns and smaller cities, universities and colleges may provide most of the economic base. An education district should be readily accessible to the surrounding residential neighborhood.

Public schools have been the target of special asbestos abatement legislation. Underground storage tanks, hazardous substances in maintenance areas, and possible radon constitute other environmental liabilities for school properties.

Historic Districts

Since 1931 when the first historic district zoning ordinance was passed in the United States, interest in preserving historically and architecturally significant properties has grown and given rise to a unique type of district.[3] The establishment of historic districts is one of the most widely applied and rapidly developing techniques for preserving cultural heritage.

Historic districts may be informally perceived by observers, or they may be formally designated by local, state, or federal agencies. Historic districts are federally certified only after stringent requirements are met, including substantial compliance with National Register criteria.[4] Once districts are federally certified, developers, investors, and renovation specialists can qualify for tax incentives such as the tax credits allowed under the Economic Recovery Tax Act of 1981. The tax credits for rehabilitating older buildings described in this legislation were reduced by Tax Reform Act of 1986.

Historic districts may include residential property, commercial property, industrial property, or other types of property alone or in combination with one another. Appraisers must become thoroughly familiar with the criteria applicable to each district's designation status and how these criteria are, or may be, applied to properties within its boundaries.

NEIGHBORHOOD AND DISTRICT ANALYSIS IN FORM REPORTS

Some organizations, businesses, and federal agencies have developed forms to standardize the reporting of appraisal data. The most widely used form is the Uniform Residential Appraisal Report (URAR) form. Appraisal forms such as the URAR include spaces for recording information on the many variables important to neighborhood analysis. (See Figure 8.1.)

A form report should not simply be construed as an exercise in checking boxes. The form is usually supplemented by comments and addenda that commu-

---

3. Russell V. Keune, ed., *The Historic Preservation Yearbook* (Bethesda, Md.: Adler & Adler, 1984), 461. See also William E. Lockard, Jr. and Dudley S. Hinds, "Historic Zoning Considerations in Neighborhood and District Analysis," *The Appraisal Journal* (October 1983).
4. Keune, 328.

Figure 8.1 Neighborhood Analysis Section of the URAR

NEIGHBORHOOD				Single family housing	Present land use %	Land use change
Location	☐ Urban	☐ Suburban	☐ Rural	**PRICE** $ (000)	One family ___	☐ Not likely ☐ Likely
Built up	☐ Over 75%	☐ 25-75%	☐ Under 25%	Low ___	2-4 family ___	☐ In process
Growth rate	☐ Rapid	☐ Stable	☐ Slow	High ___	Multi-family ___	To: ___
Property values	☐ Increasing	☐ Stable	☐ Declining	**AGE (yrs)**	Commercial ___	
Demand/supply	☐ Shortage	☐ In balance	☐ Over supply	Predominant ▨	(___)	
Marketing time	☐ Under 3 mos.	☐ 3-6 mos.	☐ Over 6 mos.			

Predominant occupancy
☐ Owner
☐ Tenant
☐ Vacant (0-5%)
☐ Vacant (over 5%)

Note: Race and the racial composition of the neighborhood are not appraisal factors.

Neighborhood boundaries and characteristics: _____

Factors that affect the marketability of the properties in the neighborhood (proximity to employment and amenities, employment stability, appeal to market, etc.): _____

_____

_____

Market conditions in the subject neighborhood (including support for the above conclusions related to the trend of property values, demand/supply, and marketing time -- such as data on competitive properties for sale in the neighborhood, description of the prevalence of sales and financing concessions, etc.): _____

_____

_____

_____

_____

nicate additional information required to complete the appraisal. In some cases narrative reports, which provide a broader scope and accommodate more detail, may better serve the needs of the appraisal.

Standard 2 of the Uniform Standards of Professional Appraisal Practice require that any report communicating the results of an appraisal comply with specific reporting guidelines.

> In reporting the results of a real property appraisal an appraiser must communicate each analysis, opinion, and conclusion in a manner that is not misleading. Each written or oral real property appraisal report must: (a) clearly and accurately set forth the appraisal in a manner that will not be misleading; (b) contain sufficient information to enable the person(s) who receive or rely on the report to understand it properly; and (c) clearly and accurately disclose any extraordinary assumption or limiting condition that directly affects the appraisal and indicate its impact on value.

SUMMARY

Through neighborhood and district analysis, an appraiser studies how value influences affect property. A neighborhood is defined as a group of complementary land uses; a district is a type of neighborhood that is characterized by homogeneous land use.

The relative uniformity of a neighborhood may result from similarities in 1) physical features and physical barriers created by either the terrain or the location of major transportation arteries, 2) population characteristics, or 3) factors affecting land use and income-producing potential. The more limited boundaries of a district depend on variations in the relevant characteristics of properties, which may be set off by proximity to an adjacent neighborhood where the land use is different or by the influence of properties nearby.

To define the boundaries of a neighborhood or district, the appraiser should inspect the physical characteristics of the area in which the subject property is located; draw preliminary boundaries on a map by connecting the points where physical characteristics change; and test these boundaries against demographic data on the ages, occupations, and income and educational levels of the occupants. The appraiser must also determine whether changes in the neighborhood are expected to exert an upward, stabilizing, or downward effect on the value of properties. Change may be evidenced by the level of maintenance or introduction of new land uses in the neighborhood or by the overall growth pattern of the metropolitan area in which the neighborhood is located.

Neighborhoods and districts often go through a four-stage life cycle, experiencing *growth, stability, decline,* and *revitalization.* Not all neighborhoods follow this cycle. The growth of a neighborhood may be interrupted, or a neighborhood may remain stable until it is revitalized, thus bypassing the decline stage.

Neighborhood analysis focuses on the four forces that influence value: social, economic, governmental, and environmental considerations. Social characteristics relate to the population's motivations for living or working in a neighborhood. Social characteristics include population density, occupant profile, safety and sanitation, the availability and quality of services, and the presence or absence of community organizations. An appraiser considers the social characteristics of a residential neighborhood only insofar as they relate to the buying public and can be objectively analyzed.

The economic characteristics of a neighborhood pertain to the occupants' financial capacity to rent or own property and to maintain and rehabilitate it. An appraiser identifies general economic trends over a three- to five-year period, isolates the economic variables that affect values in different neighborhoods, and compares the economic characteristics of competing neighborhoods. Economic characteristics include occupant income levels, the extent of occupant ownership, rent levels, property values, vacancy rates, the extent of development and construction, the effective ages of properties, and changes in property use.

The governmental characteristics considered in neighborhood analysis pertain to the regulations and taxes imposed on property and the administrative machinery needed to enforce legal compliance. Governmental characteristics include the legal tax burden relative to the services provided; any special assessments; zoning, building, housing, and sanitary codes; private restrictions relating to lot or building size, architectural style, or property use; and the quality of fire and police protection, schools, and other government services.

Environmental characteristics identify any natural or man-made features that are contained in, or exert an effect on, a neighborhood. These features, which may contribute to or detract from the desirability of a neighborhood, can be measured in terms of the differences in the sale prices of comparable properties located in different neighborhoods. Environmental characteristics include land use patterns, lot size and shape, topography and vegetation, street patterns and width, building density and the amount of open space, property maintenance, the adequacy of utilities, environmental nuisances and hazards, and time-distance *linkages*, which indicate the neighborhood's accessibility to public transportation, work areas, and other essential services and facilities.

Environmental liabilities of both natural and man-made origin are defined in legislation and regulatory statutes. Guide Note 8 of the Standards of Professional Appraisal Practice addresses the responsibility of appraisers in detecting environmental substances affecting property value. CERCLA, the legislative act passed in 1980 and commonly known as "Superfund," created a mechanism to expedite cleanup of contaminated sites. In 1985 supplementary legislation referred to as SARA was passed to remedy inequities in CERCLA. Potential environmental liability is so far-reaching that *environmental property assessments* (EPRAs) or *transactional audits* to provide limited legal protection to buyers and investors have become routine. These environmental assessments are implemented in three phases.

To analyze special types of districts, appraisers must consider their unique features. Residential districts contain single-family homes or apartments of various types.

Commercial districts are characterized by a great diversity of business services and include central business districts as well as regional and superregional shopping centers. Community shopping centers, which are often located along transportation corridors, and neighborhood shopping centers, which are frequently found along a strip or around a traffic intersection, generally provide a more limited scope of services. In valuing commercial property an appraiser should consider the size and purchasing power of the trade area, the location of the enterprise within the retail center or commercial district, linkages with the firm's clientele, the volume of traffic through the area, the direction of present and future growth, the inventory and condition of the enterprise, and the existing or anticipated competition.

Office districts may house facilities for service industries or they may contain professional and corporate offices. Heavy industry, assembly plants, and manufacturing factories and warehouses are usually found in older industrial districts. In valuing industrial districts appraisers investigate the availability of a suitable labor supply, essential raw or semifinished materials, and distribution facilities. Medical districts, research and development parks, high technology parks, and education districts are all types of specialized districts. Agricultural districts are described by the type of farming that predominates and the soil and climatic conditions that foster this use. Historic districts are designated by government agencies to preserve properties that are historically and architecturally significant.

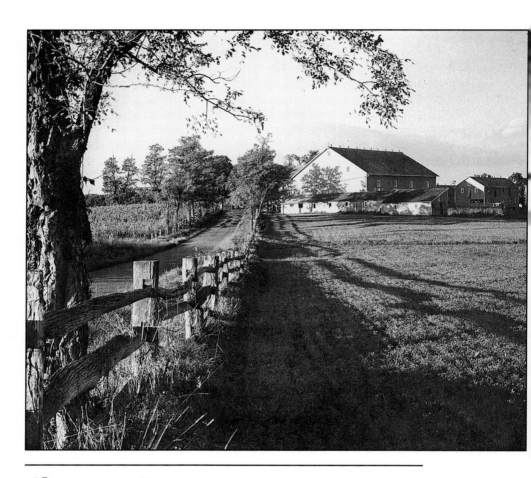

Chapter 9

LAND OR SITE DESCRIPTION

*A*ppraisal assignments may be undertaken to estimate the value of land only or the value of both land and improvements. In either case the appraiser must make a detailed description and analysis of the land. Land can be raw or improved; raw land can be undeveloped or in agricultural use. Land may be located in rural, suburban, or urban areas and may have the potential to be developed for residential, commercial, industrial, agricultural, or special-purpose use. *A site is land that is improved so that it is ready to be used for a specific purpose.* A site can have both onsite and offsite improvements which make it suitable for its intended use or development. Site improvements may include water, drainage, and sewer systems; utility lines; grading; and access to roads.

In appraising any type of property, an appraiser describes and analyzes the land or site. *A land or site description is a detailed listing of factual data, including a legal description, other title and record data, and information on pertinent physical characteristics.* A land or site analysis goes further. *A land or site analysis is a careful study of factual data in relation to the neighborhood characteristics that create, enhance, or detract from the utility and marketability of the land or site as compared with competing comparable land or sites.*

To estimate the value of improved real estate, the appraiser analyzes two distinct entities—the land and the improvements. Although the two are joined physically, it is often desirable and sometimes necessary to value them separately. Separate valuations may be required for specific purposes such as

- Local tax assessment
- Estimation of building depreciation
- Application of specific appraisal techniques
- Establishment of ground rent
- Eminent domain proceedings
- Estimation of casualty loss
- Valuation of agricultural land

One primary objective of land or site analysis is to gather data that will indicate the highest and best use of the land or site as though vacant so that land value can be estimated in terms of that use. (See Chapter 12 for a full discussion of highest and best use.) Whether a site or raw land is being valued, the appraiser must determine and evaluate its highest and best use. When the highest and best use of land is for agriculture, an appraiser usually analyzes and values the land by applying the sales comparison and income capitalization approaches. If it seems likely that the land will be developed for urban residential use, commercial use, or some other use, an appraiser may use sales comparison analysis and special techniques of the income capitalization and cost approaches.

Land or site description and analysis are conducted to provide

- A description of the property being appraised
- A basis for analyzing comparable sales
- A basis for allocating values to the land and the improvements
- An understanding of the property being appraised and its present use
- A foundation for determining the property's highest and best use

This chapter focuses on the description and analysis of the land component of real property. However, appraisers typically deal with land that has been improved to some degree, so the term *site* is used except when raw land is specified. The information required for a full site description and analysis is noted and explained, and sources for obtaining this information are presented. Throughout this discussion the property being appraised is the primary reference. However, the same type of detailed inspection and data collection are needed to analyze all comparable properties used in the appraisal.

LEGAL DESCRIPTIONS OF LAND

When land boundaries are created to differentiate separate ownerships, the land within one set of boundaries may be referred to as a *parcel, lot, plot*, or *tract*. These terms may be applied to all types of improved and unimproved land.

A parcel of land generally refers to a piece of land that may be identified by a common description and is held in one ownership. Thus, every parcel of real estate is unique. To identify individual parcels appraisers use legal descriptions. A legal description identifies a property in such a way that it cannot be confused with any other property. Because it specifically identifies and locates a parcel of real property, a legal description is often included in an appraisal report. The legal description of a property is usually entered on a deed, which may be obtained from the owner of the property or from county records.

In the United States three methods are commonly used to describe real property legally—the metes and bounds system, the rectangular survey system, and the lot and block system. An appraiser should be familiar with these forms of legal description and know which form or forms are accepted in the area where the appraisal is being conducted.

Metes and Bounds

The oldest known method of surveying land is the metes and bounds system, in which land is measured and identified by describing its boundaries. The system is centuries old, dating back to a time when property boundaries were set by a buyer and a seller walking the perimeter of a property and establishing landmarks along the way. Surveying tracts by metes and bounds was common in Western Europe and, when North America was colonized, the system was employed extensively in transferring property from crown governments to colonists and in transfers between colonists. Because this system was used when the colonies were settled, it is the primary method for describing real property in the original 13 states. Eight other states have adopted the method as well. The states using metes and bounds descriptions are: Connecticut, Delaware, Georgia, Hawaii, Kentucky, Maine, Maryland, Massachusetts, New Hampshire, New Jersey, New York, North Carolina, Pennsylvania, Rhode Island, South Carolina, Tennessee, Texas, Vermont, Virginia, parts of Ohio, and the District of Columbia. Oregon uses metes and bounds along with other surveying methods.

A metes and bounds description of a parcel of real property describes the property's boundaries in terms of reference points. To follow a metes and bounds description, one starts at the point of beginning (POB), a primary survey reference point that is tied to adjoining surveys, and moves through several intermediate reference points before finally returning to the POB. The return is called *closing* and is necessary to ensure the survey's accuracy.

Bounds refer to the POB, which is also the point of return, and all intermediate points. Points, which are sometimes called *monuments*, may refer to marked stones, trees, a creek, or the corner of another property, or they may be simply survey reference points. Metes describe the direction one moves from one reference point to another and the distances between points. One moves from point to point by knowing the courses of each point, which are identified in degrees, minutes, and seconds of an angle from the north or south. Thus, in moving from one point to another, one is moving from the vertex of one angle to the vertex of another.

Distances between angles are measured linearly in feet or meters. Sometimes, however, this measurement between angles is found to be inaccurate. When this happens, the actual distance between points or monuments is measured; actual distance takes precedence over angle measurement, especially in boundary disputes. Today more accurate determinations of points, directions, and distances have been developed. Now permanent benchmarks, which are survey markers set in heavy concrete monuments, are used to eliminate possible confusion regarding points of beginning.

The metes and bounds system is the primary method of describing real property in 21 states, and it is often used in other states as a corollary to the rectangular survey system, especially in describing unusual or odd-shaped parcels of land. Metes and bounds descriptions are frequently found in historical land grants that authorized the transfer of property from crown governments to individuals, groups, or political entities in the early years of the United States.

An example of a metes and bounds description is shown in Figure 9.1.

Rectangular Survey System

As the United States began to expand to the south and west, a more convenient system of land description was needed to facilitate the sale of large tracts of land that the federal government had acquired through purchases, treaties, and war. Because the government needed to generate revenue by selling the land quickly in a simple and orderly fashion, the U.S. Rectangular Survey System was created.

The rectangular survey system, which is also known as the *government* survey system, was established by a land ordinance passed on May 20, 1785. In 1786 the first public land surveys in the United States were made in Ohio.[1] The rectangular survey system became the principal method of land description for most land west of the Ohio and Mississippi rivers. Florida, Alabama, and Mississippi were also included in the system, but any land that was settled or colonized prior to the ordinance was not. Public lands in 30 states were surveyed in accordance with this system.

---

1. The government survey system evolved over half a century. Initially exterior township lines with sectional corners at one-mile intervals were established (1785). The sections were then numbered (1796) and subdivided into half sections (1800). The practice of allowing for excesses or deficiencies in measurement in the most westerly and northerly half mile of each township also dates back to 1800. The sections were further subdivided into quarter sections (1805) and quarter quarter sections (1832); the lines of division for half quarter sections run on an east-west axis.

Figure 9.1 Metes and Bounds System

Description of Tract: Commencing at the Northwest corner of Section 12 thence South along the section line 21 feet; thence East 10 feet for a place of beginning; thence continuing East 34 feet; thence South 62 degrees, 30 minutes East 32 feet; thence Southeasterly along a line forming an angle of 8 degrees, 04 minutes to the right with a prolongation of the last described course 29 feet; thence South 13 degrees, 0 minutes to the left with a prolongation of the last described line a distance of 49 feet; thence East to a line parallel with the West line of said Section and 180 feet distant therefrom; thence South on the last described line a distance of 65 feet; thence due West a distance of 82 feet; thence North 1 degree West 39 feet; thence North 58 degrees West a distance of 49 feet; thence Northwesterly along a line forming an angle of 163 degrees as measured from right to left with the last described line a distance of 49 feet; thence North to the place of beginning.

The initial reference points for government surveys were established under the direction of the Geographer of the United States. From each point specified, true east-west and north-south lines were drawn. The east-west lines are called *base lines* and the north-south lines are called *principal meridians*. Each principal meridian has a unique name and is crossed by its own base line. Once these base lines and principal meridians were established, land could be located accurately.

The land surveyed under the rectangular survey system is divided by north-south lines six miles apart called *range lines*, and by east-west lines six miles apart called *township lines*. The rectangles created where these lines intersect are called *townships*. The standard township is six miles square and contains 36 square miles. When applied to surveying, the term *township* has two meanings: a location on a line north or south of a base line and a square of land that measures six miles by six miles. (In some states *township* also refers to a political subdivision similar to a county.)

The intersection of a base line and a principal meridian is the starting point from which the range lines and township lines are counted to locate a specific township in a legal description. Ranges are numbered east and west from the principal meridian; townships are numbered north and south from the base line.

In Figure 9.2, the shaded township is four township rows north of the base line and three range lines east of the principal meridian. If this property were located in northern California, it would be called Township 4 North, Range 3 East, Mt. Diablo Base and Meridian, which would be abbreviated T.4N, R.3E., M.D.B.& M.

Townships are divided into 36 sections, each of which is one mile square and contains 640 acres. For a more specific description of a parcel, a section may be divided into quarter sections and fractions of quarter sections (see Figure 9.3). To accommodate the spherical shape of the earth, additional lines called *guide meridians* are drawn every 24 miles east and west of the principal meridian. Other lines, called *standard parallels*, are drawn every 24 miles north and south of the base line. These correction lines are used to adjust the rectangular townships to fit the curvature of the earth.

Sectioned land descriptions are commonly used and easily understood. A properly written legal description goes from the immediate location to the sectional boundaries—i.e., it begins with the particular site and ends with the base and meridian. The township illustrated in Figure 9.2 is called Township 4 North, Range 3 East. Similarly, Figure 9.3 shows a shaded, 20-acre parcel located in the southeast part of the section, which is properly described as follows: The west half of the northeast quarter of the southeast quarter of Section 10, Township 4 North, Range 3 East, Mt. Diablo Base and Meridian.

If this were a full-sized section, the property described would contain 20 acres. However, townships are adjusted for the curvature of the earth and some do not contain precisely 640 acres, so this section may not contain exactly 20 acres. Furthermore, the township's northern boundary is not exactly six miles long, due to the curvature of the earth and to the convergence of the meridians. This discrepancy and any others caused by errors in measurement are allowed for in the most westerly and northerly half-mile of the township. Irregular townships may also exist due to preexisting land grants and the boundaries of navigable waters.

Shortages and overages in the acreages of sections are usually found in the north and west corners of townships. Fractional sections and government lots may be found where adjustments were necessary.

Geodetic Survey Program

As part of the rectangular survey system, the U.S. government also maintains an active geodetic survey program. Geodetic surveys are performed to map large land areas, taking into account the curvature of the earth's surface. These technically sophisticated surveys are performed for a number of purposes, including the compilation of land elevation data to create topographic maps. The nation's geodetic

Figure 9.2 Government Survey System

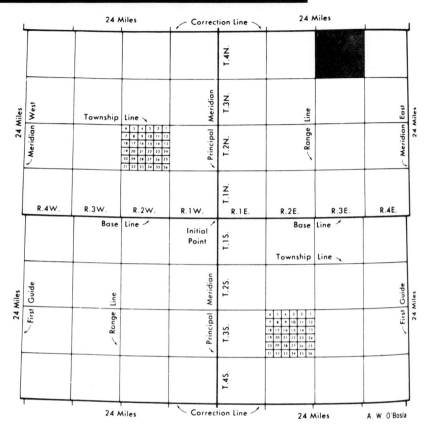

Description of the shaded township: Township 4 North, Range 3 East (T.4N.,R3E.). The township is four township rows north of the baseline and three range lines east of the principal meridian. (The township is located in northern California, so the baseline and principal meridian may be further identified as Mt. Diablo Base and Meridian.)

Source: John S. Hoag, *Fundamentals of Land Measurement* (Chicago: Chicago Title Insurance Company, 1976), p. 8 Reprinted through courtesy of Chicago Title Insurance Company.

survey effort is conducted by both the U.S. Coast and Geodetic Survey and the U.S. Geological Survey.

The topographic maps prepared under the direction of the U.S. Geological Survey, which are referred to as *quadrangles*, provide much information that is useful in land descriptions. Base lines, principal meridians, and township lines are shown along with topographic and cultural features. The topographic features commonly depicted on these maps include land elevations, which are represented by contour lines at specified intervals, rivers, lakes, intermittent streams and other bodies of water, poorly drained areas, and forest. The cultural features identified

Figure 9.3 Division of a Section of Land

← One Mile = 320 Rods = 80 Chains = 5,280 Feet →

20 Chains - 80 Rods	20 Chains - 80 Rods	40 Chains - 160 Rods		
W½ N.W¼ 80 Acres	E½ N.W¼ 80 Acres	N.E¼ 160Acres		
1320 Ft.	1320 Ft.	2640 Ft.		
N.W¼ S.W¼ 40 Acres	N.E¼ S.W¼ 40 Acres	N½ N.W¼ S.E¼ 20 Acres S½ N.W¼ S.E¼ 20 Acres 20 Chains	W½ N.E¼ S.E¼ 20 Acres 10 Chains	E½ N.E¼ S.E¼ 20 Acres 10 Chains
S.W¼ S.W¼ 40 Acres 80 Rods	S.E¼ S.W¼ 40 Acres 440 Yards	N.W¼ S.W¼ S.E¼ 10 Acres / N.E.¼ S.W¼ S.E¼ 10 Acres S.W¼ S.W¼ S.E.¼ 10 Acres / S.E¼ S.W¼ S.E.¼ 10 Acres 660 Ft. / 660 Ft.	5 Acres 5 Acres 1 Furlong 2½ Acrs / 2½ Acrs 2½ Acrs 330 Ft / 2½ Acrs 330 Ft	5 Acres 5 Chs. / 5 Acres 20 Rd. 10 Acres may be subdivided into about 80 lots of 30'x125'Each

Description of the shaded 20-acre parcel located in the southwestern part of the section: The west half of the northeast quarter of the southeast quarter of Section 10, Township 4 North, Range 3 East (Mt. Diablo Base and Meridian).

include improved and unimproved roads, highways, bridges, power transmission lines, levees, railroads, airports, churches, schools, and other buildings.

Topographic maps are published in series, which refer to the number of minutes of longitude and latitude representing the boundary of a quadrangle. The two most popular series are 7.5 minute and 15 minute, representing scales of 1:24,000 (one inch = 2,000 ft.) and 1:62,500 (one inch = approx. 1 mile), respectively. Quadrangles published in the 7.5 minute series provide greater topo-

Figure 9.4 U.S. Department of the Interior Geological Survey

Mapped, edited, and published by the Geological Survey
Control by USGS and USC&GS

Topography by photogrammetric methods from aerial
photographs taken 1958. Field checked 1960

Polyconic projection. 1927 North American datum
10,000-foot grid based on Illinois coordinate system, east zone

This Map Complies with National Map Accuracy Standards
For Sale by U.S. Geological Survey, Washington, D.C.
And by the State Geological Survey, Urbana, Illinois

A Folder Describing Topographic Maps and
Symbols Is Available on Request

Reduced from original scale 1:24,000
Contour Interval 10 Feet
Dotted Lines Represent 5-Foot Contours
Datum Is Mean Sea Level

APPROXIMATE MEAN
DECLINATION, 1960

graphic and cultural detail, but their applicability to land description depends on the nature of the appraisal assignment.[2]

Lot and Block System

The lot and block system was developed as an outgrowth of the rectangular survey system and can be used to simplify the locational descriptions of small parcels. The system was established when land developers subdivided land in the rectangular survey system and assigned lot numbers to individual sites within blocks. (The numbering of lots and blocks is illustrated in Figure 9.5.) The maps of these subdivisions were then filed with the local government to establish a public record of their precise locations. Each block was identified precisely using a ground survey or established monuments.

Figure 9.5 Lot and Block System

Description of a lot in the rectangular survey area: Lot 10 of Woodridge Creek Unit (Block) 1, a Subdivision of the Southeast quarter of Section 18, Township 10 North, Range 7 East (Mt. Diablo Base and Meridian). (Owner: Sunrise Properties, Sacramento, Calif.; Engineer: Morton and Pitalo, Sacramento, Calif.)

Applying the lot and block system to old, unsurveyed communities helped to identify each owner's site or parcel of land. Typically a surveyor located the boundaries of streets on the ground and drew maps outlining the blocks. Then lot lines were established by agreement among property owners. A precise, measured description was established for each lot and each was given a number or letter that could be referred to in routine transactions. For example, a lot in a rectangular survey area might be described as follows: Lot 5 of Block 18 of Adam's Orangegrove Colony, a Subdivision of the southwest quarter of Section 10, Township 3 North, Range 3 East, Mt. Diablo Base and Meridian.

Tax parcels

Some government authorities use a variation of the lot and block system to lay out tax parcels. Typically tax parcels are established using numerical references to the coded map books maintained by the assessing authority. Tax parcels are identified with numbers that refer to the map book, the page, the block, and the parcel number. Few jurisdictions allow tax parcels to be used as legal descriptions of property for conveyance, but an appraiser can use a tax parcel as a description when gathering data.

TITLE AND RECORD DATA

Before making an onsite inspection, an appraiser should obtain necessary property data from published sources and public documents. Most jurisdictions have a public office or depository for deeds where transactions are documented and made public. The accessibility of public records, which is legally known as *constructive notice*, ensures that interested individuals are able to research and, if necessary, contest deed transfers. Most county recorders' offices keep index books for land deeds and land mortgages, from which the book and page number of a recorded deed may be found. An appraiser might also find pertinent information in the property's *abstract of title*, which includes a summary of conveyances, transfers, and other facts used as evidence of title as well as any other public documents that may impair title. In addition, official county plat books may be examined in the county auditor's office.

Sometimes public records do not contain all relevant information about a particular property. Although official documents are the most dependable sources of information, they may be incomplete or not suited to the appraiser's purposes. Useful support data can be found in land registration systems, land data banks, and assessors' maps.

Ownership Information

A property's legal owner and type of ownership can be ascertained from the public records maintained by a county clerk and recorder. Local title or abstract companies may also provide useful information.

The most common form of property ownership is ownership in fee simple. If a property is not to be appraised in fee simple, the elements of title that are to be excluded should be indicated and carefully analyzed. If, for example, an appraiser is asked to estimate the value of a fractional ownership interest, he or she must understand the exact type of legal ownership to define the property rights to be appraised.

An appraiser must also find out if the property being appraised has any outstanding rights that may affect its value. Current Appraisal Institute standards require that appraisers investigate any previous property ownership occurring within a specified number of years.[3] The appraiser should also investigate the

---

3. See Standards Rule 1-5 of the Uniform Standards of Professional Appraisal Practice.

ownership of surface and subsurface rights. He or she may have access to a title report, an abstract of title, or other documentary evidence of the property rights to be appraised. Title data indicate easements and restrictions, which may limit the use of the property, as well as special rights and obligations such as air rights, water rights, mineral rights, obligations for lateral support, and easements for common walls.

Easements, rights of way, and private and public restrictions affect property value. Easements may provide for electrical transmission lines, underground sewers or tunnels, flowage, aviation routes, roads, walkways, and open space. Because some easements or rights of way acquired by utility companies or public agencies may not be used for many years, an appraiser's physical inspection of the property may not disclose any evidence of such use. Nevertheless, the appraiser should search diligently for information pertaining to any limitations on ownership rights.

Restrictions cited in the deed may limit the type of building or the types of business that may be conducted on the property. A typical example is a restriction that prohibits the sale of liquor or gasoline in a certain place. Often a title report will not specify the details of private restrictions; a copy of the deed or other conveyance must be obtained to identify the limitations imposed on the property.

Zoning and Land Use Information

Land use and development may be regulated by city or county government, but they are often subject to regional, state, and federal controls as well. In analyzing zoning and building codes, an appraiser considers all current regulations and the likelihood of a change in the code. Usually a zone calls for a general use, such as residential, commercial, or industrial, and then specifies a type or density of use. Zoning regulations may control the height and size of buildings, lot coverage, the number of units allowed, parking requirements, sign requirements, building setbacks, plan lines for future street widenings, and other factors of importance to the highest and best use of the site.

Most zoning ordinances identify and define the uses to which a property may be put without reservation or recourse to legal intervention. They also describe the process for obtaining nonconforming use permits, variances, and zoning changes, if permitted. Although zoning ordinances and maps are public records that are available at zoning offices, an appraiser may need help from planning and zoning staff to understand the impact of zoning regulations. Often, the appraiser must contact several agencies. Many zoning and land-use restrictions are not listed in the recorded title to a property, so confirmation from controlling agencies may be necessary.

In areas subject to floods, earthquakes, and other natural hazards, special zoning and building regulations may impose restrictions on construction. In coastal and historic districts, zoning restrictions may govern building location and design.

Probable changes in government regulations must also be considered. If, for example, a building moratorium or cessation of land use applications is in effect for a stated period, achievement of a property's highest and best use may be delayed.

Public land use and government programs in an area can also affect land uses and values. The construction of public parking garages in an area, for example, may enhance or detract from property values. Requirements for the provision of mixed low- and high-cost housing can directly affect land use.

The reasonable probability of a zoning change must be considered. If the highest and best use of a site is predicated on a zoning change, the appraiser must investigate the probability that such a change will occur. The appraiser may interview planning and zoning staff or study patterns of zoning change to assess the likelihood of a change. The highest and best use recommendation may rely on the probability of a zoning change. One of the criteria for the highest and best use conclusion is that the use must be legally permissible.

Assessment and Tax Information

Real property taxes in all jurisdictions are based on ad valorem assessments. The records of the county assessor or tax collector can provide details concerning a property's assessed value and annual tax burden. Often, an appraiser obtains the property inventory on which the property assessment is based before conducting his or her own physical inspection and inventory of the property.

Taxation levels are significant in considering a property's potential uses. From the present assessment, the tax rate, and a short history of tax rates, the appraiser can form a conclusion about future trends in property taxation. Assessed values are not good indicators of market value because mass appraisals tend to equalize the application of taxes rather than produce realistic appraisals of market value.

PHYSICAL CHARACTERISTICS OF LAND

In site description and analysis, an appraiser describes and interprets the value influences of all the physical characteristics of the site, including the physical relationship of the improvements to the land and to neighboring properties. Important physical characteristics include site size and shape, corner influence, plottage, excess land, topography, utilities, site improvements, location, and environment. Other physical characteristics are important in analyzing agricultural lands. These include soil, drainage, and irrigation.

Size and Shape

A size and shape description states a site's dimensions, street frontage, width, and depth, and sets forth any advantages or disadvantages caused by these physical characteristics. The appraiser describes the site and analyzes how its size and shape affect property value. Special attention is given to any characteristics that are unusual for the neighborhood. The effects of the size and shape of a property vary with its probable use. For example, an odd-shaped parcel may be appropriate for a dwelling, but unacceptable for certain types of commercial or industrial use.

Land size is measured and expressed in different units depending on local custom and land use. Land suitable for agriculture and large industrial tracts are described in acres. Other large tracts may be measured in miles and sometimes in rods and chains. The size of residential and commercial sites is usually expressed in square feet, although acreage may also be used. Dimensions are expressed in feet and tenths of feet for easy calculation. Metric units such as square meters and hectares may also be used to measure land.

Frontage is the measured footage of a site that abuts a street, stream, railroad, or other facility. The frontage may or may not be the same as the width of the property because a property may be irregularly shaped or have frontage on more than one side.

Often a site that is larger or smaller than normal will not have the same square foot or acreage value as neighboring sites. Size differences can affect value and are considered in site analysis. Because the functional utility of a site often results from an ideal, or optimum, size and frontage-to-depth ratio, an appraiser should recognize value tendencies when appraising sites of unusual sizes or shapes. Value tendencies can be observed by studying market sales or leases of lots of various sizes.

Corner Influence

Properties with frontage on two or more streets may have a higher or lower unit value than neighboring properties with frontage on only one street. The advantage of easier access to corner sites may be diminished by a loss of privacy or a loss of utility due to setback requirements. An appraiser must determine whether the local market considers a corner location to be favorable or unfavorable.

Corner sites can have greater utility than interior properties because they allow more flexibility in the layout of building improvements and in the subdivision of large plots. A residence situated on a corner may have a garage or carport at either the side or the rear of the property. Most interior lots have only one possible position for garages or carports. A corner location usually reduces the number of abutting owners from three to two. For commercial properties, a corner location can provide both added exposure and a convenient rear service entrance. A corner site provides advantageous ingress and egress for a drive-in business.

Corner sites can also have disadvantages. The original cost of constructing offsite improvements for corner sites is higher. Although part or all street costs are apportioned to all the lots in a development, a developer frequently demands and receives higher prices for corner sites. Residences on corner sites are exposed to more traffic noise and danger and provide less security. Owners of corner sites may pay higher costs for front-footage sidewalks and assessments, and the side street setback may affect the permitted size of the building.

For mass appraisal work such as ad valorem taxation, assessors and others compile data and derive mathematical formulas to compute how the site affects a property's value. They use corner influence tables and size adjustments based on mathematical curves. If an appraiser uses the values derived with these formulas, however, unsound value estimates can result. More accurate adjustments for site depth, corner influence, and size can be made by carefully analyzing zoning restrictions, sales data, market attitudes, and preferences.

Plottage

Plottage is an increment of value that results when two or more sites are combined to produce greater utility. Sometimes highest and best use results from assembling two or more parcels of land under one ownership. If the combined parcels have a greater unit value than they did separately, plottage value is created. Plottage value may also apply to an existing site of a special size or shape which has greater utility than more conventional, smaller lots. Neighboring land uses and values are analyzed to determine whether an appraised property has plottage value.

Plottage is significant in appraising agricultural land. Properties of less-than-optimum size have lower unit values because they cannot support the modern equipment needed to produce maximum profits. In an urban area, plottage of commercial office and retail sites and of residential apartment sites may increase the unit values of the lots assembled.

Excess Land

The portion of a property's land area that represents a typical land-to-building ratio with the existing improvements may be considered an economic unit. *Excess land, in regard to an improved site, is the surplus land not needed to serve or support the existing improvement. In regard to a vacant site or a site considered as though vacant, excess land is the land not needed to accommodate the site's primary highest and best use. Such land may have its own highest and best use or may allow for future expansion of the existing or anticipated improvement.* If the excess land is marketable or has value for a future use, its market value as vacant land is added to the estimated value of the economic entity.

Topography

Topographical studies provide information about land's contour, grading, natural drainage, soil conditions, view, and general physical usefulness. Sites may differ in value due to these physical characteristics. Steep slopes often preclude building construction. Natural drainage can be advantageous, or it can be disadvantageous if a site is downstream from other properties that have the right to direct excess flows onto it. However, adequate storm drainage systems may offset the topographic and drainage problems that would otherwise inhibit the development of such a site.

In describing topography, an appraiser must employ the terminology used in the area. What is described as a steep hill in one part of the country may be considered a moderate slope in another. In some instances, descriptions of a property's topography may be taken from published sources such as contour maps.

Surface soil and subsoil conditions are important for improved properties and for agricultural land. The soil's suitability for building is important for all types of improved property, and it is a major consideration when the construction of large, heavy buildings is being contemplated. The need for special pilings or floating foundations has a major impact on the adaptability of a site for a particular use and, therefore, on its value.

Agronomists and soil scientists measure the agricultural qualities of soil; engineers trained in soil mechanics test for soil consistency. Subsoil conditions are frequently known to local builders, developers, and others, but if there is any doubt about the soil's bearing capacity, the client should be informed of the need for soil studies. All doubts must be resolved before the land's highest and best use can be successfully analyzed.

Utilities

An appraiser investigates all the utilities and services available to a site. Offsite utilities may be publicly or privately operated, or there may be a need for onsite utility systems such as septic tanks and private water wells. The major utilities to be considered are sanitary sewers; domestic water; types of raw water for commercial, industrial, and agricultural uses; natural gas; electricity; storm drainage; telephone service; and cable television.

Although neighborhood analysis describes in general the utility systems that are available in an area, a site description and analysis should provide a detailed description of the utilities that are available to the appraised site. The exact size, location, and capacity of the utilities should be determined. It is not sufficient simply to establish which utilities are available. Any limitations resulting from a lack of utilities are important in highest and best use analysis, and all possible, alternative sources of utility service must be investigated.

The rates for utility service and the burden of any bonded indebtedness or other special utility costs should also be considered. Of particular concern to commercial and industrial users are the quality and quantity of water and its cost; the costs and dependability of energy sources; the adequacy of sewer facilities; and any special utility costs or surcharges that might apply to certain businesses.

Accurate information on public utilities can be obtained from local utility companies or agencies, local public works departments, and providers of onsite water and sewage disposal systems.

Site Improvements

In a site description an appraiser describes offsite, as well as onsite, improvements that make the site ready for its intended use or development. Then the appraiser analyzes how the site improvements affect value. The quality, condition, and adequacy of sewers, curbs, utility hookups, and other improvements influence a site's use and value. The appraiser also describes and analyzes land improvements such as grading, landscaping, fences, curbs, gutters, paving, walks, roads, and other man-made land improvements. The value of site improvements is typically considered part of site value.

The location of any existing buildings on a site must also be described and analyzed. Many appraisers make plot plans, which show all major buildings in relation to lot lines. Land-to-building ratios are usually quite significant. In a residential area where a typical building covers one-half of the lot, a four-to-one building-to-land ratio may diminish a property's value. The space allotted for parking influences a site's value for business and commercial use, so the parking space-to-building ratio in a commercial property must be analyzed.

The appraiser also notes any onsite improvements that add to or detract from a property's probable optimum use. For example, a commercial-zoned lot may be improved with an 18-unit apartment building that is too valuable to demolish. If the lot could accommodate a 24-unit building, but the present structure blocks access to the location of potential additional units, an appraiser may conclude that the site is underimproved and not being put to its highest and best use.

Location

The analysis of a site's location focuses on the time-distance relationships between the site and common origins and destinations. An appraiser describes and analyzes all forms of access to and from the property and the neighborhood. In most cases private automobile parking and the location and condition of streets, alleys, connector roads, freeways, and highways are important to land use. Industrial properties are influenced by rail and freeway access and the proximity of docking facilities. Industrial, commercial, and residential areas are all affected by the location of airports, freeways, public transportation, and railroad service.

After noting the facilities available to the site and their conditions, the appraiser analyzes how these facilities affect the site and the uses to which it can be put. Residential sites, for instance, are influenced by their access to workplaces, schools, shopping areas, recreational facilities, and places of worship. The appraiser analyzes how well the transportation facilities serve the needs of property owners in the area.

Traffic volume may be either advantageous or disadvantageous to a site, depending on other conditions that affect its highest and best use. High-volume local traffic in commercial areas is usually an asset; heavy through traffic is deleterious to most retail stores, except those that serve travelers. The volume of traffic passing a property is determined by a traffic count, which can usually be obtained from local or state road departments. Traffic counts indicate average daily traffic, peak hours, and directional flow. Observing the speed and turning movements of actual vehicles helps an appraiser judge how traffic affects a property's highest and best use.

The noise, dust, and fumes that emanate from a heavily traveled artery or freeway are detrimental to most low-density, residential lots. On the other hand, the advertising value of locations on major arteries can benefit offices and shopping centers, unless congestion restricts the free flow of traffic. The visibility of a commercial property from the street is an advertising asset; this asset is most valuable when the driving customer can easily exit from traffic and enter the property.

Median strips, left-turn restrictions, one-way streets, and access restrictions can all limit the potential uses of a parcel. In site analysis the appraiser should test any probable uses of the site in relation to the flow of traffic. Any planned changes in access should be verified with the appropriate authority and considered in the appraisal.

Environment

Appraisers also analyze land use in terms of environmental conditions. Environmental considerations include factors such as the local climate, availability of ground water, pattern of drainage, quality of air, designation in whole or in part as a federal wetland, presence of wildlife habitats, location in a floodplain or along an earthquake fault, and proximity to streams, rivers, lakes, or oceans. Air and water pollution are by-products of increased population and urbanization. Public concern over pollution has prompted political action and legislation to protect the environment. In areas subject to extreme air pollution, regulations may exclude certain industries and limit the volume of traffic; such restrictions impact land use in these jurisdictions. Industrial uses in locations near natural water sources may be prohibited while recreational uses are promoted. Environmental and climatic advantages and constraints must be thoroughly analyzed to determine the proper land use for a site. Future land uses must be compatible with the local environment.

A site in a specific location may be influenced by its exposure to the sun, the wind, or other environmental factors. A very windy location can be disastrous to a resort, but beneficial to a fossil-fuel power plant. The sunny side of the street is not always the most desirable for retail shops. In hot climates, the shady side of the street ordinarily gets more pedestrian traffic and greater sales, thus producing higher rents and higher land values.

Analysis of a site's environment focuses on the interrelationships between the appraised site and neighboring properties. The effects of any hazards or nuisances caused by neighboring properties must be considered. Of particular importance are safety concerns—e.g., the safety of employees and customers, of occupants and visitors, of children going to and from school.

A site's value is also influenced by nearby amenities and developments on adjoining sites such as parks, fine buildings, and compatible commercial buildings. The types of structures surrounding the property being appraised and the activities of those who use them can greatly influence site value.

Special Characteristics of Agricultural Resource Land

The following characteristics of agricultural resource lands should be investigated.[4]

- *Soil.* Precise soil surveys that indicate the soils found on properties, appropriate crops, and expected production are often available. These surveys are useful in comparing agricultural properties.

- *Drainage and irrigation.* The long-term dependability and cost of adequate drainage and water supplies should be analyzed.

- *Climate.* General climatic conditions and growing seasons can affect crop production and, therefore, land value.

- *Potential crops.* The crops grown on a property are related not only to climate, soil, and irrigation, but also to the availability of labor, transportation, and access to markets that make, transport, and sell the products produced from crops.

- *Environmental controls.* Cropping patterns are influenced by regulations on herbicides, insecticides, fertilizers, air and water pollution, and wildlife protection. Underground storage tanks, asbestos in farm buildings, and cattle vats are common environmental liabilities.

- *Other considerations.* The locations of minerals, wildlife habitats, and streams and lakes; the distances from populated areas; and recreational land uses are among the many other considerations to be analyzed in appraising agricultural land. Special tax provisions such as reduced taxes on agricultural or resource properties should also be studied.

---

4. For a thorough discussion of the methods used to describe and analyze the significant characteristics of land used for agricultural production, see *The Appraisal of Rural Property* (Chicago: American Institute of Real Estate Appraisers, 1983).

SUMMARY

An appraisal assignment may involve the valuation of *raw land* (i.e., land that is undeveloped, in agricultural use, or intended for development), land constituting a *site* (i.e., land improved and ready to be used for a specific purpose), or the land component of an improved property. In each of these cases, the appraiser must describe and analyze the parcel being appraised. A land or site description is a detailed listing of data that includes a *legal description*, other title and record data, and information on the physical characteristics of the land. In land or site analysis, these data are carefully studied in relation to the neighborhood characteristics that affect the utility and marketability of the land or site and comparable land or sites. The data collected in a land or site description are useful in determining the highest and best use of the land or site as though vacant and in estimating land value.

The three principal methods used to describe real property in the United States are the *metes and bounds system*, the *rectangular survey system*, and the *lot and block system*. The metes and bounds system describes the boundaries of a property in terms of reference points. *Bounds* include the point of beginning (POB), which is also the point of return, and all intermediate points, which may be survey points, benchmarks, or monuments. *Metes* describe the course or angular direction in which one moves from one reference point to another. Distances are measured in terms of the metes and bounds described. The metes and bounds system is used primarily in the eastern part of the United States and to establish the boundaries of irregularly shaped parcels of land that cannot be adequately described with rectangular surveys.

The rectangular survey system was established to facilitate the surveying and sale of public lands west of the Mississippi River. Six-mile square *townships*, each of which is called a section and contains 640 acres, are plotted along north-south meridians, called *range lines*, and east-west base lines, called *township lines*. Each section is further divided into fractional sections. In support of the rectangular survey system, the U.S. Coast and Geodetic Survey and U.S. Geological Survey publish more elaborate maps, called *quadrangles*, which take into account the curvature of the earth.

The lot and block system simplifies the description of smaller parcels within the rectangular survey system. Subdivisions of sections are divided into blocks, which are further broken down into lots. Tax parcels used for assessment are often identified using this system.

Title information can be obtained from public records kept by the county clerk and recorder. Index books to land titles and land mortgages, abstracts of title, and plat books are all useful in locating data. Using this information, an appraiser identifies the property rights to be appraised and any restrictions or special rights associated with the property.

The appraiser also considers zoning regulations, probable zoning changes, building codes, physical limitations, public land use programs, and government policies in determining the highest and best use of a land or site. The assessment on a property is rarely a reliable indication of its market value. When considered in conjunction with tax trends, however, data on the assessed value of a property may help suggest its potential uses.

To describe the physical characteristics of a land parcel or site, an appraiser must consider size and shape, corner influence, plottage, excess land, topography, utilities, site improvements, location, and environment. An appraiser describes the site's width and depth, regularity or irregularity of shape, and frontage or frontage-to-depth ratio. The advantages and disadvantages of corner influence must be weighed. For land under cultivation or land proposed for commercial and residential sites, the appraiser will recommend plottage if assemblage of the land with other parcels would produce a unit value greater than the unit value of the separate parcels. When typical land-to-building ratios for properties are observed, the combination of land and improvement components creates a functional economic unit.

An appraiser studies topographical characteristics in relation to land use. Surface soil and subsoil quality are important to agriculture, while grade, natural drainage, and soil-bearing capacity are essential to the construction of improvements. An estimate of the availability and cost of utilities helps the appraiser determine the highest and best use of a land parcel. Onsite and offsite improvements that make a site ready for its intended use or development must be described to analyze their effect on site value.

Location refers to time-distance linkages and the accessibility of a land parcel. An appraiser must consider the advantages or disadvantages of a site's proximity to major transportation arteries in terms of the intended use of the land. The appraiser also addresses any environmental conditions that affect the specific land parcel. Wind and sun exposure may affect an industrial or commercial property, and the hazards, nuisances, and amenities of adjoining properties may influence a residential or commercial property.

Chapter 10

BUILDING DESCRIPTION

*A*n important part of every appraisal is the description of the building or buildings on the site. An appraiser describes each building's design, layout, and construction details, which include structural components, materials, and mechanical systems. The appraiser also determines building size and the condition of each element described. The building description provides the basis for comparing the subject property's improvements with improvements that are considered typically in the subject property's market.

Accurate building descriptions are essential to all valuation assignments. Through them the appraiser obtains a thorough understanding of the physical characteristics of the subject property, which is needed to identify and select suitable comparables. Building descriptions also enable the appraiser to identify the extent and quality of building improvements, calculate their reproduction or replacement costs, and determine most forms of depreciation. Therefore, the quality of building descriptions directly affects the value estimate produced by applying the three approaches to value.

ELEMENTS OF BUILDING DESCRIPTION

An appraiser prepares a building description by considering a variety of specific information in sequence. Primary concerns are the type of use represented by the existing building, the codes and regulations affecting this use, and the building size, plan, and construction. Also important are the structural details of the exterior and interior of the building and its equipment and mechanical systems—both original construction and subsequent improvements. An appraiser must view a building objectively and analytically, paying careful attention to all components that ultimately contribute to the determination of the building's highest and best use as improved and any alternative highest and best uses required by the assignment.

Use Classification

Real estate is usually divided into five major use groups: residential, commercial, industrial, agricultural, and special purpose. The planning, construction, and use of buildings are restricted by various laws, codes, and regulations, which are enacted at all levels of government to protect the health, safety, and welfare of the public.

Zoning regulations establish the permitted uses of property. Existing and potential property uses must be checked against zoning regulations to determine if they are conforming or nonconforming uses. When the present use does not conform to current zoning regulations, the appraiser should consider how this fact might affect property value.

Building design and construction are controlled by building, plumbing, electrical, and mechanical codes. When violations exist, the appraiser estimates the cost to correct the deficiency and judges the effect on value.

Building Codes

Building codes are enacted at local, state, and federal levels. More than one-half of the states in the United States have codes that control the kinds of buildings that are constructed within their borders. Federal regulations are established to ensure occupational health and safety, environmental protection, pollution control, and consumer protection. Building codes establish requirements for the construction and occupancy of buildings and contain specifications for building materials, methods of construction, and mechanical systems. These codes also establish standards of performance and address considerations such as structural strength, fire resistance, and adequate light and ventilation.

To describe a building adequately, an appraiser should be familiar with the codes in the area and examine whether the building complies with all applicable codes. A building that is not in compliance probably has less value than a similar building that is. Bringing a building up to code may produce additional expenses for its owners and may limit the building's future use.

Because building codes are not uniformly established and enforced, industrial and professional groups have developed model codes, which are gradually being accepted in areas throughout the country, especially in large communities.

Size

To prepare a building description, an appraiser must determine the building's size. This may be a formidable task because the methods and techniques used to calculate building size vary regionally, differ among property types, and may reflect biases that significantly affect value estimates. The appraiser must know the measurement techniques used in the area where the building is located as well as those used to describe properties elsewhere. Appraisers must use, interpret, and report building size measurement techniques consistently within each assignment because failure to do so can impair the quality of the appraisal report.

An appraiser uses the system of measurement commonly employed in the area and includes a description of the system in the appraisal report. One of the most common measurements, gross building area, must always be calculated, but other building measurements can sometimes be ascertained from plans, if they are available. Measurements taken from plans should be checked against actual building measurements because alterations and additions are often made after plans are prepared. The areas of attached porches, freestanding garages, and other minor buildings are always calculated separately.

Standards for measuring residential property have been developed by several federal agencies, including the FHA, the VA, Fannie Mae, and Freddie Mac. Because there is a strong relationship between these agencies and the mortgage market industry, these standards have been used in millions of appraisals. The agencies use gross living area to measure single-family residences and gross building area (GBA) to measure multifamily buildings. *Gross living area is defined as the total area of finished, above-grade residential space.* It is calculated by measuring the outside perimeter of the structure and includes only finished, habitable, above-grade living space. Finished basements and attic areas are not included in total gross living area. *Gross building area is the total floor area of a building, excluding unenclosed areas, measured from the exterior of the walls.* It includes both the superstructure floor area and the substructure or basement area. Gross building area is also the standard of measurement for all industrial buildings.

Gross leasable area (GLA) is commonly used to measure shopping centers. *Gross leasable area is defined as the total floor area designed for the occupancy and exclusive use of tenants, including basements and mezzanines.* It is measured from the center of joint partitioning to outside wall surfaces.

Office buildings present special problems for appraisers because they are measured differently in different areas.[1] Office building descriptions should include measurements of gross, finished, and leasable building areas. Once most office buildings were measured in terms of net usable area, which is the area actually occupied by a tenant. Now, however, the total floor space is measured, excluding vertical openings such as elevator shafts, stairwells, and air ducts. Some methods of office measurement allocate a pro rata portion of the restrooms, elevator lobbies, and corridors to each tenant; one method also includes a pro rata portion of the ground floor main lobby in each tenant's leased area. Office building management may measure single-tenant and multiple-tenant floors in the same building differently. Because these measurements vary with occupancies, an appraiser must apply a consistent method in calculating the floor-by-floor rentable area of a building.

An appraiser should never accept a statement about the size of a subject or comparable property without personally verifying the figure and determining how it was calculated. If unverified size information is used in an appraisal, the resulting value estimate could be erroneous or misleading. Building measurement is further complicated by different description practices in local and regional markets. For example, if condominiums are compared on a square-foot basis, results may be skewed if the size of the subject property is expressed in terms of net living area while all market data are expressed in terms of gross salable area. In both cases, square footage is calculated, but the subject property's measurement must be adjusted to reflect the market standard.

Accurate measurement of building size is essential in the sales comparison approach, especially when the subject and comparable properties vary in size. The selection of units of comparison is based on market analysis, experience, and judgment. The subject property's size measurement can be adjusted to reflect the system of measurement used in the marketplace, or all the properties under consideration can be reduced to a representative unit such as square feet of gross living area or gross building area.

Building size is also important in estimating effective rent in the income capitalization approach to value. Comparable rentals rarely reflect buildings of exactly the same size. Therefore, size adjustments must be made to indicate the market rent of the appraised property. Often comparable rental information is converted into rent per square foot. The rent for the subject property is estimated by multiplying the selected adjusted rent, based on the comparable data, by the number of square feet of leasable area. Expense figures obtained from market data are also converted into square foot units, which may be used for income analysis as well.

The calculations used in the cost approach to value require measurements of the entire building and certain building components. Two similar buildings with the same square footage will have different costs if their exterior or interior walls are of different lengths. All significant differences must be considered when the

. The Building Owners and Managers Association International (BOMA) in Washington, D.C., has established a methodology for measuring office building floor area. This widely used method is described in OMA's "Standard Method for Measuring Floor Area in Office Buildings," which is periodically updated.

cost of a comparable building is used to estimate the cost of the building being appraised.

BUILDING DESCRIPTION FORMAT

A complete building description includes information about the details and condition of a building's exterior, interior, and mechanical systems. Although there is no prescribed method for describing all buildings, the following outline may be used to establish a format for building descriptions.

A. Exterior description
  1. Substructure
    a. Footings
    b. Slabs
    c. Piles
    d. Columns
    e. Piers
    f. Beams
    g. Foundation walls
  2. Superstructure
    a. Framing
    b. Insulation
    c. Ventilation
    d. Exterior walls
    e. Exterior doors
    f. Windows, storm windows, and screens
    g. Facade
    h. Roof and drain system
    i. Chimneys, stacks, and vents
    j. Special features
B. Interior description
  1. Interior walls and doors
  2. Division of space
    a. Storage areas
    b. Stairs, ramps, elevators, escalators, and hoists
  3. Interior supports
    a. Beams and columns
    b. Flooring system (subflooring)
    c. Ceilings
  4. Painting, decorating, and finishing
    a. Basements
    b. Floor coverings
    c. Molding and baseboards
    d. Fireplaces
  5. Protection against decay and insect damage
  6. Miscellaneous and special features
C. Equipment and mechanical systems
  1. Plumbing system
    a. Piping

b. Fixtures
2. Systems that use energy
   a. Hot water system
   b. Heating systems
      (1) Warm or hot air
      (2) Hot water
      (3) Steam
      (4) Electrical
   c. Heating fuels
      (1) Coal
      (2) Fuel oil
      (3) Natural gas
      (4) Electricity
   d. Air-conditioning and ventilation systems
   e. Electrical systems
3. Miscellaneous equipment
   a. Fire protection
   b. Elevators, escalators, and speed ramps
   c. Signals, alarms, and call systems
   d. Unloading facilities
   e. Attached equipment—process related

EXTERIOR DESCRIPTION

In describing a building's exterior, an appraiser provides information about the details of the building's substructure and superstructure. When a group or complex of buildings is being described, the appraiser may also need to include information about the infrastructure. *The infrastructure is the core of development in a group of buildings or in a complex and serves as the common source of utilities or support services.* For example, the infrastructure of a building complex may provide a boiler and an electrical system that serve several structures.

Substructure

Substructure usually refers to a building's entire foundational structure, which is below grade, or ground, and includes such foundation supports as footings, slabs, piles, columns, piers, and beams. Piers do extend above ground, but in general, the substructure provides a support base on which the superstructure rests.

Footings

Footings are support parts that prevent excessive settlement or movement. The most common type of footing is a perimetric base of concrete that rests on undisturbed earth below the frost line. This base distributes the load of the walls over the subgrade. Other types of footings include plain footings, which are unreinforced and designed to carry light loads, and reinforced footings, which contain steel to increase their strength. Spread footings are frequently used where the soil has poor load-bearing capacity.

Figure 10.1 Basic Systems and Components of a Building

roof systems

moisture and thermal protection

wall systems

floor systems

finish work

building materials

windows

doors

fireplaces and other special construction

foundation systems

the building site

Reprinted with permission from Frank Cheng and Cassandra Adams, *Building Construction Illustrated* (New York: Van Nostrand Reinhold, 1991).

Because footings are visible only when a building is under construction, an appraiser must obtain information about them from plans or by consulting architects, contractors, or builders. Footings that are improperly designed and constructed often cause settling and wall cracks. An appraiser must observe any structural problems in the building and evaluate their effect on the property's value. If the problems can be corrected, the cost of correction is estimated. Some defects are ignored by the market and have little effect on a property's value, while others result in substantial value decreases.

A building's foundation is made of natural or prepared material. Today most foundations are made of poured concrete walls or of concrete or cinder block walls that rest on concrete footings. The foundations of many older buildings are made of cut stone or stone and brick. Mat and raft foundations, known as *floating foundations*, are used over soils that have low load-bearing capacity. They are made of concrete slabs that are heavily reinforced with steel so that the entire foundation functions as a unit. Pile foundations are made of columnar units of concrete, metal, or wood that transmit loads through soil with poor load-bearing capacity to lower levels where the soil's load-bearing capacity is adequate. The columnar units serve as substitutes for footings. Columns, piers, and grade beams are other types of foundation supports that can be used separately or combined with other foundation supports.

Superstructure

Superstructure usually refers to *the portion of the building above grade*. However, in multipurpose buildings, components such as parking garages that are above grade but not used for habitable space are often considered part of the substructure.

Framing

The structural frame is the load-bearing skeleton of a building to which the exterior and interior walls are attached. The structural frames of most houses in the United States are made of wood, although many have brick veneer siding. The two most common types of wooden frame construction are platform and post and beam; platform framing is the more prevalent.

In *platform construction* one story of a building is constructed at a time and each story serves as a platform for the next. *Studs*, which are the vertical framing members, are cut at the ceiling height of the first story, then horizontal plates are laid on top, and more studs are cut for the second story.

Post and beam framing is composed of beams that are spaced up to eight feet apart and are supported on posts and exterior walls. The framing members used for this type of construction are much larger and heavier than those used in the other framing systems. Exposed wood construction enhances the architectural design. The post and beam system was used in colonial houses and barns and it began to regain popularity in the mid-1970s.

In *balloon framing*, once common in older, multistory, brick buildings, long studs run from the top of the foundation wall to the roof and are notched at each upper floor level to receive a horizontal framing member. Balloon framing is no longer used because long studs cost a great deal and the framing has poor fire resistance.

One relatively new method of framing employs panels of framing members and siding or subflooring that are prefabricated at a mill or built at the site. Construction begins on the ground and materials are subsequently lifted as a unit and installed in place. Some buildings are constructed with solid masonry exterior walls, which function as part of the framing system. Often interior framing is made of steel beams or reinforced concrete; older masonry buildings have interior framing of wood beams and posts.

The form of industrial buildings has changed a great deal in the past century. At the turn of the century, the most popular type of industrial building was the multistory mill building, which had exterior masonry walls and large post and heavy beam framing systems that were often supported by solid interior masonry walls and columns. After 1900 steel began to replace timber framing, and by 1910 many multistory industrial buildings were built of reinforced concrete with rectangular columns and beams and heavy slab floors. By 1920 round, mushroom-capped columns were generally used under rectangular areas of heavier slab floors. Later several other types of integral beam and slab construction became common (e.g., the tee-beam floor design with hollow tile between the tee-beams, the use of pans to form beams or waffle patterns), especially in buildings that required lower live loads.

Today large residential, commercial, and industrial buildings often have framing systems of steel beams or reinforced or precast concrete. Precast units with prestressed, reinforced steel are widely employed. Tilt-up construction uses precast concrete slabs, which can be lifted into a vertical position to become exterior bearing or curtain walls. The interior frame may consist of precast and prestressed concrete beams and columns with lighter precast slabs used for the structural roof.

There has been a trend toward constructing more functional, single-story, horizontal buildings for industrial plants. The framing for these buildings is usually made of steel. *Bays*, which are the areas between columns, have become increasingly large. Bays of 30 to 50 feet are quite common, and some aircraft plants have been built with more than 100 feet between columns. When the frame must support heavy cranes, the structural steel members used are heavier and larger.

A wood framing system that is defective can cause walls to crack, exterior walls to bulge, windows to stick, and doors to open or close improperly. In addition, the space between wall siding and a masonry chimney may be too wide. Steel framing is usually less expensive than precast or reinforced concrete, and it is easier and faster to erect. Steel framing does have one major disadvantage, however. Unless it is encased in heat-resistant, fireproof material such as plaster or concrete, the steel will buckle and bend in a fire, pulling adjacent members out of position and greatly increasing fire damage to the building. Reinforced and precast concrete framing is the most expensive and difficult to construct, but it is highly resistant to damage by fire.

Insulation

Insulation provides a number of benefits. It not only helps economize on fuel and ensure comfort in both warm and cold climates, but it also reduces noise transmission and impedes the spread of fire. The adequacy of building insulation and other energy conservation features should be noted by the appraiser in a building description.

Before World War II, most buildings were constructed without added insulation, although the heavy building materials used then provided some insulation.

Newer buildings are more energy efficient and many older buildings are being renovated to increase their energy efficiency by adding insulation. Insulation is classified by its form, which may be loose-fill, flexible, rigid, reflective, or foamed-in-place.

Loose-fill insulations, which are poured or blown by a machine into a building's structural cavities, are manufactured from mineral wool (e.g., rock, slag, or glass wool) or cellulosic fiber (e.g., recycled newsprint, wood chips, or other organic fibers).

Flexible insulations are manufactured in batt and blanket form from mineral wool or cellulosic fibers and are available in three forms. The insulation may be wrapped with kraft paper on the edges and a vapor barrier on one or both sides, faced with a vapor barrier on one side only, or friction-fit without any covering because the interlaced fibers are resilient enough to remain upright in the cavity. Flexible insulations are generally used where it is not practical to install loose-fill insulation or where the foil or kraft paper facing is needed as a vapor barrier.

Asbestos is a nonflammable, natural mineral fiber that was widely used in structures built between 1945 and 1970. Airborne asbestos fiber poses a threat to human health. Encapsulation or enclosure of asbestos is effective as a short-term solution. The Environmental Protection Agency (EPA) has guidelines for the removal of asbestos when a building is being demolished or renovated. The Asbestos Hazard Emergency Response Act (AHERA), which was amended to the Toxic Substances Control Act in 1986, empowered the EPA to regulate asbestos in public schools when it poses a hazard.

Opinions differ on the effect of asbestos on the value of income-producing properties. The presence of asbestos has hurt leasing, but there is little evidence that investors are willing to sell properties at sharp discounts because of the problem.

Rigid insulations that can be used in many parts of a building have become popular. They are available in four forms: structural wall insulation, fiberboard, structural deck insulation, and rigid board insulation. Reflective insulation made of foil reflects heat that is transferred by radiation. This type of insulation should be installed facing an air space of at least three-quarters of an inch and should remain free of dust and other materials that could reduce its reflective qualities.

There are two basic types of foamed-in-place insulation: urethane foam insulation and urea-formaldehyde foam insulation (UFFI). Both types are created by a chemical reaction that expands the mixture to approximately 30 times its original size and then solidifies it in approximately 24 hours.

In April of 1982 the Consumer Product Safety Commission banned urea-formaldehyde foam insulation in residences and schools. The ban resulted from the commission's investigation of the effects of formaldehyde gas, which can be released from the insulation at very high levels, especially immediately after installation. The ban took effect in August of 1982 and was lifted in April of 1983 by a federal court of appeals which held that the risks had not been proven. The ban was not retroactive, so it did not affect the approximately 500,000 homes in the United States that have urea-formaldehyde foam insulation.

Appraisers must recognize any effects that the presence of urea-formaldehyde foam insulation may have on the market value of a structure.[2] They should be extremely cautious in valuing properties that have or once had this type of insulation. Property sellers, real estate brokers, and salespersons representing sellers are obligated to disclose the presence of urea-formaldehyde foam insulation. Failure to fulfill this obligation could constitute a breach of a warranty of habitability and entitle the buyer to rescind his or her contract or to recover damages.

The ability of an insulation material to resist the flow of heat is measured in R values. R value is derived by measuring the British thermal units (Btus) that are transmitted in one hour through one thickness of the insulation.[3] The higher the R value, the better the insulation. There is no universal standard for the amount of insulation required in a structure because this varies with the climate and the type of building. For example, overceiling or underroof insulation with an R value of 13 might be satisfactory in a mild climate if there is gas or oil heat and no air-conditioning. In cold or hot climates, or in structures with electric heat or air-conditioning, insulation with an R value of 24 might be necessary. There has been a growing trend to superinsulate structures with insulation of much higher R values.

Ventilation

In many buildings ventilation is needed to reduce heat in closed-off areas such as attics and spaces behind walls. Ventilation also prevents the condensation of water, which collects in unventilated spaces and causes building materials to rot and decay. When condensation seeps into insulation, it reduces its R rating. Ventilation can be accomplished with holes that range in size from one inch to several feet in diameter; these holes should be covered with screening to keep out vermin. Ventilation can also be increased by using fans.

Exterior Walls

The two basic types of exterior walls are load-bearing and nonload-bearing walls. Load-bearing walls are often made of solid masonry, such as cement block, brick, or a combination of these materials. Load-bearing walls can also be made of poured concrete, prestressed concrete, steel beams covered with siding material, or wood framing heavy enough to support the weight of the roof and the upper stories. Load-bearing walls can be strengthened with masonry pilasters that are attached to the exterior of the wall.

Nonload-bearing walls, which are commonly used in larger buildings, are attached to the framing system. They can be made of porcelain enamel, steel, aluminum, precast aggregate concrete slabs, or glass. For industrial buildings less attractive, but serviceable, materials such as corrugated iron, tilt-up precast concrete slabs, asbestos board, fiberglass, and metal sandwich panels are used. When the quality of the exterior walls is below the standard for buildings in the same market, the property may suffer a loss in value.

---

2. For further information, see "Ureaformaldehyde Ban Lifted by 5th United States Court of Appeals," *The Appraiser* (May 1983); John M. Housel, "UFFI: A Potential Hazard in Residential Housing," *The Real Estate Appraiser and Analyst* (Summer 1983); and B. J. Lansink, "UFFI and Value," *The Real Estate Appraiser and Analyst* (Summer 1984).
3. Heat is measured in British thermal units (Btus). A Btu is the quantity of heat required to raise the temperature of one pound of water at or near 39.2 degrees Fehrenheit by one degree.

Exterior Doors

Exterior doors are usually made of solid wood, metal, or glass. Hollow exterior doors are a sign of poor-quality construction. Commercial and industrial buildings often have large steel truck doors. A variety of special-purpose doors are available and many have automatic door openers. Special automatic doors must be described in a building description. The presence or absence of energy-conserving material such as weatherstripping around doors should also be noted. To prevent air leakage through cracks at the bottom of a door, door shoes, weatherproof thresholds, and sweeps can be attached.

Windows, Storm Windows, and Screens

Wood was the material first used for framing windows and it is still commonly used in houses. It has good insulating properties, is readily available, can take either a natural or painted finish, and is easy to install and repair. Aluminum and steel are also used for window framing in residential, commercial, and industrial buildings. In describing a building, an appraiser notes the type of window and its material or manufacture. Window types include single- and double-hung windows, casement windows, and horizontal sliding windows as well as clerestory, fixed, awning, hopper, center pivot, and jalousie windows.

Because windows are a major source of heat and cooling loss, their design and installation is important. There is a trend toward reducing the size of windows and placing them higher to conserve energy and increase security. Windows should be tightly sealed, with caulking at the joints and between the wall and the window. The use of insulated glass, multiple glazing, and storm sashes helps keep cold air out and heat in. The appraiser should describe these energy-saving features in a building description.

Storm doors and windows provide good insulation. They can save typical home owners 10% to 20% of their fuel costs and can produce similar fuel savings when used in office buildings. Storm doors and windows are used in commercial and industrial buildings in areas with extreme weather conditions. Modern storm doors and windows are often made of aluminum and permanently installed with screens. Wooden storm doors and windows that must be removed and stored during the summer are becoming obsolete. Appraisers may find it difficult to judge how much storm windows and doors add to the value of a building, but analyzing what is typical in the market can be helpful.

In most parts of the country, screens are needed for all windows that open. Most screens have aluminum frames and, in residences, screens are often combined with storm windows. An appraiser should inventory all removable window and door screens and note if any are missing.

Facade

Many houses, stores, office buildings, and industrial buildings have a facade, or front, that differs from the design and construction of the rest of the building. Frame houses may have extra masonry veneer on the facade or contrasting siding. Retail stores often have elaborate fronts of glass and other decorative materials; even some industrial buildings have facades that are more elaborate than their exteriors. The appraiser describes a special facade and considers its cost and effect on the property's value.

In modern industry and commerce, public image is important. An attractive store, warehouse, industrial plant, or office building has advertising and public relations value to the occupant. Ornamentation, identifying signs, lighting, and landscaping all contribute to a building's attractiveness.

Roof and Drain System

A roof is designed and constructed to support its own weight and the pressure of snow, ice, wind, and rain. There are many types of roofs. Flat roofs are used extensively in industrial and commercial buildings, but are less common in residences. Lean-to roofs are used on sheds and saltbox houses, and gambrel roofs are popular for barns and Cape Ann and Dutch colonial houses. Other types of roofs include gable, hip, and mansard roofs. In industrial construction, monitor and sawtooth roofs are sometimes used.

The most prevalent systems of roof construction for houses are trusses, joists or horizontal beams, joists and rafters, post and beams, and panels. In commercial and industrial construction, the roof structure may be of steel or wood trusses, glued wood beams, or a steel or concrete frame with wood joists or purlins or with steel bar joists. These systems support the roof sheathing, which may be plywood, steel roof deck, lightweight precast concrete slabs, reinforced concrete slabs, or insulated sheathing in large sheets.

The roof covering prevents moisture from entering the structure. In most regions, residential roofs are made of asphalt shingles, which are available in various weights and styles, including lock-tab and seal-tab varieties. Other common residential roof coverings are shingles and shakes made of wood (usually cedar), asbestos, and cement. Fiberglass shingles have recently been introduced and metal, clay tiles, slate, and built-up or membrane roofs are also found on houses.

Many of these residential roof coverings are also used for commercial and industrial buildings. The flat roofs of these buildings are made of built-up layers of felt or composition material that are nailed to the sheathing and covered with tar. Gravel or another surfacing material helps keep the roof from drying out and cracking. Membrane roof assemblies are becoming popular for commercial and industrial buildings.

Joints in roofs are created where two different roof slopes meet or where the roof meets adjoining walls or projections such as chimneys, pipes, and ventilation ducts. All joints must be flashed. Flashing is usually accomplished by nailing strips of galvanized metal, aluminum, or copper across or under the point, applying a waterproofing compound or cement, and securing the roofing material over the edges to hold it permanently in place.

An appraiser investigates the condition of a roof to determine its remaining useful life. Most roofs need to be replaced several times during a building's life, so a roof's condition and age are considered in the valuation process.

The water that falls on a roof must be directed to the ground or into a drain system. Gutters and downspouts channel water from roofs to prevent damage and protect the appearance of walls when roof overhangs are not provided. Gutters or eave troughs catch rainwater at the edge of the roof and carry it to downspouts or leaders, the vertical pipes that carry the water to the ground or into sewers, dry wells, drain tiles, or splash pans. In large buildings, storm water collects in roof drains, which are connected to storm drains by pipes in the building. Even so-called flat roofs may be slightly pitched to direct water to drains and gutters. Gutters and downspouts may be made of galvanized iron, aluminum, or copper.

Chimneys, Stacks, and Vents

Chimneys, stacks, and vents should be structurally safe, durable, and smoketight; they should also be able to withstand the action of flue gases. The efficiency of any fuel-burning heating system depends on its chimney, stack, or vent. Chimneys and stacks with cracked bricks, loose mortar joints, or other leaks may be serious fire and health hazards. Exhaust systems range from simple metal vents and flues to complex masonry fireplaces, industrial chimneys, and ventilation systems. A building's chimneys, stacks, and vents and their apparent condition are described in an appraisal report.

Special Features

Some buildings have special features that must be carefully described and considered in the valuation process. Special features might include artwork, ornamentation, exterior elevators, solar and wind equipment, unique window installation, special masonry work and exterior materials, and items required for the commercial or industrial use of buildings. Unique building features can present a valuation problem. The appraiser must decide if the item or items add to the property's market value or are of value only to the current user. In the latter case, the item or items may add use value, but little or no market value. If such items are costly to remove, they can have a negative effect on value because they may not appeal to a future owner.

INTERIOR DESCRIPTION

The interior description of a building includes information about the interior walls and the areas between them, including how the space is divided and finished.

Interior Walls and Doors

In residences most interior walls are made of wood studs covered with drywall materials such as gypsum board, wood panels, ceramic tile, plywood, or hardboard. Plaster walls were once popular, but they are used less frequently now. Masonry houses often have masonry interior walls. The interior walls of commercial and industrial buildings may range from simple wire partitions to solid masonry walls that provide fire protection. Glass, wood, plywood, hardboard, metals, tiles, concrete, brick, and a number of other materials are used in wall construction. Interior walls can be painted, wallpapered, or decorated in other ways.

Types of interior doors include simple hollow-core doors, which are used in most residential construction; solid-core doors, which are found in older buildings; complex, self-closing, fire-resistant doors, which are found in commercial and industrial buildings; specialty, self-opening and closing doors, which are used in offices and commercial buildings; and special-purpose doors such as those used in bank vaults. Because hanging a door is complicated, it is often done improperly. Most poorly hung doors close improperly or fail to make contact with an edge of the frame when closed.

Division of Space

A building description provides a complete list of the number of rooms in the structure and their uses; room sizes may also be stated. The number of bedrooms and baths in a residential property usually influences the market for the property and its value. The number of units in an apartment building, and the types and sizes of the rooms within the units, significantly influence the property's income-producing potential. Similarly, the amount of office space in an industrial property and the partitioning of office suites may affect property value.

In certain parts of the United States, many types of buildings have basements. In these areas buildings without basements may have substantially less value than similar buildings with basements. If basements are not common in the area, a basement may add little or no value to a building.

Storage Areas

An appraiser must describe and consider the adequacy of a building's storage areas. Homeowners often complain about a lack of adequate storage space, especially in kitchens. Good cabinets, closets, and other storage areas are important, particularly in homes without basements. Storage problems can also exist in commercial and industrial buildings.

Stairs, Ramps, Elevators, Escalators, and Hoists

Designing and constructing even the simplest staircase is a complicated task. In public buildings codes often regulate where stairs are located, how they are designed and constructed, and how they are enclosed for fire protection. Public buildings may also have to be barrier-free to provide access for handicapped people. In a residence a well-planned stairway provides for safe ascent and descent, with adequate headroom and space for moving furniture and equipment. Railings should be installed on the sides of all interior stairways, including stairways in attics and basements where they are often omitted.

Elevators and escalators are mechanical systems that move people and freight; their adequacy must be considered by appraisers. The elevators and escalators in many multistory buildings are inadequate and do not meet current market standards. Curing these deficiencies is often extremely expensive or impossible.

Recent legislation dictates that handicapped persons be provided with access to public buildings, which may require that ramps be installed both inside and outside the building. An appraiser cannot assume that a building complies with these requirements. The enforcement of such requirements can be triggered by a change in use or a title transfer.

Special elevators and hoists are often considered part of a building, although they may be studied under the category of equipment. These building components must be carefully described, and their contribution to the value of the building must be estimated.

Interior Supports

A building description includes consideration of the building's internal supports, which include beams and columns, the flooring system, and ceilings.

Beams and Columns

Many residential, commercial, and industrial buildings have basements or crawl spaces that are too large for the first-floor joists or subfloor systems and cannot be supported by the foundation walls alone. Therefore, foundation walls are an important part of the main framing system in large buildings, and they are designed to support heavy loads. Bearing beams that rest on columns of wood, masonry, or steel provide additional support. Cracked or sagging beams may be an early indication of more serious problems in the future. If an appraiser observes these signs, he or she should consider and report them.

Flooring System

Subflooring provides safe support for floor loads without excessive deflection and an adequate base for the support and attachment of finish floor material. Bridging stiffens the joists and prevents them from deflecting.

Ceilings

In residences with gypsum walls, ceilings are often made of the same material; in other buildings, tiles may be used. In some structures, the underside of the upper story is an adequate ceiling. Ceiling height must be measured and considered by the appraiser. Ceilings that are too low or high for the property's current highest and best use as improved may be considered an item of functional obsolescence and decrease the property's value.

Painting, Decorating, and Finishing

The primary purpose of interior painting and decorating is to give the building an attractive appearance. Most buildings are decorated many times during their useful lives. An appraiser reports the condition of the painting and decorating in a structure and notes when they will need to be redone.

The attractiveness of painting and decorating is subjective. Many new owners and tenants will redecorate to suit their personal tastes. Unusual decorations and colors may have limited appeal and, therefore, may detract from a building's value. The quality of decoration is sometimes an important consideration in valuing a restaurant, store, or other commercial building.

Basements

In residences and some commercial buildings, basements may be finished and used for purposes other than storage. If these uses are accepted and typical in the area, they can add significantly to the property's value.

Dampness, which is often a problem in basements, may be caused by poor foundation wall construction, excess groundwater that is not properly drained by ground tiles, poorly fitted windows or hatches, poor venting of equipment, or poorly constructed or operating roof drains that allow water to enter. Signs that may indicate a wet basement include a powdery white mineral deposit a few inches off the floor, stains near the bottom of walls and columns or equipment that rests close to the floor, and the smell of mildew.

Flooring and Floor Coverings

A wide variety of flooring is available, and some flooring materials are selected primarily for their low cost and durability. Sand, compressed dirt, bituminous paving, brick, stone, gravel, concrete, and similar products are suitable for many industrial buildings, warehouses, garages, and basements. In many commercial and industrial buildings, floors must be especially thick or reinforced to support heavy equipment. Terrazzo flooring, which is made of colored marble chips that are mixed into cement and ground smooth, is used for high traffic areas such as the lobbies of public buildings.

Wood in various forms continues to be a popular material for floors. Planks and blocks are used for industrial floors, and many commercial buildings use wood floors to conform with their design and overall decoration. Wood planks and hardwood strips are found in many residences, although other types of flooring have become more popular. Resilient, ceramic, and quarry tiles are used in all types of buildings. Resilient flooring, which is usually a combination of vinyl and asphalt, is also produced as sheet goods.

Carpeting was once considered a luxury in residences, offices, stores, and commercial buildings, but today it is widely used in all types of buildings. An appraiser should consider whether floor coverings can endure wear and tear and how they conform to a building's design and decoration.

Molding and Baseboards

In the past architects often designed unique moldings for buildings, but now moldings are of a standard size and shape and their use is decreasing. However, beautiful, restored molding can add value to older houses. Simple baseboards are used in many types of buildings to protect the walls from damage caused by cleaning equipment or furniture.

Fireplaces

Fireplaces are popular in homes and commercial buildings such as restaurants, inns, and specialty stores. Most fireplaces do not provide a building's primary source of heat; in fact, because of their design, many have little heating power.

A typical fireplace has a single opening with a damper and a hearth. More complex designs feature two or more openings. Because fireplaces are difficult to construct, many are badly made and function poorly. One common problem is downdraft, whereby smoke is blown into the building by the wind outside. This can happen if the chimney does not extend at least two feet above any part of the roof within 10 feet of the chimney.

Many prefabricated fireplaces and flues are sold and installed in buildings that did not originally have fireplaces. Unless they are approved by Underwriters Laboratories and installed according to the manufacturer's instructions, these fireplaces can be potential fire hazards. To be safe, a fireplace should be supported with noncombustible material and have a noncombustible hearth that extends at least 16 inches in front of the opening and at least eight inches on each side. A carpet or rug that comes within a few inches of the front of a fireplace is a definite fire hazard.

Protection Against Decay and Insect Damage

All wood is susceptible to decay and insect damage. When wood is consistently exposed to moisture and water, destructive organisms propagate on or beneath its surface. The most prevalent of these organisms are aerobic fungi, which thrive where a proper combination of moisture, temperature, oxygen, and food exist. Sapwood of all species is subject to decay; heartwood varies in susceptibility from low to very high resistance, depending on the species.

Insects damage wood more rapidly and obviously than decay. Although several species of insects destroy wood, subterranean, dampwood, and drywood termites are by far the most destructive. Subterranean termites are very adaptable and are found across the United States. They colonize in moist soil and infest both damp and dry wood. Dampwood and drywood termites are more limited in their geographic distribution. Drywood termites colonize in wood and create infestations that are extremely difficult to eradicate.

To protect against decay and insect damage, builders may slope the ground away from foundations for good drainage and use vapor barriers on the interior sides of exposed walls; polyethylene as a soil cover in crawl spaces; flashing; gutters, downspouts, and splash blocks to carry water away from foundation walls; poured concrete foundation walls; concrete caps over unit masonry foundations; wood treatments; soil treatments; and metal termite shields. Using dry, naturally durable woods in construction and conducting regular maintenance inspections can also help prevent insect infestation and damage.

Miscellaneous and Special Features

Many industrial and commercial buildings are designed for special purposes. Steel mills, oil refineries, chemical plants, concrete factories, and mines are constructed for highly specialized functions. Commercial establishments often have unique design features (e.g., drive-in restaurants), or special facilities (e.g., the cooling room in a furrier's shop). Other properties with special purpose improvements include amusement parks, sports complexes, wharfs and docks, transportation terminals, and TV and radio transmission towers, studios, and theaters.

In valuing industrial and commercial properties, an appraiser may find it helpful to distinguish between two categories of equipment. The first category comprises equipment and mechanical systems that provide for human comfort. Plumbing, heating, air-conditioning, and lighting are human comfort items that will be discussed later in this chapter. The second category includes fixed building equipment that is process-related. Air hoses, process piping, craneways, bus ducts, heavy electrical lines, and freezer equipment are process-related items found in special-purpose industrial buildings. An appraiser must decide what contribution these special-purpose items make in terms of their use value, keeping in mind that their contribution may be different when measuring other types of value such as market or insurable value.

EQUIPMENT AND MECHANICAL SYSTEMS

Most buildings cannot perform the functions for which they were designed and constructed unless their equipment and mechanical systems are in good working order. Each item of equipment and each mechanical system should be inspected and described by the appraiser.

Major equipment and mechanical systems can be divided into two broad categories: those that do not consume a significant amount of energy and those that do. A plumbing system is not basically an energy consumer, although it may have pumps that use some electricity. The systems that consume energy are the hot water system, which is distinct from the plumbing system, the heating system, the air-conditioning and ventilation system, and the electrical system. Some buildings have other mechanical systems and equipment as well. Most of these systems use some electricity, but are not major energy consumers.

Figure 10.2 Mechanical Systems

Reprinted with permission from Frank Cheng and Cassandra Adams, *Building Construction Illustrated* (New York: Van Nostrand Reinhold, 1991).

Plumbing System

Plumbing is an integral part of most buildings. It consists of piping, which is usually covered or hidden except in industrial buildings, and fixtures, which are visible. Laundries, laundromats, and certain industrial buildings have elaborate plumbing systems.

Piping

Much of the cost of a plumbing system may be due to piping, which consists of pipes that carry water (and occasionally other fluids) under pressure and waste pipes that depend on the flow of gravity. The quality of the materials used, the way the pipes were installed, and how easily they can be serviced are significant considerations in estimating how long the pipes will last and how much they will cost to maintain. Worn galvanized steel, lead, or brass water pipes may need to be replaced. Copper is an excellent pipe material with a long life; cast iron is good for below-grade waste lines. In many areas and many types of buildings, a high-quality piping system will last as long as the building. However, many buildings have pipes that do not last. An appraiser describes the conditions of the pipes and notes when they will probably need to be replaced.

Plastic pipes are widely used for waste, vent, and water lines. The durability and serviceability of plastic pipes should be checked. Water pipes must be strong enough to withstand the pressure needed to move water through them. Because there is no pressure in a waste drain line, these pipes must be slanted so that waste will flow from each fixture through the main line into the sewer or sewage disposal system. Building sewers should be installed to guard against sewer backup in heavy rains.

Plumbing Fixtures

The plumbing fixtures used in bathrooms include lavatories, or washbasins; bathtubs; showers; toilets, which are known as water closets in the building trades; bidets; and urinals. High-quality fixtures are made of cast iron covered with acid-resistant vitreous enamel; fiberglass and other materials are also used.

The design of bathroom fixtures has changed substantially, and old fixtures may become obsolete during a building's economic life. An appraiser should report the need for modernization, but old fixtures of good quality, such as porcelain pedestal basins and footed tubs, are often rehabilitated.

Kitchen plumbing fixtures include single or double sinks, which should be installed in countertops and made of Monel metal, stainless steel, enameled steel, or cast iron covered with acid-resistant enamel. Other kitchen fixtures include garbage disposals, dishwashers, and instant hot water units. Some homes may have specialized plumbing fixtures such as laundry tubs, wet bars, swimming pools, or saunas.

Fittings, which are important parts of plumbing fixtures, include faucets, spigots, drains, shower heads, and spray tubes. The water in many areas is hard—i.e., it contains minerals such as calcium, magnesium, sulfates, bicarbonates, iron, and sulfur, which react unfavorably with soap and make it difficult to rinse from clothing, hair, and skin. Often hard water cannot be used until it is treated, either with simple equipment or with automatic, complex, multistage systems.

Commercial and industrial buildings have many of the same fixtures found in homes, and they also may have drinking fountains, janitor sinks, handwashing and eyewashing fountains, floor drains, and other special-purpose fixtures. An appraiser must decide which building fixtures are part of the real estate and which are personal property.

Systems That Use Energy

As mentioned earlier, the systems that consume energy are the hot water system, the heating system, the air-conditioning and ventilation system, and the electrical system.[4] An appraiser must describe all these systems and indicate the type of fuel used in the heating system.

Hot Water System

All homes and many commercial and industrial buildings need an adequate supply of hot water. A typical residential hot water system gets its heat from a self-standing water heater, which is powered by electricity, gas, or oil. Houses with inadequate hot water systems suffer from functional obsolescence. The size of the hot water tank needed in a residence is determined by the number of inhabitants and their water-using habits and by the recovery rate of the tank. Commercial and industrial buildings often require much more hot water than homes, so they often have large cast iron or steel boilers and storage tanks.

Heating Systems

Most heating systems use warm or hot air, hot water, steam, or electricity. The amount of heat a system can produce is rated in British thermal units (Btus). The heating capacity required relates to the cubic content, exposure, design, and insulation level of the structure to be heated. An appraiser describes the heating system and analyzes whether it is appropriate in the local market area.

Warm or hot air heating systems. Heating systems based on warm or hot air depend on the natural force of gravity or use a pressure blower to push heated air through the ducts. The air is heated in a furnace that is fired by gas, oil, electricity, or coal and is distributed through one or more registers directly from the furnace or through ducts connected to registers throughout the building. Air circulation is maintained with a fan and a return duct system. Thermostats, filters, humidifiers, air cleaners, and air purification devices may be included in the heating system.

In some buildings the central air-conditioning equipment uses the same ducts as the heating system. This is not always possible, however, because the air-conditioning may require ducts of a different size. Furthermore, heating registers should be placed low on the walls, while air-conditioning registers should be higher up or in the ceiling.

Some older heating systems relied on gravity and the use of larger ducts, with simple distribution patterns for circulation. Warm air systems are used in new apartment construction, especially for garden apartments and townhouse developments. When gas is used, the warm air system may function through unit heaters, radiant gas heaters, wall or floor furnaces, or individual gas furnaces. Gas-fired heating units need adequate ventilation. Indeed, all open-flame heating sources must have a sufficient air supply to support complete combustion.

Hot water heating systems. Heating systems based on hot water are called *hydronic systems*. In a hydronic system, water is heated in a cast-iron or steel boiler and moved by gravity (in older systems) or pumped by a circulator (in

---

4. Heating, ventilation, and air-conditioning systems are commonly referred to as HVAC systems.

modern systems) through pipes and radiators where the heat is transferred by convection and radiation to the areas being heated. The colder water then returns to the boiler where it is reheated and the process is repeated.

Radiant heating is a type of hot water heating system in which hot water is circulated by a pump, called a *circulator*, through narrow pipes that are embedded in floors, walls, and ceilings. This system depends primarily on heat being transferred by radiation, rather than by convection, which characterizes a conventional system. In a conventional hot water heating system, air is warmed as it passes over the heated metal of a radiator and is then circulated in an area of colder air. Radiant heat can also be produced by electric heating elements embedded in floors, walls, and ceilings.

Steam heating systems. In some structures, steam is produced in a boiler fueled by gas, oil, coal, or electricity and distributed through a piping system. In a simple, one-pipe gravity system, which may be used in small buildings, radiators are served by a single riser from the main pipe. The condensate returns to the boiler through the same riser and is used again. More complex and expensive two-pipe systems are found in larger, high-quality structures.

At one time vertical section, cast-iron boilers were used in large installations. These units were fairly efficient when covered with insulated metal casings or jackets. Steel boilers were usually of a low-pressure, fire-tube type, in which combustion gases passed through tubes inserted into a cylindrical drum that contained water. Several types of two-pass or three-pass boilers were designed for better efficiency. Recently, small, efficient "package boilers" have become popular for heating and generating process steam.

Steam systems also use radiators to transfer heat by radiation and convection. Common cast-iron radiators successfully transfer heat, but improvements are still being developed to operate steam heating more efficiently. Zone control is now widely used to stabilize the effects of different heating needs in different parts of a building. The amount of heat available for distribution can be controlled by separate temperature controls.

In many states licenses are required for certain classes of steam boilers. Appraisers must be familiar with local boiler license laws and ascertain whether boilers have current, valid licenses.

Electrical heating systems. The equipment used in electrical heating systems includes heat pumps, wall heaters, baseboard units, duct heating units, and heating units installed in air-conditioning ducts. Such equipment gives an electrical heating system both heating and cooling capacity. Radiant floors, walls, and ceilings that have panels or cables under the surface; infrared units; and electric furnaces that use forced warm air or hot water can also be used in electrical heating systems. An electrical resistance system produces heat in the immediate area or room that is to be heated. It is the least expensive system to install because it requires no furnace, furnace room, ducts, flue, or plumbing. However, it does require substantial electrical service and a great deal of wiring to each unit in the building.

Heat pumps that combine heating and cooling functions are increasingly popular. A heat pump is actually a reverse refrigeration unit. In the winter, the pump takes heat from the outside air, the ground, or well water and distributes it inside the house. When the weather is very cold, the efficiency of the unit decreases and must be supplemented with resistance heating. In the summer, the pump cools by extracting heat from inside the house like a typical air-conditioning unit.

Convectors are finned heating elements that are installed in baseboards or concealed in walls or cabinets. A convector combined with a fan becomes a unit or room heater. Unit heaters are found in commercial and industrial buildings such as stores, warehouses, and garages, where large spaces must be heated. The units are usually placed near the ceiling in the space to be heated.

The automatic regulation of a heating system helps it operate efficiently. A multiple-zone system with separate thermostats is more efficient than a single-zone system with one thermostat. Complex systems provide an individual temperature control for each room. The efficiency of certain systems can be increased by putting a thermostat on the outside of the building. This helps building operators anticipate how much heat the system will need to produce.

Heating Fuels

The type of fuel used in a building's heating system should be explained in the building description. Depending on the area and the type of building, one type of fuel may be more desirable than another. Nevertheless, many building heating systems do not use the most economical fuel. For example, during the natural gas shortage in the 1970s, a moratorium was declared on the use of natural gas. Therefore, buildings were constructed in certain areas with heating systems that use other fuels even though gas is now more economical. For any specific use, different fuels have different advantages and disadvantages, which are subject to change.

Coal. In the past coal was the most popular fuel for heating; it is still used to generate power for some industrial and commercial uses. Coal is also used in residences for stoves and fireplaces, but the burning of certain types of coal creates environmental pollution.

Fuel oil. In spite of its high cost, fuel oil is a popular energy source which is easy to transport and store. Onsite 275-gallon tanks are used in millions of houses and tanks that hold thousands of gallons of fuel oils are buried on industrial and commercial sites.

Natural gas. Natural gas is a convenient type of fuel because it is continuously delivered by pipelines; no storage tank is needed. In many parts of the United States, natural gas is the most economical fuel. Liquid petroleum gas, such as butane and propane, is used in many rural areas. It requires onsite storage tanks and is usually more expensive, but in other respects it is similar to natural gas.

Electricity. Like oil, gas, or coal, electricity can be used to produce heat in a furnace or to heat water in a boiler. In most areas electrical heating costs are high, but good insulation and control can eliminate waste.

An appraiser cannot assume that a building's existing heating system contributes maximum value to the property. The heating system that was installed when the building was constructed may not be acceptable to potential buyers today.

New technology has continued to reduce energy consumption for large heating systems. Many industrial users who once depended on gas alone now install more efficient, oil or electric systems to provide heat when the gas supply is curtailed. Electric heat has become so costly in some areas that buildings using it sell for substantially less than similar properties that use other types of fuel. *Cogeneration*, the simultaneous production of electrical energy and low-grade heat from the same fuel, is also being used in some parts of the country.

Buyers are sensitive to energy costs. Apartments in which the owner supplies heat and hot water usually sell for less than similar properties in which tenants pay for utilities. Buildings that have high ceilings, many openings, and poor insulation may be at a disadvantage in the market.

Solar heating and domestic hot water systems have attracted much interest, and many such systems are on the market. Appraisers should keep up to date on the development of solar energy and its use in particular areas. A solar heating system should be carefully described and its contribution to the property's value should be estimated. When residential appraisals are reported on Freddie Mac and Fannie Mae forms, solar heating and other special energy systems must be described and valued separately.

Air-Conditioning and Ventilation Systems

Before World War II ducts, fans, and open windows were used to reduce heat and provide fresh air in most buildings. In many buildings ducts and fans are still used to cool and provide fresh air. In certain parts of the western United States, where the humidity is low even when it is very hot, buildings can be cooled with a simple system that blows air across wet excelsior or some other water-absorbing material. Package units using this process are still manufactured for home and commercial use. These units use less power and, therefore, are less expensive to operate than conventional air-conditioning systems.

The most common type of air-conditioning system consists of an electrically powered compressor that compresses Freon from gas into liquid outside the area being cooled. The heat released in this process is either blown away or carried away by water. The compressed Freon is then directed into thin tubes in the area being cooled, where it expands and absorbs heat from the air that is directed over the tubes by one or more fans. Another type of air-conditioning system is powered by gas, rather than electricity and ammonia, not Freon, is used as the refrigerant. Air-conditioners range from small, portable units to units that provide many tons of cooling capacity. The capacity of an air-conditioning unit is rated in tons of refrigeration, which is equal to the amount of heat needed to melt a ton of ice in 24 hours, or 12,000 Btus/per hour.

Commercial and industrial air-conditioning and ventilation systems are more complex. Some simply bring in fresh air from the outside and distribute it throughout the building; others merely remove foul air. Still others combine these two functions, but do not have any cooling or heating capacity. More complex systems wash, filter, and add or remove humidity from the air. The most complex systems perform all of these functions and also heat and cool air through a complex system of ducts and fans. In larger systems that use less electricity, water cools the pipes in which the gas has been compressed. The water is then conserved in towers that cool it for reuse.

An appraiser describes the air-conditioning and ventilation system in a building and decides whether it is appropriate to the geographic area. To do this the appraiser may have to investigate whether the building's system meets current standards. If the appraiser concludes that the building has too much or too little air-conditioning, the appraisal report should include the data on which this conclusion is based.

Electrical Systems

A well-designed electrical system must be large enough to provide sufficient power for all the electrical uses in the building. Sometimes, one electrical service may supply power to more than one building.

In an electrical system power is distributed from the electrical service station through branch circuits, which are wires located throughout the building, to electrical outlets. Each branch circuit starts at a distribution box, where it is separated from the main service by a protection device such as a fuse or circuit breaker. When a short circuit or overload occurs on the branch circuit, the fuse or circuit breaker disconnects the circuit from the power supply to prevent a fire.

The wiring between the distribution boxes and the outlets may be a rigid or flexible conduit. This type of wiring is common in commercial and industrial buildings. In most houses BX or armored cable is used. Plastic-coated wire is used in certain areas, and the old knob-and-tube wiring is still used in rural areas and older buildings, although it is considered obsolete.

Most electrical wire is copper. After World War II aluminum wire became popular as the price of copper escalated, but its resistance to fire has been seriously questioned. In some sections of the country, aluminum wiring is prohibited by law.

A typical residential electrical system is a single-phase, three-wire system that provides a minimum of 100 amperes of electricity. The old 30-ampere systems are certainly obsolete and residences that have 60 amperes of service normally sell for less than those with larger services. Ampere services of 150, 200, 300, and 400 are needed when electric heating and air-conditioning are used. Most of these services can provide up to 220 volts by connecting three wires to the outlet.

Power wiring is used in commercial and industrial buildings to operate utility systems, appliances, and machinery. The electrical power is generally carried at higher voltages (e.g., 240, 480, 600 volts or more) and is usually three-phase or three-phase-four-wire, which allows both lighting and three-phase power loads to be delivered by the same supply.

Power wiring is carried in conduit or by means of plug-in bus ducts. Overhead bus ducts are frequently found in manufacturing plants where flexible service is needed. Large-capacity power wiring may contribute to the value of an industrial improvement; however, if the wiring is an uncommon type and adds to a building's operating costs or will be expensive to remove, it may result in functional obsolescence. Similarly, any building with insufficient electrical service or wiring suffers from functional obsolescence.

Switches and lighting fixtures are also part of the electrical system. Because lighting fixtures are stylized and styles change, they are often obsolete before they wear out. Fluorescent lighting, which may be suspended, surface-mounted, or recessed, is used extensively in commercial and industrial buildings. Often continuous rows are used in large spaces. Incandescent fixtures may be used for smaller rooms, accents, or special purposes.

In newer lighting design, the intensity and quality of light over working areas and display surfaces are important considerations. The degree of intensity will vary with the type of use. Sodium and mercury vapor lights are often installed in industrial buildings. Some installations are designed so that air moves past the lighting fixtures to augment the heating system.

Floor outlets or floor duct systems are extensively used in commercial and office buildings. These systems provide convenient electrical outlets for office machines and telephone outlets at desks using with a minimum number of cords. Some houses and commercial buildings have low-voltage switching systems, in which many outlets and lights can be controlled from one place.

Miscellaneous Equipment

In preparing building descriptions appraisers must also consider miscellaneous equipment, some of which is discussed below.

Fire Protection

Fire protection equipment includes fire escapes, standpipes and hose cabinets, alarm services, and automatic sprinklers. A wet sprinkler system must have adequate water pressure to ensure that the pipes are always filled. A dry system has pressurized air in the pipes. When a sprinkler head opens, the pressure is relieved and water enters. Dry systems are used on loading docks and in unheated buildings where there is a danger of water freezing.

Elevators, Escalators, and Speed Ramps

Elevators are usually classified as passenger or freight and may be either electric or hydraulic. The type, speed, and capacity of an elevator, and the number of floors it serves are related to the type of property and its utility. Hydraulic elevators are suitable for low-speed, low-rise operations. Passenger elevators that need full-time operators are costly and now practically obsolete. Most modern elevators are high-speed and completely automatic. Control systems collect signals and distribute service among all the elevators in a system. Some elevators have auxiliary controls so that they can be manually operated if necessary.

The movement of large numbers of people up and down or along horizontal or gradual slopes can be accomplished with escalators and speed ramps. This equipment must be adequate to accommodate the number of persons who use the building.

Signals, Alarms, and Call Systems

Signals, alarms, call systems, and similar devices should not be overlooked by an appraiser. Smoke detectors are increasingly common in residential and multifamily structures and are required by law in many areas. Security alarm systems, which warn occupants of forced entry, fire, or both, are available for residential, commercial, and industrial use. Because fire and safety regulations change, systems that were adequate when they were installed may later be considered substandard.

Other items to be noted by an appraiser include clocks, pneumatic tube systems, mail chutes, telephone wiring (which are subject to EPA regulations), and incinerators. In small buildings the telephone company supplies the wiring and equipment; larger buildings may have extensive systems of built-in cabinets, conduits, and floor ducts for telephone service. The telephone service in a building may be suitable for the current occupant, but unsuitable for a potential buyer.

Loading Facilities
Facilities for loading and unloading trucks and freight cars may be important in commercial and industrial buildings. Off-street loading docks are usually required by zoning ordinances. Many older buildings have only loading doors or substandard loading facilities. Loading docks may be open or covered. The floor of an efficient, one-story industrial building may be built above grade at freight car or truck-bed level. In some buildings docks are enclosed for trucks and freight cars, and leveling devices are provided to assist in loading or unloading. A properly designed industrial building has space in front of truck docks so that vehicles can maneuver.

Attached Equipment
Process-related fixed building equipment includes air hoses, process piping, industrial wiring for heavy electrical capacity, bus ducts, and freezer equipment. Although this equipment may be a part of another utility systems (e.g., plumbing or electrical), its contributory role in a specific industrial process warrants attention. The appraiser should consider attached equipment in terms of its use value.

QUALITY AND CONDITION SURVEY

A building description includes a quality and condition survey in which the appraiser analyzes and explains the quality and condition of the items described. The character, quality, and appearance of building construction are reflected in each of the three approaches to value. The quality and condition of building components have a major influence on the cost estimate, the accrued depreciation estimate, the ability of the property to produce rental income, and the property's comparability with other properties. Analysis of the quality of construction and the methods and materials used complements the appraiser's analysis of the building's structural design and architecture.

A structure can have a good, functional layout and an attractive design but be built with inferior materials and poor workmanship. These deficiencies increase maintenance and utility costs and adversely affect the property's marketability. Conversely, a building can be built too well or at a cost that cannot be justified by its utility. Most purchasers will not pay for these excess costs and only part of the original investment can be recaptured by the original owner through reduced maintenance expenses.

Practical or reasonable economy of construction results in an improvement that will produce rental income commensurate with its cost. Maintenance and operating expenses for an economically constructed building may be slightly higher than minimum expenses, but this is preferable to a building of superior construction, which would have a higher level of taxes, interest, and amortization charges. To achieve the desired level of construction quality and cost, building materials and construction methods must be chosen and used properly. An appraiser should recognize that an appropriate combination of elements results in a building that is adequate for its intended purpose.

The maintenance and age of a building affect its condition. In a quality and condition survey, the appraiser generally distinguishes between items in need of immediate repair (deferred maintenance items) and those that may be repaired or replaced at a later time (short-lived items).

Deferred Maintenance Items

An appraiser usually finds some items that need repair on the date of the appraisal, although some buildings may be in excellent condition. The following list indicates items that are commonly found to be in need of immediate attention.

- Touch-up paint on building interior and exterior and the removal of graffiti
- Minor carpentry repairs
- Leaky or noisy plumbing
- Doors and windows that stick
- Broken glass and torn screens
- Loose or damaged gutters and leaders
- Roof leaks and missing shingles, tiles, and slates
- Cracked sidewalks, driveways, and parking areas
- Infestation by vermin
- Cracked or loose tiles in bathrooms and kitchens
- Septic system problems
- Safety hazards
- Fire hazards

Short-Lived Items

During building inspection an appraiser usually encounters many items that show signs of wear and tear. It would not be economical to repair or replace most of these items on the date of the appraisal. The appraiser must decide if an item needs immediate repair or replacement or whether this work can be done later. (The consideration of deteriorated items is discussed in Chapter 17.) If the cost of the repairs adds nothing to the value of the property, the maintenance can be delayed. For example, a building with a sound, 10-year-old roof may hold up well for at least another five years. Although the roof has suffered some deterioration, replacing it probably would not add any value to the property over the cost of a new roof.

The final step in a quality and condition survey is to report on the condition of those items that should last for the remaining estimated economic life of the building, assuming they are not subject to abnormal wear and tear or accidentally damaged. The appraiser focuses on items that are not in the same condition as the rest of the building.

SUMMARY

A building description includes specific information on the size, design or layout, structural components, materials, equipment, and mechanical systems of a building. The description of a structure's physical characteristics helps an appraiser identify and select suitable comparables and estimate building costs and depreciation. In preparing a building description, an appraiser considers the current use, zoning codes that affect use, the plan and construction of the structure, building codes that affect the plan and construction, and the building's size.

Although systems of measurement vary, *gross building area (GBA)* is always calculated. For residential properties gross living area is also calculated. The *gross leasable area (GLA)* of shopping centers is commonly measured. For office buildings *GBA* and total leasable area are measured; lobby, corridor, and restroom space is allocated on a pro rata basis. All statements of size should be verified, and the method of calculation should be understood by the appraiser. Consistent units of comparison used in the sales comparison approach, and the rental and expense data used in the income capitalization approach must be based on equivalent units of area.

A building description includes an exterior description, an interior description, and a description of equipment and mechanical systems. In the exterior description, the appraiser provides information on the substructure, superstructure, and infrastructure of the building. The *substructure* is the foundational structure located below grade that provides the support base or footings on which the superstructure rests. The *superstructure* is the portion of the building above grade. The term *infrastructure* refers to a common source of utilities or support services for a complex of buildings.

In describing the substructure, the appraiser notes any problems that could cause settling or wall cracks. In examining the superstructure, the condition of the framing, insulation, ventilation, exterior walls, exterior doors, windows, facade, roof and drains, and chimneys and smoke stacks are observed.

Framing consists of vertical members called *studs*, and horizontal members called *joists*. Two forms of framing are used in wood construction: *platform*, which is the more prevalent, and *post and beam*. In large industrial and commercial buildings, the framing consists of steel beams or heat-resistant beams of reinforced or precast concrete. Defective framing can cause wall cracks. In the heat of a fire, steel beams can buckle and cause extensive damage.

Types of insulation include loose-fill insulation, which is poured or machine-blown into cavities; flexible insulation, which is attached to a foil or facing and fitted in place; and rigid insulation in board or deck form. Reflective insulation is made of foil that is chemically treated to reflect heat, and foamed-in-place insulation may be of urethane or urea-formaldehyde foam. An insulation's R value indicates its resistance to heat flow. In closed-off areas, ventilation reduces heat and prevents the condensation of water. Exterior walls may be load-bearing or nonload-bearing; their function determines the material of which they are built.

Exterior doors are made of wood, metal, or glass. An appraiser should note whether energy-saving materials such as weatherstripping are used. Window frames may be made of wood, aluminum, or steel; common types include single- and double-hung, casement, horizontal sliding, central pivot, and jalousie. The appraiser should describe window design and any installation features that conserve energy. The appraiser also considers the special contribution of an elaborate or attractive facade.

Roofs may be flat, lean-to, gable, gambrel, hip, mansard, monitor, or sawtooth. Their structural elements include trusses, joists, rafters, beams, and purlins.

Structural components and sheathing are made of wood, steel, or concrete; coverings may be of asphalt, fiberglass shingle, slate, or tile. Flashing protects a roof's structural joints against water damage, and the drain system and pitch of the roof provide for the control and disposal of rainwater. Chimneys, stacks, and vents contribute to the efficiency of the building's heating system and ensure the safety of the occupants. Any special exterior features may enhance or diminish property value.

To describe a building's interior, an appraiser investigates the condition of the interior walls and doors; space divisions; internal supports; painting, decorating, and finishing; and protection against decay and insect damage. Interior walls may be of wood, masonry, or concrete construction covered with drywall panels, plaster, tile, or brick. Doors may be hollow or solid-core, fire-resistant, or self-opening and closing.

In describing the division of space, an appraiser considers the number, function, and size of all rooms and storage areas. The appraiser also investigates the adequacy and safety of stairways, ramps, and elevators. Internal supports and subflooring should be checked for loadbearing capacity, and the functionality of ceiling heights should be considered. Painting and decorating are often a matter of taste, but the appearance of basements and floors reflects upkeep. The appraiser should check basements for dryness and ventilation. Flooring in industrial and commercial buildings may be of brick, stone block, pavement, concrete, or terrazzo mosaic. Wooden floors are common in all types of buildings. Fireplaces should be checked for potential hazards due to downdrafts and faulty flues. The appraiser must observe and describe any damage caused by fungi and termites.

Many industrial and commercial buildings have special-purpose improvements. An appraiser distinguishes between equipment and mechanical systems that provide for human comfort and fixed building equipment that is process-related. Equipment and mechanical systems can also be differentiated in terms of the amount of energy they consume. Hot water and heating systems consume energy, while plumbing is not basically energy-consuming. Plumbing consists of piping and fixtures. Piping, which may be made of galvanized steel, cast iron, copper, or plastic, should be checked for durability. Fixtures and fittings may incur obsolescence.

Hot water heaters get their heat from a furnace or are independently powered by electricity, gas, or oil. Heating systems are classified by the type of heat they produce and the kind of fuel they consume. Heating systems include hot air, in which pressure-blown heated air is circulated through ducts; hot water or hydronic, in which boiler-heated water is pumped to radiators; steam, in which boiler-heated steam is piped to radiators; and electric, in which cable-generated heat is pumped through ducts that are also used for air conditioning. Heating systems are fueled with coal, fuel oil, natural gas, or electricity.

Fuel considerations are significant in an appraisal. A zone system of temperature control provides greater energy efficiency. Technological developments such as cogeneration and solar heating promote energy conservation.

The most common type of air-conditioning system is an electrically powered Freon compressor. Complex ventilation systems distribute fresh air, filter foul air, and remove humidity. In an electrical system, power is distributed from the electrical service station with power wiring using conduits and bus ducts, branch circuits using distribution boxes and circuit breakers, and outlets. In houses BX or armored cable, single-phase wiring is common; large-capacity, three-phase wiring is used in commercial and industrial buildings. Fluorescent lighting and sodium and mercury vapor lights are found in industrial buildings.

Miscellaneous building equipment includes fire protection systems, conveyance system, signal systems, unloading systems, and attached or fixed process-related building equipment.

The appraiser performs a quality and condition survey to determine how the functional design, economy of construction, and attractiveness of a building relate to its quality of construction, economic utility, maintenance and operating expenses, and marketability. In this survey, the appraiser distinguishes among items in need of immediate repair (deferred maintenance items), items that may be repaired or replaced at a later date (short-lived items), and items that are expected to last for the remaining economic life of the building.

Chapter 11

BUILDING STYLE AND FUNCTION

*A*rchitectural style and functional utility are interrelated, and their combined effect on property value must be analyzed by appraisers. *Architectural style is the character of a building's form and ornamentation. Functional utility is the ability of a property or building to be useful and to perform the function for which it is intended, according to current market tastes and standards, as well as the efficiency of a building's use in terms of architectural style, design and layout, traffic patterns, and size and type of rooms.* Both architectural style and functional utility influence human lives by providing or withholding beauty, comfort, security, convenience, light, and air. They may also ensure reasonable maintenance expenditures, preserve valuable traditions, and indicate the need for change.

A building may have functional utility but lack architectural style, or it may have admirable style but little utility. Form and function work together to create successful architecture. Functional utility is not necessarily exemplified by minimal space or form; people's need for comfort and pleasure must also be considered in the design of offices, stores, hospitals, and houses. An appraiser must recognize and rank all market preferences regarding style and functional utility and then relate these preferences to market value.

Considerations relating to style and functional utility are integral to an appraisal. They are noted along with other physical characteristics during property inspection. Using comparable data an appraiser can analyze how style and function influence a property's market value. Style and functional utility are examined in relation to the function or use of a particular property—i.e., the use for which it was designed, its actual or contemplated use, and its most economic use. These three uses may or may not be the same.

ARCHITECTURAL STYLE AND UTILITY

Architecture is the art or science of building design and construction. It is the formal organization of three-dimensional elements on a large scale to serve various human needs. Because architecture interprets human needs, it is a fundamental reflection of culture. Architectural style affects the market value of property, so an understanding of its nature is important to appraisers. Two basic types of styles are distinguished in American architecture: formal architecture and vernacular architecture.

Formal architecture refers to the art and science of designing and building structures that meet the aesthetic and functional criteria of those trained in architectural history. Formal architectural styles are identified by common attributes of expression and are frequently named in reference to a geographic region, cultural group, or time period. Italianate, Second Empire, and Prairie School are examples of formal architectural styles.[1]

Vernacular architecture also relates to the art and science of designing and building structures, but without reference to the aesthetic and functional criteria of architectural history. Vernacular architecture refers to structures that are designed and built by individuals according to custom and in response to the envi-

---

1. Literature on American architectural history is abundant. For a description of architectural styles in a real estate appraisal context, see Judith Reynolds, *Historic Properties: Preservation and the Valuation Process* (Chicago: American Institute of Real Estate Appraisers, 1982). Other helpful sources are cited in the bibliography of this text.

ronment and contemporary life-styles. Vernacular styles share common attributes and may be technologically simple or sophisticated. However, these styles are usually unnamed because they are not formally studied by architectural historians. The sod houses built on the prairies of the American West and the mass-produced homes constructed in modern subdivisions are examples of vernacular styles. The traditional barn is another successful type of vernacular building.

Architectural style is influenced by market standards and tastes. Market standards are accepted norms, which reflect a culture's shared attitudes and beliefs. They are established forms and methods of construction that have not yet been surpassed by advances in technology or been perceived as aesthetically undesirable.

Market tastes are preferences, which may be shared by groups or expressed individually. Commonly shared tastes characterize most of the market for real estate. In a free economy, tastes shift either in reaction to, or in accordance with, market standards.

Market tastes and standards are influenced both by the desire to preserve tradition and by the desire for change, variety, and efficiency. Architectural trends respond to the market's desire to preserve tradition by including elements of past architectural styles; the market's desire for change provides the impetus for developing new elements of architectural design.

Changes in architectural trends are precipitated by the market's tolerance of current styles. When a style is too extreme, a shift to elements of past styles frequently occurs. Thus, extreme ornateness may be replaced by forms that are spare. A reactive shift, then, provides contrast to the preceding, dominant architectural style. Such changes also produce avant-garde or experimental building styles, which are ultimately tested in the market. An experimental style is eventually discarded or it becomes an accepted standard. However, design elements that are discarded in a reactive swing are not lost; old forms may disappear for a time and then reappear in a modified form.

Changes in architecture can also be generated by external forces. For example, rising energy costs have prompted new developments in the heating, ventilation, and air-conditioning systems used in office buildings. These developments include the installation of solar energy panels, the trend toward stand-alone HVAC systems, and the use of new exterior materials that conserve energy.

Architectural styles are modified over periods that are loosely related to the economic life cycles of buildings. Newly constructed buildings usually contrast in style with buildings of the previous period. Major revisions in architectural styles typically occur only after an entire building life cycle, which normally lasts 30 to 50 years. Newly constructed buildings of all architectural styles enjoy broad market appeal, whether they are professionally designed or not. When a building is no longer new, however, it is compared with other buildings in terms of the quality and usefulness of its architectural style. Form and structure, the most basic components of architectural style, limit and define a building's potential uses (and changes of use); these factors become more influential as time passes.

Architectural styles reflect a complex relationship of cultural premises and human activity over time. Thus, descriptions of architectural styles provide appraisers with a record of architectural history and a catalog of social expression. Figures 11.1 and 11.2 illustrate formal and vernacular American architectural styles.

Figure 11.1 Formal Architectural Styles

Jeffersonian

Art Deco

Georgian

Gothic Revival

Second Empire

Queen Anne

Courtesy of the United States Committee of the International Council on Monuments and Sites, the National Park Service, the National Trust for Historic Preservation, the Smithsonian Institution Traveling Exhibition Service, the Historic American Buildings Survey, the Preservation Press, and the Brown Foundation.

Figure 11.2 Vernacular Architecture

(H. Armstrong Roberts, Inc.)

Materials, Structure, Equipment, and Siting

Architectural style is reflected in a number of building components. A building's materials, structure, equipment, and siting all shape and change its style. The availability of natural materials such as wood, stone, and clay and lime for making brick was primarily responsible for the different architectural styles that emerged and prevailed in various areas of the United States. When post-and-beam construction was developed, greater spaces could be spanned. This type of construction made it possible to build the large fabricating mills of the Industrial Revolution. The evolution of lightweight balloon framing and machines to mass-produce nails changed the form of buildings in the nineteenth century. Furthermore, balloon framing allowed buildings to be constructed much more rapidly because precut components were used.

The development of the Franklin stove and central heating systems changed the shape and number of rooms in all structures because fireplaces were no longer needed to provide heat. The production of domestic equipment in the early twentieth century eliminated the need for root cellars, pantries, and large laundry rooms, which decreased the size of dwellings and changed room arrangements.

Similarly, rapid advances in computers and semiconductors, wiring networks and switching devices, and satellite communications have affected building design. In modern business facilities, much attention is devoted to the installation, routing, and expansion capabilities of communications systems.[2] Design considerations for contemporary office buildings include the capacities of feed conduit and electrical service to accommodate a wide variety of transmission linkages, the presence or absence of roof reinforcement to support satellite and microwave antennae, and the ability of HVAC systems to handle the increased heat output of office computers. These factors affect the size of conduit and risers, the amount and quality of electricity required, ceiling height, and other structural considerations.

In the mid-twentieth century, central air-conditioning and heating, made possible by modern technology, became common in residential, commercial, and industrial buildings. This resulted in a standardization of architectural styles, particularly housing styles, throughout the country and nearly obliterated the regional building styles developed in response to variations in climate.

For example, the thick, mud masonry walls and small windows of houses in the Southwest were well-suited to the hot, dry weather of the region. Houses in the rainy Northwest had overhanging roofs so that windows could be opened for ventilation without admitting the rain. The saltbox houses of New England were protected against the harsh northern wind because the windowless, steeped-roof side of the house faced north. Although regional building styles temporarily lost favor, structural defenses against climate were reincorporated into construction in the mid-1970s. Because the market has become energy-conscious, climate-

---

2. For further information, see Theodore H. Schell, "Developing Communications," *Buildings* (August 1983). Schell discusses the importance of planning for the installation of advanced communications systems in new commercial buildings. See also B.R. Jensen, "Building Efficiency: Cost and Value," *The Appraisal Journal* (January 1985) and Dean Schwanke, *Smart Buildings and Technology-Enhanced Real Estate, Vol. 1* (Washington, D.C.: Urban Land Institute, 1985).

compatible design has returned. Such design considerations are important in estimating market value because consumers increasingly desire energy-saving features.

The use of steel for framing and the invention of the elevator made the construction of taller buildings possible. Curtain walls of glass and metal are well-suited to the box-like forms of modern buildings built in the International style. Curtain-wall construction separated the functions of support and enclosure, which were inseparable in multistory buildings of heavy masonry. Curtain walls can be made of metal, masonry, precast concrete, or glass.

Steel bar joists have twice the load-bearing capacity of solid joists, so greater spaces can be spanned and pipes, ducts, and conduit can be threaded through open webbing. Lightweight structural support systems and the use of lamination and plastic glues developed in the aircraft industry have facilitated the creation of new building components such as butterfly and arcaded roofs.

Technology developed since the 1940s has allowed buildings to take new shapes because concrete can now be used in large slabs, building blocks, or beams. Elevator buildings constructed of reinforced concrete are an alternative to steel framing construction and are less vulnerable to fire. Building a structure with poured concrete is slow and must stop in cold weather, but precast concrete assembly can proceed nearly as quickly as steel construction. For additional strength, posttensioning can be used to tighten reinforcing rods while the concrete hardens. Concrete column reinforcement allows concrete buildings to be built as high as steel-framed towers. Lightweight aggregate can also be used in cement to reduce the load.

As materials, structural components, and equipment become more refined, architectural styles change. Technological advances are integrated into evolving architectural styles and may modify architectural trends.

Architectural design is also influenced by the possible placement of a building on its site. Every building has a physical setting that includes the space around it. In cities where buildings abut one another directly, there is little choice about placement. However, in some locations there is more flexibility, and a building's design, placement, and landscaping can provide a defense against the climate. High energy costs make siting an important element of compatibility, but appropriate placement on a site can also enhance a building's architectural design.

Architectural design can be adjusted to suit the climate and the individual site. Trees can provide shade, act as windbreaks and sound barriers, and filter and add moisture to the air. Deciduous trees should be placed on the western side of a property, where they can provide shade from the afternoon sun in summer and allow the sun to shine through in winter. Conifers can be planted on the northern part of a property to act as windbreaks. The effects of shade and sunlight can also be moderated by the angle and direction of overhanging roofs. These roofs deflect the high-angle rays of the summer sun and allow the low-angle rays of the winter sun to be admitted through windows.

Because increasing fuel costs have created the need for alternative energy sources, active and passive solar features have been introduced into building design to a limited extent. Active solar heating systems make use of glass roof panels or glass attached to one side of the building. Warm air is stored in a medium such as water or pumped directly into the structure. Passive solar heating techniques include strategically placed windows or glass walls, insulation, heat-retaining walls and floors, and careful siting. Rooms, roofs, and windows can be situated to allow warm air to flow freely through the structure or to provide maximum ventilation and air cooling.

A house that is built underground takes advantage of the fact that below-grade temperatures are moderate year round. The heating and cooling equipment in such houses can operate with less power, which reduces energy costs significantly. In the United States, underground housing is found primarily in the Central Plains region, where storm protection and reduced energy costs are major concerns. These earth-covered dwellings of poured concrete and concrete block are usually located on grade and bermed—i.e., set into a site that is partly or completely excavated. Berming overcomes the constraints associated with high water tables, expansive clay soils, rock strata, and flat rural sites. Usually the site is partially excavated into a hillside; the house's sod-covered roof provides additional insulation.

Underground construction, solar heating techniques, climate-specific siting, and other energy-related building style adaptations should be considered by an appraiser in terms of their acceptance in the market and their influence on sale prices, rents, and other market value indicators.

FUNCTIONAL UTILITY

To be functional an item must work and be useful. The definition of functional utility, however, is subject to changing expectations and standards. Optimal functional utility implies that the design and engineering of a building are considered to be the best in terms of perceived needs at a given time.

Functional inutility is an impairment of the functional capacity of a property or building according to market tastes and standards. It becomes equivalent to functional obsolescence when ongoing change, caused by technological advances and economic and aesthetic trends, renders building layouts and features obsolete. Functional inutility must be judged in light of market standards of acceptability, specifically the standards of buyers who make up the market for a particular type of building.

As objectives of building design, functional utility and aesthetics are sometimes in conflict; market standards generally reflect a compromise between the two. Extremely utilitarian housing designs that omitted basements, entrance halls, and dining rooms were eventually rejected by much of the market and replaced with more flexible designs. Similarly, the trend toward ultimate efficiency in office building interiors produced standard space with low ceilings, plain walls, and vinyl asbestos floors. This type of interior finish was soon considered substandard.

Functional utility represents more than practical utilitarianism. Overimprovements—i.e., superadequate structural components or space—are also items of functional obsolescence because their costs exceed their value. When an expensively finished retail space with high ceilings is included in an office building located where there is no market for retailing, the building incorporates functional obsolescence in the form of superadequacy.

Standards of functional utility vary with the type and use of property. Specific considerations for different types of property are discussed in the remainder of this chapter. Some general standards of functional utility to be considered by appraisers include

- Suitability or appropriateness
- Comfort
- Efficiency
- Safety
- Security
- Accessibility
- Ease and cost of maintenance
- Market standards
- Attractiveness
- Profitability

One additional standard must be given special consideration. In determining the functional utility and appropriateness of an architectural style, an appraiser must consider compatibility.

Compatibility

Compatibility means that a building is in harmony with its use or uses and its environment. Compatibility should extend to a building's form, materials, and scale. Styles of different periods frequently clash; a cubistic dwelling would not be in harmony with eighteenth-century colonial buildings. Similarly, a monumental or ostentatious building is often out of place in a modest setting. Two-story structures tend to be overwhelmed in a row of skyscrapers, so their market value may be diminished by incompatibility of design. There are other types of incompatibility as well. A structure can be incompatible with its function, its various elements can be incompatible with one another, or the structure can be incompatible with its site or location in the neighborhood.

Compatibility is influenced by zoning, historical districts, construction and maintenance costs, land value, physical features, architectural trends, and technology. Sometimes these factors impose conformity. Usually, the predominant uses and building styles in an area are readily observable. However, a trend in development may be more difficult to observe; an architectural style that appears atypical may actually conform to an emergency trend.

A building design that is typical in an area has less influence on value than a design that is atypical, so the impact of nonconformity must be considered carefully. A slightly unusual design that is attractive and generally in harmony with other, nearby buildings could command a higher price than its more typical neighbors. A building with an incongruous design, however, will probably be sold at a price below the general market level; if it is not, there may be offsetting qualities.

In isolated cases, assessing the value influence of a nonconforming design may require unsupported, but reasoned, appraisal judgment. In many cases, however, the effect on value can be determined from market data. For example, international style office buildings in a particular location may regularly be sold at lower prices per square foot than buildings of a different style.

Sometimes there may be sufficient demand for a nonconforming design such as a detached dwelling in a neighborhood of row houses or an art nouveau movie theater in a retail shopping district dominated by nineteenth-century buildings. If demand exists, it may support a market value equal to or greater than that of more typical structures. Functional utility may override design as a primary market requirement. If the general proportions and scale of an atypical building are in harmony with the surroundings and functional utility demands are met, there may be no design penalty.

Building materials should be in harmony with one another and with a building's architectural style. A building that is designed to be constructed of one material will not necessarily be effective when constructed of another. Building materials should not be excessively varied nor should an architectural design have too many distracting features. The design and building materials used should be well-integrated and in harmony with the site. A frame building in a wooded, hilly area will probably be in better harmony with its setting than a brick building, assuming wood is appropriate for the structure's function. A frame building in an urban area dominated by masonry usually suffers a market value penalty; an office building with a metal facade may be penalized if stone facades are typical in the area.

DESIGN AND FUNCTIONAL UTILITY BY BUILDING TYPE

Marketability is the ultimate test of functional utility. Generally, a building is functional if it successfully serves the purpose for which it was designed or adapted. Specific design considerations that affect the functional utility of residential, commercial, industrial, agricultural, and special-purpose buildings are discussed below.

Residential Properties

Trends in single-family houses and apartments change in regard to the inclusion or exclusion of building components such as porches, balconies, fireplaces, dining rooms, large kitchens, entry halls, and family rooms. Housing standards vary widely for different income levels and in different regions. Historic houses are often less functional, but they are in great demand due to their preservationist appeal. To evaluate the functional utility of residential buildings, appraisers should analyze standard expectations in the market. Nevertheless, the functional utility of a single-family or multifamily dwelling results primarily from its layout, accommodation of specific activities, adequacy, and ease and cost of maintenance.

Layout
The layout of an apartment or house relates to traffic patterns—i.e., where kitchens and bathrooms should be located for convenience and how private and public areas should be separated. A layout has functional inutility if it causes awkward traffic patterns. For example, inutility may result if people have to cross the living room to get to a bedroom, if the dining area is not adjacent to the kitchen, or if groceries have to be brought through the living room to the kitchen.

Full bathrooms, which include facilities for bathing, are most convenient, accessible, and private when they are near the bedrooms; they should be accessed directly or through a hall, not through a second bedroom. Powder rooms should be located off a hall and near, but not too near, the living room or dining room. Poor floor plans are easily recognized by those who make up the market for apartments and houses, but standards often vary with current trends in a region and neighborhood.

The location of various rooms in relation to the site can increase or diminish a dwelling's privacy, comfort, and serenity. In urban areas master bedrooms and living rooms are increasingly found in the rear of residences. Often they have access to, and views of, a garden. This trend is relatively new. Formerly it was considered desirable for the living room and best bedroom to be at the front of the house and oriented to the street. Kitchens, which were once relegated to the rear, are now just as likely to be on one side of a hall in the middle or at the front of a residence.

The popularity of condominium ownership has encouraged versatility in apartment design. Clustered, duplex, and townhouse units are designed in interesting configurations that maximize their market appeal. Structures designed for other uses are now being converted to apartments. Silos, breweries, warehouses, and schools have been successfully converted into multiunit projects. Duplexes, which often have strong market appeal, maximize salable square footage because vertical access is included in the unit, rather than the public space. Multiunit housing is also built in stacked configurations with access at more than one level to minimize stair climbing. Low-rise, multifamily housing projects can be designed in a great many ways. Elevator apartment buildings tend to have more standardized, predictable floor plans to make the best use of space within a simple rectangular configuration.

Accommodation of Specific Activities

In building design the specific activities of occupants are accommodated by providing separate areas for food preparation, eating, conversation, sleeping, hygiene, hobbies, and relaxation. The trend in American housing throughout much of this century has been toward combining the functions of many rooms into fewer rooms. The combined living room-dining room and the family room exemplify this trend.

Adequacy

Adequacy is a primary consideration in evaluating functional utility. The adequacy of building size, windows, doors, rooms, ceiling height, closets, security, privacy, and comfort are all considered in planning dwellings and in their appraisal.

Standards of adequacy vary. The one-bathroom apartment or house has, for the most part, become an anachronism. New kitchens and baths are larger, better equipped, and more expensively finished than the small, utilitarian kitchens and baths of the recent past. Dishwashers, garbage disposals, and wall ovens are usually standard in new construction and their absence may create a value penalty. Ceramic tile in baths and more elegant fixtures are becoming commonplace. The master bedroom frequently has its own compartmentalized bath with a spa tub and a separate dressing area. Closets are abundant in new apartments and houses and ceiling heights have increased, especially in living rooms, despite high energy costs.

In general more people have better housing today. Many amenities are now considered necessities and their inclusion is taken for granted. Even in periods of high construction and financing costs when average houses are smaller, the tendency is to retain extra bathrooms, labor-saving devices, and fireplaces.

Although an apartment is a dwelling unit within a larger structure, it must be seen as an integral part of the whole. Security, convenience, and ease of maintenance are primary considerations for apartments, whether they are rented or owned as cooperatives or condominiums. Amenities tend to be more important than space; apartment buyers and sellers often prefer a fireplace or an extra bathroom to an additional 200 square feet of area. Because most apartments do not have gardens or yards, they should provide light, air, and an interesting view. Amenities such as convenient parking, swimming pools, tennis courts, and exercise facilities are important to apartment projects when these features are not available nearby.

Smaller kitchens and bathrooms tend to be more acceptable to the market for apartments than the market for houses. A dining area that is an ell or a part of the living room is generally acceptable. Living rooms may be spacious to offset the smallness of other rooms and closet space must be plentiful.

Kitchen and bath finishes and equipment that are designed in response to a passing fad can quickly make an apartment less desirable to the market. Pastel ceramic tile in bathrooms and dark-colored kitchen equipment may be undesirable where all white or neutral color schemes are the norm. Dishwashers, garbage disposals, and central air-conditioning have become standard for apartments, and laundry equipment is becoming common in more expensive units.

The mix of units in an apartment project should meet market demands; an improper unit mix may indicate functional inutility.

Ease and Cost of Maintenance

The ease and cost of maintenance in a single-family dwelling or condominium unit are increasingly important to its marketability. More family members have become wage earners and less time is available for home maintenance. Interior and exterior finishes that require extensive maintenance have become noncompetitive.

The efficient use of energy is a primary consideration in the residential market because heating, cooling, lighting, and cooking fuels are expensive. As alternatives to electricity, natural gas, and oil, buyers have turned to insulation, fireplaces, wood stoves, ventilating fans, and passive solar techniques. In most markets a house that wastes fuel and electricity suffers major functional obsolescence.

Energy-conserving features are particularly important in multifamily dwellings and often make the difference between a profitable operation and an unprofitable one. A large portion of the energy used in buildings is needed to offset heat lost through cracks, window openings, and the building envelope. Insulation, properly installed windows with double or triple glazing, caulking, and weatherstripping help reduce heat loss in the winter; shade trees, blinds, and solar screens can help keep units cooler in the summer. Energy-efficient equipment and controls also help meet new standards of functional utility in multifamily buildings.

Commercial Properties

Commercial buildings are used for offices, stores, banks, restaurants, and service outlets. Hotels constitute an important subcategory of commercial property. Frequently, two or more commercial uses are combined in a single building.

The structural and design features of commercial buildings are constantly changing. Developers want the most competitive building possible, within the cost constraints imposed by economic pressures, so they incorporate technological changes to meet the demand for innovation whenever possible.

The efficiency use of commercial construction today is much greater than it was in the past. Greater utility can be observed both in the portion of the total area enclosed by the structure, which produces direct income in the form of rent, and in the structural facilitation that has evolved out of new materials and construction methods. No single method of commercial building construction predominates; methods vie with one another, and one may surpass others in a given area at a particular time. Steel and reinforced concrete are the most commonly used structural materials.

An appraiser examines a number of specific elements of functional utility in commercial buildings. An additional concern—i.e., safety and security—may be affected by the treatment of the specific elements listed below.

- Column spacing
- Bay depth
- Live-load floor capacity
- Ceiling height
- Module width
- Elevator facilities
- The work letter
- HVAC adequacy
- Energy efficiency
- Public amenities
- Parking ratios

Column Spacing

Column placement relates to a building's total height, and greater spans are more expensive to construct. Closely spaced columns limit the possibilities for interior partitioning. In some areas columns are typically placed at 20 to 22 feet on center, but this placement is far more limiting than column placement at 28 to 30 feet on center. Tenants usually prefer the wider spacing, but the cost to construct it may prove prohibitive.

Bay Depth

Bay depth is the distance from the tenant side of the corridor wall to the exterior wall. Bay depth controls the layout of interior space and is dictated by the depth and width of the site, which prescribes the building's configuration. The box-like configuration of contemporary office buildings is cost efficient because the ratio of perimeter wall to enclosed area is optimized. A long, thin building is more expensive to construct than a square one with the same area. The shallower bays of older buildings are more adaptable to the needs of smaller tenancies, but greater bay depths are more profitable to build if they do not exceed market demand. Tenants are often more concerned with the configuration of the space and its ability to house staff and equipment than with the amount of square foot area.

Live-Load Floor Capacity

Floor load capacity is measured in live-load pounds per square foot. Inadequate floor load capacity is a type of functional obsolescence that often decreases a building's marketability and is expensive to cure. Live load includes everything that can be moved, excluding parts of the structure. A floor load capacity of 100 pounds per square foot, up from 70 pounds a generation ago, is generally considered adequate for commercial buildings. Microfilm and microfiche record storage and the use of small-frame computer equipment have reversed the trend toward ever-increasing, live-load floor capacity.

Ceiling Height

New commercial buildings usually have finished ceilings. Finished ceiling heights depend on the building heights permitted by zoning and on market standards and preferences. Higher ceiling heights within a normal range are generally preferred for office space.

Module Width

Building modules are based on the distance between window mullions, which determines the size of partitioned offices in a building. Ceiling tiles and other finish components also determine the dimensions of contemporary office space modules.

When older commercial buildings have architectural charm or other desirable structural qualities, it may be cost-effective to retrofit them with modern lighting, ventilation, and elevators, even if their design does not conform to contemporary standards. Structures with high ceilings, narrow bay depths, wide public corridors, tall doors, and elaborate woodwork may be successfully preserved and adapted to meet the demand of markets that do not require streamlined space.

Elevators

The elevators in multilevel office buildings should be adequate in terms of speed, load capacity, safety, and number, and they should be able to meet peak period demands. Appraisers judge the adequacy of elevators using established standards. A building should have one elevator for every 25,000 to 40,000 square feet of leasable area. The elevators should be able to transport from 10% to 30% of the building's occupants within five minutes at speeds of 300 to 350 feet per minute.

The standards for elevators vary with a building's tenants. For example, a building that houses a single organization may require more elevator service due to heavy interfloor traffic. Many building codes require that elevators accommodate handicapped persons, so control panels should be accessible and interior corridors and doors should be wide enough for wheelchairs.

Elevator capacity is expressed in weight and number of occupants. Electric elevators are faster than hydraulic ones and serve multistory buildings better; hydraulic elevators are sometimes used to connect two or more floors.

In assessing the functional utility of elevator service, an appraiser should consider the number of tenants, the number of floors, and the total building area served by the elevators, as well as the quality of elevator service in competing buildings.

Work Letter

A work letter is an agreement, usually part of a lease, that specifies the level of interior finish and equipment that the landlord is to provide to the tenant, including lighting, partitioning, door allowance, and electrical capacity. The quality and dollar value of these standard installations vary. A typical work letter may include the following specifications:

- One linear foot of partitioning for every 12 to 15 square feet of office space
- One suite entrance door for every 5,000 square feet of office space and one interior door for every 200 to 300 square feet of space
- One 2-by-4-ft., lighting fixture for every 80 square feet of office space
- One light switch for each room
- One duplex receptacle for every 125 square feet of space
- One telephone outlet for every 150 square feet of space
- One linear foot of closet door for every 800 square feet of space and one bifold closet door for every 5,000 square feet of space

Inadequacies or superadequacies in the level of finish specified in a work letter can result in market value penalties; variations may result in a tenant payment or credit, or in a rental addition or concession.

HVAC Adequacy

Another aspect of a building's functional utility is the adequacy of the heating, ventilation, and air-conditioning (HVAC) systems. It is particularly important that a building's principal use matches its mechanical equipment. For example, medical office buildings usually have substantially more plumbing lines and connections, ventilating diffusers, electrical wiring, and partitioning than typical office structures.

Energy Efficiency

Energy consumption is increasingly significant for commercial buildings. To remain competitive, office buildings must incorporate technological advances such as computer-programmed controls, zoned heating and cooling, and highly efficient mechanical equipment. Public pressure to economize on energy consumption has increased due to rising energy costs, peak load pricing policies, and the threat of energy allocation.

In inefficient commercial buildings energy expenditures range from 125,000 to 150,000 Btus per square foot per year. In buildings that house computers, energy costs are significantly higher. With improved building design, energy consumption can be reduced to 60,000 to 80,000 Btus per square foot per year; experimental buildings can operate on less than 50,000 Btus per square foot per year.

Most newer commercial buildings in urban areas have been constructed with fixed-sash windows, but some are now being built with windows that open to admit fresh air and regulate temperatures. If energy allocation occurs and certain fuels become scarce or unavailable at times, fixed-sash windows could become functionally obsolete.

Public Amenities in Retail Space

Amenities can contribute to a building's functional utility. Building amenities may include attractive public areas, well-kept grounds, and adequate, well-located restroom facilities. The type and use of a property may dictate building amenities. For example, a retail center must have good delivery access, suitable traffic patterns for shoppers, strong lighting, adequate column spacing, and a sufficient number of escalators. Surface and finish elements should be durable and easily maintained. A retail center must also have areas for shoppers and workers to rest, ample restroom facilities, and attractive, coordinated signs.

The specialty shopping center is the newest type of retail grouping; it houses a number of retailers, most of which offer nonessential goods and services. A specialty shopping center usually has no anchor tenants, so it must project its image with a central feature, integrated design elements, or attractive landscaping. Restaurants and entertainment facilities such as movie theaters are also included in specialty shopping centers.

The quality and distribution of public amenities in shopping centers are important appraisal concerns. The need for adequately distributed amenities influences the design of shopping centers, which are as competitive in the market as office buildings. The configuration of the typical shopping center has changed even more drastically than the design of the typical office building.

Trends in shopping centers change so rapidly that many structures become functionally obsolete before they deteriorate physically. Because retail space is relatively easy to renovate, many centers are streamlined and modernized when they lose their market appeal. Shopping centers have evolved from the small strip centers developed after World War II into huge regional and superregional centers, which may occupy up to 100 acres of land and include more than one million square feet of building area. Despite the trend toward greater size, however, most existing and newly built shopping centers have less than 200,000 square feet of space; more than half have less than 100,000 square feet of area.

Supermarkets and drugstores were once the anchor tenants of large suburban shopping centers. They now tend to be freestanding structures located near, but not within, shopping centers. This change is the result of increased merchandising competition between supermarkets, department stores, drugstores, and smaller stores. Large suburban shopping centers are frequently town centers, where people go to shop, socialize, be entertained, and attend civic meetings.

Parking Ratios

Parking ratios are crucial to the success of all retail centers, except those located in dense urban areas. The emergence of multiuse shopping centers and the trend toward smaller cars have increased the ratio between gross leasable store area and parking spaces. One parking space for every 180 square feet of gross leasable store area is usually adequate. Orientation to a means of access is crucial for all commercial buildings.

Users of commercial space tend to occupy separate structures in areas of low-density development. These buildings are usually accessed by automobile, so sufficient, adjacent parking is essential. Pedestrian traffic from buildings to parking areas should also be accommodated. Access to both public transportation and parking is important for commercial buildings located in densely developed urban areas.

Security and convenience govern the placement of parking facilities; the route between a commercial facility and its parking area must be direct and visible. The amount of parking provided is determined by the proximity and availability of alternative sources of access, such as public transportation, and the amount of parking provided by similar buildings. Some commercial buildings in urban areas do not include onsite parking because other forms of transportation are convenient or adequate parking facilities are located nearby.

In an efficiently designed parking garage, columns are placed every 28 feet, which permits three cars to be parked between columns. The popularity of small cars has given outdoor parking lots greater capacity; more cars can be accommodated by restriping spaces. Parking garage design has not changed fundamentally because columns are still needed, but, when possible, drive aisles have been reduced from 26 to 25 feet in width.

The standard parking space has been reduced from an area of 9 feet by 18 feet to $8^3/4$ feet by $17^1/2$ feet. A compact car needs a space approximately $8^1/4$ feet by $16^1/2$ feet. Most self-park garages allow 300 to 350 gross leasable square feet per car, which includes aisles and ramps; garages with attendant parking allow substantially less than 300 square feet per car. The most efficient configuration for a garage is 90-degree-angle parking. A typical parking ratio in an area without good public transit is one parking space for every 200 square feet of leasable area.

Hotels

Hotels range from tiny inns with fewer than a dozen rooms to huge convention hotels with more than a thousand rooms.[3] All hotels and motels were once measured against standard, current designs; this tendency continues, particularly for medium-priced hotels. In appraising older facilities and luxury hotels, however, variation in architectural styles and interior finish must be considered.

Many older hotels and apartment buildings that have been rehabilitated as hotels have unique architectural styles and a sense of luxury that is difficult to replicate in newer structures. The desire to rehabilitate older buildings is widespread, affecting large, historic structures in urban centers as well as small inns in picturesque country settings.

All lodging facilities benefit from suitable fireproofing, soundproofing, and security systems. Beyond these basic considerations, the physical configuration of a hotel or motel is determined by the type of patrons it serves. A motor hotel, or motel, must be oriented to the needs of drivers who wish to spend a minimum amount of time on the premises; a resort hotel, on the other

---

3. For a thorough discussion of hotels, see Stephen Rushmore, *Hotels, Motels, and Restaurants: Valuation and Market Studies* (Chicago: American Institute of Real Estate Appraisers, 1983) and *The Computerized Income Approach to Hotel-Motel Market Studies and Valuations* (Chicago: Appraisal Institute, 1990).

hand, must provide a variety of entertainment facilities for its guests. Although automobile parking is still needed at resorts, it is usually situated away from direct view.

Functional inutility in hotel structures, like other types of buildings, can be categorized in terms of overimprovements, inadequacies, poor layout, inappropriate structural quality or finishes, and inefficient equipment.

The amount of hotel space devoted to guest rooms varies. A hotel that is a major meeting and entertainment center has a much lower proportion of guest rooms to public areas than an apartment hotel. Many apartment hotels are successful transient operations which consist entirely of suites with small equipped kitchens, living rooms, and separate bedrooms. These hotels usually have small lobbies and restaurants.

The layout of guest rooms also varies with the clientele. Large rooms, separate dressing areas, and large closets are needed when most guests stay for several nights. Room size is usually geared to the necessary amount of furniture; the room should be large enough to provide ample space around and between the pieces of furniture. Business travelers need desks, while vacationers usually do not. The trend toward larger beds requires larger rooms, but rooms that are too large do not use space efficiently.

Support space for guest rooms includes hotel office and operations areas, restaurants, lounges, public meeting rooms, and often athletic facilities.

Industrial Properties

Like all properties, an industrial property must have a site, buildings, and equipment that function as an operating unit. Inutility is measured against the standard of optimal efficiency for similar properties in the market.

Some industrial properties are designed and equipped to meet the needs of a specific occupant and have limited appeal to others. Buildings used for industries that involve bulky or volatile materials and products have specialized equipment and building designs, so they have few potential users. Buildings used for research and development or for light fabricating and processing are less limited in their appeal.

All industrial buildings are measured in terms of gross building area *(GBA)*. To make comparisons and measurement buildings in terms of market standards, the *GBA* can be divided into finished and unfinished space. The most flexible design for industrial buildings, and the one with the greatest appeal on the open market, is a one-story, square or nearly square structure that complies with all local building codes.

Industrial buildings can be constructed of many types of material, but concrete and steel are used most often. The building method commonly applied is tilt-up construction, which incorporates concrete walls that are cast horizontally and put in place vertically. The walls are often designed to be load-bearing. Flat roofs supported by steel bar joists are also common. Prefabricated steel buildings are less expensive to build, and their appearance is now considered more acceptable than it was in the past. Plastic skylights can be installed for natural light instead of expensive monitor and sawtooth roofs.

Industrial properties must have land-to-building ratios that allow plenty of space for parking, truck maneuvering, yard storage, and expansion. Other locational considerations include reasonable real estate taxes, an available supply of labor, adequate utility service, beneficial zoning, proximity to supply sources and customers, and ease of transportation which is vital to the receipt of raw materials and the distribution of finished products.

Industrial parks are groups of industrial buildings that have similar uses. With good landscaping, ample setbacks, building and lot size minimums, and professional architecture, engineering, and management, industrial parks provide an environment that is acceptable to occupants as well as government land-planning groups.

The combination of old and new industrial space may have substantial functional obsolescence if the new construction contributes less than its cost to the value of the whole. The layout of industrial space should allow operations to be carried out with maximum efficiency. Typically receiving functions are performed on one side of the building, shipping functions on the other, and processing or storage functions in the middle. Some industrial buildings include special features such as sprinkler systems, scales, loading dock levelers, refrigeration areas, conveyor systems, process piping (for compressed air, water, and gas), power wiring, and employee lockers and lunchrooms.

Storage Buildings

Storage structures range from simple cubicles, known as *miniwarehouses*, to huge regional warehouses with one million square feet of area. Functional utility and location have a major impact on the market value of storage buildings; obsolescence usually occurs before the structures deteriorate physically. The functions of warehouses are

- To store materials in a protected environment
- To organize materials so that they can be easily inventoried and removed
- To provide facilities for efficient delivery
- To provide facilities for efficient access and shipping

For optimal functional utility, warehouses should have adequate access, open areas, ceiling height, floor load capacity (often 300 pounds or more for heavy-duty industrial storage buildings), humidity and temperature controls, shipping and receiving facilities, fire protection, and protection from the elements.

The primary consideration in warehouse location is good access. Trucking is the most common means of transporting goods, but certain warehouse operations also need access to rail, water and air transportation. Operations that depend on trucks to transport goods should be near an arterial highway. The highway's access street or frontage road and the truck maneuvering area at the warehouse loading dock must allow for efficient use of loading facilities at all times. If a warehouse site slopes downward from a frontage road, the loading dock can be constructed at truck-bed level. For rail access, one portion of the site must be long and level.

Forklifts, conveyor belts, and automatically guided vehicle conveyor systems are used to move materials inside warehouses. Truck docks must be wide enough to accommodate truck widths and the interior servomechanism used to move goods and materials. If electric trucks are used, a battery-charging area should be included. Most storage operations are palletized—i.e., pallets, or portable platforms, are used for moving and storing materials. Therefore, ceiling heights in warehouses should accommodate an ideal number of pallets. Because wide spans provide maximum flexibility, a square structure generally is the most cost-effective.

Office space in warehouses may constitute as little as 1% of the total area, but generally approximately 5% of the total gross building area is used for offices. In distribution facilities, office space may comprise 35% to 50% of the total gross building area. Office space in warehouses should be adequately heated, cooled, and lighted, but its finish is generally utilitarian.

Sprinkler systems are needed in warehouses where flammable goods are stored. The nature of the stored material determines whether the system should be wet or dry, using water or chemicals.

Miniwarehouses are usually combined in one-story rectangular structures located near those who will use them. These properties should be visible, accessible, and include sufficient land for parking and maneuvering. The sizes of the individual units within miniwarehouses vary; they usually include small storage units, which have passage doors, and larger units, which have roll-up truck doors.

Buildings on Agricultural Properties

In most of the United States, there is a trend toward fewer, larger farms. Therefore, the contribution of farm buildings to the total value of farm real estate has been steadily decreasing. Statistics from the U.S. Department of Agriculture indicate that farm buildings represent less than 20% of the total value of farm property. The number of farm buildings per acre of farmland has also decreased.

Farms are operated by families and by large, specialized business operations. The equipment and management needed to run agricultural operations have become increasingly specialized.

Farming operations are conducted in fewer types of farm buildings because each operation is responsible for fewer functions. Farm buildings must accommodate the type of machinery and equipment used in farming today. More large machine sheds are needed to house tractors, combines, discs, plows, harrows, cultivators, pickers, trucks, and other equipment. Pipeline milking machines and overhead feed bins dictate the requirements for milking parlors and loafing sheds where livestock are sheltered. Changes in the care and feeding of poultry have substantially modified the design of poultry farm buildings.

The history of the United States has been shaped by certain types of buildings. Barns are second only to houses in their influence on American culture. Barns have successfully combined functional utility with picturesque design. Form, function, and materials have come together in a unique way to make the barn the most successful type of vernacular building. Some barns have traditionally been multifunctional, providing animal shelter, grain storage, and a threshing floor. Other farm structures, such as tobacco barns and modern farm buildings, serve a single, specialized function.

The typical American barn is 60 feet long and 30 feet wide, with two gable ends, a loft, and double doors on the wide sides. Most barns are built of wood, but some are made of stone, logs, or brick. Old barns are suitable for modern, general-purpose farming if they are sufficiently adaptable. The use of baled, rather than loose, hay and the increased use of ensilage have lessened the need for barn storage. Silos, however, have become more prevalent and larger.

Animal shelters should be dry and clean, provide protection from the wind and sun, and be adaptable to equipment storage. To be useful each farm building must contribute to the operating efficiency of the entire farm. Each building's usefulness relates to the type and size of the farm. Functional inutility can result from having too many farm buildings when fewer would be more efficient.

Special-Purpose Buildings

The architecture of special-purpose buildings tends to limit them to a single use. Although most buildings can be converted to other uses, the conversion of special-purpose buildings generally involves extra expense and design expertise. Special-purpose structures include churches, synagogues, theaters, sports arenas, and other types of auditoriums.

The functional utility of a special-purpose building depends on whether there is continued demand for the use for which the building was designed. When there is demand, functional utility depends on whether the building conforms to competitive standards. For example, there is a continued demand for movie theaters, but their design has changed due to high maintenance and utility costs. Ornate movie theaters have been replaced with simple, unembellished structures. However, there is a trend to convert older movie theaters into concert halls and legitimate theaters.

The design and materials used in synagogues and churches are simpler today to keep maintenance and utility costs down. The functional utility of these structures, like sports and concert arenas, is primarily related to seating capacity. Nevertheless, the structure's support facilities, general attractiveness, and appeal must also be considered.

The adaptive-use movement has generated public awareness of the conversion potential of special-purpose buildings. Buildings usually outlive their function, and energy shortages, the decline of modernism, and disproportionate construction costs have contributed to the preservation movement. Railroad stations, schools, firehouses, and grist mills are popular structures for conversion. The functional utility of these buildings relates to how much they deviate from building codes and to how the cost of rehabilitation relates to the potential economic return. A typical item of functional inutility in adaptive-use projects is an insufficient number of staircases to meet building codes. By contrast, a high ceiling in a specialty property does not indicate functional inutility if it is a desirable architectural quality that contributes to net income.

Mixed-Use Buildings

Many buildings successfully combine two or more uses. The construction of mixed-use buildings, which began in the late 1950s and 1960s, reflects postwar developments such as the suburban shopping center and the planned business and residential communities of urban America. One prevalent example is the mixed-use development (MUD), which comprises at least three revenue-producing uses such as retail, office, and residential or hotel/motel facilities.

Mixed-use developments are characterized by the physical and functional integration of their components. They are megastructures built around centrally located shopping galleries or hotel courtyards. Walkways, plazas, escalators, and elevators provide an interconnecting pedestrian thoroughfare with easy access to parking facilities underground, at street level, or aboveground. Because mixed-use developments bring together diverse participants, they require extensive, extraordinarily coherent planning.[4]

In mixed-use buildings each type of use reflects a number of design criteria, which must be analyzed separately. The structure must also be considered as a whole to determine how successfully it combines uses. The uses combined should be compatible, but minor incompatibilities can be alleviated with separate entrances, elevators, and equipment. In a mixed-use building without separate entrances and elevators, the residential units on upper floors and the office units below would both suffer. Only in a rather large building can the extra expense of separate features be justified. A hotel located in an office building should have its own entrance and elevators. In general security and privacy should characterize a building's residential area; a professional, prestigious image is sought for the office portion of the structure.

Mixed-use buildings are an architectural challenge. Traditional residential and commercial buildings look different and are easily distinguished from one another. These differences have been diminished, however, by the eclecticism of postmodern architecture.

SUMMARY

Architectural style, the character of a building's form and ornamentation, and *functional utility*, the usefulness of the building and its ability to perform its intended function according to current market standards and the efficiency of layout, are interrelated. Both affect the attractiveness, comfort, and maintenance of buildings because form and function work together to create successful architecture.

Architecture is the art or science of building design and construction in which three-dimensional elements are organized on a large scale to serve human needs. American architectural style is divided into *formal architecture*, which conforms to the aesthetic and functional criteria of architectural historians, and *vernacular architecture*, which reflects conventional norms and adaptations made in response to the environment or contemporary life-styles.

Market tastes and preferences are influenced by the desire to preserve tradition and by desires for innovation, which precipitates a shift away from the predominant style, and improved efficiency, which motivates energy conservation. Major changes in architectural style generally occur at the end of building cycles, about every 30 to 50 years. As the economic life of a building progresses, utility and function become the principal factors affecting its value.

Architectural style depends on the availability of natural materials, the state of technology, and the versatility of the site. Innovations that have affected building

4. For a comprehensive analysis of mixed-use developments, see Robert E. Witherspoon, Jon P. Abbett, and Robert M. Gladstone, *Mixed-Use Developments: New Ways of Land Use* (Washington, D.C.: Urban Land Institute, 1976).

design and construction include balloon and post-and-beam framing, the Franklin stove, central heating, computer and communications installations, air-conditioning, and elevators. The shape of buildings has also been influenced by the use of structural components such as steel bar joists with increased load-bearing capacity and steel and reinforced concrete framing (post-tensioning and tube bundling), which facilitate the construction of curtain walls. Technological advances have resulted in the standardization of residential and office building styles.

Climate and physical setting also affect building design and placement. The placement of trees as windbreaks, the installation of solar heating systems and heat-retaining materials, and the use of underground construction and berming are examples of environmental adaptations.

Functional inutility is an impairment of the functional capacity of a building according to market standards. It corresponds to functional obsolescence brought on by technological advances, trends in style, or superadequacies in structural components.

Functional utility is not necessarily found in the most utilitarian or efficient design, although these features are important. Suitability, comfort, safety and security, ease and cost of maintenance, market standards, attractiveness, and profitability all contribute to functional utility. The *compatibility* of a building with its use and environment must also be considered. Building compatibility involves the integration of style, form, scale, design, material, function, site, and neighborhood. Marketability is the ultimate test of functional utility.

The functional utility of a single-family or multifamily residential property depends on its layout, accommodation of special activities, adequacy, and ease and cost of maintenance. Layout considerations focus on how effectively the location of rooms within a dwelling satisfies the occupants' desire for accessibility and seclusion. Versatility of configuration is particularly evident when townhouses, lofts, and duplex apartments are converted into condominiums.

In modern residential design, the functions of many rooms are combined into fewer rooms (e.g., the living room-dining room and the family room). The adequacy of a dwelling is considered in terms of size, rooms, storage area, security, privacy, and comfort. Amenities such as well-equipped kitchens and bathrooms, parking, and recreational facilities are now often considered necessities. More family members have become wage earners, so less time is available for home maintenance. Due to rising energy costs, more attention is being focused on energy-conserving features.

In commercial buildings functional utility is considered in terms of column spacing, bay depth, live-load capacity, ceiling height, module width, elevator facilities, HVAC adequacy, energy efficiency, public amenities, parking ratios, safety, and security. The *work letter* is an agreement, usually part of a lease, that specifies which equipment and installations the landlord is to provide the tenant.

Hotels, which are a special subcategory of commercial buildings, vary according to location, the clientele served, and design. In evaluating the functional utility of hotels, fire- and sound-proofing, security, the efficient use of space, adequate facilities, and possible overimprovements are important factors.

Some industrial buildings house technical processes that involve hazardous materials and specialized equipment; others accommodate more generalized uses such as research and development. To measure the functional utility of an industrial building, an appraiser applies the market standard of optimum efficiency for comparable buildings. Reinforced concrete and steel framing with steel bar joists for greater load-bearing capacity is common in industrial construction. All industrial buildings are measured in *gross building area (GBA)*. The land-to-building ratios of industrial properties must allow space for parking and truck maneuvering. Operating layouts should facilitate efficient processing—i.e., receiving, fabricating, storage, and shipping operations.

Warehouses provide for the storage, organization, inventory, access, and delivery of materials. For functional utility, warehouses must have adequate loading facilities, ceiling height, floor load capacity, temperature and humidity control, and protection against fire and the elements.

Farm buildings include machinery sheds and barns, which provide for animal shelter, grain storage, and threshing. The mechanization of dairy and poultry farming has necessitated changes in the buildings where animals are sheltered. Farm buildings must contribute to the efficiency of the entire farm, although they generally account for less than 20% of the value of farm property.

The functional utility of special-purpose buildings depends on whether there is continued demand for their intended use and how well they conform to competitive standards for that use. Special-purpose buildings are limited because they are designed for a single use. The conversion of movie theaters, firehouses, mills, and other special-purpose properties is costly, but feasible, if the quality and design of the structures can ensure enhanced property income.

Mixed-use developments (MUDs) accommodate at least three different types of income-producing uses and are usually located in a megastructure. The functional utility of MUDs depends both on the efficiency of the individual facilities and how well the stucture as a whole combines uses.

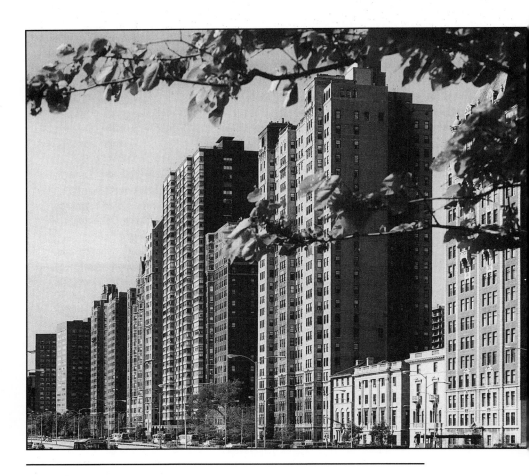

Chapter 12

HIGHEST AND BEST USE ANALYSIS

The economic principles of supply and demand, substitution, balance, and conformity are basic tools for analyzing the relationships between economic behavior and appraisal. The interdependent factors that influence value—i.e., utility, scarcity, desire, and effective purchasing power—are also economic in origin because modern value and appraisal theory has evolved from neoclassical economic thought.

The relationships between economic behavior and appraisal are clearly evident in real estate markets. In these markets where buyers and sellers of property rights interact, market value has great significance to debt and equity capital investors and to professional appraisers. In all types of property transactions, market value estimates based on careful analyses of market behavior are needed to shape financial decisions that affect individuals, neighborhoods, businesses, and governments.

An understanding of market behavior is essential to the concept of highest and best use. Market forces create market value, so the interaction between market forces and highest and best use is of crucial importance. When the purpose of an appraisal is to estimate market value, highest and best use analysis identifies the most profitable, competitive use to which the property can be put. Therefore, highest and best use is a market-driven concept.

Analyzing the highest and best use of a property may require detailed study. Elaborate studies of highest and best use are typically performed for consulting or evaluation assignments. In many appraisals, however, the nature of the assignment sets limits on the extent of the analysis to be undertaken, and the characteristics of the property restrict the number of alternative uses to be considered.

DEFINITION

Highest and best use may be defined as

the reasonably probable and legal use of vacant land or an improved property, which is physically possible, appropriately supported, financially feasible, and that results in the highest value.

To clarify the distinction between the highest and best use of 1) land or a site as though vacant, and 2) property as improved, consider a single-family residential property. If the property is located in an area zoned for commercial use, the maximum productivity of the land as though vacant will most likely be based on commercial use. If, however, the competitive level of demand is sufficient for a residential use, then the highest and best use of the property as improved will be for residential use. As long as the value of the property as improved is greater than the value of the site as unimproved, the highest and best use is use of the property as improved. Once the value of the vacant land exceeds the value of the improved residential property, the highest and best use becomes use of the land as though vacant.

The highest and best use of a specific parcel of land is not determined through subjective analysis by the property owner, the developer, or the appraiser; rather, highest and best use is shaped by the competitive forces within the market where the property is located. Therefore, the analysis and interpretation of highest and best use is an economic study of market forces focused on the subject property.[1]

Market forces also shape market value. The general data that are collected and analyzed to estimate property value are also used by the appraiser to formulate an opinion of the property's highest and best use as of the appraisal date. In all valuation assignments, value estimates are based on use. The highest and best use of a property to be appraised provides the foundation for a thorough investigation of the competitive positions of market participants. Consequently, highest and best use can be described as the foundation on which market value rests.

When potential buyers contemplate purchasing real estate for personal use or occupancy, their principal motivations are the perceived benefits of enhanced enjoyment, prestige, and privacy. Purchasers of investment property are frequently motivated by the promise of net income or capital accumulation and certain tax advantages. Investors are directly concerned with *feasibility, an indication that a project has a reasonable likelihood of satisfying explicit objectives*. These objectives may include assured occupancy, low management costs, and potential value enhancement.

Like highest and best use and market value, highest and best use and feasibility are interrelated. However, feasibility analyses may involve data and considerations that are not directly related to highest and best use determinations. A feasibility study may involve different data and have a somewhat different focus. Generally, the feasibility of developing real estate under a variety of alternative uses is studied. (See Figure 12.1.)

Figure 12.1 Relationship of Market Analysis, Feasibility Analysis, and Highest and Best Use

Market Analysis	Feasibility Analysis	Selection of Highest and Best Use
to identify demand for alternative uses	to determine respective values on the basis of criterion variables (e.g., residual land value, rate of return, capitalized value of overall property)	i.e., the use resulting in the maximum value
Supply and demand analysis to forecast absorption rate and probable rents for:	Calculation of *NOI*/cash flows and selection of appropriate cap rate/discount rate to determine property value based on criterion variables for:	Specification in terms of use, timing, and market participants
use no. 1, use no. 2, use no. 3, use no. 4	use no. 1, use no. 2, use no. 3, use no. 4	(i.e., user of the property, equity investor or debt investor)

1. The benefit a real estate development produces for a community or the amenity contribution provided by a planned project (i.e., the public space in a park-like area) are not considered in the appraiser's analysis of highest and best use.

The use that maximizes the value represents the highest and best use.

Traditionally highest and best use analysis has been associated with land residual analysis, which is derived from classical economics. In a classic land residual analysis, value is attributed to the income that remains after improvement costs are compensated. Highest and best use of the land as though vacant indicates only how the land should be used if it were vacant. Although it is primarily a tool for land valuation, it is also used by appraisers to measure a building's value contribution on the rationale that property value minus land value under highest and best use equals improvement value.

While buildings can be changed, the essential characteristics of sites cannot. The income to any particular site depends on the use decision. When an individual site can be substituted for another site in a particular market, the difference in value between the two sites is attributable to the superior features of one of the parcels of land. From this vantage point, therefore, land value is the driving force and property values in a specific market are a function of the income to the land.

The highest and best use of property as improved is a distinct concept elaborated by valuation theorists and practitioners. The concept was developed to answer an important question that the original concept does not address. How should the property as improved be used? Should the existing improvements continue to be used, or should they be demolished so new improvements can be constructed?

HIGHEST AND BEST USE OF LAND AS THOUGH VACANT

Highest and best use of land or a site as though vacant assumes that a parcel of land is vacant or can be made vacant by demolishing any improvements. With this assumption uses that create value can be identified, and the appraiser can begin to select comparable properties and estimate land value. Land as though vacant is a fundamental concept of valuation theory and the basis for the cost approach. Because many appraisals include an allocation of value between the land and the buildings associated with it, a highest and best use analysis of the land as though vacant is frequently performed.

The questions to be answered in this analysis are: If the land is, or were, vacant, what use should be made of it? What type of building or other improvement, if any, should be constructed on the land and when?

When a reasonable forecast of a property's highest and best use indicates a change in the near future, the present highest and best use is considered an interim use. For example, the highest and best use of a farm in the path of urban growth would be for interim use as a farm, with a potential future highest and best use as a residential subdivision. If the farm is ready for development at the time of the appraisal, there is no interim use. If the farm has no subdivision potential, its highest and best use is as a farm with no interim use.

In some cases an appraiser may conclude that the highest and best use of a parcel of land is to be held for speculation—i.e., to remain vacant until development is justified by market demand. This occurs frequently when real estate markets are oversupplied. For many parcels of land, however, achieving the highest and best use requires some change or improvement. The highest and best use of land as though vacant may call for its subdivision into smaller parcels of land or its assemblage with other land.

If an improvement is needed to realize the highest and best use of the land, the appraiser must determine the type and characteristics of the improvement to be constructed. For example, should the parcel of land be improved with an office building, a retail building, or a hotel? If an office building would be the highest and best use, how many stories should it have? How many offices should it contain? What size should the offices be? Which features should be included? What rental should be charged, and what level of operating expenses would be incurred? How much would such a building cost? In short, the conclusion of highest and best use for a parcel of land should be as specific as the marketplace suggests. General categories such as "an office building," "a commercial building," or "a single-family residence" may be adequate in some situations, but in others the use demanded by market participants may be more specific.

Even when a site is not vacant, it is often analyzed as though it were. Such analysis seeks to determine how desirable the current use is and whether it should be continued or superseded. The appraiser considers the site as if it were vacant to determine whether a building with the same use, size, quality, and function as the existing building should be constructed on it. If this new improvement were to be the highest and best use of the land as though vacant, it presumably would have no physical deterioration or functional obsolescence. Thus, any difference in value between the existing improvement and the new improvement would be attributable to these forms of depreciation. The appraiser also must consider external obsolescence, which would affect the existing and new improvement equally.

The present use of a site may not be its highest and best use. The land may be suitable for a much higher, or more intense, use. For instance, the highest and best use of a parcel of land as though vacant may be for a 10-story office building, while the office building that currently occupies the site has only three stories.

HIGHEST AND BEST USE OF PROPERTY AS IMPROVED

Highest and best use of a property as improved pertains to the use that should be made of an improved property in light of its improvements. For example, should a 30-year-old hotel building be maintained as it is or should it be renovated, expanded, or partly demolished? Should it be replaced with a different type or intensity of use?

The use that maximizes an investment property's value, consistent with the long-term rate of return and associated risk, is its highest and best use as improved. If potential uses require no capital expenditures for remodeling, their estimated returns can be compared directly. If capital expenditures would be required to convert the structure from its existing use to other potential uses, rates of return must be calculated for these property uses, considering the total investment in the property and all capital expenditures. These rates of return can then be compared with rates of return for uses that do not require capital expenditures.

In analyzing the highest and best use of owner-occupied properties, appraisers must consider any rehabilitation or modernization that is consistent with market preferences. For example, the highest and best use of a luxury residence should reflect all rehabilitation that would be required for maximum enjoyment of the property.

PURPOSE OF HIGHEST AND BEST USE ANALYSIS

An appraiser should distinguish between highest and best use as though vacant and highest and best use as improved in the appraisal analysis, and the appraisal report should clearly identify, explain, and justify the purpose and conclusion for each type of use.

Highest and Best Use of Land as Though Vacant

The value of land is generally estimated as though vacant.[2] When land is already vacant, the reasoning is obvious; an appraiser values the land as it exists. When land is not vacant, however, land value depends on how the land can be utilized. Therefore, the highest and best use of land as though vacant must be considered in relation to its existing use and all potential uses.

Land value can be determined by potential, rather than actual, use. For example, consider a valuable commercial site in an excellent location that is currently improved with a service station that has not had any negative environmental impact.[3] A purchaser who wants to build a high-rise office building on the site may pay a price for the property that includes no value, or even negative value, for the existing improvements. The potential use, not the existing use, usually governs the price that will be paid.

Any building can be demolished; the fact that most buildings are not does not negate the possiblity. The possibility of removing existing improvements is the premise for the concept of highest and best use of land as though vacant. Land values are not penalized so long as the existing buildings have economic value. If the buildings no longer have value, demolition is appropriate. As mentioned earlier, buildings can be changed, but the basic physical characteristics of sites cannot.

Historic district zoning controls have made demolition permits difficult if not impossible to obtain in some areas. Furthermore, special tax incentives for older buildings can substantially enhance their value and alter the highest and best use of the property in many cases.

Several appraisal techniques require a separate estimate of land value; the highest and best use of land must be identified to estimate land value under its optimal use. The highest and best use of comparable properties should be the same or similar to that of the subject property since land use influences value. Therefore, there are two reasons to identify the highest and best use of land as though vacant in an appraisal: to estimate a separate land value and to identify comparable sales of vacant land.

. Standards Rule 1-3 (b) recognizes "that land is appraised as though vacant and available for development ɔ its highest and best use and that the appraisal of improvements is based on their actual contribution to ne site." The comment explains "This guideline may be modified to reflect the fact that, in various legal nd practical situations, a site may have a contributory value that differs from the value as if vacant."
. When the highest and best use of the land as though vacant is different from that of the property as ɔrrently improved, demolition may be recommended. At this time the costs of demolition as well as the ɔsts of curing any environmental problems—e.g., the removal of underground storage tanks, the abatement f asbestos, the replacement of transformers containing PCBs—must be considered.

Highest and Best Use of Property as Improved

There also are two reasons to analyze the highest and best use of a property as improved. The first is to identify the property use that can be expected to produce the highest overall return for each dollar of capital invested. This information is important to a buyer who is economically motivated and fully informed. If, for example, a property is currently being used as rental apartments, will this use continue to provide maximum benefits or would the rate of return be increased by converting the property to an apartment hotel? The value of the property will differ under these two use assumptions, and the use that provides the highest present value is the highest and best use.

The second reason to estimate the highest and best use of property as improved is to help identify comparable properties. The highest and best use of land as though vacant and property as improved should be the same or similar for each comparable property as for the subject property. For example, it may be inappropriate to use a comparable property that has a highest and best use as offices in appraising a subject property that has a highest and best use as a hotel.

CRITERIA IN HIGHEST AND BEST USE ANALYSIS

The highest and best use of both land as though vacant and property as improved must meet four criteria. The highest and best use must be legally permissible, physically possible, financially feasible, and maximally productive. These criteria are often considered sequentially.[4] Tests of legal permissibility and physical possibility *must* be applied before the remaining tests of financial feasibility and maximal productivity. A use may be financially feasible, but this is irrelevant if it is physically impossible or legally prohibited. Only when there is a reasonable possibility that one of the prior, unacceptable conditions can be changed is it appropriate to proceed with the analysis. If, for example, current zoning does not permit a potential highest and best use, but there is a possibility that the zoning can be changed, the proposed use can be considered on that basis. Physical limitations that prevent a site from achieving its optimal use may often be overcome by applying additional capital.

Legally Permissible

In all cases an appraiser must determine which uses are legally permissible. (Nonconforming uses are discussed later in this chapter.) Private restrictions, zoning, building codes, historic district controls, and environmental regulations must be investigated because they may preclude many potential uses.

A long-term lease can also affect a property's highest and best use because, over the remaining term of the lease, property use may be limited by lease provisions. If a property is subject to a land lease that has 12 more years to run, for example, it may not be economically possible to construct a new building with a 40-year remaining economic life.[5] In such a case the appraisal report should state that the highest and best use determination is influenced by the lease's impact on

---

4. The four criteria interact and therefore may also be considered in concert. Matrix analysis is used to plot their interaction.
5. If a lease buyout were possible, the cost of the buyout plus the cost of demolition or conversion would have to be considered.

future utility. A distinction, however, must be made between the highest and best use of property and a legal requirement to use property for a particular purpose beyond its economic life.

Private restrictions and deed restrictions relate to the covenants under which properties are acquired. These restrictions may prohibit certain uses or specify building setbacks, heights, and types of materials. If deed restrictions conflict with zoning laws or building codes, the most restrictive guidelines usually prevail.

If there are no private restrictions, the property uses allowed by the zoning typically reflect the available choices in most highest and best use determinations. However, the possiblity of a change in zoning should also be considered by the appraiser. If the highest and best use of the site or property is not allowed under current zoning, but there is a reasonable probability that a change in zoning could be obtained due to shifting economic and social patterns, these conditions can be considered in determining highest and best use. However, the appraiser must fully disclose all pertinent factors relating to a possible zoning change, including the time and expense involved and the risk that the change will not be granted.

Building codes can prevent land from being developed to its highest and best use by imposing burdensome restrictions that increase the cost of construction. This is particularly common in metropolitan areas that include municipalities or jurisdictions with different building codes. Residential development in metropolitan areas has been greatly influenced by different offsite requirements in building codes. Less restrictive codes typically result in lower development costs and, therefore, attract developers; more restrictive codes tend to discourage development. Some areas limit growth by using building codes to slow new construction.

Increasing concern over the effects of land use has resulted in environmental regulations, which also must be considered in highest and best use analysis. Appraisers must be familiar with environmental regulations pertaining to clear air, clean water, and wetlands, and be sensitive to the public's reaction to proposed development projects. Resistance from local residents and the general public have stopped many real estate developments.

Physically Possible

The size, shape, area, terrain, and accessibility of a parcel of land and the risk of natural disasters such as floods or earthquakes affect the uses under which it can be developed. The utility of a parcel may also depend on its frontage and depth. Irregularly shaped parcels can cost more to develop and, after development, may have less utility than regularly shaped parcels of the same size. Ease of access enhances the utility of a site.

Certain parcels can achieve their highest and best use only as part of an assemblage. In such a case the appraiser must either determine the feasibility and probability of assembly or make the highest and best use determination and other appraisal decisions conditioned on such an assembly. For example, a large petro-chemical plant may be constructed on a site that has been created by assembling smaller tracts. The individual tracts may not have had utility for industrial use and, therefore, may have had much lower unit values.

An appraiser also considers the capacity and availability of public utilities. If a sewer main located in front of a property cannot be tapped because of a lack of capacity at the disposal plant, the property does not have access to the public sewerage system and its use is limited.

When the topography or subsoil conditions of a site make development difficult or costly, its potential use is adversely affected. All sites available for a particular use compete with one another. If the cost of grading or constructing a foundation on the site being appraised is higher than is typical for sites in the area, the subject site may be economically unusable for the highest and best use that is otherwise indicated.

The highest and best use of a property as improved also depends on physical considerations such as size, design, and condition. The condition of the property and its ability to continue in its current use may be relevant. If the property should be converted to another use, the cost of conversion must be analyzed in light of the returns to be generated by the new use. Obviously the costs of conversion depend on the property's existing physical condition.

Financially Feasible

In determining which uses are legally permissible and physically possible, an appraiser eliminates some uses from consideration. Then the uses that meet the first two criteria are analyzed further to determine which are likely to produce an income, or return, equal to or greater than the amount needed to satisfy operating expenses, financial obligations, and capital amortization. All uses that are expected to produce a positive return are regarded as financially feasible. Analyses of supply and demand and of location are needed to identify those uses that are financially feasible as well as the use that is maximally productive.

To determine financial feasibility an appraiser estimates the future gross income that can be expected from each potential highest and best use. Vacancy and collection losses and operating expenses are then subtracted from each gross income to obtain the likely net operating income *(NOI)* from each use. A rate of return on the invested capital can then be calculated for each use. If the net revenue capable of being generated from a use is sufficient to satisfy the required rate of return on the investment and provide the requisite return on the land, the use is financially feasible.

Maximally Productive

Of the financially feasible uses, the use that produces the highest residual land value consistent with the rate of return warranted by the market for that use is the highest and best use. To determine the highest and best use of land as though vacant, an appropriate rate of return that reflects the associated risk is often used to capitalize income streams from different uses into their respective values. This procedure is suitable if all competing uses have similar risk characteristics. The use that produces the highest residual land value is the highest and best use.

The residual land value can be found by estimating the value of the proposed use (land and improvements) and subtracting the cost of the labor, capital, and coordination expended to create the improvements. Alternatively the land value can be estimated by capitalizing the residual income to the land.

The land income that is capitalized into value is the residual income remaining after operating expenses and the return attributable to the creation of the improvements are allocated a market-determined portion of the property's income. Using a land residual technique, the value of the improvements is multiplied by a building capitalization rate determined in the market. The income attributable to the improvements is then subtracted from the net operating income for the total property, and the remaining income is allocated to the land. This procedure is illustrated in the next section of this chapter.

The potential highest and best uses of land are usually long-term land uses, which are expected to remain on the site for the normal economic, or useful, life of the improvements. Depending on building type, quality of construction, and other factors, most buildings are expected to last at least 25 years; some may have useful lives of more than 100 years. The stream of benefits, or income, produced by the buildings reflects a carefully considered, and usually very specific, land use program.

TESTING HIGHEST AND BEST USE

To test the highest and best use of land as though vacant or a property as improved, an appraiser analyzes all feasible alternatives. The market usually limits the number of property uses to a few logical choices. Each alternative use must first meet the tests of physical possibility and legal permissibility. The uses that meet the first two tests are then analyzed to ascertain how many financially feasible alternatives must be considered.

For example, market analysis may indicate the need for a large office building in a community. If the subject site is surrounded by modern, single-family residential developments, however, a large, multistory office building would probably not be logical, even if it were legally permitted. Similarly, a housing development for the elderly might be a permissible use for a site, but if most residents of the area are under 40 years old, this use may be illogical and would probably not meet the criterion of financial feasibility.

An appraiser must exercise caution in performing market analysis to support an estimate of highest and best use. Although a given site may be particularly well-suited for a specific use, there may be a number of other sites that are equally or more appropriate. Therefore, the appraiser must test the highest and best use conclusion to ensure that existing and potential competition from other sites has been fully recognized.

The examples that follow are presented to illustrate the determination of the highest and best use of property as though vacant and as improved.

Highest and Best Use of Land as Though Vacant

Example 1. Single-Family Residence

Consider a site zoned for detached, single-family residences. A builder has narrowed the logical development alternatives to two types of houses, both of which are compatible with other houses in the neighborhood. Use A calls for the construction of a large house with an estimated market value of $125,000, including the lot value. Use B calls for the construction of a smaller house which would be worth approximately $100,000 with the lot. Similar sites in the area have been selling for approximately $30,000. The estimated costs of constructing the two houses and their respective value estimates can be used to identify the highest and best use of the appraised land. The calculations are in the table that follows.

	Use A	Use B
Market value	$125,000	$100,000
Cost to construct new	–80,000	–75,000
Developer's fee	–15,000	–12,000
Land value	$ 30,000	$ 13,000

The larger house, Use A, is the highest and best use of the alternatives considered (assuming other alternatives were eliminated earlier in the analysis). It is the use that results in the highest residual land value. Similar sites can be expected to sell for about $30,000. Thus, if $30,000 was paid for the lot and the smaller house was built, the builder would incur a financial loss.

Example 2. Income-Producing Use
To estimate highest and best use among various income-producing uses, the available uses are generally considered in terms of their potential rates of return and perceived income stability. For example, consider a 150-ft.-by-150-ft. site in a strip commercial area that has been valued at $160,000 using the sales comparison approach. Development trends in the area suggest that the site be developed as either a retail convenience store or a commercial office building. The development costs, potential net operating incomes, and overall rates of return for the two uses are shown below.

	Retail Use	Office Use
Potential *NOI*	$55,000	$60,000
Overall capitalization rate	11%	10%
Capitalized *NOI*	500,000	600,000
Development costs	–300,000	–450,000
Residual land value	$200,000	$150,000

Of the two alternatives, the retail use requires a smaller investment and produces a greater residual land value. Thus, it is the highest and best use.

Example 3. Income-Producing Use: Alternative Approach
In the previous example, land value was calculated by deducting development costs from the estimated property value. Land value was the residual amount. An alternate approach is to assume that the income available to the land is the residual. Consider a 100-ft.-by 200-ft. site that is zoned for apartment, office, or retail use. If the logical, alternative uses are an apartment building, an office building, and a retail building, the appraiser must assemble data on the construction costs, net operating income, and market rate of return that can be anticipated for each alternative use. Cost and income figures are shown on the following page. The market capitalization rate for the improvements is 12% and the capitalization rate for the land is 10%. (Market-derived land and building capitalization rates are discussed in depth in Chapter 20.)

	Apartment Building	Office Building	Retail Building
Cost to construct	$1,200,000	$950,000	$800,000
NOI	162,000	135,000	110,000
Income to improvement (12%)	−144,000	−114,000	−96,000
Income to land	$ 18,000	$ 21,000	$ 14,000
Residual land value (income to land capitalized at 10%)	$ 180,000	$210,000	$140,000

The site's highest and best use would be represented by the office building because this use produces the greatest residual value for the land. The land residual technique is useful in testing highest and best use alternatives, but it is rarely employed to measure land value.

As the examples indicate, highest and best use is not determined by a single item such as cost, size, total income, or rate of return. Highest and best use results when an optimal combination of factors creates a maximum residual land value.

Highest and Best Use of Property as Improved

An analysis of the highest and best use of a property as improved may indicate that little or no capital expenditure is required, or it may suggest that significant expenditures are required to convert the property to a different use or to rehabilitate or remodel the existing use.

Example 1. No Capital Expenditure

Consider a single-family residence that could be converted into a combination apartment-rooming house or could be used for single-family occupancy. The first use would require no capital expenditure. The first floor could be rented to a family, while the three upstairs bedrooms would be rented as is to college students.

The downstairs could be rented for $500 per month and each of the three upstairs rooms could be rented for $100 per month. Property expenses for heat, power, repairs and maintenance, real estate taxes, insurance, and additional management cost would be approximately $2,000 per year. These expenses would be paid by the owner. Some vacancy or collection loss must be anticipated for both the downstairs and upstairs rentals.

As an alternative, the property could be rented as a single-family residence for $575 per month net— i.e., the renters would pay all property-related expenses, including property taxes and insurance. Some vacancy or collection loss must be anticipated for this use also.

Assume that an overall capitalization rate of 10% would be appropriate for either use. The calculations for comparing these alternative uses are in the following table.

	Combination Apartment-Rooming House Use	Single-Family Occupancy Use
Gross income	$ 9,600	$ 6,900
Vacancy or collection losses (5%)	−480	−345
Effective gross income	$ 9,120	$ 6,555
Expenses	−2,000	−0
NOI	$ 7,120	$ 6,555
Overall capitalization rate*	10%	10%
Value	$71,200	$65,550

*Overall capitalization rates are discussed in Chapter 20.

The figures suggest that the highest and best use of the property as improved would be a combination apartment-rooming house.

Example 2. Capital Expenditure Required

A warehouse property can be rented for $75,000 total net to the owners. However, the owners are considering converting some of the warehouse space into office space and increasing the rent. The conversion would cost approximately $125,000 and would probably add to the market value of the property, which is currently $600,000. An appraiser estimates that with the new office space the annual rent could be increased to $85,000, even though the amount of warehouse space would be reduced. The highest and best use is calculated as follows:

	Warehouse Use Only	Warehouse With Office Space
NOI	$ 75,000	$ 85,000
Overall capitalization rate	12.5%	12.5%
Capitalized NOI	$600,000	$680,000
Conversion cost	0	−125,000
Property value	$600,000	$555,000

The warehouse without offices is the highest and best use of the property as improved.

HIGHEST AND BEST USE STATEMENTS

All appraisal reports should contain summary statements that describe the appraiser's analyses and conclusions pertaining to the highest and best use of the land or site as though vacant or of the property as improved; both must be described in market value assignments where a separate site valuation is always included. When the highest and best use conclusion is the primary objective of an evaluation report, the income and return calculations and the reasoning employed should be included. If an appraiser concludes that the highest and best use of an improved property is different from its existing use, justification for this conclusion should be included in the market value appraisal report. When the highest and best use conclusions are based on techniques applied to identify the highest and best use among two or more potential uses, the full analysis is usually included in the appraisal report.

If land value is estimated separately in an appraisal, it is appropriate for the report to discuss the highest and best use of the land as though vacant as well as the highest and best use of the property as improved. If land value is not estimated separately and the appraisal is conditioned on continued use of the property as improved, the appraiser usually discusses only the highest and best use of the property as improved. In such cases the existing improvements may not represent the highest and best use of the site, but they are expected to continue in use and thus add value to the site.

Each parcel of real estate may have a highest and best use of the land or site as though vacant and a different highest and best use of the property as improved. If an appraiser comments on both the highest and best use of the land as though vacant and the property as improved, each highest and best use must be identified separately in the highest and best use section of the appraisal report. The highest and best use of the land or site is presented first, with a statement that the determination was made under the theoretical presumption that the land is vacant and available for development. Then the highest and best use of the property as improved is given with a statement that the determination was based on the future potential of the land and the existing improvements.

If the land is already improved to its highest and best use, the two statements may be combined. Nevertheless, the report should specifically state that the determination is the same for both the land as though vacant and the property as improved, or that the land is improved to its highest and best use.

An appraisal report should also identify the highest and best uses of the comparable sale properties both as though vacant and as improved. If the improved comparable properties have different highest and best uses of the land as though vacant and of the property as improved, this must also be explained. The difference could affect value, especially in the sales comparison approach.

The following examples illustrate highest and best use statements for single-family residences and income-producing properties. Obviously the statements used in a particular appraisal report should be tailored to the situation.

Example 1. Single-Family Residence—Highest and Best Use of Land as Though Vacant

This type of highest and best use is analyzed to estimate the value of land separately. The appraiser recognizes that any significant elements of physical deterioration and functional obsolescence would not be replicated if the land were vacant and a new building were constructed on the site. However, external obsolescence still must be considered. The highest and best use determination is being used in this appraisal to identify comparable properties.

The existing structure is not the highest and best use of the land as though vacant. The house was constructed approximately 10 years ago and, like most existing structures, it contains measurable elements of physical deterioration and functional obsolescence. If the site were vacant, a new single-family residence would be its highest and best use.

The architecture of the new house would be more compatible with other houses in the neighborhood. The house would contain approximately 2,000 square feet and have three bedrooms and two baths, a larger living room, and more electrical outlets. None of the elements of physical deterioration found in the existing structure would be present in the new structure.

Example 2. Single-Family Residence—Highest and Best Use of Property as Improved

In analyzing this type of highest and best use, an appraiser recognizes that existing improvements should continue to be used until it is financially advantageous to remodel the structure or demolish it and build a new one. The present use of the property as a single-family residence is its highest and best use as improved. No other use of the property would be as beneficial or as profitable.

The existing structure is well maintained and in good repair. It has an effective age of about eight years and a remaining economic life of approximately 50 years. The structure is compatible with the neighborhood, which is zoned for single-family residential occupancy only. The structure was designed as a single-family residence, and no other use would be legally or financially feasible.

Example 3. Income-Producing Property—Highest and Best Use of Land as Though Vacant

The existing structure is not the highest and best use of the land as though vacant. To analyze this type of highest and best use, an appraiser recognizes that any significant elements of physical deterioration and functional obsolescence would not be replicated if the site were vacant and a new building were constructed. The income attributable to the land under its highest and best use is capitalized to estimate the value of the land separate from the improvements. (At this point, the appraiser might state, "The valuation procedure is shown in the section titled Land Valuation.")

If the present building were razed and the site were vacant, a new commercial building would be its highest and best use. The new building would contain 16 store units, the maximum permitted by the zoning, and each store would contain about 2,000 square feet. The building would be of concrete block construction with a poured concrete floor, a flat built-up roof, and an attractive facade. It would have adequate parking facilities. No physical deterioration would be evident in the new building, and in functional layout and design it would be similar to other modern buildings of this type.

Example 4. Income-Producing Property—Highest and Best Use of Property as Improved

The existing property should be converted from office use to commercial use to maximize its productivity and value. The property currently contains 12 office units that have experienced high vacancy rates during the past two years. The units would have to be renovated and remodeled to regain a competitive position in the local office market. However, the surrounding area is in transition from residential and office uses to commercial and light industrial uses. Because substantial expenditures would be required to retain the present use or convert the structure to another use, it is recommended that the space be converted to commercial use as soon as possible.

The following calculations show the additional capital investments required to retain the existing use and to convert to commercial use, and the estimated value for each use.

	Office Use	Commercial Use
Additional capital investment	$ 50,000	$100,000
Total capital investment (initial investment of $250,000 plus cost to retain or convert to use)	$300,000	$350,000
NOI	$ 30,000	$ 50,000
Overall capitalization rate	10%	10%
Capitalized NOI	$300,000	$500,000
Renovation cost	–50,000	–100,000
Residual value	$250,000	$400,000

The figures indicate that conversion would be profitable at this time. Conversion would provide a substantially higher return on both the current investment and new capital funds. Moreover, the income produced by the commercial use would probably be less risky and longer lasting; vacancy rates for the commercial space would probably be lower.

SPECIAL SITUATIONS IN HIGHEST AND BEST USE ANALYSIS

The premises of highest and best use analysis are fundamental to all studies of the uses to which vacant land or improved properties can be put. In identifying and testing highest and best uses, however, special considerations are required to address single uses, interim uses, legally nonconforming uses, uses that are not highest and best, multiple uses, special-purpose uses, speculative uses, and excess land.

Single Uses

The highest and best uses of land or sites as though vacant and property as improved are generally consistent with, and similar to, surrounding uses. For example, a single-family residential use is usually not appropriate in an industrial neighborhood.

However, a property's highest and best use may be unusual or even unique. For example, market demand may be adequate to support one large, multistory office building in a community, but it may not support more than one. A special-purpose property such as a museum may be unique and highly beneficial to the site, but it may not be supported by surrounding land uses or comparable properties. Land value should be based on the highest and best use of property, regardless of its most likely use as suggested by surrounding land uses and comparable properties.

Interim Uses

In many instances a property's highest and best use may change in the foreseeable future. A tract of land at the edge of a city might not be ready for immediate development, but current growth trends may suggest that the land should be developed in a few years. Similarly, there may not be enough demand for office space to justify the construction of a multistory office building at the present time, but increased demand may be expected within five years. In such situations, the immediate development of sites or conversion of improved properties to their future highest and best uses is usually not financially feasible.

The use to which a site or improved property is put until it is ready for its future highest and best use is called an *interim use*. Thus, interim uses are current highest and best uses that are likely to change in a relatively short time. Farms, parking lots, old buildings, and temporary buildings may be interim uses.

Parking lot as an interim use of property
(H. Armstrong Roberts, Inc.)

An interim use may or may not contribute to the value of the site or improved property. Farming vacant land does not contribute to the site's value unless the income produced exceeds a typical return for similar vacant land that is not used for agricultural purposes. If old buildings or other uses cannot produce gross revenues that exceed reasonable operating expenses, they do not contribute to property value. If the net return is less than the amount that could be earned by the vacant land, the buildings do not have contributory value. Indeed, the value of such improved properties may be less than the value of their sites as though vacant when demolition costs are considered. The value of these sites is based entirely on their potential highest and best uses.

Many outmoded improvements clearly do not meet the tests of highest and best use, but they do create increments of value over the value of the vacant land. These improvements may appear to violate the consistent use theory but, in fact, the market simply acknowledges that, during transition to a new use, old improvements may make a property worth more than the vacant land.

Interim uses such as farming operations, parking lots, and golf courses may be contributory uses. In comparing a subject property with other properties, differences in their interim uses must be taken into account even though their future highest and best uses are identical. For example, consider two sites that are expected to be economically ready for high-rise office building construction in about five years. One property has a commercial interim use that produces $40,000 more net operating income per year than the other property, which has a parking lot as its interim use. The site with the commercial interim use might be worth $150,000 more than the other site ($40,000 for five years discounted at 10.5% with a factor of 3.743).

If the demolition costs for the two present uses are different, this must be considered and an adjustment must be made. If the present value of the future cost to demolish the commercial building is $50,000, and the parking lot will entail no demolition cost, the difference in values could be only $100,000 ($150,000 − $50,000). An appraiser must identify the interim uses of the property being appraised and all comparable properties. Differences in the prices paid may be due to different return requirements and different anticipated demolition costs.

Legally Nonconforming Uses

A legally nonconforming use is a use that was lawfully established and maintained, but no longer conforms to the use regulations of the zone in which it is located. This kind of use frequently results from new zoning laws or a change in the zoning ordinance. Zoning changes may create underimproved or overimproved properties.[6] A single-family residence located in an area that is subsequently zoned for commercial use is an underimproved property. In this case the residence will most likely be removed so that the site can be improved to its highest and best use, or the house will be considered an interim use until conversion to commercial use is financially feasible.

Nonconforming, overimproved property results when zoning changes reduce the permitted intensity of property use. For example, an old country store may be located in a neighborhood that has been rezoned for low-density residential use. Nonconforming uses may also result from changes in the permitted density of development and changes in development standards that affect features such as landscaping, parking, setbacks, and access. Zoning ordinances vary with the jurisdiction; they usually permit a preexisting use to continue, but prohibit expansion or major alterations that support the nonconforming use. When the nonconforming use is discontinued or terminated, it usually cannot be reestablished.

When valuing land with a legally nonconforming use, an appraiser must recognize that the current use may be producing more income, and thus have more value, than the property could produce with a conforming use. It may also produce more income and have a higher value than comparable properties that conform to the zoning. Therefore, to estimate the value of a legally nonconforming-use property by comparing it with similar, competitive properties in the sales comparison approach, the appraiser should make an adjustment to reflect the higher intensity of use allowed for the subject property.

In most nonconforming use situations, the property value estimate reflects the nonconforming use. Land value, however, is based on the legally permissible use,

---

6. J. Mark Quinlivan and Vance R. Johnson, "Nonconforming-Use Properties: The Concept of Positive Economic Obsolescence," *The Appraisal Journal* (January 1981). Other sources of information on highest and best use analysis are *Readings in Highest and Best Use Analysis* (Chicago: American Institute of Real Estate Appraisers, 1981), and Lincoln W. North, *The Concept of Highest and Best Use* (Winnipeg: Appraisal Institute of Canada, 1981).

assuming that the land is vacant. The difference between the property value and the land value reflects the contribution of the existing improvements and possibly a bonus for the nonconforming use. The appraiser may find it helpful to allocate value separately to the nonconforming improvements and the bonus created by the nonconforming use.

Usually any bonus resulting from a nonconforming improvement and use is directly related to the existing improvements. Therefore, the extra income or benefit should be capitalized over the economic life of the improvements.

Legally nonconforming uses that correspond to the highest and best use of the property as improved are often easy to recognize. Sometimes, however, it is not clear whether an existing nonconforming use is the site's highest and best use. The question can only be answered by carefully analyzing the income produced by the nonconforming use and the incomes that would be produced by alternative uses if the property were brought into conformity with existing regulations. Some jurisdictions specify a time period for phasing out legally nonconforming uses. In most jurisdictions, a nonconforming use must be eliminated if the property suffers major damage.

Uses That Are Not Highest and Best

Many existing buildings and other improvements do not represent the highest and best use of their sites as though vacant. Nevertheless, the highest and best use is generally in the same category as the existing use. For example, the highest and best use of a site improved with a 10-year-old apartment building may be for a new, more functional apartment building. Similarly, the highest and best use of a residential site improved with a 20-year-old house may be for a new, more modern, single-family residence. In such cases the improvement does not suffer from external obsolescence, so its value need not be discounted for inappropriate use of the site.

For certain sites the general category of highest and best use may have changed—e.g., from apartment to industrial use or from single-family residential to commercial use. The improvements on these sites suffer from external obsolescence, so they are worth less than similar improvements on more appropriate sites. It would be incorrect to value such an improvement as if it were located on an appropriate site. According to the concept of consistent use, an improvement must be valued on a basis that is consistent with the site's highest and best use.

To understand the importance of valuing a site and its improvements according to a consistent use, consider the following situation. An apartment building is located on a site that has an industrial use as its highest and best use. The land as though vacant is worth approximately $1 million, considerably more than it would be worth if its highest and best use were for apartment use. The existing apartment building on the site is worth $1.5 million, which reflects a penalty on its value; its value would be $2 million if it were located on a site appropriate for apartment use. Because both the site and the improvement must be valued according to the same highest and best use, the appraiser must consider the building's value to be $1.5 million. Consequently, the total value of the property would be $2.5 million. If the appraiser had used $2 million as the building value (and a lower land value consistent with the apartment use), an erroneous total property value would have resulted.

Multiple Uses

Highest and best use often includes more than one use for a parcel of land or a building. A large tract of land might be suitable for a planned unit development with a shopping center in front, condominium units around a golf course, and single-family residential sites on the remainder of the land. Industrial parks often have sites for retail stores in front and warehouse or light manufacturing structures in the rear.

One parcel of land may serve many functions. Timberland or pastureland may also be used for hunting, recreation, and mineral exploration. Land that serves as a right of way for power lines can double as open space or a park. Public streets with railroad siding are also considered multiple-use land.

A building can have multiple uses too. A hotel may contain a restaurant, a bar, and retail shops in addition to its guest rooms. A multistory building may house offices, apartments, and retail stores. An office building may contain retail stores and a restaurant as well as offices; a single-family, owner-occupied home may have an apartment upstairs.

Appraisers can often estimate the contributory value of each use on a multiple-use site or in a multiple-use building. If, for example, the market value of a timber tract that can be leased for hunting is compared on a unit basis with the value of another timber tract that cannot, the difference should be the value of the hunting rights. In oil-producing areas, appraisers are often asked to segregate the value of mineral rights from the value of other land uses. Some properties may have mineral rights value; others may not. In multiple-use assignments, appraisers must make sure that the sum of the separate use values does not exceed the value of the total property.

Special-Purpose Uses

Because special-purpose properties are appropriate for only one use or for a very limited number of uses, appraisers may encounter practical problems in specifying their highest and best uses. The highest and best use of a special-purpose property as improved is probably the continuation of its current use, if that use remains viable. For example, the highest and best use of a plant now used for heavy manufacturing is probably continued use for heavy manufacturing, and the highest and best use of a grain elevator is probably continued use as a grain elevator.

If the current use of a special-purpose property is physically or functionally obsolete and no alternative uses are feasible, the highest and best use of the property as improved may be realized by demolishing the structure and selling the remains for their scrap or salvage value.

Sometimes a special-purpose property must be analyzed and appraised on the basis of two highest and best uses—i.e., continuation of the existing, special-purpose use (value in use) and conversion to an alternative use (value for an alternative use). For example, a church may first be analyzed on the basis of its highest and best use as a church; in this analysis the contributory value of the improvements may be supported by cost or sales comparison data. If the demand for churches is low, the appraiser may also project a highest and best use as commercial office space. The estimated value of the improvements for conversion to this use would probably be derived from a detailed cost study or from sales data on churches converted to commercial uses.

Speculative Uses

Land that is held primarily for future sale may be regarded as a speculative investment. The purchaser or owner may believe that the value of the land will increase, but there may be considerable risk that the expected appreciation will not occur while the speculator holds the land. Nevertheless, the current value of the land is a function of its future highest and best use, so the appraiser should discuss its potential future highest and best use. The appraiser may not be able to predict the exact future highest and best use, but the general *type* of future use (e.g., as a shopping center or industrial park) is often known or indicated by the zoning or surrounding land-use patterns. Because there may be several types of potential highest and best uses (e.g., single-family or multifamily residential developments), appraisers usually cannot identify a specific future highest and best use they can, however, discuss logical alternative uses and anticipated income and expense levels.

Excess Land

Some parcels of land are too large for their principal highest and best uses. Improved sites may have excess land that does not support the existing improvement. Vacant sites or sites considered as though vacant may have land that is not needed to accommodate the site's primary highest and best use. In some cases the highest and best use of excess land is for open space or nondevelopment. In other situations the highest and best use of excess land may be for future expansion of the existing or anticipated buildings or for future development as a separate entity.

The land required to support the property's primary use, such as a parking lot for an office building or a playground for a school, is not excess land. Only land beyond the normal needs of a particular use, as determined in the market, can be considered excess land. The appraiser should clearly identify the excess land and, if appropriate, indicate its unit value separately.

Some large sites are not considered to have excess land because the acreage that is not needed for the particular use cannot be used separately. For instance, an overly large lot in an area that is 100% built up does not have excess land nor does a site that cannot be divided because of the location of its buildings.

SUMMARY

In highest and best use analysis, an appraiser identifies the most profitable, competitive use to which a property can be put. Like value, *highest and best use* is a market-driven concept. It may be defined as the reasonably probable and legal use of vacant land or an improved property, which is physically possible, appropriately supported, financially feasible, and results in the highest land value.

Highest and best use analysis is an economic study of market forces that is focused on the subject property. The general data collected and analyzed to estimate property value provide the evidence on which the highest and best use conclusion is based. Highest and best use is the basis for all valuation assignments. The concept is also linked to *feasibility*, the reasonable likelihood that a project will satisfy specific objectives. Feasibility generally pertains to income-producing property and relates to investment objectives such as stabilized occupancy, budget management, and potential value enhancement. Feasibility analyses often address considerations that are beyond the scope of highest and best use analysis.

Highest and best use is associated with the land residual concept of the classical economists—i.e., the idea that land value is equivalent to the portion of property income that remains after improvement costs are paid. Buildings can be changed, but the characteristics of sites cannot. The use decision is fundamental to determining how much income a site can produce. From this vantage point, the income to the land is the driving force of property value.

Appraisal theorists and practitioners have elaborated the highest and best use concept to address property as improved. Analyzing the highest and best use of property as improved addresses whether the existing improvement should be maintained, adapted, or demolished to make way for a new improvement.

The highest and best use of land or a site as though vacant assumes that the land parcel is vacant or can be made vacant by demolishing the existing improvements. An appraiser considers what use should be made of the land, what type of improvement should be constructed, and when. The highest and best use of land or a site as though vacant forms the basis for the cost approach.

When a property's highest and best use is expected to change in the near future, the present use is considered an *interim use*. The highest and best use of vacant land may be an exisiting use, a projected development, a subdivision, an assemblage, or a speculative holding. The highest and best use conclusion for a parcel of vacant land should be as specific as the market suggests. The highest and best use of improved property considered as though vacant may be the existing improvement, a similar improvement, or demolition of the existing building to construct a different improvement.

The highest and best use of a property as improved may be continued maintenance, renovation, expansion, partial or total demolition, or a combination of these uses. The appraiser's goal is to find the use that maximizes the value of the property. If some potential uses require capital expenditures for conversion or rehabilitation, the value of the each use minus any required renovation costs must be compared to determine which use maximizes the residual value.

The purpose of determining the highest and best use of land as though vacant is to identify a site's potential use, which governs its value. The fact that any existing improvement can be demolished validates the concept of the highest and best use of land as though vacant. The highest and best use of land as though vacant must be determined when a separate estimate of land value is required, and it is useful for identifying comparable parcels of vacant land that have been sold recently.

The purpose of determining the highest and best use of property as improved is to identify the use that is expected to produce the greatest value and to help the appraiser select comparable properties.

A property's highest and best use must be legally permissible, physically possible, financially feasible, and maximally productive. These criteria should be considered sequentially and conditionally.

Legal permissibility depends on public restrictions such as zoning, building codes, historic preservation regulations, and environmental controls as well as the private or contractual restrictions found in deeds and long-term leases. If there is a reasonable probability of a zoning change, an appraiser may consider highest and best uses that are not now legally permitted. All pertinent factors supporting the presumed zoning change must be disclosed.

The size, shape, terrain, soil conditions, and accessibility of a parcel of land affect its physical utility and adaptability. The size, design, and condition of an improved property may suggest that rehabilitation, conversion, or demolition are in order.

Financially feasible uses produce returns that exceed the income required to satisfy operating expenses, financial obligations, and capital amortization. To calculate the rate of return on invested capital, net operating income *(NOI)* is estimated by subtracting vacancy and collection losses and operating expenses from the property's gross income. Among financially feasible uses, the use that produces the highest price or value consistent with the rate of return warranted by the market is the maximally productive use.

Depending on the particular situation, various indicators may identify the highest and best use of land as though vacant. If, for example, the use decision is limited to one type of improvement, but the size of the improvement is in question, the profits produced by improvements of various sizes can indicate highest and best use. The highest and best use of income-producing property may depend solely on the overall rate of return on the investment, or it may depend on achieving an optimal relationship among investment, income, and rate of return to maximize the return to the land and the capital invested.

One capitalization rate can be used to capitalize income streams from different uses into values if the associated risks are similar. A *land residual* procedure may be used to estimate the income attributable to the land. The value of the improvements (cost to construct) is capitalized at a market-determined building rate and then subtracted from the total property income.

In determining the highest and best use of property as improved, the appraiser may consider uses for which additional capital expenditures are and are not required. In all cases the *residual value* is derived from the relationship between value and the additional capital investment.

The market usually limits the number of logical and feasible highest and best uses. The existing and potential competition from other properties suited to the same or similar uses should also be considered.

All appraisal reports should contain statements summarizing the highest and best use of land as though vacant, property as improved, or both if land value is estimated separately. In some situations the highest and best use of land as though vacant may be different from the highest and best use of the property as improved. In these cases, each determination must be stated separately; when the land is already improved to its highest and best use, the two statements may be combined.

Statements of the highest and best use of land as though vacant, for both income-producing and non-income-producing property, often indicate that land value would be maximized by demolishing an existing improvement, to eliminate accrued depreciation, and constructing a new improvement. Statements of the highest and best use of property as improved may recommend that the existing improvements be maintained for the same use or converted to a different use.

Special considerations are involved in the determination of highest and best use in appraising single uses, interim uses, legally nonconforming uses, uses that are not highest and best, multiple uses, special-purpose uses, speculative uses, and excess land.

In *single-use* situations the highest and best use may be unusual or unique. Land value should be based on this use, not the most likely use. The *interim uses* of sites or improved properties are highest and best uses that are anticipated to change within a short time. Interim uses may or may not contribute to value, and demolition costs and the costs to cure any environmental problems must be considered for improvements with interim uses.

A *legally nonconforming use* is a use that was lawfully established and maintained, but no longer conforms to the use regulations of the zone in which it is located. Zoning changes often result in underimproved or overimproved properties with legally nonconforming uses. A nonconforming use may produce more income for the property than a conforming use, and more income than is produced by comparable properties that conform with zoning. Both the economic life of the improvements and any regulations pertaining to nonconforming uses must be considered.

The existing use is not the highest and best use of a site when the use provided by the improvement is inconsistent with changes in neighborhood use patterns. In such cases the appraiser should apply *consistent use* criteria when valuing the land and improvements. Highest and best use may indicate *multiple uses* for a parcel of land or a building. In multiple-use situations, the appraiser estimates the *contributory value* of each use, making sure that the sum of the individual values does not exceed the value of the total property.

Properties with *special-purpose uses* may sometimes be considered in terms of both their *value in use* and their potential *alternative use value*. A *speculative land* investment is created when a buyer holds land in anticipation of appreciation. Although the specific future highest and best use of such land may not be predictable, logical alternatives can usually be identified. *Excess land* is land not needed to support the existing improvement or to accommodate the primary highest and best use of a vacant site or site considered as though vacant. Excess land should be clearly identified.

Chapter 13

LAND OR SITE VALUATION

$\mathcal{T}$he supply of land is relatively stable. Although vast changes have occurred in the earth's surface over the ages, and slight modifications in the supply and quality of land may occur over a lifetime, these natural events rarely affect the land with which appraisers are concerned.

There are, however, a few notable exceptions to the permanence of land, such as the accretion or erosion of land along a shoreline, the pollution of land with harmful wastes, the exhaustion of agricultural land through improper farming methods, and the transformation of arable land into desert due to ecological imbalances. Earthquakes may change the surface of the earth and faults beneath the surface can create vast sinkholes. Fortunately, these occurrences are rare.

Land has value because it provides potential utility as the site of a structure, recreational facility, agricultural tract, or right-of-way for transportation routes. If land has utility for a specific use and there is demand for that use, the land has value to a particular category of users. Beyond the basic utility of land, however, there are many principles and factors that must be considered in land valuation. Although it is sometimes considered the simplest of appraisal tasks, the valuation of land requires careful analysis of a complex variety of factors.

LAND VALUATION THEORY

Value Concepts and Principles

Anticipation, change, supply and demand, substitution, and balance are appraisal principles that influence land value. Anticipation means that value is created by the expectation of benefits to be derived in the future. Therefore, if buyers anticipate that sites in a certain location will be in demand for office use within the next five years, they may be motivated to acquire land for development even though the development of office space is not presently tenable. The competition among buyers who make up the market for these sites creates a price level for the land that may have little to do with its current use. In such circumstances the highest and best use of the sites could be speculative holding for eventual office development.

The supply of and demand for sites in a particular location tend toward equilibrium. If supply declines and demand remains stable or increases, prices rise. Conversely, if the supply of sites for a particular use increases and demand remains stable or declines, prices fall. Temporary imbalances between supply and demand are usually resolved and equilibrium is reestablished. The price of property reflects this relationship. When prices drop sufficiently, supply will contract because existing uses will be retained. When prices rise, a new supply may be created through rezoning, annexation, or abandonment of existing uses.

Although the supply of and demand for sites tend toward ultimate equilibrium, this principle may not apply in the short run. If one type of site is very scarce in a particular location, the pressure of intense market competition may increase the value of a site beyond the level indicated by its profitability. For example, the rents that can be obtained for office space in a particular location may not justify the high prices being paid for office sites. Similarly, the prices that can be obtained for improved residential properties may not justify the high prices paid for the last few lots in a popular location. Nevertheless, market value is generally the most probable price the market can sustain. Eventually, the equilibrium among rents, prices, and land values will be reestablished; if all other factors remain constant, rents will rise or prices will fall.

Land value is substantially affected by the interplay of supply and demand, but it is the economic use of a site that determines its value in a particular market. For example, the price that a developer can afford to pay for a warehouse site is determined by the net income that the warehouse will earn and the cost of constructing it. Intense competition for choice sites or for the last remaining sites in a particular location can cause prospective owners or owner-occupants to pay more for a particular site than is indicated by the broad spectrum of market activity and the highest and best use of the site.

The principle of substitution, which holds that a buyer will not pay more for one site than for another that is similar or equal, applies to land values and indicates that the greatest demand will be for the lowest-priced sites. The principle of balance is also applicable to land values. When the various elements of a particular economic mix or a specific environment are in a state of equilibrium, value is sustained; when the balance is upset, values change. If, for example, a district has too much industrially zoned land, property values will probably fall. Because prices are usually quoted in inflated, not constant, dollars, prices may appear to be increasing when they are actually falling or remaining level.

Definition of the Appraisal Problem

At the start of a valuation assignment, an appraiser identifies the real estate and property rights to be valued, specifies the date and use of the appraisal, defines the type of value, and states the limiting conditions that govern the appraisal report. The next step is the selection and analysis of comparable data. The appraiser must identify all property rights, legal encumbrances, physical characteristics, and site improvements that pertain to the land in question.

Property Rights and Public Controls

The appraisal of land focuses on valuing the property rights attached to the land. These include the rights to develop the land within certain limits, to lease it to others, to farm it, to mine it, to alter its topography, to subdivide it, to assemble it, and to use it for waste disposal. Whenever possible, an appraiser should consult public records to identify easements, rights-of-way, and private or public restrictions that affect the subject property.

Because the supply of land cannot keep pace with the demand for it, governments regulate how land can be used and developed. Most municipalities and counties have some form of zoning that specifies how a parcel of land can be developed. In addition to zoning, many jurisdictions now have master plans that specify long-term development goals. Developers frequently must provide public amenities such as open space, streets, and adjacent or offsite public improvements to acquire development rights. Sometimes developers can proceed with development only after they submit approved site plans. In some areas citizen groups may protest a development they do not like, and their wishes frequently influence the type of development that is finally approved.

Through the power of eminent domain, the government can remove land from private use to augment the supply of public land or to modify land use through urban renewal programs. In some rural jurisdictions land use is influenced by government-sponsored transferable development rights (TDRs), which compensate farmers for retaining land in agricultural use and shift the cost of development to developers. Lower ad valorem taxes on agricultural land also affect rural land use; this form of tax subsidy tends to extend the duration of agricultural uses.

A significant amount of land in the United States has been encumbered with open space or conservation easements in perpetuity. These permanent encumbrances limit or prohibit the subdivision of land to prevent further development. Land subject to perpetual open space or conservation easements is usually restricted to its existing use, as specified in the deed of easement. These deeds are vested in preservation or conservation trusts. Other encumbrances prohibit the demolition or alteration of historic structures.

Physical Characteristics and Site Improvements

The physical characteristics of land, the available utilities, and site improvements affect land use and value. The physical characteristics of a parcel of land that an appraiser must consider are size and shape, frontage, topography, location, and view. Topographical characteristics include the land's contour, grade, and drainage.

The availability of utilities such as water, sewers, electricity, natural gas, and telephone service also influences the use and development potential of a parcel of land. Utilities may be provided by offsite facilities such as public water mains, sewers, and power lines or by onsite facilities such as spring basins, drilled domestic wells, and septic tanks.

A parcel of land becomes a *site* when it is improved and ready to be used for a specific purpose. A site may have both onsite and offsite improvements that make it suitable for its intended use or development. Necessary onsite improvements include grading, landscaping, paving, and utility hookups for water, gas, electricity, and telephone. Essential offsite improvements include streets, curbs, sidewalks, drains, and connecting utility lines. Site improvements are typically considered part of site value; only rarely are they valued with other property improvements. Like buildings and other structures, site improvements are subject to physical and functional obsolescence.

Highest and Best Use

Land value must always be considered in terms of highest and best use. Even if the site has improvements, the value of the land is based on its highest and best use as though vacant and available for development to its most economic use. Consideration of the land as though vacant is a commonly accepted procedure which facilitates the orderly analysis and solution of appraisal problems that require land to be valued as a separate component. Land has first claim to any income generated by the property and priority over any return on the improvements. Land value may be equal to, or even greater than, total property value, even when substantial improvements are located on the site.

Highest and best use is also affected by how much existing improvements contribute to property value. The contribution of the improvements is estimated by subtracting the value of the land from the value of the total property. Land is said to *have value*, while improvements *contribute to value*. When improvements do not contribute to property value, demolition is indicated. In this case the cost of converting the property into a vacant site is a penalty, or negative building contribution, to be deducted from the value of the land.

In some circumstances the appraisal of a property may require that the site be considered in terms other than its highest and best use. In an appraisal to estimate the use value or legal, nonconforming use value of an improved site, an appraiser may need to value the site according to its specified use or the existing improvements, not its highest and best use. In this case the appraiser should value the site both in terms of its highest and best use and its conditional use.

LAND VALUATION TECHNIQUES

The six procedures used to value land are:

1. Sales comparison
2. Allocation
3. Extraction
4. Subdivision development
5. Land residual
6. Ground rent capitalization

All six procedures are derived from the three basic approaches to value. Sales comparison and income capitalization (i.e., ground rent capitalization) can be directly applied to land valuation. Allocation and extraction procedures reflect the influence of the sales comparison and cost approaches; the land residual technique is based on the income capitalization and cost approaches. Subdivision development draws on elements of all three approaches.

Sales Comparison

The sales comparison approach may be used to value land that is actually vacant or land that is being considered as though vacant for appraisal purposes. Sales comparison is the most common technique for valuing land and it is the preferred method when comparable sales are available. To apply this method, sales of similar parcels of land are analyzed, compared, and adjusted to provide a value indication for the land being appraised. In the comparison process the similarity or dissimilarity of the parcels is considered.

The appraiser gathers data on actual sales and ground leases as well as listings, offers, and renewal options; identifies the similarities and differences in the data; ranks the data according to their relevance; adjusts the sale prices of the comparables to account for the dissimilar characteristics of the land being appraised; and forms a conclusion as to the most reasonable and probable market value of the subject land.

Elements of comparison include property rights, legal encumbrances, financing terms, conditions of sale (motivation), market conditions (sale date), location, physical characteristics, available utilities, zoning, and highest and best use. The most variable elements of comparison are the physical characteristics of the site, which include its size and shape, frontage, topography, location, and view. (A more complete discussion of elements of comparison appears in Chapter 17.) The units of comparison applied in the analysis may be acres, square feet, front feet, lots, or any other units used in the market. For example, land value may be expressed in dollars per apartment unit, per apartment room, or per square foot of net or gross building area. It is usually wise to correlate the results of two or more units of comparison in arriving at a land value estimate—e.g., dollar per acre and per lot or dollars per unit and per square foot.

If sale prices have been changing rapidly over the past several years and an adequate amount of sales data are available, the sales selected for comparison should take place as close to the effective appraisal date as possible. If an appraiser must choose between transactions involving properties close to the subject property that occurred several years ago and recent transactions in more distant locations, a balance must be struck. The more recent sales will probably be most indicative.

Size is generally a less important element of comparison than date and location. Most types of development have an optimal site size; if the site is larger, the value of the excess land tends to decline at an accelerating rate. Because sales of different sizes may have different unit prices, appraisers ordinarily give more weight to comparables that are approximately the same size as the subject property.

Zoning is often the most basic criterion in selecting comparables. Sites zoned the same as the subject property are the most appropriate comparables. If sufficient sales in the same zoning category are not available, data from similar categories can be used after adjustments are made. As a general rule, the greater the dissimilarity between the subject and the comparables, the more potential there is for distortion and error in sales comparison.

In addition to recorded sales and signed contracts, appraisers should consider offers to sell, offers to purchase, and other incomplete transactions. Offers provide less reliable data than signed contracts and recorded sales. Usually the final sale price is lower than the initial offer to sell, but higher than the initial offer to buy. Negotiation can take place in several stages.

Data on land sales are available from sources such as electronically transmitted and printed data services, newspapers, and records of deeds and assessments. Interviews with the parties involved in transactions—i.e., the buyers, sellers, lawyers, and brokers—can provide more direct information. After comparable data are collected and categorized and the comparable properties are examined and described, sales data can be assembled in an organized, logical manner. Sales are commonly arranged on a market data grid that has separate columns for important categories of property characteristics. Adjustments for dissimilarities between the subject property and the comparable properties are made to the sale prices of the comparables. Paired data and patterned analyses may be used to isolate the effects of individual variables. (Paired data analysis and valuing land with the sales comparison approach are discussed in Chapter 17.)

Generally separate adjustments are made to the comparable sale prices for each unit of comparison. The magnitude of each adjustment is indicated by the data. Land parcels of different sizes sell at different unit prices because the optimal size of a parcel depends on its use. Unit prices also vary with the sale date and location. If the data selected are not sufficient to indicate the magnitude of the adjustments required, the appraiser must gather and analyze additional comparable data.

A sale price adjustment can be simply an acknowledgment of a property's superior or inferior quality, or it may be a precise dollar sum or percentage. Adjustments can also be totaled and factored into the comparable sale prices. Typically, adjustments are made in a particular order—i.e., adjustments for property rights, financing, and sale and market conditions are made before adjustments for location and physical characteristics. All adjustments should be presented in a logical and understandable manner in the appraisal report.

Allocation

Vacant sites in densely developed urban locations may be so rare that their values cannot be estimated by direct comparison. Similarly, sales of vacant sites in remote rural areas may occur so seldom that comparable data are inadequate. In such cases land value can be estimated by allocation or extraction.

The allocation method is based on the principle of balance and the related concept of contribution, which affirm that there is a normal or typical ratio of land value to property value for specific categories of real estate in specific locations. This ratio is generally more reliable when the subject property includes relatively new improvements. With older improvements the ratio of land value to total value increases. The allocation method does not produce conclusive value indications, but it can be used to establish land value when the number of vacant land sales is inadequate.

For example, allocation could be used in an appraisal assignment to value parcels of lakefront land used as sites for vacation homes. Assume that no sales of vacant land have occurred recently, but the appraiser has ascertained that houses on the lake have sold for $150,000 to $200,000. A developer of lakefront houses in a nearby area can purchase a lot of the same size for $60,000, build a house for $90,000, and make $30,000 in profit and overhead. The developer's total improvement contribution is $120,000 and the total property value is $180,000, of which the land represents one third.

The appraiser must recognize that, in such an enterprise, the profit and overhead accrue from the developer's expertise and assumption of risk. No profit or overhead is imputable to the land, which is appraised as vacant, unimproved, and available for development. None of the developer's profit or overhead can be allocated to the unimproved lot, and none can be attributed to the seller of the lot. In short, the lot price paid to the seller does not include profit or overhead.

The ratio of land value to total property value in the completed development is 0.33 1/3 to 1.0. The indicated land values for homes around the lake range from $50,000 (0.33 1/3 x $150,000) to approximately $66,600 (0.33 1/3 x $200,000). This is a rough estimate because more expensive and less expensive dwellings may be built on equally valuable lakefront lots.

Extraction

Extraction is a variant of the allocation method in which land value is extracted from the sale price of an improved property by deducting the value contribution of the improvements, which is estimated from their depreciated costs. The remaining value represents the value of the land. Improved sales in rural areas are frequently analyzed in this way because the building's contribution to total property value is generally small and relatively easy to identify.

For example, an appraiser takes on an assignment that requires an estimate of the site value of a vacant lot in a fully developed, older neighborhood. No vacant lots have been sold in the neighborhood recently, and the allocation procedure yields inconclusive results. Three improved properties on lots near the subject have recently been sold and these lots are identical to the subject in size. From the sale price of each property, the appraiser deducts the contribution of the depreciated improvements (improvement cost new less depreciation) to establish a range of site values. It is reasonable to assume that the value of the subject site will fall within this range.

The land value estimates produced with the extraction method can also be used with the data gathered from vacant land sales in sales comparison. Sometimes, the extraction technique is applied to assessment ratios rather than specific numerical amounts. However, a value indication derived in this way is generally not persuasive because the assessment ratios may be unreliable and the extraction method does not reflect market considerations.

Subdivision Development

The subdivision development method is used to value land when subdivision and development represent the highest and best use of the appraised parcel and sales data on finished lots are available. Subdivision development analysis may involve industrial, residential, or recreational land. The subdivision of land is the normal pattern of real estate development. A landowner divides a large plot into smaller parcels to sell or lease them. A planned subdivision can create a higher, better, and more intense property use when zoning, available utilities, community conditions, access, and other influential elements are favorably combined. Traditionally subdivision developers divide large tracts into smaller plots and create roads, drainage systems, public utilities, and other improvements that are required by local law and zoning ordinances.

An appraiser begins to analyze a subdivision development by determining the number and size of the lots that can be created from the appraised land physically, legally, and economically. The proposed lots must conform to jurisdictional and zoning requirements with regard to size, frontage, topography, soil quality, and land improvements— e.g., water facilities, drainage, sewage, streets and curbs. The lots must also meet the demands of the market in which the property is located. Without surveys and engineering studies, an appraiser cannot know exactly how many lots can be created from a particular parcel of land. However, a reasonable estimate of the number of potential lots can be deduced from zoning and subdivision ordinances or, preferably, from the number of lots created in similar subdivisions. Allowance must also be made for land needed for streets and green space.

A sales comparison analysis of finished lots is then undertaken. After adjusting the comparable sales for differences, the appraiser estimates the most likely retail sale prices of the lots, the probable development period, and the absorption rate.

All direct and indirect costs associated with developing and marketing the lots must be deducted from the sum of their projected sale prices. These costs may include the engineering expenses to clear, grade, and finish the land; to build streets, roads, and sidewalks; and to install utilities. Carrying costs such as taxes, insurance premiums, overhead expenses, and inspection fees must be considered along with marketing costs for sales commissions and advertising. Further deductions must be made to provide an appropriate return on the total investment during the development period and an entrepreneurial profit for the developer.

Development and marketing costs and entrepreneurial profit are deducted from the projected gross sale price to arrive at the net sales proceeds. The periodic net sales proceeds are then discounted to present value at an appropriate yield rate over the estimated period required for project development and market absorption. The result is an indication of the value of the raw land. The discount rate selected should reflect the risk involved and be supportable in the market.

To illustrate the subdivision development procedure, consider a 10-acre tract of land that a developer wants to subdivide into 25 residential lots. The projected gross sale prices of the developed lots total $500,000. The following costs will be incurred in site development.

Development costs for grading, clearing, paving, and curbing; sewage and water lines; and design engineering	$150,000
Management and supervision	7,500
Contractor's overhead and profit*	50,000
Sales expenses	17,500
Taxes	10,000
Entrepreneurial profit†	30,000
Total	$265,000

* Contractor's profit must be distinguished from entrepreneurial profit. Contractor's profit is considered a direct cost in site development.
† Entrepreneurial profit is generally treated as a line item and may be estimated differently in different markets. In this example it is approximately 13% of total hard and soft costs ($30,000/$235,000).

If all sales and development costs were incurred at once, the indicated land value would be the difference between the total projected gross sale price and all anticipated development costs, carrying and sales costs, and entrepreneurial profit ($500,000 - $265,000 = $235,000). However, development is projected to take four years, so discounting must be employed. The discount rate selected should reflect the risk incurred during the anticipated selling period. In this example, a 10% discount rate was selected. The average, annual return on the net income is calculated as follows.

$$\$235,000/4 = \$58,750$$

The present value of $58,750 can be obtained by applying the present value of $1 per period factor for four years at 10%, which is 3.1699.

$$\$58,750 \times 3.1699 = \$186,230 \text{ (rounded)}$$

(The application of present value factors is covered in Chapter 21.)

So, the developer can afford to pay $186,230 for the land in view of antici-
pated development costs, carrying and sales costs, and entrepreneurial profit. As
an additional check, this land value can be compared with the prices being paid
for similar parcels of raw land that have subdivision development as their highest
and best use. There are several, more sophisticated variations of this procedure in
which the timing of cost and income flows are itemized on a year-to-year basis.
These techniques also involve the application of growth rates.

The subdivision development method of land valuation is used in feasibility
studies and in appraisals when comparable sales are scarce. Nevertheless, bona
fide sales data provide a better indication of value than a subdivision development
prospectus.

Land Residual

The land residual technique may also be used to estimate land value when sales
data on similar parcels of vacant land are not available. This technique is based
on the principle of balance and the related concept of contribution, which are
concerned with equilibrium among the agents of production—i.e., labor, capital,
coordination, and land. The land residual technique can be used to estimate land
value when 1) building value is known or can be accurately estimated, 2) stabilized, annual net operating income to the property is known or can be estimated,
and 3) both building and land capitalization rates can be extracted from the market. Building value can be estimated for new or proposed buildings that represent
the highest and best use of the property and have not yet incurred physical deterioration or functional obsolescence.

To apply the land residual technique, an appraiser first determines what actual or hypothetical improvements represent the highest and best use of the site.
Then the stabilized, annual net operating income to the property is estimated
from market rents and operating expenses as of the date of the appraisal. Next,
the appraiser calculates how much of the income is attributable to the building
and subtracts this amount from the total net operating income. The remainder is
the residual income to the land, which is capitalized at a market-derived capitalization rate to provide an estimate of land value.

To illustrate the application of the land residual technique, assume that a
developer engages an appraiser to estimate the value of a site that he plans to
purchase. The developer intends to use the site to construct a professional office
building, which is considered the highest and best use of the site. The appraiser's
investigation of the local market indicates that the total property can be expected
to produce a net operating income of $100,000 per year. The market indicates a
building capitalization rate of 8% and a land capitalization rate of 6%. The value
of a new building with no depreciation is estimated to be $350,000.

NOI	$100,000
Less income to the building	
$(I_B = V_B \times R_B)$ $350,000 \times 0.08$ =	28,000
Income attributable to the land	$72,000
Land value	
$(V_L = I_L/R_L)$ $72,000/0.06$ =	$1,200,000

In this example the property is assumed to be free and clear of debt. If the purchase of the land or the construction of the improvement were to be finance other items would have to be considered. With sufficient market data to indica the value of the building, the property's anticipated net operating income, and land and building capitalization rates, the value of the land can be calculated.

There are several variations of the land residual technique. In one variation the property is valued as improved and the cost of the improvements and any profit are deducted. The sum remaining is the residual value of the land. The land residual technique can be used when comparable sales are lacking and as check on the sales comparison approach. It may be most useful in testing the feasibility of alternative uses of a particular site.

Ground Rent Capitalization

Ground rents can be capitalized at an appropriate rate to indicate the market value of a site. *Ground rent is the amount paid for the right to use and occupy the land according to the terms of the ground lease.* It corresponds to the value the landowner's interest in the land, the leased fee interest. Market-derived cap talization rates are used to convert ground rent into market value. This procedu is useful when an analysis of comparable sales of leased land indicates a range rents and capitalization rates. If the current rent corresponds to market rent, th value indication obtained by applying a market capitalization rate will be equiv lent to the market value of the fee simple interest in the land. If the ground ren paid under the terms of the existing contract does not correspond to market re the ground rent must then be adjusted for the difference in property rights to obtain an indication of the market value of the fee simple interest.

Ground leases can have different terms and escalation clauses, so the appraiser should consider all benefits to the lessor during the term of the lease an the option periods and determine when the reversion of the property will take place. An alternative method of ground rent capitalization involves discounting anticipated cash flows (rental income) over the holding period and the reversion or lump-sum benefit, received upon termination of the investment.

SUMMARY

The supply of land is relatively stable. Although physical and ecological change may result in the accretion or destruction of land, these occurrences are rare. Land has value because it has specific utility and is in demand. Several apprais concepts and principles contribute to the formation of land value. Anticipation the expectation of increased demand for sites suitable to a particular use, moti vates speculators to acquire land. The supply of and demand for sites tend tow equilibrium in the long run, but short-term imbalances do occur. Intense mark competition can create land values that exceed profitability. The principle of su stitution holds that the greatest demand is generated for the lowest-priced sites. Balance implies that value is sustained when the various elements in an econom or environmental mix are in equilibrium.

The first steps in land valuation are identification of the real estate and pro erty rights to be valued, specification of the date and use of the appraisal, and definition of the value and limiting conditions that govern the appraisal. Encum brances on property rights include easements, rights of way, and restrictions in private deeds and public zoning ordinances. Governments adopt master plans to direct development, sponsor transferable development rights to preserve agricultural or conservation uses, and take land for public use through the power of eminent domain.

An appraiser collects and analyzes data on the subject and comparable land parcels, identifying the property rights involved, any legal encumbrances, the physical characteristics of the sites, and all available utilities and site improvements that may affect the site's development potential. The value of a site or parcel of land is based on its highest and best use as though vacant and available for development to its most economic use. Land is assumed to have prior claim to the income generated by the property before any return to the improvements. Land is said to have value, while improvements contribute to value. Improvements that make no contribution to property value constitute a value penalty equal to the cost of their demolition. A site's highest and best use may be the existing use or a different use. The statement of highest and best use should be as specific as the market warrants.

The six procedures used in land valuation are all derived from the three approaches to value. *Sales comparison* is the most commonly used and preferred method to value land when comparable data are available. Using this technique, data on sales of similar parcels of land are analyzed, compared, and adjusted for their dissimilarity to the subject property.

Elements of comparison include property rights, legal encumbrances, financing terms, sale and market conditions, location, physical characteristics, available utilities, zoning, and highest and best use. The units of comparison applied should be those used in the market. Two or more units of comparison may be correlated. Generally, sale prices are adjusted for each unit of comparison and a market data grid is used to organize the data.

Data on land sales that are most similar to the subject are given the greatest weight. Appraisers analyze data on actual transactions and relevant listings and offers. The *allocation* procedure is based on the typical ratio of land value to improvement value for specific categories of real estate in specific locations. When the improvements are recent, the ratio is more dependable; as improvements age, the ratio of land value to total value increases. Allocation is less conclusive than other procedures, but it is useful when data on comparable transactions are not available.

Extraction is a similar procedure in which the contribution of the improvements is deducted from the total property value. The land value derived with this procedure should be compared with any available data on vacant land sales. Extraction is used to estimate the land value of improved properties in rural areas and in situations in which the building contributes little to total property value.

The *subdivision development* procedure is used to value land when subdivision and development represent the highest and best use of the land being appraised and sales data on finished lots are available. The appraiser begins by determining the number and size of the lots that can physically, legally, and economically be created from the parcel of land. Then finished lots are analyzed to estimate the likely sale price, development period, and absorption rate for the projected lots. From the anticipated gross sale price, the appraiser deducts all direct and indirect costs and an entrepreneurial profit. The net sales proceeds are discounted to present value with a market-derived yield rate for the period required for project development and market absorption. The resulting value indication should be compared with the prices being paid for similar parcels of raw land that have subdivision and development as their highest and best use. There are several, sophisticated variations of this procedure.

The *land residual* procedure is used when sales data on similar parcels of vacant land are not available. To apply this procedure, known or estimable building value, known or estimable property *NOI*, and market-extracted building and land capitalization rates are needed. The appraiser determines what actual or hypothetical improvements represent the highest and best use of the site and the stabilized annual *NOI* to the property is estimated. The portion of the *NOI* attributable to the building is deducted from total *NOI* and the remainder, the residual income to the land, is capitalized at a market-derived rate to provide an estimate of land value. In another variant of the land residual procedure, the appraiser simply values the property as improved and deducts the cost of the improvements and an entrepreneurial profit from the total property value.

Ground rent capitalization is used to value land when the ground rent corresponds to the value of the landowner's interest in the property. Market-derived capitalization rates are used to convert ground rent into an indication of the market value of the land. This procedure is useful when comparable sales of leased land indicate a range of rents and capitalization rates.

Chapter 14

THE COST APPROACH

$\mathcal{T}$he cost approach to value, like the sales comparison and income capitalization approaches, is based on comparison. In the cost approach the cost to develop a property is compared with the value of the existing property or a similarly developed property. When applicable, the cost approach reflects market thinking by recognizing that market participants relate value to cost. Buyers tend to judge the value of an existing structure by considering the prices and rents of similar buildings and the cost to create a new building with optimal physical condition and functional utility. Moreover, buyers adjust the prices they are willing to pay by estimating the costs to bring an existing structure up to the physical condition and functional utility they desire.

Therefore, in applying the cost approach, an appraiser attempts to estimate the difference in worth to a buyer between the property being appraised and a newly constructed building with optimal utility. The appraiser estimates the cost to construct a reproduction of, or replacement for, the existing structure and site improvements (including direct costs, indirect costs, and an appropriate entrepreneurial profit), and then deducts all accrued depreciation in the property being appraised from the reproduction or replacement cost of the structure as of the effective appraisal date. When the value of the site is added to this figure, the result is an indication of the value of the fee simple interest in the property.

The data used in the sales comparison approach reflect the market's reaction to items of accrued depreciation. One way to estimate the total amount of accrued depreciation in a comparable property is by allocating its sale price between the land and the improvements and then deducting the contribution of the improvements from the estimated reproduction or replacement cost. If the price allocated to the improvements is less than their current reproduction or replacement cost, there is accrued depreciation. In applying the cost approach, an appraiser attempts to identify and quantify the causes of accrued depreciation and relate them to the subject property. The development of appraisal methodology is an evolving process, and practitioners who apply the cost approach must adapt it to the needs of the appraisal problem as well as the conventions of contemporary appraisal practice.

RELATION TO APPRAISAL PRINCIPLES

Substitution

The principle of substitution is basic to the cost approach. This principle affirms that no prudent buyer would pay more for a property than the cost to acquire a similar site and construct improvements of equal desirability and utility without undue delay. Older properties can also be substituted for the property being appraised, and their value is measured relative to the value of a new, optimal property. Consequently, the reproduction cost of a property on the effective date of the appraisal plus its site value provides a measure against which prices for improved properties may be judged.

Supply and Demand

Although markets tend toward equilibrium, market forces change and as they change different points of equilibrium (i.e., prices) result. Shifts in supply and demand cause prices to increase or decrease. Thus, one property may have different values over time. If costs do not shift in proportion to price changes, the construction of buildings will be more or less profitable and the value of existing buildings will increase or decrease commensurately.

Balance

The principle of balance holds that the agents of production and the various property components must be in proper proportion if optimum value is to be achieved or sustained. An improper economic balance may result in an underimprovement or an overimprovement. An underimprovement is created by too little investment in the improvements relative to the value of the site; an overimprovement is created by too much investment.

Any excess or deficiency in the proportionate contributions of the site and the improvements results in a loss in value relative to their cost. An imbalance in the various components of the improvements also produces a loss in value. In the cost approach the value differential resulting from an excess or deficiency is measured by deducting depreciation from the estimated reproduction or replacement cost of the improvements as of the effective appraisal date.

Externalities

When supply and demand are in balance and credit is available, the cost of new improvements plus an appropriate entrepreneurial profit minus depreciation plus the value of the site equals market value. However, properties can gain or lose value due to external conditions or events. Gains or losses in value caused by externalities may accrue to both land and buildings. Rising construction costs can significantly affect the market value of new construction and, in turn, the market value of older, substitute properties.

In the cost approach a loss in building value due to external causes is ascribed to external obsolescence, one of the three major types of accrued depreciation. If, for example, an industrial plant that depends on trucks to transport its product is located a great distance from a recently completed highway, the property may suffer from external obsolescence.

External conditions can cause a newly constructed building to be worth more or less than its cost. If a certain type of property is scarce or it is difficult to construct new competitive properties, the value of a newly constructed building may be higher than its reproduction or replacement cost. On the other hand, an economic recession might create an oversupply of a certain type of property, which would cause the value of a new property to be less than its reproduction or replacement cost. In the late 1980s and early 1990s, external obsolescence most often has been attributed to declining market conditions. Externalities may have an especially strong effect on older properties.

Highest and Best Use

The concept of highest and best use is fundamental to real property value. In one application of the concept, a site is valued as though vacant and available for its highest and best use; in the other application, the highest and best use of the property as improved is estimated. Thus, a site may have one highest and best use as though vacant, and the existing combination of site and improvements may have another highest and best use. Existing improvements have a value equal to the amount they contribute to the site or they may penalize value by an amount equal to the cost to remove them from the site.

Existing improvements that do not develop the site to its highest and best use are worth less than their reproduction or replacement cost. A new building that is poorly designed is worth less than its reproduction cost due to the functional obsolescence in its design. Thus, the improvement that constitutes highest and best use is the one that adds the greatest value to the site.

HISTORICAL BACKGROUND

The appraisal procedures that are now identified as the three approaches to value were developed after the stock market crash of 1929. The economic crisis that ensued had an immediate impact on the appraisal practices of the time. The collapse of the real estate market in the 1930s seemed to discredit the concept that market price is central to value. The role of cost in the formation of property value also came into question. There was not enough construction activity to derive accurate cost estimates for many types of property. Although the supply of capital and real estate was adequate, investors were wary of risking their money in new developments. The primary consideration was economic feasibility—i.e., whether effective demand could transform cost into value.

The depression era was characterized by a public backlash against the speculative excesses of the 1920s. Before the stock market crash in 1929, lending institutions competed to provide speculative real estate loans in a business environment devoid of government regulation. During the depression, however, the federal government entered the picture. The Federal Housing Administration (FHA) was established by the National Housing Act of 1934.

By insuring mortgages, the FHA created a more stable mortgage market. It also promoted better-quality single-family housing by requiring builders to comply with government housing standards. As a precaution, the FHA required property appraisals before purchase so that it would not be left holding unsalable properties if the mortgagors defaulted.

Federal policy guidelines for appraisals specifically endorsed use of the replacement cost approach. By this means the FHA intended to stimulate construction because the cost of building new dwellings was clearly greater than the value of these dwellings in the market at the time. The emphasis on quality construction during this period was reinforced by the background of many appraisers, whose appraisal skill was based on a direct knowledge of building costs and quality.

In the building boom that followed World War II, the real estate industry again became disillusioned with the cost approach. Some critics argued that it was not practical to estimate the reproduction or replacement cost of an existing structure. Others found it difficult to keep up with increasingly complex construction costs. Nevertheless, the building costs services established before World War II helped maintain the validity of the cost approach throughout the 1940s, 1950s, and 1960s.

As investment analysis techniques became more sophisticated and the real estate industry grew more income-oriented, the position of the cost approach was further jeopardized. In the 1980s appraisal clients were mainly interested in the investment potential of properties, so the cost approach was not of direct relevance to many real estate investors. Proponents of the cost approach rightly contend that the approach imparts a unique understanding of the economics of real estate. On the other hand, the usefulness of the cost approach in valuing existing improvements has been criticized on the grounds that cost information is better computed by building professionals than by appraisers. Furthermore, due to technical and procedural developments, modern appraisal places far greater emphasis on the income and market characteristics of properties than on their reproduction or replacement cost. Yet the cost approach still shows vitality. As markets became oversupplied in the late 1980s and early 1990s, some speculative investors purchased buildings because their prices were "a fraction of replacement cost."

APPLICABILITY AND LIMITATIONS

Because cost and market value are usually closely related when properties are new, the cost approach is important in estimating the market value of new or relatively new construction. The approach is especially persuasive when the site value is well supported and the improvements are new or suffer only minor accrued depreciation and, therefore, represent a use that approximates the highest and best use of the land or site as though vacant. The cost approach can also be applied to older properties when adequate data are available to measure accrued depreciation.

The cost approach is used to estimate the market value of proposed construction, special-purpose properties, and other properties that are not frequently exchanged in the market. Buyers of these properties often measure the price they will pay for an existing building against the cost to build a replacement, minus accrued depreciation, or the cost to purchase an existing structure and make any necessary modifications. If comparable sales are not available, they cannot be analyzed to estimate the market value of such properties. Therefore, current market indications of depreciated cost, or the costs to acquire and refurbish an existing building, are the best reflections of market thinking and, thus, of market value.

In any market building value can be related to the cost to reproduce or replace the building. The cost approach is particularly important when a lack of market activity limits the usefulness of the sales comparison approach and when the properties to be appraised—e.g., single-family residences—are not amenable to valuation by the income capitalization approach. To estimate market value in these situations, an appraiser can calculate the cost of a replacement or reproduction of the building and then make a deduction for the amount of depreciation present in the existing improvement.

When the physical characteristics of comparable properties differ considerably, the relative values of these characteristics can sometimes be identified more precisely with the cost approach than with sales comparison. Because the cost approach starts with the cost to construct a substitute property with optimal physical and functional utility, it can help an appraiser determine accurate adjustments for physical differences in comparable sale properties. If, for example, an appraiser must make an adjustment for inadequate elevators in a comparable property, the cost to cure the deficiency can be used as a basis for this adjustment.

Because the cost approach requires that land and improvements be valued separately, it is also useful in appraisals for insurance purposes, when noninsurable items must be segregated from insurable items, and in appraisals for accounting purposes, when depreciation must be estimated for income taxes.

The cost approach is especially useful when building additions or renovations are being considered. The approach can be used to determine whether the cost of an improvement will be recovered through an increased income stream or anticipated sale price; its use can prevent the construction of overimprovements.

Finally, an estimate of probable building and development costs is an essential component of feasibility studies, which test the investment assumptions on which land-use plans are based. Financial feasibility is indicated when a property's market value exceeds its total building and development costs, including a reasonably market-supported entrepreneurial profit.

When improvements are older or do not represent the highest and best use of the land as though vacant, the physical deterioration, functional obsolescence, and external obsolescence of the structure are more difficult to estimate. Furthermore, relevant comparable data may be lacking or the data available may be too diverse to indicate an appropriate estimate of entrepreneurial profit.

In valuing investment properties, the persuasiveness of the cost approach is seriously diminished by the premise that improvements be constructed without "undue delay." The development and construction of investment properties may take several months to several years; in the eyes of some investors, this constitutes an unacceptable delay.

When value estimates derived with the cost approach are not supported by market data, they must be regarded with caution. Because the estimation of accrued depreciation and entrepreneurial profit is difficult, the cost approach may be of limited usefulness in valuing older improved properties. Moreover, the cost approach results in an indication of the value of the fee simple interest in a property. To value real estate held in leased fee or property subject to other partial interests, appraisers must make adjustments to reflect the specific real property rights being appraised.

PROCEDURE

After inspecting the neighborhood, the site, and the improvements and gathering all relevant data, an appraiser follows a series of steps to derive a value indication by the cost approach. The appraiser will

1. Estimate the value of the land as though vacant and available to be developed to its highest and best use.
2. Estimate the reproduction or replacement cost of the primary structure(s) as of the effective appraisal date. The estimate includes both direct (hard) costs and indirect (soft) costs.
3. Estimate other costs (indirect costs) incurred after construction to bring the new, vacant primary structure(s) up to market conditions and occupancy levels.
4. Estimate an appropriate entrepreneurial profit from an analysis of the market.

5. Add estimated replacement or reproduction cost, indirect costs, and the entrepreneurial profit, often expressed as a percentage of total direct and indirect costs, to arrive at the total replacement or reproduction cost of the primary structure(s).

6. Estimate the amount of accrued depreciation in the structure, which is divided into three major categories: physical deterioration, functional obsolescence, and external obsolescence.

7. Deduct the estimated accrued depreciation from the total reproduction or replacement cost of the primary structure(s) to derive an estimate of the depreciated reproduction or replacement cost.

8. Estimate reproduction or replacement costs and depreciation for any accessory buildings and site improvements, and then deduct the estimated depreciation from the reproduction or replacement costs of these improvements. Site improvements and minor buildings are often appraised at their net value—i.e., directly on a depreciated-cost basis.

9. Add the depreciated reproduction or replacement costs of the primary structure(s), the accessory buildings, and the site improvements to obtain the estimated total depreciated reproduction or replacement cost of all the improvements.

10. Add the site value to the total depreciated reproduction or replacement cost of all the improvements to arrive at the indicated value of the fee simple interest in the property.

11. Adjust the indicated fee simple value to reflect the property interest being appraised, if necessary, to arrive at the indicated value of the interest in the subject property being appraised.

Site Value

In the cost approach the estimated market value of the site is added to the depreciated cost of the improvements. The value of the site is strongly influenced by its potential highest and best use. Site value can be estimated using various techniques: sales comparison, allocation, extraction, subdivision development analysis, the land residual technique, or ground rent capitalization. (For a full discussion of the procedures used to estimate site value, see Chapter 13.) Appraisers must remember that the site value estimates produced with these techniques reflect the value of the fee simple interests in the site. If another interest is being appraised, the site value indication must be adjusted.

Reproduction or Replacement Cost of the Improvements

The cost to construct an improvement on the effective appraisal date may be developed as the reproduction or replacement cost of the improvement. The theoretical base for the cost approach is reproduction cost, but replacement cost may also be used. An important distinction must be made between the terms.

Reproduction cost is the estimated cost to construct, at current prices as of the effective appraisal date, an exact duplicate or replica of the building being appraised, using the same materials, construction standards, design, layout, and quality of workmanship, and embodying all the deficiencies, superadequacies, and obsolescence of the subject building.

Replacement cost is the estimated cost to construct, at current prices as of the effective appraisal date, a building with utility equivalent to the building being appraised, using modern materials and current standards, design, and layout.

The use of replacement cost eliminates the need to estimate *some* forms of functional obsolescence, but other forms of functional obsolescence, physical deterioration, and external obsolescence must still be measured.

Reproduction cost is sometimes difficult to estimate because identical materials may be unavailable and construction standards may have changed. Nevertheless, reproduction cost usually provides a basis for measuring depreciation from all causes.

Even a well-built, sound improvement with considerable remaining economic life may have a significant amount of functional obsolescence. Although use of a replacement cost estimate automatically eliminates the need to measure some forms of functional obsolescence, an appraiser who uses a replacement cost estimate must consider the added costs of removing items of curable functional obsolescence (i.e., items that can be corrected at costs that do not exceed their value contributions) and any excess operating costs associated with superadequate construction. Estimating replacement cost also eliminates the need to measure accrued depreciation due to excessive or superadequate construction.

The decision to use replacement cost or reproduction cost is often related to the purpose of the appraisal. An appraiser using replacement cost should indicate that the estimate is based on substitute materials because they are functional and the structure's value would not be diminished by their use. If reproduction cost is used, the excess reproduction cost of a superadequacy such as unusually thick walls is considered an item of functional obsolescence.

In estimating reproduction cost appraisers must ensure that their data sources are thorough and reliable. This function may be best delegated to an engineer or builder.

Types of Costs

To provide complete building cost estimates, appraisers must consider direct, or hard, costs and indirect, or soft, costs. Both types of costs are essential to reliable reproduction or replacement cost estimates. An incentive sufficient to induce an entrepreneur to undertake the risk associated with building the project must also be estimated. Interviews with developers regarding anticipated profit may help in estimating entrepreneurial incentive.

Direct construction costs include the costs of material and labor as well as the contractor's profit required to construct the improvement on the effective appraisal date. Indirect costs are other costs not included in the direct construction of improvements—e.g., professional fees, financing costs, taxes during construction, and carrying charges such as leasing commissions, sales commissions, and absorption expenses during the lease-up or sellout period. Three methods may be used to estimate construction costs: the comparative-unit method, the unit-in-place method, and the quantity survey method. These methods are discussed in Chapter 15.

An anticipated profit is often the primary motivation for developing a property. The total cost of a project before entrepreneurial profit should be less than the market value of the completed property; entrepreneurial profit rewards investors for their risk. The difference between the cost of development and the value of a property after completion is the entrepreneurial profit (or loss) realized. Whether the entrepreneur actually realizes a profit depends on how successful he or she has been in selecting the site, constructing the improvements, obtaining the proper tenant mix, and negotiating the leases, and on how well he or she has analyzed the market demand for the property. An in-depth discussion of entrepreneurial profit is provided in Chapter 15.

Accrued Depreciation

Accrued depreciation is the difference between the reproduction or replacement cost of the improvements on the effective date of the appraisal and the market value of the improvements on the same date. Depreciation is caused by deterioration or obsolescence in the property. Deterioration is evidenced by wear and tear on the structure. Functional obsolescence is caused by internal property characteristics such as a poor floor plan, inadequate mechanical equipment, or functional inadequacy or superadequacy due to size or other characteristics. External obsolescence is caused by conditions outside the property such as a lack of demand, changing property uses in the area, or national economic conditions. Some types of depreciation interact with one another, and the analysis of depreciation from all causes is cumulative.

Several methods may be used to estimate accrued depreciation: the economic age-life method, the modified economic age-life method, the breakdown method, cost-to-cure estimates, sales comparison techniques, and income capitalization techniques. These procedures are discussed and illustrated in Chapter 16.

Final Value Indication

To complete the final steps in the cost approach, an appraiser uses the methods cited above to make depreciated cost estimates of all site improvements and accessory buildings on the effective appraisal date. The depreciated reproduction or replacement costs of all the improvements are combined and entrepreneurial profit is added to produce the estimated value of the improvements. Then the appraiser adds the site value estimate to this figure to obtain an indication of the total value of the fee simple estate.

The appraiser should make sure that the value indicated by the cost approach is estimated as of the effective appraisal date and that it is consistent with value indications derived from the other approaches to value. For example, an appraiser may be asked to estimate the market value of the fee simple interest in an income-producing property both upon completion of the building improvements and when stabilized occupancy is achieved. The cost estimates used in the cost approach should reflect the construction time required to complete the improvements as well as all marketing, sales, or lease-up costs incurred to achieve stabilized occupancy or required sales in a normal market. Thus, an adjustment for external obsolescence or prolonged absorption should be made to reflect current occupancy if the building has not achieved stabilized occupancy as of the effective appraisal date. *Stabilized occupancy or income is defined as occupancy or income at that point in time when abnormalities in supply and demand or any additional transitory conditions cease to exist and the existing conditions are those expected to continue over the economic life of the property*. The concept of value at stabilization is based on stabilized occupancy or income—i.e., occupancy or income without significant fluctuations.

Care must be taken to reconcile the value indications from the various approaches to value to ensure consistency with the effective appraisal date and the purpose of the appraisal. This is especially important when the appraiser is reconciling prospective value indications.

Similarly, any unusual physical deterioration or functional or external obsolescence evidenced in the subject property but not in the comparable sales should be reflected in the adjustments made in the sales comparison approach. Such factors should also be reflected in the income approach and accounted for with a temporary or permanent rent loss or an appropriate adjustment to the final value indication.

Finally, an adjustment for property rights should be made to the indicated value, if appropriate, to reflect the property interest being appraised.

SUMMARY

The cost approach is based on a comparison between the cost to develop a property and the value of the existing property or a similarly developed property. Because the market relates value to cost, the cost approach reflects market thinking. Buyers tend to compare the value of existing structures with the prices and rents obtained for similar buildings and with the cost to create new buildings with optimal physical and functional utility. Buyers adjust the prices they are willing to pay by estimating the cost to bring an existing structure up to desired levels of physical and functional utility.

To apply the cost approach, an appraiser estimates the cost to construct a new reproduction of, or replacment for, the subject property and deducts all accrued depreciation in the property from that cost. Accrued depreciation can be broken down into physical deterioration, functional obsolescence, and external obsolescence. When site value and an entrepreneurial profit are added to this figure, an indication of the value of the fee simple interest in the property is produced. Appraisers may use data from the sales comparison approach to measure the market's reaction to items of accrued depreciation. An appraiser estimates accrued depreciation by allocating the sale price of a comparable property between the site and the improvements and deducting the value contribution of the improvements from an estimate of their cost new as of the date of sale. The appraiser can then relate this estimate of depreciation to the subject property.

The cost approach is generally most applicable in valuing new or relatively new construction when improvements represent the highest and best use of the site, site value is well supported, and no functional or external obsolescence is evident. The cost approach is also used to estimate the value of proposed construction, additions, and renovations; special-purpose properties; and properties that are not frequently exchanged in the market.

The cost approach can be used to estimate adjustments for the physical differences between comparable properties in the sales comparison approach. The cost approach is also useful in appraisals that require separate valuations of the site and the improvements—e.g., when insurable items must be segregated from non-insurable items and when depreciation must be estimated for income taxes. The cost approach is essential in feasibility studies to determine whether market value will exceed development costs and allow a suitable margin for entrepreneurial profit.

The difficulty of estimating the accrued depreciation in older improvements diminishes the reliability of the cost approach, unless adequate data are available. It is also difficult to estimate how much entrepreneurial profit will be realized in a proposed development. The value indication produced with the cost approach represents a fee simple interest. If the real estate being appraised is held in leased fee or involves partial interests, an adjustment may be needed to reflect the specific property rights being appraised.

The procedure for valuing property with the cost approach includes the following steps: 1) estimate the value of the land (site) as though vacant and available for development to its highest and best use; 2) estimate the reproduction or replacement cost of the primary structure(s) as of the effective appraisal date, including direct and indirect costs; 3) estimate other costs (indirect costs) to bring the new, vacant primary structure(s) to market conditions and occupancy levels; 4) estimate an entrepreneurial profit; 5) add reproduction or replacement costs, other costs, and the entrepreneurial profit to arrive at the total cost of the primary structure(s); 6) estimate accrued depreciation due to physical deterioration, functional obsolescence, and external obsolescence; 7) deduct estimated accrued depreciation from the total cost of the primary structure(s) to derive an estimate of the depreciated cost; 8) estimate the depreciated cost of accessory buildings and site improvements; 9) add the depreciated costs of the primary structure(s), the accessory buildings, and site improvements to obtain the total cost of all the improvements; 10) add site value to the total depreciated cost of the improvements to obtain a value indication for the fee simple estate; and 11) adjust the fee simple value to reflect the interests being appraised, if necessary.

Various techniques can be used to estimate site value: sales comparison using paired data set and patterned analyses, allocation, extraction, subdivision development analysis, the land residual technique, and ground rent capitalization. The site value derived with the first five techniques is the fee simple value, which may need to be adjusted if other interests are being appraised.

The distinction between reproduction cost and replacement cost is important. *Reproduction cost* is the estimated cost to construct an exact duplicate or replica of the building with the same materials, construction standards, layout, and quality of workmanship as the subject building on the effective appraisal date. *Replacement cost* is the estimated cost to construct a building with utility equivalent to the subject building, using modern materials, standards, and layout as of the effective appraisal date. Reproduction cost includes the cost of constructing superadequate features that may be functionally obsolete. The use of replacement cost eliminates the need to estimate *some* forms of functional obsolescence, but the cost of removing items of curable functional obsolescence and the excess operating costs of superadequacies must still be considered. The use of replacement or reproduction cost estimates often depends on the purpose of the appraisal.

Costs are broken down into direct costs, indirect costs, and the entrepreneurial profit. Direct costs include the costs of material and labor and the contractor's profit. Indirect costs include professional fees, financing charges, taxes during construction, and carrying charges during the lease-up or sellout period. Entrepreneurial profit (or loss) is the difference between the cost of development and the value of the completed property.

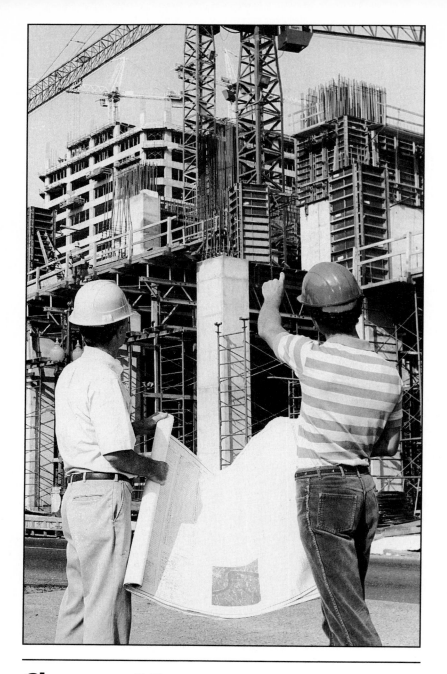

Chapter 15

BUILDING COST ESTIMATES

$\mathcal{T}$o apply the cost approach to value, an expert cost estimator or an appraiser who understands construction plans, specifications, materials, and techniques must first prepare an estimate of the cost of the improvements as of the effective appraisal date. Existing improvements should be carefully inspected and described by all individuals responsible for the cost estimate. Proposed improvements may be valued per plans and specifications, provided the appraiser discloses that the improvements do not exist and that the appraisal is conditioned on their completion as detailed.

This chapter explains the distinction between estimates of reproduction and replacement cost and identifies and discusses the components of cost: direct costs, indirect costs, and entrepreneurial profit. It also briefly describes sources of cost data and presents three methods appraisers use to estimate cost: the comparative-unit method, the unit-in-place method, and the quantity survey method.

REPRODUCTION AND REPLACEMENT COST ESTIMATES

From a theoretical standpoint, the cost estimate used in applying the cost approach to value is the cost to create duplicate improvements as of the effective appraisal date. This is known as an estimate of *reproduction cost*. An existing building, however, may incorporate materials, construction techniques, or design elements that are now out-of-date and would not be reproduced. Or a structure may exhibit a combination of features that diverge from the current standards for building components, for which cost estimates are readily available. In these situations it is common appraisal practice to estimate the cost to create improvements that would provide comparable utility. This produces an estimate of *replacement cost*. Obviously, cost estimates can vary significantly depending on whether reproduction cost or replacement cost is used; the concept selected for a particular appraisal must be clearly explained in the report to avoid misunderstanding.

Reproduction cost is the estimated cost to construct, at current prices as of the effective appraisal date, an exact duplicate or replica of the building being appraised, using the same materials, construction standards, design, layout, and quality of workmanship, and embodying all the deficiencies, superadequacies, and obsolescence of the subject building.

Replacement cost is the estimated cost to construct, at current prices as of the effective appraisal date, a building with utility equivalent to the building being appraised, using modern materials and current standards, design, and layout.

COSTS

Capital expenditures that are directly related to the construction of the physical improvements (e.g., contract costs) are called *direct* or *hard costs*. Capital costs that are indirectly related to the construction of the improvements (e.g., financing) are called *indirect* or *soft costs*. It is the entrepreneur who provides the inspiration, drive, and coordination involved in the overall project. The difference between the cost of development and the value of a property after completion is the *entrepreneurial profit* that is realized. The true measure of entrepreneurial profit is determined by surveying profit expectations in the market. The estimate of reproduction cost or replacement cost is not complete until all costs, including entrepreneurial profit, have been considered.

Direct Costs

Direct costs are expenditures for the labor and materials used in the construction of improvements. The overhead and profit of the general contractor and various subcontractors are part of the usual construction contract and represent direct costs that should always be included in the cost estimate. Direct costs also include the cost of:

- Building permits
- Materials, products, and equipment
- Labor used in construction
- Equipment used in construction
- Security during construction
- Contractor's shack and temporary fencing
- Material storage facilities
- Power line installation and utility costs
- Contractor's profit and overhead, including job supervision; worker's compensation; and fire, liability, and unemployment insurance
- Performance bonds

A building can cost substantially more than is typical if items such as walls and windows are insulated or thicker slabs are used to accommodate higher floor loads. Because the quality of materials and labor greatly influences costs, the appraiser should be familiar with the costs of the materials used in the subject property. The competitive situation in the local market can also affect cost estimates. Actual contractor bids based on the same set of specifications can vary substantially. A contractor who is working at capacity is inclined to make a high bid; one who needs the work is likely to submit a lower figure.

Indirect Costs

Indirect costs are expenditures or allowances that are necessary for construction, but are not typically part of the construction contract. Indirect costs may include:

- Architectural and engineering fees for plans, plan checks, surveys to establish building lines and grades, and environmental studies
- Appraisal, consulting, accounting, and legal fees
- The cost of carrying the investment in land and contract payments during construction (If the property is financed, the points, fees or service charges, and interest on construction loans are indirect costs.)
- All-risk insurance and ad valorem taxes during construction
- The cost of carrying the investment in the property after construction is complete, but before stabilized occupancy is achieved (return on investment, plus operating expenses, offset by operating income)
- Supplemental capital investment in tenant improvements or leasing commissions
- Marketing, sales commissions, or title transfers
- Administrative expenses of the developer
- Cost of title change

The items cited above reflect typical indirect costs incurred in a balanced market. In markets that are out of balance, higher costs may result from a prolonged absorption period—e.g., additional carrying costs, tenant improvements, leasing commissions, and marketing and administrative expenses. These costs should be considered as part of the estimate of external obsolescence.

Some indirect costs, such as architectural fees and property taxes, are generally related to the size and cost of the project; these are best estimated as a percentage of direct costs. Other costs, such as leasing and sales commissions, are related to the type of property or market practice. Still others, such as appraisal fees and environmental studies, are a function of the time required to carry out the assignment. The indirect costs of carrying an investment during and after construction is a combination of all of the above. Total indirect costs are sometimes estimated as a percentage of direct costs. More detailed studies of these costs are recommended. These should become easier to compile as computer applications are developed.

Entrepreneurial Profit

Entrepreneurial profit is a market-derived figure that refects the amount an entrepreneur expects to receive for his or her contribution. It represents the degree of risk and expertise associated with the development of a project.

If the cost of developing a property is used to provide an indication of value, the appraiser must recognize the contribution of the entrepreneur and consider the inclusion of entrepreneurial profit in addition to direct and indirect costs. However, this does not mean that the entrepreneur is guaranteed a reward for his or her efforts. Expenditures do not guarantee value. There is no certainty that any component of cost will create commensurate value and the residual nature of an entrepreneurial reward makes it the least certain. Nevertheless, entrepreneurship represents a legitimate cost of development and should be included in the estimate of development costs.[1] Entrepreneurial profit can take the form of profit on a sale, additional return on an investment in an operating property, or use value to the entrepreneur.

---

1. In analyzing the components of reward and compensation anticipated by an entrepreneur, some appraisers differentiate between the concepts of entrepreneurial incentive and developer's fee. In such an analytical framework, *entrepreneurial incentive* reflects the projected return that is required to attract an entrepreneur to invest capital in a project, based on market expectations. Entrepreneurial incentive may be expressed as a rate or percentage of cost. The concept of *developer's fee* is distinct from entrepreneurial incentive. It represents compensation for the time, energy, and experience a developer invests in a project as well as a reward for the risks the developer takes. The developer's fee is equivalent to the salary the developer might otherwise obtain. The developer's fee may also be expressed as a rate. Care should be taken to distinguish the developer's fee from the fee paid to a project management firm for the supervision of onsite contractors or subcontractors in the event the developer has assumed the construction management role.

Practitioners who draw this analytical distinction identify *project profit* as the difference between the total cost of the project and its sale price or market value. In a well-conceived enterprise, project profit may be expected to cover both entrepreneurial incentive and the developer's fee. In a poorly conceived project, there may be no project profit, and perhaps even a project loss. In such a scenario entrepreneurial incentive may not be realized.

To avoid confusion, it is advisable to define *entrepreneurial profit* and *developer's fee* specifically in the appraisal report. Sometimes the terms are used interchangeably. *Developer's fee* is another term that is subject to multiple interpretations. Some practitioners associate the term primarily with subdivision development. Others associate developer's fee with the overseeing of the development of a project from inception to completion, and include it among the direct and indirect costs of development.

In depressed markets the appraiser's attention should focus on whether diminished entrepreneurial profit or entrepreneurial loss represents a form of external obsolescence. Considering entrepreneurship as a component of cost in a depressed market helps establish a basis for estimating the level of rent required to induce new construction, which may in turn provide some insight into problems of absorption and stabilized occupancy.

Depending on market practice, entrepreneurial profit may be estimated as a percentage of direct costs, direct and indirect costs, direct and indirect costs plus site value, or the value of the completed project. In the following example, the dollar amounts and ratios, or relative percentages, of entrepreneurial profit are presented only for purposes of illustration.

Base	% Applied		Entrepreneurial Profit
Direct cost	$ 400,000 × 30.0%	=	$120,000
Direct cost + indirect cost	$ 400,000 200,000		
	$ 600,000 × 20.0%	=	$120,000
Direct cost + indirect cost + land value	$ 400,000 200,000 200,000		
	$ 800,000 × 15.0%	=	$120,000
Direct cost + indirect cost + land value + entrep. profit	$ 400,000 200,000 200,000 120,000		
	$ 920,000 × 13.0%	=	$120,000 (rounded)

Presumably the entrepreneurial profit would be the same amount regardless of how it is calculated—i.e., as 30%, 20%, 15%, or 13% of the base cost selected. The final calculation, of entrepreneurial profit as a percentage of the value of the completed project, would actually be accomplished as follows: ($ 800,000 × 0.13)/(1 − 0.13) = $ 120,000 (rounded).

Potential entrepreneurial profit should be derived from market analysis and through interviews with developers to determine the expectations of profit required as motivation or incentive to undertake a particular development.

Less emphasis should be given to historical profit margins. Historical profits are records of results and often differ from the anticipated profit which originally motivated the entrepreneur to proceed with a project. Estimating an appropriate amount of entrepreneurial profit is a continued challenge for appraisers because expectations of profit vary with different market conditions and property types and typical relationships between profit and other costs are difficult to establish.

COST DATA SOURCES

Construction contracts for buildings similar to the building being appraised are primary sources of comparable cost data, but in their absence local building con-

tractors and professional cost estimators are often reliable sources. Some appraisers maintain comprehensive files of current cost data that include current costs for
completed houses, apartments, hotels, office buildings, retail buildings, and industrial buildings. These costs can provide a basis for calculating the cost to construct an existing or proposed building.

Many cost-estimating services publish data for estimating the current cost of
improvements. A few of these services are Marshall and Swift Publication Company; Boeckh Publications, a division of American Appraisal Associates; and the
F. W. Dodge Corporation.

Published cost manuals usually include direct unit costs, but an appraiser
must research the market to find which costs are most applicable to the appraisal.
Manuals almost always include some indirect costs such as escrow fees, legal fees,
interest on construction loans, financing fees, carrying charges, and property
taxes, but the costs of these items may not be included: permanent financing fees
and lease-up, sales, marketing, or carrying costs on the investment after construction, but before reaching stabilized occupancy. The costs furnished by national
cost services often do not include site improvement costs—e.g., the costs of demolition, roads, storm drains, rough grading, soil compaction, utilities, and jurisdictional utility hookup fees and assessments. Entrepreneurial profit is rarely, if ever,
included in cost service data. The appraiser must estimate such costs separately
and include them in the total reproduction or replacement cost estimate.

Computer-assisted cost-estimating services may also provide useful data.

Cost-Index Trending

Cost services often include information on cost indexes, which are used to convert
a known historical cost into a current cost estimate. The manuals identify base
year and regional multipliers for specific building components.

The following situation illustrates the application of cost-index trending. The
contract cost for constructing a building in January of 1988 was $1,000,000. The
index for January of 1988 is 285.1 and the current index is 327.3. To trend the
historical cost into a current cost, the current cost index is divided by the historical cost index and the result is multiplied by the historical cost. In this case the
current cost is calculated as follows:

$$327.3 \; / \; 285.1 \; = \; 1.148$$
$$1.148 \; \times \; \$ \; 1,000,000 \; = \; \$1,148,000$$

Problems can arise when cost index data are used to estimate current reproduction or replacement cost. The accuracy of the figures cannot always be ascertained, especially when it is not clear which components are included in the data
(i.e., only direct costs or direct costs and some indirect costs). Furthermore, historical costs may not be typical for the time period, and the construction methods
used at the time of the historical cost may differ from those used on the effective
appraisal date. Although cost-index trending may be helpful in confirming a cost
estimate, it is not a reliable substitute for the cost-estimating methods described in
the following section.

COST-ESTIMATING METHODS

The three traditional cost-estimating methods are the comparative-unit method, the unit-in-place method, and the quantity survey method. The quantity survey method produces a cost estimate based on a detailed inventory of the materials and equipment used in the subject improvements. The comparative-unit and the unit-in-place methods provide less detail, but they are the basis for the cost estimates used in most appraisals.

Measurement

Although buildings can be measured in several ways, appraisers should measure buildings according to local custom. To use cost service data effectively, an appraiser must understand the measurement technique used by the service.

Area measurement is widely used for all types of structures, particularly one-story houses, apartments, and small office buildings. It is most appropriate for buildings constructed to meet basic standards of height.

A building's outside measurements are used to compute gross area. Then the area of all projections or cantilevers are added, and the areas of insets or recesses are subtracted. The gross building area is the sum of the areas of all floor levels in the structure. In certain locations dwellings are measured in terms of the area of ground floor coverage; in others the gross area of living space is calculated. For example, a two-story house that measures 24 feet by 24 feet with an unfinished basement and attic has an area of 1,152 square feet ($24 \times 24 \times 2$). Guidelines established by the Federal National Mortgage Association (Fannie Mae) call for the measurement of gross living area, which is defined to include finished and habitable, above-grade living area only. On Fannie Mae residential appraisal forms, finished basement or attic areas must be calculated and shown separately in the cost estimate.

Because ceiling heights, roof pitches, and similar building components have a significant effect on the quantity of materials used in construction, the volume of space in a particular building may be a more accurate means of estimating its reproduction cost. In measuring warehouses, loft buildings, places of worship, and similar structures, volume measurement may be most appropriate.

To estimate the volume of a building, an appraiser multiplies the gross area of the structure by its mean height. The mean height is measured from six inches below the basement floor surface to the mean height of the roof. Thus, the mean height of a gable roof is one-half the distance from the top of the ceiling joists to the ridge; the mean height of a hip roof is one-third of this distance. If the subject building does not have a basement, the mean height used in determining volume is measured from one foot below the surface of the first floor or from grade, whichever is lower.

Comparative-Unit Method

The comparative-unit method is used to derive a cost estimate in terms of dollars per unit of area or unit of volume. The method employs the known costs of similar structures adjusted for market conditions and physical differences. Indirect costs may be included in the unit cost or computed separately. If the comparable properties and the subject property are in different markets, the appraiser may need to make an adjustment for location.

Unit costs vary with size; all else being equal, unit costs decrease as buildings increase in area or volume. This reflects the fact that plumbing, heating units, elevators, doors, windows, and similar items do not usually cost proportionately more in a larger building than in a smaller one.

The comparative-unit method is relatively uncomplicated, practical, and widely used. Unit-cost figures are usually expressed in terms of gross building dimensions converted to square feet or cubic feet. Total cost is estimated by comparing the subject building with similar, recently constructed buildings for which contract prices are available. The trend in costs between the date of the contract (or construction) and the effective appraisal date must be factored into the comparison.

In the absence of contract prices, an indication of the total cost new of a building can be extracted from sales of similar, newly constructed buildings so long as these tests are met: 1) the improvements reflect the highest and best use of the site; 2) the property has reached stabilized occupancy; 3) supply and demand are in balance; and 4) site value is reasonably ascertainable. The value of the site is subtracted from the sale price of each comparable property and the residual indicates the cost new of the improvements.

Most appraisers using the comparative-unit method apply unit-cost figures developed with data from a recognized cost service. Unit costs for the benchmark buildings found in cost-estimating manuals usually start with a base building of a specified size—i.e., base area or volume—to which additions or deductions are made to approximate the actual area or volume involved. If the subject building is larger than the benchmark building, the unit cost is usually lower; if the subject building is smaller, its unit cost will probably be higher.

Because few buildings are identical in terms of size, design, and quality of construction, the benchmark building is often different from the subject building. Different roof designs and irregular perimeters and building shapes can affect comparative-unit costs substantially. The following example illustrates this situation:

	Building A	**Building B**
Building dimensions	100 × 100	50 × 200
Building area in square feet	10,000	10,000
Perimeter walls in linear feet	400	500
Ratio: area to perimeter	25:1	20:1
Cost of walls		
Per linear foot	$50	$50
Total cost	$20,000	$25,000
Per building square foot	$2.00	$2.50

To develop a reliable conclusion with the comparative-unit method, an appraiser should calculate the unit cost from similar improvements or adjust the unit-cost figure to reflect variations in size, shape, finish, and HVAC equipment. The unit cost applied should also reflect any changes in cost levels between the date of the benchmark unit cost and the effective appraisal date.

The ratio between the costs of equipment and the basic building shell has increased consistently through the years. Equipment tends to increase unit building costs and depreciate more rapidly than other building components.

To use area or volume cost estimates, an appraiser assembles, analyzes, and catalogs data on actual building costs. These costs should be divided into general construction categories and separate figures should be used to account for special finishes or equipment. The overall area or volume unit cost can then be broken down into its components, which may help the appraiser adjust a known cost for the presence or absence of items in later comparisons.

The apparent simplicity of the comparative-unit method can be misleading. To develop dependable unit-cost figures, an appraiser must exercise judgment and carefully compare the subject building with similar or standard structures for which actual costs are known. Errors can result if an appraiser selects a unit cost that is not comparable to the building being appraised. However, when it is correctly applied, the method produces reasonably accurate reproduction or replacement cost estimates.

The warehouse shown in Figure 15.1 will be used to illustrate the comparative-unit method (and later the other two methods of estimating costs). A detailed description of the warehouse follows Figure 15.1.

Figure 15.1 Plan of a Warehouse

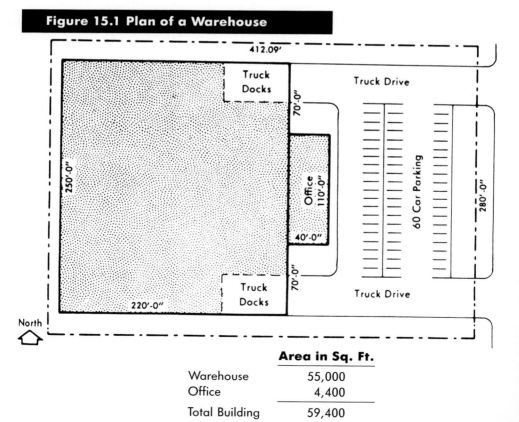

Area in Sq. Ft.	
Warehouse	55,000
Office	4,400
Total Building	59,400

Basic Construction

Exterior walls, block and brick facade; structural steel columns, steel deck; rigid insulation; built-up tar and gravel roofing. Structure has full sprinkler system. Other details are typical.

Warehouse Area

Heating to 65°F at −10°F outside temperature; clear ceiling height, 18 feet; bays, 41 1/2 × 36 1/2 feet; structural steel framing; insulated roof deck and slab over steel bar joists; 6-in. concrete floor slab at grade, waterproofed; electric service, 600 amperes, 120/240 volts. Four overhead wood truck doors; one washroom that contains three fixtures.

Office Area

Heated, with air-conditioning equipment rated at 15 tons; ceiling height, 9 feet; flooring, asphalt tile over concrete slab; illumination, 60 foot-candle intensity, fluorescent lighting; ceiling, acoustic tile; partitions, stud and drywall; two washrooms that contain six fixtures.

Table 15.1 shows how comparative-unit costs from a published cost manual can be applied to the warehouse building illustrated in Figure 15.1. Calculations such as those shown can be used to confirm a cost indication obtained from construction contracts for similar properties in the same market as the property being appraised on or about the effective appraisal date. Published data can be used independently when no local cost data are available.

In Table 15.1 an adjustment for a sprinkler system was made using a square-foot unit cost. In other cases similar adjustments may be appropriate for observed physical differences in the amount of office area, construction features, or specific equipment.

Cost manuals rarely include all indirect costs or an allowance for entrepreneurial profit, so adjustments must often be made to obtain an indication of the total cost new. In Table 15.1 adjustments are made for: 1) indirect costs not included in the base price quoted in the cost manual; 2) indirect costs after construction but before stabilized occupancy is reached; and 3) entrepreneurial profit calculated as a percentage of total direct and indirect costs. The estimate of the value of the site and site improvements was derived through sales comparison.

Table 15.1 indicates the cost new of the warehouse building plus the site value, but the result shown is more likely to represent the value of a close substitute than a duplicate structure. Cost services use typical buildings for their base cost, so an appraiser can apply the comparative-unit method, develop reliable adjustment amounts and factors, and produce a reasonable property value estimate.

Construction contracts normally include other improvements to the land such as auxiliary buildings, driveways, pools, underground drainage facilities, rail sidings, fences, and landscaping. The possible combinations and varied value contributions of these improvements can cause a wide range in unit cost if the total contract is related to the size of the major improvement only. Therefore, when

Table 15.1 Warehouse Property— Comparative-Unit Method

Base cost per sq. ft.	$27.22
Add for sprinkler system per sq. ft.	1.14
Subtotal	$28.36
Adjustment for 18-ft. ceiling	× 1.086
Subtotal	$30.80
Adjustment for area/perimeter	× 0.895
Subtotal	$27.57
Current cost multiplier	× 1.120
Subtotal	$30.88
Local cost multiplier	× 0.980
Total cost per sq. ft. (from manual)	$30.26
Indirect costs not included in cost manual data*	× 1.050
Subtotal	$31.77
Indirect costs from completion to stabilized occupancy*	× 1.070
Subtotal	$33.99
Entrepreneurial profit: 10.0% of total direct & indirect costs ($33.99 × 0.10)/(1−0.10) =	+ 3.78
Subtotal	$37.77
Plus site value & site improvements per sq. ft. of building $650,000/59,400 sq. ft.	+ 10.94
Total project cost per sq. ft.	$48.71

Total cost new for warehouse building:

59,400 sq. ft. @ $37.77	$ 2,243,538	
	2,244,000	(rounded)
Plus site value & site improvements		
59,400 sq. ft. @ $10.94	$ 650,000	(rounded)
Total project value	$ 2,894,000	
	$ 2,895,000	(rounded)

Source: *Marshall Valuation Service* (Los Angeles: Marshall and Swift Publication Co.), Section 14, March 1988, pp. 16, 24, and 25; Section 44, March 1988, p. 3; Section 99, March 1991, pp. 3 and 6.

* Note: Contractor's overhead and profit and some other indirect costs are included in these base costs and adjustments. The source of published cost data should be studied for a complete understanding of what is included in the quoted costs.

For purposes of simplicity, a percentage was applied for indirect costs. A breakdown of costs which comprise these estimates should be itemized by the appraiser to support the percentages applied.

actual contract costs from the local market are used in the comparative-unit method, it is imperative that the costs of these other improvements be excluded from the base price.

Unit-in-Place Method

In the unit-in-place, or segregated-cost, method unit costs for various building components as installed are applied to the number of components or to linear, area, volume, or other appropriate measures of these components. Using this method the appraiser computes a unit cost based on the actual quantity of materials used plus the labor of assembly required for each square foot of area. For example, the cost can be applied on the basis of square feet of floor area or linear feet of wall of a certain height. The same procedure is applied for other structural components.

Unit-in-place cost estimates are made using standardized costs for structural components as installed. Excavating costs are typically expressed in dollars per cubic yard; foundation costs may be expressed in dollars per linear foot or cubic yard of concrete. Floor construction may be reduced to dollars per square foot and interior partitions may be expressed in dollars per linear foot. The basic unit for roofing is called a *square*, which represents 100 square feet. The unit in place measure on which the cost is based may be the measure employed in a particular trade, such as the cost per ton of air-conditioning; alternatively, any appropriate unit of measurement may be selected. All constituent unit costs are totaled to provide the estimated direct cost of the entire improvement. Contractor's overhead and profit may be included in the unit cost figures provided by some cost services, or they may be computed separately. The appraiser must ascertain exactly what is included in any unit price quoted. Indirect costs are usually computed separately.

The following example shows how the cost of a brick veneer wall would be calculated on a unit-in-place basis. (Costs such as these vary with market conditions and location; the figures shown are used only for purposes of illustration.)

Cost	Unit	Description
$460.00	per 1,000	4-in. face brick, installed: common bond, 1/2-in. struck joints, mortar, scaffolding, and cleaning included
$360.00	per 1,000 bd. ft.	Dimension lumber, erected: 2-in.- x -4-in. wood stud framing, 16 inches on center
$0.42	per sq. ft.	Sheathing, installed: impregnated 4-ft. x 8-ft., 1/2-in.
$0.22	per sq. ft.	Insulation, installed: 2 1/2-in. foil backing, one side
$0.30	per sq. ft.	Drywall: 1/2-in. with finished joints
$0.25	per sq. ft.	Paint: primer and one coat flat

From these data the cost per square foot of wall can be estimated as follows:

Cost	Unit	Description
$3.45	per 7 1/2	Bricks
0.24	per 2/3 bd. ft.	Wood stud framing
0.42	per sq.ft.	Sheathing
0.22	per sq.ft.	Insulation
0.30	per sq.ft.	1/2-in. drywall
+ 0.25	per sq.ft.	Paint
$4.88	per sq.ft.	Total for finished wall

After calculating the unit cost of $4.88 per square foot, the appraiser can estimate the total cost of a veneer wall that meets these standards without detailing the quantities of material and labor. In practice a cost analyst would refine the procedure by adjusting for waste and for extra framing for windows and doors which require wall openings, lintels, and facing corners.

The unit costs for all components can be calculated in a similar fashion and, once these are established, the appraiser can estimate the cost of an entire building. However, specialized knowledge may be required to assemble the basic costs of equipment, material, and labor and to combine these costs into a final cost estimate. When fully developed, the unit-in-place method provides a substitute for a complete quantity survey and produces an accurate reproduction or replacement cost estimate with considerably less effort.

The concept of unit-in-place is not limited to cubic, linear, or area units. It may also be applied to the cost of complete, installed components such as the cost of a roof truss that is fabricated off site, delivered, and erected. Unit-in-place cost estimates may be based on an appraiser's compiled data or be obtained from a cost-estimating service that provides updated monthly figures.

Table 15.2 illustrates how the unit-in-place method can be used to estimate the reproduction cost of the warehouse shown in Figure 15.1.

In Table 15.2 adjustments are made for: 1) indirect costs not included in the cost manuals base price; 2) indirect costs after construction but before stabilized occupancy is reached; and 3) entrepreneurial profit calculated as a percentage of total direct and indirect costs.

Quantity Survey Method

The most comprehensive and accurate method of cost estimating is the quantity survey method. A quantity survey is a computation that reflects the quantity and quality of all materials used and all categories of labor hours required. Unit costs are applied to these figures to arrive at a total cost estimate for materials and labor; then the contractor adds a margin for contingencies, overhead, and profit.

Depending upon the size of the project and the resources of the contractor, the quantity survey and cost calculations may be accomplished by a single cost estimator or by a number of subcontractors whose bids are compiled by a general contractor and submitted as the final cost estimate. In either instance, the analysis

Table 15.2 Warehouse Property—Unit-in-Place Method

Excavation			
Site	59,400 cu. ft. @ $ 0.24	=	$ 14,256
Foundation	115,385 sq. ft. @ $ 0.17	=	19,615
Framing	59,400 sq. ft. @ $ 1.79	=	106,326
Floor (concrete)	59,400 sq. ft. @ $ 4.82	=	286,308
Floor (asphalt tile)	59,400 sq. ft. @ $ 3.12	=	185,328
Ceiling (acoustical tile)	4,400 sq. ft. @ $ 1.02	=	4,488
Plumbing (3 rooms)	4,400 sq. ft. @ $ 4.35	=	19,140
Fixtures	9 fixtures @ $2,525	=	22,725
Drains	6 units @ $ 380	=	2,280
Sprinkler system	59,400 sq. ft. @ $ 1.48	=	87,912
HVAC	55,000 sq. ft. @ $ 0.84	=	46,200
	4,400 sq. ft. @ $ 4.20	=	18,480
Electrical & lighting	59,400 sq. ft. @ $ 1.70	=	100,980
Exterior wall			
Concrete block	15,180 sq. ft. @ $12.09	=	183,526
Brick facade	5,060 sq. ft. @ $13.80	=	69,828
Partitions			
Walls	8,650 sq. ft. @ $ 3.70	=	32,005
Doors	10 sq. ft. @ $ 103	=	1,030
Overhead doors			
(10 ft. × 12 ft. × 4 ft.)	480 sq. ft. @ $18.25	=	8,760
Roof joists & deck	59,400 sq. ft. @ $6.86	=	407,484
Roof cover & insulation	59,400 sq. ft. @ $2.18	=	129,492
Misc. specified items			30,000
Subtotal			$1,776,163
Current cost multiplier			
(Different base from Table 15.1)			× 1.030
Subtotal			$1,829,448
Local cost multiplier:			× 0.980
Total cost			
(From manual—$ 30.18 per sq. ft.)			$1,792,859
Indirect costs not included in cost manual*			× 1.100
Subtotal			$1,972,145
Indirect costs from completion to date			
of stabilized occupancy*			× 1.050
Subtotal			$2,070,752
Entrepreneurial profit: 10.0% of total direct & indirect costs			
($2,070,752 × 0.10)/(1 − 0.10)			230,084
Total cost new ($38.73 per sq. ft.)			$2,300,836
Rounded			$2,301,000
Plus site value & site improvements			650,000
Total project value			$2,951,000

Source: *Marshall Valuation Service* (Los Angeles: Marshall and Swift Publication Co.), Segregated Cost Method, Section 44, March 1986.

* Note. Contractor's overhead and profit and some indirect costs are included in the base costs; architect's fees and other indirect costs are not. The source of published cost data should be studied for a complete understanding of what is included in the quoted costs.

For purposes of simplicity, a percentage was applied for indirect costs. A breakdown of costs which comprise these estimates should be itemized by the appraiser to support the percentage applied.

Table 15.3 Warehouse Property—Contractor's Breakdown

General conditions of contract	$ 7,854
Excavating & grading	24,781
Concrete	182,053
Carpentry	25,473
Masonry	194,231
Structural steel	280,343
Joist, deck, & deck slab	329,827
Roofing	57,494
Insulation	32,378
Sash	5,256
Glazing	11,329
Painting	7,611
Acoustical material	5,803
Flooring	3,333
Electric	75,334
HVAC	67,560
Piping	6,458
Plumbing & sprinkler system	77,464
Subtotal	$1,394,58
Contingencies @ 5.0%	69,72
Contractor's overhead & profit @ 12.0%	167,35
Total proposed contract costs ($27.46 per sq. ft.)	$1,631,66
Rounded	$1,631,70
Indirect costs before, during, and after construction*	× 1.2
Subtotal	$2,072,25
Entrepreneurial profit ($2,072,259 × 0.10)/(1 − 0.10)	+ 230,25
Total reproduction cost	$2,302,51
Plus site value & site improvements	+ 650,00
Total project value	$2,952,51
Rounded	$2,950,00

* For purposes of simplicity, a percentage was applied for indirect costs. A breakdown of costs which comprise these estimates should be itemized by the appraiser to support the percentages applied.

details the quantity, quality, and cost of all materials furnished by the general contractor or subcontractor and the appropriate cost allowances.

A general contractor's cost breakdown for the warehouse shown in Figure 1? is summarized in Table 15.3. This is only a summary; the specific quantities and costs are not indicated.

Contractor bids do not usually include indirect costs or entrepreneurial prof The analysis illustrated in Table 15.3 reflects indirect costs and the calculation c entrepreneurial profit as a percentage of total direct and indirect costs. In the ex amples presented, indirect costs are considered in various stages of the cost estimating procedure.

Although site improvements such as parking facilities, landscaping, and signage are commonly included in a general contractor's bid, they are not detailed in Table 15.3. They should be included in a cost estimate of all improvements. In a cost estimate of an existing building, however, a separate itemization of site improvements facilitates the consideration of accrued depreciation.

Because the quantity survey method produces a cost estimate of a duplicate building, Table 15.3 indicates the reproduction cost of the warehouse building as of the effective appraisal date.

In recent years the percentage of a general contract that is subcontracted has increased. Subcontractors have become more efficient in their specializations. Subcontractor unit-in-place costs compare favorably with the cost of work done by employees of the general contractor, and the general contractor can operate with reduced overhead. For estimates prepared by quantity survey, each contractor and subcontractor can provide a breakdown of materials, labor, overhead, and profit. The contractor's profit may depend on the volume of work that the contractor has lined up.

Although the quantity survey method produces a complete cost analysis of the improvements being appraised, it is time-consuming, costly, and frequently requires the services of an experienced cost estimator. For these reasons this method is seldom used in routine appraisal assignments.

SUMMARY

The cost approach to value starts with an estimate of the current cost to reproduce or replace the improvements as of the effective appraisal date. The estimate of cost must be prepared by a knowledgeable party because if it is not accurate, the value conclusion will be flawed. Cost estimates are based on either *reproduction cost* or *replacement cost* and are composed of *direct and indirect costs, developer's fee,* and *entrepreneurial profit.*

Reproduction cost refers to the cost of a duplicate structure as of the effective appraisal date. Theoretically the cost approach always starts with reproduction cost. *Replacement cost* refers to the cost of a substitute property with equal desirability, rather than a duplicate, as of the effective appraisal date. Replacement cost is used in most appraisals as a practical alternative to preparing a costly and time-consuming customized estimate.

Direct costs are capital expenditures that are directly related to the physical construction of improvements, e.g., contract cost. Contractor's overhead and profit are direct costs.

Indirect costs are capital expenditures that are indirectly related to the physical construction of improvements—e.g. architectural and engineering fees, property taxes during construction, and financing.

Entrepreneurial profit is that portion of cost that reflects the contribution of the entrepreneur. It is the incentive behind the inspiration, drive, and coordination that go into creating a project. Entrepreneurial profit should definitely be considered a real cost, but it does not necessarily result in value. Entrepreneurial profit should be measured and included as an item in both replacement and reproduction cost estimates. An estimate of the cost to replicate or create an improvement is not complete unless all costs are considered. Where markets are characterized by an imbalance in supply and demand, an entrepreneurial loss may occur and should be considered as a part of the estimate of external obsolescence.

Entrepreneurial profit can be estimated as a percentage of direct costs, direct and indirect costs, direct and indirect costs plus site value, or the value of the completed project. The estimate is most often based on a percentage of direct and indirect costs. Estimates of entrepreneurial profit should reflect market analysis and interviews with developers to determine their expectations of profit. Because anticipations of profit vary with economic conditions, project size, and property type, it is difficult to establish a typical relationship between entrepreneurial profit and other costs.

Cost data can be obtained from construction contracts, building contractors, cost estimators, and computer programs and manuals from cost-estimating services. To use the data effectively, an appraiser must understand the measurement technique employed by the cost-estimating service. Gross building area (*GBA*) and building volume are calculated from outside measurements; ground floor coverage and gross living area may be based on interior measurements. Area units of measure are applied to most structures, while volume is measured when vertical dimensions vary significantly.

Cost-estimating services also provide data for cost-index trending, which is used to convert historical costs into current estimates. Cost manuals list base years and regional multipliers to accomplish this conversion, but appraisers should recognize that recent costs are generally more accurate than historical costs adjusted with a cost index.

Building costs can be estimated with the *comparative-unit method, the unit-in-place method, or the quantity survey method.* The comparative-unit and unit-in-place methods are less detailed than the quantity survey method, but they are generally adequate for appraisals in which greater reliance is placed on the sales comparison or income capitalization approaches.

The comparative-unit method expresses cost in terms of dollars per unit of area or volume, usually gross square feet or cubic feet. Costs are calculated for standard structures or derived from known costs found in local construction contracts for similar improvements. These costs must be adjusted for market conditions, location, and physical differences. All else being equal, unit costs vary substantially for buildings of different proportions or size. Although the comparative-unit method appears simple, experience and familiarity with construction materials and techniques are needed to apply it successfully.

Cost manuals provide data for benchmark buildings. The standard structures used are rarely identical to the building being appraised, so a cost estimate prepared with published data is most likely an estimate of typical replacement cost, even though adjustments for size, design, quality and type of construction, equipment, and other variables can be made. These costs, which are compiled and published periodically, also must be adjusted for market conditions and location.

The unit-in-place, or segregated-cost, method employs unit costs for various building components as installed, and may reflect linear, area, or volume measurements. Specialized knowledge may be needed to derive unit-in-place costs, but they are generally available from various cost services. A unit-in-place estimate can be a reasonable substitute for a detailed quantity survey.

The quantity survey method is the most comprehensive way to estimate building cost. This method closely follows a contractor's bid preparation. All quantities of materials and hours of labor required to construct the improvements are estimated. Costs consistent with the quality of construction are applied to these estimates and a margin for contingencies and contractor's overhead and profit is added to produce a contract price. The appraiser must add estimates of any costs of improvements omitted from the bid as well as indirect costs and entrepreneurial profit, if appropriate. The practical application of this method is limited due to the expertise, time, and expense required to prepare a complete quantity survey cost breakdown.

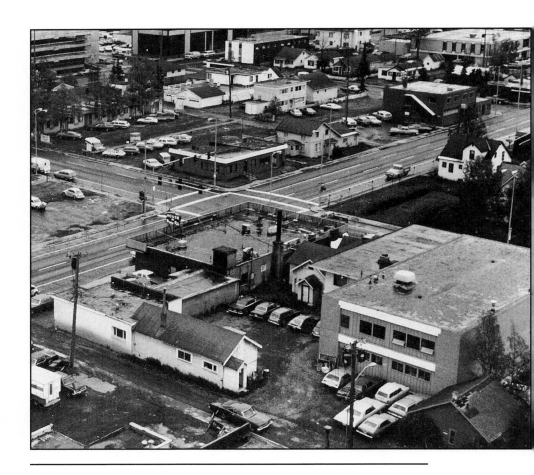

Chapter 16

ACCRUED DEPRECIATION

$\mathcal{A}$ccrued depreciation is a loss in value from the reproduction or replacement cost of improvements that may emanate from physical deterioration, functional obsolescence, external obsolescence, or any combination of these sources. After separate elements of accrued depreciation are identified and measured, the appraiser deducts the dollar amounts of all applicable types of depreciation from the reproduction or replacement cost of the improvements. The result is the estimated depreciated reproduction or replacement cost of the improvements.

Theoretically, depreciation can begin to accrue the moment construction is completed, even in a functional building that represents the highest and best use of its site. Although most forms of physical deterioration can be corrected or temporarily halted, physical deterioration tends to persist. As a building ages, functional obsolescence may occur. Even new buildings can have various forms of functional obsolescence such as obsolescence attributable to poor design.

In the cost approach depreciation from all causes is subtracted from current reproduction or replacement cost. However, depreciation is a penalty only insofar as it is recognized by the market as a loss in value. For older buildings the value loss may be offset by a temporary scarcity relative to demand or by a building's historical or architectural significance.

If an appraiser uses replacement cost rather than reproduction cost to derive the current cost estimate, the estimate of accrued depreciation will be affected. Some forms of functional obsolescence are automatically eliminated when replacement cost is used. An appraiser who uses a replacement cost estimate must consider the added costs of removing items of curable functional obsolescence and any excess operating costs associated with superadequate construction.

DEFINITIONS

To analyze accrued depreciation an appraiser should understand these essential terms: *depreciation, accrued depreciation, book depreciation, economic life, remaining economic life, effective age,* and *actual age.*

Depreciation is a loss in property value from any cause. It may also be defined as the difference between the reproduction cost or replacement cost of the improvement and its market value. Deterioration, or physical depreciation, is evidenced by wear and tear, decay, dry rot, cracks, infestation, or structural defects in a building. Other types of depreciation are caused by obsolescence, which may be either functional or external. Functional obsolescence may be caused by the inadequacy or superadequacy of a building's size, style, or mechanical equipment. Physical deterioration and functional obsolescence can usually be observed in an improvement. External obsolescence is caused by factors outside the property such as changes in demand, general property uses in the area, zoning, financing, and government regulations.

To measure accrued depreciation, an appraiser identifies and measures the loss in value experienced by the subject structure in its present condition and compares its present value with the value it would have if it were new. Accrued depreciation is sometimes referred to as *diminished utility.*

Book depreciation is an accounting term that refers to the amount of capital recapture written off on an owner's books. Generally, it is the amount that a particular owner can provide for the retirement or replacement of an asset under the tax laws. Book depreciation is not market-derived; traditionally accountants have based depreciation on book value or original cost. In current cost accounting, however, some assets may be carried at current value, which is the same as market value measured with accepted valuation methods.

Economic life is the period of time over which improvements to real estate contribute to property value. Economic life and physical life can differ widely; physical life is expected to exceed economic life. For example, improvements with varying degrees of physical utility are ordinarily replaced with new structures. However, renewing or remodeling older properties usually extends their economic lives. At any given point in time, a property's economic life cannot exceed its physical life. Rehabilitation can extend the physical life of real estate.

Remaining economic life is the estimated period during which improvements continue to contribute to property value. An appraiser determines a property's remaining economic life by interpreting the attitudes and reactions of typical buyers of competitive properties.

Actual age, sometimes called historical or chronological age, is the number of years that have elapsed since construction was completed. Effective age is the age indicated by the condition and utility of a structure. The effective age of a building may be less than its actual age if it has had above-average maintenance or is of superior quality or design, or if there is a scarcity of such buildings in the market. For example, a 40-year-old building may have an effective age of 20 years due to rehabilitation, modernization, or strong market demand. However, if the building has not been adequately maintained, its effective age may be greater than its actual age.

METHODS OF ESTIMATING ACCRUED DEPRECIATION

An appraiser identifies depreciation due to physical deterioration, functional obsolescence, and external obsolescence by analyzing similar improvements and the market's reaction to their observed condition. The amount of depreciation to be deducted from an improvement's current reproduction or replacement cost is typically indicated by the difference between the improvement's contribution to the current market value of the property and the market-value contribution of a similar improvement constructed new on the date of the appraisal.

Several methods can be applied to estimate accrued depreciation; each is acceptable if the appraiser applies it consistently and logically and if it reflects an informed, prudent buyer's reaction to the condition of the structure being appraised. To produce an accurate and supportable estimate of accrued depreciation with any method, the appraiser must consider all elements that may diminish value and account for each element only once. The methods for estimating accrued depreciation are the economic age-life method, the modified economic age-life method, the breakdown method, sales comparison techniques, and income capitalization techniques. An additional method, the physical age-life method, can be used to estimate physical deterioration *only.*

Accrued depreciation is applied to improvements only because the site is included in the value estimate at its current market value. External forces can cause the site to lose value, but the effects of externalities on site value are reflected in the current market value of the site.

Table 16.1 Estimating Accrued Depreciation by the Economic Age-Life Method

	Reproduction Cost
Cost new	$222,725
Total economic life	50 yrs.
Remaining economic life	32 yrs.
Effective age	18 yrs.
Ratio applied to current cost: 18/50	36%
Less total accrued depreciation	$ 80,181
Depreciated value of improvements	$142,544
Plus land value	60,000
Indicated value by the cost approach	$202,544
Rounded	$202,500

Economic Age-Life Method

To estimate accrued depreciation with the economic age-life method, the ratio between the effective age and total economic life of a building is applied to the cost of the improvements as of the effective appraisal date to obtain a lump-sum deduction for accrued depreciation. (See Table 16.1.) The formula is

$$\frac{\text{Effective age}}{\text{Total economic life}} \times \text{reproduction or replacement cost} = \text{accrued depreciation}$$

This method appears simple, but many items of accrued depreciation are obscured because they are grouped together. One major weakness of the economic age-life method is that curable items of depreciation are not treated separately. Furthermore, the method does not recognize that some building components may have shorter remaining physical lives than the total economic life of the structure.

The economic age-life concept normally pertains to overall depreciation. This method does consider functional and external obsolescence and physical deterioration, but it does not differentiate between the separate causes of accrued depreciation.

Modified Economic Age-Life Method

The effect of curable items of accrued depreciation is recognized in the modified economic age-life method. To apply the method, the appraiser first estimates the cost to cure all curable items of physical deterioration due to deferred maintenance and functional obsolescence. This sum is deducted from the cost of the improvements as of the effective appraisal date. The appraiser then arrives at a percentage, lump-sum deduction that covers all incurable items by applying the ratio of effective age to total economic life to the cost of improvements minus all curable physical and functional obsolescence estimated as of the effective appraisal

Table 16.2 Estimating Accrued Depreciation by the Modified Economic Age-Life Method

	Reproduction Cost
Cost new	$222,725
Less physical and functional curable items	2,250
Depreciated cost	$220,475
Total economic life	50 yrs.
Remaining economic life*	33 yrs.
Effective age*	17 yrs.
Ratio applied to cost less physical and functional curable items: 17/50	34%
Less incurable items	$220,475
from all causes	× 0.34
	$74,962
Depreciated value of improvements	$145,513
Site value	60,000
Indicated value by the cost approach	$205,513
Rounded	$205,500

* After curable physical deterioration and curable functional obsolescence have been accounted for, the remaining economic life of the structure may increase and/or its effective age may decrease depending on the magnitude of the changes.

date. (See Table 16.2.) In applying the modified economic age-life method, the appraiser must recognize that when curable items are cured, the structure's remaining economic life may increase and/or the effective age may decrease.

Although immediately curable items of depreciation are recognized in the modified economic age-life method, the method does not allow for differences in the remaining economic lives of individual structural components, particularly short-lived items. The method is predicated on the assumption that a single age-life ratio can be applied to the entire structure.

The modified economic age-life method presumes that utility is reduced on a straight-line basis, which makes the method simple, but perhaps unrealistic. Careful estimation of effective age based on thorough investigation of the property can often overcome this weakness. The modified economic age-life method provides a convenient means for relating properties to one another and for making comparisons within a set of properties.

Breakdown Method

To apply the breakdown method of estimating accrued depreciation, an appraiser analyzes each cause of depreciation separately, measures the amount of each, and then totals the estimates to derive a lump-sum figure that is deducted from the estimated reproduction or replacement cost. If the appraiser is using replacement

Table 16.3 Breakdown Method of Estimating Accrued Depreciation

Item	Reproduction Cost	Replacement Cost
Physical deterioration		
Curable	Cost to cure	Same
Incurable	Physical age-life or economic age-life (with effective age adjusted)	Same
Functional obsolescence		
Curable		
Deficiency requiring		
Addition	Cost to add less cost if included in new building today	Same
Substitution or modernization	Cost of existing item in cost new less physical deterioration previously charged plus cost to remove less salvage value	Same
Superadequacy	Current cost new less physical deterioration charged plus cost to remove less salvage value	Cost to remove less salvage value
Incurable		
Deficiency		
Item not included in cost new but should be	Capitalized (PV) net rent loss @ R_B less cost if included in cost new	Same
Item in cost new but should not be	Current cost new less physical deterioration charged less value added	Same
Superadequacy	Current cost new less physical deterioration charged plus PV of added cost of ownership less value added	PV of added cost of ownership less value added
External obsolescence	Capitalization of property's net income loss due to external obsolescence; proportionate allocation to improvement	Same

cost, some forms of functional obsolescence are automatically eliminated. (See Table 16.3.)

The five basic types of accrued depreciation that affect structures are

1. Curable physical deterioration
2. Incurable physical deterioration
3. Curable functional obsolescence
4. Incurable functional obsolescence
5. External obsolescence (which may be temporary if caused by depressed market conditions)

The various types of accrued depreciation are discussed in this chapter in the order in which they are traditionally treated in appraisal reports. However, an appraiser may find it more convenient to measure all curable physical and functional items first and then analyze physical, functional, and external incurable items. Generally, incurable items cannot be measured properly until all curable items have been measured due to the nature of curable and incurable deterioration.

The valuation of single-family properties generally does not require the amount of detail used in the breakdown method. To estimate accrued depreciation for a single-family property, an appraiser may sometimes use a simple cost per square foot derived from a national cost service or a lump-sum accrued depreciation estimate derived with an age-life method. These procedures are distillations of the method illustrated in the following pages. Although certain appraisal problems can be resolved with simple cost-per-square-foot estimates, many appraisals require the use of the breakdown method. Appraisers should be familiar with the more exacting, detailed method to apply the simple procedures accurately.

SAMPLE APPLICATION

The tables that follow illustrate applications of the breakdown method. The site value indicated in the tables is supported by market analysis. The tables are based on a hypothetical two-story office building with 4,667 square feet of gross building area and 3,770 square feet of net leasable area. The building is located on a 2,372- sq.-ft. site and contains most forms of accrued depreciation.

Table 16.4 is a summary of the reproduction cost estimate of the office building. In the subsequent tables, estimates of each category of depreciation are calculated on a reproduction cost basis.

Curable Physical Deterioration

Curable physical deterioration refers to items of deferred maintenance; the estimate of curable physical deterioration applies only to items in need of repair on the effective appraisal date. This element of accrued depreciation is measured as the cost of restoring the item to new or reasonably new condition—i.e., the cost to cure. Table 16.5 shows the calculations for estimating curable physical items of deterioration.

An observed condition in the improvements being appraised is considered curable if the cost of correcting the condition, including any reasonable profit, would be offset by an equal or greater increase in value. Most structural defects,

Table 16.4 Reproduction Cost by the Quantity Survey Method

	Reproduction Cost
Direct costs (including labor, materials, equipment, and contractor's overhead and profit)	
Excavation and site preparation	$ 395
Foundation	4,685
Exterior walls	53,275
Roof structure	9,720
Roof cover	2,505
Frame	19,590
Floor structure	12,925
Floor cover (carpeting)	5,995
Ceiling	5,505
Interior partitions	33,300
Painting (exterior and interior)	1,250
Plumbing system	5,675
Plumbing fixtures	2,135
Electrical system	6,560
Electrical fixtures	3,415
HVAC	13,580
Total direct costs	$180,510
Indirect costs (including architect's fees, survey, legal fees, permits and licenses, insurance, taxes, financing charges, selling expenses, leasing expenses, and holding expenses)	$ 15,215
Entrepreneurial profit	$ 27,000
Total reproduction cost	$222,725
Cost per sq. ft. of gross building area	$ 47.72

Table 16.5 Reproduction Cost: Curable Physical Deterioration (Deferred Maintenance)

	Reproduction Cost	Cost to Cure	Remainder
Roof cover (repair)	$2,505	$ 250*	$2,255
Painting	1,250	1,350†	0
Total curable physical deterioration		$1,600	

* The roof was damaged in a storm; the cost to cure the roof is $250.
† The cost to cure the painting exceeds its current cost because additional labor and preparation are required that are not involved in new construction.

deficiencies, and superadequacies can be corrected with new construction technology, but the crucial consideration is economic. Will curing the condition restore the structure's function and is it prudent to cure it at this time?

Appraisers differ in how they categorize a curable building component that is only partly worn. For example, a five-year-old roof that is expected to have a total physical life of 25 years obviously contributes less value than it would if it were new. Some appraisers opine that the 20% loss in value cannot economically be cured as of the date of the appraisal; others believe that deteriorated roofs are indeed curable. The pro rata loss in value due to such an item may be deducted as incurable or curable deterioration; the appraiser's choice of either category will not affect the market value opinion.

Incurable Physical Deterioration

Incurable physical deterioration identifies items of deterioration that cannot be practically or economically corrected at present. This type of depreciation is calculated for all structural components that are not included in the curable physical category. Because the cost to cure curable physical items of deterioration has already been deducted from the total reproduction or replacement cost estimate, incurable physical deterioration does not apply to the total cost estimate. Incurable physical deterioration must be based on the reproduction or replacement cost of the entire structure that remains *after the cost to cure the components treated as physically curable has been deducted*. Otherwise, the cost of incurable physical deterioration would also be charged to curable items.

For purposes of analysis, items that have incurable physical deterioration are classified as long-lived and short-lived. A long-lived item is a building component that is expected to have a remaining economic life that is the same as the remaining economic life of the entire structure. A short-lived item is a component that is expected to have a remaining economic life that is shorter than the remaining economic life of the structure.

Whether items of physical deterioration that are not due to deferred maintenance are classified as curable or incurable, the deterioration in short-lived items must be measured consistently and each element of the structure must be measured only once. Tables 16.6 and 16.7 show the calculations for estimating the physical deterioration evident in short- and long-lived items.

In the tables incurable physical deterioration for both short- and long-lived components is usually estimated with *the physical age-life method.*

To estimate the depreciation charged for incurable physical deterioration in short-lived components, the appraiser applies *the ratio of actual age to estimated total physical life* to the reproduction or replacement cost of each incurable physical short-lived component that remains after the cost to correct curable physical deterioration has been deducted from the total cost estimate. The depreciation evident in all the items is added to obtain an estimate of the total incurable physical deterioration in short-lived building components.

To calculate the amount of depreciation to be charged to incurable physical long-lived components, the total reproduction or replacement cost of the curable physical items (or cost to cure in some instances) and incurable physical short-lived components must be deducted from the estimated reproduction or replace-

Table 16.6 Reproduction Cost: Incurable Physical Deterioration, Short-Lived Components

	Reproduction Cost Remaining	Actual Age	Total Physical Life	Ratio Applied to Cost		Incurable Physical Depreciation
Roof cover	$ 2,255*	10 yrs.	15 yrs.	10/15	(67%)	$ 1,511
Floor cover	5,995	7 yrs.	10 yrs.	7/10	(70%)	4,197
Ceiling	5,505	5 yrs.	15 yrs.	5/15	(33%)	1,817
Painting	0	New	5 yrs.	0		0
Plumbing fixtures	2,135	10 yrs.	20 yrs.	10/20	(50%)	1,068
Electrical fixtures	3,415	8 yrs.	10 yrs.	8/10	(80%)	2,732
HVAC	4,750†	10 yrs.	15 yrs.	10/15	(67%)	3,183
	$24,055					
Total incurable physical deterioration, short-lived components						$14,508
Rounded						$14,510

* Of the current reproduction cost of $2,505, $250 was cured in the treatment of physical curable deterioration, leaving a remainder of $2,255. The appraiser may choose to use the entire $2,505 if repairing the damaged item will not increase the remaining life of the building component.
† Of the current reproduction cost of $13,580 for the entire HVAC system, $4,750 is attributable to short-lived items such as fans, controls, and other mechanical components that will need to be repaired or replaced before the end of the structure's estimated economic life. The $8,830 remainder is included in the long-lived category.

Table 16.7 Reproduction Cost: Incurable Physical Deterioration, Long-Lived Components

Reproduction cost		$222,725
Less reproduction cost of curable physical items	$ 1,500*	
and incurable physical short-lived items	$24,055	
		−25,555
Reproduction cost of long-lived items		$197,170
Actual age—5 yrs.		
Total physical life (new): 75 yrs.		
Ratio applied to cost: 5/75		× 0.06667
Total incurable physical deterioration, long-lived components		$13,145

* This figure consists of the cost to cure the roof ($250) and the reproduction cost of the painting ($1,250). The reproduction cost of the painting is used because the cost to cure exceeds reproduction cost.

ment cost. If this step is not completed, the charges for curable and incurable physical deterioration in short-lived components will be duplicated. After subtracting these figures, an appraiser may use one of two methods to estimate incurable physical deterioration in the long-lived components.

The first method involves use of a ratio of actual age to estimated total physical life. This ratio is applied to the remaining replacement or reproduction cost of incurable physical long-lived building components. The use of this ratio ensures that components of functional or external obsolescence are not included in the estimate of physical deterioration. The problem with this method is the difficulty of estimating total physical life from the market. Physical life is typically longer than economic life.

The second method employs a ratio of effective age to economic life. This ratio is applied to the remaining replacement or reproduction cost of the incurable physical long-lived building components. In applying this method, the effective age has to be adjusted so that the ratio does not include curable physical deterioration, incurable physical deterioration of short-lived components, functional obsolescence, or external obsolescence. Accordingly, the effective age used in the ratio is shorter than the effective age used in the economic age-life method of estimating total depreciation.

The economic age-life method should be applied with great care to derive a separate estimate of the incurable physical deterioration of long-lived items. The economic age-life concept normally pertains only to overall depreciation. A distorted estimate may result if the economic age-life method is used to measure the incurable physical deterioration of long-lived items separately without proper adjustment of effective age to reflect deductions for curable physical deterioration, incurable physical deterioration of short-lived items, and functional or external obsolescence.

Curable Functional Obsolescence

Functional obsolescence is a loss in value resulting from defects in design. It can also be caused by changes that, over time, have made some aspect of a structure, such as its materials or design, obsolete by current standards. The defect may be curable or incurable. *To be curable, the cost of replacing the outmoded or unacceptable aspect must be the same as or less than the anticipated increase in value.* Curable functional obsolescence is measured as the cost to cure the condition. Deficiencies requiring additions are not included in either reproduction or replacement cost, and some items of functional obsolescence due to superadequacies are not present when depreciation is estimated on a replacement cost basis. Curable functional obsolescence may be divided into three subcategories.

1. *Deficiency requiring addition*, which is measured by how much the cost of the addition exceeds the cost of the item if it were installed new during construction

2. *Deficiency requiring substitution or modernization*, which is measured as the cost of the existing component in the cost estimate minus physical deterioration already charged against the existing component and salvage value, plus the cost to remove existing component and the added cost of installation. *Salvage value* is defined as the value attributed to an item to be removed from the property, usually for use elsewhere.

3. *Superadequacy,* which is measured as the current reproduction cost of the item minus any physical deterioration already charged plus the cost of removal, minus the salvage value, if any. A superadequacy is curable if correcting it on the date of the appraisal is economically feasible; otherwise it is considered incurable. For example, a superadequacy is curable when the added value of curing it is greater than the cost to cure. The measure for a superadequacy when using replacement cost is the cost to remove minus the salvage value.

Tables 16.8, 16.9, and 16.10 show the calculations for measuring curable functional obsolescence when reproduction cost is used.

The office building being appraised has no lavatory on the second floor, which has made it difficult to rent this space. Adequate space is available for the addition of the lavatory. Although space allocation is included in the reproduction cost estimate, fixtures are not. The calculation is necessary because it would be improper to deduct a component from the reproduction cost that was not included in this cost.

Table 16.8 Reproduction Cost: Curable Functional Obsolescence—Deficiency Requiring Addition

Cost to install a lavatory in the existing structure	$1,200
Less cost to install a lavatory in the existing structure if the structure were being built new on the date of the appraisal	900
Loss in value	$300

The light fixtures in the subject office building are outdated. Table 16.9 shows the loss in value attributable to this item.

Table 16.9 Reproduction Cost: Curable Functional Obsolescence—Deficiency Requiring Substitution or Modernization

Cost of existing fixtures already included in cost estimate	$1,000
Less physical deterioration previously charged	800
Less salvage value	0
Plus removal costs	200
Plus cost to install new fixtures	400
Loss in value	$800

The office building includes 150 square feet of lighted and climate-controlled storage area. Demand for office space indicates the storage area should be converted to office use. This superadequacy is considered curable only if it is economically feasible to cure on the effective appraisal date, i.e., if the added value of curing it is greater than the cost to cure.

Table 16.10 Reproduction Cost: Curable Functional Obsolescence—Superadequacy

Determination of Feasibility

Cost to finish storage area	$750
Less salvage value	0
Total cost to cure	$750
Potential gain in *NOI*	$900
(150 square feet × $6.00)*	
Less increased operating expenses or plus reduced operating expenses	0
Gain in *NOI*	$900
Change in *NOI* capitalized at the building capitalization rate of 10.5%†	$8,571
Rounded	$8,570

The capitalized gain in *NOI* to the building that results from curing the superadequacy is greater than the cost to cure, so it is feasible to convert the storage area to office space.

Depreciation Estimate

Current reproduction cost of the storage area‡	$6,400
Less physical deterioration already charged	427
Subtotal	$5,973
Plus net cost to cure	750
Loss in value	$6,723
Rounded	$6,725

---

* The market rent for office space is $10 per square foot. Current storage space is leased for $4 per square foot. The increase in *NOI* is $6 per square foot for the 150 square feet.
† The appraiser estimates a building capitalization rate of 10.5%.
‡ The appraiser estimates the current reproduction cost of the storage area to be $6,400.

Functional Obsolescence in Replacement Cost Estimates

If the current cost estimate is based on a replacement rather than a reproduction, the cost of excess or superadequate items is not included. Therefore, no expenditure to reproduce them and no charge for physical deterioration need be deducted. However, the cost to cure the superadequacy is still a valid charge. The $750 shown in Table 16.10 as the cost to cure (convert) the storage area represents the extent of curable functional obsolescence due to the superadequacy that must be applied to the replacement cost estimate. Tables 16.11, 16.12, and 16.13 illustrate appropriate procedures for calculating curable functional obsolescence when a replacement cost estimate is used. As in the preceding tables, these calculations are based on the conditions observed in the subject office building.

Table 16.11 Replacement Cost: Curable Functional Obsolescence—Deficiency Requiring Addition

Cost to install a lavatory in the existing structure	$1,200
Less cost to install a lavatory in the existing structure if the structure were built new on the date of the appraisal	900
Loss in value	$300

The curable functional obsolescence evidenced by the outdated light fixtures is measured by the cost to cure the defect after the contributory value of the deteriorated items, if any, is deducted (see Table 16.12). If a structure contains an obsolete component that must be removed at a separate cost, the cost of removal would be added to the cost of the repairs.

Table 16.12 Replacement Cost: Curable Functional Obsolescence—Deficiency Requiring Substitution or Modernization

Cost of existing fixtures already included in cost estimate	$1,000
Less physical deterioration previously charged	800
Less salvage value	0
Plus removal costs	200
Plus added cost to install new fixtures	400
Loss in value	$800

Table 16.13 Replacement Cost: Curable Functional Obsolescence—Superadequacy

Cost to finish the storage area into office space less salvage value	$750*

* This is the only charge because the storage area was not included in the replacement cost estimate.

Incurable Functional Obsolescence

Incurable functional obsolescence may be caused by a deficiency or a superadequacy. Two types of deficiencies may be involved: an item not included in the cost new that should be, or an item included in the cost new that should not be. Incurable functional obsolescence due to a deficiency that *is not* included in the cost

Table 16.14 Reproduction or Replacement Cost: Incurable Functional Obsolescence— Deficiency

Estimated *NOI* loss due to the deficiency	$1,274
Building capitalization rate applicable to subject property (developed in the income capitalization approach)	10.5%
NOI loss divided by building capitalization rate ($1,274/0.105)	$12,133
Less cost if included in cost new estimate	7,500
Estimated incurable functional obsolescence due to the deficiency (rounded)	$4,635

estimate but should be, is measured as the net income loss attributed to the deficiency, capitalized at the building capitalization rate (developed in the income capitalization approach), less the cost of the item if it was included in the cost estimate. Incurable functional obsolescence due to a deficiency that *is* included in the cost estimate but should not be, is measured as the current cost new, less physical deterioration previously charged, less value added.

The calculations for measuring incurable functional obsolescence due to a deficiency are the same whether a reproduction or replacement cost basis is used (see Table 16.14).

The office building being appraised has no fire protection system. Other office buildings in the neighborhood have fire protection and sprinkler systems in place. Market analysis indicates a differential of $0.75 per square foot of net leasable area between office buildings with adequate fire protection systems and those without adequate systems. The subject property has 3,770 square feet of net leasable area, which indicates an annual gross income loss of $2,830, minus vacancy losses and expenses of $1,556, to produce a net operating income loss of $1,274 per year. The cost to add a sprinkler system is $15,000.

In many cases the net income loss as a percentage of gross income loss attributable to functional obsolescence differs from the general income and expense ratio for the property because certain expenses, such as utilities and insurance, are not affected by the deficiency, while other expenses, such as taxes and management, may be affected.

Incurable functional obsolescence due to a superadequacy is measured differently depending on whether a reproduction or replacement cost estimate is used. If reproduction cost is the base, the appraiser must consider the cost to construct a building that contains the same superadequacy. The superadequacy is measured as the reproduction cost of the superadequate component, minus any physical deterioration already charged, plus the present value of any added cost of ownership due to the presence of the superadequacy, less any value added such as in-

Table 16.15 Reproduction Cost: Incurable Functional Obsolescence—Superadequacy

Current reproduction cost of the superadequacy	$6,900
Less physical deterioration already charged*	460
Subtotal	$6,440
Plus present value of added cost of ownership†	0
Less value added‡	0
Estimated incurable functional obsolescence due to superadequacy	$6,440

* A 6²/3% charge was made for incurable physical deterioration, long-lived. Therefore, 6²/3% of the reproduction cost of the excess component must be deducted to avoid a double charge.
† No extra ownership expenses are incurred for this type of superadequacy.
‡ There is no increased rent resulting from the superadequacy. Therefore, no value added is attributable to this component.

creased rent. The charge for this burden of ownership is based on items such as additional taxes, insurance, maintenance, and utility charges. The excess depreciated reproduction cost of the item, over and above the cost that may be supported by an increase in market rent as a result of the superadequacy, is added to the capitalized net income loss to derive an indication of the total depreciation caused by incurable functional obsolescence due to a superadequacy.

To estimate incurable functional obsolescence due to a superadequacy when reproduction cost is the base, the appraiser must review the estimates of curable and incurable physical deterioration. If the superadequate component has been included in either of these categories, the reproduction cost of the superadequacy must be reduced by the amount of physical depreciation already charged. Such a charge is often made in estimating the incurable physical deterioration in long-lived components, but it could also be made in estimating curable or incurable physical deterioration in short-lived components. All charges made in estimating physical deterioration must be reviewed to ensure that charges for items of accrued depreciation are not made twice.

Replacement cost does not include the cost to construct a superadequacy, so no loss in the value of a superadequacy due to physical deterioration is considered when replacement cost is used. However, a charge is required if the superadequacy causes a monetary burden of ownership for items such as additional taxes, insurance, maintenance, and utility charges. The capitalized value of these additional expenses, over and above any increase in market rent resulting from the superadequacy (value added), represents the loss in value caused by incurable functional obsolescence due to the superadequacy.

Incurable functional obsolescence caused by a superadequacy is calculated in Table 16.15.

The office building was designed and built to accommodate three stories, but only two stories were constructed. It is not economically feasible to add the additional floor. The framing cost new of a three-story building would be $19,590, while the framing cost new of a two-story building would be $12,690. Therefore, the cost of the superadequacy is $19,590 − $12,690, or $6,900.

Because replacement cost does not include the cost of the superadequacy, no loss in value for incurable functional obsolescence caused by a superadequacy is considered except a charge for any burden of ownership created by the superadequacy. This particular superadequacy does not cause additional expenses for the subject property, so there is no loss in value due to the superadequacy in this case

External Obsolescence

External obsolescence, the diminished utility of a structure due to negative influences emanating from outside the building, is usually incurable on the part of the owner, landlord, or tenant. External obsolescence can be caused by a variety of factors— e.g., neighborhood decline; the property's location in a community, state, or region; or local market conditions. Any estimate of external obsolescence must be based on a thorough neighborhood analysis and justified in the neighborhood analysis section of the appraisal report.

External influences can cause any property to lose value. In the cost approach the total loss in value due to external obsolescence is allocated to the improvements. Therefore, an appraiser must first estimate the income attributable to the improvements. Then the income imputable to the improvements is capitalized at the building capitalization rate to estimate external obsolescence.

Two methods can be used to measure external obsolescence. The appraiser should select the procedure that is best supported by market evidence. The appraiser can either 1) capitalize the income or rent loss attributable to the negative influence, or 2) compare sales of similar properties that are subject to the negative influence with others that are not. If pertinent sales data are abundant, the second procedure is preferred. However, an appraiser may encounter significant practical problems in attempting to account for other differences between the subject property and the comparable properties. Care should be exercised when this method is used.

To estimate external obsolescence by capitalizing the resulting loss in property income, the appraiser first estimates the income loss to the entire property that is attributable to external forces. Then the loss in income attributable to the improvements is capitalized at the building capitalization rate.

Appraisers can often find market data to help break down an overall capitalization rate (R_O) into a building capitalization rate (R_B) and land (or site) capitalization rate (R_L). It is much more difficult to find an income or rent multiplier that reflects the proportions of building and site.

When net operating income and appropriate capitalization rates are used, the net income loss imputable to the building can be capitalized at the building capitalization rate. The resulting figure is an estimate of depreciation due to external obsolescence.

Appraisers should recognize that conditions in temporarily depressed markets may dictate measuring external obsolescence by discounting the net income loss for the time frame over which the negative externality is expected to exist rather than by capitalizing the loss, which would assume the condition is permanent.

Table 16.16 Reproduction or Replacement Cost: External Obsolescence

Estimated annual NOI not subject to external obsolescence after physical deterioration and functional obsolescence are cured	$23,940
Less subject's current NOI after physical deterioration and functional obsolescence are cured	−21,490
Estimated annual NOI loss due to external influences	$ 2,450
NOI imputable to the land (land value of $60,000 at R_L of 8.5%)	$ 5,100
NOI imputable to the building (total property NOI of $21,490 minus NOI imputable to the land)	$16,390
Income loss attributable to the building (building proportion* of 76.3% × $2,450)	$ 1,869
Building capitalization rate	0.105
Capitalized net income loss to building ($1,869/0.105)	$17,800
Amount of external obsolescence applicable to building	$17,800

* To derive the proportion of NOI to the building, NOI to the land is divided by NOI to the overall property: $5,100/$21,490 = 23.7%. The resulting percentage was then subtracted from 1; 1 − 23.7% = 76.3%.

The appraiser may capitalize the remaining income at the market-derived land or site capitalization rate to derive an indication of the loss in value attributable to the site. If this percentage of the loss in site value approximates the adjustment that was made for location in the sales comparison analysis of site value,[1] the appraiser can have greater confidence in both the location adjustment and the estimate of external obsolescence attributed to the building in the cost approach.

Table 16.16 illustrates one procedure for estimating external obsolescence. The procedure can be used with either a reproduction or replacement cost estimate.

The subject building in Table 16.16 is adjacent to an operating landfill. On windy days the neighborhood and property experience an annoying stench. Office buildings a few blocks away are not affected by this nuisance and have a greater annual net operating income of approximately $0.65 per square foot. The subject suffers an annual net operating income loss of $2,450 (3,770 square feet × $0.65).

TOTAL ESTIMATES OF ACCRUED DEPRECIATION

After each element of depreciation is accurately estimated, the results of the analysis are summarized. (See Table 16.17.)

FINAL VALUE INDICATION

When accrued depreciation is measured with the breakdown method, the appraiser derives a final value indication in the cost approach by deducting the estimate of accrued depreciation from the reproduction or replacement cost of the improvements on the effective appraisal date and then adding the market value of the site on the same date. When appropriate, this total represents a fee simple

---

1. This procedure assumes that an adjustment for location has been made in the sales comparison approach. If a comparable property in proximity to the subject has recently been sold, there is no need for a location adjustment.

Table 16.17 Reproduction Cost: Total Estimate of Accrued Depreciation, Breakdown Method

Physical deterioration		
Curable, deferred maintenance	$ 1,600	
Incurable, short-lived items	14,510	
Incurable, long-lived items	13,145	
Total		$29,255
Functional obsolescence		
Curable ($300 + $800 + $6,725)	$ 7,825	
Incurable ($4,635 + $6,440)	11,075	
Total		$18,900
External obsolescence		17,800
Total accrued depreciation		$65,955

value indication, which may have to be adjusted to reflect the specific property rights being appraised. An adjustment to reflect rents above or below market levels is made to obtain the value of the leased fee. An example appears below. The final calculations are shown in Table 16.18.

It is assumed that the office building being appraised is rented to a single tenant for six more years at an annual net rent of $38,000. Market rent is $44,000 per year net. The present value of the tenant's leasehold interest is $24,668, which was obtained by discounting the $6,000 difference between market rent and contract rent for the six-year term at the 12% discount rate currently sought by equity investors—i.e., $6,000 × 4.111407 (present value of $1 per period) = $24,667.

ESTIMATING ACCRUED DEPRECIATION BY THE SALES COMPARISON APPROACH

When accrued depreciation is measured with sales comparison techniques, the reproduction or replacement cost of the property on the valuation date minus the value contribution of the improvements on the same date should equal the total accrued depreciation. Table 16.19 illustrates the procedure for estimating accrued depreciation through analysis of comparable sales.

The accuracy of this method depends on the availability of truly comparable sales of both improved properties and vacant sites. The real property interests conveyed in the improved properties used for comparison should be the same as the real property interests being valued in the subject property. Sales of partial interests should be used with caution because vast differences can exist among leased fee or leasehold interests. Any adjustment for differences in real property interests must be well supported with market data.

The sales used in Table 16.19 are current and similar to the subject property in terms of physical, functional, and external elements of accrued depreciation. Adjustments should be made for any dissimilarities. The sales indicate a narrow range for accrued depreciation of between 33% and 37% of total replacement

Table 16.18 Cost Approach Value Indication Using Reproduction Cost

	Reproduction Cost	
Direct	$180,510	
Indirect	15,215	
Entrepreneurial profit*	27,000	
Total	$222,725	
Accrued depreciation		
Curable physical	$1,600	
Incurable physical, short-lived	14,510	
Incurable physical, long-lived	13,145	
Subtotal†	$29,255	
Curable functional, deficiency	$300	
Curable functional, deficiency	800	
Curable, functional superadequacy	6,725	
Subtotal	$7,825	
Incurable functional, deficiency	$4,635	
Incurable functional, superadequacy	6,440	
Subtotal	$11,075	
External obsolescence	$17,800	
Total accrued depreciation	$65,955	(29.6%)
Depreciated value of improvements	$156,770	
Site value	60,000	
Fee simple value indication	$216,770	
Adjustment for tenant's leasehold interest‡	−24,668	
Leased fee value indicated by cost approach	$192,102	
Rounded	$192,100	

* This estimate is derived from market evidence of the profits accruing to investors in properties similar to the subject property.

† At this intermediate stage, some appraisers employ physical value, which is the value that would be calculated if the property had no functional or external obsolescence. Physical value is obtained by deducting all physical deterioration from the reproduction or replacement cost estimate.

‡ There are times when the contract rent may be higher than the market rent, necessitating a positive adjustment rather than a negative adjustment as shown above.

Table 16.19 Estimating Accrued Depreciation with Sales Comparison Techniques (All sales are of fee simple interests.)

	Sale 1	Sale 2	Sale 3
Sale price	$215,000	$165,000	$365,000
Estimated site value	−60,000	−40,000	−127,750
Present value of improvements	$155,000	$125,000	$237,250
Estimated replacement cost on date of sale	$230,000	$195,000	$375,000
Less present value of improvements	−155,000	−125,000	−237,250
Indicated total accrued depreciation in dollars	$ 75,000	$ 70,000	$137,750
Indicated total accrued depreciation as percentage of current replacement cost (rounded)	33%	36%	37%

cost. The total percentage of depreciation estimated by the other methods are shown below.

	Reproduction Cost
Economic age-life	36%
Modified economic age-life	34%
Breakdown	28%

When sales comparison techniques are used to estimate depreciation, various types of depreciation—i.e., physical, functional, and external—are not distinguished. If the sale is an open-market transaction involving a fee simple interest, site value is market supported, and the estimate of current replacement or reproduction cost is accurate, the percentage derived from comparative analysis will represent all types of accrued depreciation.

However, this method for measuring accrued depreciation has certain limitations. An adequate quantity of reliable comparable sales data is needed. Truly comparable sales are not always available and certain special-purpose properties are not frequently exchanged in the open market. When data are not available, the method is of little use. Furthermore, the allocation of comparable sale prices between site value and improvement value may be difficult to justify, particularly when the ratio of site value to building value varies.

SUMMARY

Depreciation is a loss in property value from any cause as of the effective appraisal date. In other words, it is the difference between reproduction or replacement cost of an improvement and its market value as of the effective date of appraisal. Depreciation can emanate from three sources: physical deterioration, functional obsolescence attributable to a deficiency or a superadequacy, and external obsolescence caused by changes in the overall economy, demand patterns, or general property use in the neighborhood. Physical deterioration and functional obsolescence can usually be observed in an improvement. Depreciation represents a penalty because the market recognizes it as a value loss. A temporary undersupply of properties relative to demand may offset the value loss older buildings generally experience. Historic or architectural significance may also compensate for the value penalty that time imposes.

Several important terms are associated with depreciation. To measure *accrued depreciation*, an appraiser estimates the amount of value loss incurred by the subject structure in its present condition, as compared with the value of the property if it were new. *Book depreciation*, the amount of capital recapture written off on an owner's books, is based on original cost; it is not derived from the market. *Economic life* is the period over which improvements to real estate contribute to property value. Generally, the economic life of a property is shorter than its *physical life* if the property is not rehabilitated. *Remaining economic life* is an estimate of how long improvements will continue to contribute to property value.

Actual age (i.e., historical or chronological age) is the number of years that have elapsed since construction was completed. *Effective age* is the age indicated by the condition and utility of the structure. If a building has been well maintained, has an especially good design, or happens to be in an undersupplied market, its effective age may be less than its actual age.

To measure accrued depreciation, an appraiser considers all elements that may cause a loss in value and treats each element only once. Accrued depreciation can be estimated with *the economic age-life method, the modified economic age-life method, the breakdown method,* or *sales comparison and income capitalization techniques*. To estimate physical deterioration *only, the physical age-life method* may be used.

To apply *the economic age-life method*, the ratio of effective age to total economic life is applied to the current reproduction or replacement cost of the improvements. Although this is the simplest method of estimating accrued depreciation, it does not distinguish between curable and incurable items of depreciation, or between short- and long-lived building components. The economic age-life method should not be used to derive estimates of the incurable physical deterioration of short-lived items in the breakdown method.

The modified economic age-life method recognizes the effect of curable items of physical deterioration due to deferred maintenance and functional obsolescence. An appraiser estimates the curable depreciation in physical and functional items, and deducts this amount from the current reproduction or replacement cost of the improvements. To estimate incurable depreciation, the appraiser determines the ratio of effective age to total economic life and applies it to the cost of the improvements as of the effective appraisal date, minus the estimated curable depreciation. The appraiser must recognize that correcting curable items may increase the remaining economic life and/or decrease the effective age of the improvements. The modified economic age-life method does not distinguish between short- and long-lived items of depreciation.

The breakdown method analyzes each cause of depreciation separately and measures its effect. The separate estimates are totaled to arrive at a lump-sum amount, which is deducted from the reproduction or replacement cost of the improvements as of the effective appraisal date. When this method is applied to a replacement cost estimate, deductions for certain forms of functional obsolescence (i.e., superadequacies) in the improvements are not included. The five types of accrued depreciation that this method considers are 1) curable physical deterioration, 2) incurable physical deterioration, 3) curable functional obsolescence, 4) incurable functional obsolescence, and 5) external obsolescence.

An appraiser may choose to consider all curable physical and functional items before measuring incurable items, because the depreciation in incurable items cannot be properly measured until the depreciation in curable items has been calculated. The cost to correct curable items is offset by a resulting increase in value; the cost to cure incurable items exceeds the resulting increase in value.

Curable physical deterioration applies to items of deferred maintenance that are in need of repair on the effective appraisal date. An item is curable if the cost of curing it is less than or equal to the increase in property value. Appraisers differ on how a partly worn item should be categorized. Some opine that the value loss cannot be cured as of the date of the appraisal, so the item is incurable; others contend that deterioration is curable. In any case the prorata loss must be deducted as either curable or incurable physical deterioration.

Incurable physical deterioration refers to deterioration that cannot be practically or economically cured. The estimate of incurable physical deterioration is based on the reproduction or replacement cost of the entire structure after the cost to cure physically curable components has been deducted. Items of incurable physical deterioration are classified as long-lived and short-lived. A long-lived item is expected to have a remaining economic life equal to the life of the entire structure; a short-lived item is expected to have a remaining economic life that is shorter than the life of the structure. The physical age-life method should be used with short-lived items and can be used with long-lived items. The ratio of actual age to estimated total physical age is applied to the reproduction or replacement cost of the short- and long-lived items to derive an estimate of incurable physical deterioration. An alternative method for estimating the physical deterioration in long-lived items is an economic age-life method in which the effective age is adjusted for all other components of depreciation found in the property. This ratio of effective age to estimated economic life is applied to the replacement or reproduction cost of long-lived items to derive an estimate of incurable physical deterioration. Great care should be taken in applying this method to avoid including other components of depreciation in the ratio.

Curable functional obsolescence is caused by defects in design or changes in structural standards and building materials. To be curable the cost of replacing the outmoded or unacceptable aspect must be less than or equal to the anticipated increase in value. Curable functional obsolescence can result from a deficiency requiring additions, a deficiency requiring substitution or modernization, or a superadequacy. If the cost is based on replacement rather than reproduction of the improvements, the cost of superadequate items is not included.

Incurable functional obsolescence may be caused by a deficiency or a superadequacy. When it is caused by a deficiency that is not included in the cost estimate but should be, incurable functional obsolescence is estimated by capitalizing the net income loss attributable to the deficiency—i.e., by dividing the net income loss by the building capitalization rate minus the cost of the item if included in the estimate of cost new. Incurable functional obsolescence due to a deficiency that is included in the cost estimate but should not be is measured as the current cost new, less physical deterioration previously charged, less value added. When caused by a superadequacy, incurable functional obsolescence may be measured two different ways, depending on whether reproduction or replacement cost is used.

If reproduction cost is the base, the superadequacy is measured as the reproduction cost of the superadequate component, minus any physical deterioration already charged, plus the present value of the added costs of ownership (e.g., for taxes, insurance, maintenance, and utilities) minus value added, if any. If replacement cost is the base, the superadequacy is represented only by a charge for the extra monetary burden of ownership minus value added.

External obsolescence is caused by negative influences outside the site; it is usually incurable on the part of the owner. The total income loss due to external obsolescence must be allocated between the site and the improvements. In one method, the loss in income allocated to the improvement is capitalized at the building capitalization rate to determine the extent of external obsolescence as of the effective appraisal date. The effect of external obsolescence on site value is considered separately in site value analysis by the adjustment for location. The proportionate share of external obsolescence allocated to the site is *not* applied to the site value, but it may be used to test the reasonableness of the value loss charged to the property's location in the site valuation section of the appraisal report.

An appraiser may also apply sales comparison techniques, analyzing sales of similar properties that are subject to the negative influence and others that are not. With this method, practical problems may arise in isolating and quantifying other differences between the subject and the comparable properties.

To derive a final value indication, the appraiser totals the estimates of each form of accrued depreciation, subtracts the total from the reproduction or replacement cost of the improvements, and adjusts this figure, if appropriate, to reflect the specific property rights being appraised.

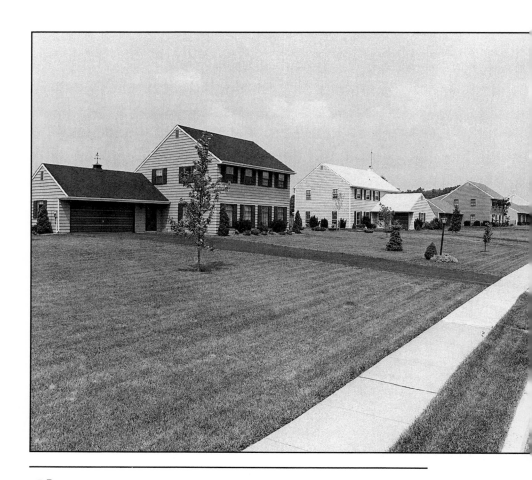

Chapter 17

THE SALES COMPARISON APPROACH

$\mathcal{T}$he sales comparison approach is the process in which a market value estimate is derived by analyzing the market for similar properties and comparing these properties to the subject property. Estimates of market rent, cost, depreciation, and other value parameters may be derived in the other approaches to value using comparative techniques. Often these elements are also analyzed in the sales comparison approach to determine the adjustments to be made to the sale prices of comparable properties. The comparative techniques of analysis applied in the sales comparison approach are fundamental to the valuation process.

In the sales comparison approach, market value is estimated by comparing the subject property to similar properties that have recently sold, are listed for sale, or are under contract (i.e., recently drawn up purchase offers accompanied by a cash or equivalent deposit). A major premise of the sales comparison approach is that the market value of a property is directly related to the prices of comparable, competitive properties.

The comparative analysis performed in the approach focuses on similarities and differences among properties and transactions that affect value. These may include differences in the property rights appraised, the motivations of buyers and sellers, financing terms, market conditions at the time of sale, size, location, physical features, and, if the properties produce income, economic characteristics. Elements of comparison are tested against market evidence to determine which elements are sensitive to change and how they affect value.

RELATIONSHIP TO APPRAISAL PRINCIPLES

The concepts of anticipation and change, together with the principles of supply and demand, substitutions, balance, and externalities, are basic to the sales comparison approach. Guided by these principles, an appraiser attempts to consider all issues relevant to the valuation problem in a manner that is consistent and reflects local market conditions.

Supply and Demand

Property prices are determined by the market; they result from negotiations between buyers and sellers. Buyers constitute market demand and the properties offered for sale make up the supply. If the demand for a particular type of property is high, prices tend to increase; if demand is low, prices tend to decline. Shifts in the supply of improved properties frequently lag behind shifts in demand because supply is created by time-consuming construction and reduced by conversion to other uses, while satisfiable demand can change rapidly. The analysis of real estate markets at a specific time may seem to focus on demand, but the supply of properties must also be considered. Proposed construction, conversion and demolition may change the supply-demand relationship and affect prices. To estimate demand appraisers consider the number of potential users of a particular type of property, their purchasing power, and their tastes and preferences. To analyze supply appraisers focus on existing properties that are unsold or vacant as well as properties that are being constructed, converted, or planned. Shifts in any of these elements may cause the prices of the subject property and comparable properties to vary.

Substitution

As applied in the sales comparison approach, the principle of substitution holds that the value of a property tends to be set by the price that would be paid to acquire a substitute property of similar utility and desirability within a reasonable amount of time. This principle implies that the reliability of the sales comparison approach is diminished if substitute properties are not available in the market.

Balance

The forces of supply and demand tend toward equilibrium, or balance, in the market, but absolute equilibrium is almost never attained. The balance between supply and demand changes continually. Due to shifts in population, purchasing power, and consumer tastes and preferences, demand varies greatly over time. The construction of new buildings, conversion to other uses, and the demolition of old buildings cause supply to vary as well.

Another aspect of this principle holds that the relationship between land and improvements and the relationship between a property and its environment must both be in balance for a property to reflect its actual market value. If, for example, a property has too much land in relation to its improvements or too many expensive amenities for its location, an imbalance is created. Appraisers must watch for imbalances in the market and within properties because they can cause the market to impute different prices to otherwise comparable properties.

Externalities

Positive and negative external forces affect all types of property. A period of economic development or economic depression influences property values. An appraiser analyzes the neighborhood of a subject property to identify all significant external influences. To a great extent these external forces are reflected in the adjustments made for property location. Two properties with identical physical characteristics may have quite different market values if one of the properties has less attractive surroundings. The condition and lighting of streets, the convenience of transportation facilities, the adequacy of police protection, the enforcement of municipal regulation, and the proximity to shopping and restaurant facilities vary with location. These factors must be considered by the appraiser to determine if they have a positive or negative effect on the value of the property being appraised.

APPLICABILITY AND LIMITATIONS

The sales comparison approach is applicable to all types of real property interests when there are sufficient recent, reliable transactions to indicate value patterns or trends in the market. For property types that are bought and sold regularly, the sales comparison approach often provides a supportable indication of market value. When data are available, this is the most direct and systematic approach to value estimation.

When the number of market transactions is insufficient, the applicability of the sales comparison approach may be limited. For example, the sales comparison approach is rarely applied to special-purpose properties because few similar properties may be sold in a given market, even one that is geographically broad. This may also be true of the income approach. To value special-purpose properties, the cost approach may be more appropriate and reliable. Nevertheless, data on sales and offers for similar properties may establish broad limits for the value of the property being appraised and help verify the findings of other value approaches.

The sales comparison approach has broad applicability and is persuasive when sufficient data are available. It usually provides the primary indication of market value in appraisals of properties that are not purchased for their income-producing characteristics. Single-family residences provide the best example of this kind of property. Most single-family residential properties are amenable to direct sales comparison because many similar properties are commonly bought and sold in the same market, and many prospective buyers do not choose to rent or build. Typically, the sales comparison approach also provides the best indication of value for small, owner-occupied commercial and industrial properties.

Buyers of income-producing properties usually concentrate on a property's economic characteristics, most often focusing on the rate of return for an investment made in anticipation of future cash flows. Thoroughly analyzing comparable sales of large, complex, income-producing properties is difficult because information on the economic factors influencing buyers' decisions is not readily available from public records or buyers and sellers. For example, an appraiser may not have sufficient knowledge of the terms of the existing leases applicable to a multi-tenanted, class A office building that is comparable to the subject. Or the appraiser may not be fully informed of the investment parameters of the buyer. Sales data on the comparable will only be of limited use to the appraiser. Without complete information it will be difficult to arrive at a reliable indication of value for the subject property.

Rapidly changing economic conditions and legislation can limit the reliability of the sales comparison approach. For example, changes in income tax laws and zoning regulations, the availability and cost of financing, or moratoriums on building and infrastructure development may result in a lack of recent comparable sales that reflect the impact of such changes over a given time period. An appraiser will have difficulty finding reliable market data on which to base an adjustment for the change. Rapid inflation or deflation can also jeopardize the reliability of an appraiser's adjustments.

Little comparable data will exist for the first property to be renovated in an area of deteriorated buildings or for the only property of a given type in a neighborhood. The appraiser may need to expand the search for sales data to other comparable neighborhoods.

To ensure the reliability of value conclusions derived by applying the approach, the appraiser must verify the market data obtained and fully understand the behavioral characteristics of the buyers and sellers involved in property transactions. Caution should be exercised when relying on sales data provided by someone other than a party to the transaction. Incorrect assumptions and conclusions may result if the appraiser relies on cold statistical data without regard for the motivation of the parties to the transactions. Similarly, errors can result if the characteristics of the databases, anticipated income and expense schedules, or potential changes in use are not considered.

It is imperative that the appraiser identify and analyze the strengths and weaknesses of the data compiled and the comparative analyses undertaken in the application of the sales comparison approach. All relevant facts and opinions must be communicated in the appraisal report. Statements concerning the reliability of the data, the analyses performed, and the final conclusion of value should be presented in both the reconciliation section of the sales comparison approach and the final reconciliation of the value estimate.

The sales comparison approach is a significant and essential part of the valuation process, even when its reliability is limited. In situations where the dissimilarities in factors affecting property value cannot be properly determined or quantified, the sales comparison approach may still provide a probable range of value that can support a primary value indication derived from the application of one of the other approaches. Furthermore, data needed to apply the other approaches (e.g., overall capitalization rates for the income approach or depreciation estimates for the cost approach) are often obtained in the comparative process.

REQUIRED DATA AND SOURCES

To apply the sales comparison approach, an appraiser gathers data on sales, contracts, offers, refusals, options, and listings of properties considered competitive with, and comparable to, the subject property. First, the appraiser thoroughly researches the prices, real property rights conveyed, financing terms, motivations of buyers and sellers, and dates of the property transactions. Then details on each property's location, physical and functional condition, and economic characteristics must be examined.

Most appraisers maintain data files on the details of market transactions and add information as other transactions occur. Potential sources of sales data are many and varied. Primary sources of sales data include courthouse records, commercially available data from electronic reporting and multiple listing services, real estate periodicals, and interviews with the parties to the transaction, their employees, attorneys, counselors, brokers, property managers, and lenders. In many cases appraisers must contact other sources to obtain and verify information and to understand the motivation behind a transaction. Sales that are not arm's-length market transactions should be identified and treated with caution. To verify sales data an appraiser confirms statements of fact with the principals to the transaction and, if possible, with any brokers, closing agencies, and lending institutions involved. The owners and tenants of neighboring properties may also provide helpful information.

The geographic limits of the appraiser's search for sales data depend on the nature and type of real estate being valued. The boundaries of the market define the area in which potential buyers of comparable properties would look. If similar properties are commonly bought and sold in the same neighborhood or market area as the subject property, the search will probably be relatively limited. At times, however, the appraiser must extend the search to similar neighborhoods or market areas. Certain types of properties have regional, national, and even international markets. To appraise regional shopping malls, office buildings, resort hotels, large multi-use complexes, and large industrial properties, appraisers may scrutinize data from a wide geographic area within which the competitive proper-ties are located.

A sale price reflects many different factors that affect a property's value in varying degrees. Qualitative and quantitative techniques are employed to deter-mine the relative significance of these factors. Such techniques include relative comparison analysis, trend analysis, paired data set analysis, statistical and graphic analysis (e.g., regression and curve fit analysis to best represent a data set), and sensitivity analysis (to isolate the effect of individual variables on value). Appraisers employ the mathematical applications of such techniques to derive quantitative adjustments. When sufficient data to support a quantitative adjust-ment are not available, appraisers investigate qualitative relationships through direct comparison of market data and analysis of market trends.

After sales information has been collected and analyzed, it can be organized in a variety of ways. One convenient and commonly used method is to arrange the data on a market data grid. Each important difference between the subject property and the comparable properties that could affect property value is consid-ered an element of comparison; each element is assigned a row on the grid and total property prices or unit prices of the comparables are adjusted to reflect the value of these differences. The adjustments made reflect the thought process and judgments formed by a typical buyer before an offer to buy or an actual purchase is made. A sample market data grid and the procedures used to make adjustments on such a grid are presented later in this chapter.

PROCEDURE

To apply the sales comparison approach, an appraiser follows a systematic proce-dure. A general outline of the basic procedure follows.

1. Research the market to obtain information on sales transactions, listings, and offers to purchase or sell properties that are similar to the subject property in terms of characteristics such as property type, date of sale, size, location, and zoning.

2. Verify the information by confirming that the data obtained are factually accurate and that the transactions reflect arm's-length market considerations. Verification may also elicit additional information about the market.

3. Select relevant units of comparison (e.g., income multipliers or dollars per acre or per square foot) and develop a comparative analysis for each unit.

4. Compare comparable sale properties with the subject property using the elements of comparison and adjust the sale price of each comparable appropriately to the subject property *or* eliminate the sale property as a comparable.

5. Reconcile the various value indications produced from the analysis of comparables into a single value indication or a range of values. In an imprecise market subject to varying occupancies and economies, a range of values may be a better conclu-sion than a single value estimate.

Units of Comparison

After sales data have been gathered and verified, systematic analysis begins. Be-cause like units must be compared, each sale price should be stated in terms of appropriate units of comparison—i.e., the components into which a property may be divided for purposes of comparison. The units of comparison selected depend on the appraisal problem and nature of the property. Apartment properties are often analyzed on the basis of price per apartment unit and price per room, but price per square foot of gross building or leasable building area is also widely used. When analyzing apartments, attention should be paid to average unit size. Warehouses and industrial properties may be considered on the basis of price per square foot or cubic foot of gross building area. Hotels and motels are typically analyzed in terms of price per guest room; restaurants, theaters, churches, and auditoriums in price per seat; golf courses in price per acre and hole, round, and member; mobile home parks in price per parking pad; tennis and racquetball facilities in price per playing court or member; marinas in price per slip; automobile repair facilities in price per bay; and rights of way in price per front foot, per square foot, or per acre. For single-family residential property, the typical units of comparison are total property price and price per square foot of gross living area.

Units of comparison are used to facilitate comparison of the subject and comparable properties. Because most properties can be analyzed with several units of comparison, the appraiser should apply all reasonably appropriate units of comparison, compare the results of each application, and examine the reasons for any wide variation in the results. This will help the appraiser choose the most appropriate and reliable unit or units of comparison to use in the sales comparison approach section of the report. If the volume of data permits, a basic statistical analysis using means, medians, and standard deviations may also be developed. The unit(s) of comparison selected can have a significant bearing on the reconciliation of value indications in this approach.

Adjustments can be made either to total property prices or to appropriate units of comparison. Often adjustments for the property rights conveyed, financing, conditions of sale (motivation), and date of sale (market conditions) are made to the total sale price. The adjusted price is then converted into a unit price (e.g., per square foot, per apartment unit, or per acre) and adjusted for other elements of comparison such as location and physical characteristics.

Units of comparison such as income multipliers and income rates are not adjusted in sales comparison analysis, but the appraiser should consider why these units vary among the sale properties. The comparable sales are analyzed to extract these units of comparison, and an appropriate unit or units are chosen based on the economic or other characteristics of the property. For example, an appraiser may analyze sales of income-producing properties to derive potential and effective gross income multipliers, overall and equity capitalization rates, and even total property and equity yield rates (i.e., current yield or dividend rates as well as yield-to-maturity rates). These units of comparison are not adjusted. Instead, the appraiser considers their ranges and the similarities and differences between the subject and comparable sale properties that cause the multipliers and rates to vary. Then the appraiser chooses the multiplier(s) and rate(s) appropriate to the property being appraised.

Income multipliers, capitalization rates, and yield rates are applied in the income capitalization approach to value. It is appropriate to extract such rates and factors from comparable properties in sales comparison analysis.

Elements of Comparison

Elements of comparison are the characteristics of properties and transactions that cause the prices paid for real estate to vary. The appraiser considers and compares all reasonable differences between the comparable properties and the subject property that could affect their values. Market evidence should be tested to identify the variable elements to which property values are especially sensitive. Adjustments for differences are made to the price of each comparable property to make the comparables equal to the subject on the effective date of the value estimate. Adjustments for differences in elements of comparison may be made to the total property price, to a common unit price, or to a mix of both, but the unit prices used must be consistently applied to the subject and comparable properties. The amount of adjustment made for each element of comparison depends on the extent to which each comparable property differs from the subject property. Appraisers must be sure to consider all appropriate elements of comparison and avoid adjusting for the same difference more than once.

There are nine basic elements of comparison that should always be considered in sales comparison analysis.

1. Real property rights conveyed
2. Financing terms
3. Conditions of sale
4. Market conditions
5. Location
6. Physical characteristics
7. Economic characteristics
8. Use
9. Non-realty components of value

In most cases these nine elements of comparison cover all the significant factors to be considered, but on occasion additional elements may be relevant. Other possible elements of comparison include access to the property, governmental restrictions such as conservation or preservation easements, water and riparian rights, onsite environmental conditions, and offsite improvements required for the development of a vacant site. Often a basic element of comparison is broken down into subcategories that specifically address the property factor being analyzed. For example, physical characteristics may be broken down into subcategories for age, condition, size, etc.

If the appraiser's investigation uncovers only a few truly comparable properties or none at all, less similar properties with more divergent characteristics may be included among the market evidence. A broad sample of more diverse properties, if properly analyzed and adjusted, may offer an enhanced perspective on the value of the subject property. More extensive market evidence can give the appraiser greater insight into differences in property values attributable to elements such as zoning, site size, or location (e.g., corner vs. interior lot). A small sample of comparable sales is often insufficient to support adjustments for differences in several elements of comparison; a range of value indications based on small samples of comparable data may distort the appraiser's conclusions and the final value estimate.

Real Property Rights Conveyed

A transaction price is always predicated on the real property interest conveyed. Many types of real estate, particularly income-producing property, are sold subject to existing leases. The revenue-generating potential of a property is often fixed or limited by the terms of existing leases. In the valuation process adjustments must be made to reflect the difference between properties leased at market rent and those leased at rent either below or above market levels. The lengths of the remaining lease terms affect these adjustments.

Market rent and the financing currently available are used to estimate the value of a fee simple estate. When a property is considered free and clear of all existing leases and loans, its value is normally based on the market rent that it can command and the financing that can be obtained for it. The transaction price of a property that is sold subject to existing leases reflects the contract rent that it will generate during the term of each lease and the market rent that will likely be achieved thereafter. In these situations the real property interest that is sold or being appraised is the leased fee estate as subject to the existing leases.

A preliminary step in the valuation process is to determine the real property interest to be appraised. Once this is established, the appraiser can relate the market data to the subject property. The appraiser must precisely identify the real property rights conveyed in each comparable transaction selected for analysis.

One of the first adjustments to be considered is the adjustment for differences in real property rights. For example, assume that the fee simple interest in an office building is being appraised. The subject building is being compared to a building that was fully leased at the time of sale; the leases were long term and the credit ratings of the tenants were good. To compare a fee simple estate to a leased fee estate, the appraiser must determine if the contract rent of the sale property was above, below, or equal to market rent. If the market rent for office space is $25 per square foot, and the average rent for the sale property was $24 per square foot, the difference between market and contract rent is $1 per square foot.

For purposes of illustration, assume the sale property is a 100,000-sq.-ft. office building. The market indicates that 10% is an appropriate overall capitalization rate, the vacancy rate for the market in which the subject property is located is 5%, and 4% of effective gross income is a reasonable management expense.[1] The effective difference between the market rent of $25 per square foot and the contract rent of $24 per square foot is estimated by deducting the vacancy allowance (5%) and management expenses (4%) from the actual difference between these rents ($1). Then this amount is multiplied by the total area of the sale property and the product is capitalized at the overall rate. Calculation of the adjustment is illustrated below.

$$\$1.00 - 0.05 \ (5\% \text{ vacancy}) = \$0.95$$
$$\$0.95 - 0.04 \ (4\% \text{ management}) = \$0.91 \text{ (rounded)}$$

---

1. The appraiser should make sure that the operating expenses of the properties are comparable. Generally the higher the rent the tenant pays, the more services the landlord provides.

$$\$0.91 \times 100,000 \text{ sq. ft.} = \$91,000$$
$$\$91,000/10\% \ (R_o) = \$910,000$$

Other expenses are not considered because the leases are net leases and expenses do not constitute percentage charges against income.

The adjustment for the difference in real property rights is an upward adjustment of $910,000. If there were no difference between market rent and contract rent, the adjustment for real property rights would be zero. Similarly, if contract rent exceeded market rent, an appropriate downward adjustment would be required.

Note that if the market typically uses a 10% overall capitalization rate for a building that is leased at market rent, the market may apply a lower overall capitalization rate to derive an indication of the purchase value when rents are below market levels. Conversely, the market may apply a higher overall capitalization rate if rents are above market levels, particularly in a depressed economy where the risk of declining income stream is greater.

An alternative method for calculating an adjustment for real property rights conveyed is to discount the difference in the income stream over the remaining term of the lease. Assume that in the above example the lease has 10 more years to run, and the market indicates that an appropriate discount rate is 12%. Discounting of the $91,000 annual loss in income over 10 years at 12% yields an indicated upward adjustment of $514,000. The present value of the $91,000 annual loss for 10 years at 12% is calculated below.

$$5.650223^* \times \$91,000 = \$514,170, \text{ or } \$514,000$$

*PV of $1 per period factor, 10 years @ 12%

The two methods demonstrated for calculating the property rights adjustment yield different answers, $910,000 under the first hypothesis and $514,000 under the second. In the first scenario, an overall capitalization rate is used to capitalize the rent loss in perpetuity. Provided the lease term is sufficiently long, this method is appropriate. In the second situtation the rent loss is discounted over the remaining lease term of 10 years. Thus a smaller adjustment is indicated. Discounting is an appropriate method in this case because the remaining lease term is only 10 years. Capitalizing the annual $91,000 rent loss would unduly penalize the property by $396,000 (i.e., the difference between $910,000 and $514,000).

Calculating an adjustment for differences in real property rights is also necessary when just the leasehold interest is to be conveyed. For example, consider an office building that is sold separately from its site, which is subject to a 99-year lease. Assume that the 100,000- sq.-ft. building is sold for $7,500,000, or $75.00 per square foot. To determine the value of the fee simple estate in the total property, the value of the leased fee estate (the land) must be added to the value of the leasehold estate (the building).

One way to calculate the value of the leased fee estate is to capitalize the rent that accrues to the land. Assuming that the annual ground rent is $200,000 and the market indicates a land capitalization rate of 8%, the calculation is

$$\text{Income to the land divided by } R_L = \$200,000/0.08$$
$$\text{Value of the leased fee} = \$2,500,000$$

Typically the capitalization rate for the land will be lower than the rate for the building because the building incurs physical depreciation. In the sales comparison grid, the adjustment for property rights conveyed is an upward adjustment of $2,500,000.

In many situations there may be an advantage associated with a leasehold interest in the land. For example, if the market value of the land in fee simple exceeds the market value of the land in leased fee, a leasehold owner with not only an interest in the building but also a long-term ground lease is at an advantage. In many U.S. cities (e.g., New York, Los Angeles, Houston), ground leases typically are long term. An adjustment for the advantage accruing from a long-term leasehold in the land can be derived by capitalizing the difference between contract rent and market rent.

If no numerical adjustment is made in the sales comparison approach for differences in the real property rights conveyed among the subject and comparable properties, this dissimilarity must be addressed elsewhere in the appraisal report—e.g., in the reconciliation of value indications from the sales comparison approach or in the reconciliation and final value estimate section. The appraiser should also consider these differences in the income capitalization approach and estimate how they affect the value indication derived in this approach.

Financing Terms

The transaction price of one property may differ from that of an identical property due to different financing arrangements. For example, the purchaser of a comparable property may have assumed an existing mortgage at a favorable interest rate. In another case a developer or seller may have arranged a buydown, paying cash to the lender so that a mortgage with a below-market interest rate could be offered. In both cases the buyers probably paid higher prices for the properties to obtain below-market financing. Below-market rates might also be extended to individuals who have substantial bank accounts and are therefore especially creditworthy. Conversely, interest rates at above- market levels often result in lower sale prices.

Other nonmarket financing arrangements include installment sale contracts, in which the buyer pays periodic installments to the seller and obtains legal title only after the contract is fulfilled, and wraparound loans, which are superimposed on existing mortgages to preserve their lower interest rates. These loans offer below-market overall or blended interest rates to borrowers (buyers), but they yield market or above-market interest rates to lenders (sellers).

A financing adjustment may or may not include an adjustment for conditions of sale. A condition of sale adjustment recognizes that some sales are transacted by parties under duress, who are at a disadvantage. A combined adjustment results when favorable financing is a function of the seller's need to sell the property quickly. Appraisers should recognize that, in some situations, these factors are interdependent.

In cash equivalency analysis an appraiser investigates the sale prices of comparable properties that were sold with apparent nonmarket financing to determine whether adjustments to reflect typical market terms are warranted. First, sales with nonmarket financing are compared to other sales transacted with market financing to determine whether an adjustment for cash equivalency can be made.

If the market evidence is insufficient to support an adjustment based on the comparable sales, but trend or linear regression analysis indicates a value variance attributable to the difference in terms, then numerical adjustments can be made. There are precise, mathematical calculations for analyzing cash equivalency, but the financing adjustments derived from these calculations must be rigorously tested against market evidence.

More often than not, the cash discount indicated by the calculations is not fully recognized by buyers and sellers. The market evidence itself must support whatever adjustment is made. The definition of market value recognizes cash-equivalent terms provided the calculation is based on market evidence. Furthermore, conditions of sale may reveal other noneconomic interests on the part of buyers or sellers. Therefore, appraisers must use cash equivalency calculations with caution and remember that the final adjustment is always derived from the market.

Cash equivalency calculations vary depending on the kind of financing arrangement that requires adjustment.[2] Two common situations involve points that the seller pays and loans that the seller finances. When the seller rather than the buyer pays points—i.e., the percentage of a loan that a lender charges for making the loan—the appraiser often deducts the full dollar amount from the sale price.

Appraisers may calculate adjustments for atypical financing by analyzing paired data sets or discounting the cash flows (e.g., payments and balloons) created by the mortgage contract at market interest rates. Discounting can be accomplished with present value factors from financial tables, or it can be calculated directly with a financial function calculator or computer for the full loan term or the term a typical mortgage is held. In discounting it should not be assumed that the buyer will hold the property for the life of the mortgage. Market evidence often indicates otherwise. (Sources such as the reports of the Crittenden Institute and the American Council of Life Insurance can provide information on the behavior of market participants.) Therefore a mortgage is often discounted for a shorter term, but the balloon payment must still be included.

Buyers of real estate consciously commit to 1) the amount to be invested in the equity and 2) the fixed periodic dollar payment to amortize the debt and meet the interest. Thus, debt components vary with the periodic loan payment and the constant debt cost. Differences in loan amounts and terms warrant the adjustment of sales prices. Estimating cash equivalency employs direct market evidence to make the appropriate adjustments. The appraiser tries to locate sales with and without atypical financing, makes adjustments for other differences, and attributes the remaining price differential to the financing terms. This method can be used as a guide if substantial data on transactions with and without special financing are available.

When paired data set analysis is used to derive a cash equivalency adjustment, the calculations for discounting and adjusting for atypical conditions of sale are often combined. In other words, when a cash equivalency adjustment is derived

---

2. For further discussion and examples of cash equivalency calculations, see Harold D. Albritton, "Use of Cash Equivalency in Valuation," *Controversies in Real Property Valuation: A Commentary* (Chicago: American Institute of Real Estate Appraisers, 1982), 96-100; David C. Lennhoff, "Defining the Problem," *The Appraisal Journal* (April 1986); and Halbert C. Smith and John B. Corgel, "Adjusting for Nonmarket Financing: A Quick and Easy Method," *The Appraisal Journal* (January 1984).

through paired data set analysis, the adjustments for financing and conditions of sale can be represented by a single figure.

For example, consider a house that sells for $125,000 with a down payment of $25,000 and a seller-financed mortgage of $100,000 at 8% interest. The mortgage is amortized over 25 years with a balloon payment due in 8 years. To determine the appropriate discount rate, the appraiser checks the market for sales financed by similar mortgage arrangements, and finds that an $80,000, 8% note has sold for $65,000. The discount rate for this note is calculated as follows:

$$(\$80,000 - \$65,000)/\$80,000 = 0.1875 \text{ or } 18.75\%$$

This discount rate may then be applied to the given loan of $100,000 to arrive at the cash equivalent value of the mortgage.

$100,000 − ($100,000 × 0.1875)	=	$ 81,250
Plus down payment	=	$ 25,000
Sale price adjusted for financing		$106,250

Calculating a cash equivalency adjustment by discounting cash flows can be accomplished in different ways. When a seller finances a mortgage at a below-market interest rate, the appraiser can estimate the present value of the mortgage by applying a present value factor to the monthly mortgage payment at the market interest rate for the stated term of the mortgage. For example, an appraiser might find a comparable sale of a single-family residence that was sold for $110,000 with a down payment of $25,000 and a seller-financed mortgage of $85,000 for a 20-year term at 10% interest. If the market-derived rate is 13%, the sale can be adjusted to cash equivalency as follows:

Mortgage: $85,000, 20 years, 10%
Monthly payment: $820.27
Present value of $820.27 per month for 20 years @ market rate of 13%
85.355132* × $820.27 = $70,014

PV of mortgage, rounded	$70,000
Plus down payment	$25,000
Sale price adjusted for financing	$95,000

*PV of $1 per period factor, 20 years @ 13%, compounded monthly

Another way to calculate the present value of the mortgage is to divide the monthly payment or annual constant at the contract interest rate by the monthly payment or annual constant at the market interest rate and multiply the mortgage by the result. In this case, 0.00965/0.011715 = 0.82373; 0.82373 × $85,000 = $70,017.

Discounting cash flows to calculate a cash equivalency adjustment may also take into account the expectation of a balloon payment. The following example incorporates the same assumptions set forth in the previous example, except that the mortgagor (borrower) holds the mortgage for only seven years. (The average mortgage life for loans on different types of properties can be ascertained from sales data on loans that were paid off or refinanced rather than assumed by a buyer.) In the following example, the present value of the mortgage is computed as the sum of two components: the present value of the mortgage payments at the market interest rate for the expected life of a mortgage and the present value of the future mortgage balance at the market interest rate. One way to obtain the latter is to first calculate the value in seven years of the remaining 13 years of monthly payments at the contract rate and then calculate the present value of that lump sum.

Monthly payment: $820.27
Present value of $820.27 per month for 7 years @ 13%
    54.969328* × $820.27 = $45,090, rounded $ 45,000
Value of remaining mortgage payments in 7 years
    PV of $820.27 per month for 13 years @ 10%
    87.119542† × $820.27 = $71,462
PV of mortgage balance
    0.425061‡ × $71,462 = $30,376, rounded   30,000
PV of mortgage $ 75,000
Plus down payment   25,000
Sale price adjusted for financing $100,000

*PV of $1 per period factor, 84 months @ 13% (monthly frequency)
†PV of $1 per period factor, 156 months @ 10% (monthly frequency)
‡PV of $1 factor, 7 years @ 13% (annual frequency)

Note: When the cash flow is realized at the end of the year, the annual frequency of the PV of $1 factor should be chosen. When the payments are made on a monthly basis, the monthly frequency should be used. The quantitative difference resulting from the choice of a discount factor at an annual frequency rather than a discount rate at a monthly frequency is insignificant. If the monthly frequency of the PV of $1 factor for 7 years @ 13% (0.404499) had been used in the above example, the adjusted sale price would have come to $99,000 (rounded). Errors in discounting are generally attributable to the choice of the discount rate, not the frequency of that rate.

Alternatively, the outstanding mortgage balance at the end of seven years can be calculated. Although these methods require more calculation, they are preferable because they reflect the typical holding period more accurately.

Sometimes this type of adjustment can convert a puzzlingly inconsistent sale into a usable comparable. Consider a shopping center that is sold for $2,580,000. Routine investigation of the sale indicates that the 10-year-old shopping center has a gross leasable area of 60,110 square feet, gross rents of $238,259, and a net income of $202,222. Thus, the property has a 15% expense ratio. The sale appears to reflect a price of $42.92 per square foot, a gross rent multiplier of 10.83, and an overall capitalization rate of 7.84%. Because these pricing units are inconsistent with the local market, the appraiser may be tempted to discard the sale as a comparable.

However, further inquiry reveals that the seller financed the transaction with a 39.5-year mortgage loan of $1,850,000 at a 9% interest rate payable monthly. The current market interest rate for this type of property is 12% and the typical mortgage is held for 15 years. The adjustment technique illustrated above is applied as follows:

Mortgage payments for 39.5 years @ 9%: $14,288.84
Present value of mortgage payments for 15 years @ 12%
    83.321664*×$14,288.84 = $1,190,570, rounded $1,190,000
Mortgage balance in 15 years
    $14,288.84 for 24.5 years @ 9%
    $14,288.84×118.511817† = $1,693,396
PV of $1,693,396 in 15 years @ 12%
    0.182696‡×$1,693,396 = $309,377, rounded $ 310,000
                                                $1,500,000

Down payment $ 730,000

Adjusted sale price $2,230,000

*PV of $1 per period factor, 180 months @ 12% (monthly frequency)
†PV of $1 per period factor, 294 months @ 9% (monthly frequency)
‡PV of $1 factor, 15 years @ 12% (annual frequency)

Note: If the payments are made on a monthly basis, the monthly frequency of the PV of $1
     factor for 15 years @ 12% (0.166783) would be used; the adjusted sale price would
     come to $2,202,400 (rounded).

After adjusting for financing, the units of comparison are price per gross leasable square foot, $37.10; gross rent multiplier, 9.36; overall capitalization rate, 9.1%. Because these figures are reasonably consistent with other local market data, the appraiser can include the sale in the data file.

Transactions involving mortgage assumptions can be adjusted to cash equivalency with the same method applied to seller-financed transactions. However, the appraiser should be certain that the existing loan was assumed, not paid off. Other atypical mortgage terms include payments of interest only, followed by payments that include principal repayment. This type of mortgage can also be adjusted to its cash equivalent value using the adjustment procedure described here. The present values of the payments (monthly, quarterly, semi-annual, or annual) at the market rate, year by year, are derived using present value factors. If balloon payments are involved, present value factors may be applied to isolate the contributory market value of the unpaid balance of the mortgage.

The cash equivalency of any set of financing terms can be computed, but adjustments are needed to reflect the market conditions and financing terms under which the property is expected to be sold. These adjustments may indicate that the effect of the financing terms suggests a value that differs from the cash equivalency calculation.

Cash equivalency adjustments are based on precise mathematical calculations, but appraisers must make sure that they reflect market perceptions. In selecting an appropriate adjustment for use in cash equivalency analysis, the appraiser gives greater emphasis to the market-derived adjustment than to one derived by calculation.

Conditions of Sale
Adjustments for conditions of sale usually reflect the motivations of the buyer and the seller. In many situations the conditions of sale significantly affect transaction prices. For example, a developer may pay more than market value for lots needed in a site assemblage because of the anticipated incremental value, or plottage

value, resulting from the greater utility of a larger site. A sale may be transacted at a below-market price if the seller needs cash in a hurry. A financial, business, or family relationship between the parties to a sale may also affect the price of property. Interlocking corporate entities may record a sale at a nonmarket price to serve their business interest. One member of a family may sell a property to another at a reduced price, or a buyer may pay a higher price for a property because it was built by his ancestors.

When nonmarket conditions of sale are detected in a transaction, the sale can be used as a comparable only with great care. The circumstances of the sale must be thoroughly researched before an adjustment is made, and the conditions must be adequately disclosed in the appraisal.

Although conditions of sale are often perceived as applying only to sales that are not arm's-length transactions, some arm's-length sales may reflect atypical motivations or sale conditions due to unusual tax considerations, lack of exposure on the open market, or the complexity of eminent domain proceedings. If the sales used in the sales comparison approach reflect unusual situations, an appropriate adjustment must be made for motivation or conditions of sale. Again, the circumstances of the sale must be explained in the appraisal report.

Market Conditions

Comparable sales that occurred under different market conditions than those applicable to the subject on the effective date of the value estimate require adjustment for any differences that affect their values. A common adjustment for market conditions is made for differences occurring since the date of sale. Since the time the comparable sales were transacted, general values may have appreciated or depreciated due to inflation or deflation and investors' perceptions of market conditions may have changed.

Changes in market conditions may also result from other factors such as changes in income tax laws, building moratoriums, and fluctuations in supply and demand. Sometimes several economic factors working in concert cause a change in market conditions. A recession tends to deflate all real estate prices, but different property types will be affected differently. A decline in demand may affect only one category of real estate. If the demand for a specific type of property falls during a period of inflation, appraisals made during that period may not provide a reliable indication of the value of a similar property in a different period unless appropriate adjustments are made. Sales of other types of real estate transacted during the same period may better reflect the market conditions for the specific property under consideration. In a depressed economy, recent sales are often difficult to find. Older sales may be discounted over a reasonable holding period, corresponding to the length of time estimated for the market segment to recover. Declining office rents over a specified period may also be compared when there are few recent sales data.

Although the adjustment for market conditions is often referred to as a "time" adjustment, time is not the cause of the adjustment. Market conditions which shift over time create the need for an adjustment, not time itself. If market conditions have not changed, no adjustment is required even though considerable time may have elapsed.

Appraisers must also recognize that the sale of a property may be negotiated months or even years before the sale or final disposition of the property. In this case an adjustment for changes in market conditions between the date the contract is signed and the effective date of value may be appropriate.

Changes in market conditions are usually measured as a percentage of previous prices. If the physical and economic characteristics of a property remain unchanged, analyzing two or more sales of the same property over a period of time will indicate the rate of price change. An appraiser should always attempt to examine several sets of sales to arrive at an appropriate adjustment. An adjustment supported by just one paired data set may be unreliable.

Sales and resales of the same properties provide the best indication of the change in market conditions over time. If data on resales are unavailable, sales of similar properties in the same market must be used. Even when data on property sales and resales are available, the transactions must be examined very carefully. The sale and rapid resale of the same property may indicate that nonmarket sale conditions were involved in one or both transactions.

Location

An adjustment for location may be required when the locational characteristics of a comparable property are different from those of the subject property. Excessive locational differences may disqualify property from use as a comparable. Location adjustments are usually expressed as percentages that reflect the increase or decrease in value attributable to the property's location or neighborhood.

Most comparable properties in the same neighborhood have similar locational characteristics, but variations may exist within a neighborhood. Consider, for example, the difference between a property with a pleasant view of a park and one located two blocks away with an unattractive view. Adjustments for location may also be needed to reflect the difference in demand for various office suites within a single building, the retail advantage of a corner location, the privacy of the end unit in a residential condominium, or the value contribution of an ocean view.

A property's location is analyzed in relation to the location of other properties. Although no location is inherently desirable or undesirable, an appraiser can conclude that the market recognizes that one location is better than, equal to, or worse than another. To evaluate the desirability of one location relative to other locations, appraisers must analyze sales of physically similar properties located in different locations. Although the sale prices of properties in two different areas may be similar, properties in one area may be sold more rapidly than properties in the other.

For example, consider two recent sales of vacant lots that are identical in every way except for location. Comparable A, which is a corner lot with frontage on two streets, was sold for $12 per square foot; Comparable B, which is an interior lot with frontage on only one street was sold for $9 per square foot. The value of Comparable A in relation to that of Comparable B can be shown as:

$$\$12.00 / \$9.00 \ = \ 1.33 \text{ (rounded)}$$

Thus, it can be concluded that a corner lot is worth 1/3 more than an interior lot. The subject of the appraisal is an interior lot. The percentage adjustment that must be applied to Comparable A to adjust for its corner location may be derived in two ways. One is to divide Comparable A by 1.33:

$$\$12.00/1.33 \;=\; \$9.00 \text{ (rounded)}$$

The sales price of Comparable A adjusted downward for corner location is $9.00 per square foot. Another way of expressing this relationship is to say that Comparable A is 1/3 better than the subject.

$$\text{Value of Comparable A} = \text{value of subject} \times 1.33$$
$$\text{Value of Comparable A}/1.33 = \text{value of subject}$$
$$1/1.33 = 0.75 \text{ (rounded)}$$

Thus, the value of Comparable A may be adjusted for corner location by multiplying its sale price by 0.75.

$$\$12.00 \times 0.75 \;=\; \$9.00$$

In the absence of external obsolescence, the adjustment for difference in location between two otherwise comparable properties may be equivalent to the difference in the land values of the two properties. The appraiser must take care, however, to avoid adjusting a comparable sale for the same value influence under both location and physical characteristics.

Physical Characteristics

If the physical characteristics of a comparable property and the subject property differ in many ways, each of these differences may require comparison and adjustment. Physical differences may include differences in building size, quality of construction, architectural style, building materials, age, condition, functional utility, site size, attractiveness, and amenities. Onsite environmental conditions are also considered.

The value added or lost by the presence or absence of a differing item in a comparable property does not usually equal the cost of installing or removing the item. Buyers may be unwilling to pay a higher sale price that includes the extra cost of adding an amenity. Conversely, the addition of an amenity sometimes adds more value to a property than the extra cost of its installation.

Economic Characteristics

Economic characteristics include all the attributes of a property that affect its net operating income. This element of comparison is usually applied to income-producing properties. Characteristics that affect a property's net operating income include operating expenses, quality of management, tenant mix, rent concessions, lease terms, lease expiration dates, renewal options, and lease provisions such as expense recovery clauses. Investigation of these characteristics is critical to proper analysis of the comparables and to the final value estimate.

An appraiser must take care not to attribute differences in real property rights conveyed or changes in market conditions to different economic characteristics. Furthermore, the sales comparison analysis must not be presented simply as a variation of income approach, applying the same techniques and reaching an identical value indication.

Use

An appraiser must address any difference in the use or the highest and best use of a potential comparable and the subject property. The appraiser must recognize this difference and determine whether the sale is an appropriate comparable and whether an adjustment is required. In most cases the buyer or his or her agent must confirm the ultimate use for which the comparable was purchased.

For example, an apartment complex purchased for conversion to condominiums may reflect a sale price that is above the market level for apartment properties. This property would not be an appropriate comparable for the "as is" valuation of an apartment complex for which no change in use is intended or one for which the highest and best use remains an apartment use.

In the valuation of vacant land, zoning is one of the primary factors in determining the best use of the property—i.e., zoning serves as the test of legal permissibility. Thus zoning is typically a primary criterion in the selection of market data. When comparable properties with the same zoning as the subject are lacking or scarce, parcels with slightly different zoning that have a similar highest and best use to that of the subject may be used as comparables. These comparables must be adjusted for the difference in utility if the market indicates that this is appropriate.

A difference in the uses permitted under the two zoning classifications does not necessarily require an adjustment if the parcels have the same use. When sale prices are reduced to compatible units (e.g., price of land per square foot of permissible building area), however, there may still be dissimilarities due to the different zoning classification requirements. For example, because of differences in parking requirements or landscaping requirements, site development costs for two parcels under different zoning classifications may differ even if the parcels have the same highest and best use. These dissimilarities must be considered.

Non-Realty Components of Value

Non-realty components of value include personality, business concerns, or other items that do not constitute real property but are included in the sale price of either the comparable or the subject property. These components should be analyzed separately from the realty. In most cases the economic lives, associated investment risks, rate of return criteria, and collateral security for such non-realty components differ from those of the realty.

Furniture, fixtures, and equipment in a hotel or restaurant are typical examples of personality. In the appraisal of properties in which the business operation is essential to the use of the realty, the value of the non-realty component must be recognized, estimated, and reported. Properties such as hotels and timeshare condominiums which have high expense ratios attributable to the business operation typically include a significant business value component.

Identification and Measurement of Adjustments

Various analytical techniques may be used to identify and measure adjustments. The techniques of comparative analysis can be grouped into two categories: quantitative and qualitative. Several of these techniques are listed below.

Quantitative

- Paired data set analysis
- Statistical analysis
- Graphic analysis
- Trend analysis
- Cost-related analysis
- Secondary data analysis

Qualitative

- Relative comparison analysis
- Ranking analysis
- Personal interviews

The first step in comparative analysis is to identify which elements of comparison affect property values in the subject market. Each of the basic elements of comparison must be tested by one or more of the techniques listed above to determine whether an adjustment is required. For example, in appraising a vacant, 50-acre parcel of land, an appraiser finds sales data on comparables that range in size from 35 acres to 65 acres. The market data may indicate that there is no significant difference in the comparables' price per acre. The appraiser must be careful not to assume that an element of comparison affects value unless its influence is indicated by the market data.

Quantitative Techniques

When quantitative analytical techniques are applied, mathematical processes are used to identify which elements of comparison require adjustment and to measure the amount of these adjustments.

Paired data analysis is a process in which two or more market sales are compared to derive an indication of the size of the adjustment for a single characteristic. Ideally the sales being compared will be identical in all respects except for the element being measured. However, this is rarely the case. Frequently an appraiser must undertake a series of paired data analyses to isolate the effect of a single characteristic. A detailed example of paired data analysis is presented on pages 394-397 of this chapter.

Although paired data analysis is a theoretically sound method, it is sometimes impractical because only a narrow sampling of sufficiently similar properties may be available and it is difficult to quantify the adjustments attributable to all the variables present. An adjustment derived from a single paired data set is not necessarily indicative, just as a single sale does not necessarily reflect market value. However, even when only limited data are available, the appraiser should not discard the technique. Rather, he or she should determine the amount of adjustment indicated by the limited data and use other analytical procedures to test the reasonableness of the adjustment derived from the paired data sets. It is imperative that the appraiser use all analytical tools appropriate to the appraisal problem.

Statistical analysis of market data is becoming increasingly common in appraisal literature and appraisal practice. Appropriate statistical methods include statistical inference and regression analysis. Linear and multiple regression are excellent tools for analyzing certain market situations. The effectiveness of regression analysis is limited by the number of elements or factors influencing a sale price; the more factors a sale reflects, the less applicable is quantitative analysis. Regressions for specific elements, however, may be used in conjunction with other techniques. Full discussion of the statistical methods applicable to the sales comparison approach is beyond the scope of this text. Appendix B provides a review of basic statistical techniques.[3]

Graphic analysis is a variant of statistical analysis in which the appraiser arrives at a conclusion through either visual interpretation of a graphic display of data or statistical curve fit analysis of the data. A simple graphic display of grouped data may provide a picture of how the market views variations in the elements of comparison. In curve fit analysis different formulas are employed to determine the best fit for the market data being analyzed. The resulting equation of the best fit curve can be plotted, or the equation can be solved to derive an adjustment.

Trend analysis is applicable when large amounts of market data are available. It is especially useful when there is a lack of closely comparable sales data, but a broad database on properties with less similar characteristics. The various elements influencing a sale price can be tested to determine market sensitivity. Once the appraiser has determined which elements show market sensitivity, patterns for their adjustment can be analyzed.

In cost-related analysis cost indicators such as depreciated building cost or permit fees are used as a basis for adjustments. The appraiser should make certain that such adjustments are reasonable and approximate market expectations.

Secondary data analysis is a method for determining adjustments based on data that do not directly pertain to the subject or comparable properties. These secondary data describe the general real estate market and are usually collected by a research firm or government agency.

Qualitative Techniques

Relative comparison analysis is the study of the relationships indicated by market data without recourse to quantification. Many appraisers use this technique because it reflects the imperfect nature of real estate markets. To apply the technique the appraiser analyzes comparable sales to determine whether the comparables' characteristics are inferior, superior, or equal to those of the subject property. The analysis is very similar to paired data analysis, except that the adjustments are not expressed as dollar or percentage amounts. A detailed example of relative comparison analysis is presented on pages 397-402 of this chapter.

Ranking analysis is a variant of relative comparison analysis. In ranking analysis the comparable sales are ranked in descending or ascending order of desirability. Then the appraiser analyzes each sale to determine the relative position of the subject in the array. An example of such an array is provided on page 401.

---

3. Two texts that can help an appraiser apply statistical analysis to an appraisal are Freeman F. Elzey's *A First Reader in Statistics*, second edition (Belmont, California: Brooks/Cole Publishing Company, a division of Wadsworth Publishing Company, Inc., 1974) and Norman R. Benedict and Ted H. Szatrowski's *Statistical Primer for Real Estate Problem Solving* (Chicago: American Society of Real Estate Counselors, 1989). *The Appraisal Journal* has also published numerous articles on advanced statistical applications.

Personal interviews can also shed light on the opinions of knowledgeable individuals participating in the subject's market. This information can be used to determine adjustments, but it must be regarded as secondary data and should not be used as the sole criterion for estimating adjustments to derive a market value indication.

Comparative Analysis

Comparative analysis is the general term used to identify the process that employs either paired data set analysis or relative comparison analysis to derive a value indication in the sales comparison approach. These are the most commonly used techniques in appraisal practice. In a comparative analysis, the two techniques may be used separately or in combination.

When the adjustments derived in comparative analysis are applied to the sale prices of the comparables they may be expressed as percentages, as dollar amounts, in qualitative terms (e.g., inferior, superior, greatly inferior, greatly superior), or in any other descriptive terms that clearly convey the magnitude and quality of the difference in the element of comparison between the subject and the comparable.

Whether quantitative or qualitative techniques are used, four general steps are involved in the analytic process.

1. Identify the elements of comparison that affect the value of the type of property being appraised.

2. Compare the attributes of each comparable with those of the subject property and measure the difference in each element of comparison between the subject and the comparable either quantitatively or qualitatively. Each adjustment must be adequately explained to ensure that a third party will understand the reasoning behind the adjustment.

3. Derive a net adjustment for each comparable and apply it to the sale price (or rent) of the comparable to arrive at an indication of the adjusted value (or rent) of the subject property. (A net adjustment is calculated as the difference between total positive and negative adjustments.)

4. Make a summary or overall comparison of the adjusted or ranked comparables and reconcile the array of value indications into a single value indication.

When quantitative adjustments are being applied, the appraiser considers the array of value indications obtained in the third step to be the range of probable value indications for the subject property. The appraiser then determines the most probable position of the subject within this range of indications and reaches a single value indication. In this way the comparables that are most similar to the subject are given the greatest weight.

Applying the qualitative method, the appraiser will normally divide the adjusted comparables into two groups: those that are superior overall to the subject and those that are inferior. The adjusted prices of these two groups will bracket the value of the subject by indicating the probable range of values. By considering those comparables most similar to the subject, the appraiser can conclude a single value indication for the subject property. If all the comparables are either rated as superior or as inferior to the subject, it may not be possible to determine a reliable range of value and reach a single value indication by means of the qualitative method.

Quantitative relationships are investigated based on direct comparison, trend analysis, or statistical and graphic analysis. Qualitative adjustments can be weighted if market evidence is sufficient to support the weighting.

In performing comparative analysis, an appraiser may use quantitative and qualitative techniques in combination. However, care must be exercised to ensure that the reader of the appraisal report will not be confused. Appraisal reports that utilize qualitative relationships often require more extensive discussion of the reasoning that the appraiser applied.

TYPES OF ADJUSTMENTS

The adjustments derived with quantitative techniques can be applied to a comparable property as either percentage or dollar amounts. The manner in which the adjustment is derived from the market determines how it is expressed. Percentages are usually converted into dollar amounts that may be added to or subtracted from the price of the comparable on the market data grid.

Adjustments can be applied in several ways depending on how the relationship between the properties (i.e., subject and comparable, comparable and subject, or comparable and comparable) is expressed or perceived by the market. This relationship is expressed as an algebraic equation which is solved to determine the amount of adjustment to be made for the differences between the properties.

An appraiser uses logical calculations to make an adjustment, but the mathematics should not control the appraiser's judgment. Using computer and software technology an appraiser can effectively apply mathematical techniques that were once prohibitively time-consuming. These techniques can be used to narrow the range of value, but a market value estimate is not determined by a set of precise calculations. Appraisal has a creative aspect in that appraisers use their judgment to analyze and interpret quantitative data. Quantification helps the appraiser analyze market evidence and identify how various factors affect property value; qualitative adjustments also contribute to the process by limiting the range of values and identifying a *bracket* in which the final value estimate should fall. Preparing an organized grid that includes both quantitative and qualitative adjustments can ensure that all elements of comparison are considered. Qualitative adjustments may be weighted on the basis of market evidence. If market evidence is inconclusive, the grid should clearly indicate this.

Percentage Adjustments

Adjustments for differences between a subject property and a comparable property are frequently expressed in percentages. Appraisers often use percentage adjustments to reflect changes in market conditions and differences in location.

For example, the data may indicate that market conditions have resulted in a 5% increase in overall prices during the past year, or that prices for a particular category of property have recently increased 0.5% per month. Similarly, an appraiser may analyze market data and conclude that properties in one location bring prices that are approximately 10% higher than the prices of similar properties in another location. These percentages may be converted into dollar amounts, which are then added to or subtracted from the price of the comparable. The percentages may also be directly applied to the price or unit price of the comparable.

If the subject and the comparable are equal for all practical purposes, no adjustment is necessary; otherwise, an adjustment is required. Algebraic statements that express how percentage adjustments are derived appear below. These statements indicate that when the comparison is stated in terms of the subject (i.e., "The subject is. . ."), the proper procedure is multiplication; when the comparison is stated in terms of the comparable (i.e., "the comparable is. . ."), the proper procedure is division. In these equations, X equals the unknown value of the subject and 1.0 equals the known value of the comparable.

"*The subject is 10% superior to the comparable*" may be expressed as

$$
\begin{aligned}
X &= 1.0 + (10\% \times 1.0) \\
&= 1.0(1 + 0.1) \\
&= 1.1
\end{aligned}
$$

The price of the comparable is multiplied by 1.1 to estimate the value of the subject. The percentage adjustment to the price of the comparable is plus 0.1, or 10%.

"*The subject is 10% inferior to the comparable*" may be expressed as

$$
\begin{aligned}
X &= 1.0 - (10\% \times 1.0) \\
&= 1.0(1 - 0.1) \\
&= 0.9
\end{aligned}
$$

The price of the comparable is multiplied by 0.9 to estimate the value of the subject. The percentage adjustment to the price of the comparable is minus 0.1, or 10%.

"*The comparable is 10% superior to the subject*" may be expressed as

$$
\begin{aligned}
1.0 &= X + (10\% \times X) \\
1.0 &= X(1 + 0.1) \\
1.0 &= X(1.1) \\
1.0/1.1 &= X \\
0.909 &= X
\end{aligned}
$$

The price of the comparable is divided by 1.1 to estimate the value of the subject. This is the same as multiplying by 0.091. The percentage adjustment to the price of the comparable is minus 0.091, or 9.1%.

"*The comparable is 10% inferior to the subject*" may be expressed as

$$
\begin{aligned}
1.0 &= X - (10\% \times X) \\
1.0 &= X(1 - 0.1) \\
1.0 &= X(0.9) \\
1.0/0.9 &= X \\
1.111 &= X
\end{aligned}
$$

The price of the comparable is divided by 0.9 to estimate the value of the subject. This is the same as multiplying by 1.111. The percentage adjustment to the price of the comparable is plus 0.111, or 11.1%.

The appraiser must be consistent in stating the relationship between the subject and the comparable. Percentage adjustments can be stated in terms of differences in the subject property in relation to the comparable property or in terms of differences in the comparable in relation to the subject. *However, only the price of the comparable is known, so the adjustment must be made to this price in order to arrive at an indication of value for the subject.*

When percentage adjustments are stated in terms of the differences in the subject in relation to the comparable (e.g., "The subject is a certain percentage superior or inferior to the comparable."), the appropriate percentages can be applied directly to the known value of the comparable. This relationship is expressed in the first two algebraic statements presented. If the appraiser finds it more convenient to state percentage adjustments in terms of the differences in the comparable in relation to the subject (e.g., "The comparable is a certain percentage superior or inferior to the subject."), the more oblique algebraic procedure expressed in the third and fourth algebraic statements may be followed. *The relationship between the subject property and the comparable property should be stated in a manner that corresponds to the way it is perceived by the market.*

Dollar Adjustments

Adjustments can also be computed in dollars. For example, an appraiser may conclude that the favorable financing terms involved in the sale of a comparable property resulted in a $100,000 premium paid by the buyer. In analyzing major investment properties, an appraiser can frequently use discounting to derive a dollar adjustment for financing terms. Adjustments for many physical characteristics may also be estimated in dollar amounts, which are added to or subtracted from the sale price of the comparable.

SEQUENCE OF ADJUSTMENTS

The sequence in which adjustments are applied to the comparables is determined by the market data and the appraiser's analysis of those data. The sequence presented in Table 17.1 is provided for purposes of illustration.[4] This sequence is often applicable when percentage adjustments are calculated and added, either in conjunction with other percentage adjustments or in combination with dollar adjustments. However, this is not the only order in which quantitative adjustments may be made. Adjustments may be applied in other sequences if so indicated by the market and the appraiser's analysis of the data. Using the adjustment sequence the appraiser applies successive adjustments to the prices of comparable properties. The percentage adjustments applied in the illustration have been rounded. The percentage adjustments made to the price of a comparable property reflect the comparable's superiority or inferiority with regard to the real property rights conveyed, financing, conditions of sale, market conditions, location, physical characteristics, economic characteristics, use, and non-realty components. Table 17.1 relates to a subject property that is a certain percentage superior or inferior to the comparable with respect to several elements of comparison. This

---

4. This sequence of adjustments was first presented by Halbert C. Smith in *Real Estate Appraisal* (Columbus, Ohio: Grid, Inc., 1976).

Table 17.1 Sequence of Adjustments

Element of Comparison	Market-Derived Adjustments	Adjustment to Price of Comparable Sale
Sale price		$100,000
Adjustment for property rights conveyed	+5%	+5,000
Adjusted price		$105,000
Adjustment for financing terms	−2%	−2,100
Adjusted price		$102,900
Adjustment for conditions of sale*	+5%	+5,145
Adjusted price		$108,045
Adjustment for market conditions	+5%	+5,402
Adjusted price		$113,447
Adjustment for		
Location	+3%	+3,403
Physical characteristics	−5%	−5,672
Economic characteristics	−5%	−5,672
Use	+2%	+2,269
Non-realty components	+3%	+3,403
Indication of value of the subject		$111,178

* The conditions of sale adjustment may be combined with another adjustment depending on how it is extracted from the market.

treatment of the relationship between the comparable and the subject property is presented strictly for purposes of illustration.

The first adjustment, which is made for the property rights conveyed, is applied to the transaction price. This adjustment accounts for differences in the legal estates of the subject property and the comparable property. The second adjustment converts the transaction price of the comparable into its cash equivalent price or modifies it to match the financing terms of the subject property. The third adjustment is made for conditions of sale and reflects the difference between the actual sale price of the comparable and its probable sale price if it were currently sold in an arm's-length transaction. If the financing terms or conditions of sale of the comparable had been the same as those typical in the market for the subject property, adjustments of zero would have been shown in the chart. At this stage in the sequence, the price figure is $108,045, which represents the amount for which the comparable property would have been sold under normal financing and sale conditions. This figure is approximately 108% of the actual transaction price.

The next adjustment is for market conditions. It reflects the change in the prices paid for real property due to changes in market conditions and the purchasing power of money over time. This adjustment is applied after the adjustments for property rights conveyed, financing, and conditions of sale. The adjustment would be distorted if it were applied directly to the actual transaction price, which was influenced by nonmarket considerations such as atypical financing. The adjustment for market conditions results in a figure of $113,447, which represents the amount for which the comparable property would be sold as of the date of appraisal on the open market. The adjusted price is approximately 113.4% of the transaction price.

The adjustments for location, physical characteristics, economic characteristics, use, and non-realty components account for these differences between the comparable property and the subject property. In this particular example, no other adjustments are required. After all adjustments have been made to the sale price of the comparable, the resulting value indication for the subject property is $111,178.

The adjustment procedure described above calls for the addition and subtraction of percentage adjustments. However, the multiplication and division of percentages may be appropriate under certain conditions. Cumulative percentage adjustments, which are obtained by multiplying percentage adjustments, are used when the basis for one adjustment is the result of a previous adjustment. In other words, cumulative percentage adjustments are causally interrelated. Although a sequence may not be required when adjustments are multiplied, its use helps to clarify the procedure followed in this special application of the sales comparison approach.

For example, consider a comparable property that was sold one year ago for $100,000. Current financing terms and conditions of sale are the same for the comparable and the subject property. A positive adjustment of 10% is made for the superior market conditions under which the subject is being valued, and a 10% negative adjustment is made to account for the inferior location of the subject property. The difference in market conditions affects the base to which the subsequent adjustment for location is applied. Thus, a cumulative percentage adjustment is appropriate. The calculation is:

$$110\% \times 90\% = 99\%$$
$$0.99 \times \$100,000 = \$99,000$$

SAMPLE MARKET DATA GRID

The sample market data grid shown in Table 17.2 reflects the elements of comparison and a typical sequence of adjustments. The sample grid includes lines for all elements of comparison. If the subject and comparable sales are similar in regard to an element of comparison, no adjustment is required for that element. The grid may include separate lines for comparison and adjustment to ensure that adjustments are made in a consistent manner.

The section labeled "For reconciliation purposes" is provided to help the appraiser analyze the degree of comparability of each sale which will indicate the

Table 17.2 Sample Market Data Grid: Comparison and Adjustment of Market Data

Element	Subject	Sale 1	Sale 2	Sale 3	Sale 4
Sale price	?	_____	_____	_____	_____
Real property rights conveyed adjustment	_____	_____	_____	_____	_____
Adjusted price*					
Financing adjustment	_____	_____	_____	_____	_____
Conditions of sale adjustment	_____	_____	_____	_____	_____
Adjusted price†	_____	_____	_____	_____	_____
Market conditions adjustment	_____	_____	_____	_____	_____
Adjusted price‡	_____	_____	_____	_____	_____
_____	_____	_____	_____	_____	_____
_____	_____	_____	_____	_____	_____
_____	_____	_____	_____	_____	_____
Final adjusted sale price	_____	_____	_____	_____	_____
For reconciliation purposes:					
Total adjustment	_____	_____	_____	_____	_____
Total adjustment as % of sale price	_____	_____	_____	_____	_____

* Sale price further adjusted for property rights conveyed
† Sale price further adjusted for financing and conditions of sale
‡ Sale price further adjusted for market conditions

relative reliability of the separate value indications derived. Each final adjusted sale price is a possible value indication for the subject property; together these sale prices constitute a range of value within which the value of the subject property will likely fall. Each of these adjusted sale prices can be analyzed to show the total, or absolute, adjustment to the sale price of the comparable and the percentage of the sale price that is reflected by this total adjustment. With these figures an appraiser can rank the comparability of the sales to the subject and select an appropriate estimate of value, if the value conclusion is to be reported as a point estimate. The sale that requires the lowest total, or absolute, adjustment (regardless of sign) is often the most comparable and generally should be given more weight in reconciling the value indications from the sales comparison approach.[5] In reconciling the value indications derived in the sales comparison approach, the appraiser must also consider the reliability of the data used to make adjustments.

SAMPLE APPLICATIONS

In the following two examples, the sales comparison approach is applied to the appraisal of a single-family residence and an office building. These examples demonstrate the two most common techniques for identifying and estimating adjustments: paired data analysis and relative comparison analysis. Paired data analysis is illustrated in the single-family residence example; relative comparison analysis is demonstrated in the office building example.

Illustration of other techniques used to identify and estimate adjustments is beyond the scope of this text. The appraiser should consider all applicable techniques to determine the ones most appropriate for the appraisal of the subject property. Generally, the more complex the property, the greater the number of techniques that may be applicable to its valuation.

Paired Data Analysis

The property being appraised is a single-family residence with 1,200 square feet of gross living area and a finished basement. It has six rooms, three bedrooms, one and one-half baths, and no garage. The site covers 10,000 square feet. Site improvements are average for the neighborhood; all improvements are in average condition. Five comparables are used in this analysis and all are located in the same neighborhood as the subject. The comparable properties are described below.

Comparable A is a 1,200-sq.-ft., frame ranch house situated on a 10,000-sq.-ft. lot with an unfinished basement and an attached, two-car garage. It has six rooms, three bedrooms, and one and one-half baths. It was sold three weeks before the date of the appraisal for $67,000 with financing at a below-market interest rate, which resulted in a price that was $5,000 higher than it would have been otherwise.

Comparable B is a 1,450-sq.-ft., frame ranch house situated on a 12,000-sq.-ft. lot with an unfinished basement and an attached, two-car garage. It has seven rooms, three bedrooms, and one and one-half baths. It was sold one month before the date of the appraisal for $75,000 with financing at a below-market inter-

---

5. Weighting is a technique used to rate data according to their reliability relative to the subject property or their similarity to the subject property. Applications include weighted mean analysis (see following example), band of investment, and compatibility matrixes.

Weighted Mean Analysis

	Sale 1	Sale 2	Sale 3
Indicated value per square foot	$40	$50	$45
Reliability weighting (3 = most reliable; 1 = least reliable)	× 3	× 1	× 2
	120	50	90

The sum of the products is then divided by the sum of the weights:
$$260/6 = 43.33 \text{ or } \$43 \text{ per square foot (rounded)}$$

est rate, which resulted in a price that was $5,000 higher than it would have been otherwise.

Comparable C is a 1,200-sq.-ft., frame ranch house situated on a 10,000-sq.-ft. lot with an unfinished basement and an attached, two-car garage. It has six rooms, three bedrooms, and one and one-half baths. It was sold one year before the date of the appraisal for $56,500 with market financing.

Comparable D is a 1,450-sq.-ft., frame ranch house situated on a 12,000-sq.-ft. lot with a finished basement and an attached, two-car garage. It has seven rooms, three bedrooms, and one and one-half baths. It was sold one year before the date of the appraisal for $70,000 with market financing.

Comparable E is a 1,200-sq.-ft., frame ranch house situated on a 10,000-sq.ft. lot with an unfinished basement and no garage. It has six rooms, three bedrooms, and one and one-half baths. It was sold one year before the date of the appraisal for $53,200 with market financing.

The summary grid is shown in Table 17.3. The comparable properties differ from the subject property in terms of financing, market conditions at time of sale, size (i.e., living area, number of rooms), lot size, and the presence or absence of a garage and a finished basement. The following discussion explains how paired data analysis is used to derive the adjustments for differences in these elements of comparison.

The adjustment for financing terms is derived by comparing the sale prices of the comparables with favorable financing to the sale prices of other comparables with market financing. To perform the analysis, the appraiser interviewed buyers and sellers of the comparable properties and calculated the effect of the favorable financing terms on the sale price by discounting the buyer's advantage to present value. In this case the appraiser based the adjustment for financing terms on the actual price required to recapture the seller's buydown payment to the lender. The appraiser concluded that the adjustment to Comparables A and B for favorable adjustment terms is $5,000.

Comparables A and C differ only in their financing terms and the market conditions at the time of sale. After the adjustment was made to Comparable A for financing terms, the adjustment for market conditions (date of sale) could be calculated as follows:

$$(\$62,000 - \$56,500)/\$56,500 \quad = \quad .097345.$$

This 9.7% adjustment may be rounded to 10%.

The difference in size between Comparables A and B can be attributed to the additional room in Comparable B. (The lot on which Comparable B is located is also 20% larger than the lot in Comparable A.) A size adjustment was made after each price had been adjusted $5,000 downward for financing terms. The adjustment for size was calculated as follows:

$$\$70,000 - \$62,000 \quad = \quad \$8,000$$

Comparison of Comparables C and E indicated that the adjustment for the lack of a garage in Comparable E could be calculated as $62,150 - $58,520 = $3,630, rounded to $3,600.

The adjustment for the finished basement in Comparable D was calculated by comparing Comparables B and D after adjusting Comparable D $7,000 upward

Table 17.3 Market Data Grid for Paired Data Analysis: Single-Family Residence Appraisal

	Subject	Comparable				
		A	B	C	D	E
Sale price	—	$67,000	$75,000	$56,000	$70,000	$53,200
Real property rights conveyed	Fee simple	Fee simple	Fee simple	Fee simple	Fee simple	Fee simple
Adjusted price		$67,000	$75,000	$56,000	$70,000	$53,000
Financing terms	—	Nonmarket	Nonmarket	Market	Market	Market
Adjustment for financing		-$5,000	-$5,000	0	0	0
Conditions of sale	—	Arm's-length	Arm's-length	Arm's-length	Arm's-length	Arm's-length
Adjustment for conditions of sale		0	0	0	0	0
Adjusted price		$62,000	$70,000	$56,500	$70,000	$53,200
Market conditions	—	-3 weeks	-1 month	-1 year	-1 year	-1 year
Adjustment for market conditions		0	0	+10%	+10%	+10%
Adjusted price		$62,000	$70,000	$62,150	$77,000	$58,520
Location	—	Similar	Similar	Similar	Similar	Similar
Adjustment for location		0	0	0	0	0
Size in sq. ft.	1,200	1,200	1,450	1,200	1,450	1,200
Adjustment for size		0	-$8,000	0	-$8,000	0
Garage	None	2-car	2-car	2-car	2-car	None
Adjustment for garage		-$3,600	-$3,600	-$3,600	-$3,600	0
Finished basement	Yes	No	No	No	Yes	No
Adjustment for basement		+$7,000	+$7,000	+$7,000	0	+$7,000
Adjustment price		$65,400	$65,400	$65,550	$65,400	$65,520

For reconciliation purposes:

	A	B	C	D	E
Total net adjustment	$1,600	$9,600	$9,050	$4,600	$12,320
Total net adjustment as % of sale price	2.4%	12.8%	16.0%	6.6%	23.2%
Total gross adjustment	$15,600	$23,600	$16,250	$18,600	$12,320
Total gross adjustment as % of sale price	23.3%	31.5%	28.8%	26.6%	23.2%

for market conditions and adjusting Comparable B $5,000 downward for financing terms. The adjustment was calculated as $77,000 − $70,000 = $7,000.

Next, the value indications derived for each comparable must be reconciled into a single value indication. Appraiser's sometimes find it preferable to *derive a range of values* and *then conclude a single value indication*. In this step the appraiser considers the range of value indications, the number of adjustments applied to each comparable, the total percentage adjustment to each comparable calculated in absolute values (i.e., the gross adjustment), the total percentage adjustment to each comparable calculated as the difference between positive and negative adjustments (i.e., the net adjustment), any particularly large adjustments applied to the comparables, and any other factors indicating that a particular comparable should be given greater weight.

In this case the appraiser considered the narrowness of the range of value indications ($65,400 to $65,550) and gave the greatest weight to the comparable that required the least amount of adjustment. The fewest adjustments (only two) were applied to Comparable E, which also required the lowest gross adjustment ($12,320). The adjusted sale price of Comparable E indicated the subject's value to be $65,520. Thus, Comparable E was given the most emphasis and the value of the subject was estimated to be $65,500.

Relative Comparison Analysis

The property being appraised is a five-year old, multitenanted office building with 36,000 square feet of gross building area and 31,800 square feet of rentable area (88% of *GBA*). Its occupancy rate is 90%, which is considered stable in the subject market. The amount of space occupied by tenants ranges from 2,500 square feet to 7,000 square feet. The building is average in construction (Class B) and average in condition. The ratio of rentable area to gross building area is low according to the average for the subject market area which is approximately 93%. The site is appropriately landscaped. The open space parking provided is both adequate and in compliance with the zoning code. The location, which may also be considered average, is an interior site accessed from a major arterial highway.

Current base rents range from $12 per square foot to $13 per square foot of rentable area. Rent for the overall building averages $12.60 per square foot. With the exception of telephone service, the landlord pays all expenses including janitorial and electrical. Operating expenses are typical for the market. The leases have three- and four-year terms; they contain an option to renew for three more years at the then-current market rent. All leases are less than 18 months old, and the rents and terms they specify are standard for the current market. Leasehold positions in the subject property do not accrue any particular advantage. The leased fee interest in the property is the interest to be appraised. The quality of the tenants is good.

Five comparable sales are used in the analysis. All the comparables are midrise, multitenanted office properties located in the subject's market area and all were financed at market rates. All comparables were sold in leased fee. The unit of comparison employed in this analysis is price per square foot of rentable area. The five comparables are described below.

Comparable A was sold five months ago for $2,930,000. It is six years old and in average condition. The building contains 40,000 square feet of gross building area and 37,600 square feet of rentable area (94% of GBA). The indicated price per square foot of rentable area is $77.93. Average rent is $12.80 per square foot of rentable area. The landlord pays all expenses and occupancy is 87%. The rents, lease terms, and expenses of the property are at market levels. The site is located at the intersection of a major arterial highway and a collector road. Parking is adequate. The ratio of parking spaces to rentable area in Comparable A is approximately the same as that of the subject.

Comparable B was sold four months ago for $2,120,000. The building is four years old and contains 32,000 square feet of gross building area and 29,700 square feet of rentable area (93% of GBA). Its unit price is calculated to be $71.38 per square foot of rentable area. Site improvements are average, and the ratio of parking area to rentable area is similar to that of the subject property. The property is in average condition. The leases provide tenants with full services. Occupancy is a 85% and the effective rents are below market levels. The average base rent is $11.80 per square foot of rentable area. The lengths of the leases and property expenses are considered to be at market levels. The property is located on an interior site accessed from a major collector street. Parking is adequate.

Comparable C was sold nine months ago for $2,450,000. The building contains 35,000 square feet of gross building area and 32,200 square feet of rentable area (92% of GBA). Its unit price is $76.09 per square foot of rentable area. The improvements were constructed five years ago and are in average condition. Rent averages $12.60 per square foot of rentable area. All tenant services are provided by the landlord. The building has an occupancy rate of 90%, and all rents and lease terms are at market levels. The total expenses for the building are slightly higher than typical for the market because two tenants who occupy 15% of the total space use excessive electricity; they do not pay additional rent to compensate for the extra expense. The property's location is an interior site accessed from a major arterial highway. The property has a parking ratio similar to that of the subject.

Comparable D was sold two months ago for $2,160,000. The building is six years old and in average condition. It contains 30,000 square feet of gross building area and 26,700 square feet of rentable area (89% of GBA). The unit price is $80.90 per square foot of rentable area. The rent averages $13.00 per square foot of rentable area, and the lease terms and building expenses are at market levels. The occupancy rate is 95%. The site is located at the intersection of two major arterial highways in a district zoned for higher-density development than is permitted in the subject district. Thus, the ratio of parking area to rentable area is lower than that of the subject property.

Comparable E was sold six months ago for $2,470,000. The building was constructed four years ago and is in average condition. It contains 38,000 square feet of gross building area and 33,800 square feet of rentable area (89% of GBA). Its unit price is $73.08 per square foot of rentable area. The location is an interior site accessed by a major collector street. The occupancy rate for the building is 90%. Rents average $12.30 per square foot of rentable area. Full tenant services are provided by the landlord. Rents, lease terms, and property expenses are at market levels. The property has adequate parking, and the parking ratio is similar to that of the subject property.

To perform a relative comparison analysis of the sales, the appraiser must apply the same logic applied in paired data analysis. The difference between the two techniques is the appraiser's interpretation of market data. Relative comparison analysis is employed when the market data may not be sufficient to derive dollar or percentage adjustments. It is essential, therefore, that the appraiser explain the logic followed in arriving at the adjustments so that readers of the appraisal report will understand how they were derived.

In the office building example, the appraiser first analyzes the market data and determines that all sales involved the transfer of a leased fee interest. No adjustment for differences in property rights conveyed is necessary (the below-market rent of Comparable B will be considered subsequently). All sales were transacted with market financing, so no adjustment for this element of comparison is required. All of the transactions were conducted at arm's length, so there is no adjustment for conditions of sale. The comparables used were recent transactions, occurring within nine months of the date of valuation, and there were no significant changes in rent levels and occupancy; therefore, no adjustments are warranted for market conditions. The relative comparative analysis of dissimilar elements is described below. (See Table 17.4.)

Comparable A has an indicated unit price of $77.93 per square foot of rentable area. Its location at the intersection of a major arterial highway and a collector road is superior to the location of the subject property. Thus, a downward adjustment to the price of Comparable A is required for location. The building has an average rentable area ratio, but it is a more efficient building than the subject. Thus, another negative adjustment is required for building efficiency. The building occupancy rate for Comparable A is slightly lower than the subject's and lower than is considered typical for stabilized occupancy in the market. Thus, a small positive adjustment to the price of the comparable is required for this element of comparison. The overall net adjustment applied to the price of Comparable A is negative because the negative location adjustment is considered the most significant. The negative adjustments for the superior location and superior rentable area ratio of Comparable A outweigh the positive adjustment for its lower occupancy rate.

Comparable B has an indicated unit price of $71.38 per square foot of rentable area. Effective contract rent is lower than market rent, so a positive adjustment must be made to the price of Comparable B. The location of this property on a major collector street is inferior to the subject property's location on a major arterial highway. Thus a second positive adjustment to the price of this comparable is required for location. Comparable B also has a superior rentable area ratio, indicating that the property will yield a higher net income. Thus, a negative adjustment is required for this dissimilarity. The occupancy rate for the comparable, which is below the market rate for stabilized occupancy, necessitates a positive adjustment to the price of the property. In all, Comparable B requires three positive adjustments and only one negative adjustment. Furthermore, in this particular case the difference in the rentable area ratios may be considered to have the least impact on value. Therefore, the overall adjustment to the comparable must be

Table 17.4 Market Data Grid for Relative Comparison Analysis: Multitenanted Office Building

Element of Comparison	Subject	Comparable A	Comparable B	Comparable C	Comparable D	Comparable E
Sale price	—	$2,930,000	$2,120,000	$2,450,000	$2,160,000	$2,470,000
Property interest	Leased fee	Leased fee	Leased fee	Leased fee	Leased fee	Leased fee
Age	5 years	6 years	4 years	5 years	6 years	4 years
Sq. ft. of GBA	36,000	40,000	32,000	35,000	30,000	38,000
Sq. ft. of rentable area	31,800	37,600	29,700	32,200	26,700	33,800
Rental area ratio	88%	94%	93%	92%	89%	89%
Price/sq.ft. of rentable area	—	$77.93	$71.38	$76.09	$80.90	$73.08
Occupancy rate	90%	87%	85%	90%	95%	90%
Construction quality and condition	Average	Average	Average	Average	Average	Average
Ratio of parking spaces to rental area	Good	Same	Same	Same	Inferior	Same
Average rent per sq. ft. of rentable area	$12.60	$12.80	$11.80	$12.60	$13.00	$12.30
Location	Average	Superior	Inferior	Average	Superior	Inferior
Expense ratio	Market norm	Similar	Similar	Higher	Similar	Similar
Net adjustment	—	Negative	Positive	Negative	Negative	Positive

positive. The adjusted price of Comparable B indicates that the subject has a unit value greater than $71.38 per square foot of rentable area.

Comparable C has a unit price of $76.09 per square foot of rentable area. The location of the comparable is similar to that of the subject, so there is no need for a location adjustment. The comparable has a superior rentable area ratio, so a negative adjustment to its price is required. The expense ratio for the property is slightly higher than typical, resulting in a lower net income. Thus a small positive adjustment must be made to the price of the property for this difference. The net adjustment to this comparable is negative because the higher rentable area ratio has a greater effect on value than the higher expense ratio.

Comparable D indicates a unit price of $80.90 per square foot of rentable area. Because it is situated at the intersection of two major arterial highways, the property has a significantly superior location compared to that of the subject. Therefore a negative adjustment to the price of the property is required for location. The availability of parking is more limited, requiring a positive adjustment. Comparable D has a higher occupancy rate than the stabilized occupancy rate that characterizes the market for this type of property, so a negative adjustment is required for this difference. The negative adjustments for superior location and higher occupancy outweigh the positive adjustment for limited parking spaces, so the net adjustment is negative.

Comparable E indicates a unit price of $73.08 per square foot of rentable area. The location of the property on a major collector street is inferior to that of the subject. A positive adjustment is required for this difference. The property is similar to the subject in all other elements of comparison. A positive net adjustment indicates that the price of the subject is greater than $73.08 per square foot of rentable area.

The value indications derived from the comparable sales are reconciled into a single value indication by arranging the five sales in an array relative to the subject.

Comparable	Price Per Square Foot	Net Adjustment
D	$80.90	Negative
A	$77.93	Negative
C	$76.09	Negative
Subject	—	—
E	$73.08	Positive
B	$71.38	Positive

Comparables A, C, and D have unit values greater than that of the subject; Comparables B and E have unit values less than that of the subject. The lowest value indication in the first group is $76.09 per square foot of rentable area for Comparable C. The higher value indication in the second group was $73.08 per square foot of rentable area for Comparable E. Therefore, the indicated range of value for the subject is between $73.08 and $76.09 per square foot of rentable area. Comparable E is the property most similar to the subject and therefore may be accorded the greatest weight. On the basis of the indicated range of value and the weight placed on Comparable E, a single point indication of $74.00 per square foot of rentable area may be concluded.

The total value indication for the subject property may then be calculated by multiplying the unit value of $74.00 per square foot of rentable area by the 31,800 square feet of rentable area, resulting in a value indication of $2,353,200, which may be rounded to $2,350,000.

In an appraisal report a value indication derived with relative comparison analysis will usually require a greater degree of narrative explanation than an indication derived through paired data set analysis. In applying either technique, the appraiser must ensure that his or her reasoning is clear. The appraiser must adequately explain how the sales comparison approach was used to arrive at the final value indication. The extent of narrative explanation required depends on the complexity of the property being appraised. In practice the appraiser's analysis would normally be explained in greater detail than is indicated in the sample application because more data would be available. The more complex the property, the greater the number of factors that must be considered.

RECONCILIATION

Reconciliation is the last phase of any valuation analysis in which two or more value indications have been derived from market data. In reconciliation, the appraiser summarizes and reviews the data and analyses that resulted in each of the value indications. These value indications are then resolved into a range of value or a single value indication or point estimate. It is important that the appraiser consider the strengths and weaknesses of each value indication derived, examining the reliability and appropriateness of the market data compiled and the analytical techniques applied. The appraisal report should clearly communicate the reasoning by which the appraiser arrived at the value conclusion.

In the sales comparison approach, reconciliation may involve two levels of analysis. The first level of analysis pertains to the derivation of a value indication from the adjusted prices of two or more comparables that are expressed in terms of a single unit of comparison. The reconciliation process at this level of analysis was demonstrated in the sample applications of paired data set analysis and relative comparison analyses. A second level of analysis in reconciliation is required when the appraiser derives two or more value indications that are expressed in different units of comparison. For example, value indications expressed in price per square foot and price per dwelling must be reconciled into a value range or a single value indication for the sales comparison approach.

Reconciliation is also required when value indications are derived using two or more approaches to value. At this final point in the valuation process, reconciliation results in the value estimate identified in the problem definition. Final reconciliation is discussed in Chapter 23.

Two related points should be stressed in any discussion of the reconciliation process. They apply both to the reconciliation of value indications within the sales comparison approach and to the reconciliation of indications derived from the sales comparison approach and other approaches. In arriving at a final value indication in the sales comparison approach, the appraiser must ensure that the value concluded is consistent with the purpose of the appraisal and the value indications derived from the other approaches to value. This is especially important in regard to *date of prospective value* estimates. For example, an appraiser may seek market value estimates of an income-producing property at two different points in the future—e.g., upon project completion (fee simple) and upon stabilized occupancy (leased fee). The only market data available, however, may pertain to comparable properties at or near stabilized occupancy. Typically, these data are appropriate only for an analysis of the market value of the subject property at the point of stabilized occupancy. Thus, the appraiser has to reconcile the prospective value indication based on these data with value indications derived form the other approaches for the corresponding date of stabilized occupancy (leased fee). These data should *not* be used to derive a value indication for the date of completion (fee simple) unless other truly comparable sales can be identified.

The appraiser must also consider any differences in the property rights appraised between the comparables and the subject property since the comparable sales may include the transfer of a leased fee estate. If the data are not properly analyzed, the value indication concluded in the sales comparison approach for the leased fee estate in the subject property upon the achievement of stabilized occupancy might be lower than the value for the fee simple estate. This value indication would not be compatible with the corresponding value indications derived from the cost and income approaches for the fee simple estate in the subject property unless adjustments had been made. Failure to recognize that the value indications may apply to different property rights would likely result in an incorrect value conclusion.

SUMMARY

The sales comparison approach is the process by which a market value estimate is derived by analyzing the market activity of similar properties and comparing these properties to the subject property. Comparative analysis techniques are fundamental to the valuation process and are used in the other approaches to value.

The sales comparison approach is based on the premise that the market value of a property is directly related to the prices of comparable, competitive properties. The value of a property in the market is set by the availability of substitute properties of similar utility and desirability. Value is sustained when the relationships between land and the improvements on land, and between property and its environment are in balance. Externalities such as the neighborhood and the economy can affect property value positively or negatively.

The sales comparison approach is applicable when there are sufficient data on recent market transactions to indicate value patterns; it is less useful when data are scarce. Changes in economic conditions, zoning regulations, income tax laws, and the availability of financing may also limit the reliability of the approach. Sales comparison is commonly used to value single-family residential properties. Thorough analysis of comparable sales of complex, income-producing properties is more difficult. Sales comparison does provide information on capitalization rates and depreciation that are applied in the income and cost approaches.

To apply the sale comparison approach, the appraiser considers data from sales, contracts, offers, refusals, and listings of competitive properties. These data are used to establish the prices, real property rights conveyed, financing terms, motivations, transaction dates, locations, physical and functional conditions, and economic characteristics of the properties under consideration. Sources of information may include public records, commercially available data from reporting services, real estate periodicals, and interviews with the parties involved in transactions. The geographic limits of the data search depend on the nature and type of real estate being valued. Market boundaries are set by the range of competitive properties.

A systematic, five-step procedure for applying the sales comparison approach involves: 1) researching the market for data on sale transactions, listings, and offerings to purchase or sell comparable properties; 2) verifying that the data are accurate and representative of arm's-length transactions; 3) determining relevant units of comparison; 4) comparing the subject with the comparables and adjusting the comparables for differences; and 5) reconciling the multiple value indications into a single value or a range of values.

Units of comparison, the components into which properties may be divided for purposes of comparison, vary with the appraisal problem. The use of units of comparison facilitates the comparative analysis of the subject and the comparables, but the units applied should be appropriate, reliable, and consistent. Some adjustments can be made to the total property price; others are made to the price per unit of comparison. Income multipliers and income rates may also be used as units of comparison. Appraisers do not adjust these units; rather, they explain any similarities or differences in reconciling separate value indications.

Elements of comparison are the characteristics of properties and transactions that cause the prices paid for real estate to vary. They are used to help identify differences between the subject and comparable properties so that adjustments can be made. An appraiser must not adjust for the same difference more than once. The most common elements of comparison are real property rights conveyed, financing terms, conditions of sale, market conditions, location, physical characteristics, economic characteristics, use, and non-realty components of value. Other possible elements include access, governmental restrictions, onsite environmental conditions, and offsite improvements.

An adjustment for real property rights conveyed reflects the difference in the income-generating and use potential of a property encumbered with leases and that of an unencumbered property. The adjustment is needed to account for the difference between the market rent that an unencumbered property is capable of commanding, and the contract rent that a property subject to existing leases will generate until the termination of each lease. If an adjustment is not made for differences in property rights in the sales comparison approach, any difference must be addressed in the reconciliation of the separate value indications.

Financing arrangements such as mortgage assumptions, buydowns, installment sale contracts, and wraparound loans affect sale prices. Although cash equivalent prices can be computed mathematically, the financing adjustments derived with these calculations must be rigorously tested against market conditions and perceptions.

Cash equivalency calculations are commonly used to adjust sales in which the seller pays points or finances the loan at a rate that differs from the market rate. Cash equivalency adjustments for atypical financing may be calculated by analyzing paired data sets or by discounting the cash flows created by these mortgage contracts at market interest rates. The financing adjustment may or may not include an adjustment for conditions of sale; a combined adjustment results when favorable financing is a function of the seller's need to sell the property quickly.

An adjustment for conditions of sale is used to reflect the motivations of buyers or sellers in sales that are not arm's-length transactions due to duress or special relationships. Such an adjustment may also be required in transactions influenced by unusual tax considerations or a lack of market exposure.

An adjustment for market conditions is derived by analyzing changes that have occurred over time and determining their effect on a specific type of property during that period. Changes in market conditions may result from appreciation or depreciation in value due to inflation or deflation, fluctuations in supply and demand, building moratoriums, or changes in income tax laws. Analysis of two or more arm's-length sales of a single property over a period when no changes in physical or economic characteristics have occurred may indicate the rate of price change; several paired sets will provide a more reliable indication of the rate of price change.

An adjustment for location is required when the neighborhoods or environments of the subject and comparables differ significantly, creating variances in demand. Adjustments for physical characteristics account for differences in the size of improvements or sites, the quality and condition of the improvements, the construction materials used, the functional utility of the improvements, and the amenities provided.

Adjustments for economic characteristics reflect differences in management quality, tenant mix, and contractual terms such as rent concessions, lease expiration dates, renewal options, and special lease provisions such as expense recovery clauses. The appraiser must take care not to report differences in real property rights conveyed or changes in market conditions as dissimilarities involving economic characteristics.

An adjustment for difference in use may be made when properties differ in terms of intended use, highest and best use, or zoning. Non-realty property components include personalty and the business value.

Both quantitative and qualitative techniques may be used to identify and measure adjustments. *Quantitative techniques* include paired data analysis, statistical analysis, graphic analysis, trend analysis, cost-related analysis, and secondary data analysis. *Qualitative techniques* include relative comparison analysis, ranking analysis, and personal interviews.

Paired data analysis can be used to isolate the effect of a particular variable on price when sufficient data are available and other variables can be quantified. When sufficient data are not available, the technique may be employed to suggest the size of an adjustment, which can then be tested for reasonableness. *Statistical analysis* includes statistical inference and regression analysis. *Graphic analysis* involves visual interpretation of a graphic display of data or curve fit analysis of data. *Trend analysis* is useful when a broad database of properties is available. *Cost-related* and *secondary data analysis* rely on special types of data such as cost indicators and market analyses prepared by research firms or governmental agencies.

In *relative comparison analysis* an appraiser studies the relationships indicated by market data without recourse to quantification. Typically the appraiser analyzes comparable sales to determine whether their characteristics are inferior, superior, or equal to those of the subject property. The process is similar to paired data analysis, but no quantitative analysis is involved. *Ranking analysis* arrays properties according to their degree of similarity to the subject. *Personal interviews* of market participants also may provide useful information for making qualitative adjustments.

Comparative analysis refers to the basic analytical process, which may employ quantitative techniques, qualitative techniques, or a combination of both to derive a value indication. The process consists of four steps: 1) identification of the elements of comparison affecting the value of the property being appraised; 2) comparison of each comparable with the subject and measurement of the difference in each element of comparison, either quantitatively or qualitatively; 3) derivation of a net adjustment for each comparable; and 4) review of the comparable prices after adjustment or ranking and reconciliation of the various indications into a single value estimate.

The adjustments derived through quantitative techniques may be applied to a comparable property either as percentages or dollar amounts. The relationship between the subject and the comparable should be expressed as it is perceived by the market. The relationship between the subject and a comparable property is converted into an algebraic statement to determine the percentage adjustment to be applied to the price of the comparable. The appraiser should express this relationship consistently.

The application of qualitative adjustments involves separating the comparables into those that are overall superior to the subject and those that are inferior. The adjusted prices of these two groups *bracket* the probable value range of the subject. By studying the comparables most similar to the subject, the appraiser concludes a single value indication for the subject.

The sequence in which adjustments are applied to the comparables is determined by the market data and the appraiser's analysis of those data. The following sequence of adjustments is provided for purposes of illustration: 1) real property rights conveyed adjustment, adjusted price; 2) financing terms adjustment, adjusted price; 3) conditions of sale adjustment, adjusted price; 4) market conditions adjustment, adjusted price; and 5) adjustments for location, physical characteristics, economic characteristics, use, and non-realty components. Each final adjusted price is an indication of the value of the subject property.

Use of a market data grid ensures that adjustments are made in a consistent manner. The grid should include a section for reconciling the separate value indications derived in the sales comparison approach. Collectively these indications constitute a range of value. The market data grid can be used to rank sales in terms of their comparability to the subject property and to find which sales require the least total adjustment. The sales that occurred nearest to the appraisal date, those that require the least adjustments, and those that are most similar to the subject are given the most weight in the sales comparison approach.

The last phase of the valuation analysis is reconciliation. Because different indications are derived in the sales comparison approach, reconciliation may be carried out on two levels. Value indications expressed in terms of a single unit of comparison may differ. Value indications expressed in terms of different units of comparison may also diverge. Furthermore, indications derived through two or more approaches to value must be reconciled. In reconciliation the appraiser should ensure that value indications are estimated as of the same date, especially in regard to prospective value,—i.e., date of project completion vs. date of stabilized occupancy. Value indications must also apply to the same property rights (fee simple vs. leased fee).

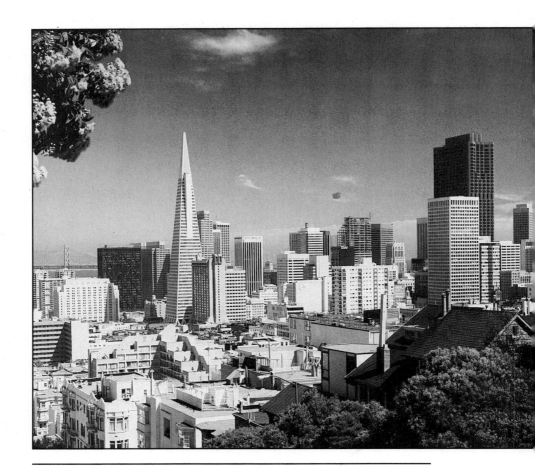

Chapter 18

THE INCOME CAPITALIZATION APPROACH

*I*ncome-producing real estate is typically purchased as an investment, and from an investor's point of view earning power is the critical element affecting property value. One basic investment premise is that the higher the earnings, the higher the value. An investor who purchases income-producing real estate is essentially trading present dollars for the right to receive future dollars. The income capitalization approach to value consists of methods, techniques, and mathematical procedures that an appraiser uses to analyze a property's capacity to generate benefits (i.e., usually the monetary benefits of income and reversion) and convert these benefits into an indication of present value.

The income capitalization approach is one of three traditional approaches that an appraiser may use in the valuation process. However, it is not an independent system of valuation that is unrelated to the other approaches. The valuation process as a whole is composed of integrated, interrelated, and inseparable techniques and procedures designed to produce a convincing and reliable estimate of value, usually market value.

The analysis of cost and sales data is often an integral part of the income capitalization approach, and capitalization techniques are frequently employed in the cost and sales comparison approaches. Capitalization techniques are commonly used to analyze and adjust sales data in the sales comparison approach; in the cost approach, obsolescence is often measured by capitalizing an estimated rent loss. The income capitalization approach is described here as part of the systematic valuation process, but the various methods, techniques, and procedures used in the approach are general-purpose analytical tools applicable in the valuation and evaluation of income-producing properties.

This chapter provides a broad overview of the income capitalization approach and discusses the rationale, methods, and history behind it. Chapters 19 through 22 continue this discussion with detailed explanations of the specific methods, techniques, and procedures used to project and capitalize future benefits.

RELATIONSHIP TO VALUE INFLUENCES AND APPRAISAL PRINCIPLES

The income capitalization approach is based on, and consistent with, the basic value influences and principles of real estate appraisal.

Anticipation and Change

The principle of anticipation is fundamental to the approach. Because value is created by the expectation of benefits to be derived in the future, value may be defined as the present worth of all rights to these future benefits. All income capitalization methods, techniques, and procedures attempt to consider anticipated future benefits and estimate their present value. This may involve either forecasting the anticipated future income or selecting a capitalization rate that implicitly reflects the anticipated pattern of change in income over time.

The approach must also consider how change affects the value of income-producing properties. To provide sound value indications, investors' expectations of changes in income levels, the expenses required to ensure income, and probable increases or decreases in property value must be carefully addressed and forecast. The capitalization procedure used to value the property must reflect the fact that the actual change in income, expenses, and property values may be different than originally anticipated by investors at the time of the appraisal. The more uncertainty there is about how these variables will change, the riskier the property investment. Investors expect to earn a higher rate of return on investments that are riskier. This should be reflected in the discount rate or capitalization rate selected by the appraiser.

Supply and Demand

The principle of supply and demand and the related concept of competition are particularly relevant in forecasting future benefits and estimating rates of return in the income capitalization approach. Both income streams and rates of return are determined in the market. The rents charged by the owner of a motel, a shopping center, an office building, an apartment building, or any income-producing property usually do not vary greatly from those charged by owners of competing properties that offer the same quality of service.

If the demand for a particular type of space exceeds the existing supply, owners may be able to increase rents. Vacancy rates may fall and developers will find new construction profitable. Property values may increase until supply and demand are in balance. On the other hand, if the demand for space is less than the existing supply, rents may decline, and vacancy rates may increase. Therefore, to estimate rates of return and forecast future benefits, appraisers consider the demand for the particular type of property and how this demand affects supply.

Substitution

The prices, rents, and rates of return for property tend to be set by the prevailing prices, rents, and rates of return for equally desirable substitute properties. The principle of substitution is market-oriented and provides the basis for estimating rents and expenses and selecting an appropriate discount rate or capitalization rate for the subject property. The principle of substitution may also be used to test the validity of the income capitalization approach and the reliability of the assumptions and data used in its application.

Balance

The principle of balance and all related concepts are especially significant in applying the income capitalization approach. A good balance between the types and locations of income-producing properties creates and sustains value; an imbalance in efficient land use may result in a decline in value. Efficient land use is facilitated by good planning and zoning laws.

The concept of contribution suggests that a reasonable balance among the four agents of production in an income-producing property creates and sustains maximum profitability. If a property is overimproved or underimproved, its rate of profit may be adversely affected.

Externalities

Positive and negative external forces affect the value of income-producing property. Apartments and office buildings are subject to the same types of external forces (e.g., the availability and quality of public transportation and shopping facilities) that affect single-family residences. Similarly, commercial establishments are enhanced by attractive, spacious, accessible surroundings and damaged by unattractive, poorly maintained, dirty surroundings. The negative externalities imposed by high crime rates have affected all types of income-producing property in recent years. External conditions such as pollution, unattractive surroundings, and high crime rates can even affect the value of property used for factories housing heavy industry.

INTERESTS TO BE VALUED

The rights of ownership in income-producing real estate are seldom held in fee simple by individual owners. An investor may hold title to real property rights as an individual, a corporate shareholder, or a general or limited partner. In addition, the interest in the real estate is often subject to mortgage financing, which further divides the real property rights into debt and equity interests. Finally, income-producing real estate is usually leased, which creates legal estates of the lessor's interest (i.e., the leased fee) and the lessee's interest (i.e., the leasehold).

As the flowchart in Figure 18.1 illustrates, the appraiser follows a logical sequence to identify the real property rights being appraised. The three main components of real property rights are ownership entities, financial interests, and legal estates. In a typical market value appraisal, the appraiser values an ownership entity's financial interest in a legal estate. By properly identifying all three catego-

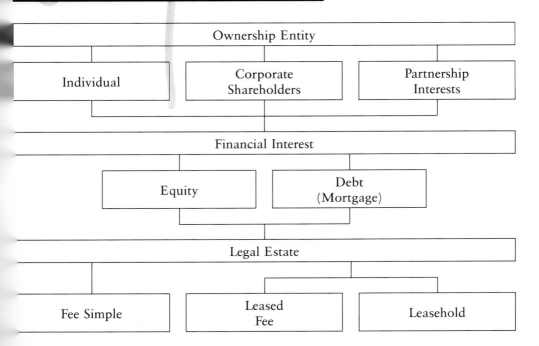

Figure 18.1 Components of Real Property Rights

ries of rights, the appraiser pinpoints the specific real property rights to be appraised.

Market valuation assignments relating to income-producing real estate often concern 100% ownerships of equity interests in a leased fee estate. A 100% ownership includes all shareholders or partners in a real estate venture. A typical example is the valuation of an existing, multitenant office building for a prospective buyer. The real property rights to be valued may be free and clear of mortgage debt or they may be subject to specified financing terms. The scope of the assignment may require a value estimate of the equity interest alone or it may call for a total value including the mortgage. In the latter case, the final conclusion may be reported in cash, in terms equivalent to cash, or in other precisely revealed terms depending on the nature of the assignment and applicable professional standards.

Appraisers do not only value fee simple, leased fee, and leasehold estates. They are often called upon to value real property rights complicated by other factors. For example, appraisers may value

- Minority shareholder or partnership interests
- Equity interests subject to various layers of debt, some of which may contribute to pre-tax cash flow and reversion
- Participation mortgages for lenders
- Master leasehold, sandwich leasehold, or subleasehold estates

Real property rights may be further affected by the specific requirements of the client, who may ask an appraiser to value a property subject to anticipated rezoning, planned renovation or rehabilitation, or the completion of construction. It is essential that the client and the appraiser begin with a clear understanding of the fundamentals of the appraisal assignment—i.e., the valuation of specified real property rights as of a specific date expressed in clearly defined terms.

Non-Realty Interests

Appraisers are often asked to value properties that include property components that are not "real property." For example, hotels include a significant amount of furniture, fixtures, and equipment which would often be classified as personal property. When there is a business enterprise associated with the property (as in the case of a hotel), the price investors are willing to pay for the property may also include a premium over the value of the real property for what is referred to as *business value*.

Business value is a value enhancement that results from items of intangible personal property such as marketing and management skill, an assembled work force, working capital, trade names, franchises, patents, trademarks, contracts, leases, and operating agreements. Going-concern value is the value created by a proven property operation. It consists of the total value of the real property plus intangible personal property, or business value. Properties that might have a business value component in addition to the real property include hotels and motels, restaurants, bowling alleys, industrial enterprises, retail stores and shopping malls, and similar properties.

Market Value and Investment Value

The income capitalization approach is typically used in market value appraisals of income-producing property. The approach may also be used to estimate investment value, which is the value of a property to a particular investor. Market value and investment value may coincide if the client's investment criteria are typical of investors in the market. In this case, the two value estimates may be the same number, but the two types of value are *not* interchangeable.

Market value is objective, impersonal, and detached; investment value is based on subjective, personal parameters. To estimate market value with the income capitalization approach, the appraiser must be certain that all data and assumptions used are market-oriented and reflect the motivations of a typical investor who would be willing to purchase the property at the time of the appraisal. A particular investor may be willing to pay more than market value, if necessary, to acquire a property that satisfies investment objectives unique to that investor. Similarly, a particular investor may place a higher investment value on a property he or she already owns than the current price for which property could be sold.

This text discusses the income capitalization approach as it is applied to estimate the market value of a fee simple or leased fee interest. The conclusions reached reflect the use and analysis of market data; they should be consistent with the value indications reached in the other valuation approaches.

Future Benefits

The benefits of owning specific rights in income-producing real estate include the right to receive all profits accruing to the real property over the holding period (i.e., the term of ownership) plus the proceeds from resale or reversion of the property at the termination of the investment. Various measures of future benefits are considered in the income capitalization approach. Commonly used measures include potential gross income, effective gross income, net operating income, pre-tax cash flow, and reversionary benefits.

Potential gross income (PGI) is the total potential income attributable to the real property at full occupancy before operating expenses are deducted. Potential gross income may refer to the level of rental income prevailing on the date of the appraisal or expected during the first full month or year of operation, or to the periodic income anticipated during the holding period.

Effective gross income (EGI) is the anticipated income from all operations of the real property adjusted for vacancy and collection losses. This adjustment covers losses incurred due to unoccupied space, turnover, and nonpayment of rent by tenants.

Net operating income (NOI) is the actual or anticipated net income remaining after all operating expenses are deducted from effective gross income, but before mortgage debt service and book depreciation are deducted. Net operating income is customarily expressed as an annual amount. In certain income capitalization applications, a single year's net operating income may represent a steady stream of fixed income that is expected to continue for a number of years. In other applications the income may represent the starting level of a stream of income that is expected to change in a prescribed pattern over the years. Still other applications may require that net operating income be estimated for each year of the analysis.

Pre-tax cash flow is the portion of net operating income that remains after debt service is paid, but before ordinary income tax on operations is deducted. Like net operating income, a single year's pre-tax cash flow may represent a steady stream of fixed income, the starting level of a changing income stream, or the equity income for a particular year of the analysis. Pre-tax cash flow is also referred to as *equity dividend* or *before-tax cash flow.*

After-tax cash flow is the portion of pre-tax cash flow that remains after ordinary income tax on operations has been deducted. The amount of ordinary income tax paid by the owner depends on the taxable income accruing from ownership of the property. This is affected by the amount of interest and tax depreciation that can be deducted from *NOI* in the calculation of taxable income.

Reversion is a lump-sum benefit that an investor receives at the termination of an investment. Depending on the real property rights being valued, the benefits may be calculated before or after deduction of the mortgage balance and income taxes. For example, the reversionary benefits for a fee simple estate are the expected proceeds from resale of the property at the end of the investment holding period. Depending on the method adopted, this may be gross proceeds or some form of net proceeds; in either case the type of proceeds must be identified and explained. For a mortgagee or lender, reversion consists of the balance of the mortgage when it is paid off.

Reversionary benefits are usually estimated either as an anticipated dollar amount or as a relative change in value over the presumed holding period. A dollar estimate of the reversion might be based on a lessee's option to purchase the property at the end of the lease. Alternatively, the value of the reversion at the end of the holding period might be estimated by applying a capitalization rate to the income that a buyer might expect to receive at the time of resale. Reversionary benefits may or may not require separate measurement, depending on the purpose of the analysis and the method of capitalization employed.

RATES OF RETURN

In applying the income capitalization approach, an appraiser assumes that the investor's ultimate objective is a total return that exceeds the amount invested. Therefore, the investor's expected return consists of 1) full recovery of the amount invested (i.e., the return *of* capital), and 2) a profit or reward (i.e., a return *on* capital). Many rates, or measures of return, can be used in capitalization.

All rates of return can be categorized as either *income rates* (also referred to as *cash flow rates*) or *yield rates.* The overall capitalization rate and equity capitalization rate are income rates. The interest rate, discount rate, internal rate of return, and equity yield rate are yield rates.

Under certain conditions the yield rate for a particular property may be numerically equivalent to the corresponding income rate; nevertheless, the rates are not conceptually the same nor are they interchangeable. An income rate is the ratio of one year's income to value;[1] a yield rate is applied to a series of individual incomes to obtain the present value of each.

In the income capitalization approach, both income rates and yield rates can be derived for, and applied to, any component of real property rights or the underlying physical real estate. For example, an appraiser may analyze total property income in terms of income to the land and income to the building or in terms of income to the mortgage and equity interests in the property. Similarly, an appraiser may seek the total investment yield or may analyze the separate yields to the land and the building or to the mortgage and the equity interests. Finally, an appraiser may want to know the value of the unencumbered fee simple, the leased fee, or the leasehold interest.

Income Rates

An income rate expresses the relationship between one year's income and the corresponding capital value of a property. Several types of income rates are discussed below.

An overall capitalization rate (R_O) is an income rate for a total property that reflects the relationship between a single year's net operating income expectancy and the total property price or value; it is used to convert net operating income into an indication of overall property value. An overall capitalization rate is not a rate of return on capital or a full measure of investment performance. It may be more than, less than, or equal to the expected yield on the capital invested, depending on projected changes in income and value.

An equity capitalization rate (R_E) is an income rate that reflects the relationship between a single year's pre-tax cash flow expectancy and the equity investment. When used to capitalize the subject property's pre-tax cash flow into value, the equity capitalization rate is often referred to in the real estate market as the *cash on cash rate, cash flow rate,* or *equity dividend rate.* Like the overall capitalization rate, the equity capitalization rate is not a rate of return on capital; it may be more than, less than, or equal to the expected equity yield rate, depending on projected changes in income, value, and amortization of the loan.

Yield Rates

A yield rate is a rate of return on capital; it is usually expressed as a compound annual percentage rate. The yield rate considers all expected property benefits, including the proceeds from sale at the termination of the investment. The term *interest rate* usually refers to the yield rate for debt capital, not equity capital.

A discount rate is a yield rate used to convert future payments or receipts into present value. The resulting present value represents the amount of capital to be invested so that the investor's expected yield equals the specified discount rate.

Internal rate of return (IRR), refers to the yield rate that is earned or expected for a given capital investment over the period of ownership. The internal rate of return for an investment is the yield rate that equates the present value of the future benefits of the investment to the amount of capital invested. The internal rate

---

1. The rate is usually calculated with the income for the first year, although the income for the previous year may be used. In some cases the incomes for several years might be averaged to obtain a representative income figure.

of return applies to all expected benefits, including the proceeds from resale at the termination of the investment. It can be used to measure the return on any capital investment, before or after income taxes.

An overall yield rate (Y_O) is a rate of return on the total capital invested. It takes into consideration changes in income over the investment holding period as well as the reversion at the end of the holding period. It does not, however, consider the effect of debt financing; it is calculated as if the property was purchased with no debt capital. The overall yield rate can be viewed as the combined yield on both the debt and equity capital. Conceptually it is a weighted average of the equity yield rate, which is discussed below, and the mortgage yield, or mortgage interest, rate.[2]

An equity yield rate (Y_E) is a rate of return on equity capital. It may be distinguished from a rate of return on debt capital, which is usually referred to as an *interest rate*. The equity yield rate is the equity investor's internal rate of return; it considers the effect of debt financing on the cash flow to the equity investor (equity dividend).

Return on and Return of Capital

The notion that an investor is entitled to complete recovery of invested capital plus a payment for the use of capital prevails in the real estate market just as it does in other markets. The term *return of capital* refers to the recovery of invested capital; the term *return on capital* refers to the additional amount received as compensation for use of the investor's capital until it is recaptured. Investors are concerned with both return of capital and return on capital. The rate of return on capital is analogous to the yield rate or the interest rate earned or expected.

In real estate investments capital may be recaptured in many ways. (The term *recapture* was coined at a time when investors assumed that property values could only decline due to economic depreciation. Today appraisers use the term when some income provision must be made to compensate for the loss of invested capital.) Investment capital may be recaptured through annual income or it may be recaptured all or in part through resale of the property at the termination of the investment. If the property value does not change between the time of the initial investment and the time the property is sold, the investor can recapture all the capital invested at its sale. Thus the annual income can all be attributed to the return on capital. In this case, the indicated income rate—i.e., the overall capitalization rate—will equal the return on capital.

If, on the other hand, the property value is expected to decrease over time and the investor does not expect to recapture all of the original investment at the time of resale, some of the income stream must be used for the repayment of capital. In this case the rate of return on capital will be somewhat less than the indicated income rate (i.e., the overall capitalization rate in direct capitalization). The difference between the rate of return on capital and the indicated capitalization rate will be the rate of return of capital. The recapture rate is considered positive.

---

2. In practice the overall yield rate is not usually calculated by averaging the equity yield rate and the mortgage interest rate because the ratio of debt and equity changes each year as the loan is amortized and the property value changes.

Finally, if the investor expects to receive more than the original investment at resale, the rate of return on capital is more than the indicated income rate; in this case the recapture rate appears to be negative because the annual income is not providing all of the expected return on capital.

In yield capitalization the distinction between return on and return of capital is always definite and precise. The discount rate is selected to provide a specified return on capital. Direct capitalization, on the other hand, uses income rates such as overall capitalization rates that must implicitly allow for both the return on and return of capital. That is, when the capitalization rate is applied to the income of the subject property, the estimated present value must represent a price that would allow the investor to earn a market rate of return on, in addition to recapture of, the capital invested. Thus, the capitalization rate selected and applied to value property must reflect the way that capital is expected to be recaptured.

RATE SELECTION

Whether it is an income rate or a yield rate, the rate of return used to convert income into property value should represent the annual rate of return necessary to attract investment capital. This rate is influenced by many factors, including the degree of apparent risk, market attitudes toward future inflation, the prospective rates of return for alternative investments, the rates of return earned by comparable properties in the past, the supply of and demand for mortgage funds, and the availability of tax shelters. Because the rates of return used in the income capitalization approach represent *prospective* rates, not historical rates, the market's perception of risk and changes in purchasing power are particularly important.

The suitability of a particular rate of return cannot be proven with market evidence, but the rate selected should be consistent with the available data. Rate selection requires appraisal judgment and knowledge about prevailing market attitudes and economic indicators.

Risk

An appraiser must consider the element of risk in applying the income capitalization approach. The anticipation of receiving future benefits creates value, but the possibility of losing future benefits detracts from value. Higher rewards are required in return for accepting higher risk. This belief is fundamental to the real estate market and the valuation of income-producing properties. It is generally accepted that all investments are predicated on the expectation of receiving a return on capital that represents the time value of money with an appropriate adjustment for perceived risk. The minimum rate of return for invested capital is sometimes referred to as the safe, or riskless, rate. Theoretically the difference between the total rate of return on capital and the safe rate may be considered a premium to compensate the investor for risk, the burden of management, and the illiquidity of invested capital.

To a real estate investor, risk is the chance of incurring a financial loss and the uncertainty of realizing projected future benefits. Most investors avoid excessive risk; they prefer certainty to uncertainty and expect a reward in return for assuming a risk. Appraisers must recognize investors' tendencies in analyzing market evidence, projecting future benefits, and applying capitalization procedures.

The appraiser must be satisfied that the income or yield rate used in capitalization is consistent with market evidence and reflects the level of risk associated with receiving the anticipated benefits.

Expected Inflation and Deflation

The amount of inflation or deflation expected affects the forecast of future benefits and the selection of an appropriate income or yield rate. If inflation, the erosion of the purchasing power of currency, is anticipated, the desired nominal rate of return on invested capital will tend to increase to compensate for lost purchasing power. That is, the required nominal rate will increase to offset the expected inflation. It is the *real* rate of return that investors try to protect over time.

In theory the total desired rate of return on capital includes any expected inflation rate. Therefore, the anticipated yield rate generally varies directly with the expected inflation rate. When discount rates that do not include a specific allowance for inflation are applied, the income streams and reversions calculated are expressed in constant, or uninflated, dollars.

Because the inflation rate and the yield rate tend to fluctuate together, there is no proof that a particular combination of rates provides the best reflection of current market attitudes. Nevertheless, the combination chosen must be consistent with general market expectations and the relationship or difference between the two rates must be plausible and supportable. In market value appraisals, the appraiser's objective is to simulate the expectations of a typical investor, not necessarily to make the most reliable prediction of yield and inflation rates.

Appraisers should be aware of the difference between inflation and appreciation in real value. Inflation is an increase in the volume of money and credit, a rise in the general level of prices, and the consequent erosion of purchasing power. Appreciation in real value results from an excess of demand over supply, which increases property values.

Inflation and appreciation have a similar effect on future dollars, but different effects on discount rates. Inflation tends to increase discount rates because investors require a higher nominal rate of return to offset the loss in value due to inflation. Appreciation will not affect the discount rate unless the risk associated with the property has changed. Inflation does, however, tend to lower capitalization rates because these rates are applied to the income at the time of the appraisal, which has not increased due to inflation. Although inflation does not create true value, certain properties are better hedges against inflation than others. Also, real estate may tend to increase in value in an inflationary environment whereas other investments such as stocks and bonds do not. Thus the outlook for inflation may affect property value.

An appraiser can account for the effects of inflation in capitalization by expressing future benefits in constant dollars, which are adjusted to reflect constant purchasing power, and by expressing the discount rate as a *real*, uninflated *rate* of return on capital. In practice, however, appraisers usually project income and expenses in unadjusted, inflated dollars and express the discount rate as a nominal, or apparent, rate of return on capital that includes an allowance for inflation.

Because lease terms often allow for inflation with CPI adjustments and expense pass-throughs, it is convenient and customary to project income and expenses in dollars just as they are expected to occur, not to convert the amounts to constant-dollar equivalents. Unadjusted discount rates rather than real rates of return are used so that these rates can be compared with other rates quoted in the open market—e.g., mortgage interest rates and bond yield rates. Fixed income securities like bonds do not respond to unexpected inflation in the same way as real estate because the interest rate and face value are fixed at the time the bond is issued.

Thus, projecting income from real estate in nominal terms allows the analyst to consider whether or not the income potential of the property and the resale price will increase with inflation. If the income and resale price are expected to increase with inflation, the present value of the projected cash flows will be affected. Any projected increases in income and property value due to inflation must be realistic. Furthermore, the appraiser must be consistent and not discount inflated dollars at real, uninflated rates. When inflated nominal dollars are projected, the discount rate must also be a nominal discount rate that reflects the anticipated inflation.

Unexpected Inflation

A distinction must be made between expected inflation and unexpected inflation. Expected inflation refers to changes in price levels that are expected at the time the investment is made or the property is being appraised. As discussed above, anticipated inflation should be reflected in expected rates of return. However, actual inflation may differ from what was anticipated at the time the investment was made. Depending on how the investment responds to the actual change in price levels, its value may increase or decrease over time at a different rate than originally anticipated. If the return on the investment does not increase with unexpected inflation, the investor's real rate of return will be less than originally projected. Investors often include an additional risk premium in the rate of return required on investments that do not respond well to unexpected inflation. As indicated, the net operating income and resale value of income-producing real estate may increase with unexpected inflation. Thus, investors may not require as great a premium for the risk due to unexpected inflation in discount rates for real estate as they would for fixed income investments like corporate bonds.

INCOME CAPITALIZATION APPROACH METHODS

Two capitalization methods—direct capitalization and yield capitalization—are described below. These methods are based on different measures of expected earnings and include different assumptions concerning the relationship between expected earnings and value.

Direct Capitalization

Direct capitalization is a method used to convert an estimate of a single year's income expectancy into an indication of value in one direct step—either by dividing the income estimate by an appropriate income rate or by multiplying the income estimate by an appropriate factor. The income expectancy considered is frequently the anticipated income for the following year. The rate or factor selected represents the relationship between income and value observed in the market and is derived through comparable sales analysis. The income from a property, usually annual net operating income or pre-tax cash flow, is divided by its sale or equity price to obtain the income rate. A factor or multiplier can be derived by dividing a property's sale price by its annual potential or effective gross income.

Direct capitalization is market-oriented; an appraiser analyzes market evidence and values property by inferring the assumptions of typical investors. Direct capitalization does not explicitly differentiate between the return on and return of capital because investor assumptions are not specified. However, it is implied that the selected multiplier or rate will satisfy a typical investor and that the prospects for future monetary benefits, over and above the amount originally invested, are sufficiently attractive.

Direct capitalization may be applied to potential gross income, effective gross income, net operating income, or pre-tax cash flow (equity dividend). The income selected for capitalization depends on the purpose of the analysis and the data available.

Yield Capitalization

Yield capitalization is a method used to convert future benefits into present value by discounting each future benefit at an appropriate yield rate or by developing an overall rate that explicitly reflects the investment's income pattern, value change, and yield rate. Like direct capitalization, yield capitalization should reflect market behavior. The method is profit- or yield-oriented, simulating typical investor assumptions with formulas that calculate the present value of expected benefits assuming specified profit or yield requirements.

The procedure used to convert periodic income and reversion into present value is called *discounting*; the required yield rate of return is called the *discount rate*. The discounting procedure presumes that the investor will receive a satisfactory return on the investment and complete recovery of the capital invested. The method is referred to as *yield capitalization* because it analyzes whether an investment property will produce the particular level of profit or yield required. Yield capitalization is also called *discounted cash flow analysis* because a discount rate is used to calculate the present value of anticipated future cash flows.

Appraisers distinguish between contract rent and market rent in analyzing income. Market rent is used to value a fee simple estate. If a leased fee estate is being valued, the appraiser considers contract rent for the existing leases and market rent for lease renewals.

A number of analytical techniques and procedures can be used to value an entire property, specific property benefits, or partial interests in property. Present value can be calculated with or without considering the impact of financing and income taxes as long as the specific rights being appraised are clearly identified. The techniques and procedures selected are determined by the purpose of the analysis, the availability of data, and the practices common in the marketplace.

Direct Capitalization, Yield Capitalization, and Discounting Compared

Direct capitalization is simple and easily understood. The capitalization rate or factor is derived directly from the market. Direct capitalization does not require explicit estimates of future income as long as the capitalization rate is extracted from comparable sales that reflect similar expectations for changes in income and property value.

Yield capitalization, on the other hand, is based on assumptions about expected changes in income and property value. To select a market-oriented discount rate, market attitudes and expectations must be interpreted. In yield capitalization specific investment goals for the return on and of invested capital are considered. The property's projected income stream and reversion are capitalized into a present value by applying the investor's anticipated yield rate in the discounting procedure. Discounting can be performed with formulas and factors that are obtained from financial tables or calculated and applied with hand-held financial calculators or programmable computers. There are also a variety of software programs for personal computers that can be used for discounting cash flows.

The income capitalization approach need not be limited to a single capitalization method. With adequate information and proper use, direct and yield capitalization methods should produce similar value indications. Both methods are market-derived and, therefore, should reflect a typical investor's view of market value.

Residual Techniques

Residual techniques are employed in the income capitalization approach so that physical value components (land and building), financial value components (mortgage and equity), or legal estates (leased fees and leaseholds) can be considered separately. Residual techniques presume that the value of a component or portion of the property is known or can be estimated. The income attributed to this component is then deducted from total property income to reveal the residual income, which is capitalized to ascertain the value of the unknown portion of the property. Residual techniques can be used in both direct and yield capitalization. In Chapter 12 (Highest and Best Use Analysis), the land residual technique was introduced as a means to determine which land use maximizes the residual value of the land. In Chapter 20 (Direct Capitalization), the land residual technique will be explored in greater depth.

HISTORY OF THE APPROACH

To understand the development of the various methods, techniques, and procedures used in the income capitalization approach, it may be helpful to examine its history. The following discussion is divided into two time periods: the early years, when the theoretical bases for direct and yield capitalization were established, and the modern era, when specific techniques and procedures were developed and refined.[3]

---

3. See James H. Burton, *The Evolution of the Income Approach* (Chicago: American Institute of Real Estate Appraisers, 1982).

Early Writings

The mathematical foundation for discounting can be traced to John Newton, who was among the first to provide a theory of compound interest, and Edmund Halley, the noted astronomer who published the first present value tables in 1693. John Smart is credited with providing the first comprehensive set of tables and the first partial payment table in 1726. His book, *Tables of Interest and Annuities*, included tables identical to the present value and compound interest tables found in modern appraisal texts.

In 1811 William Inwood published tables that had originally appeared in the works of others, such as John Smart. Of particular significance to appraisers, Inwood used real estate valuation examples to illustrate the use of Smart's tables. Inwood's example postulated that the present value of an annuity was based on a single discount rate. Inwood's book also contained a table for calculating the present value of an income in perpetuity, which seems to mark the first time an author converted an interest rate into a coefficient. Inwood multiplied the coefficient by the investment's annual income, which was assumed to be perpetual, to calculate the current value of the investment. The Inwood premise has been used by real estate appraisers ever since.

In 1890 Alfred Marshall became the first economist to address valuation techniques specifically. He identified the interest rate as the link between income and value and offered the formula

$$\text{Value} = \frac{\text{Income}}{\text{Interest rate}}$$

In the early 1900s Irving Fisher contributed to capitalization theory by analyzing the proposition that value is the present worth of future benefits. This concept is fundamental to modern appraisal theory and is recognized directly in discounted cash flow analysis. Thus, by the early 1900s the mathematical and conceptual foundations of direct and yield capitalization were established. In the years that followed, these concepts were applied in a manner consistent with prevailing investor attitudes and behavior.

Modern Era

Pre-1959

In the history of the income capitalization approach, two characteristics distinguish the years before 1959 from the periods that followed. First, prior to 1959 property was usually valued by dividing it into its land and improvement components. During this period the land and building residual techniques dominated appraisal practice. Their use reflected investors' concern with the physical components of property and the need to recapture the cost of depreciating improvements.

Second, before 1959 property value was estimated without considering financing. An all cash market value transaction was assumed without recognizing that a purchaser might use borrowed funds. Although band-of-investment techniques were available to synthesize an overall capitalization rate from the required returns of debt and equity investors, capitalization was dominated by physical residual techniques.

Real estate investors at this time were concerned with the productive economic life of the improvements, not with investment attributes such as financing. Prices were relatively stable and the effects of physical deterioration were not obscured by inflation. Capital gains were not seen as a significant source of equity return. Loan-to-value ratios and interest rates were relatively low, and creative financing, variable interest rates, and lender participation were not common. Because real estate financing was predictably regular, its effect on value was of little concern.

1959 to Mid-1970s

The year 1959 is especially significant to the income capitalization approach and serves as a transitional point in appraisal history. With the publication of *The Ellwood Tables*, L. W. Ellwood signaled the shift from reliance on physical residual techniques to techniques based on the debt and equity components of real estate investment.

Ellwood's contribution to the income capitalization approach was monumental because his system allowed for the capitalization of a stream of cash flows and provided a basis for analyzing specific investment assumptions in the valuation process. Ellwood popularized the notion that the total value of a property should reflect both the value of the mortgage and the value of the equity and he included financing in his formula. He recognized that the property appreciation or depreciation reflected in the proceeds of resale or reversion was a potentially important benefit of real property investment. Ellwood's formula explicitly considered reversion and the effects of mortgage amortization. Ellwood also recognized that a finite, relatively short holding period was the proper framework for analysis and valuation. Although the Ellwood formula is essentially a way to solve a discounted cash flow problem, Ellwood simplified the discounting procedure by publishing tables of precalculated rates that could be combined into a representative overall capitalization rate. These tables were particularly useful before electronic calculators and personal computers became available.

In the 1960s many appraisers began to use investment component, or band-of-investment, techniques to synthesize overall capitalization rates. (For further discussion of band-of-investment techniques, see Chapter 20.) Soon many appraisers applied a band-of-investment technique that employed the loan constant and the equity capitalization rate as the appropriate returns to the lender and the equity investor. This technique, which is similar to one introduced by S. Edwin Kazdin in 1944, was especially significant during the 1970s and 1980s.

Ellwood techniques were popular at this time for several reasons. First, stable income streams became less common because inflation and real increases in property values began to overtake the effects of physical depreciation. Thus, capital gains became more significant. Second, investors were becoming increasingly sophisticated. They began to think in terms of leveraging and shorter holding periods rather than the economic lives of properties, recapture rates, and long-term investments. During this period major appraisal organizations first recognized the effect of financing in their definitions of market value.

Mid-1970s to the Present

Since the mid-1970s capitalization theory and practice have been influenced by inflation and recurring national recessions. Recent developments in the real estate market include

- The marketing of partial interests such as limited partnerships and joint ventures
- Rapid increases in market rent levels until the mid-1980s, followed by declining rent levels in many metropolitan areas
- Use of complex participation mortgages, creative financing, and seller financing
- Fluctuating mortgage interest rates, which resulted in a preponderance of all-cash transactions in periods of high interest rates
- More foreign investment in U.S. real estate
- Numerous changes in tax laws which have drastically changed the treatment of real estate relative to other investments
- Cycles of overbuilding, underbuilding, excess demand, and a lack of sufficient demand

In recent years appraisers have focused on market participants' reactions to the dynamics of the market and relied on capitalization methods, techniques, and procedures to simulate investor decision making.

The methods that are most useful today include direct capitalization based on equity capitalization rates derived from comparable sales and yield capitalization that employs DCF analysis. In many circumstances these methods best reflect the behavior of market participants. The availability of computers has also had a major effect on investment analysis and valuation. Computers process data quickly and can be used for statistical analysis, DCF analysis, and business accounting, as well as the storage of comparable sales data.

Appraisers do not always agree on which income valuation techniques are appropriate. There is ongoing debate on the relevance of traditional capitalization techniques and the validity of DCF analysis. However, market participants use both traditional techniques and DCF analysis, so both are valid and relevant tools for real property appraisers.

SUMMARY

From an investor's perspective, the earning power of a real estate investment is the critical element affecting its value. The fundamental investment premise is the higher the earnings, the higher the value. Investment in an income-producing property represents the exchange of present dollars for the right to receive future dollars.

In the income capitalization approach to value, an appraiser analyzes a property's capacity to generate benefits and converts these benefits into an indication of present value. The income capitalization approach is an integral part of the valuation process. Income capitalization techniques and procedures are employed to analyze and adjust sales data in the sales comparison approach and to measure functional and external obsolescence by capitalizing an estimated income loss in the cost approach.

The three main components of real property rights are ownership entities, financial interests, and legal estates. A market value appraisal of income-producing property most often involves 100% ownership of equity interests (either free of debt or subject to specified financing) in a leased fee estate.

Appraisers may be called on to value complex property rights such as minority shareholder or partnership interests; equity interests subject to various layers of debt; participation mortgages; and master leasehold, sandwich leasehold, and subleasehold estates. Clients may also ask an appraiser to value property rights subject to anticipated rezoning, rehabilitation, or project completion. When a business enterprise is associated with a property, the value of the property may reflect a premium for the *business value* created by profitable management, operations, or franchises. *Going concern value* refers to the value of the realty plus business value.

The income capitalization approach is typically applied to derive an indication of market value, but it can also be employed to estimate investment value, which is the value of a property to a particular investor. Although the criteria of the investor and the market may coincide and the numerical estimates may be equivalent, market value and investment value are not interchangeable.

In the income capitalization approach, future benefits are commonly measured as *potential gross income (PGI)*, the total potential income attributable to the real property at full occupancy before operating expenses are deducted; *effective gross income (EGI)*, the anticipated income from all real property operations adjusted for vacancy and collection losses; *net operating income (NOI)*, the actual or anticipated net income remaining after all operating expenses are deducted from effective gross income, but before mortgage debt service and book depreciation are deducted; *pre-tax cash flow*, the portion of net operating income that remains after debt service is paid, but before ordinary income tax on operations is deducted; *after-tax cash flow*, the portion of pre-tax cash flow that remains after ordinary income tax on operations is deducted; and *reversion*, the lump-sum benefit that an investor receives at the termination of an investment.

An investor's total expected return includes full recovery of the amount invested, the *return of capital*, and a profit, the *return on capital*. Rates of return can be categorized as either *income rates* or *yield rates*. An income rate is the ratio of one year's income to value; it may be used as a capitalization rate to convert income into value. A yield rate is applied to a series of individual incomes to obtain the present value of each. Both income and yield rates can be used to analyze components of real property rights and the physical real estate by applying residual techniques in the capitalization procedure.

Overall capitalization and equity capitalization rates are income rates. They are not rates of return on capital and do not reflect the eventual equity yield rate. *An overall capitalization rate* (R_O) is an income rate for a total property that reflects the relationship between its annual net income expectancy and total property value; it is used to convert net operating income into an indication of overall property value. An *equity capitalization rate* (R_E) is an income rate that reflects the relationship between the annual pre-tax cash flow expectancy and the equity investment. It is also referred to as a *cash on cash rate, cash flow rate,* or *equity dividend rate*.

A *yield rate* is a rate of return on capital. It is usually expressed as a compound annual percentage rate. The yield rate considers all expected benefits, including the proceeds from sale at the termination of the investment. An *interest rate* is a yield rate for debt capital. A *discount rate* is a yield rate used to convert future payments into present value.

An *internal rate of return (IRR)* refers to the yield rate that is earned or expected for a given capital investment over the period of ownership. The *IRR* equates the present value of the future benefits of the investment to the amount of capital invested. The *overall yield rate* (Y_o) is a rate of return on the total capital. It represents a weighted average of the equity yield rate and the mortgage yield rate. An *equity yield rate* (Y_E) is the rate of return on equity capital, as distinguished from the rate of return on debt capital.

Return of capital refers to the recovery of invested capital; *return on capital* refers to the additional amount received as compensation for use of the investor's capital until it is recaptured. In real estate investments, capital may be recaptured in many ways (e.g., through annual income or resale of the property).

If property value does not change over the period of the investment, the investor can recapture all the capital at the sale of the property and the indicated income rate (R_o) will equal the return on capital. If the investor does not expect to recapture all of the original investment, some of the income must be used to repay the capital, and the return on capital will be less than the income rate (R_o). If the investor expects to receive more than the original investment, the rate of return on capital will exceed the income rate (R_o).

In yield capitalization, the distinction between return on and return of capital is always explicit, and a discount rate is selected to provide a specified return *on* capital. In direct capitalization the income rates used must allow for both a return on and return of capital. An estimate of value derived by applying an overall capitalization rate to property income reflects both the return on and recapture of the capital invested.

The capitalization rate selected for valuation may be an income rate or a yield rate, but it should represent the annual rate of return necessary to attract investment capital. Because rates of return are prospective, market perceptions of risk and changes in purchasing power due to inflation or deflation are important considerations. The capitalization rates chosen should simulate market expectations.

All investments are predicated on the expectation of receiving a return on capital that represents the time value of money plus an appropriate adjustment for risk. Risk reflects the chance of incurring financial loss and the uncertainty of realizing future benefits. Investors expect a reward for assuming risk. The rate of return on capital thus combines a safe, riskless rate with a premium to compensate the investor for risk, the burden of management, and the illiquidity of invested capital.

Inflation erodes purchasing power and jeopardizes the rate of return that an investor anticipates. Because lease terms often allow for inflationary adjustments, appraisers usually project income and expenses in inflated, unadjusted dollars and express the discount rate as a nominal, apparent rate of return on capital that includes an allowance for inflation. The use of unadjusted discount rates allows for comparison with other rates quoted in the open market (e.g., mortgage interest and bond yield rates).

Appreciation in real value results from an excess of demand over supply and increases property values. Inflation and appreciation have a similar effect on future dollars, but different effects on discount rates. Inflation tends to increase discount rates because investors require a higher nominal rate of return to offset any loss in value due to inflation. Appreciation does not affect the discount rate unless the risk of the property changes. Inflation tends to lower capitalization rates. Actual inflation may differ from the inflation anticipated at the time the investment was made. *Unexpected inflation* is reflected in the rate of return on capital used to value the property.

Direct capitalization is a method used to convert an estimate of a single year's income expectancy into an indication of value in one direct step—either by dividing the income estimate by an appropriate income rate or by multiplying the income estimate by an appropriate income factor.

Yield capitalization is a method used to convert future benefits into present value by discounting each future benefit at an appropriate yield rate or by developing an overall rate that explicitly reflects the investment's income pattern, value change, and yield rate. Yield capitalization is also called *discounted cash flow analysis* because a discount rate is applied to calculate the present value of anticipated future cash flows.

Appraisers distinguish between contract rent and market rent in analyzing income. Market rent is used to value a fee simple estate. In valuing a leased fee estate, the appraiser considers contract rent for existing leases and market rent for lease renewals.

Direct capitalization does not require explicit estimates of future income because the capitalization rate is extracted from comparable sales that reflect similar expectations as to changes in income and property value.

Yield capitalization is based on assumptions about expected changes in income and property value. The property's projected income stream and reversion are capitalized into present value by applying the investor's anticipated yield rate in the discounting procedure. With adequate data and proper use, direct and yield capitalization should provide similar value indications.

Since the mid-1970s the income capitalization approach has been influenced by macroeconomic conditions and specific developments within the real estate market. Current valuation methods draw on equity capitalization using rates derived from comparable sales and yield capitalization with computer-assisted *DCF* analysis.

Chapter 19

INCOME ESTIMATES

To apply any capitalization procedure, a reliable estimate of income expectancy must be developed. Although some capitalization procedures are based on the actual level of income at the time of the appraisal rather than a projection of future income, an appraiser must still consider the future outlook. Failure to consider future income would contradict the principle of anticipation, which holds that value is the present worth of future benefits. Historical income and current income are significant, but the ultimate concern is the future. The earning history of a property is important only insofar as it is accepted by buyers as an indication of the future. Current income is a good starting point, but the direction and expected rate of income change are critical to the capitalization process.

Four types of income can be converted into value in the income capitalization approach: potential gross income (PGI), effective gross income (EGI), net operating income (NOI), and pre-tax cash flow ($PTCF$). Reliable projections of income are important because large value differences can result when the same rate or factor is used to convert different income estimates into value. If, for example, a potential gross income multiplier of 6.0 is applied to potential gross income estimates of $50,000 and $55,000, values of $300,000 and $330,000 result. A $5,000 difference in potential gross income produces a $30,000 difference in value. Similarly, when an overall capitalization rate of 10.0% is applied to net operating income estimates of $35,000 and $40,000, values of $350,000 and $400,000 result. In this example a $5,000 difference in net operating income results in a $50,000 value difference. Thus, income forecasting is a sensitive and crucial part of income capitalization.

An appraiser may estimate income for a single year or series of years depending on the data available and the capitalization method employed. The analysis can be based on the actual level of income at the time of the appraisal, a forecast of income for the first year of the investment, a forecast of income over a specified holding period, or a stabilized, average annual income over a specific holding period. If a market value estimate is sought, the income forecast should reflect the expectations of market participants. In an assignment to estimate investment value, an appraiser may base the income forecasts on the specific ownership or management requirements of the investor.

If an investment in a partial interest—e.g., an equity interest in a fee simple or leased fee estate—is being valued, pre-tax cash flow is usually capitalized. The appraiser must deduct mortgage debt service from net operating income to calculate pre-tax cash flow. Sometimes debt service is based on an existing mortgage and the amount is specified; in other cases debt service must be estimated based on the typical mortgage terms indicated by current market activity.

LEASE ANALYSIS

The income to various lease interests is generally derived through the conveyance and operation of leases. *A lease is a written document in which the rights to use and occupy land or structures are transferred by the owner to another for a specified period of time in return for a specified rent.* An appraiser begins to develop an income and expense forecast for investment real estate by studying all existing and proposed leases that apply to the subject property. These leases provide information on rent and other income and on the division of expenses between the landlord and the tenant.

If leases exist and the income estimate is based on the continuation of lease income, the appraiser examines lease provisions that could affect the quantity, quality, and durability of property income. The appraiser must either read the leases or rely on the client or another authorized party to disclose all pertinent lease provisions. The appraiser also analyzes the leases of competitive properties to estimate contract rent, market rent, and other forms of income. Because lease analysis is important, the characteristics of leases must be fully understood.

LEASE TYPES

Although a lease can be drawn to fit any situation, most leases fall into one of several broad classifications: flat rental, graduated rental, revaluation, index, and percentage. Leases may be applied on a *gross rental basis*, with the lessor paying all the operating expenses of the real estate, or a *net rental basis*, with the tenant paying all expenses. Lease terms frequently fall between these extremes and specify the division of expenses between the lessor and the lessee. Leases can also be categorized by their terms of occupancy—e.g., month-to-month, short-term (of five years or less), or long-term (of more than five years).

Flat Rental
A flat rental lease specifies a level of rent that continues throughout the duration of the lease. In a stable economy, this type of lease is typical and acceptable. In a changing economy, however, leases that are more responsive to fluctuating market conditions are preferred. When flat rental leases are used in inflationary periods, they tend to be short-term.

Graduated Rental
Graduated rental leases provide for specified changes in the amount of rent at one or more points during the lease term. A step-up lease, which allows for smaller rent payments in the early years, can be advantageous to a tenant establishing a business in a new location. This type of lease can also be used to recognize tenant expenditures on a property that are effectively amortized during the early years of the lease. Long-term ground leases may include provisions for increasing rent to reflect the expectation of future increases in property value and protect the purchasing power of the landlord's investment. Because property value is usually expected to increase, tenants are expected to pay commensurately higher rents.

Step-down leases are less common than step-up leases. They are generally used to reflect unusual circumstances associated with a particular property such as the likelihood of reduced tenant appeal in the future or capital recapture of interior improvements during the early years of a long-term lease.

Revaluation
Revaluation leases provide for periodic rent adjustments based on revaluation of the real estate under prevailing market conditions. Although revaluation leases tend to be long-term, some are short-term with renewal option rents based on revaluation of the real estate when the option is exercised. When the parties to a lease cannot agree on the revaluation, revaluation through appraisal or arbitration may be stipulated in the lease.

Index

Index leases are generally long-term leases that provide for periodic rent adjustment based on the change in a specific index such as a nationally published, cost-of-living index. The Consumer Price Index (CPI) is frequently the index selected.

Percentage

In percentage leases some or all of the rent charged is based on a specified percentage of the volume of business, productivity, or use achieved by the tenant. Percentage leases may be short- or long-term and are most frequently used for retail properties. A straight percentage lease may have no minimum rent, but most specify a guaranteed minimum rent with the percentage, or graduated percentage, rent payable on sales that exceed a specified level.

Lease Data

The data contained in a typical lease include

- Date of the lease
- Reference information, if the lease is recorded
- Legal description or other identification of the leased premises
- Name of lessor—i.e., owner or landlord
- Name of lessee—i.e., tenant
- Lease term
- Occupancy date
- Commencement date for rent payment
- Rent amount, including any percentage clause, graduation, escalation provisions, and payment terms
- Rent concessions, including any discounts or benefits
- Landlord's covenants—i.e., items such as taxes, insurance, and maintenance for which the owner or landlord is responsible
- Tenant's covenants—i.e., items such as taxes, insurance, maintenance, utilities, and cleaning expenses for which the tenant is responsible
- Right of assignment or right to sublet— i.e., whether the leasehold, or tenant's interest, may be assigned or sublet, under what conditions, and whether assignment relieves the initial tenant of future liability
- Option to renew, including the date of required notice, term of renewal, rent, and other renewal provisions
- Options to purchase
- Escape clauses
- Security deposits, including advance rent, bond, or expenditures by the tenant for items such as leasehold improvements
- Casualty loss—i.e., whether the lease continues after a fire or other disaster and on what basis
- Lessee's improvements, including whether they can be removed when the lease expires and to whom they belong

- Condemnation, including the respective rights of the lessor and the lessee if all or any part of the property is appropriated by a public agency
- Revaluation clauses
- Special provisions

A sample form for analyzing a typical office lease is shown in Figure 19.1. Special attention should be paid to lease data on rent, rent concessions, the division of expenses, renewal options, escalation clauses, purchase options, escape clauses, and tenant improvements.

Rent

The quantity of income to be paid by the tenant is basic lease data. An appraiser considers rent from all sources, which may include base, or minimum, contract rent, percentage rent, and escalation rent. The source of rental income should be clearly identified.

Rent Concessions

When real estate markets are oversupplied, landlords may give tenants concessions such as free rent for a specified period of time or extra tenant improvements. In shopping center leases, retail store tenants are sometimes given rent credit for interior store improvements. All rent concessions result from market conditions and the relative negotiating strengths of the landlord and the tenant.

Lessor/Lessee Division of Expenses

Most leases outline the obligations of the lessor and the lessee to pay for taxes, utilities, heat, repairs, and other expenses required to maintain and operate the leased property. An appraiser should identify the division of expenses in each lease analyzed and compare the rents and estimated rental value of the subject space to those of comparable space.

Renewal Options

Renewal options that allow a tenant to extend the lease term for one or more prescribed periods of time are frequently included in short- and long-term leases. A typical renewal option requires that the tenant provide advance notice of the intention to exercise the option and identifies the length of the renewal period or periods as well as the rent or method of determining the rent to be paid. The option rent may be set at the original rent or at a level determined when the lease was negotiated, or it may be calculated with an established procedure or formula when the option is exercised. Renewal options are binding on the lessor, but allow the tenant to reach a decision in light of the circumstances prevailing at the time of renewal. Thus, they are generally considered favorable to the tenant, not the lessor.

Escalation Clauses

Expense-stop clauses are often added to traditional gross or flat rental leases. Expense-stop clauses provide that increases in specified operating expenses are the obligations of the lessee. In multitenanted retail or office buildings, increased expenses are usually prorated among the tenants in proportion to the area they occupy or on some other equitable basis. The prorated shares are then added to the

Figure 19.1 Office Space Rental Worksheet

Building: _____

_____

Lessor: _____

Lessee: _____

Premises: Floor _____ Rentable area _____ Usable area _____ Loss factor _____

Term: Commencement _____ Expiration _____

Base rent: _____ CPI _____

Graduations: _____

_____

Escalations:

Real estate taxes _____

Porter wage _____

Operating expenses _____

Energy _____

Work letter (cost): _____

Special provisions (e.g., repainting, etc.): _____

Who pays:	Lessor	Lessee	Stop	Base Amount per Square Foot
Tenant electric	( )	( )	( )	( )
Building electric	( )	( )	( )	( )
Tenant HVAC	( )	( )	( )	( )
Building HVAC	( )	( )	( )	( )
Tenant space cleaning	( )	( )	( )	( )
Public space cleaning	( )	( )	( )	( )
Fuel	( )	( )	( )	( )
Repairs and maintenance				
Exterior	( )	( )	( )	( )
Interior	( )	( )	( )	( )
Fire insurance (building)	( )	( )	( )	( )

Renewal options:

How many _____ Years each_____

New rent

_____

_____

New escalation (and base year): _____

New rentable area or loss factor: _____

New work letter: _____

Occupancy (or status) of building when lease was originally signed: _____

_____

Comments: _____

_____

_____

tenants' rents; the expenses allocated to vacant space are normally paid by the owner.

Sometimes a single stop provision is used to cover all the expenses to be passed through to the tenants. Alternatively, an expense stop might be specified for individual expense items. For example, tax-stop clauses provide that any increases in taxes over a specified level be passed on to the tenant. When there is more than one expense stop, it is likely that expenses will be passed through because an increase in one category of expenses is not offset by a reduction in another.

Escalation payments are frequently based on changes in a local wage rate or index such as the Consumer Price Index (CPI). In New York City, for example, the porter wage escalation formula is frequently used. Each one cent increase in the porter wage rate, the hourly wage paid to office workers who are members of the porters' union, produces a one to one and one-half cent increase in expense charges per square foot of space. Some escalation clauses are drawn so broadly that the lease is almost applied on a net rental basis.

Purchase Options

Certain leases include a clause granting the lessee an option to purchase the leased property. In some cases this option must be exercised on the lease termination date or at some point or points during the lease term; in other cases this option may be available at any time. The option price may be fixed or it may change periodically based on an empirical formula or a depreciated book value. A purchase option may only give the lessee the right to purchase the property if an offer to purchase is made by a third party. This provision is referred to as a *right of first refusal*.

In any case a purchase option restricts marketability and, unless the property is being appraised in fee simple, the option price may represent a limit on the market value of the leased fee estate.

Escape Clauses

An escape clause permits a tenant to cancel a lease under circumstances that would not ordinarily be considered justification for lease cancellation. For example, a condemnation or casualty clause might allow the tenant to cancel the lease if the condemnation or casualty loss creates a serious obstacle to continued operations. A casualty clause may stipulate that the lessor be allowed a reasonable amount of time to make necessary repairs and provide for appropriate abatement of rent in the interim. A landlord might include a demolition clause in a lease to preserve the prospects for sale or redevelopment of the site. This type of escape clause can affect rent levels and market value.

Continued Occupancy Clauses

Multitenanted properties may be subject to leases that condition the continued occupancy of one tenant on the provision that another tenant is in occupancy. An anchor tenant's decision to vacate during the lease term can precipitate the departure of other tenants as well. In appraising shopping centers, the probability of an anchor tenant leaving at or before expiration of the current lease must be carefully analyzed. This is true whether or not the satellite stores have a lease condi tioning their occupancy on the continued occupancy of the anchor tenant. Small stores are often unable to continue operation if the anchor leaves the center.

Tenant Improvements

Extensive tenant improvements can influence lease rent. When capital expenditures are made by the lessor, reimbursement may be accomplished through rent increases that amortize the lessor's expenditures over all or part of the lease period. If capital expenditures are made by the tenant, the lessor may lower the tenant's rent below market levels for all or part of the lease term.

RENT ANALYSIS

The income to investment properties consists primarily of rent. Different types of rent affect the quality of the income studied in the income capitalization approach to value. The five types of rent are contract rent, market rent, excess rent, percentage rent, and overage rent.

Contract rent is the actual rental income specified in a lease. It is the rent agreed on by the landlord and the tenant and may be higher, lower, or the same as market rent.

Market rent is the rental income that a property would most probably command in the open market; it is indicated by the current rents paid and asked for comparable space as of the date of the appraisal. Market rent is sometimes referred to as *economic rent*.

Excess rent is the amount by which contract rent exceeds market rent at the time of the appraisal. Excess rent is created by a lease that is favorable to the lessor and may reflect an advantageous location, unusual management, or a lease negotiated in a stronger rental market. Excess rent can be expected to continue for the remainder of the lease but, due to the higher risk associated with the receipt of excess rent, it is often calculated separately and capitalized at a higher rate. Because excess rent is a result of the lease contract rather than the income potential of the underlying real property, the incremental value created by a lease premium is sometimes considered a non-realty component of value.

Percentage rent is rental income received in accordance with the terms of a percentage clause in a lease. Percentage rent is typically derived from retail store tenants and based on a certain percentage of their retail sales. The emergence of new competition in the area or the departure of an anchor tenant from a shopping center may reduce or eliminate anticipated percentage rent.

Overage rent is percentage rent paid over and above the guaranteed minimum rent or base rent. This type of rent should not be confused with excess rent. Overage rent is a contract rent; it may be market rent, part market and part excess rent, or excess rent only.

To a certain extent the interest being appraised determines how rents are analyzed and estimated. The valuation of fee simple interests in income-producing real estate is based on the market rent the property is capable of generating. To value proposed projects without actual leases, properties leased at market rent, and owner-occupied properties, only market rent estimates are used in the income capitalization approach.

To value a lessor's marketable interest in real estate, the leased fee, the appraiser generally must consider existing contract rent for leased space, which may or may not be at market levels, and market rent for vacant and owner-occupied space. When discounted cash flow analysis is used, future market rent estimates are also required to estimate income after existing leases expire. It should be emphasized that the discounting of contract rents does *not* result in a market value estimate of the fee simple interest.

Appraisers usually estimate the market value of income-producing property in one of two ways. An appraiser can value a fee simple interest in property at the market rent the property is capable of generating and deduct the present value of the rent loss, calculated as market rent less contract rent. To use this technique the appraiser may extract capitalization rates or factors from comparable sales of fee simple real property interests, but such sales of multitenant buildings are rare. Therefore, the appraiser may need to analyze a number of property sales subject to leases to find properties that were sold with market rents or with rent structures that can be easily adjusted for market rent equivalency.

To apply the second technique, an appraiser values a leased fee property by estimating the existing contract rent for leased space and market rent for vacant and owner-occupied space. Because most real estate transactions reflect similar income characteristics, market-derived capitalization rates and factors may adequately reflect the estimated value of lessors' marketable interests. If adequate comparable data exist, rent loss analysis is unnecessary.

Rent analysis begins with study of the subject property's present rent schedule. By examining audits and leases and interviewing selected tenants during property inspection, an appraiser can verify the rent schedule. Further verification may be necessary if the owner's or manager's representation of the schedule is in doubt.

The sum of the scheduled, current rents may be compared with previous totals using operating statements for the past several years. Statements of rents, including the rent paid under percentage leases or escalation clauses, should be examined for all building tenants. After analyzing the existing rent schedule for the subject property, the appraiser reduces all rents to a unit basis for comparison. All differences in rents within the property are described and explained. Then rental data for comparable space in the market are assembled so that market rents can be adjusted to an equivalent rent basis if necessary and reduced to a unit of comparison.

When a market rent estimate is required, the appraiser gathers, compares, and adjusts market data to form a sound conclusion as to market rent for the subject property. The parties to each lease should be identified to ensure that the party held responsible for rent payments is actually a party to the lease or, by endorsement, the guarantor. It is also important to ascertain that the lease represents a freely negotiated, arm's-length transaction. Leases that do not meet these criteria do not provide reliable indications of the rental terms typical in the market.

The rents of comparable properties can provide a basis for estimating market rent for a subject property once they have been reduced to a unit basis equivalent to the unit applied to the subject property. The appraiser may need to adjust comparable rents just as the transaction prices of comparable properties are adjusted in the sales comparison approach.

The elements of comparison for rental analysis are the real property rights being appraised, conditions of rental (i.e., arm's-length lease terms), market conditions, location, physical characteristics, economic characteristics stipulated in the lease, use of the property, and non-realty components. Rents for comparable properties are analyzed and adjusted for differences in these elements of comparison to develop a market rent estimate for the subject property.

The amount of data needed to support a market rent estimate for a subject property depends on the complexity of the appraisal problem, the availability of comparable rentals, and the extent to which the pattern of adjusted rent indications derived from the comparables varies from the income pattern of the subject property.

When sufficient, closely comparable rental data are not available, the appraiser should include data that require adjustment. First, the real property rights and conditions that affect the rent paid must be analyzed and adjustments must be made. Rentals that do not reflect arm's-length negotiations might have to be eliminated as comparables. Each rental is then analyzed to determine a possible adjustment for market conditions. Economic conditions change and leases negotiated in the past may not reflect prevailing rents.

The stability of the location or trends in the market's attitude toward property location might also affect income potential and therefore require adjustment. Physical differences such as the functionality of the building are then analyzed and adjustments are made for these differences. Next the appraiser examines the economic (e.g., income-producing) characteristics of the lease to determine who pays operating expenses and to make adjustments for any differences. Market rents might also have to be adjusted for the intended use of the subject property when it differs from that of the comparable. Finally, adjustments may be needed to account for differences in non-realty components, which can result in differences in the income of the properties. For example, the income of a hotel that is part of a national chain may be higher than that of a hotel that is not in a chain because of the franchise value associated with the name of the hotel rather than any difference in the income potential of the real property. If an appraiser uses proper judgment in making adjustments, a reasonably clear pattern of market rents should emerge.

DEVELOPING INCOME ESTIMATES

To assess the earning power of a property, an appraiser must first analyze its net operating income expectancy. The appraiser estimates income and expenses after researching and analyzing 1) the income and expense history of the subject property; 2) income and expense histories of competitive properties; 3) recently signed leases, proposed leases, and asking rents for the subject and competitive properties; 4) actual vacancy levels for the subject and competitive properties; 5) management expenses for the subject and competitive properties; 6) published operating data; 7) market expectations; and 8) tax assessment policies and projected changes in utility rates.

Appraisers often present this information in tabular form to assist the reader of the report. Income and expenses are generally reported in annual or monthly dollar amounts and analyzed in terms of total dollar amounts, dollars and cents per unit of rentable area, or dollar and cents based on another unit of comparison. Table 19.1 summarizes a subject property's operating expense history, Table

Table 19.1 Subject Property Operating Expense History
(Based on 435,146 rentable square feet)

	1990 Actual		1991 Actual		1992 Actual		1993 Budget	
	Dollars	Per Square Foot	Dollars	Per Square Foot	Dollars	Per Square Foot	Dollars	Per Square Foot
Fixed expenses								
Real estate taxes	$1,689,600	$ 3.88	$1,973,722	$ 4.54	$2,279,860	$ 5.24	$2,347,500	$ 5.39
Insurance	18,948	0.04	17,956	0.04	46,861	0.11	50,000	0.11
Variable expenses								
Electricity	$1,453,482	$ 3.34	$1,569,948	$ 3.61	$1,534,296	$ 3.53	$1,800,000	$ 4.14
Steam heat	575,599	1.32	519,203	1.19	525,646	1.21	619,190	1.42
Cleaning	848,260	1.95	797,455	1.83	935,544	2.15	990,000	2.28
Payroll	62,441	0.14	73,553	0.17	82,350	0.19	90,000	0.21
Repairs and maintenance	125,417	0.29	222,074	0.51	283,215	0.65	381,996	0.88
Water and sewer	19,638	0.05	23,444	0.05	16,958	0.04	33,600	0.08
Administrative, legal, and accounting	8,603	0.02	13,712	0.03	77,397	0.18	77,400	0.18
Management fees	33,240	0.08	36,105	0.08	36,643	0.08	38,400	0.09
Miscellaneous	22,492	0.05	511	0.001	3,862	0.01	3,600	0.01
Total operating expenses	$4,857,720	$11.16	$5,247,683	$12.05	$5,822,632	$13.39	$6,431,686	$14.79

Note. Figures have been rounded.

19.2 presents comparable rental data, and Table 19.3 analyzes the operating expenses of comparable properties.

After thoroughly analyzing property and lease data for the subject and comparable properties, the appraiser develops a net operating income estimate for the subject property. If the appraiser is focusing on the benefits accruing to the investment before taxes, he or she also estimates the pre-tax cash flow. A sample outline for estimating net operating income and pre-tax cash flow is presented in Table 19.4. Both these estimates are developed from the gross income estimate.

Potential Gross Income

Potential gross income is the total income attributable to a real property at 100% occupancy before operating expenses are deducted. Appraisers usually analyze potential gross income on an annual basis. Potential gross income comprises rent for all space in the property, rent from escalation clauses, and all other income to the real estate.

Scheduled Rent

Scheduled rent is the portion of potential gross income derived from the rent stipulated in the leases in effect on the date of the appraisal. Some appraisers refer to this income as *existing lease* or *contract income* or *rent*. Scheduled rent may or may not coincide with the rent that could currently be obtained in the local market if the space were vacant and available for leasing.

In calculating scheduled rent, an appraiser must adjust for rent concessions, discounts, or other benefits that may induce a prospective tenant to enter into a lease. These concessions, or offsets, usually take the form of rent-free months at the beginning of the lease term, but they may also be reflected in extra services or tenant benefits. Such benefits might include higher tenant improvement allowances, reduced expense or base rent escalations, below-market renewal options, tenant cancellation clauses, or building naming rights.[1]

Escalation Income

Escalation income is derived from lease escalation clauses. Escalation income consists of additional charges to tenants for part or all of the increases in operating expenses or charges that result from exercising a specific escalation formula contained in an existing lease.

Market Rent

Rent for vacant or owner-occupied space is usually estimated at market rent levels and distinguished from scheduled rent in the income estimate. In fee simple valuations, all rentable space is assumed to be leased at market rent; no rent attributable to specific leases is included in the income estimate. In developing market rent estimates, the appraiser assumes that property management is competent.

Other Income

Other income covers all income generated by the operation of the real property that is not derived directly from space rental. It includes income from services supplied to the tenants such as switchboard service, antenna connections, and

---

Kenneth Barnes, "Rental Concessions and Value," *The Appraisal Journal* (April 1986).

Table 19.2 Actual Rentals of Competitive Office Buildings in Downtown CBD of Major U.S. City

I.D. Number	Location	Tenant	Commence-ment Date	Rentable Area (in Square Feet)	Term (in Years)	Rent per Square Foot	Leases (Net Subject to Escalation)	Work Letter/ Miscellaneous
1	180 Main Street	Law firm	7/1/91	11,600	15	$22.00*	Pro rata share of operating expenses and real estate taxes in excess of base year	$20.00 work letter; 4 months free rent; one 5-year renewal option at $5.00 below market rent
		Oil company	8/15/91	15,600	10	$23.00 (5 years) $26.50 (5 years)	Pro rata share of operating expenses and real estate taxes in excess of base year	Building standard; 6 months free rent; one 5-year renewal option
		Stock brokerage company	9/1/92	15,600	10	$29.00 (5 years) $41.50 (5 years)	Pro rata share of operating expenses and real estate taxes in excess of base year	Building standard; three 5-year renewal options
		Accounting firm	7/1/92	31,200	10	$28.00	Pro rata share of operating expenses and real estate taxes in excess of base year	Not available
2	33 Broad Street	Bank	7/1/91	25,000	10	$ 8.00† $35.00‡ $22.00§	Pro rata share of operating expenses and real estate tax increases in excess of a $4.00 base for each	Building standard; 3 months free rent
		Computer services firm	7/1/92	10,000	10	$25.00‖	Pro rata share of operating expenses and real estate tax increases in excess of a $4.00 base for each	$20.00 work letter

* For 10 years, then $2.00 below market rent for 5 years; minimum rent set at $29.00
† Basement
‡ Ground floor
§ Floors 2 through 4
‖ For 7 years, then market rent for 3 years

Table 19.2 (continued)

I.D. Number	Location	Tenant	Commence- ment Date	Rentable Area (in Square Feet)	Term (in Years)	Rent per Square Foot	Leases (Net Subject to Escalation)	Work Letter/ Miscellaneous
3	One Exchange Place	Stock brokerage firm	7/1/91	10,200	10	$26.50	Pro rata share of operating expenses and real estate tax increases in excess of a $4.00 base for each	$22.00 work letter plus $6.00 work letter for computer room; 3 months free rent; one 5-year renewal option
3	One Exchange Place	Law firm	7/1/92	15,000	10	$26.00	Pro rata share of operating expenses and real estate tax increases in excess of a $4.00 base for each	$22.00 work letter
4	101 Front Street	Accounting firm	1/1/92	25,000	3	$22.00	Pro rata share of real estate taxes in excess of first full assessment; $.01 per square foot for each $.01 increase in the porter wage	Building standard
5	One Commercial Plaza	Bank	7/1/92	88,823#	20	$27.10 (5 years) $30.81 (5 years) $35.65 (5 years) $40.93 (5 years)	25.0% of real estate taxes in excess of $2.85 per square foot**; 25.0% of operating expenses in excess of $3.42 per square foot	$25.00 work letter

Includes 4,600 square feet of retail space
** Tenant's contribution to real estate escalations is reduced 50% in Year 1, 40% in Year 2, 30% in Year 3, 20% in Year 4, and 10% in Year 5
Note. Base year is year of lease commencement.

Table 19.3 Analysis of Operating Expense Comparables (Per Square Foot)

Property I.D.	Subject Property Pro Forma	Comparable A 130 Main Street	Comparable B 110 Second Avenue	Comparable C 717 Fourth Avenue	Comparable D 133 Third Avenue	Comparable E One Commerce Plaza
Operating year	1993	1992	1992	1992	1992	1992
Year built	1986	1986	1975	1968	1971	1985
Rentable area in square feet	60,000	75,000	49,411	56,411	52,000	66,000
Operating Expenses						
Fixed expenses						
Real estate taxes	$ 3.50	$ 3.51	$ 3.48	$ 3.01	$ 3.47	$3.35
Insurance	0.11	0.06	0.09	0.10	0.17	0.09
Variable expenses						
Cleaning	$ 1.40	$ 1.61	$ 1.38	$ 1.27	$ 1.28	$1.30
Payroll, payroll taxes, and benefits	0.60	0.45	0.52	0.98	0.93	0.41
Electricity	2.50	3.03	2.47	2.31	2.25	2.45
HVAC	1.50	1.25	1.60	1.35	1.75	1.55
Repairs and maintenance	0.25	0.25	0.43	0.78	0.79	0.18
Water and sewer	0.04	0.02	0.02	0.02	0.03	0.04
Administrative and general	0.27	0.19	0.19	0.26	0.08	0.11
Management	0.30	0.25	0.20	0.40	0.35	0.30
Total operating expenses	$10.47	$10.62	$10.38	$10.48	$11.10	$9.78

Table 19.4 Income Estimate

Potential gross income		
Scheduled rent*	$XXXX	
Escalation income	XXXX	
Market rent†	XXXX	
Other income	XXXX	
Total potential gross income		$XXXX
Vacancy and collection loss		–XXXX
Effective gross income		$XXXX
Operating expenses		
Fixed	$XXXX	
Variable	XXXX	
Replacement allowance	XXXX	
Total operating expenses		–XXXX
Net operating income		$XXXX
Total mortgage debt service		–XXXX
Pre-tax cash flow (equity dividend)		$XXXX

* Rent from existing leases, adjusted for rental concessions if appropriate
† Rent attributed to vacant space, lease renewals, and owner-occupied space; in fee simple valuation, rent attributable to the whole property

garage space; income from coin-operated equipment and parking fees is also included. Because service-derived income may or may not be attributable to the real property, an appraiser might find it inappropriate to include this income in the property's potential gross income. The appraiser may treat other income as business income or real property income, depending on how the market perceives it.

Vacancy and Collection Loss

Vacancy and collection loss is an allowance for reductions in potential income attributable to vacancies, tenant turnover, and nonpayment of rent. Annual rent collections are typically less than annual potential gross income, so an allowance for vacancy and collection loss is usually included in the appraisal of income-producing property. The allowance is usually estimated as a percentage of potential gross income, which varies depending on the type and characteristics of the physical property, the quality of its tenants, current and projected supply and demand relationships, and general and local economic conditions.

Published surveys of similar properties under similar conditions may indicate an appropriate percentage allowance for vacancy and collection loss. An appraiser should survey the local market to support the vacancy estimate, but his or her conclusion may differ from the current level indicated by primary or secondary data because it reflects typical investor expectations over the specific holding period assumed or projected in the income capitalization approach.

Effective Gross Income

Effective gross income is the anticipated income from all operations of the real property after allowance is made for vacancy and collection loss.

Operating Expenses

In the income capitalization approach, a comprehensive analysis of the annual expenses of property operation is essential whether the value indication is derived from estimated net operating income or pre-tax cash flow. *Operating expenses are the periodic expenditures necessary to maintain the real property and continue the production of the effective gross income.*

An operating statement that conforms to this definition of operating expenses is used for appraisal purposes; this statement may differ from a statement prepared for an owner or an accountant. Because operating statements are prepared on either a cash or accrual basis, the appraiser must know the accounting basis used in the operating statements for the property being appraised. Operating statements provide valuable factual data and can be used to identify trends in operating expenses.

Expenses may be recorded in categories selected by the property owner, or the records may follow a standard system of accounting established by an association of owners or by accounting firms that serve a particular segment of the management market. In any case an appraiser analyzes and reconstructs expense statements to develop a typical expense expectancy for the property on an annual accrual basis.

Operating expense estimates usually list fixed expenses, variable expenses, and a replacement allowance. These classifications have long been in use, but there are other valid systems that an appraiser can employ.

Fixed Expenses

Fixed expenses are operating expenses that generally do not vary with occupancy and have to be paid whether the property is occupied or vacant. Real estate taxes and building insurance costs are typically considered fixed expenses. Although these expenses rarely remain constant, they generally do not fluctuate widely from year to year, do not vary in response to changing occupancy levels, and are not subject to management control. Therefore, an appraiser can usually identify a trend and legitimately estimate these expense items.

Tax data can be found in public records and the assessor's office may provide information about projected changes in assessments or rates and their probable effect on future taxes. If a property is assessed unfairly, operating expenses may need to be adjusted for the reconstructed operating statement used in the appraisal. If the subject property is subject to an unusually low assessment or appears to deviate from the general pattern of taxation in the jurisdiction, the most probable amount and trend of future taxes must be thoroughly analyzed. Any past changes in the assessment of the subject property should be studied. If the assessment is low, the assessor may raise it sooner or later; if the figure is high, however, a reduction may not be easily obtained. In projecting real estate taxes, an appraiser tries to anticipate tax assessments based on past tax trends, present taxes, the municipality's future expenditures, and the perceptions of market participants.

For proposed properties or properties that are not currently assessed, appraisers can develop operating statement projections without including real estate taxes. The resulting estimate is net operating income before real estate taxes, but a provision for real estate taxes is included in the capitalization rate used to convert net income into property value. For example, assume that real estate taxes are typically 2% of market value and net operating income after real estate taxes would normally be capitalized at 11% to derive a market value estimate for the subject property. In this case the estimated net operating income before real estate taxes could be capitalized at 13% (i.e., 11% + 2%) to derive a property value indication. Alternatively, the appraiser may choose to estimate real estate taxes for a proposed project based on building costs or the taxes paid by recently constructed, competitive properties.

An owner's operating expense statement may show the insurance premiums paid on a cash basis. If the premiums are not paid annually, they must be adjusted to an annual accrual basis before they are included in the reconstructed operating statement. Fire, extended coverage, and owner's liability insurance are typical insurance items, but depending on the type of property elevators, boilers, plate glass, or other items may also be insured. The appraiser must determine the amount of insurance and, if it is inadequate, adjust the annual cost to indicate appropriate coverage for the property.

Insurance on business inventory and other personal property is the occupant's responsibility and, therefore, cannot be charged to the operation of the real estate. When questions concerning co-insurance or terms of coverage arise, an appraiser might need to obtain professional insurance counsel.

Variable Expenses

Variable expenses are operating expenses that generally vary with the level of occupancy or the extent of services provided. Individual variable expense items may vary greatly from year to year, but similar types of property may reflect a reasonably consistent pattern of variable expenses in relation to gross income. Because fewer services are provided to the tenants of retail and industrial properties, these properties usually have a much lower ratio of expenses to gross income than apartment and office buildings.

Operating statements for large properties frequently list many types of variable expenses. Typical categories include

- Management charges
- Leasing fees
- Utilities—e.g., electricity, gas, water, and sewer
- Heat
- Air-conditioning
- General payroll
- Cleaning
- Maintenance and repair
- Decorating

- Grounds and parking area maintenance
- Miscellaneous—e.g., security, supplies, rubbish removal, and exterminating

Management charges. Management charges are proper expenses of operation, whether management services are contracted or provided by the property owner. The expense of management is usually expressed as a percentage of effective gross income and reflects the local pattern for such charges.

The operation of multitenant properties requires a considerable amount of supervision, accounting, and other services. Larger properties may have onsite offices or apartments for resident managers and corresponding expenses for their maintenance and operation. Other management expenses may include the cost of telephone service, clerical help, legal or accounting services, printing and postage, and advertising.

Leasing fees. Leasing fees are commissions paid to agents for negotiating and securing property leases. When these fees are spread over the term of a lease or lease renewal, they are included in the operating statement. However, initial leasing fees, which may be extensive in a new shopping center or other large development, are usually treated as part of the capital expenditure for developing the project. In these cases initial leasing fees are not included as periodic expenses. When a net income or pre-tax cash flow forecast is developed, leasing fees can be deducted in the year they are payable or spread over the lease term, depending on local practice.

Utilities. Utility expenses for an existing property are usually projected based on an analysis of past charges and current trends. The subject property's utility requirements can be compared with known unit utility expenses for similar properties to estimate probable future utility expenses. Hours of tenant operation may prove to be significant in the analysis. For example, the number of nights per week that a shopping center is open and the hours of after-dark operation will directly affect electricity consumption, and may indirectly affect expenses for maintenance and garbage removal. In analyzing utility expenses, appraisers recognize local circumstances and the increasing cost of all types of energy.

Although the cost of electricity for leased space is frequently a tenant expense, and therefore not included in the operating expense statement, the owner may be responsible for lighting public areas and for the power needed to run elevators and other building equipment.

Gas. When used for heating and air-conditioning, gas can be a major expense item that is frequently paid by the tenant or reflected in the rent.

Water. The cost of water is generally not a major consideration except for laundries, restaurants, taverns, hotels, and similar operations. The leases for these properties may stipulate that the tenant pay this expense. If the owner typically pays for gas and water, these charges should be included in the expense statement.

Sewer. In municipalities with sewerage systems, a separate charge for use of the system may be paid by the tenant or the owner of the real estate.

When the property owner is responsible for all utility charges, the total expense may be substantial, particularly for hotels, motels, recreation facilities, apartments, and office buildings.

Heat. The cost of heat is generally a tenant expense in single-tenant properties, industrial or retail properties, and apartment projects with individual heating units. It is a major expense item shown in operating statements for office buildings and many apartment properties. The fuel consumed may be coal, oil, gas, electricity, or public steam. Heating supplies, maintenance, and workers' wages are included in this expense category under certain accounting methods. Public steam suppliers and gas companies maintain records of fuel consumption in terms of degree days from year to year. (One degree day is equal to the number of degrees, during a 24- hour day, that the mean temperature falls below 65° Farenheit, which is the base temperature in the United States.) An appraiser can use these records and fuel cost data to compare the property's heating expense for the most recent year or years with a typical year. Probable changes in the cost of the fuel used should be reflected in the appraiser's projection.

Air-conditioning. Air-conditioning expenses may be charged under the individual categories of electricity, water, payroll, and repairs, or heating and air-conditioning may be combined under the category of heating, ventilating, and air-conditioning (HVAC). The cost of air-conditioning varies substantially with local climatic conditions and the type of system installed. A projection of this expense may be based on typical unit charges for the community or the property type. Most office buildings and many apartment buildings have central HVAC systems and operating expenses are included in their annual statements. Most commercial properties and many apartment buildings have individual heating and air-conditioning units that are operated by the tenants. However, the maintenance and repair of these units, particularly in apartments, may continue to be obligations of the property owner.

General payroll. General payroll expenses include payments to all employees whose services are essential to property operation and management, but whose salaries are not included in other specific expense categories. In some areas the cost of custodial or janitorial service is based on union wage schedules; in others the charge is negotiated based on local custom and practice. If a custodian or manager occupies an apartment as partial payment for his or her services, the apartment's rental value may be included as income and an identical amount deducted as an expense. In certain properties additional expenses are incurred to pay the salaries of watchmen, doormen, porters, and elevator operators. Unemployment and social security taxes for employees may be included under general payroll expenses or listed in a separate expense category.

Cleaning. In office buildings the cost of cleaning is a major expense. It is usually estimated in terms of cents per square foot of rentable area, whether the work is done by payroll personnel or by an outside cleaning firm. This expense is equivalent to maid service or housekeeping in hotels and furnished apartments. In hotels and motels, cleaning expenses are attributed to the rooms department and may be based on a percentage of the department's gross income. The percentage established reflects the property's previous experience and industry standards.

Cleaning may be an owner or tenant expense, depending on the property type and lease provisions.

Maintenance and repair. Maintenance and repair expenses may cover roof repair, window caulking, tuckpointing, exterior painting, and the repair of heating, lighting, and plumbing equipment. There may be a contract for elevator maintenance and repair, but because these contracts vary, an appraiser must determine any additional operating expense not covered by the maintenance contract. A contract that covers air-conditioning equipment would probably be included in the air-conditioning expense category.

Alterations may be considered capital expenditures and, therefore, are not included as a periodic expense under repair and maintenance. If the lessor makes alterations in the rented space, the expense may or may not be amortized by additional rental; in some cases the tenant may pay for alterations.

The total expense for property maintenance and repair is affected by the extent to which building component and equipment replacements are covered in the replacement allowance. If an extensive replacement allowance is included in the reconstructed operating statement, annual maintenance and repair expenses will be reduced. However, maintenance and repair expenses for the main portion of the building should always be listed in the maintenance and repair category.

Decorating. Decorating expenses may include the cost of interior painting, wallpapering, or wall cleaning in tenant or public areas. Lease provisions may stipulate that the owner is only responsible for decorating vacant space to attract new tenants. Decorating expenditures may vary with local practice and the supply and demand for space.

Grounds and parking area maintenance. The cost of maintaining grounds and parking areas can vary widely depending on the type of property and its total area. Hard-surfaced public parking areas with drains, lights, and marked car spaces are subject to intensive wear and can be costly to maintain. These expenses may be entirely or partly compensated with an increment added to the rents of tenants served by the facility. In this case both the added income and the added expenses are included in the appraiser's reconstructed operating statement.

Miscellaneous. Expenses for miscellaneous items vary with property type. If this expense category represents a significant percentage of effective gross income, however, it may be wise to explain individual expense items or reallocate them to specific categories.

Security. Certain types of buildings in some areas may require security provisions, the cost of which will vary according to the number of employees needed to control entry and exit and to circulate through the property. Maintenance and energy expenses may also be incurred if security provisions include electric alarm systems, closed circuit television, or flood lighting.

Supplies. The cost of cleaning materials and miscellaneous items not covered elsewhere may be included under supplies.

Rubbish removal and exterminating. Garbage and pest control services are usually contracted and their cost is included in the expense statement. The cost of snow removal may be substantial in northern states, particularly if properties have outdoor parking in addition to sidewalks and driveways.

Replacement Allowance

A replacement allowance provides for the periodic replacement of building components that wear out more rapidly than the building itself and must be replaced periodically during the building's economic life. These components may include

- Roof covering
- Carpeting
- Kitchen, bath, and laundry equipment
- Compressors, elevators, and boilers
- Specific structural items and equipment that have limited economic life expectancies
- Interior improvements to tenant space that are made periodically by the landlord, usually at lease renewal
- Sidewalks
- Driveways
- Parking areas
- Exterior painting

The annual allowance for each component is usually estimated as the anticipated cost of its replacement prorated over its anticipated remaining economic life, provided this does not exceed the remaining economic life of the structure. Some appraisers use simple averaging, while others prefer to show the actual cost and timing of these replacements. New elevators or other components that are expected to have economic lives that equal or exceed the remaining economic life of the structure do not require an allowance for replacement.

If an appraiser is using a short projection period in applying the income capitalization approach, items that will not require replacement during this period need not be considered in the replacement allowance, particularly if market evidence indicates that market participants follow a similar practice. Rather, the effect of these items is reflected in the anticipated resale price. When a long-term projection is being considered, however, the appraiser may need to identify future expenditures for replacements. An annual reserve could then be set up to cover the cost of these replacements. Alternatively, if a discounted cash flow analysis is being used to estimate value, the cash flow in the year the replacement is projected to occur could be reduced by the cost of the replacement. In any case, appraisers should attempt to reflect market practice in the use of replacement allowances.

The scope of items to be covered in a replacement allowance is a matter of appraisal judgment based on market evidence; however, the extent of the replacement allowance is based on the annual repair and maintenance expenses of the property. Historical operating statements prepared on a cash basis may include periodic replacement expenses under repair and maintenance. If extensive provisions for replacement are made in the reconstructed operating statement, these charges may be duplicated unless the annual maintenance expense estimate is reduced.

In certain real estate markets, space is rented to a new tenant only after substantial interior improvements are made. If this work is performed at the landlord's expense and is required to achieve market rent, the expense of these improvements should be included in the reconstructed operating statement as part of the replacement allowance.

A total expense estimate that provides for all items of repair and replacement may exceed the actual expenditures shown in the owner's operating statements for recent years. This is particularly common when the building being appraised is relatively new and the owner has not set up a replacement allowance. In preparing a reconstructed operating statement for a typical year, an appraiser recognizes that replacements must be made eventually and that replacement costs affect operating expenses; these costs can be reflected in increased annual maintenance costs or, on an accrual basis, in an annual replacement allowance.

The appraiser must understand whether or not a replacement allowance is included in an operating statement to derive a market capitalization rate for use in the income capitalization approach. A capitalization rate derived from a comparable sale property is valid only if it is applied to the subject property on the same basis. Consequently, a rate derived from a sale with an expense estimate that does not provide for a replacement allowance cannot be applied to an income estimate for the subject property that includes such an allowance.

Total Operating Expenses

Total operating expenses are the sum of fixed and variable expenses and the replacement allowance cited in an appraiser's operating expense estimate.

Net Operating Income

Net operating income is the anticipated net income remaining after all operating expenses are deducted from effective gross income but before mortgage debt service and book depreciation are deducted.

Total Mortgage Debt Service

Total mortgage debt service is the periodic payment for interest on and retirement of the mortgage loan (principal). Mortgage debt service is deducted from net operating income to derive pre-tax cash flow, which is used in certain capitalization procedures. The definition of market value assumes financing terms compatible with those found in the market. Thus, in estimating market value, the mortgage debt service to be deducted from the net operating income must be based on market terms. In some cases the appraiser may be asked to estimate the value of the equity investor's position based on existing financing. Here the debt service would reflect the terms specified in the existing mortgage.

Pre-Tax Cash Flow

Pre-tax cash flow (equity dividend) is the income that remains after total mortgage debt service is deducted from net operating income. It is also referred to as *before-tax cash flow.*

Expense and Income Ratios

The ratio of total operating expense to effective gross income is the *operating expense ratio*. The complement of this ratio is the *net income ratio*—i.e., net operating income to effective gross income. These ratios tend to fall within limited ranges for specific categories of property. Experienced appraisers recognize appropriate ratios, so they can identify statements that deviate from typical patterns and require further analysis.

Nationwide studies of apartment and office building properties conducted by the Institute of Real Estate Management (IREM) and the Building Owners and Managers Association (BOMA) can often be used as general guides in selecting operating expense ratios. Sometimes local BOMA or IREM chapters, or real estate appraisal organizations and their chapters, conduct and publish studies of operating expenses that can be used as market indicators. Published studies are useful, but the appraiser must still develop operating expense ratios from comparable properties in the subject property's market or verify the applicability of published ratios in this market.

Exclusions from Reconstructed Operating Statements

The operating statements prepared for real estate owners typically list all expenditures made during a specific year. Owners' statements may include nonrecurring items that should not be included in an expense estimate intended to reflect typical annual expenses. They may also include items of business expense or costs associated with the specific circumstances of ownership.

A reconstructed operating statement represents an opinion of the probable future net operating income of an investment.[2] Certain items included in operating statements prepared for property owners should be omitted in reconstructed operating statements prepared for appraisal purposes. These items include book depreciation, income tax, special corporation costs, and additions to capital.

Book Depreciation

The book depreciation for the improvements on a parcel of real estate is based on historical cost or another previously established figure that may have no relation to current market value. Moreover, book depreciation may be based on a formula designed for tax purposes. The capitalization method and procedure selected provide for the recapture of invested capital, so including depreciation in the operating expense statement would be redundant.

Income Tax

The amount of income tax varies with the type of property ownership; the property may be held by a corporation, a partnership, a public utility, or an individual. The income tax obligation of the owner is not an operating expense of the property.

---

2. Some practitioners use the term *pro forma* synonymously with *reconstructed operating statement*. Technically a pro forma is a financial statement—e.g., a balance sheet or income statement used by a business. The term *reconstructed operating statement* is unique to appraisal practice. A reconstructed operating statement is developed to conform to the appraiser's definition of net operating income, which generally differs from the definition of income used by accountants. Thus a reconstructed operating statement drawn up by an appraiser will probably differ from a pro forma income statement prepared by an accountant.

Special Corporation Costs

The expenses attributable to corporate operation also pertain to the type of ownership. Corporate expenses are not part of a reconstructed operating statement developed for appraisal purposes.

Additions to Capital

Expenditures for capital improvements do not recur annually and, therefore, should not be included in an estimate reflecting the typical annual expenses of operation. Capital improvements may enhance value by increasing the annual net operating income or economic life of the property, but the capital expenditure is not a periodic operating expense.

The exclusion of expenditures is specific to reconstructed operating statements, which are used to calculate net operating income. When cash flows are estimated for a discounted cash flow analysis, capital expenditures may be deducted from the net operating income in the year the expenditure is expected to occur. This is particularly important when the property's future net operating income is based on the assumption that the capital expenditure will be made. In this case failure to account for the capital expenditure could result in an overstatement of value.

SAMPLE ONE-YEAR INCOME FORECAST

The property being appraised, ABC Apartments, is a 55-unit apartment project with a potential annual rent of $147,600 at 100% occupancy. Open parking is included in the rent. Additional income from coin-operated equipment averages about $1,150 per year, so total potential annual gross income at 100% occupancy is $148,750. Annual vacancy and collection loss is estimated at 4% and local management services are available for 5% of rent collections. The building superintendent receives an annual salary of $4,200, including fringe benefits.

Last year's tax bill was $16,250, but taxes are expected to be $17,000 by the end of this year. The owner carries $1 million in fire and extended coverage insurance and pays a three-year premium of $4,300. The appraiser believes that this coverage should be increased to $1,200,000. The additional expense for other insurance coverage is $700 per year.

The payroll to cover site maintenance and snow removal averages $5,400 per year. Trash removal costs $40 per month and miscellaneous supplies are estimated at $300 per year. Pest control costs $60 per month and other miscellaneous expenditures are projected at $300 per year.

Building tenants pay their own utilities, including the gas and electricity for individual apartment heating and air-conditioning units. Based on experience and anticipated rate changes, the electricity for public space is expected to total $2,000 in the coming year. Expenses for other utilities, including water, consistently run about $900 each year.

Repair and maintenance expenses are $12,000 to $13,000 per year, including replacement expenditures. The appraiser anticipates that replacement expenses will increase, and the reconstructed operating statement should include a separate replacement allowance in addition to normal repair and maintenance expenses. Exterior painting, which is estimated to cost $4,200 in the present market, is scheduled to be done every three years.

Most of the apartments are rented on three-year leases, with a typical redecorating cost of $200 per apartment at lease renewal. Public space is minimal, and redecorating this space costs about $240 every third year. All the apartments have stoves, refrigerators, dishwashers, garbage disposals, and exhaust fans, so a replacement allowance of $1,300 per apartment is required. The economic lives of these items vary, but they are estimated to average 10 years. The replacement of carpeting costs the owner about $900 per unit, and the average economic life of carpeting is six years. The roof is considered to have a 20-year life and a replacement cost of $18,000.

The operating statement shown in Table 19.5 reflects these figures. The precision of each entry is set by the appraiser, but rounding to the closest $5 or $10 is well within the estimated accuracy of the data.

SAMPLE MULTIYEAR INCOME FORECAST

In certain appraisals, such as those in which discounted cash flow analysis is used, the appraiser forecasts the expected future monetary benefits of the investment over the total projected holding period. The anticipated benefits may include the net operating income and the pre-tax cash flow for each year of the expected holding period plus the reversion—i.e., the resale price after the expenses of sale and any mortgage balance are deducted. The analysis that follows is based on a 10-year forecast of the future benefits from an office building investment. Both net operating income and pre-tax cash flow are estimated for each year. The proceeds from resale of the property at the end of the tenth year are also estimated.[3]

All the techniques discussed in this chapter are used to develop a net operating and pre-tax cash flow estimate for the first year of the forecast. Estimates for the other years are based on existing lease provisions and assumptions regarding lease renewals and growth rates applied to other income and operating expenses.

Property Analysis

The subject property is a 50,000-sq.-ft. site improved with a 50-year-old, 25-story office building in a secondary location north of the downtown commercial district. The rentable area totals 951,049 square feet of office and retail space. The retail space is small, consisting of 13,293 square feet of space covered by five leases. The building is fully occupied by 19 tenants under 21 leases. Many of the leases are old and will expire soon. The leases for approximately 58.4% of the building's rentable area will expire and be available for renewal or re-leasing in 1995 and 1996. The last existing lease will expire in 2014. Hence, all of the leases will roll over in 22 years. (Lease expiration and subsequent re-leasing is referred to as lease rollover.) The property's lease expiration profile is summarized in Table 19.6.

The current average gross rent per square foot of rentable area is $8.57. Appraisers estimate current average market rents at $18 per square foot for office space and $25 per square foot for retail space. The weighted-average market rent is estimated to be $18.10 per square foot. Therefore, the market differential (i.e.,

---

3. This example has been adapted from an article by Peter F. Korpacz and Mark I. Roth titled "Changing Emphasis in Appraisal Techniques: The Transition to Discounted Cash Flow," *The Appraisal Journal* (January 1983).

Table 19.5 ABC Apartments: Reconstructed Operating Statement

Potential gross annual income		
Rents	11 units @ $2,400/yr.	$26,400
	12 units @ $2,580/yr.	30,960
	16 units @ $2,760/yr.	44,160
	16 units @ $2,880/yr.	46,080
		$147,600
Other income		+1,150
Total potential gross income @ 100% occupancy		$148,750
Less vacancy and collection loss @ 4%		−5,950
Effective gross income		**$142,800**
Operating expenses		
Fixed		
Real estate taxes		$17,000
Insurance—Fire and extended coverage		
($4,300 × 1.2)/3		1,720
Other		+700
Subtotal		$19,420
Variable		
Management ($142,800 × .05)		$7,140
Superintendent		4,200
Payroll		5,400
Electricity		2,000
Other utilities		900
Repair and maintenance		6,500
Exterior paint ($4,200/3)		1,400
Interior decorating		3,750*
Miscellaneous		
Trash removal ($40 × 12)		480
Pest control ($60 × 12)		720
Supplies		300
Other		300
Subtotal		$33,090
Replacement allowance		
Kitchen and bath equipment		
($1,300 × 55)/10		$7,150
Carpeting		
($900 × 55)/6		8,250
Roof		
$18,000/20 yrs.		900
Subtotal		$16,300
Total operating expenses		**−$68,810**
Operating expense ratio		
($68,810/$142,800) = 48.2%		
Net operating income		**$73,990**
Net operating income ratio		
($73,990/$142,800) = 51.8%		

---

* 55 units × $200 = $11,000; $11,000 + $240 = $11,240; $11,240/3 = $3,750 (rounded). This entry could be included under replacement allowance.

the difference between potential gross income at market rent and existing contract rent) is $9.53 per square foot ($18.10 − $8.57), and the total actual rent is 47.35% of market rent. The market for office space is in balance and there is above-average demand for space in this building. Although the building is old, it has been remodeled and extensive capital expenditures have been made to improve

Table 19.6 Lease Expiration Profile

Year	No. of Expiring Leases	Rentable Area in Sq. Ft.	Percent of Total Area Available for Leasing (Cumulative)
1993	0	0	
1994	0	0	
1995	7	268,458	28.2
1996	6	286,706	58.4
1997	2	51,302	63.8
1998	2	22,730	66.2
1999	1	7,930	67.0
2000	1	45,979	71.8
2001-2002	0	0	71.8
2003	1	924	71.9
2004-2013	0	0	71.9
2014	1	267,020	100.0
Total	21	951,049	

its mechanical systems and maintain its competitive position. It is located in a good secondary area and is ideally suited to back office, computer, bookkeeping, or storage operations that require a large, contiguous space.

Rationale for the Forecast

The appraiser determines that investors in office buildings similar to the subject property typically forecast net operating incomes or pre-tax cash flows over a 10-year projected holding period. To establish a purchase price that will justify the risk inherent in the proposed investment, the forecast net operating incomes or pre-tax cash flows and the reversion are discounted at an appropriate yield rate.

To simulate typical investor analysis an appraiser performs the following tasks:

1. Analyzes current income, establishes the market rent level for each tenant's space, and forecasts future income for each year of a 10-year period based on existing leases, probable lease renewal at market rent, and expected vacancy experience
2. Forecasts other income, including income from escalation clauses contained in existing leases and assumed escalation provisions in new leases
3. Forecasts future property expenses after analyzing historical operating expenses, the experience of competitive properties, and the current budget for the property
4. Forecasts mortgage debt service based on existing or proposed financing terms
5. Estimates the net operating incomes or pre-tax cash flows to be generated by the property in each year of the forecast holding period
6. Estimates the reversionary benefits to be received at the end of the forecast holding period

Table 19.7 Comparable Sales Data

Sale No.	1
Address	110 Main St.
	Subject city, subject state
Date of sale	June 1992
Sale price	$60 million
Seller	XYZ Investment Co.
Purchaser	110 Main Street Co.
Description	A 32-story, multitenant office building that was built in 1966 and contains 748,701 square feet of area on floors that range in size from 8,100 square feet to 30,600 square feet situated on a 32,609-sq.-ft. plot
Comments	The property was sold on an all-cash basis; the buyer expects above-average increases in net income.
Sale price per sq. ft.	$80.14
Average scheduled rent per sq. ft. at sale date	$12.44

Anticipated financial data for Year 1
(buyer's estimate)

Average market rent per square feet	$27.50
Average scheduled rent per square feet	$12.44
Fixed expenses per square feet	$2.67
Variable expenses per square feet	$4.79
Replacement allowance	$0.00
Net operating income per square feet	$4.98
Overall capitalization rate*	6.2%
Equity capitalization rate	6.2%
Anticipated 10-year yield (*IRR*)	13.5%

Purchaser's assumptions

Market rent rate	Averages 27.50 per square feet in Years 1 and 2, increasing 8% per year thereafter
Escalation income	Typical total rent will closely approximate market rent rates.
Expense increases	Real estate taxes assumed to increase 2% per year; energy expenses assumed to increase 5% per year; other operating expenses assumed to increase 4% per year

* Because the property is not mortgaged, the equity capitalization rate is the same as the overall capitalization rate.

Table 19.7 (continued)

Re-leasing	All space assumed to be re-leased for successive 5-year terms
Vacancy	75% of space being re-leased assumed to be vacant for 3 months
Leasing fees	Standard commission schedule payable in first year of lease
Interior improvements to tenant space	$20.00 per square foot for new leases; $7.50 per square foot for renewal of existing leases
Resale	Computed by applying a 10% overall capitalization rate to the net operating income in Year 11 after deducting 2.5% for selling expenses

In a market value appraisal, these steps must be applied to reflect the thinking of market participants. In this sample application, the appraiser begins by assembling pertinent information on recent sales of office buildings in the same market as the subject property. To verify each sale, the appraiser interviews the participants, usually the buyer, to determine the net operating income or pre-tax cash flow forecast assumptions associated with each sale. Table 19.7, which lists information on Comparable Sale 1, illustrates the type of detailed information that must be gathered for each comparable sale.

Assumptions for the Subject Property

After gathering and analyzing data on local market conditions and the income and expense expectations of comparable properties, the appraiser develops assumptions about the subject property.

Forecast Period
The forecasts are based on an assumed 10-year holding period commencing on the date of valuation. A 10-year forecast is typical in this market. This forecast considers the effects of re-leasing 71.9% of the building space; a lease for the other 28.1% of the building is held by one major tenant and does not expire until the year 2014. Income for the eleventh year of the investment is forecast to estimate the resale price of the property at the end of the 10-year projection period. The income for Year 11 of this forecast is the income for the first year of operation under the new owner.

Existing Rents
Contract rents and rent adjustments are forecast in light of existing leases and escalation provisions.

Escalation Income
Escalation income is calculated in accordance with the specific terms of existing leases. For anticipated new leases, escalation income is based on a pro rata share

of the amount by which operating expenses and real estate taxes exceed these expenses in the base year. The base year is defined as the year of lease commencement. By local custom, escalation income is assumed to be collected in the year after it accrues.

Although specific escalation provisions vary, the appraiser's analysis reveals that prospective investors use a combination of escalation provisions which, taken together, increase tenant collections annually so that total collections in any given year do not lag far behind market rents.

Renewal Options

It is assumed that the renewal options contained in existing leases, which specify new contract rents or escalation provisions, will be exercised; the income specified under these renewals is incorporated into the forecast. One lease has a seven-year renewal option beginning in 1994 that specifies an annual rent that is less than the expected market rent for that year ($18.00 market rent compared with $13.00 contract rent). Other renewal options that do not specify contract rent or escalation provisions are also assumed to be exercised; in these cases market rental rates and new escalation provisions are applied.

Tenant Turnover

Approximately 35% of the space in the building is occupied by three major corporations that are likely to remain. It is assumed that this space will be re-leased to the existing tenants. Another 50% of the building is assumed to be re-leased to other existing tenants; the remaining 15% will be leased to new tenants. These assumptions are consistent with comparable sales data, given the character of the property and its tenants.

New Lease Terms

When the existing leases and any renewal options expire, all space is assumed to be re-leased for successive 10-year terms. In this market 10-year leases are customary for this type of space.

Market Rental Rates

The market rental rates applied to leasing activity are set forth below.

Office space: For two years beginning January 1, 1993, rent will average $18 per square foot; the market rate is assumed to increase 5% per year thereafter.

Retail space: For the year beginning on January 1, 1993, average rent will be $25 per square foot; the market rate is assumed to increase 5% per year.

The office rental rate assumptions are supported by an analysis of actual leases for office space in competitive buildings. Assumptions pertaining to rate increases are consistent with the assumptions made by the buyers of all but one of the comparable sales (see Table 19.8).

Vacancy and Collection Loss

Fifteen percent of the building space is being leased to new tenants and is assumed to remain vacant for an average of four months. The other 85% is assumed to be re-leased by existing tenants, so no vacancy is anticipated. The appraiser has considered the rent loss associated with vacancies by not accruing

Table 19.8 Analysis of Growth Rate Assumptions Derived from Office Building Data

Sale No.	Date	Market Rent Growth Rates					Expense Growth Rates		
		1st Period		2nd Period			Variable Operating	Energy	Real Estate Taxes and Insurance
		%	No. of Years	%	No. of Years	Thereafter			
1	9/92	0.0	2	—	—	5.0%	4.0%	5.0%	2.0%
2	9/92	4.0	—	—	—	4.0	4.5	4.5	3.0
3	6/92	0.0	2	4.0	2	5.0	4.5	5.0	3.0
4	7/91	0.0	3	—	—	5.0	4.0	4.0	4.0
5	3/92	0.0	2	4.0	2	5.0	4.0	5.0	4.0
6	3/92	0.0	3	—	—	5.0	4.0	4.0	4.0
7	4/91	5.0	—	—	—	5.0	5.0	5.0	4.0
8	4/91	0.0	2	—	—	5.0	4.5	4.5	4.0
9	7/91	5.0	—	—	—	5.0	5.0	6.0	5.0
10	10/91	0.0	3	—	—	5.0	4.0	5.0	4.0
11	8/92	0.0	2	4.0	2	5.0	4.0	4.0	5.0

contract rent or escalation income for the space for a four-month period beginning at the expiration of each lease. Furthermore, an additional allowance for the underlying level of vacancy and collection loss inherent in any multitenant office building is estimated at 0.5% of total gross revenue, as indicated by comparable sales data.

Real Estate Taxes and Insurance
Real estate taxes and insurance are estimated at $998,000, or $1.03 per square foot of rentable area, for the year ending in December 1993. The combined real estate tax and insurance expense is assumed to increase at a rate of 4% per year thereafter.

Management
Management fees are estimated at $75,000 for 1993 and are expected to increase 4.5% each subsequent year. Although the building is large, the small number of tenants and the significant leasing activity scheduled for the near term should attract competent management at this rate.

Leasing Fees
To estimate leasing fees the appraiser applies a weighted-average leasing commission rate of 17.15% of the first year's base rent to all re-leasing activities. This estimate assumes that 35% of the space will be re-leased to the three major tenants at a commission rate of 14% of the first year's contract rent; 50% of the space will be re-leased to existing tenants at a commission rate of 14% of the first year's contract rent; and 15% of the space will be leased to new tenants at a commission rate of 35% of the first year's contract rent. Commissions are assumed to be paid in full upon occupancy and are deducted from income. This commission schedule is consistent with the typical rates obtained by local real estate brokers.

Variable Operating Expenses
Variable operating expenses, excluding leasing fees and management which are treated separately in this case, are estimated to be $2,161,000 in 1993, or $2.23 per square foot of rentable area (see Table 19.9). The expense estimates are supported by an analysis of the recent operating histories of competitive buildings. The HVAC estimate is decreased from 1992 to 1993 because the building is being converted from steam to oil heat (see Table 19.9). Expenses for energy-related items are expected to increase 4.5% per year, and other expenses are estimated to increase 4% per year. These rate increases are based on the expense rate increase assumptions indicated by comparable sales. Expenses for tenant electricity and the cleaning of tenant space are not included because existing tenants pay for their own cleaning and electricity. This is not unusual in leasing back office space, and the market rent estimate of $18 per square foot is based on the assumption that future tenants will continue this practice.

Replacement Allowance
The replacement allowance consists of the cost of preparing tenant space and the cost of replacing building components that wear out over time. All space being leased to new tenants is assumed to require decorating at a cost of $20.00 per square foot. Space being re-leased to existing tenants is assumed to incur decorating expenses of $7.50 per square foot. The cost per square foot is expected to increase 5% per year. In addition, the cost to replace building improvements (e.g.,

Table 19.9 Estimate of Variable Operating Expenses for Subject Property*

	1992 Budget	1993 Estimate
HVAC	$ 500,000	$ 400,000†
Payroll	154,000	175,000
Repairs and maintenance	385,000	440,000
Building electricity	600,000	660,000
Security	175,000	200,000
Cleaning public areas	25,000	30,000
Garbage collection	5,000	6,000
Administrative and general	185,000	200,000
Water and sewer	44,000	50,000
Total	$2,073,000	$2,161,000
Total per rentable sq. ft.	$2.18	$2.27

* Excluding management expenses and leasing fees, which are estimated separately
† Reflects conversion to oil heat for part of year

roof, HVAC equipment, and structural components) is forecast at $100,000 for Year 1, increasing 5% each year thereafter.

Reversion

There are several ways to estimate a resale price. A market-derived capitalization rate can be applied to the appropriate income for the last year of the forecast or the year following the end of the forecast. In this case the resale price is forecast by applying a 10% overall capitalization rate to the net operating income for the year after the projection period (Year 11). The net operating income for Year 11 represents the projected income for Year 1 under the next owner. When an overall capitalization rate is used to estimate a resale price, it is sometimes referred to as a *terminal capitalization rate*. In this application sales expenses of 2.5% are deducted to arrive at the net resale price; then the balance of the mortgage is deducted to calculate the owner's net sale proceeds, or equity reversion.

Forecast Results

Mathematical calculations based on the assumptions set forth in this sample application result in the forecast shown in Table 19.10. The future benefits are converted into a value indication for the subject property using an appropriate capitalization procedure.

This example demonstrates one method for forecasting future benefits, but this is not the only acceptable forecasting procedure. The rent levels, growth rates, expense levels, and other economic and financial information described here are particular to the specific property being appraised and the real estate market under consideration. In market value appraisals, the forecasting of future benefits should be based on market-derived information. In assignments to estimate investment value, the appraiser has more latitude in interpreting market attitudes and specific investor preferences.

Table 19.10 Income Estimates

	1993	1994	1995	1996	1997	1998	1999	2000	2001	2002	2003†
Income											
Contract and market rents*	$8,149,802	$8,149,802	$8,986,591	$12,645,178	$15,241,645	$16,035,714	$16,485,322	$17,432,668	$19,487,680	$20,291,478	$20,291,478
Escalation income	153,078	283,867	360,523	528,617	625,906	772,808	1,074,136	1,455,791	1,816,841	2,061,857	2,336,857
Vacancy and collection loss	(40,749)	(40,749)	(44,933)	(63,226)	(76,208)	(80,179)	(82,427)	(87,163)	(97,438)	(101,457)	(101,457)
Effective gross income	$8,262,131	$8,392,920	$9,302,181	$13,110,569	$15,791,343	$16,728,343	$17,477,031	$18,801,296	$21,207,083	$22,251,878	$22,526,878
Operating expenses											
Fixed expenses											
Real estate taxes	$926,671	$963,738	$1,002,287	$1,042,379	$1,084,074	$1,127,437	$1,172,534	$1,219,436	$1,268,213	$1,318,942	$1,371,699
Insurance	71,329	74,182	77,149	80,235	83,445	86,783	90,254	93,864	97,619	101,523	105,584
Variable expenses											
HVAC	400,000	420,000	441,000	463,050	486,203	510,513	536,038	562,840	590,982	620,531	651,558
Payroll	175,000	182,875	191,104	199,704	208,691	218,082	227,896	238,151	248,868	260,067	271,770
Repair and maintenance	440,000	459,800	480,491	502,113	524,708	548,320	572,994	598,779	625,724	653,882	683,307
Electricity	660,000	693,000	727,650	764,033	802,234	842,346	884,463	928,686	975,121	1,023,877	1,075,070
Security	200,000	209,000	218,405	228,233	238,504	249,236	260,452	272,172	284,420	297,219	310,594
Cleaning	30,000	31,350	32,761	34,235	35,776	37,385	39,068	40,826	42,663	44,583	46,589
Garbage removal	6,000	6,270	6,552	6,847	7,155	7,477	7,814	8,165	8,533	8,917	9,318
Water	50,000	52,250	54,601	57,058	59,626	62,309	65,113	68,043	71,105	74,305	77,648
Administrative and general	200,000	209,000	218,405	228,233	238,504	249,236	260,452	272,172	284,420	297,219	310,594
Management	75,000	78,375	81,902	85,587	89,439	93,464	97,670	102,065	106,658	111,457	116,473
Leasing fees	0	0	870,166	976,026	183,356	85,293	31,239	190,196	0	0	4,424
Replacement allowance	100,000	104,500	1,508,943	1,676,378	411,366	259,884	179,535	434,857	454,426	474,875	162,148
Total operating expenses	$3,334,000	$3,484,340	$5,911,416	$6,344,111	$4,453,081	$4,377,765	$4,425,522	$5,030,252	$5,058,752	$5,287,397	$5,196,776
Net operating income	$4,928,131	$4,908,580	$3,390,765	$6,766,458	$11,338,262	$12,350,578	$13,051,509	$13,771,044	$16,148,331	$16,964,481	$17,330,102

Resale price	$173,301,020
Less sales expenses @ 2.5%	(4,332,526)
Net resale price	$168,968,494

* Reflects added vacancy associated with lease rollovers, as discussed under vacancy and collection loss
† For calculation of resale price in 2002

SUMMARY

An estimate or scheduled projection of future income is fundamental to the income capitalization approach. Historic and current income are relevant to the forecast, but the future direction of income is the critical concern. Appraisers can estimate and capitalize four levels of income: *potential gross income (PGI), effective gross income* (EGI), *net operating income (NOI),* and *pre-tax cash flow.* Depending on the data available and the capitalization method to be used, income analysis may be based on the actual income level at the time of the appraisal, a forecast of the first year's income, a forecast of property income over a specified holding period, or the stabilized, or average, annual income over a holding period. To value investments in partial interests, pre-tax cash flow is usually capitalized.

An income and expense forecast begins with lease analysis. *Gross rental* leases are leases in which the lessor pays all operating expenses of the real estate. In *net rental* leases the tenant pays all such expenses. Leases can be classified as flat rental, with a specific level of rent that continues for the duration of the lease; graduated rental, in which the rent undergoes specified changes at one or more points during the lease term (e.g., step-up and step-down); revaluation, in which rent is adjusted at periodic intervals based on a revaluation of the real estate; index, in which periodic rent adjustments are tied to a specific index; and percentage, in which a portion of the rent is based on a specified percentage of the volume of business or productivity.

Typical lease data include the lease date, a legal description of the leased property, the names of the lessor and the lessee, the lease term, the dates of occupancy and the commencement of payments, the amount and source of the rent, escalation clauses (e.g., tax- and expense-stop clauses), rent concessions, landlord and tenant covenants regarding the division of expenses, the right of assignment or right to sublet, renewal options, purchase options (e.g., the right of first refusal), escape clauses, stipulated advance rent or bonding, provisions for casualty or condemnation loss, continued occupancy clauses, specifications concerning tenant improvements, and revaluation clauses.

Five different types of rent can affect income: *contract rent*, the actual rental income specified in a lease; *market rent* or *economic rent,* the rental income a property would most probably command in the open market; *excess rent*, the amount by which contract rent exceeds market rent at the time of the appraisal; *percentage rent*, rental income received in accordance with the terms of a percentage clause in a lease; and *overage rent*, rent paid over and above the guaranteed minimum rent.

The valuation of a fee simple interest such as an owner-occupied property is based on the market rent the property is capable of generating. However, most income-producing properties are leased. To value a leased fee interest, the appraiser must examine existing contract rent for leased space and market rent for vacant or owner-occupied space. If discounted cash flow analysis is used, future market rents are estimated.

Appraisers can estimate market value either by valuing the fee simple property at market rent and deducting the present value of the rent loss (i.e., market rent less contract rent), or by valuing the leased fee property subject to existing contract rent for leased space and market rent for vacant and owner-occupied space.

The scheduled current rent for the subject property is reduced to a unit basis so that it can be compared with the rent for similar properties. When the market rents of comparable properties are adjusted to an equivalent rental basis and reduced to the same unit of comparison, a clear indication of market rent should result. Rents are adjusted in the same way the transaction price of a comparable property is adjusted in the sales comparison approach. Comparable rents must be similar to the subject rent in terms of lessor/lessee obligation, conditions of rental, time of renting, property location, and physical and income-producing characteristics.

The net operating income and pre-tax cash flow expectancy of a property are analyzed to determine its earning power. The appraiser examines the income and expense history of the subject property; the income and expense histories of competitive properties; recently signed leases, proposed leases, and asking rents for the subject and competitive properties; actual vacancy levels for the subject and competitive properties; management expense budgets for the subject and competitive properties; published operating data; market expectations; and tax assessment policies and utility company projections for rate changes. This information is often presented in tabular form when income and expenses per rentable area are analyzed on a monthly or annual basis.

To develop a net operating income estimate for the subject property, the appraiser begins by computing the potential gross income from the scheduled rent specified in existing leases, rent from escalation clauses, market rent attributable to vacant and owner-occupied space, and other income. Income generated by the operation of the real property but not directly attributable to rent is considered other income; depending on market practice, this income may also be treated as business income. *Vacancy and collection loss*, which allows for reductions in potential income due to vacancies, tenant turnover, and nonpayment of rent, is deducted from potential gross income to obtain effective gross income.

Next the appraiser undertakes a comprehensive analysis of *operating expenses*, the periodic expenditures necessary to maintain the real property and continue the production of income. The appraiser should know whether the operating statements examined were prepared on a cash or accrual basis. An operating expense estimate includes *fixed expenses*, which generally do not vary with occupancy and must be paid whether the property is occupied or not; *variable expenses*, which generally do vary with the level of occupancy or the extent of services provided; and a replacement allowance, which provides for the periodic replacement of building components during the economic life of the building.

Fixed expenses include taxes and premiums for fire and owner's liability insurance. Variable expenses include charges for management services that are contracted or provided by the owner; leasing fees or commissions to agents who negotiate and secure property leases; utility expenses incurred by the owner for electricity, gas, water, and sewerage; heat charges; air-conditioning costs; general payroll for all employees whose services are essential to property operation and management but whose salaries are not included in other specific categories; cleaning charges; maintenance and repair costs; decorating expenses; charges for grounds and parking area maintenance; and miscellaneous expenses for security, supplies, and rubbish and snow removal.

A replacement allowance provides for items that wear out, including roofing; carpeting; kitchen, bath, and laundry equipment; elevators and boilers; interior improvements in tenant space at lease renewal; sidewalks; driveways; parking lots; and exterior painting. The annual allowance for each item is calculated as its anticipated replacement cost prorated over its remaining economic life. Discounted cash flow analysis may also be applied to the actual costs of these items and the timing of payments.

Fixed expenses, variable expenses, and the replacement allowance cited in the operating expense estimate are added together to calculate *total operating expenses*. The anticipated net income remaining after all operating expenses are deducted from effective gross income, but before mortgage debt service and book depreciation are deducted, is net operating income.

The appraiser deducts *mortgage debt service*, the periodic payment for interest on and retirement of the mortgage loan principal, from net operating income to derive *pre-tax cash flow*, or equity dividend, which is used in certain capitalization procedures. The value definition used in the appraisal may assume existing financing or market financing; the mortgage debt service deducted should be consistent with the value definition applied.

The appraiser may use an *operating expense ratio*, the ratio of total operating expenses to effective gross income, or a *net income ratio*, the ratio of net operating income to effective gross income, to identify income or expense statements that do not conform to typical patterns and require further analysis.

A *reconstructed operating statement* represents an opinion of the probable future net operating income of an investment. The following items are often included in operating statements for property owners, but should be omitted from reconstructed operating statements for appraisal purposes: book depreciation, which may have little relation to market value and could be redundant in light of provisions for capital recapture; income tax, which varies with the type of property ownership and is not considered an operating expense; special corporation costs; and additions to capital, which are one-time expenditures for capital improvements.

Once the future net operating income or pre-tax cash flows and the reversion are estimated, they may be discounted to obtain an indication of the present value of the investment.

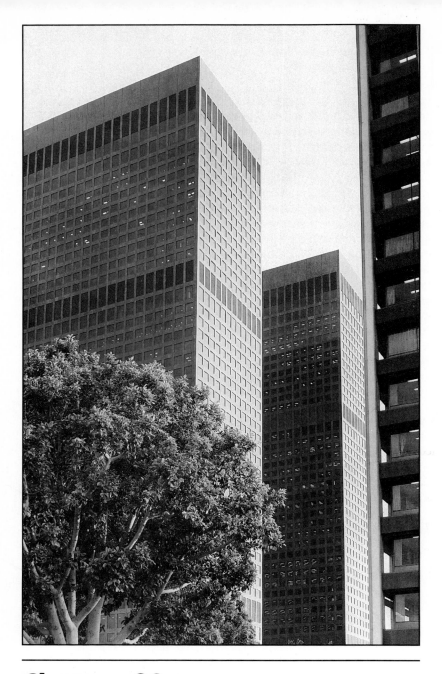

Chapter 20

DIRECT CAPITALIZATION

$\mathcal{D}$irect capitalization is a method used in the income capitalization approach to convert a single year's income estimate into a value indication. This conversion is accomplished in one step, either by dividing the income estimate by an appropriate income rate or by multiplying it by an appropriate income factor.

In direct capitalization no precise allocation is made between the return on and the return of capital because the method does not simulate investor assumptions or forecasts concerning the holding period, the pattern of income, or changes in the value of the original investment. However, a satisfactory rate of return for the investor and recapture of the capital invested are implicit in the rates or factors applied in direct capitalization because they are derived from similar investment properties.

Direct capitalization may be based on potential gross income, effective gross income, net operating income, equity income, mortgage income, land income, or building income. Therefore, the income rates used in direct capitalization include the overall (property) capitalization rate (R_O); the mortgage capitalization rate (R_M); the equity capitalization, or equity dividend, rate (R_E); the land capitalization rate (R_L); and the building capitalization rate (R_B). Income factors include the potential gross income multiplier $(PGIM)$, the gross rent multiplier (GRM), and the effective gross income multiplier $(EGIM)$.

The income rates and factors reflect the relationship between income and value and are derived from market data. It is essential that the properties used as comparables reflect risk, income, expense, and physical and locational characteristics that are similar to the property being appraised. Consequently, income multipliers and rates must be extracted from properties that reflect similar income-expense ratios, land-to-building ratios, risk characteristics, and expectations as to change in income and value over a typical investment holding period.

In addition to direct capitalization procedures in which a rate or factor is directly applied to the income estimate, physical, financial, economic, and legal residual techniques may be used.

DERIVATION OF OVERALL CAPITALIZATION RATES

Any interest in real estate that has an income stream can be valued by direct capitalization, but the interest most commonly appraised is the fee simple estate, which includes all property rights in the real estate. The direct capitalization formula that applies to this type of valuation is

$$\text{Value} = \frac{\text{Net operating income}}{\text{Overall capitalization rate}}$$

An appraiser can estimate an overall capitalization rate with various techniques; the techniques used depend on the quantity and quality of data available. Accepted techniques include 1) derivation from comparable sales, 2) derivation from effective gross income multipliers, 3) band of investment—mortgage and equity components, 4) band of investment—land and building components, and 5) the debt coverage formula.

Derivation From Comparable Sales

Deriving capitalization rates from comparable sales is preferred when sufficient data on sales of similar, competitive properties are available. Data on each property's sale price, income, expenses, financing terms, and market conditions at the time of sale are needed. In addition, the appraiser must be certain that the net operating income of each comparable property is calculated and estimated in the same way that the income of the subject property is estimated and that neither nonmarket financing terms nor different market conditions have affected the prices of the comparables. When these requirements are met, the appraiser can estimate an overall rate by dividing each property's net operating income by its sale price. Table 20.1 illustrates this procedure using data from four comparable sales.

Table 20.1 Derivation of Overall Capitalization Rates From Comparable Sales

| | Comparables | | | |
	A	B	C	D
Price	$368,500	$425,000	$310,000	$500,000
Net operating income	50,000	56,100	42,718	68,600
Indicated R_O	0.1357	0.1320	0.1378	0.1372

If all four transactions are equally reliable and comparable, the appraiser might conclude that an overall rate of 0.1320 to 0.1378 should be applied to the subject property. The final rate selected depends on the appraiser's judgment as to how comparable each sale is to the subject property.

If there are differences between a comparable property and the subject property that could affect the overall capitalization rate selected, the appraiser must account for these differences. In such cases the appraiser must decide whether the rate chosen for the subject property should be higher or lower than the rate in a specific sale. Appraisal judgment is also needed to determine whether the rate selected for the subject should fall within the range established by the sales or, as in certain cases, be set above or below the range.

When rates derived from comparable sales are used, the overall capitalization rate is applied to the subject property in a manner consistent with the rate derivation. In other words, if the market-derived capitalization rates are based on the properties' net operating income expectancies for the first year, the capitalization rate for the subject property should be applied to its anticipated net operating income for the first year of operation. *To capitalize prospective income for the subject property, an analyst should not apply retrospective capitalization rates from comparable sales.*

The net income to be capitalized may be estimated before or after an annual allowance for replacements is considered. Again, it is imperative that the appraiser analyze comparable sales and derive their capitalization rates in the same manner used to analyze the subject property and capitalize its income.

The examples that follow illustrate the importance of deriving and applying rates consistently. In the first example, the replacement allowance for the subject property is estimated at $2,500. The overall rate indicated by comparable sales in which a replacement allowance was not deducted as an operating expense was 0.0850. If the replacement allowance were deducted as an operating expense, the indicated overall rate would be 0.0825. In the first calculation, the allowance is included as an expense item to be deducted from effective gross income. Therefore, the net operating income here is $2,500 more than in the second calculation. The valuation conclusions produced by the two calculations are identical.

Before Deducting Allowance for Replacements

Net operating income	$ 85,000
Overall rate	0.0850
Capitalization: $85,000/0.0850	$1,000,000

After Deducting Allowance for Replacements

Net operating income	$ 82,500
Overall rate	0.0825
Capitalization: $82,500/0.0825	$1,000,000

This simple technique for estimating overall capitalization rates is preferred and will produce a reliable indication of value by the income capitalization approach if three conditions are met.

1. Income and expenses must be estimated on the same basis for the subject property and all comparable properties.
2. Market expectations concerning resale prices, tax benefits, and holding periods must be similar for all the properties.
3. The financing terms and market conditions that affect the comparables must be similar to those affecting the subject property or an adjustment must be made for any dissimilarities.

Derivation From Effective Gross Income Multipliers

Sometimes an overall capitalization rate cannot be derived directly because the stringent data requirements cannot be met, but reliable transaction data and *gross* income data can be obtained from several comparable sales. In such cases an effective gross income multiplier can be derived and used in conjunction with an operating expense ratio (*OER*) to produce an overall capitalization rate. (The derivation of income multipliers is discussed later in this chapter.)

The operating expense ratio is the ratio of operating expenses to effective gross income. Although effective gross income multipliers can be based on annual or monthly income, annual income is used unless otherwise specified. Monthly income is primarily used for single-family or small multifamily residential properties. Frequently an appraiser can obtain marketwide averages of operating expense ratios as well as the effective gross income multipliers indicated by comparable sales.

The formula for deriving an overall rate from a effective gross income multiplier and operating expense ratio is

$$R_O = \frac{1 - OER}{EGIM}$$

According to Table 20.1, Comparable A was recently sold for $368,500. Assume the property's potential gross income is $85,106, its effective gross income is $80,000, and its operating expenses are $30,000. Thus, the effective gross income multiplier is 4.6063 ($368,500/$80,000) and the operating expense ratio is 0.3750 ($30,000/$80,000). The overall capitalization rate extracted from the effective gross income multiplier of Comparable A is

$$R_O = \frac{1 - 0.3750}{4.6063}$$

$$= 0.1357$$

After this calculation is performed for all the comparables, an estimated overall capitalization rate is reconciled from the overall capitalization rate indications derived. The effective gross income multiplier is supportable if the property comparability requirements that apply to the direct derivation of an overall rate are met.

Band of Investment—Mortgage and Equity Components

Because most properties are purchased with debt and equity capital, the overall capitalization rate must satisfy the market return requirements of both investment positions. Lenders must anticipate receiving a competitive interest rate commensurate with the perceived risk of the investment or they will not make funds available. Lenders also require that the loan principal be repaid through periodic amortization payments. Similarly, equity investors must anticipate receiving a competitive equity cash return commensurate with the perceived risk or they will invest their funds elsewhere.

The capitalization rate for debt is called the *mortgage constant* (R_M). It is the ratio of the annual debt service to the principal amount of the mortgage loan. If the loan is paid off more frequently (e.g., with monthly payments), the mortgage constant is calculated by multiplying each period's payment by the frequency of payment and then dividing this amount by the amount of the loan. For example, the annual constant for a monthly payment loan is obtained by multiplying the monthly payment by 12 and dividing the result by the amount of the loan. Of course, the same result can be obtained by multiplying the ratio of monthly payments to the mortgage amount (i.e., the monthly constant) by 12.

The mortgage constant is a function of the interest rate, the frequency of amortization, and the term of the loan. It is the sum of the interest rate and sinking fund factor; when the loan terms are known, the mortgage constant can be found in financial tables. (Appendix C contains financial function tables for selected rates.) An appraiser must take care to use a table that corresponds to the frequency of amortization (e.g., monthly, quarterly, or annual).

The equity investor also seeks a systematic cash return. The rate used to capitalize equity income is called the *equity capitalization rate* (R_E). It is the ratio of annual pre-tax cash flow to the amount of equity investment. This rate is not simply a rate of return on capital, rather it is a rate of return both on and of capital. The equity capitalization rate may be more or less than the eventual equity yield rate. For appraisal purposes, a property's equity capitalization rate is the anticipated return to the investor, usually for the first year of the holding period.

The overall capitalization rate must satisfy both the mortgage constant requirement of the lender and the pre-tax cash flow requirement of the equity investor. It is a composite rate, weighted in proportion to the total property investment represented by debt and equity. The overall capitalization rate is a weighted average of the mortgage constant (R_M) and the equity dividend rate (R_E). The loan-to-value ratio (M) represents the loan or debt portion of the property investment; the equity ratio is expressed as $(1-M)$. Typical mortgage terms and conditions may be obtained by surveying lenders active in the market area. Equity capitalization rates are derived from comparable sales by dividing the pre-tax cash flow of each sale by the equity investment. The equity capitalization rate used to capitalize the subject property's pre-tax cash flow ultimately depends on the appraiser's judgment.

When the mortgage constant and equity capitalization rates are known, an overall rate may be derived with the band-of-investment, or weighted-average, technique using these formulas.

Mortgage component $\qquad$ $M \times R_M =$

Equity component $\qquad$ $(1 - M) \times R_E = \quad +$

$R_O = $ CAP rate

To illustrate how the overall capitalization rate is calculated with the band-of-investment technique, assume that the following characteristics describe the subject property.

Available loan	75% ratio, 13.5% interest, 25-year amortization period, 0.1399 constant (R_M)
Equity capitalization rate	12.0% (derived from comparable sales)

The overall rate is calculated as follows:

$$
\begin{aligned}
R_O &= (0.75 \times 0.1399) + (1 - 0.75)(0.1200) \\
&= 0.1049 + 0.0300 \\
&= 0.1349
\end{aligned}
$$

Although this technique is frequently used to derive overall capitalization rates, appraisers should be careful when using it for this purpose. The technique is particularly applicable in real estate markets where sufficient market data are available and it can be demonstrated that the equity capitalization rate is the primary investment criterion used by buyers and sellers. A capitalization rate used to estimate market value should be justified and supported by market data, but such data often are not available to derive information for mortgage-equity analysis. Therefore, survey and opinion data about equity capitalization rates, available loan terms, and loan-to-value ratios are often substituted for market data. When survey and opinion data or other data not derived from market transactions are used, mortgage-equity techniques are more appropriately used to test market-derived capitalization rates.

Band of Investment—Land and Building Components

A band-of-investment formula can also be applied to the physical components of property—i.e., the land or site and the buildings. Just as weighted rates are developed for mortgage and equity components in mortgage-equity analysis, weighted rates for the land and buildings can be developed if accurate rates for these components can be estimated independently and the proportion of total property value represented by each component can be identified.

The formula is

$$R_O = L \times R_L + B \times R_B$$

where L = land value as a percentage of total property value, R_L = land capitalization rate, B = building value as a percentage of total property value, and R_B = building capitalization rate.

Assume that the land represents 45% of the value of the property and the building represents the other 55%. The land capitalization rate derived from comparable sales data is 0.1025; the building capitalization rate is 0.1600. The indicated R_O is calculated as follows:

$$\begin{aligned} R_O &= (0.45 \times 0.1025) + (0.55 \times 0.1600) \\ &= 0.0461 + 0.0880 \\ &= 0.1341 \end{aligned}$$

Debt Coverage Formula

In addition to the traditional terms of lending (i.e., the interest rate, loan-to-value ratio, amortization term, maturity, and payment period), real estate lenders sometimes use another constraining factor—the debt coverage ratio (DCR). This is the ratio of net operating income to annual debt service, the payment that covers interest on and retirement of the outstanding principal of the mortgage loan (I_M).

$$DCR = \frac{NOI}{I_M}$$

This measure of constraint is frequently used by institutional lenders, who are generally fiduciaries. They manage and lend the money of others, including depositors and policyholders. Because of their fiduciary responsibility, institutional lenders are particularly sensitive to the safety of loan investments, especially the safety of principal. They are concerned with safety and profit and are anxious to avoid default and possible foreclosure. Consequently, when they underwrite income property loans, institutional lenders try to provide a cushion so that the borrower will be able to meet the debt service obligations on the loan even if building income declines.

To estimate an overall rate, the debt coverage ratio can be multiplied by the mortgage constant and the loan-to-value ratio.[1] The formula is

$$R_O = DCR \times R_M \times M$$

---

1. See Ronald E. Gettel, "Good Grief, *Another* Method of Selecting Capitalization Rates?!" *The Appraisal Journal* (January 1978).

Assuming that a property's net operating income is $50,000 and annual debt service is $43,264, the debt coverage ratio is calculated as follows.

$$DCR = \frac{\$50,000}{\$43,264}$$
$$= 1.1557$$

If R_M equals 0.1565 and M is 0.75, R_O is estimated as

$$R_O = 1.1557 \times 0.1565 \times 0.75$$
$$= 0.1357$$

RESIDUAL TECHNIQUES

Residual techniques allow an appraiser to capitalize the income allocated to an investment component of unknown value once all investment components of known value have been satisfied. The physical, or land and building, residual techniques and the financial, or mortgage and equity, residual techniques are the primary residual techniques used in direct capitalization.

Regardless of which known and unknown, or residual, components of the property are being analyzed, the appraiser starts with the value of the known item(s) and the net operating income. The appraiser

1. Applies an appropriate capitalization rate to the value of the known component to derive the annual income needed to support the investment in that component
2. Deducts the annual income needed to support the investment in the known component from the net operating income to derive the residual income available to support the investment in the unknown component
3. Capitalizes the residual income at a capitalization rate appropriate to the investment in the residual component to derive the present value of this component
4. Adds the values of the known component and the residual component to derive a value indication for the total property

Building Residual Technique

An appraiser using the building residual technique assumes that land or site value can be estimated independently. The appraiser applies the land capitalization rate to the known land value to obtain the amount of annual net income needed to support the land value. Then this amount is deducted from the net operating income to derive the residual income available to support the investment in the building(s). The appraiser capitalizes this residual income at the building capitalization rate to derive an indication of the present value of the building(s). Finally, the land value and the building value are added to derive an indication of total property value. The land and building capitalization rates derived from the market are applied to the subject property with the calculations shown below.

Estimated land value		$200,000
Net operating income	$85,500	
Land value × R_L ($200,000 × 0.09)	−18,000	
Residual income to building	$67,500	
Building value (capitalized: $67,500/0.15)		+450,000
Indicated property value		$650,000

To apply the building residual technique, the appraiser must obtain information on present land value, current net operating income, and land and building capitalization rates. This technique is simple, but its applicability and usefulness are extremely limited.

When the required data are available, the building residual technique can be used in valuing properties with improvements that have suffered substantial accrued depreciation. In fact, current reproduction or replacement cost minus the present value of the improvements provides an estimate of total accrued depreciation. In addition, the building residual technique directly measures the contribution of the improvements to total property value, so it can help an appraiser determine when demolition or major renovation of property improvements is economically feasible.

Land Residual Technique

The land residual technique assumes that the value of the building(s) can be estimated separately. In land residual applications, an appraiser will often consider a new highest and best use for the building that does not exist. Thus, building value is usually estimated as the current cost to construct a new building that represents the highest and best use of the land or site.

The building capitalization rate is applied to the building value to obtain the amount of annual net income needed to support the value of the building. This amount is then deducted from net operating income to indicate the residual income available to support the investment in the land. The residual income is capitalized at the land capitalization rate to derive an indication of the value of the land. Finally, the building value is added to the land value to derive a total property value indication. As in the building residual technique, the land and building capitalization rates derived from the market are applied to the subject property. The calculations are shown below.

Estimated building value		$450,000
Net operating income	$85,500	
Building value × R_B ($450,000 × 0.15)	−67,500	
Residual income to land	$18,000	
Land value (capitalized: $18,000/0.09)		+200,000
Indicated property value		$650,000

The land residual technique allows an appraiser to estimate land values when recent data on land sales are not available. The technique can be applied to proposed construction to test the highest and best use of the land or site or to new structures that do not suffer from accrued depreciation. However, the land residual technique is not applicable when the cost to produce a new building is inconsistent with the amount of value such a new building contributes to property value.

Equity Residual Technique

To apply the equity residual technique, an appraiser deducts annual debt service from net operating income to obtain the residual income for the equity interest. An appraiser who uses this technique assumes that mortgage loan terms can be obtained from the market and that the dollar amount of the debt can be estimated. The residual equity income is then capitalized into value with a market-derived equity capitalization rate as shown below. This technique is especially useful for appraising the fee simple interest in a newly constructed property or the equity interest in a property subject to a specific mortgage.

Mortgage amount		$375,000
Mortgage interest rate	12.0%	
Mortgage amortization term	25 yrs.	
Monthly amortization payment		
($375,000 × 0.0105322)	$3,950	
Net operating income	$60,000	
Mortgage × R_M ($375,000 × 0.12639)	−47,400	
Residual income to equity	$12,600	
Equity value (capitalized:		
$12,600/0.09)		+140,000
Indicated property value		$515,000

Mortgage Residual Technique

When the mortgage residual technique is applied, the amount of available equity is the known component and the mortgage amount or value is unknown. The income needed to satisfy the equity component at the equity capitalization rate is deducted from the net operating income to obtain the residual income to the mortgage component. The residual mortgage income is then capitalized into value at the mortgage capitalization rate. These calculations are demonstrated as follows:

Available equity		$140,000
Net operating income	$60,000	
Equity × R_E ($140,000 × 0.09)	−12,600	
Residual income to mortgage	$47,400	
Mortgage value (capitalized:		
$47,400 / 0.1264)		+375,000
Indicated property value		$515,000

The mortgage residual technique assumes that the amount of funds the equity investor is willing to invest in the property has already been determined. It further assumes that the equity investor requires a specified equity dividend rate from the property. This implies that the loan amount depends on the residual cash flow available for mortgage debt service and the mortgage constant.

As with any capitalization method, residual techniques should only be used to estimate market value when they reflect market behavior. The importance of this point is especially apparent in the case of the mortgage residual technique because lenders are generally unwilling to make a loan unless net operating income exceeds the mortgage debt service by a specified amount. Thus, the mortgage amount implied may not reflect the behavior of lenders.

It should also be noted that once the loan is made, the lender has the legal right to receive the agreed-upon debt service. Any residual cash flow goes to the equity investor. Thus, the mortgage residual technique would not normally be appropriate for estimating the value of a property subject to a specific mortgage.

GROSS INCOME MULTIPLIERS

Gross income multipliers are used to compare the income-producing characteristics of properties in the sales comparison approach. Nevertheless, converting a potential or effective gross income stream into a lump-sum capital value by applying a gross income multiplier is capitalization. Therefore, the derivation and use of multipliers are discussed in direct capitalization.

To derive a gross income multiplier from market data, sales of properties that were rented at the time of sale or were anticipated to be rented within a short time must be available. The ratio of the sale price to the annual gross income *at the time of sale* or projected over the first year or several years of ownership is the gross income multiplier.

Appraisers who attempt to derive and apply gross income multipliers for valuation purposes must be careful for several reasons. First, the properties analyzed must be comparable to the subject property and to one another in terms of physical, locational, and investment characteristics. Properties with similar or even identical multipliers can have very different operating expense ratios and, therefore, not be comparable for valuation purposes.

Second, the term *gross income multiplier* is used because some of the gross income from a property or type of property may come from sources other than rental. A *gross rent multiplier* applies to rental income only.

Third, the appraiser must use similar income data to derive the multiplier for each transaction. The sale price can be divided by either the potential or effective gross income, but the data and measure must be used consistently throughout the analysis to produce reliable results. Different income measures may be used in different valuation studies and appraisals, however. The income measure selected is dictated by the availability of market data and the purpose of the analysis.

To illustrate the difference between different gross income multipliers, data from Comparable A in Table 20.1 are used in the following calculations:

$$\text{Potential gross income multiplier} = \frac{\text{sale price}}{\text{potential gross income}}$$

$$= \frac{\$368,500}{\$\ 85,106}$$

$$= 4.3299^*$$

*In actual practice, multipliers are typically rounded to two decimal places.

$$\text{Effective gross income multiplier} = \frac{\text{sale price}}{\text{effective gross income}}$$

$$= \frac{\$368,500}{\$\ 80,000}$$

$$=\ 4.6063^*$$

*In actual practice, multipliers are typically rounded to two decimal places.

After the gross income multiplier is derived from comparable market data, it must be applied on the same basis it was derived. In other words an income multiplier based on effective gross income can only be applied to the effective gross income of the subject property; an income multiplier based on potential gross income can only be applied to the potential gross income of the subject property. The timing of income also must be comparable. If sales are analyzed using next year's income expectation, the multiplier derived must be applied to next year's income expectation for the subject property.

SUMMARY

Direct capitalization is used to convert an estimate of a single year's income expectancy into an indication of value in one step, either by dividing the income estimate by an appropriate rate or multiplying it by an appropriate factor. The method does not distinguish between the return on and the return of capital because investor assumptions are not simulated. Because the rates or factors used in direct capitalization are derived from similar investment properties, a satisfactory rate of return on and of capital may be assumed.

In addition to *PGI, EGI,* and *NOI,* direct capitalization may be based on equity income, mortgage income, land income, or building income. Thus, the income rates that may be used include the overall property capitalization rate (R_O), the equity capitalization rate (R_E), the mortgage capitalization rate (R_M), the land capitalization rate (R_L), and the building capitalization rate (R_B). The income factors include the potential gross income multiplier *(PGIM)*, the gross rent multiplier *(GRM)*, and the effective gross income multiplier *(EGIM)*. The income rates and factors must be derived from data on comparable properties that reflect similar income-expense ratios, land-to-building ratios, risk characteristics, and expectations as to change in income and value over a typical investment holding period.

The direct capitalization formula is

$$\text{Value} = \frac{\text{Net operating income}}{\text{Overall capitalization rate}}$$

The techniques that can be used to estimate an overall capitalization rate include derivation from comparable sales, derivation from effective gross income multipliers, band of investment—mortgage and equity components, band of investment—land and building components, and the debt coverage formula.

When reliable data on similar, competitive properties are available, an appraiser can derive overall capitalization rates by dividing the *NOI* of each property by its sale price. If a comparable sale and the subject property differ, the appraiser must decide whether the rate for the subject property should be higher or lower. The overall rate should be applied to the subject property in a manner consistent with the way the rates were derived from comparable sales. Deriving rates from comparable sales is the preferred technique when the income and expenses of the subject and comparable properties are estimated on the same basis, market expectations for all the properties are similar, and the market conditions affecting the comparables are similar to those affecting the subject.

If adequate data to derive an overall capitalization rate are not available, but reliable data on sales transactions and gross incomes are, an *effective gross income multiplier* can be used with the operating expense ratio (*OER*) to estimate an overall capitalization rate. The formula for this procedure is

$$R_O = \frac{1 - OER}{EGIM}$$

This calculation is performed for all the comparable properties and an overall capitalization rate is reconciled from the different rate indications.

Lenders of mortgage funds expect both a return on capital, in the form of interest, and a return of capital through amortization of the principal. Similarly, equity investors expect a return on equity commensurate with the investment risk. Accordingly, one band-of-investment technique considers the overall capitalization rate as a composite rate, weighted by the proportions of debt and equity in the property investment.

The mortgage constant (R_M), which is the capitalization rate for debt, represents the ratio of annual debt service to the principal amount of the mortgage loan. The mortgage constant is a function of the interest rate, the frequency of amortization, and the term of the loan. Given the interest rate and the loan terms, the mortgage constant can be found in published financial tables.

The equity capitalization rate (R_E) is the ratio of annual pre-tax cash flow to the amount of equity investment. The equity capitalization rate reflects the anticipated return to the investor, usually for the first year of the holding period.

The overall capitalization rate must satisfy the requirements of both the mortgage constant and the pre-tax cash flow. The overall capitalization rate is a weighted average of the mortgage constant (R_M) and equity dividend (R_E). In addition to R_M and R_E, the loan-to-value ratio (M) and the equity ratio ($1 - M$) are needed to weight the mortgage components. The formula for this band-of-investment, or weighted-average, technique is

$$R_O = M \times R_M + [(1 - M) \times R_E]$$

This technique can only be used when reliable, market-derived data on equity capitalization rates, available loan terms, and loan-to-value ratios are available.

A second band-of-investment technique considers the overall capitalization rate as a composite rate weighted by the proportions of land and building components in the property. The formula is

$$R_O = L \times R_L + B \times R_B$$

where L represents the percentage that land contributes to the overall property, and B is the percentage contribution represented by the building.

In making loan decisions, institutional lenders use the *debt coverage ratio* (*DCR*), which is the ratio of *NOI* to annual debt service (I_M). The *DCR* may also be used to estimate the overall capitalization rate with the formula

$$R_O = DCR \times R_M \times M$$

where M represents the percentage of the mortgage component.

Residual techniques allow an appraiser to capitalize the income allocated to an investment component of unknown value after all investment components of known value have been satisfied. There are both physical (i.e., land and building) and financial (i.e., mortgage and equity) residual techniques.

Four procedures are common to all residual techniques. The appraiser 1) applies an appropriate capitalization rate to the value of a known component to obtain the annual income needed to support the investment in that component, 2) deducts this amount from the *NOI* to derive the residual income available to support the unknown, or residual, component, 3) capitalizes the residual income at a capitalization rate appropriate to the investment in the residual component to derive the present value of this component, and 4) adds the values of the known and residual components to derive a value indication for the total property.

In the building and land residual techniques, either land or building value is estimated independently and converted into the annual net income required to support this component by applying an appropriate capitalization rate. This income is deducted from the *NOI* to derive the residual income available to support the investment in the unknown component. The residual income is then capitalized and added to the value of the known component to obtain an indication of overall property value. The building residual technique is limited in its applicability. The land residual technique may be applied to proposed construction to test the highest and best use of the land or to new construction that shows little accrued depreciation.

In the equity and mortgage residual techniques, either the mortgage or the equity amount is converted into net annual income by applying an appropriate capitalization rate. This income is deducted from *NOI* to derive the residual income available to support the investment in the unknown component. The residual income is then capitalized and added to the value of the known component to obtain an indication of overall property value.

The equity residual technique is especially useful in valuing a newly constructed property or an equity interest subject to a specific mortgage. It is unlikely that the mortgage residual technique will reflect market behavior since lenders extend loans in situations where *NOI* exceeds mortgage debt service, and lenders exercise a legal claim to debt service before the residual cash flow is paid to the equity investor.

Gross income multipliers may be used to compare the income-producing characteristics of properties in the sales comparison approach and to convert gross income streams into property value in direct capitalization. The ratio of the sale price of a property to its annual gross income at the time of sale or projected over the first year or several years of ownership is the gross income multiplier. The appraiser must be sure that the properties used to derive gross income multipliers are comparable, that the gross income multipliers obtained apply only to rental income, that similar income data on either potential or effective gross income are used to derive the multipliers, and that the gross income multiplier obtained is applied to the same income base from which it was derived.

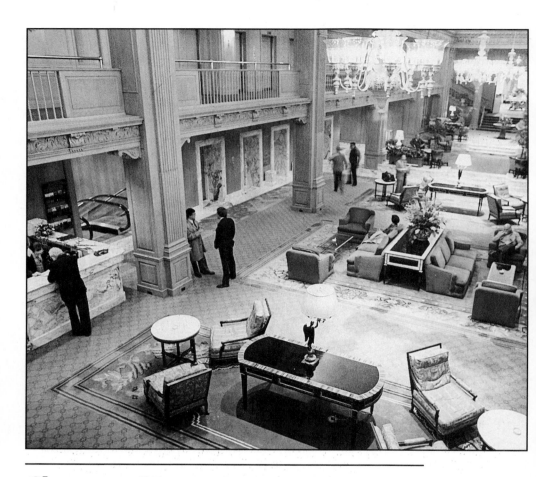

Chapter 21

YIELD CAPITALIZATION—
THEORY AND BASIC
APPLICATIONS

$\mathcal{Y}$ield capitalization is used to convert future benefits into present value by applying an appropriate yield rate. To select an appropriate yield rate for a market value appraisal, an appraiser analyzes market evidence of the yields anticipated by typical investors. When investment value is sought, the yield rate used should reflect the individual investor's requirements, which may differ from the requirements typical in the market.

To perform yield capitalization, an appraiser 1) selects an appropriate holding period; 2) forecasts all future cash flows or cash flow patterns; 3) chooses an appropriate yield, or discount, rate; and 4) converts future benefits into present value by discounting each annual future benefit or by developing an overall rate that reflects the income pattern, value change, and yield rate. The application of capitalization rates that reflect an appropriate yield rate, the use of present value factors, and discounted cash flow analysis are all yield capitalization procedures. Mortgage-equity formulas and yield rate or value change formulas may be used to derive overall capitalization rates. Like direct capitalization, yield capitalization may also employ residual techniques. To apply the discounting procedure, the appraiser must be familiar with income patterns, capital return concepts, the mathematics of discounting, investor requirements or assumptions (i.e., holding period, anticipated market growth, and inflation), and the appropriateness of discount rates.

THE NATURE OF ANNUITIES

Although the word *annuity* means an annual income, it is used to refer to a program or contract specifying regular payments of stipulated amounts. Payments need not be annual, but the interval between payments must be regular. An annuity can be level, increasing, or decreasing, but the amounts must be scheduled and predictable. Income that has the characteristics of an annuity is expected at regular intervals and in predictable amounts. Obviously real estate income or rental income can have the characteristics of an annuity.

The income expected from a real estate investment may take the form of a regular or irregular pattern. Various capitalization techniques can be applied to different patterns of income streams.

DISCOUNTING

Periodic income and reversions are converted into present value through discounting, a procedure based on the assumption that benefits received in the future are worth less than the same benefits received today. The return on an investment compensates the investor for foregoing present benefits (i.e., the immediate use of capital) and accepting future benefits and risks. This return is usually called *interest* by lenders and *yield* by equity investors. The discounting procedure includes the assumption that the return of capital will be accomplished through periodic income, the reversion, or a combination of both. In some instances, tax benefits may contribute to the investment yield.

An investor seeks a total return that exceeds the amount invested. The present value of a prospective benefit must be less than its expected future value. A future payment is discounted to present value by calculating the amount that, if invested today, would grow with compound interest at a satisfactory rate to equal the future payment. The standard formula for discounting future value to present value is

$$\text{Present value} = \frac{\text{Future value}}{(1+i)^n}$$

where i is the rate of return on capital per period that will satisfy the investor and n is the number of periods that the payment will be deferred. The two examples that follow illustrate applications of the discounting formula.

Problem 1. *What is the present value of $115 due one year hence discounted at 15% per year?* To solve this problem, the amount that should be invested now to grow to $115 with compound interest at the rate of 15% per year must be calculated.

$$\text{Present value} = \$115/1.15^1 = \$100$$

Problem 2. *What is the present value of $1,000 due in three years discounted at 10% per year?* This problem can be solved by calculating the amount that should be invested now to grow to $1,000 in three years with compound interest at 10% per year.

$$\text{Present value} = \$1,000/1.10^3 = \$751.31$$

If a series of future payments is expected, each payment is discounted with the standard formula, and the present value of the payments is the sum of all the present values. This standard discounting procedure is the foundation for all yield capitalization techniques.

The amount deposited or received can be in the form of a single lump sum, a series of periodic installments such as rental income, or a combination of both. When amounts are compounded or discounted, the rate used is the effective interest rate; on an annual basis, this rate is identical to the *nominal interest rate*. If amounts are compounded or discounted more often than annually (e.g., semiannually or monthly), the nominal interest rate is divided by the number of compounding or discounting periods. For example, a nominal rate of 12% is an effective rate of 6% for semiannual conversion periods, or an effective rate of 1% for monthly conversions. Standard tables of factors or preprogrammed financial calculators can be used to facilitate the application of factors, but the user must select the appropriate conversion frequency (i.e., monthly, quarterly, or annually).

Each precomputed factor and yield capitalization formula have specific built-in investment assumptions that are implied when the table is used or the factor is calculated. Therefore, the appraiser must identify the assumptions applicable to the subject property and use the factor table and capitalization formula that correspond to these assumptions. Thus, to apply compounding or discounting procedures, the appraiser must know the basic formulas, how the various factors relate to one another, and how they may be used or combined to simplify income capitalization.[1]

Tables and factors allow appraisers to solve many arithmetic problems that are fundamental to the valuation process, thus they are useful in applying capitalization techniques. However, in the final analysis, a value estimate reflects the ap-

---

1. See Appendix C for a discussion of financial tables.

praiser's judgment based on appropriate research of the subject property and the market.

Discounted Cash Flow Analysis

Discounted cash flow (DCF) analysis can be used both to estimate present value and to extract a discount rate from a comparable sale. In DCF analysis the quantity, variability, timing, and duration of cash flows are specified. *Cash flow* refers to the periodic income attributable to the interests in real property. Each cash flow, including the reversion if any, is discounted to present value and then all the present values are totaled to obtain the value of the real property interest being appraised. The future value of that interest, the reversion, is forecast at the end of the projection period (i.e., the holding period or remaining economic life) and is also discounted. The cash flows discounted with the DCF formula may be the net operating income to the entire property or the cash flows to specific interests— e.g., the pre-tax cash flows to the equity interest (equity dividends), the after-tax cash flows to the equity interest, or debt service for the mortgage interest.

The DCF formula is a yield formula expressed as

$$PV = \frac{CF_1}{1 + Y} + \frac{CF_2}{(1 + Y)^2} + \frac{CF_3}{(1 + Y)^3} + \ldots + \frac{CF_n}{(1 + Y)^n}$$

where PV = present value; CF = the cash flow for the period specified; Y = the appropriate periodic yield, or discount, rate; and n = the number of periods in the projection.

With the DCF formula an appraiser can discount each payment of income separately and add all the present values together to obtain the present value of the property interest being appraised. The formula treats the reversion as a cash flow that can be valued separately from the income stream. The formula can be used to estimate total property value (V_O), loan value (V_M), equity value (V_E), leased fee value (V_{LF}), leasehold value (V_{LH}), or any other interest in real property.

When a series of periodic incomes varies in an irregular pattern, the basic DCF formula is used in its analysis and valuation. Any series of periodic incomes, with or without a reversion, can be valued with the basic formula. Formulas for valuing level annuities and increasing and decreasing annuities, which are introduced later in this chapter, are merely shortcuts to be used in these special situations.

Selection of a Yield Rate for Discounting

The selection of a yield rate is critical to DCF analysis. To select an appropriate rate an appraiser must verify and interpret the attitudes and expectations of market participants, including buyers, sellers, advisers, and brokers. Although the actual yield on an investment cannot be calculated until the investment is sold, an investor may set a target yield for the investment before or during ownership. Historical yield rates derived from comparable sales may be relevant, but they reflect past, not future, benefits in the mind of the investor and may not be reliable indicators of current yield. Therefore, the selection of yield rates for discounting cash flows should focus on the prospective or forecast yield rates anticipated by typical buyers and sellers of comparable investments. An appraiser can verify investor assumptions directly by interviewing the parties to comparable sales transactions or indirectly by estimating the income expectancy and likely reversion for a comparable property and deriving a prospective yield rate.

The appraiser narrows the range of indicated yield rates and selects an appropriate rate by comparing the physical, economic, and financial characteristics (risk) of the comparable properties with the property being appraised and assessing the competition for capital in other financial markets. In some situations there may be reason to select a yield rate above or below the indicated range. The final selection of a yield rate requires judgment, just as an appraiser uses judgment to select an overall rate or equity capitalization rate from the range indicated by comparable sales. In selecting a yield rate, the appraiser should analyze current conditions in capital and real estate markets and the actions, perceptions, and expectations of real estate investors.

Different Rates

Yield rates are primarily a function of perceived risks. Different portions of forecast future income may have different levels of risk and, therefore, different yield rates. In lease valuation, for example, one rate might be applied to discount the series of net rental incomes stipulated in the lease and a different rate might be applied to discount the reversion. One rate reflects the creditworthiness of the tenant as well as the benefits, constraints, and limitations of the lease contract, while the other is subject to free, open-market conditions. The decision to apply a single yield rate to all benefits or to apply different rates to different benefits should be based on investors' actions in the market. It may be prudent for an appraiser to check a bond rating service such as Moody's for the specific rating of the company leasing a property. Typically, long-term leases are underwritten on this basis.

INCOME STREAM PATTERNS

After specifying the amount, timing, and duration of the cash flows to the property interest being appraised, the appraiser should identify the pattern that the income stream is expected to follow during the projection period. These patterns may be grouped into the following basic categories—variable annuity, level annuity, and increasing or decreasing annuity.

Variable Annuity: Nonsystematic Change

A variable annuity is an income stream in which payment amounts vary per period. To value a variable annuity, the present value of each income payment is calculated separately and these values are totaled to obtain the present value of the entire income stream. This procedure is discounted cash flow analysis.

Any income stream can be valued as if it were a variable annuity. Level annuities and annuities that change systematically are special cases which can also be handled with special formulas that reflect the systematic pattern of the income stream. These shortcut formulas can save time and effort in certain cases, but valuing an income stream as a variable annuity with a hand-held calculator or computerized program may be just as easy.

Level Annuity

A level annuity is an income stream in which the amount of each payment is the same; it is a level, unchanging flow of income over time. The payments in a level annuity are equally spaced and regularly scheduled. There are two types of level annuities: ordinary annuities and annuities payable in advance.

Ordinary Annuity

An ordinary annuity, which is the most common type of level annuity, is distinguished by income payments that are received at the *end* of each period. Standard fixed-payment mortgage loans, many corporate and government bonds, endowment policies, and certain lease arrangements are ordinary annuities.

Annuity Payable in Advance

An annuity payable in advance is a level annuity in which the payments are received at the *beginning* of each period. A lease that requires payments at the beginning of each month creates an annuity payable in advance.

Increasing or Decreasing Annuity

An income stream that is expected to change in a systematic pattern is either an increasing annuity or a decreasing annuity. Three basic patterns of systematic change are reflected in step-up and step-down annuities, straight-line (constant dollar) change per period annuities, and exponential-curve (constant ratio) change per period annuities.

Step-Up and Step-Down Annuities

A step-up or step-down annuity is usually created by a lease contract that calls for a succession of level annuities of different amounts to be paid in different periods of the lease term. For example, a lease might call for monthly payments of $500 for the first three years, $750 for the next four years, and $1,200 for the next six years. Over the 13-year term of the lease, there are three successive level annuities—one for three years, one for four years, and one for six years.

Straight-Line (Constant-Amount) Change per Period Annuity

An income stream that increases or decreases by a fixed amount each period fits the pattern of a straight-line (constant-amount) change per period annuity. These income streams are also called *straight-line increasing* or *straight-line decreasing annuities*. For example, a property may have an estimated first-year net operating income of $100,000 that is forecast to increase by $7,000 per year. Thus, the second year's net operating income will be $107,000, the third year's net operating income will be $114,000, and so forth. Similarly, the income stream of a straight-line decreasing annuity is expected to decrease by a constant amount each period.

Exponential-Curve (Constant-Ratio) Change per Period Annuity

An income stream with an exponential-curve (constant-ratio) change per period is also referred to as an *exponential annuity*. This type of income stream increases or decreases at a constant ratio and, therefore, the increases or decreases are compounded. For example, a property with an estimated first-year pre-cash tax flow of $100,000 that is forecast to increase 7% per year over each preceding year's cash flow will have a pre-tax cash flow in the second year of $107,000 ($100,000 × 1.07). However, the third year's pre-tax cash flow will be $114,490 ($107,000 × 1.07) and the fourth year's cash flow will be $122,504 ($114,490 × 1.07).

REVERSION

As mentioned previously, income-producing properties typically provide two types of financial benefits— periodic income and the future value obtained from sale of the property or reversion of the property interest at the end of the holding period. The length of the holding period usually may be determined by reviewing the property's lease expiration date(s). This future cash flow is called a *reversion* because it represents the anticipated return of a capital sum at the end of the investment. (Tax benefits are not considered in this discussion.)

A single property may include one or more property interests that have their own streams of periodic benefits and reversions. For example, a property may have an equity interest with equity capitalization, or equity dividend, as the periodic benefit and the equity reversion (i.e., property reversion minus the mortgage balance at loan maturity or property resale) as the reversionary benefit. The same property could have a mortgage with debt service as the periodic benefit and the mortgage balance (called a *ballon payment*) as the reversionary interest. A single property also comprises both building and land components. In situations involving long-term ground leases, annual ground rent should be deducted before capitalizing *NOI*. Table 21.1 shows several possible investment positions in an income-producing property and identifies the income streams and reversions associated with each interest.

The reversion is often a major portion of the total benefit to be received from an investment in income-producing property. If the investor's capital is not recaptured through some combination of cash flow and (possibly tax-oriented) reversion proceeds, the effective rate of return *on* the investment will always be negative or zero. For certain investments, *all* capital recapture is accomplished through the reversion, indicating higher risk; for other investment properties, part of the recapture is provided by the reversion and part is provided by the investment's income stream. For those properties in which the net present value of the reversion exceeds the net present value of the income stream, a higher discount rate should be applied to reflect the additional risk associated with the investment.

To judge how much of the return of an investment will be provided by the reversion, an appraiser acknowledges that three general situations could result from the original investment. First, the property may increase in value over the holding period. Second, the property's value may not change—i.e., the value of the property at the end of the holding period or remaining economic life may be equal to its value at the beginning of the period. Third, the property may decline in value over the period being analyzed. Because these possible outcomes affect the potential yield of the investment and the amount of income considered acceptable, the appraiser must estimate the change, if any, that will occur in the original investment or the property value over the holding period. (For leveraged invest-

Table 21.1 Summary of Incomes and Reversions Associated with Various Real Property Interests in Income-Producing Property

Real Property Interest	Income	Reversion
Fee simple	Net operating income	Proceeds of resale
Mortgage (lender's position)	Mortgage debt service	Balance if paid prior to maturity, or balloon payment if paid at maturity
Equity	Cash flow (equity dividend)	Equity proceeds of resale
Leased fee	Net operating income based on contract rents	Property reversion or proceeds of resale of leased fee estate
Leasehold	Rental advantage when contract rent is below market rent; rental disadvantage when contract is above market rent	None if held to end of lease or proceeds of resale of leasehold estate

Note. Incomes and reversions may be calculated before or after income taxes.

ments, equity build-up may also occur through periodic debt service payments that include amortization.)

When a property is expected to be sold, the appraiser projects the reversion amount as the proceeds of resale. The term *proceeds of resale* refers to the net difference between the transaction price and the selling expenses, which may include brokerage commissions, legal fees, closing costs, transfer taxes, and possibly penalties for the prepayment of debt.

An appraiser judges the likely value of the reversion in light of the expectations of investors in the market for the type of property being appraised. The appraiser may ask: Do investors expect a change in the value of this type of property in this particular locale? By how much will values change and in which direction? The appraiser analyzes and interprets the market and estimates the value of the future reversion based on the direction and the amount or percentage of change that investors expect. The use of personal computers and software to perform lease-by-lease analysis allows appraisers to predict future cash flows, which are the basis for the reversion amount, more accurately.

DISCOUNTING MODELS

The present value of any pattern of increasing, level, or decreasing income or of any irregular income can be calculated with DCF analysis. Specific valuation models, or formulas, categorized as either income models or property models have been developed for application to the corresponding pattern of projected benefits. Income models can be applied only to a stream of income including a reversion. The present value of an expected reversion or any other benefit not already included in the income stream must be added to obtain the investment's total present value. When a property model is used, an income stream and a reversion are valued in one operation. Other present value models employ mortgage-equity concepts and discounted cash flow analysis; these are discussed in Chapter 22.

Income Models

Valuation models can be applied to the following patterns of income: variable or irregular income, level income, straight-line (constant-amount) change per period income, and exponential-curve (constant-ratio) change per period income.

Variable or Irregular Income

As mentioned previously, the present value of an uneven stream of income is the sum of the discounted benefits treated as a series of separate payments or reversions. This model simply totals all present values using the standard discounting formula. The routine can be applied as a property valuation model as well as an income valuation model because it can be adapted to include the final reversion as part of the final cash flow expected at the end of the last, or *n*th, period.

Level Income

When a lease provides for a level stream of income or when income can be projected at a stabilized level, one or more capitalization procedures may be appropriate depending on the investor's assumptions with respect to capital recovery. Capitalization can be accomplished using capitalization in perpetuity, the Inwood premise, or the Hoskold premise.

Capitalization in perpetuity. Capitalization in perpetuity can be considered a property valuation model or an income valuation model. If, for example, a property is expected to generate level net operating income for a finite period of time and then be resold for the original purchase price, the property could be valued with capitalization in perpetuity simply by dividing the expected periodic income by an appropriate discount rate. In this model the discount rate and the overall capitalization rate are the same because the original investment is presumed to be recovered at the termination of the investment.

The Inwood premise. The Inwood premise applies to income that is a level ordinary annuity. It holds that the present value of a stream of income is based on a single discount rate. Each installment of income is discounted with a single discount rate, and the total discounted values of the installments are accumulated to obtain the present value of the income stream. The present value of a series of $1 payments can be found in compound interest tables for a given rate and a given period of time. It is assumed that the income will be sufficient to return all investment capital to the investor and to pay the specified return on the investment.

In most mortgages the amount of interest is assumed to decline gradually over the holding period and is calculated as a specified percentage of the unrecaptured capital. Any excess over the required interest payment is considered a return of capital and reduces the amount of capital remaining in the investment. Because the installments are always the same amount, the principal portion of the payments increases by the same amounts that the interest portion of the payments decreases. It is also valid, but not customary, to see the interest payments as constant, always amounting to the specified return on the original investment, with any excess over the required, fixed-interest payments credited to a hypothetical sinking fund that grows with interest at the same rate.

An Inwood capitalization rate can be constructed by adding the interest rate to a sinking fund factor $(1/S_n)$ that is based on the same interest rate and duration as the income stream. The resulting capitalization rate is simply the reciprocal of the ordinary level annuity (present value of $1 per period) factor found in financial tables. Thus, the Inwood premise is consistent with the use of compound interest tables to calculate the present value of the income stream.

The Inwood premise applies only to a stream of income. Therefore, the present value of any expected reversion or other benefit not included in the income stream must be added to obtain the total present value of the investment. For example, assume that the *NOI* of a property is $10,000 per year for five years. What is the value of the property assuming an overall yield rate (Y_O) of 10% under the Inwood premise?

Solution 1

Apply the *PV* of $1 per period (ordinary level annuity) factor to the *NOI*:

$$3.79079 \times \$10,000 = \$37,908 \text{ (rounded)}$$

Solution 2

Use the general yield capitalization formula for a level income with a percentage change in value:

$$R_O = Y_O - \Delta_O \, 1/S_n$$

Because there is no reversion, the property will lose 100% of its value. Δ_O is thus −1.0 and the yield capitalization formula becomes:

$$R_O = Y_O + 1/S_n$$

This equation represents the Inwood premise. By substituting the data given in the example, we may arrive at R_O:

$$R_O = 0.10 + .163797$$
$$R_O = 0.263797$$

The value of the property may be estimated using the basic valuation formula.

$$V_O = NOI/R_O$$
$$V_O = \$10,000/0.263797$$
$$V_O = \$37,908 \text{ (rounded)}$$

Note that the sinking fund factor $(1/S_n)$ is based on a 10% discount rate, which implies that a portion of the *NOI* could be reinvested at 10% to replace the investment. It can be said that Y_O represents the return *on* capital and $1/S_n$ represents the return *of* capital.

The Inwood premise assumes a constant rate of return on capital each year with the return of capital being reinvested in a sinking fund at the same yield rate as Y_O. The amount accumulated in this sinking fund can be used to replace the asset at the end of its economic life. Using the assumptions applied in the preceding example, the *NOI* for the first year may be allocated as follows:

NOI	$10,000.00
Return on capital (10% of $37,908)	$ 3,790.80
Return of capital	$ 6,209.20

If the return of capital ($6,209.20) is placed in a sinking fund earning 10%, the fund will accumulate to $37,908 over five years. The sinking fund accumulation factor (future value of $1 per period), S_n, is applied to the return of capital: 6.1051 x $6,209.20 = $37,908. This is the exact amount required to replace the asset.

The Hoskold premise. The Hoskold premise differs from the Inwood premise in that it employs two separate interest rates: a speculative rate, representing a fair rate of return on capital commensurate with the risks involved, and a safe rate for a sinking fund designed to return all the invested capital to the investor in a lump sum at the termination of the investment. It is assumed that the stream of income is of limited duration and is sufficient to 1) pay a fair return on capital at the speculative rate, and 2) contribute necessary installments to a conservative, minimum-risk sinking fund, which will grow with interest at a safe rate and repay the investor in full at the termination of the investment.

In contrast to the Inwood premise, the Hoskold premise assumes that the portion of *NOI* needed to recover or replace capital (the return of capital) is reinvested at a "safe rate" (i.e., the prevailing rate for insured savings accounts or government bonds) which is lower than the yield rate (Y_O) used to value the other portion of *NOI*. Like the Inwood premise, the Hoskold technique was designed to be applied when the asset value of the investment decreases to zero over the holding period. However, Hoskold assumed that funds would have to be set aside at a lower, safe rate to replace the asset at the end of the holding period. Hoskold suggested that this technique might be appropriate for valuing wasting assets such as a mine where the value is reduced to zero as minerals are extracted; thus funds have to be set aside to invest in a new mine once the minerals are totally depleted (the reversion equals zero). In some cases this premise might apply to personal property, depending on whether investors typically set up cash reserves for replacements.

Using the same *NOI*, yield, and term set forth in the previous example, assume that a portion of *NOI* has to be set aside at a 5% safe rate to allow for the recovery of capital at the end of every five years. All other assumptions remain the same. This problem may be solved with the same yield capitalization formula applied in the Inwood calculation, but the sinking fund factor ($1/S_n$) is based on the safe rate of 5% rather than the yield rate of 10%. Thus, the overall rate is calculated as follows:

$$R_O = Y_O + 1/S_n$$
$$= 0.10 + 0.180975$$
$$= 0.280975$$

Because the sinking fund factor $(1/S_n)$ is calculated at a 5% rate rather than the 10% rate, the capitalization rate is higher and the value is lower. The value is calculated as:

$$V_O = NOI/R_O$$
$$= \$10,000/0.280975$$
$$= \$35,590 \text{ (rounded)}$$

The lower value is a result of setting aside the portion of *NOI* earning 5% to allow for the recovery of capital ($35,590) at the end of five years. The income allocation for the first year can be shown as follows:

NOI	$10,000
Return on capital (10% of $35,590)	$ 3,559
Return of capital	$ 6,441

To find the future value of $6,441 at 5% for five years, apply the sinking fund accumulation factor (future value of $1 per period), S_n, to the return of capital: $5.525631 \times \$6,441.00 = \$35,590$. The result is the exact amount required to recover the capital invested.

The Hoskold premise has become less popular and is now considered appropriate only for certain types of investments. A Hoskold capitalization rate can be easily constructed by adding the speculative rate to the sinking fund factor for the safe rate. Generally the prevailing rate for insured savings accounts or government bonds is considered an appropriate safe rate.

Straight-Line (Constant-Amount) Change per Period in Income

When income is expected to increase or decrease by a fixed amount per period, the periodic income over time can be graphically portrayed as a straight line. Hence the term *straight-line* is used to describe this type of income pattern.

To obtain the present value of an annuity that has a starting income of *d* at the end of the first period and increases *h* dollars per period for *n* periods, the following equation is used.

$$\text{Present value} = (d + hn)a_n - \frac{h(n - a_n)}{i}$$

where a_n is the present value of $1 per period at a rate of *i* for *n* periods. In the formula, *h* is positive for increases and negative for decreases.

This formula for valuing straight-line income patterns should not be confused with straight capitalization with straight-line recapture. Although straight capitalization with straight-line recapture may be seen as a model for valuing a particular income stream, the procedure can also be applied to properties in which the expected change in value is commensurate with the expected change in income. Therefore, straight capitalization with straight-line recapture and related concepts are discussed with property models later in this chapter. Again, the preceding formulas apply to income streams only. Special tables of present value factors based on these formulas are available.[2]

Exponential-Curve (Constant Ratio) Change per Period in Income

In the absence of lease-by-lease analysis, often the best way to reflect market expectations is to project income to change at a constant rate. In soft markets, slower rates of growth or even no growth is often projected for the first few years of cash flow. In active markets, higher rates of growth may be projected for the first few years of cash flow. Portrayed graphically, this type of income stream follows an exponential curve rather than a straight line. To obtain the present value of an annuity that starts at $1 at the end of the first period and increases each period thereafter at a rate of x for n periods, the following equation is used.

$$\text{Present value} = \frac{1 - (1 + x)^n / (1 + i)^n}{i - x}$$

where i is the annual discount rate and x is the ratio of the increase in income for any period to the income for the previous period. The formula for calculating the present value of a stream of income that declines at a constant rate is similar, but the sign of x is reversed to indicate a negative rate of change. Thus, the formula for calculating the present value of an annuity starting at $1 and declining thereafter at a rate of x may be rewritten as

$$\text{Present value} = \frac{1 - (1 - x)^n / (1 + i)^n}{i + x}$$

Property Models

When both value and income changes are expected to follow a regular or predictable pattern, one of the yield capitalization models for property valuation may be applicable. The common yield capitalization models employ a capitalization rate, R, which is also used in direct capitalization. There is a difference, however, between direct capitalization and yield capitalization. In direct capitalization R is derived directly from market data, without addressing the expected rate of return on capital or the means of recapture; in yield capitalization R cannot be determined without taking into account the income pattern, the anticipated rate of return on capital, and the timing of recapture. This does not mean that yield capitalization procedures are not market-oriented. On the contrary, for some property types yield capitalization procedures may represent the most realistic simulation of decision making in the marketplace.

Real estate investors are greatly influenced by expectations of change in the value of a property. When an investor looks forward to property appreciation as a component of the eventual investment yield, he or she is anticipating that the total yield rate will be higher than the expected rate of income—i.e., the overall capitalization rate. The total yield rate is a complete measure of performance that includes any property appreciation. Therefore, the capitalization rate for an appreciating property equals the total yield rate minus an adjustment for expected

---

2. See James J. Mason, MAI, ed. and comp., *American Institute of Real Estate Appraisers Financial Tables*, rev. ed. (Chicago: American Institute of Real Estate Appraisers, 1982), Table No. 5, Ordinary Annuities Changing in Constant Amount.

growth. Similarly, the capitalization rate for a depreciating property can be seen as the yield rate plus an adjustment for expected loss.

If the adjustment for growth is treated as a positive change and the adjustment for loss is treated as a negative change, the capitalization rate (R) can be expressed in terms of the yield rate (Y) and an adjustment rate (A) with the simple formula

$$R = Y - A$$

Note that when A is deducted from Y, a gain is indicated; when A is added to Y, a loss is indicated. Because A is often expressed as a function of the relative change in property value, the Greek letter delta (Δ) is used to denote relative change in value. To calculate A it is usually necessary to multiply Δ by a conversion factor such as an annual sinking fund factor or an annual recapture rate to convert the total relative change in value into an appropriate periodic rate of change. If we call the annualizer a, the general formula for R may be expressed as

$$R = Y - \Delta a$$

where R is the capitalization rate, Y is the yield rate, and Δ is the relative change in value.

This general formula for the capitalization rate can be adapted for use with typical income/value patterns for the property as a whole or for any property components. In the general formula, R, Y, and Δ apply to the total property and are expressed without subscripts. However, if there is a possibility of confusing the total property with any of its components, subscripts should be used for clarification. Once the appropriate capitalization rate has been determined, an indication of property value can be obtained by applying the universal valuation formula

$$\text{Value} = \frac{\text{Income}}{\text{Cap rate}} \quad \text{or} \quad V = \frac{I}{R}$$

Level Income

Level income with no change in value. When both income and value are expected to remain unchanged, a property may be valued by capitalization in perpetuity, which was explained in the discussion of income models. According to the general formula $R = Y - \Delta a$, the capitalization rate (R) becomes the yield rate (Y) when there is no change in value because Δ equals zero.

Level income with change in value. When level income with a change in value is projected over a period of n years, the general formula for R can be adapted by using the sinking fund factor for rate Y over n years for the conversion factor (a). For example, consider a commercial property that will generate a stable *NOI* of $25,000 per year for the next 10 years. Total property appreciation of 50% is expected during this 10-year period. The appraiser is asked to value the property to yield 15%. To solve this problem, the formula $R = Y - \Delta a$ is used with the sinking fund factor for 15%, over 10 years as a. According to the tables, the sinking fund factor is 0.049252, so R is calculated as follows:

$$R = 0.15 - (0.50 \times 0.049252) = 0.125374$$
$$\text{Value} = NOI/R$$
$$\text{Value} = \$25,000/0.125374 = \$199,403$$

Straight-Line (Constant-Amount) Changes in Income and Value

When income and value are expected to increase or decrease by fixed amounts per period according to the standard, straight-line pattern, property value can be estimated using straight capitalization with straight-line recapture. The general formula for the capitalization rate (R) can be adapted for use with the standard, straight-line income/value pattern by using the straight-line recapture rate as the conversion factor (a). The straight-line recapture rate is simply the reciprocal of the projection period. For example, if income is projected over a period of 25 years, the annual, straight-line recapture rate is 1/25, or 4%. Depreciation of 100% would indicate that the projection period is equal to the property's remaining economic life. The concept of a limited remaining economic life does not apply to appreciating properties, but 100% appreciation would indicate a projection period equal to the amount of time required for the property to double in value.

Classic straight-line recapture. Straight-line capitalization has historically been used to value wasting assets. This classic procedure has limited applicability due to its underlying assumptions, but it should be thoroughly understood to ensure its proper use. The classic straight-line procedure presumes that capital is recaptured in equal amounts during the economic life of the investment and that net income always consists of a fixed amount that represents the return of capital, plus a declining return on the capital remaining in the investment. Total income, therefore, diminishes until the asset is worthless and all capital has been recovered.

The presumption that value and income will decline steadily is frequently inconsistent with market behavior; nevertheless, the procedure has important uses. Straight-line recapture is appropriate whenever the projection of income and value in an investment corresponds with the assumptions implicit in the procedure. Classic straight-line recapture is most easily understood when it is applied to an investment in a wasting asset such as a perishable structure, a stand of timber, or a mineral deposit. The procedure is not appropriate for valuing an investment in land or another asset that can sustain value indefinitely.

For example, consider an investment in a partial interest in real estate such as a leasehold in which all improvements must be written off during the term of the lease. Assume that $50,000 is invested in a 10-year leasehold to earn 8% per year as a yield on capital. What flow of income to the investor would be required to return the entire amount of the investment on a straight-line basis during the 10-year period and, in addition, yield 8% per year to the investor?

Yearly recapture would, of course, be one-tenth of $50,000, or $5,000. The investor is entitled to a return on unrecaptured capital amounting to 8% of $50,000 in the first year, 8% of $45,000 in the second year, 8% of $40,000 in the third year, and so forth. In other words, the income flow starts at $9,000 the first year and drops $400 each year after that. The total income payable at the end of the tenth and final year would be $5,400, of which $5,000 would be the last installment of the return of capital and the other $400 would be the interest due on the capital remaining in the investment during the tenth year. Thus the investor achieves 100% capital recovery plus an 8% return on the outstanding capital.

Note that the recapture rate amounts to 10% of the original investment and is simply the reciprocal of the economic life. Also, all income is presumed to be payable at the end of each year and the yields are always computed at the end of the year on the amount of capital outstanding during the year. Based on the starting income, the capitalization rate in this example would be $9,000/$50,000, or 18%. The 18% capitalization rate could also be calculated by adding the 10% recapture rate to the 8% yield rate.

The straight-line capitalization procedure reflects some useful mathematical relationships.

First period return on investment = original value × yield rate
Periodic change in value = original value × periodic rate of change
Periodic change in income = periodic change in value x yield rate

When the decline in income and value reflects these relationships, the periodic rate of change is the recapture rate and the reciprocal of the recapture rate is the economic life.

Expanded straight-line concept. The traditional concept of straight-line capitalization can be expanded to remove some of its theoretical constraints and facilitate a broader range of practical applications. The assumption of a predictable decline in income can be expanded to include any predictable change, which allows the appraiser to consider growing assets as well as wasting assets. Presuming a predictable rate of change within the foreseeable future can also eliminate the need to consider the full economic life of a property. Although there are significant theoretical differences, the expanded straight-line concept corresponds mathematically to classic straight-line recapture.

Under both the expanded and classic straight-line concepts, changes in value and income are presumed to occur on a straight-line basis. The basic requirements for a satisfactory return on, and complete recovery of, invested capital are also preserved. The expanded concept does not presume, however, that capital is recaptured in annual installments throughout the economic life of a property. Rather, the property could be resold for a predictable amount at some point during its economic life, thereby providing for partial or complete return of the invested capital at the time of resale.

The straight-line capitalization rate is simply a combination of the yield rate and the straight-line rate of change, which is expressed in the general formula $R = Y - \Delta a$, where Δ is the relative change in value in n periods and a is $1/n$. For example, consider a leasehold that will produce NOI of $19,000 the first year. This NOI is expected to decline thereafter in the standard straight-line pattern and value is expected to fall 25% in 10 years. To appraise the leasehold to yield 12%, use the formula $R_{LH} = Y_{LH} - \Delta_{LH} a$, where the subscript LH denotes the leasehold.

$$R_{LH} = 0.12 - (-0.25 \times 0.1) = 0.145$$
$$\text{Value} = NOI/R$$
$$\text{Value} = \$19,000/0.145 = \$131,034$$

The classic and expanded straight-line concepts are popular because they are simple and do not require the use of compound interest tables. However, straight-line concepts have theoretical and practical limitations. The straight-line premise does not always represent a realistic pattern of changing income and changing value.

Exponential-Curve (Constant-Ratio) Changes in Income and Value

When both income and value are expected to change at a constant ratio, the capitalization rate can be determined without tables using the general formula

$$R = Y - \Delta a$$

where Δa is the relative change in value and income for one period. Thus, Δa can be replaced with the periodic compound rate of change (CR). The formula then becomes

$$R = Y - CR$$

where Y is the yield rate per period and CR is the rate of change per period. An expected loss is treated as a negative rate of change, and the formula becomes

or

$$R = Y - (-CR)$$
$$R = Y + CR$$

If both income and value are expected to change at the same rate, the capitalization rate is expected to remain constant. Therefore, this pattern of growth or decline is sometimes referred to as the *frozen cap rate* pattern. For example, assume an income-producing property is expected to produce NOI of $50,000 for the first year. Thereafter both NOI and value are expected to grow at a constant ratio of 2% per year. In other words, 2% is the expected ratio of the increase in income for any year to the income for the previous year; the ratio of the increase in value for any year to the value for the previous year is also 2%. To appraise the property to yield 11%, the formula is $R_o = Y_o - CR_o$

$$R_o = 0.11 - 0.02 = 0.09$$
$$\text{Value} = \$50,000 / 0.09 = \$555,556$$

Variable or Irregular Income and Value Changes

When income and value are not expected to follow a regular pattern of change, the present value of a property can be obtained by applying the standard discounting formula separately to each projected benefit, including the final reversion.

To illustrate a variable or irregular pattern of change in income, the reader is referred to the income estimate for the office building that was developed in Chapter 19. The projected NOI and reversion are shown in Table 19.10. It is assumed that a typical buyer projects income for a 10-year holding period. Net operating income for Year 11 is also projected to estimate the resale price of the property. The reversion is calculated by applying a 10% capitalization rate typically to the NOI for Year 11. Care should be taken to note variations in NOI subsequent to Year 11, which may warrant use of a different capitalization rate or different annual income to calculate the reversion. The value of the property can be estimated by calculating the present value of the NOI for each year of the 10-year holding period and adding the present value of the cash flow from the sale of

Table 21.2 Discounting of Income Streams and Reversion for Office Building in Table 19.10

Year	NOI	PV of $1 factor (15%)	Discounted Value
1993	$4,928,131	0.869565	$4,285,330
1994	$4,908,580	0.756144	$3,711,593
1995	$3,390,765	0.657516	$2,229,482
1996	$6,766,458	0.571753	$3,868,743
1997	$11,338,262	0.497177	$5,637,123
1998	$12,350,578	0.432328	$5,339,501
1999	$13,051,509	0.375937	$4,906,545
2000	$13,771,044	0.326902	$4,501,782
2001	$16,148,331	0.284262	$4,590,357
2002	$16,964,481	0.247185	$4,193,365
			$43,263,821
Reversion of $168,968,494 discounted at 0.247185			$41,766,478
Value of office building as of January 1, 1993			$85,030,299

the property in Year 10 (the net resale price). Suppose the typical investor requires an overall yield rate (Y_E) of 15%. At a 15% discount rate the present value of the NOI and reversion is $85,030,299 (see Table 21.2). This means that the investor would expect to earn a 15% rate of return if $85,030,299 is paid for the property.

Although property value was estimated by discounting the projected cash flow for each year rather than by applying a formula to develop an overall capitalization rate, an overall capitalization rate is implied in the solution. In this case the overall capitalization rate (R_O) for Year 1 is 5.8% ($4,928,131/$85,030,299). This overall capitalization rate is considerably lower than the 10% capitalization rate applied to the estimated NOI for Year 11 to estimate the resale price. The difference is attributable to the fact that the NOI for Year 1 in this example is relatively low due to the impact of existing leases. The overall capitalization rate of 5.8% implied by a value estimate of $85,030,299 was calculated using only the NOI for Year 1. In this example, many of the existing leases specify a contract rate that is below the market rate. As these leases are renewed at market levels during the 10-year holding period, the NOI is projected to increase. By the end of the holding period, most of the leases will have been renewed. Thus, the projected increase in NOI from Year 11 onward should closely parallel changes in the market rental rate, and the 10% capitalization rate used to estimate the resale price would reflect this assumption.

For example, if NOI is projected to increase 5% per year from Year 11 onward and the discount rate is still assumed to be 15%, then the exponential-curve property model discussed earlier in this chapter, which implies a capitalization rate of 10%, would be appropriate. In addition, all else being equal, terminal capitalization rates are usually higher than first-year capitalization rates because of the increased risk associated with projecting income several years into the future.

Recapture requirements for older properties are generally also higher because of the greater associated risk.

The estimated present value of the property, $85,030,299 in this example, reflects the projected increase in *NOI* due to lease renewals and increases in the market rental rate and the estimated resale price. The resulting value estimate for the property is high relative to the *NOI* for the first year, which explains the relatively low overall capitalization rate of 5.8%. Although many investors base their purchase decisions on total expected yield (discount rate), most have minimum first-year return requirements (capitalization rate).

The long-term projections of income and expenses developed by appraisers will almost always differ from actual property income and expenses. However, rather than attempt to forecast the peaks and troughs that will occur during an anticipated holding period, appraisers simulate how market participants expect the property to perform over the extended holding period.

The preceding example illustrates the need to consider carefully the anticipated pattern of *NOI* when selecting an overall capitalization rate to be used in direct capitalization or a property model for yield capitalization. Capitalization rates can differ significantly for properties with different patterns of *NOI* beyond the first year and different resale potential.

However, the absence of a regular income pattern does not necessarily mean that detailed DCF analysis is the only method that should be considered. The appraiser may discover that one of the standard valuation models can be adjusted to compensate for a deviation from the regular income pattern or that a special valuation model can be devised to solve the problem at hand.

MORTGAGE INTERESTS

The purchase and ownership of real property nearly always involves debt capital secured with the real estate as collateral. Appraisers use mortgage information in the form of dollar amounts and rates or factors, depending on the data available, to value income-producing properties. Mortgage information may include 1) the monthly or periodic payments and annual debt service on a level-payment, fully amortized loan; 2) the accompanying partial payment factors and annual constants (R_M); and 3) the balance outstanding (B) on an amortized loan at any time before it is fully amortized, expressed as a dollar amount or a percentage of the original loan amount. The percentage or proportion of the principal amount paid off before full amortization (P) must also be calculated, especially if mortgage-equity analysis is used.

Mortgage investments have a great impact on real property value and equity yield rates. Because yield is a significant consideration in the lender's decision to invest in a mortgage interest in real estate, the lender's yield must be understood and often calculated. In the absence of any points and participation or accrual feature the lender's yield equals the interest rate.

Types of Mortgage Loans

A mortgage is a legal document pledging a described property as security or collateral for the repayment of a loan under certain terms and conditions. There are various types of mortgage loans and many are identified by their repayment characteristics—e.g., interest only, direct reduction, variable rate, and equity participation mortgages.

An interest-only mortgage is a nonamortizing loan in which the lender receives interest only during the term of the loan and recovers the principal in a lump sum at the time of maturity.

A direct reduction mortgage is a mortgage loan that is repaid in periodic, usually equal, installments that include repayment of part of the principal and the interest due on the unpaid balance. Although the payments are level, the amount of principal and interest varies with each payment. In the most common type of direct reduction mortgage, the interest component decreases with each payment while the principal or amortization component increases.

An adjustable variable-rate mortgage is a mortgage with an interest rate that may move up or down following a specified schedule or in accordance with the movements of a standard or index to which the interest rate is tied.

A wraparound mortgage is a mortgage that is subordinate to, but inclusive of, any existing mortgage(s) on a property. Usually, a third-party lender refinances the property, assuming the existing mortgage and its debt service which are wrapped around a new, junior mortgage. A wraparound lender gives the borrower the difference between the outstanding balance on the existing mortgage(s) and the face amount of the new mortgage.

A participation mortgage is a mortgage in which the lender receives a share of the income and sometimes the reversion from a property on which the lender has made a loan. Some variants give the lender a share of annual income.

A shared appreciation mortgage is a mortgage in which the borrower receives assistance in the form of capital when buying the real property in return for a portion of the property's future appreciation in value.

A convertible mortgage is a mortgage in which the lender may choose to take an equity interest in the real estate in lieu of cash amortization payments by the borrower. In this way the mortgage interests of the lender may be converted into equity ownership at specified times during the life of the mortgage.

A graduated-payment mortgage is a mortgage designed to aid borrowers by matching mortgage payments to projected increases in income; the periodic payments start out low and gradually increase. Because the borrower's payments in the early years of the loan are not sufficient to pay the entire interest due or to amortize the mortgage, the borrower actually borrows the difference between the payments and the current interest due.

A zero-coupon mortgage is a debt secured by real estate with interest payments accruing rather than being paid by the borrower; in some circumstances, a rate of interest may be imputed—e.g., for income taxation.

Mortgage Components

Periodic (Monthly) Payment

The monthly payment factor for a fully amortized, monthly payment loan with equal payments is the direct reduction loan factor, or monthly constant, for the loan given the interest rate and amortization term. Thus, the monthly payment factor for a 30-year, fully amortized, level monthly payment loan at 10.5% interest is 0.009147. This number can be obtained from a direct reduction loan table or by solving for the monthly payment (PMT) on a preprogrammed financial calculator given the number of periods (n), the interest rate (i), and the principal loan amount.

Assume that the loan described above had an initial principal amount of $160,000. The monthly payment required to amortize the principal over 30 years and provide interest at the nominal rate of 15.5% on the outstanding balance each month would be

$$\$160,000 \times 0.013\,045 = \$2,087.20$$

Annual Debt Service and Loan Constant

Cash flows are typically converted to an annual basis for real property valuation, so it is useful to calculate the amount of annual debt service as well as the monthly payments. For a 30-year, fully amortized, level monthly payment loan of $160,000 at a 15.5% interest rate, the annual debt service is

$$\$2,087.20 \times 12 = \$25,046.40$$

The annual loan constant is simply the ratio of annual debt service to the loan principal. (The annual loan constant, often called the mortgage constant, describes a rate although it is actually the annual debt service per dollar of mortgage loan outstanding which may be expressed as a dollar amount.) The annual loan constant is expressed as R_M to signify that it is a capitalization rate for the loan or debt portion of the real estate investment. For the loan mentioned, the annual loan constant can be calculated as follows:

$$
\begin{aligned}
R_M &= \frac{\text{Annual debt service}}{\text{Loan principal}} \\
&= \frac{\$25,046.40}{\$160,000.00} \\
&= 0.156540
\end{aligned}
$$

The annual loan constant can also be obtained when the amount of the loan principal is not known. In this case the monthly payment factor is simply multiplied by 12.

$$
\begin{aligned}
R_M &= \text{monthly payment factor} \times 12 \\
&= 0.013045 \times 12 \\
&= 0.156540
\end{aligned}
$$

Although these figures are rounded to the nearest cent, in actual practice most loan constants are rounded up to make sure that the loan will be repaid during the stated amortization period.

Outstanding Balance

Properties are frequently sold, or loans may be refinanced, before the loan on the property is fully amortized. Furthermore, loans often mature before the completion of loan amortization. In such cases there is an outstanding balance or balloon payment due on the note; from the lender's point of view, this is the loan or debt reversion to the lender.

The outstanding balance (B) on any level-payment, amortized loan is the present value of the debt service over the *remaining* amortization period discounted at the interest rate. Thus, at the end of 10 years, the balance for the 30-year note discussed above would be the present value of 20 years of remaining payments. The balance is calculated by multiplying the monthly payment by the present value of $1 per period factor (monthly) for 20 years at the interest rate. Alternatively, the balloon payment, or future value, may be calculated.

$$B = \$2,087.20 \times 73.861752$$
$$= \$154,164.25$$

Similarly, the outstanding balance at the end of 18 years would be equal to the monthly payment times the present value of $1 per period factor (monthly) for 12 years at the interest rate.

$$B = \$2,087.20 \times 65.222881$$
$$= \$136,133.20$$

The outstanding balance on a loan can also be expressed as a percentage of the original principal. This is useful, and sometimes necessary, if dollar amounts are not given or are unavailable.

For a 10-year projection with 20 years remaining on the note,

$$B = \frac{\$154,164.25}{\$160,000.00}$$
$$= 0.963527$$

For an 18-year projection with 12 years remaining on the note,

$$B = \frac{\$136,133.20}{\$160,000.00}$$
$$= 0.850833$$

A percentage balance can also be calculated as the ratio of the present value of $1 per period factor for the remaining term of the loan at the specified interest rate divided by the present value of $1 per period factor for the full term of the loan at the interest rate. This can be expressed as

$$B = \frac{PV\ 1/P\ \text{remaining term}}{PV\ 1/P\ \text{full term}}$$

where P is the percentage of the loan paid off over the given term.

In the case of the 30-year, 15.5% loan, the balance for a 10-year projection with 20 years remaining is calculated as

$$B = \frac{73.861752}{76.656729}$$
$$= 0.963539$$

For a 18-year projection with 12 years remaining, the balance would be

$$B = \frac{65.222881}{76.656729}$$
$$= 0.850844$$

These results are similar to those obtained using dollar amounts.

Percentage of Loan Paid Off

It is often necessary to calculate the percentage of the loan paid off before full amortization over the projection period, especially in Ellwood mortgage-equity analysis. The percentage of the loan paid off is expressed as P and is most readily calculated as the complement of B.

$$P = 1 - B$$

For the 30-year note, P is calculated as follows:

$$P_{10} = 1-0.963539$$
$$= 0.036461$$
$$P_{18} = 1-0.850844$$
$$= 0.149156$$

The percentage of the loan paid off prior to full amortization over the projection period (P) can also be calculated directly. There are many different procedures for this operation, but they are not all presented here. The simplest and most direct procedure is to calculate P as the *ratio* of the sinking fund factor for the full term (monthly) divided by the sinking fund factor for the projection period (monthly).

$$P = \frac{1/S_n}{1/S_{nP}}$$

For the 30-year monthly payment note at 15.5%, the calculations are

$$P_{10} = \frac{0.000129}{0.003524}$$
$$= 0.036606$$

$$P_{18} = \frac{0.000129}{0.000862}$$
$$= 0.149652$$

Any differences are due to rounding.

Lender's Yield

The monetary benefits that accrue to the lender are similar to the benefits received by the equity owner—i.e., periodic income from debt service and the reversion represented by the outstanding principal paid off prior to or at maturity. In calculating the lender's yield, discounting formulas must be applied.

To illustrate how the lender's yield on a mortgage loan investment is calculated, consider a mortgage loan with the following characteristics.

Loan amount	$100,000
Interest rate	13.5%
Term	25 years
Payment	Monthly
Balance in five years	$96,544
Points	3
Other costs	Borrower to pay all other costs

If the mortgage runs full term, the yield can be obtained using a calculator.

$$n = 300$$
$$PMT = \$1{,}165.65$$
$$PV = \$97{,}000 \ (\$100{,}000 \text{ less 3 points, or } \$3{,}000)^*$$
$$i = 13.97\%$$

* Each point is equal to 1% of the loan amount: $100,000 × 0.01 = $1,000.

The lender's yield is greater than the nominal interest rate because of points paid by the borrower. In effect, the lender only loaned $97,000 ($100,000 – $3,000 which was paid by the borrower), yet received a stream of debt service payments based on $100,000. If the mortgage is paid off in five years, the lender's yield is calculated with these figures.

$$n = 60$$
$$PMT = \$1{,}165.65$$
$$PV = \$97{,}000$$
$$i = 14.36\%$$

If there were no points in either of these examples, the yield to the lender would be 13.5% in each case. Points or any other monetary payments that reduce the lender's investment are important considerations in calculating the lender's yield. It should also be noted that the lender's yield may be supplemented through the syndication process.

In some depressed markets lenders may find that the property securing the loan has declined in value to the point that the loan balance exceeds the property's value. In this case there is no longer any equity interest in the property, and the value of the loan may often be calculated based on the actual cash flows to the property rather than the cash flows projected when the loan contract was obtained. To do otherwise would be to estimate the value of the mortgage interest as greater than the value of the property.

EQUITY INTERESTS

Equity in real property is the owner's interest after all claims and liens have been satisfied. An equity interest, like a mortgage loan, represents a financial interest in real property.

Equity ownership in real property can be legally accomplished in many ways—e.g., as an individual owner, joint owner, partner, or shareholder in a corporation. The legal form of equity ownership does not affect property value in most appraisal assignments. However, an appraiser is sometimes called upon to estimate the value of a specific legal form of equity interest.

For example, an appraiser may be asked to value a limited partner's equity interest in a partnership which was created solely to make the individual the legal owner of the real property. Partial interests must usually be valued at less than their pro rata share of ownership, especially if the holder of the partial interest does not have any voice in the management or control of the asset. An assignment to value a limited partnership interest may be undertaken to appraise assets for estate tax purposes or for sale or purchase decisions.

Because the equity side of the real estate market dominates sales activity, appraisers must thoroughly understand the benefits that accrue to equity owners and know how equity yield is calculated.

Benefits of Equity Ownership

Equity owners look for two kinds of benefits: income, usually on an annual basis, and reversion at the end of the ownership period. Income is the annual cash flow before or after taxes and the reversion is the pre- or after-tax equity proceeds of resale after any outstanding mortgage balance and all selling expenses have been paid. Any refinancing benefits taken during the ownership period are usually viewed as a form of early reversion. In investment analysis assignments the sum of all benefits received over the ownership period is analyzed in comparison to the equity invested to reveal the equity yield rate. In valuation assignments an equity yield rate is applied to the forecast benefits to produce a present value conclusion. If market value is sought, the equity yield rate is derived from the market.

Equity Yield Rate

For the investor the prime measures of investment performance are the equity yield rate and the first-year dividend, usually expressed as the equity capitalization rate (or equity dividend rate), and, to a lesser extent, the price per square foot. An investor may compare the expected equity yield on a real property investment with the yields on alternative investments with commensurate risk (e.g., stocks and bonds) and with a lender's yield on mortgages secured by similar real property. Usually the equity investor will seek a higher yield than the lender because the lender has a more secure position. The lender can foreclose the mortgage and take title to the real property if the mortgage terms are not fulfilled.

The equity yield rate must be distinguished conceptually from the equity capitalization rate. The equity yield rate (Y_E) is a rate of return *on* equity capital; the equity capitalization rate is simply the relationship between one year's equity income or cash flow and equity capital (cash on cash). The equity yield rate is a full measure of investment performance, but the equity capitalization rate is not. The equity capitalization rate is *not* a rate of return on capital. It may be more or less than the eventual equity yield on the capital invested, depending on future changes in equity income and equity value. Although it cannot be considered a full measure of performance, the equity capitalization rate is useful and important. In certain markets and at certain times, it is the preferred measure of investment performance.

Derivation of the Equity Yield Rate

To estimate equity yield rates, appraisers must do market research. This research can take many forms and may include one or more of the following analyses.

- Direct comparison with equity yield rates abstracted from recent comparable sales (For an example, see the two-variable algebraic method of rate abstraction described in Chapter 22.)
- Verification of the prospective equity yields considered by market participants, particularly buyers, in recent or anticipated sales
- Comparison with the equity yield rates achieved in alternative investments of comparable risk such as stocks and bonds
- Review of published investor surveys, which can provide guidelines for appraisers

Appropriate equity yield rates vary with property characteristics. To develop an equity yield rate from recent comparable sales, an appraiser analyzes the forecast benefits of equity ownership in relation to the equity capital invested. This process will be covered in the next chapter.

Leverage

The term *leverage* is often used to show how borrowed funds increase or decrease the amount that would be considered the equity return free and clear. In the recent past leverage has been used almost exclusively to analyze equity capitalization rates in relation to overall and mortgage capitalization rates. However, leverage may also be considered in the analysis of equity yield rates. The underlying principles are the same in both cases. (See Table 21.3 and the example that follows.)

Table 21.3 Leverage Analysis

Type of Leverage	Equity Cap Rate (R_E)	Equity Yield Rate (Y_E)
Positive	R_O greater than R_M	Y_O greater than Y_M
Zero	R_O equals R_M	Y_O equals Y_M
Negative	R_O less than R_M	Y_O less than Y_M

In analyzing cash flows, positive leverage is indicated when the overall capitalization rate is greater than the mortgage capitalization rate. The difference between the two rates directly benefits the equity owner, so the equity capitalization rate is higher than it would be if there were no mortgage. For example, assume a property was sold for $100,000 and analysis of the transaction indicates a net operating income of $10,000, an equity investment of $25,000, and a mortgage of $75,000 payable in annual installments of $7,125.00. The indicated capitalization rates are:

Overall (R_O)	10.0%
Mortgage (R_M)	9.5%
Equity (R_E)	11.5%

Because the mortgage capitalization rate is less than the overall capitalization rate, the equity interest receives a benefit that is reflected in the equity capitalization rate. If there were no mortgage, the equity capitalization rate would be 10.0%, the same as the overall capitalization rate. When the overall capitalization rate exceeds the mortgage capitalization rate, positive leverage results. Similarly, when the overall yield rate exceeds the mortgage yield rate, positive leverage is indicated and the equity yield rate must exceed the overall yield rate. However, if the overall capitalization rate is less than the mortgage capitalization rate or the overall yield rate is less than the mortgage yield rate, negative leverage results. The leverage is zero when the overall rate, the mortgage capitalization rate, and the yield rate are equal.

The analysis of leverage is important because positive or negative leverage can affect the level of risk associated with a real property investment and the yield required to satisfy an investor willing to assume the risk. Often negative leverage on early cash flows may suggest the need to achieve a greater equity yield rate. Conversely, positive leverage on early cash flows may reduce the equity yield rate required. On a yield basis, positive equity yield leverage is expected due to the greater risk associated with equity interest as compared to the more secure mortgage interest. If negative equity yield leverage is anticipated, the equity buyer may consider the investment to be inappropriate.

SUMMARY

Yield capitalization is used to convert future benefits into present value by discounting each future benefit at an appropriate yield rate or by applying an overall rate that explicitly reflects the investment's income pattern, change in value, and yield rate. For market value appraisals, the analysis focuses on the yield anticipated by typical investors. In yield capitalization an appraiser 1) selects an appropriate holding period; 2) forecasts all future cash flows or cash flow patterns; 3) selects the appropriate yield, or discount, rate; and 4) converts the future benefits into present value by discounting each annual future benefit or applying an overall rate.

The application of rates that reflect an appropriate yield, the use of present value factors, and discounted cash flow analysis are yield capitalization procedures. To derive overall capitalization rates, mortgage-equity formulas and yield rate/value change formulas may be applied; residual techniques may also be used in yield capitalization.

A knowledge of *income patterns* and *capital return concepts* is fundamental to the discounting process. An *annuity* is literally an annual income, but it has come to mean a program or contract of regular payments in stipulated amounts. An annuity can be level, increasing, or decreasing, but it must be scheduled at regular intervals in predictable amounts. Real estate or rental income may have the characteristics of an annuity.

The *return on* an investment induces investors to forego the present benefits of the immediate use of capital for future benefits. To a lender this return is interest, to equity investors it is yield. The investor's objective is a total return that exceeds the amount invested. The discounting procedure assumes that *the return of the investment* is accomplished through periodic income, the reversion, or a combination of both. Tax shelter is a less important by-product of some investments.

An appraiser converts periodic income and reversion into present value through the discounting procedure. The present value of a prospective benefit is less than the future value of that benefit. A future payment is discounted to present value by calculating the amount that should be invested today to grow with compound interest to equal the future payment. The standard discounting formula is:

$$\text{Present value} = \frac{\text{Future value}}{(1+i)^n}$$

where i is the rate of return on capital per period and n is the number of periods that payment will be deferred. If a series of future payments is expected, the total present value of the series is the sum of all the present values.

When amounts are compounded or discounted, the *effective interest* rate is used. On an annual basis, this rate is identical to the *nominal interest rate*. When amounts are compounded or discounted more often than annually, the nominal interest rate is divided by the number of compounding or discounting periods. In *discounted cash flow (DCF) analysis*, the quantity, variability, timing, and duration of cash flows are specified. The cash flows that constitute the periodic income (i.e., the NOI for the entire property or the cash flows to a specific property interest) and the reversion are discounted with the DCF formula:

$$PV = \frac{CF_1}{1+Y} + \frac{CF_2}{(1+Y)^2} + \frac{CF_3}{(1+Y)^3} + \ldots + \frac{CF_n}{(1+Y)^n}$$

where Y represents the appropriate periodic yield, or discount rate and n is the number of periods in the projection. The formula can be used to estimate total property value (V_O), loan value (V_M), equity value (V_E), leased fee value (V_{LF}), or leasehold value (V_{LH}). Any series of periodic incomes, with or without a reversion, can be valued with this basic formula.

The actual yield on an investment cannot be calculated until the investment is sold, but investors anticipate yields. Although historical yield rates are relevant, they are not necessarily reliable indicators of current yield. The appraiser should select a *yield rate* that reflects the rates currently anticipated by typical market buyers and sellers for the property being appraised.

Rates can be selected by researching the expectations of market participants and directly analyzing comparable sales transactions or indirectly estimating the income expectancy and likely reversion of comparable properties. To select an appropriate yield rate, the appraiser should also assess the competition for capital in other financial markets. The yield rates applied to discount net rental incomes subject to lease contracts may differ from those applied to the reversion because the resale value is subject to open-market conditions and different risks.

Once the appraiser has specified the amount, timing, and duration of all cash flows, the *income stream pattern* over the projection period can be forecast. There are three major types of annuities. A *variable annuity* is an income stream in which the payment amounts vary per period; a *level annuity* is an income stream in which the payment amounts are equal and unchanging; and an *increasing or decreasing annuity* is an income stream that is expected to change in a systematic pattern. There are two types of level annuities—ordinary annuities and annuities payable in advance. There are three types of increasing or decreasing annuities— step-up or step-down annuities, straight-line (constant-amount) change per period annuities, and exponential-curve (constant-ratio) change per period annuities.

Periodic income and the *reversion,* the future value obtained by selling the property at the end of the holding period, are the prime financial benefits of income-producing property. The reversion may be considered a future cash flow because it is the anticipated return of capital upon termination of the investment. The number of periodic income streams and reversions for a property varies according to the property interests involved (e.g., fee simple, mortgagee [lender], equity investor, leased fee, and leasehold).

The reversion often represents a major portion of the benefits provided by income-producing property. In deciding what portion of the return of the investment the reversion provides, the investor considers three possible outcomes. The property may increase in value over the holding period, it may not change in value, or it may decline in value.

An appraiser projects the reversion to a property when the property is expected to be sold. The projected *proceeds of resale* are equal to the net difference between the future transaction price and all selling expenses such as brokerage commissions, legal fees, closing costs, transfer taxes, and possible penalties for the prepayment of debt.

Specific valuation models, or formulas, categorized as income or property models have been developed to project patterns of benefits. Income models are applied only to income streams, not to anticipated reversions. Property models can be used to value an income stream and the reversion in one operation. *Income models* describe patterns of *variable or irregular income*, in which each benefit is separately discounted: *level income, straight-line (constant-amount) change per period income, and exponential-curve (constant-ratio) change per period income.*

The present value of level income can be estimated by capitalization in perpetuity, in which the discount rate equals the overall capitalization rate; by capitalization under the Inwood premise, which employs a single discount rate and is the basis of compound interest tables; or by capitalization under the Hoskold premise, which employs the sum of two separate rates—a speculative rate for risk and a safe rate for the sinking fund. The Hoskold premise is not generally used.

The formula used to calculate the present value of an income pattern characterized by a straight-line (constant-amount) increase per period is:

$$\text{Present value} = (d + hn)a_n - \frac{h(n-a_n)}{i}$$

where d is the starting income at the end of the first period, h is the dollar increase per period, n is the number of periods, and a_n is the present value of $1 per period at rate i for n periods. The formula for straight-line income patterns should *not* be confused with straight capitalization with straight-line recapture, which is a property model formula.

To obtain the present value of an annuity with an income pattern subject to exponential-curve (constant-ratio) increases per period, the following formula is used:

$$\text{Present value} = \frac{1-(1+x)^n/(1+i)^n}{i-x}$$

where the annuity starts at \$1 at the end of the first period, increases at the rate of x per n periods, and is discounted at the annual rate of i. In the formula x is positive for increase and negative for decrease.

Property models can be used when changes in both property value and income can be projected according to a regular or predictable pattern. In yield capitalization a capitalization rate (R) is determined by considering the prospective rate of return on capital and the timing of capital recapture. Real estate investors consider property appreciation or depreciation, if any, as part of the eventual yield. An investor usually anticipates that the total eventual yield rate, which is a complete measure of profit, will be higher than the expected income rate (R_O).

The capitalization rate for an appreciating property equals the total yield rate minus an adjustment for expected value growth $(R = Y-A)$. The capitalization rate for a depreciating property equals the yield rate plus an adjustment for expected value loss $(R = Y + A)$. The symbol A is used to express a function of the relative change in property value, represented by the Greek letter delta (Δ). To calculate the adjustment, Δ must be multiplied by a conversion factor (e.g., an annual sinking fund factor or an annual recapture rate) expressed as a. Thus, $R = Y-\Delta a$ and $R = Y + \Delta a$. Once the appropriate capitalization rate is obtained, it can be used in the general formula $V = I/R$.

Property models describe *properties with level income and unchanging value* with capitalization in perpetuity $(R = Y)$; *properties with level income and changing value* $(a = \text{sinking fund})$; *properties in which income and value are increasing or decreasing in straight-line, constant amounts* with straight capitalization with straight-line recapture $(a = \text{straight-line recapture rate})$; *properties in which income and value are increasing or decreasing at an exponential-curve, constant ratio* $(\Delta a = \text{periodic compound rate of change, or } CR)$; and *properties with income and value changes that do not follow a regular pattern,* in which each benefit must be separately discounted.

The mortgage information needed to value income-producing properties includes the *periodic (monthly, quarterly, semi-annual, or annual) payment factor,* or direct reduction loan factor, for the given loan interest rate and amortization term; the *annual debt service* used to compute the partial payment factor or annual constant $(R_M = \text{annual debt service/loan principal and } R_M = \text{monthly payment factor} \times 12)$; the *outstanding balance* (B) at any time prior to full amortization $(B = PV$ of the debt service over the remaining amortization period discounted at the interest rate and $B = \text{monthly payment} \times PV$ of \$1 per period factor for the remaining years at the interest rate); and the *percentage of the principal amount paid off* (*P*) prior to full amortization ($P = 1 - B$ and P = the sinking fund factor for the full term/the sinking fund factor for the projection period

$$P = \frac{1/S_n}{(1/S_{nP})}$$

Mortgages affect real property values and equity yield rates. The *lender's yield* influences a lender's decision to invest in a real estate mortgage.

A *mortgage* is a legal document in which a described property is pledged as security or collateral for the repayment of a loan under certain terms and conditions. Many types of mortgages are identified by their repayment characteristics— e.g., *interest-only, direct reduction, adjustable or variable-rate, wraparound, equity participation, shared appreciation, convertible, graduated-payment*, and *zero-coupon* mortgages.

Real estate *equity* is the owner's interest after all claims and liens are satisfied. Equity ownership can be held by an individual owner, joint owner, a partnership, or corporate shareholders. At least two benefits are received by equity owners: income in the form of annual pre- or after-tax cash flows and reversion, the equity proceeds of resale. When an equity yield rate is applied to forecast benefits, a present value conclusion results.

An *equity yield rate* (Y_E) is a rate of return *on* equity capital and, thus, is a full measure of investment performance. It should not be confused with an equity capitalization rate, which is simply the relationship between one year's equity income and equity capital. Equity yield rates can be derived directly by comparing the equity yield rates of recent comparable sales, by verifying prospective equity yields with the participants in recent or anticipated sales, by discussing market expectations with market participants and reviewing published materials, or by comparing the equity yield rates achieved on alternative investments with commensurate risks such as certain stocks and bonds.

Leverage describes how borrowed funds increase or decrease the equity return. Leverage is analyzed in conjunction with equity capitalization rates and equity yield rates. The characteristic relationships between R_O and R_M and Y_O and Y_M, and the indicated leverage of R_E and Y_E are shown below:

Type of Leverage	Equity Capitalization Rate(R_M)	Equity Yield Rate (Y_E)
Positive	R_O greater than R_M	Y_O greater than Y_M
Zero	R_O equals R_M	Y_O equals Y_M
Negative	R_O less than R_M	Y_O less than Y_M

The analysis of leverage is important because positive or negative leverage can affect the risk of an investment and the yield required to satisfy an investor willing to assume that risk.

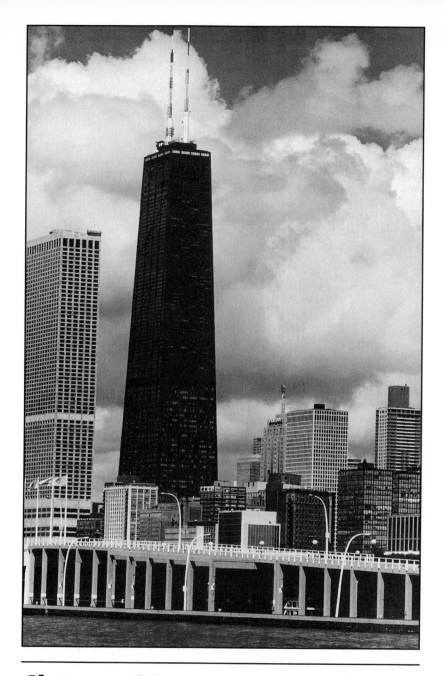

Chapter 22

YIELD CAPITALIZATION—
ADVANCED APPLICATIONS

*L*W. Ellwood was the first to organize, develop, and promulgate the use of mortgage-equity analysis in yield capitalization for real property valuation. He theorized that mortgage money plays a major role in determining real property prices and values. Ellwood saw real property investments as a combination of two components—debt and equity—and held that the return requirements of both components must be satisfied through income, reversion, or a combination of the two. Thus, Ellwood developed an approach for estimating property value that made explicit assumptions as to what a mortgage lender and an equity investor would expect from the property.

In general mortgage-equity analysis involves estimating the value of a property on the basis of both mortgage and equity return requirements. The value of the equity interest in the property is found by discounting the pre-tax cash flows available to the equity investor. The equity yield rate (Y_E) is used as the discount rate. The total value of the property is equal to the present value of the equity position plus the value of the mortgage. This is true whether the value is found using discounted cash flow analysis or yield capitalization formulas that have been developed for mortgage-equity analysis.

MORTGAGE-EQUITY ANALYSIS

Applications

Mortgage-equity analysis can facilitate the valuation process in many ways. It may be used 1) to compose overall rates, 2) to derive building and land capitalization rates for residual techniques, 3) to analyze and test the capitalization rates obtained with other capitalization techniques, 4) as an investment analysis tool to test the values indicated by the sales comparison and cost approaches, and 5) to analyze a capitalization rate graphically.

Given a set of assumptions concerning the *NOI*, mortgage (amount, rate, and term), reversion (rate of appreciation or depreciation), equity yield rate, and projection period, mortgage-equity analysis may be employed to estimate the present value of the equity and to arrive at the total property value. The following example illustrates a general approach to mortgage-equity analysis.

Given:	
Annual *NOI* (level)	$25,000
Projection period	10 years
Loan amount	$168,000
Loan terms*	
Interest rate	9%
Amortization term	
(monthly payments)	25 years
Estimated reversion	$201,600
Equity yield rate	15%

* Contract terms are at current market rates

Using these assumptions, cash flow to the equity investor can be projected as follows:

Annual Cash Flow from Operations—Years 1-10	
Annual net operating income	$25,000
Annual debt service	16,918
Pre-tax cash flow	$8,082
Cash Flow from Reversion—Year 10	
Estimated resale price	$201,600
Mortgage balance	139,002
Cash flow from reversion	$62,598

Using the present value factor for a 15% yield rate and a 10-year holding period, we may calculate the present value of the cash flows to the equity investor as follows:

Years	Cash Flow	Present Value Factor	Present Value
1-10	$8,082	5.018769*	$40,562
10	$62,598	0.247185†	15,473
Present value of equity			$56,035

*Ordinary level annuity (present value of $1 per period) factor
†Reversion (present value of $1) factor

The total property value can now be found by adding the present value of the equity to the present value of the loan.[1]

Present value of the equity	$56,035
Present value of the loan	168,000
Total value	$224,035

This example illustrates a fairly straightforward application of mortgage-equity analysis. The present value of the equity was easily calculated by discounting the dollar estimates of the cash flows. The assumptions in this example were simplified in several ways. First, the income was assumed to be level. In a more complex situation, income may be expected to change over the holding period. Second, the loan amount was specified in dollars.[2] If the loan amount were assumed to be based on a loan-to-value ratio, the dollar amount of the loan would depend on the property value being calculated. In such a case the cash flows to the equity investor could not be specified in dollars and discounted as they were in the example. Third, the resale price was specified in dollars.[3] Investors often

---

1. Because the loan is assumed to be at current market rates, the face amount of the loan is equal to the value of the loan to the lender.
2. This might be the case if the property were being valued subject to an existing loan. Such a situation is illustrated later in this chapter. Alternatively, the dollar amount may have resulted from a separate calculation of the maximum amount that could be borrowed to meet a minimum debt coverage ratio.
3. This situation might occur if there is a purchase option in a lease that the appraiser believes will be exercised. Alternatively, a dollar estimate may be the result of a separate estimate of the resale price calculated by applying a capitalization rate to the income at the end of the holding period. This situation is illustrated later in this chapter.

assume that property values will change by a specified percentage amount over the holding period (see Chapter 21). Thus the resale price depends on the property value being calculated. Finally, in the preceding example the total property value is greater than the loan amount. If the opposite were true, the value of the loan could *not* exceed the combined debt and equity interests in the property.

When either the loan amount or the resale price depends on the value of the property, the cash flows cannot be projected in dollar amounts and discounted. An alternative procedure must be used to solve for the present value. One such alternative is to use a yield capitalization formula that has been developed to solve this type of problem.[4] This is what L. W. Ellwood did when he developed the Ellwood equation, which is illustrated in the following section.

Mortgage-Equity Formula

The general mortgage-equity formula is:

$$R_O = \frac{Y_E - M\,(Y_E + P\,1/S_n - R_M) - \Delta_O\,1/S_n}{1 + \Delta_I\,J}$$

where:

R_O = overall capitalization rate
Y_E = equity yield rate
M = loan-to-value ratio
P = percentage of loan paid off
$1/S_n$ = sinking fund factor at the equity yield rate
R_M = mortgage capitalization rate or mortgage constant
Δ_O = change in total property value
Δ_I = total ratio change in income
J = J factor (This symbol is discussed later in the chapter.)

The part of the formula represented as $Y_E - M\,(Y_E + P\,1/S_n - R_M)$ can be referred to as the *basic capitalization rate* (r), which satisfies the lender's requirement and adjusts for amortization. It also satisfies the investor's equity yield requirement before any adjustment is made for income and value changes. Therefore, the basic rate starts with an investor's yield requirement and adjusts it to reflect the effect of financing. The resulting basic capitalization rate is a building block from which an overall capitalization rate can be developed with additional assumptions.

If level income and no change in property value are anticipated, the basic rate will be identical to the overall capitalization rate. The last part of the numerator, $\Delta_O\,1/S_n$, allows the appraiser to adjust the basic rate to reflect an expected change in overall property value. If the value change is positive, sometimes referred to as property *appreciation*, the overall capitalization rate is reduced to reflect this an-

---

4. A computer can be programmed to handle this type of valuation problem. For a discussion of this procedure, see Jeffrey D. Fisher, "Using Circular Reference in Spreadsheets to Estimate Value," *The Quarterly Byte*, vol. 5, no. 4, fourth quarter 1989.

ticipated monetary benefit; if the change is negative, referred to as *depreciation*, the overall capitalization rate is increased.

Finally, the denominator, $1 + \Delta_i J$, accounts for any change in income. The J factor is always positive. Thus, if the change in income is positive, the denominator will be greater than one and the overall rate will be reduced. If the change in income is negative, the overall rate will be increased. For level-income applications, $\Delta = 0$, so the denominator is $1 + 0$, or 1.

Akerson Format

The mortgage-equity procedure developed by Charles B. Akerson substitutes an arithmetic format for the algebraic equation in the Ellwood formula.[5] This format is applicable to level-income situations; when modified with the J factor, it can also be applied to changing-income situations.

The Akerson format is

Loan ratio × annual constant	= _____
Equity ratio × equity yield rate	= + _____
Loan ratio × % paid off in projection period × $1/S_n$	= - _____
Basic rate (r)	= _____
+ dep or - app × $1/S_n$	= + _____
Overall capitalization rate	= _____

where $1/S_n$ is the sinking fund factor at the equity yield rate for the projection period and dep/app denotes the change in value from property depreciation or appreciation during the projection period.

Level-Income Applications

Mortgage-equity analysis can be used to value real property investments with level income streams or variable income streams converted to level equivalents using overall capitalization rates and residual techniques.

Use of Overall Capitalization Rates

In the simplest application of the mortgage-equity formula and the Akerson format, a level income and a stable or changing overall property value are assumed. The following example illustrates the application of the mortgage-equity formula using an overall capitalization rate applied to a level flow of income.

NOI (level)	$25,000
Projection period	10 years
Loan terms	
Interest rate	9%
Amortization term (monthly payments)	25 years
Loan-to-value ratio	75%
Property value change	10% loss
Equity yield rate	15%

---

5. The format was first presented by Charles B. Akerson in "Ellwood without Algebra," *The Appraisal Journal* (July 1970).

The overall rate is calculated as follows:

$$R_O = \frac{Y_E - M\,(Y_E + P1/S_n - R_M) - \Delta_O\,1/S_n}{1 + \Delta_I\,J}$$

$$R_O = \frac{0.15 - 0.75\,(0.15 + 0.1726 \times 0.04925 - 0.1007) - (-0.10 \times 0.04925)}{1 + 0 \times J}$$

$$R_O = \frac{0.15 - 0.75\,(0.057801) + 0.004925}{1}$$

$$R_O = 0.15 - 0.043350 + 0.004925$$

$$R_O = \frac{0.111575}{1}$$

$$R_O = 0.1116 \text{ (rounded)}$$

The capitalized value of the investment is $25,000/0.1116 = $224,014

Using the same data and assumptions, an identical value can be derived by applying the Akerson format.

0.75 × 0.100704	=	0.075528
0.25 × 0.15	=	+0.037500
−0.75 × 0.172608 × 0.049252	=	−0.006376
Basic rate (r)	=	0.106652
0.10 × 0.049252	=	+0.004925
R_O	=	0.111577
The capitalized value is $25,000/0.1116	=	$224,014

Note that the answer derived in this example is virtually the same as the answer to the first problem in this chapter in which the cash flows were discounted in dollars. This is true because the dollar amount of the loan and resale price are approximately the same in both examples. That is, the implied amount of the loan is 75% of $224,014, or approximately $168,000 and the implied resale price is 90% of $224,014, or approximately $201,600. It is important to realize, however, that this was not known until the problem was solved. The examples were designed to produce the same answer to demonstrate that both problems are based on the same concepts of discounted cash flow analysis. In fact, it is possible to check the answer found with the Ellwood formula by discounting the implied cash flows, the procedure used to solve the first problem.

Use of Residual Techniques

Land and building residual techniques can be applied with land and building capitalization rates based on mortgage-equity procedures. The general mortgage-equity formula or the Akerson format is applied to derive a basic rate, which is used to develop land and building capitalization rates.

For example, assume that a commercial property is expected to produce level annual income of $15,000 per year over a 10-year term. Mortgage financing is available at a 75% loan-to-value ratio, and monthly payments at 11% interest are made over an amortization term of 25 years. The land is currently valued at $65,000 and is forecast to have a value of $78,000 at the end of the projection period, indicating a 20% positive change in land value. The building is expected to have no value at the end of the projection period and the equity yield rate is 15%.

The first step in valuing this property is to derive the basic rate (r) using the Ellwood formula.

$$r = Y_E - M (Y_E + P \, 1/S_n - R_M)$$
$$= 0.15 - 0.75 (0.15 + 0.137678 \times 0.049252 - 0.117614)$$
$$= 0.15 - 0.029375$$
$$= 0.120625$$

The Akerson format can also be used to derive the basic rate.

0.75×0.117614	=	0.088211
0.25×0.15	=	0.037500
$0.75 \times 0.137678 \times 0.049252$	=	-0.005086
Basic capitalization rate (r)	=	0.120625

Next, the land and building capitalization rates are calculated. To solve for the land capitalization rate, R_L, the calculations are

$$R_L = r - \Delta_L \, 1/S_n$$
$$= 0.120625 - (0.20 \times 0.049252)$$
$$= 0.120625 - 0.009850$$
$$= 0.110775$$

The building capitalization rate, R_B, is calculated as follows:

$$R_B = r - \Delta_B \, 1/S_n$$
$$= 0.120625 - (-1.0 \times 0.049252)$$
$$= 0.120625 + 0.049252$$
$$= 0.169877$$

These rates can be used to value the property with the building residual technique.

NOI		$ 15,000
Land income		
($V_L \times R_L$) = $65,000 × 0.110775		7,200
Residual income attributable to building		$ 7,800
Capitalized value of building		
($I_B \div R_B$) = $7,800/0.169877		$ 45,916
Plus land value		+ 65,000
Indicated property value		$110,916

When the rates are used in the land residual technique, a similar property value is indicated.

NOI		$ 15,000
Building income		
($V_B \times R_B$) = $46,000 × 0.169877		7,814
Residual income attributable to land		$ 7,186
Capitalized value of land		
($I_L \div R_L$) = $7,186/0.110775		$ 64,870
Plus building value		+ 46,000
Indicated total property value		$110,870

Changing-Income Applications

The general mortgage-equity formula can be applied to income streams that are forecast to change on a curvilinear or exponential-curve (constant-ratio) basis by using a J factor for curvilinear change or a K factor for constant-ratio change. The J factor, used in the stabilizer $(1 + \Delta_I J)$, may be obtained from precomputed tables or calculated with the J-factor formula.[6] The K factor, an income adjuster or stabilizer used to convert a changing income stream into its level equivalent, can be calculated with the K-factor formula.

Use of the J Factor

The J-factor formula for curvilinear income reflects an income stream that changes from time zero in relation to a sinking fund accumulation curve. The formula is

$$ J = 1/S_n \times \frac{n}{1-1/(1 + Y)^n} - \frac{1}{Y} $$

where:

$$ 1/S_n = \text{sinking fund factor at equity yield rate} $$
$$ n = \text{projection period} $$
$$ Y = \text{equity yield rate} $$

Consider the facts set forth in the level annuity example on page 518, but substitute a 20% overall property value gain for the 10% loss and assume a 20% increase in income. Note that the J factor is applied to the income in *the year prior to the first year* of the holding period.

$$ R_O = \frac{0.15 - 0.75 \,(0.15 + 0.172608 \times 0.049252 - 0.100704) - (0.20 \times 0.049252)}{1 + (0.20 \times 0.3259)} $$

$$ = \frac{0.15 - 0.043348 - 0.009850}{1 + 0.0652} $$

$$ = \frac{0.096802}{1.0652} $$

$$ = 0.09088 $$

The capitalized value is $25,000/0.09088 = $275,088

The net operating incomes for the projection period that are implied by the curvilinear J-factor premise are calculated on the following page.

---

6. James J. Mason, ed., comp., *American Institute of Real Estate Appraisers Financial Tables*, rev. ed. (Chicago: American Institute of Real Estate Appraisers, with tables computed by Financial Publishing Company, 1982.)

Period	1st Year Adjustment*		S_n		Periodic Adjustment		Base NOI†		NOI
1	$246.26	×	1/1.000000	=	$246	+	$25,000	=	$25,246
2	$246.26	×	1/0.465116	=	$529	+	$25,000	=	$25,529
3	$246.26	×	1/0.287977	=	$4,855	+	$25,000	=	$25,855
4	$246.26	×	1/0.200265	=	$1,230	+	$25,000	=	$26,230
5	$246.26	×	1/0.148316	=	$1,660	+	$25,000	=	$26,660
6	$246.26	×	1/0.114237	=	$2,156	+	$25,000	=	$27,156
7	$246.26	×	1/0.090360	=	$2,725	+	$25,000	=	$27,725
8	$246.26	×	1/0.072850	=	$3,380	+	$25,000	=	$28,380
9	$246.26	×	1/0.059574	=	$4,134	+	$25,000	=	$29,134
10	$246.26	×	1/0.049252	=	$5,000	+	$25,000	=	$30,000

* This adjustment was derived by multiplying the NOI ($25,000) by the assumed increase in the NOI (20%); the resulting figure ($5,000) was then multiplied by the sinking fund factor for the anticipated 15% equity yield rate over the 10-year projection period ($1/S_n$ = 0.049252)
† The base NOI is the income for the year prior to the beginning of the projection period.

Mathematical proof of the example is provided below.

Valuation of Equity

Period	NOI		Debt Service		Cash to Equity		PVF at 15%		PV
1	$25,246	−	$20,772	=	$4,474	×	0.869565	=	$3,890
2	$25,529	−	$20,772	=	$4,757	×	0.756144	=	$3,597
3	$25,855	−	$20,772	=	$5,083	×	0.657516	=	$3,342
4	$26,230	−	$20,772	=	$5,458	×	0.571753	=	$3,121
5	$26,660	−	$20,772	=	$5,888	×	0.497177	=	$2,927
6	$27,156	−	$20,772	=	$6,384	×	0.432328	=	$2,760
7	$27,725	−	$20,772	=	$6,953	×	0.375937	=	$2,614
8	$28,380	−	$20,772	=	$7,608	×	0.326902	=	$2,487
9	$29,134	−	$20,772	=	$8,362	×	0.284262	=	$2,377
10	$30,000	−	$20,772	=	$9,228	×	0.247185	=	$2,281
					$159,365*	×	0.247185	=	$39,393

Value of equity at 15% = $68,789

Check: $275,028 × 0.25 = $68,757

* The reversion is calculated as follows:

Resale ($275,028 × 1.20)	$330,034
Loan balance ($275,028 × 0.75)(1 − 0.1726)	170,669
Equity proceeds	$159,365

Use of the K Factor

The *K*-factor formula, which is applied to income that changes on an exponential-curve (constant-ratio) basis, is expressed as

$$K = \frac{1 - (1 + C)^n / S^n}{(Y - C)a_n}$$

where:

$$K = \text{factor}$$
$$C = \text{constant-ratio change in income}$$
$$S = \text{future value factor}$$
$$Y = \text{equity yield rate}$$
$$a_n = \text{present value factor for ordinary level annuity}$$

When the general mortgage-equity formula is used to derive an overall capitalization rate applicable to an income expected to change on a constant-ratio basis, K is substituted for the denominator $(1 + \Delta_I J)$. The following example is based on a property with a 70% mortgage at 11% interest, a 20-year amortization period, and monthly mortgage payments. The property has a starting net operating income of $50,000 that will increase by 3% per year. A 10% increase in property value and a 14% equity yield are assumed.

This property can be valued using the K factor in the mortgage-equity formula.

$$R_O = \frac{Y_E - M(Y_E + P\,1/S_n\,R_M) - \Delta_O\,1/S_n}{K}$$

$$= \frac{0.14 - 0.70\,(0.14 + 0.0919 \times 0.1513 - 0.1239) - (0.1 \times 0.1513)}{1.0537}$$

$$= 0.098573$$

The capitalized value of the investment is $50,000/0.098573 = $507,238$

Proof:

Year	Property	Mortgage	Equity
0	−$507,238	−$355,067	−$152,171
1	$50,000	$43,980	$6,020
2	$51,500	$43,980	$7,520
3	$53,045	$43,980	$9,065
4	$54,636	$43,980	$10,656
5	$56,275 + 557,959	$43,980 + 322,450	$12,295 + 234,512
Y_E =	14.0%		

Solving for Equity Yield

Given an actual or proposed equity sale price and a forecast of equity benefits, an equity yield rate can be estimated. When level income is forecast, a formula is used. The calculations can be performed by iteration or with the financial functions of a calculator. When income is expected to change on a curvilinear basis or a constant-ratio basis, formulas must be used to solve for the yield. A calculator cannot be used to solve the problem conveniently, and the iteration technique is too time-consuming.

Level-Income Example

Consider a property that is purchased for $250,000. The net operating income is forecast to remain level at $35,000 per year and the buyer believes that property value will decline 15% over a five-year ownership period. The mortgage amount is $200,000 and monthly payments are at 10% interest with an amortization term of 20 years. The investment forecast is outlined below.

Purchase		Holding Period	
Sale price	$250,000	NOI	$35,000
Mortgage	200,000	Debt service	23,161*
Equity	$50,000	Pre-tax cash flow	$11,839

Resale After 5 Years	
Sale price	$212,500
Mortgage balance	$179,605†
Equity reversion	$32,895
Original equity	$50,000
Equity change	-$17,105

* $200,000 × 0.115803 mortgage constant
† Unamortized portion of $200,000 mortgage at end of 5-year projection period.

$$R_E \text{ (equity capitalization rate)} = \frac{\$11,839}{\$50,000} = 0.236780$$

$$E \text{ (equity change)} = \frac{-\$17,105}{\$50,000} = -0.342100$$

The equity yield rate may now be computed through iteration or by using the formula and interpolation.

Iteration is performed using the formula

$$Y_E = R_E + \Delta_E \, 1/S_n$$

Because the sinking fund factor for 10 years at the Y_E rate cannot be identified without knowing Y_E, a trial-and-error procedure must be used to develop Y_E. Without discounting, the 34.21% equity decline over the five-year holding period would subtract 6.84% each year from the equity capitalization rate of 23.67%. Consequently, Y_E will be less than 23.87% and more than 16.83% (23.67% − 6.84%).

The first computation is performed with a Y_E of 18%. When the correct equity yield rate is applied, the equation will balance.

Estimated Y_E	R_E	+	Δ_E	×	$1/S_n$	=	Indicated Y_E
0.1800	0.2368	+	(−0.3425)	×	0.139778	=	0.1889
0.2000	0.2368	+	(−0.3425)	×	0.134380	=	0.1908
0.1900	0.2368	+	(−0.3425)	×	0.137050	=	0.1899

Therefore, $Y_E = 0.1900$, or 19.0%

This procedure for computing Y_E is correct because Y_E is defined as the rate that makes the present value of the future equity benefits equal to the original equity. The future benefits in this case are the pre-tax cash flow of $11,839 per year for five years and the equity reversion of $32,895 at the end of the five-year period.

If Y_E is 19%, the present value of the two benefits can be computed.

$$\$11,839 \times 3.057635 = \$36,199$$
$$\$32,895 \times 0.419049 = \underline{13,785}$$
$$\$49,984$$

Thus, the equity yield rate has been proven to be 19.0%. Precision to 0.03% represents a level of accuracy in keeping with current practice and the normal requirements of the calculation. This example is based on level income, but the same procedure can be applied to changing income streams by incorporating J and K factors into the formula.

J-Factor Premise Example

Consider the information set forth in the previous example, but assume that income is expected to decline 15% according to the J-factor premise.

$$R_O = \$35,000/\$250,000 = 0.14, \quad M = \$200,000/\$250,000 = 0.80$$

$$Y_E = R_E + \frac{\Delta_E}{S_n} + \frac{R_O \Delta_I}{1-M} J$$

Try 15%,

$$0.2368 + -0.3421 \times 0.1483 + \frac{0.14 \times -0.15}{0.2} \times 0.4861 = 0.135$$

Try 12%,

$$0.2368 + -0.3421 \times 0.1574 + \frac{0.14 \times -0.15}{0.2} \times 0.5077 = 0.130$$

Try 13%,

$$0.2368 + -0.3421 \times 0.1543 + \frac{0.14 \times -0.15}{0.2} \times 0.5004 = 0.131472$$

Therefore, $Y_E = 13.15\%$ (rounded)

K-Factor Premise Example

Consider the same information, but assume that income is expected to decrease at a compound rate of 3% per year, indicating a constant-ratio change in income.

$$Y_E = R_E + \Delta_E \, 1/S \, \Delta \, n + \frac{R_O \, (K-1)}{1-M}$$

Try 13%,

$$0.2368 + -0.3421 \times 0.1543 + \frac{0.14 \times 0.9487 - 1}{0.2} = 0.148$$

Try 15%,

$$0.2368 + -0.3421 \times 0.1483 + \frac{0.14 \times 0.9497 - 1}{0.2} = 0.151$$

Therefore, $Y_E = 15.1\%$

Rate Analysis

Rate analysis allows an appraiser to test the reasonableness of the value conclusions derived through the application of overall capitalization rates. Once an overall capitalization rate has been developed with mortgage-equity analysis or another technique, its reliability and consistency with market expectations of equity yield and value change can be tested using Ellwood graphic analysis.

To create a graph for rate analysis, the appraiser chooses equity yield rates that cover a realistic range of rates expected and demanded by investors. It is often wise to include a rate that is at the low end of the range of market acceptance as well as a rate at the high end of the range. For the analysis to be useful to the client, the range of yield rates chosen should be in line with investors' perceptions of the market.

In most real estate investments, there is no assurance that the investment can be liquidated at the convenience of the equity investor or on the terms dictated by the investor. For example, in the early 1990s most liquidity evaporated from the market. Moreover, in negotiating a purchase price, the prospects for profit within a plausible range of possibilities may be greater than the chance of achieving a specific equity yield rate, which cannot be determined until the property is resold. However, the appraiser's value judgments can easily be subjected to realistic tests. The appraiser should ask the following questions.

- What resale prices correspond to various yield levels?
- Can the property suffer some loss in value and still produce an acceptable profit?
- How sensitive is the equity yield rate to possible fluctuations in value?
- What percentage of the investor's return is derived from annual cash flows, and what percentage comes from the reversion? (Reversion is generally considered riskier.)
- What prospective equity yield rates can be inferred from the overall capitalization rates found in the marketplace?

Many of these questions focus on the relationship between the change in property value and the equity yield rate.

The unknown variable in rate analysis is the change in property value (Δ_o). The formula for the required change in property value in a level-income application is

$$\Delta_o = \frac{r - R_o}{1/S_n}$$

Level-Income Example

Consider an investment that will generate stable income and has an overall capitalization rate of 10%. The purchase can be financed with a 75% loan at 10% interest amortized over 25 years with level monthly payments. If the investment is held for 10 years, what levels of depreciation or appreciation should be expected with equity yield rates of 9%, 12%, and 15%?

To solve this problem the appraiser must first find the basic rate (r) and the sinking fund factor for each equity yield rate. The Ellwood Tables are the source of the figures listed below.

Y_E	r	$1/S_n$
9%	0.096658	0.065820
12%	0.105185	0.056984
15%	0.113584	0.049252

When the difference between r and the overall rate (R_O) is divided by the corresponding sinking fund factor, the result is the expected change in property value. If r is greater than R_O, a value increase is indicated; if r is less than R_O, value loss is indicated. Analysis of the 10% overall capitalization rate is shown below.

Y_E	$\dfrac{r - R_o}{1/S_n}$
9%	−0.0508 (5.1% depreciation)
12%	0.0910 (9.1% appreciation)
15%	0.2758 (27.6% appreciation)

The formula produces answers consistent with the notion that a loss is negative and a gain is positive. In some texts the numerator in this formula is expressed as $R_O - r$. Use of this formula results in a change of sign—i.e., positive answers indicate depreciation and negative answers indicate appreciation.

J-Factor Premise
A similar analysis can be performed when income is presumed to change commensurately with value according to the J-factor premise. In this case the expected change in overall property value is calculated by dividing $(r - R_O)$ by $(R_O J + 1/S_n)$.

Graphic Rate Analysis
Various systems have been developed to employ mortgage-equity concepts in graphic rate analysis. The graphic analysis of capitalization rates is a helpful analytical tool used by practicing appraisers and investment analysts. Rate analysis in graphic or tabular form is particularly useful in interpreting market data. Although analyzing a market-oriented overall capitalization rate cannot reveal a property's eventual equity yield rate or resale price, the analysis can reveal combinations of Y_E and Δ_O implicit in the overall rate. Thus, an appraiser can use rate analysis to decide whether a particular combination of Y_E and Δ_O is consistent with market behavior.

The accompanying figures illustrate two types of graphic analysis. Figure 22.1 shows Ellwood-style graphic analysis, with time on the horizontal axis and the percentage change in property value on the vertical axis. Figure 22.2 illustrates another type of graphic analysis with the equity yield rate on the horizontal axis and the percentage change in value on the vertical axis. Graphs like these can be constructed manually by plotting three or more key points and connecting the points with a smooth curve; they can also be constructed using a computer.

The graph in Figure 22.1 shows change in value and income under the J-factor premise with respect to time for equity yield rates of 5%, 10%, 15%, 20%, and 25%. It is assumed that $R_O = 0.11$, $I = 0.125$, $R_M = 0.135$, $M = 0.7$, and $\Delta_O = \Delta_I$.

Figure 22.1 Ellwood-style Graphic Analysis

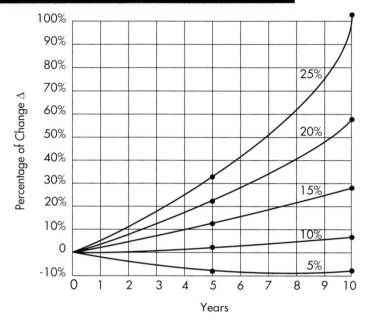

The graph in Figure 22.2 shows the change in value and income under the *J*-factor premise for equity yield rates ranging from 5% to 25% over a 10-year holding period. Again, it is assumed that $R_O = 0.11$, $I = 0.125$, $R_M = 0.135$, $M = 0.7$, and $\Delta_O = \Delta_I$.

Figure 22.2 Alternative Graphic Analysis

After a graph is created, it must be interpreted by the appraiser. Usually the appraiser determines the range of property value changes (Δ_o) anticipated by the market, and then forms an opinion as to the reasonableness of the overall capitalization rate. If the value changes are in line with the expectations of market participants and there is nothing unusual about the subject property, the overall rate being tested may be reasonable. If the value changes are not within the range expected by the marketplace, the overall capitalization rate should either be considered unreasonable and in need of further analysis or must be explained and accounted for.

Rate Extraction

Rate extraction is a technique that allows an appraiser to infer the market's expectation of yield and change in property value from a market-oriented overall capitalization rate. The key is to determine what assumptions about the yield rate and the change in property value are consistent with the overall capitalization rates derived from comparable sales. Although an analyst cannot identify a specific yield rate or change in value using this approach, he or she can determine what change in property value is needed to produce a given yield rate. That is, for each assumed yield rate, there is only one assumption about the change in property value that can be used with that rate to obtain the overall capitalization rate implied by comparable sales.

The following example illustrates this technique. The subject property is an apartment complex. Data on three comparable properties are given.

Factual Data on Three Apartment Complexes

	Sale 1	Sale 2	Sale 3
Number of units	240	48	148
Sale price	$4,678,000	$811,000	$3,467,000
Cash down payment	$1,300,000	$462,145	$1,370,000
Gross income	$594,540	$126,240	$507,120
NOI	$368,600	$71,500	$293,400

Comparative Factors

	Sale 1	Sale 2	Sale 3
Price per unit	$19,492	$16,896	$23,426
Gross income per unit			
Annually	$2,477	$2,638	$3,426
Monthly	$206	$219	$285
Gross income multiplier (GIM)	7.870	6.420	6.830
Overall capitalization rate (R_O)	0.079	0.088	0.085
Loan-to-value ratio (M)	0.722	0.430	0.605
Mortgage constant (R_M)	0.107	0.127	0.136
Percent paid off (P)	−0.125	0.016	0.032
Equity capitalization rate (R_E)	0.006	0.059	0.006
Debt coverage ratio (DCR)	1.021	1.610	1.030

Using the mortgage-equity J-factor formula, pairs of Y_E and Δ_O can be extracted for each comparable sale. The formula for change in income and value is

$$\Delta_{O=I} = \frac{Y_E - M\,(Y_E + P\,1/S_n - R_M) - R_O}{R_O\,J + 1/S_n}$$

The overall rate for each of the sales can be used in this formula to solve for the combinations of Y_E and Δ_O that would produce that overall capitalization rate. These data are shown in the table below.

Calculated Required Changes for the Three Sales (Five-Year Projection)

%Y_E	Sale 1	Sale 2	Sale 3
	% $\Delta_{O=I}$		
10	19.9	10.7	16.1
12	23.2	16.8	20.8
14	26.7	23.3	25.7
16	30.5	30.3	31.0
18	34.5	37.8	36.6
20	38.8	45.8	42.7
22	43.4	54.3	49.1
24	48.3	63.4	55.9
26	53.7	73.2	63.2
28	59.0	83.4	70.9
30	64.9	94.6	79.2

Note that the rate of change in property value is assumed to equal the rate of change in income. This reflects the appraiser's belief that this assumption is consistent with market perceptions. The relationship between equity yield and change in value and income can now be graphed (see Figure 22.3).

Once the graph is completed, the appraiser can draw certain conclusions. If the sales used accurately reflect market perceptions, every pair of equity yield rate and change in property value is a perfect pair. When the figures are inserted into the mortgage-equity formula to derive an overall capitalization rate, the resulting value estimate will be market-oriented.

In this case any pair of Y_E and Δ_O that does not coincide with the lines on the graph is not market-oriented. The lines have different slopes and cross at some point because each sale has a different loan-to-value ratio (M). Furthermore, because of the differences in the loan-to-value ratios, we would expect some variation in the yield rate that equity investors would require for each of the sales. For example, Sale 1 had the highest loan-to-value ratio and, therefore, probably had the highest required yield rate because of its greater risk. The curves indicate reasonable assumptions about yield rates and changes in value that are consistent with the prices paid for comparable sales and the manner in which they were financed.

The graph can also be used to reflect the most likely pair of Y_E and Δ_O for developing an overall capitalization rate. By verifying current investor perceptions of the yield anticipated for the type of property being appraised, the appraiser can

Figure 22.3 Graphic Illustration of the Relationship Between Equity Yield and Total Change in Value and Income

determine the necessary property value change. Then, with the mortgage-equity formula, the overall capitalization rate can be calculated. This overall rate will reflect typical investor assumptions for both yield and change in property value.

Discounted Cash Flow Analysis

The Ellwood formula illustrated above is applicable only to properties with stable or stabilized income streams and properties with uneven income streams that are expected to change according to the J- or K-factor pattern. Discounted cash flow (DCF) analysis does not have these constraints; it is appropriate for any pattern of regular or irregular income[7]. In many markets DCF analysis is the technique preferred by most investors. Advanced computer technology makes DCF analysis a practical tool for everyday appraisal work. That is, the need for a specialized yield capitalization formula is eliminated by the use of appropriate computerized programs.

Generally, DCF analysis is used to solve for present value given the rate of

Guide Note 4 to the Standards of Professional Appraisal Practice addresses criteria for proper DCF nalysis as well as unacceptable practices.

return or to solve for the rate of return given the purchase price. In typical appraisal work, the appraiser begins by developing detailed spreadsheets with computer software. These spreadsheets show itemized incomes, expenses, and cash flows year by year, or occasionally month by month, over the presumed period of ownership. The cash flows, including the net resale price, are then discounted at a required rate of return to derive an indication of present value. In this way the appraiser can account for all cash flows in and out of the real property interest being appraised and the timing of these cash flows so that the time value of money is properly recognized in the analysis.

Critics point out that projections not warranted by market evidence can result in unsupported market values and that the results of the analysis can be subtly affected by minor leaning. These problems, like the problems associated with the Ellwood formula, reflect misuse by individual appraisers; they do not undermine the soundness of the technique. Other critics object to the uncertainty of projecting financial results five or 10 years into the future and cite this as a reason for not using or relying on the DCF technique. However, this argument ignores the reality of the real estate marketplace. Investors do make forecasts and rely on DCF analysis, particularly in regard to investment-grade, multitenanted properties such as shopping centers and office buildings.

In keeping with the principle of anticipation, forecasting is the essence of valuation. Hence, forecasting must be approached in the same way that all market data extractions are accomplished—i.e., with diligent research and careful verification. Discounted cash flow analysis can only provide accurate results if the forecasts developed are based on accurate, reliable information. Rather than attempt to forecast peaks and troughs over the holding period, a level of precision that is virtually impossible to achieve, appraisers reflect market expectations as to how the subject property will perform over a reasonably long time frame. For example, an appraiser may assume that inflation-driven expense items will increase at an average annual rate of $X\%$ over the next Y years.

Forecasting

In making forecasts an appraiser employs the same procedure applied by investors who use DCF analysis in their decision making. The procedural steps typically include forecasting income, vacancy, operating and capital expenses, and pre-tax cash flow over ownership periods of five to 15 years. (Ten years is often cited as an average or standard period of ownership.) When appropriate, debt service and after-tax cash flow may also be forecast. In addition, the residual income from the sale of the property at the end of the forecast period is estimated.

Typical forecast categories to be addressed in DCF analysis include:

- Current market rental rates and expected rate changes
- Existing base rents and contractual base rent adjustments
- Renewal options
- Existing and anticipated expense recovery (escalation) provisions
- Re-leasing assumptions including new lease terms; vacancy loss and sometimes free rent at existing lease expirations; tenant space preparation costs; and leasing commissions
- Tenant turnover
- Operating expenses

- Reversion and any selling or transaction costs
- Changes in inflation (Consumer Price Index)
- Discount rate(s)
- Business cycle—i.e., the state of the economy and economic trends
- Monetary cycle—i.e., the expansion or contraction of the money supply

Applications

The two DCF analyses that follow concern a shopping center and an office building. The first example provides an overview of the procedures used to forecast and discount cash flows into value. The second example presents more detailed market research of cash flow assumptions and a more complicated valuation procedure.

Shopping Center Example

The property being appraised is a strip center consisting of five units of 2,000 square feet each. Market rents are currently $8.00 per square foot per year and are increasing at a compound rate of 4% per year. The landlord is responsible only for real estate taxes and exterior maintenance; tenants are responsible for all other expenses.

Taxes are currently $7,000 per year. The tax assessor reviews and reassesses each property every three years. The subject property was reviewed one year ago and taxes are expected to increase by about $800 with each subsequent review.

General exterior maintenance including cleanup and landscaping costs $100 per month; this expense is expected to increase each year by $10 per month. The roof should be replaced during the second year at a cost of $12,500, but no other exterior repairs or replacements are expected during the projection period.

Management fees, which include lease-up costs, are set at 5% of the rents collected plus 5% of the repair and maintenance expense negotiated. No vacancy or collection loss is anticipated.

The lease on Store A will run for two more years at a rent of $825 per month. The tenant will re-lease at market rent when the lease expires. Store B has a 10-year lease with five years remaining. The rent is currently $1,223 per month and will increase at a rate of 5% per year or one-half the change in the Consumer Price Index (CPI), whichever is greater. The CPI is expected to increase 7% per year over the next five years. Stores C, D, and E were recently leased for 10 years. These leases and all new leases are set at market rent with provisions to keep the rents at market rates throughout the projection period.

The net resale price of the property in five years is expected to be approximately $485,000 (*NOI* for Year 5 capitalized at 15% minus sales expenses). The appraiser has determined that a discount rate of 15% is proper and is using a five-year discounted cash flow analysis to estimate the value of the owner's interest—i.e., the leased fee estate.

Five-Year DCF Analysis

	Year 1	Year 2	Year 3	Year 4	Year 5
Income					
Store A	$ 9,900	$ 9,900	$17,306	$17,999	$18,718
Store B	14,676	15,410	16,180	16,989	17,839
Store C	16,000	16,640	17,306	17,999	18,718
Store D	16,000	16,640	17,306	17,999	18,718
Store E	16,000	16,640	17,306	17,999	18,718
Total	$72,576	$75,230	$85,404	$88,985	$92,711
Expenses					
Taxes	$ 7,000	$ 7,000	$ 7,800	$ 7,800	$ 7,800
Maintenance	1,200	1,320	1,440	1,560	1,680
Management	3,689	4,453	4,342	4,527	4,720
Replacement	0	12,500	0	0	0
Total	$11,889	$25,273	$13,582	$13,887	$14,200
NOI	$60,687	$49,957	$71,822	$75,098	$78,511

Present Value of Income Stream

Cash Flow		PV of $1		Present Value
$60,687	×	0.869565	=	$52,771
$49,957	×	0.756144	=	$37,775
$71,822	×	0.657516	=	$47,224
$75,098	×	0.571753	=	$42,938
$78,511	×	0.497177	=	$39,034
Subtotal			=	$219,742

Present Value of Reversion

$485,000	×	0.497177	=	$241,131

Total present value $460,873

Office Building Example

An appraiser has been engaged to estimate the current market value of the leased fee interest in a property on an all-cash basis as if 1) free and clear of existing financing and 2) subject to two existing mortgages. The property being appraised is a 45,000-sq.-ft. site improved with a four-year-old, three-story suburban office building in a desirable location several miles from a major city. The property has 11,000 square feet of rentable office space and 4,000 square feet of retail space. Leases are held by three tenants: RKM Insurance Corporation, ABC Appraisal Company, and BMI Computer Center.

Leases. The insurance corporation's lease, which covers 5,000 square feet of rentable area, was signed four years ago and expires on June 30 of Year 6. The base rent is set at $18.00 per square foot through December 31 of Year 3 and $20.00 per square foot thereafter. There are no renewal options. The tenant also pays:

- A pro rata share of any increases in real estate taxes that exceed $1.50 per square foot
- A pro rata share of total energy-related expenses
- A pro rata share of all other operating expenses that exceed $1.50 per square foot plus a 15% administrative charge

The lease held by ABC Appraisal Company covers 6,000 square feet of rentable area. It was signed recently and expires on March 31 of Year 7. The base rent is $24.50 per square foot and there are no renewal options. In addition to base rent, the tenant pays:

- A pro rata share of any increases in real estate taxes that exceed $2.05 per square foot
- A pro rata share of all energy expenses that exceed $2.50 per square foot
- A pro rata share of all increases in other operating expenses that exceed $2.60 per square foot

BMI Computer Center leases 4,000 square feet of ground floor retail space. The lease is one year old and expires on December 31 of Year 8. Base rent is $23.00 per square foot until December 31 of Year 4; thereafter it is $26.00 per square foot. This tenant pays percentage rent based on 6% of sales in excess of $600,000. Sales for the current year totaled $468,000 and are forecast to increase 7% per year. In addition, the tenant pays:

- A pro rata share of all increases in real estate taxes that exceed $1.75 per square foot
- Thirty percent of all increases in energy expenses that exceed $2.20 per square foot
- Thirty percent of all increases in other operating expenses that exceed $2.35 per square foot

Other revenue. Parking revenue is expected to be $15,000 per year for the next two years, increasing 5% per year thereafter.

Property expenses. Property expenses for Year 1 are forecast as follows:

Real estate taxes	$2.05 per square foot
Utility-related expenses	$2.50 per square foot
Other operating expenses	$2.60 per square foot
Replacement reserves	$0.10 per square foot
Management expenses	2.5% of effective gross revenue

In this market neither management expenses nor replacement reserves are reimbursed by the tenants.

Mortgage information. The two mortgages on the property are summarized below. The terms are the same as those available today.

First Mortgage

Outstanding balance	$1,100,000
Annual interest rate	11.25%, payable monthly
Amortization term	32 years
Payments	Level payment, self-amortizing

Second Mortgage

Outstanding balance	$250,000
Annual interest rate	13.5% for Years 1 and 2, 14% thereafter; payable quarterly
Amortization term	25 years
Payments	Interest only for Years 1 and 2; level payment, self-amortizing for balance of term

Miscellaneous Assumptions

Leasing commissions	For a new tenant, 3% of base rent per year payable in the first year of the lease; for a renewal tenant, 1.5% per year
Tenant turnover	The RKM Insurance Corporation is expected to move out when its lease expires; the other tenants are expected to re-lease their space.
Lease terms	All new leases will have four-year terms
Tenant improvement costs	For a new tenant, $15.00 per square foot; for an existing tenant, $5.00 per square foot in Year 1 dollars
Growth rate	6%
Selling expense at resale	2.5%

Market research. Eight recent sales of competitive office buildings have been researched and verified. The information derived from each sale is summarized in Tables 22.1 and 22.2.

The comparable sales are analyzed to extract capitalization rates, discount rates, growth rates, and other pertinent information. The appraiser has formed the following conclusions.

Forecast period	10 years		
Market rent	$24.50 per sq. ft.		
Market rent growth rate	6% per year	Overall capitalization rate	
Vacancy and collection loss	3.0% + 3 months vacancy at rollover	for calculating reversion	11.0%
		Discount rates	
Expense growth rates		Free and clear of	
Real estate taxes	5.0%	financing	13.0%
Utility costs	8.0%	Subject to existing financing	14.0%
Other operating expenses	6.0%		

Based on these investment assumptions, a 10-year cash-flow forecast was prepared for the subject property (see Table 22.3). The values indicated by DCF analysis are shown on page 541.

Table 22.1 Comparable Office Building Sales

Sale	Rentable Area (Sq. Ft.)	Sale Price	Sale Price per Sq. Ft.	Equity	Mortgage Amount	Mortgage Interest Rate	NOI* Ratio	EGRM†	First Year		Forecast	
									Cash Flow Rate	Overall Rate	Equity IRR‡	Period (Years)
1	16,000	$2,464,000	$154.00	$1,000,000	$2,464,000	10.50%	45.5%	6.0	6.50%	7.58%	13.8%	10
2	23,000	$3,500,000	$152.17	$1,250,000	$1,500,000 (1st) $750,000 (2nd)	12.00% 13.25%	52.5%	7.5	2.10%	7.00%	14.0%	11
3	12,500	$1,950,000	$156.00	$1,500,000	$450,000	9.00%	60.0%	8.0	5.50%	7.50%	13.8%	10
4	25,000	$4,050,000	$162.00	$1,500,000	$1,500,000 (1st) $1,050,000 (2nd)	11.50% 13.50%	50.5%	7.0	4.30%	7.21%	14.5%	10
5	16,000	$2,550,000	$159.38	$2,550,000	0	—	55.0%	7.7	7.14%	7.14%	13.0%	5
6	15,000	$2,265,000	$151.00	$1,500,000	$765,000	9.50%	48.0%	7.5	6.20%	6.40%	14.0%	10
7	9,000	$1,575,000	$175.00	$1,575,000	0	—	43.0%	5.0	8.60%	8.60%	13.0%	10
8	35,000	$5,075,000	$145.00	$1,600,000	$3,000,000 (1st) $475,000 (2nd)	12.50% 14.0%	65.0%	7.5	3.00%	8.67%	14.0%	10

* NOI ratio = net operating income/effective gross revenue
† EGRM = effective gross revenue multiplier; sale price/effective gross revenue
‡ IRR = prospective internal rate of return or discount rate

Table 22.2 Analysis of Cash Flow Assumptions for Comparable Office Building Sales

Sale	Market Rent Growth Rate	Expense Growth Rate			Resale Price (OAR)	Vacancy	Terms of New Leases (Years)	Re-Leasing Escalation Provisions		
		R.E. Taxes	Utility Items	Other Operating Expenses				R.E. Taxes	Utility Items	Other Operating Expenses
1	6.0%	5.0%	8.0%	8.0%	11.0%	3 months plus 2.0%	3	*	*	*
2	5.5%	5.0%	10.0%	6.0%	11.0%	3 months plus 3.0%	5	*	*	*
3	6.0%	4.5%	7.5%	6.0%	12.0%	5.0%	5	*	*	*
4	6.0%	5.0%	8.0%	7.0%	10.5%	3 months plus 3.0%	3	*	*	*
5	5.5%	5.0%	8.0%	6.0%	12.0%	4 months plus 2.0%	3	*	*	*
6	6.5%	6.0%	8.5%	6.0%	10.5%	3 months plus 3.0%	3	*	*	*
7	6.0%	5.0%	7.5%	5.0%	11.0%	3 months plus 3.0%	5	*	*	*
8	6.0%	4.5%	9.0%	6.0%	11.0%	2 months plus 2.5%	5	*	*	*

* Pro rata share of increases over base year—i.e., year in which lease commences

Table 22.5 Cash Flow Forecast

	Year 1	Year 2	Year 3	Year 4	Year 5	Year 6	Year 7	Year 8	Year 9	Year 10	Year 11*
Revenue											
Base rent	$329,000	$329,000	$329,000	$339,000	$351,000	$369,305	$443,698	$476,455	$515,636	$529,334	$586,231
Real estate tax escalation	3,950	5,487	7,102	8,797	10,577	9,655	5,689	6,703	3,752	4,848	3,221
Utilities escalation	13,850	16,950	20,298	23,914	27,819	22,853	11,622	14,341	8,731	11,525	7,939
Other operating expense escalation	7,450	9,985	12,672	15,520	18,540	16,049	8,698	10,495	6,058	7,885	5,303
Percentage rent	0	0	0	807	3,384	6,141	9,090	12,247	0	0	0
Parking	15,000	15,750	16,537	17,364	18,233	19,144	20,101	21,107	22,162	23,270	24,433
Total revenue	$369,250	$377,172	$385,609	$405,402	$429,553	$443,147	$498,897	$541,348	$556,339	$576,862	$627,127
Less vacancy	11,077	11,315	11,568	12,162	12,887	13,294	14,967	16,240	16,690	17,306	18,814
Effective gross revenue	$358,173	$365,857	$374,041	$393,240	$416,666	$429,853	$483,930	$525,108	$539,649	$559,556	$608,313
Property expenses											
Real estate taxes	30,750	32,287	33,902	35,597	37,377	39,246	41,208	43,268	45,432	47,703	50,089
Utilities	37,500	40,500	43,740	47,239	51,018	55,100	59,508	64,268	69,410	74,963	80,960
Other operating expenses	39,000	41,340	43,820	46,450	49,237	52,191	55,322	58,642	62,160	65,890	69,843
Management	8,954	9,146	9,351	9,831	10,417	10,746	12,098	13,128	13,491	13,989	15,208
Replacement reserve	1,500	1,590	1,685	1,787	1,894	2,007	2,128	2,255	2,391	2,534	2,686
Total expenses	$117,704	$124,863	$132,498	$140,904	$149,943	$159,290	$170,264	$181,561	$192,884	$205,079	$218,786
Net operating income	$240,469	$240,994	$241,543	$252,336	$266,723	$270,563	$313,666	$343,547	$346,765	$354,477	$389,527

* For calculating the resale price in Year 10

Table 22.3 (continued)

	Year 1	Year 2	Year 3	Year 4	Year 5	Year 6	Year 7	Year 8	Year 9	Year 10
Other deductions:										
Tenant improvements	0	0	0	0	0	55,737	70,898	0	53,107	70,367
Leasing commissions	0	0	0	0	0	13,115	16,682	0	12,496	16,557
Total other deductions						$68,852	$87,580		$65,603	$86,924
Cash from operations	$240,469	$240,994	$241,543	$252,336	$266,723	201,711	226,086	$343,547	288,874	302,603
Debt service										
Interest	157,246	156,616	126,039	125,358	124,609	123,786	122,878	121,878	120,773	119,551
Amortization	5,057	5,688	13,835	14,516	15,264	16,088	16,995	17,996	19,101	20,322
Total debt service	$162,303	$162,304	$139,874	$139,874	$139,873	$139,874	$139,873	$139,874	$139,874	$139,873
Pre-tax cash flow	$78,166	$78,690	$101,669	$112,462	$126,850	$61,837	$86,213	$203,673	$149,000	$162,730
Resale price										$3,541,154†
Selling expenses										88,529
Loan balance										1,205,137
Net pre-tax residual										$2,247,488

† NOI for Year 11 ($389,527) capitalized at 11%; this reversion technically occurs on December 31 of Year 10.

Free and Clear of Financing (All Cash)

Equity discount rate*	13.0%
Present value of equity	$2,393,094
Mortgage	0
Total real property value	$2,393,094

*Because there is no loan, this is equivalent to the overall yield rate (Y_o).

Subject to Existing Financing (Cash and Terms) at Market Rates

Equity discount rate	14.0%
Present value of equity	$1,160,196
First mortgage balance	1,100,000
Second mortgage balance	250,000
Total real property value	$2,510,196

Several observations can be made from this example. First, note that the yield rate used to discount the property on an all-cash (free-and-clear) basis is lower than the rate used to value the property subject to existing financing. This reflects the greater risk of the equity position when there is a loan because available income must be used to pay the mortgage first. The discount rate is not significantly higher (14% versus 13%) because the existing loans are only about 54% of the property value. The value estimates are fairly close under the different assumptions although the value is still slightly higher when estimated subject to existing financing.[8]

Second, note that there is an overall rate implied by each estimated value. For example, on a free-and-clear basis the implied overall capitalization rate is about 10% ($240,469/$2,393,094). To check on the reasonableness of the value estimated with the discounted cash flow analysis, this overall rate could be compared to available information concerning the overall rates derived from comparable sales.

Third, note that the implied overall capitalization rate (10%) is less than the overall capitalization rate used to estimate the resale price, which was assumed to be 11%.[9] Higher capitalization rates are often used to estimate the future resale price because of the greater risk associated with income estimated at the end of the investment holding period. The relationship between these two capitalization rates appears to be reasonable.

Critique of the Internal Rate of Return

Limitations and Pitfalls

Without question, the internal rate of return (IRR) is a significant measure of investment performance. It is widely used and its popularity is well deserved. The IRR can be simply defined as *that rate of discount that makes the net present value of an investment equal to zero.* (Net present value is the difference between

---

8. In theory the total value of the real estate should not increase due to the use of market-rate debt financing. Any apparent premium due to favorable financing does not increase the value of the real property; it only increases the price an investor would be willing to pay to buy the property subject to the existing loan.
9. An overall capitalization rate used to estimate the resale price of an investment is usually referred to as a *terminal* or *residual capitalization rate.*

the present value of all positive cash flows and the present value of all negative cash flows.) *The IRR discounts all returns from an investment, including returns from its termination, to equal the original investment.* The IRR has limitations and appraisers may encounter pitfalls in its use. By understanding these shortcomings, practitioners can avoid wasted effort and false conclusions. The search for a single IRR within a plausible range is not always successful. Unusual combinations of cash flows may produce strange results and more than one IRR or no IRR may be indicated.

More than one IRR. Consider a real estate investment with the cash flows set forth below. Assume that the investor borrows $10,000 and pays 10% interest only, with the principal to be repaid in a lump sum at the end of 10 years. The investor's net cash flows are tabulated as follows:

Year	Cash Flow Before Loan/Interest	Loan	Interest	Net Cash Flow
0	-$12,300*	$10,000	$ 0	-$2,300
1	$2,000	0	-$1,000	$1,000
2	$2,000	0	-$1,000	$1,000
3	$2,000	0	-$1,000	$1,000
4	$2,000	0	-$1,000	$1,000
5	$1,000	0	-$1,000	0
6	$1,000	0	-$1,000	0
7	$1,000	0	-$1,000	0
8	$1,000	0	-$1,000	0
9	$1,000	0	-$1,000	0
10	$9,000†	-$10,000	-$1,000	-$2,000

* Initial cash outlay
† Income and proceeds from sale

The IRR for the net cash flows after financing can be obtained through graphic analysis. Net present values are calculated for even discount rates between 0% and 24% and plotted on a graph. The table and graph that follow indicate not one, but two, IRRs. With a computer the two IRRs are calculated as 4.50839% and 18.3931%.

Multiple rates like these are interesting from a theoretical point of view, but it is difficult to accept more than one IRR as a useful measure of performance. In real estate investment analysis, the presence of more than one IRR usually suggests that some other measure of performance would be more appropriate or that the cash flows or time frame should be adjusted to permit a more meaningful analysis. Close examination of the example presented here reveals some characteristics of the IRR that may not be apparent in ordinary examples.

Negative net present value at zero rate of return. The cumulative value of the net cash flows in the example is negative. Negative net cash flows total $4,300, while positive net cash flows total $4,000. Therefore, the net present value—i.e., the difference between the present value of expected benefits, or positive cash flows, and the present value of capital outlays, or negative cash flows—with no discounting or at a zero discount rate—is -$300 (see graph). This should be a

Table of Net Present Values

Discount Rate	Net Present Value
0	-$300
2	-$133
4	-$21
6	$48
8	$86
10	$99
12	$93
14	$74
16	$45
18	$8
20	-$34
22	-$80
24	-$128

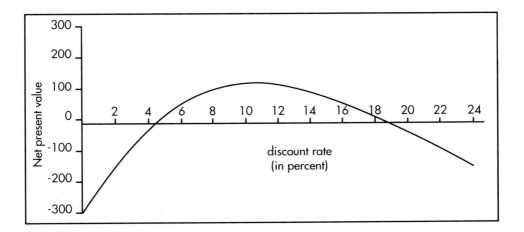

warning sign to the analyst. Whenever the total capital invested over a period of time is equal to or more than the total income for the same period, the *IRR* should be viewed with suspicion.

Under these conditions, the *IRR* cannot be positive unless the mixture of positive and negative cash flows over time is such that the net present value increases with increases in the discount rate until the net present value reaches zero. This phenomenon can be seen in the preceding example. This kind of reverse discounting is mathematically valid, but it is contrary to the practical notion of reducing net present value by increasing the discount rate. It is not surprising that the *IRR* in such cases is difficult to comprehend and of questionable practical use.

Negative IRR. If the net present value of an investment at a 0% rate of return is negative, a negative *IRR* may be indicated. A negative *IRR* may be interpreted as a rate of loss, but the *IRR* is generally understood to be a positive rate of return. Any prospective rate of loss will normally discourage capital investment.

The concept of a negative *IRR* has theoretical, as well as practical, limitations. A glance at the *IRR* equation reveals that a negative *IRR* of 100% or more has no meaning because it involves division by zero or powers of a negative number.

Little or no equity. Because the *IRR* is a measure of the return on invested capital, it cannot be used to measure the performance of opportunities that require no investment of capital. Some investments can be "financed out"—i.e., financed with loans that cover 100% or more of the capital required. If the projected net cash flows are all positive, there is no *IRR*. Obviously, no discount rate can make a series of exclusively positive benefits equal zero.

The same rationale can be applied to investments that call for very low equity or a very small down payment in relation to expected returns. For example, a profit of $1 on an investment of $1 amounts to a 100% rate of return; a return of $100 on an investment of $1 indicates a 10,000% rate of return. When the investment is very small, slight changes in income can cause astronomical changes in the rate of return or rate of loss. The *IRR* is an impractical yardstick for such investments.

However, the *IRR* can be a valuable indicator in analyzing investments that are 100% financed at the start and then expected to operate at a loss for a period of time. In these arrangements, the early negative cash flows may represent a significant investment of equity capital and the prospective *IRR* may be the best measure of performance. It may also be useful to compare the prospective *IRR* before financing with an interest rate that reflects the cost of capital. The difference can be used as a measure of prospective leverage.

Reinvestment Concepts

The *IRR* is an *internal* rate of return on the capital *within* an investment. No consideration is given to the rate of return on reinvested capital after it has been withdrawn from the investment. The income from a real estate investment may be reinvested in another project at another rate of return, stored in a vault, or spent, but the *IRR* is not affected. Thus, no assumptions about a reinvestment rate are needed to understand and use the *IRR*.

Although investment rates are not relevant to the *IRR*, some analysts choose to envision the reinvestment of income at a rate equal to the *IRR*. This assumption is implied if the objective is to measure the total return on a fixed capital sum over a fixed period of time and the fruits of reinvestment are not otherwise taken into account. This is a popular premise, but it can be misleading.

It is correct to assume that if all the dollars withdrawn from a project are reinvested at the same *IRR*, the final composite rate of return will be equal to the *IRR* of the investment. It is also correct to assume that if all the dollars withdrawn from a project are reinvested at a rate of return that is not equal to the *IRR*, the final composite rate of return will not be equal to the *IRR* of the investment. It does not follow, however, that the final composite rate of return on invested and reinvested dollars must equal the original *IRR* of the investment.

If an investor wants to find the *IRR* associated with a *capital sum* at work over a period of time, the reinvestment of income must be considered. If, on the other hand, the objective is to find the *IRR* associated with a *particular property*, the reinvestment of income may be irrelevant. Therefore, unless instructed otherwise by a client, an appraiser need not therefore address reinvestment assumptions when valuing property on the basis of an *IRR*.

An *IRR* is an independent, informative statistic that reflects the amount of earnings for each dollar invested over a specific unit of time for a particular set of cash flows. It can be applied to a single property or to an entire investment portfolio. If an overall *IRR* that reflects the combined results of project earnings and reinvestment is sought, the reinvestment cash flows can be incorporated into the analysis. In short, there is no automatic or implicit assumption in the *IRR* regarding reinvestment. The *IRR can*, however, accommodate reinvestment assumptions by including the expected costs and benefits of reinvestment in the projection of cash flows if so desired.

Reinvestment assumptions are sometimes made to prevent multiple *IRR*s such as those found in the preceding example. If it is assumed that all income is reinvested at a known rate and withdrawn in a lump sum at the termination of the investment, there can be only one overall *IRR* that represents the combined results of project earnings and reinvestment.

IRR Before Taxes Versus IRR After Taxes

The *IRR* is generally seen as a measure of an investment's ultimate net financial performance after all expenses, including income taxes, have been paid. It is a convention among real estate analysts, however, to analyze property on a *pre-tax* basis. The *IRR* can be used to measure profit before income taxes. In fact, the *IRR* is applicable to any level of financial return; it is a general-purpose comparative measure with no arbitrary restrictions.

Comparing the after-tax performance of one investment opportunity to the after-tax performance of another is only one of its many applications. As mentioned earlier, the *IRR* before financing for a particular investment can be compared to the *IRR* after financing to assess the effects of leverage produced by borrowing. Similarly, the *IRR* before taxes can be compared to the *IRR* after taxes to determine the impact of taxation and any tax-shelter benefits. Although the *IRR* is not restricted to a particular use, there is considerable debate regarding its proper use in the analysis of real estate investments.

Arguments in favor of the IRR before income taxes. Income taxes depend on the tax bracket of the individual investor as well as the earning power of the real estate. Therefore, many analysts feel that the *IRR* before taxes is a better measure of intrinsic performance because it is not dependent on outside influences. This argument is often raised when market value is sought and the tax bracket of the investor is not known.

The market for real estate investments is influenced, to some extent, by decision makers who are tax-exempt or do not pay income taxes directly (e.g., charitable foundations, pension funds, real estate investment trusts). Consequently, the *IRR* before taxes is more meaningful in comparisons that involve this segment of the market.

The *IRR* before taxes also has the advantage of simplicity. Projecting cash flow before taxes is less complicated and less subject to error because many calculations are eliminated. Including assumptions regarding tax brackets and allowable deductions introduces more uncertainties and weakens the credibility of the forecast. Furthermore, yields on stocks, bonds, and mortgages are reported in terms of a rate of return before income taxes. Real estate must compete for capital with these alternative investment opportunities, so the *IRR* before income taxes provides a logical basis of comparison.

Arguments in favor of the IRR after income taxes. Tax shelter was once a major attraction for real estate investors. Some analysts argue that any yardstick that does not reflect the full effect of taxes and tax-shelter benefits is deficient. (For a discussion of how the Tax Reform Act of 1986 has affected tax shelters, see Chapter 25.)

The fact that income taxes vary with the tax bracket of the investor may be seen to encourage, rather than discourage, the use of the *IRR* after taxes. The tax bracket of the investor is an important variable that cannot be ignored in any complete analysis. If an estimate of market value is sought and the investor's tax bracket is unknown, the analyst can simulate the decision-making process of a typical investor by using a typical tax rate.

Computer models are readily available and can be used to produce detailed after-tax cash flow analyses. The required calculations can be automated without significant effort or expense. However, the appraiser or analyst must know the assumptions of the analysis, especially the manner in which the program calculates taxes. Similarly, the reported yields on stocks, bonds, and mortgages can easily be converted to reveal equivalent yields after taxes for purposes of comparison. The yields reported for tax-exempt municipal bonds need not be converted at all, but can be compared directly to the *IRR* after taxes.

Clearly, there are valid arguments for using either the *IRR* before taxes or the *IRR* after taxes. The *IRR* selected depends on the application and the objective of the analysis.

Conclusion

The *IRR* can be as important to the real estate investor as the interest rate is to the mortgage lender; in fact, the two measures are equivalent. The interest rate on a mortgage is the same as the mortgagee's yield, or the *IRR*. The *IRR* is not a meaningful measure of all investments and, even when it is meaningful, it is not the only possible criterion. It is, however, a fundamental and pure measure of the financial performance of a particular investment. In general the *IRR* is an extremely valuable analytical tool if the decision maker understands its attributes and limitations and has access to complementary or alternative analytical techniques.

OTHER MEASURES OF PERFORMANCE

The *IRR* is not the only measure of financial performance or profitability. Other popular alternatives such as the payback period, the profitability index or cost/benefit ratio, the net present value or dollar reward, and the time-weighted rate are discussed in Chapter 25. *These yardsticks do not measure performance or profit on the same scale or under the same assumptions as the IRR* and other measures. The usefulness of these measures depends on the situation and the preferences of the user. Neither the *IRR* nor any alternative measure is superior in all situations. The two measures described below represent specific modifications of the IRR.

IRR with Reinvestment

This variation of the IRR was mentioned in the discussion of reinvestment concepts. The assumption underlying this concept is that all income from a project can be immediately reinvested at a specified rate and left to grow at that rate until the end of the investment holding period. The combined results of the investment's earnings and reinvestment are then reflected in one overall rate of return. This measure traces the presumed total performance of a capital sum at work in more than one investment, rather than the performance of a single real estate project. This measure can also be used to prevent multiple solutions to the IRR equation. The IRR with reinvestment is often called the adjusted IRR.

IRR with a Specified Borrowing Rate

The IRR with a specified borrowing rate is another variation of the IRR that can be used to prevent multiple rates. It is sometimes called *the IRR* for investment. The IRR for investment specifies an interest rate for the borrowed funds needed during the period when the investment is producing negative cash flows; thus it prevents the use of the IRR as a borrowing rate. Stipulating a fixed borrowing rate modifies the cash flows as well as the IRR and prevents the possibility of more than one IRR. Like the IRR with reinvestment, the IRR with a specified borrowing rate is a measure of the performance of a capital sum, not the returns generated exclusively by a real estate investment.

SUMMARY

Mortgage-equity analysis as developed by L. W. Ellwood is based on the premise that mortgage financing strongly influences real property prices and values. Ellwood believed that both the debt and equity components of an investment have return requirements that must be satisfied through income and reversion. Mortgage-equity analysis involves estimating the value of both the mortgage and equity interests in a property. The value of the equity interest is found by discounting the pre-tax cash flows available to the equity investor. The equity yield rate (Y_E) is used as the discount rate. The total value of the property is equal to the present value of the equity position plus the value of the mortgage, which may or may not be equal to the balance outstanding on the mortgage principal.

Mortgage-equity analysis can be used to derive overall capitalization rates, to calculate land and building capitalization rates for use in residual techniques, to test the rates obtained with other capitalization techniques, to test the values indicated by other approaches, and to examine capitalization rates with graphic analysis.

The general mortgage-equity formula is:

$$R_O = \frac{Y_E - M\ (Y_E + P1/S_n - R_M) - \triangle_O 1/S_n}{1 + \triangle_I J}$$

The first part of the numerator, $Y_E - M\ (Y_E + P1/S_n - R_M)$, is the basic capitalization rate (r), which satisfies the requirements of both the lender and the equity investor. The last part of the numerator, $\triangle_o 1/S_n$, allows the basic rate to be adjusted for a change in overall property value. The denominator, $1 + \triangle_I J$ allows adjustment for an anticipated change in income. An arithmetic format developed by Charles B. Akerson can be substituted for the algebraic equation in the Ellwood formula. This format is directly applied to level-income situations and, when modified with the J factor, can be applied to changing-income situations as well.

The Akerson format is

Loan ratio × annual constant	=	_____
Equity ratio × equity yield rate	=	+ _____
Loan ratio × % paid off in		
projection period × $1/S_n$	=	− _____
Basic rate (r)	=	_____
+ dep or − app × $1/S_n$	=	+ _____
Overall capitalization rate	=	_____

Mortgage-equity analysis is applied to real property investments with level income streams through the use of overall capitalization rates and residual techniques. The general mortgage-equity formula can be used to value income streams that are anticipated to change on a curvilinear basis by incorporating the J factor into the formula. Exponential-curve (constant-ratio) change can be handled with the K factor. The J factor is used in the stabilizer $(1 + \triangle_I J)$ and can be obtained from precomputed tables or calculated with the formula

$$J = 1/S_n \times \frac{n}{1 - 1/(1 + Y)^n} - \frac{1}{Y}$$

The K factor is an income adjuster or stabilizer that is used to convert a changing income stream into its level equivalent. The K factor can be calculated with the formula

$$K = \frac{1 - (1 + C)^n/S^n}{(Y - C)a_n}$$

where C is the constant-ratio change in income. When the general mortgage-equity formula is applied to an income expected to change on a constant-ratio basis, the K factor is substituted for the denominator $(1 + \triangle_I J)$.

Given an actual or proposed equity sale price and a forecast of equity benefits, an equity yield rate can be estimated. These computations are accomplished through iteration or with a calculator. When income is forecast to be level, the formula for Y_E is

$$Y_E = R_E + \triangle_E 1/S_n$$

When income is forecast to change on a curvilinear basis,

$$Y_E = R_E + \frac{\triangle_E}{S_n} + \frac{R_O \triangle_I}{1 - M} J$$

If income is forecast to change on an exponential-curve (constant-ratio) basis,

$$Y_E = R_E + \triangle_E \, 1/S_n + \frac{R_O \, (K-1)}{1-M}$$

An appraiser can test the reasonableness of value conclusions derived with overall capitalization rates by analyzing the rates graphically. For this analysis, the appraiser selects equity yield rates that cover the full range of realistic expectations.

There is no assurance that a real estate investment can be liquidated upon the initiative of the equity investor. Furthermore, at the conclusion of the holding period, the likelihood of achieving a profit may be greater than the chance of achieving a specific equity yield rate. The relationship between the equity yield rate and the change in property value is very significant. Rate analysis is used to determine the requisite change in property value ($\triangle_O$). The formula for calculating the required property value change in a level-income application is:

$$\triangle_O = \frac{r - R_O}{1/S_n}$$

When level income is forecast, the difference between the basic rate (r) and the overall rate (R_O) divided by the sinking fund factor is the anticipated change in property value. If r is greater than R_O, appreciation is indicated; if r is less than R_O, depreciation is indicated.

When value and income are presumed to change at the same rate, the J factor is used. In this situation the formula for anticipated change in overall property value is:

$$\triangle_O = \frac{r - R_O}{R_O J + 1/S_n}$$

Graphic rate analysis reveals combinations of Y_E and $\triangle_O$ that are implicit in the market capitalization rate. Using this type of analysis, an appraiser can test whether a particular combination of Y_E and $\triangle_O$ is consistent with market evidence. The reasonableness of overall capitalization rates is scrutinized against the range of property value changes anticipated by market participants.

Rate extraction is a technique that allows an appraiser to infer the market's expectation of yield and change in property value from a market-oriented overall capitalization rates. Use of this technique allows the analyst to determine what change in property value would be needed to achieve a given yield rate. Overall capitalization rates can be obtained for specific combinations of Y_E and $\triangle_O$. When the anticipated rate of change in property value equals the anticipated rate of change in income, the formula used to determine $\triangle_O$ is

$$\triangle_{O=I} = \frac{Y_E - M \, (Y_E + P1/S_n - R_M) - R_O}{R_O \, J + 1/S_n}$$

By graphically analyzing the relationship between equity yield and change in property value, an appraiser can identify pairs of Y_E and $\triangle_O$ that are market-oriented. Any pair not suggested by the lines on the graph is not market-oriented and should be thoroughly investigated before being used to derive an overall capitalization rate with the mortgage-equity formula.

The Ellwood formula can only be applied to stable or stabilized income streams, but discounted cash flow (DCF) analysis is appropriate for any pattern of regular or irregular income. Discounted cash flow analysis can be used to solve for present value given the rate of return or for the rate of return given the purchase price. This type of analysis accounts for all cash flowing in and out of the real property interest over time, so the time value of money is recognized. A specialized yield capitalization formula is not needed when an appropriate computer program is used. Discounted cash flow analysis is commonly used for investment forecasts in the commercial real estate market. Appraisers must be careful to always use market-extracted data in DCF analysis.

In making forecasts appraisers apply the procedure used by investors in DCF analysis. Forecasts typically include data on income, vacancy and collection losses, operating expenses, debt service when appropriate, pre- or after-tax cash flow over the ownership period, and the residual income from sale of the property at the end of the forecast period. The ownership period commonly used is 10 years.

The *internal rate of return* (IRR) is the rate of return that makes the net present value of an investment equal to zero. It is a highly significant measure of investment performance, but it has limitations. In rare situations a single IRR cannot be determined because unusual combinations of cash flows can produce multiple IRRs or no IRR at all. If more than one IRR is found, another measure of performance may be more appropriate, or the cash flows or projection period should be adjusted to permit more meaningful analysis.

An investment's net cash flows may have a negative cumulative value. When the total capital outlay over a period is equal to, or more than, the total income for the same period, the IRR should be viewed with suspicion. A negative net present value at a 0% rate of return may indicate a negative IRR, which suggests a loss that would discourage investment.

The IRR measures the return on invested capital, but it cannot measure the performance of investments that are 100% financed by investors or investments that call for very low equity in relation to the expected returns. The IRR can, however, be a valuable indicator for investments that are initially "financed out" and expected to operate at a loss for a finite period of time. Comparing a project's IRR before financing with its IRR after financing is useful in assessing the effects of leverage produced by borrowing.

The IRR can be used to forecast the investment performance of a single property or an entire investment portfolio. Cash flows that are reinvested can be incorporated into the analysis to reflect the combined results of earnings and reinvestment. However, the IRR includes no automatic or implicit assumption regarding reinvestment. When all income from a project is reinvested to grow at a known rate and then withdrawn in a lump sum at the end of the holding period, only one IRR can represent the combined results of project earnings and reinvestment.

By comparing the IRR before taxes with the IRR after taxes, an investor can assess how taxation and tax shelters affect the profitability of an investment.

Some practitioners favor the *IRR* before taxes because it is simpler, less prone to error, independent of outside influence, and can be compared with investment yields that are reported on a pre-tax basis. Those who favor the *IRR* after taxes argue that the income-tax bracket of the investor is an important variable that must be included if the analysis is to simulate the decision-making process of the typical investor.

Other yardsticks of investment performance measure profitability under different assumptions. Two of these measures are specific modifications of the *IRR*: the *IRR with reinvestment*, also called the *adjusted IRR*, and the *IRR with a specified borrowing rate*, or the *IRR for investment*, which specifies a fixed borrowing rate.

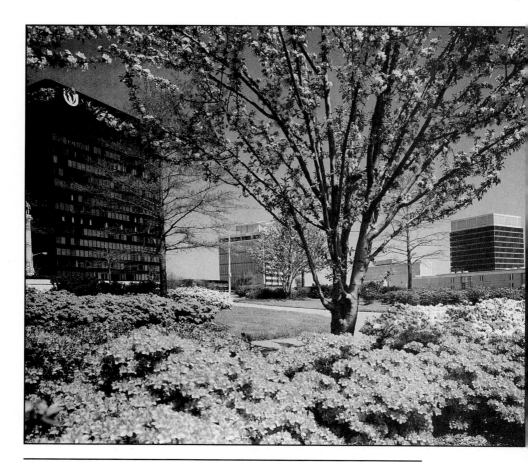

Chapter 23

RECONCILING VALUE INDICATIONS

*A*n appraisal is performed to answer a client's question about real estate. To answer the question, the appraiser follows the valuation process. In the course of this process, the appraiser identifies, gathers, and analyzes general and specific data; determines the property's highest and best use; and applies the cost approach, sales comparison approach, and income approach (direct capitalization and discounting), as warranted by the question and as suggested by the available data.

Usually more than one approach is applied, and typically each approach results in a different indication of value. Therefore, if two or more approaches are used, the appraiser must reconcile at least two value indications. Moreover, several value indications may be derived in a single approach. In the sales comparison approach, for example, the analysis of each comparable sale produces an adjusted sale price, which is an indication of value; when the sales are considered together, the various units of comparison may also produce different value indications. For example, apartment properties may be analyzed in terms of price per dwelling, price per room, price per square foot of *GBA*, or price per square foot of rentable area. In an analysis of income, different indications of value may result from applying gross income multipliers to income streams, directly capitalizing net income, and discounting cash flows.

The appraiser often resolves multiple value indications within a single approach as part of the application of the approach. In other cases, however, an appraiser may choose to resolve these differences after reviewing the entire appraisal. This is acceptable so long as the integrity of each approach is maintained. Resolving the differences among various value indications is called reconciliation. *Reconciliation is the analysis of alternative conclusions to arrive at a final value estimate.*

REVIEW

To prepare for reconciliation the appraiser reviews the entire appraisal, making sure that the data available and the analytical techniques, rationales, and logic applied have led to consistent judgments. Data are reviewed to ensure that they are authentic, pertinent, and sufficient. The value defined, the legal estate appraised, and the qualifying conditions imposed are carefully reconsidered to ascertain whether the methods and techniques used in the analysis specifically address each of these items. The appraiser should examine the differences in the conclusions derived from the various approaches, apply tests of reasonableness to these primary conclusions, and resolve any inconsistencies. For example, is the effective age of the property used in the cost approach consistent with the physical condition reported? Is the same physical condition used as the basis for adjustments to rent comparables, expense comparables, and sales comparables in the income and sales comparison approaches? Are the results of all the approaches consistent with the appraiser's determination of highest and best use?

All mathematical calculations should be verified, preferably by someone other than the person who derived them originally. Significant errors can lead to incorrect value indications, but even minor errors can destroy the client's confidence in the appraisal. Finally, the logic employed throughout the valuation process should be scrutinized. Do the approaches and methods applied consider all the available data, and systematically lead to meaningful conclusions that relate directly to the purpose of the appraisal? Does the appraisal provide the type of advice required to solve the client's problem? For example, if the client wants to establish a depreciation basis to compute federal income tax, does the appraisal give separate values for the improvements and the land? If the client contemplates remodeling, have the costs and benefits of this plan been explored? If the client needs insurance coverage, does the appraisal contain a well-supported insurable value estimate that is consistent with the carrier's definition? If the client is considering an offer to purchase, has the appraiser adequately analyzed the terms of the proposed contract?

RELATIONSHIP TO THE VALUATION PROCESS

The resolution of differences among valuation procedures may depend on subtle differences in the objectives of the appraisal or in the interests being appraised. For example, if an appraiser is estimating the market value of a proposed office tower both as completed and occupied and as completed but unoccupied, the value contribution represented by stabilized occupancy must be carefully weighed in each approach.

In all appraisals, and particularly in appraisals required for litigation, the definition of the appraised value should be reexamined in reconciliation. Does the client-specified definition call for the value to be expressed in terms of cash equivalent financing or in simple cash? Does it call for the most probable price or the highest price available in the open market? Does it call for the value to be commensurate with all the uses to which the property is adaptable, or merely the highest and best use? The appraiser should consider the use of the appraisal. Should the value be commensurate with the current highest and best use or with all of the uses to which the property could be put or to which it could be physically, legally, and economically adapted?

Appraisers may also need to answer questions that relate to the potential users of property. Can the investment value of a property as part of a plot assemblage be reasonably reconciled with an estimate of the property's market value to a typical purchaser? Can the intrinsic value of a new office property be reasonably reconciled with an estimate of its market value for a mortgagee who is contemplating foreclosure? Must an opinion of the insurable value of a property be reconciled with the market value contribution of the insurable improvements?

RELATIONSHIP TO THE MARKET

Appraisers should keep in mind that an appraisal client seeking a professional opinion often wants to know the basis for that opinion as well. The final value estimate represents the application of the appraiser's judgment to mathematical results. An appraiser should employ the quantity of data that market participants would consider appropriate to solve the appraisal problem at hand. These data should be applied consistently in each approach that is relevant to the appraisal problem. The valuation process is a collection of available tools from which an appraiser selects the most appropriate in any given case.

Approaches that are not of primary importance in a specific assignment may be useful in reconciliation. In some cases, for example, the cost approach may not be useful to the appraiser and is thus omitted; nevertheless, the reconciliation may consider the difference between 1) the sum of the reproduction cost and the land value, and 2) the final opinion of market value. A discussion of the degree of apparent depreciation is often instructive.

All estimates used in the approaches to value must be consistent with market perceptions. The appraisal conclusion should reflect market value and the data analyzed should support the appraiser's final value opinion, but the data alone do not produce the value estimate. By combining data analysis with professional training and experience, the appraiser is able to exercise good judgment and form a sound value opinion. Sometimes an appraiser must offer substantive, albeit subjective, judgments when precise market information is not available. The effect of these judgments must be evaluated in the reconciliation process. When an appraisal assignment calls for an estimate of market value but market data are scarce, the opinion of an impartial appraiser who has pertinent training and experience may be relied on.

RECONCILIATION CRITERIA

Reviewing an appraisal helps substantiate its accuracy, its consistency, and the logic leading to the value indications. However, an appraiser relies more on professional experience, expertise, and judgment in reconciliation than in any other part of the valuation process. In reconciliation an appraiser considers and evaluates varying value indications to arrive at a final value estimate. The appraiser weighs the relative significance, applicability, and defensibility of each value indication and relies most heavily on the approach that is most appropriate to the nature of the appraisal. All factors that influence the assignment are brought into focus and related to the client's question, which ultimately guides the appraiser's deliberations.

Reconciliation requires appraisal judgment based on a careful, logical analysis of the procedures that lead to each value indication. Appropriateness, accuracy, and quantity of evidence are the criteria with which an appraiser forms a meaningful, defensible final value estimate. These criteria are used to analyze multiple value indications within each approach and to reconcile the indications produced by the different approaches into a final estimate of defined value.

Appropriateness

Using the criterion of appropriateness, an appraiser judges how pertinent each approach is to the purpose and use of the appraisal. The appropriateness of an approach is usually most directly related to property type and market viability. For example, an appraisal to estimate the market value of a 30-year- old community shopping center will ordinarily employ procedures associated with the income capitalization approach—e.g., the derivation of a gross rent multiplier, net income capitalization, and the discounting of cash flows. The cost approach might not be useful in valuing obsolete improvements, but it may be applied to estimate land value and determine, through an analysis of highest and best use, whether demolition of all or part of an improvement is appropriate. The sales comparison approach can be used to obtain value indications through analysis of physical units of comparison.

Although the final value estimate is based on the approaches that are most applicable, the final value opinion need not be identical to the value produced by the most applicable approach. If two approaches are applicable, the final estimate of value may be closer to one value indication than to the other. For example, assume that the value indication derived from the income capitalization approach is lower than the value derived from the sales comparison approach. If market participants are primarily interested in income-earning potential, the final estimate may be closer to the value indicated by the income capitalization approach than the value derived from sales comparison. For a different type of property such as an owner-occupied dwelling, the sales comparison approach is likely to be of primary relevance.

The criterion of appropriateness is also used to judge the relevance of each comparable property and each significant adjustment made in an approach. The appraiser asks whether this comparable property is a valid and reliable indicator of the value of the subject property. Is it similar in terms of physical characteristics and location? Was it developed, rented, or sold in the same market? Are the characteristics of the transaction similar to those expected for the subject property? If relevant, are the expenses of the comparables appropriate indicators of the expenses of the appraised property? Similarly, if relevant, are the estimates of accrued depreciation in the subject justified by comparison of comparable costs and comparable sales?

Accuracy

The accuracy of an appraisal is measured by the appraiser's confidence in the correctness of the data, the calculations performed in each approach, and the adjustments made to the sale price of each comparable property. For example, are the cost data and estimates of accrued depreciation used in the cost approach as accurate as the adjustments made in the sales comparison approach, or as the income, expenses, and capitalization rates applied in the income capitalization approach? An appraiser may have more confidence in the accuracy of the data and calculations used in one approach than in the others.

The number of comparable properties, the number of adjustments, and the gross and net dollar amounts of adjustments may suggest the relative accuracy of a particular approach. If a large number of comparable properties are available for one approach and seem to conform to a reasonably close pattern of market activity, greater accuracy may be indicated and the appraiser may place more reliance on this approach than would otherwise be the case. For example, if there are many properties competitive with the subject property, an appraiser can extract income and expense data and capitalization rates from these properties. In this instance, the appraiser might attribute greater accuracy and confidence to the income capitalization approach and less to the cost approach or to estimates of price per square foot.

If fewer total adjustments must be made to one or two comparable properties than to other comparables within an approach, an appraiser may attribute greater accuracy and weight to the value indications obtained with fewer adjustments, particularly if the magnitude of the adjustments is approximately the same. Although the number of adjustments among comparable properties may be similar, the gross dollar amount of the total adjustments might vary considerably. For example, in the sales comparison approach an appraiser may analyze five comparable properties that each require nine adjustments. However, the gross dollar amount of adjustments for one comparable property may total 15% of the sale price, while the gross dollar amount of the adjustments for the other four properties may be less than 5% of each sale price. If the sales are otherwise similar, less accuracy will probably be attributed to the comparable properties that require large adjustments.

In some cases, however, one large adjustment may be more accurate and supportable in the market than many smaller adjustments. For example, an appraiser may find abundant market evidence in a community to indicate the amount of value diminution caused by an atypical vacancy rate in one of the comparable buildings. Even though a large adjustment is required, the appraiser might impute greater accuracy to this sale because reliable market evidence supports the adjustment.

Usually the net dollar amount of adjustments is a less reliable indicator of accuracy. The net adjustment is calculated by totaling the positive and negative adjustments to a sale and then subtracting the smaller amount from the larger amount. This figure may be misleading because one cannot assume that any inaccuracies in the positive and negative adjustments will cancel each other out. Several adjustments that are all positive (or all negative) may be more accurate and produce a smaller total gross adjustment than a combination of positive and negative adjustments.

Inaccuracies may be compounded when several adjustments are added or multiplied. The precise arithmetic conclusion derived from adjusted data should support, rather than control, the appraiser's judgment.

Quantity of Evidence

Appropriateness and accuracy affect the *quality* and relevance of the value indication derived from a comparable or an approach. Although these criteria are considered separately in reconciliation, both must be studied in relation to the *quantity* of evidence provided by a particular comparable or approach. Even data that meet the criteria of appropriateness and accuracy can be weakened by a lack of sufficient evidence.

To illustrate the importance of the quantity of evidence, assume that an appraiser is attempting to extract an overall capitalization rate from three comparable sales. The properties are considered appropriate in terms of their physical and locational characteristics and the similarity of the transactions. The available data for each sale are verified and considered reliable, and seemingly each comparable could produce an accurate indication of value. However, the available data for one comparable include an income and expense forecast for a 12-year holding period and a detailed report of the property's expenses and income for the preceding three years. The data on the two other comparables are less detailed. Only total income and expense data for three years are available for one comparable; for the other, detailed data are available for only one year. Because more data are available for the first comparable, the appraiser will have greater confidence in the value indication obtained from it than the indications obtained from the other two sales. In statistical terms, the confidence interval in which the true value lies may be said to be narrowed by additional data.

Regardless of the quantity of evidence available, the responsibility of the appraiser goes beyond the manipulation of numerical data. It is the appraiser's duty to provide a value estimate that fits the definition of value used in the assignment.

Finally, although the evidence from comparable sales may be accurate and appropriate, these data relate to events that took place before the effective date of the appraisal. Reported building sales, land sales, rentals, expenses, development costs, and vacancy and absorption rates all reflect the *past*. These data are relevant only insofar as they help the appraiser estimate the *future* anticipated benefits of the property and the *present* value of these benefits. Market data are important; they should help, but not hamstring, the appraiser's analyses.

FINAL VALUE ESTIMATE

In an appraisal report the final value estimate may be stated as a single figure, as a range of values, or as both. Traditionally a value estimate is reported as a single dollar amount called a *point estimate*. This figure is the appraiser's best estimate of the value of the property. A point estimate is required for many purposes—e.g., real estate taxation, calculating depreciation deductions for federal income tax, estimating compensation in condemnation cases, determining value-based rent, and making property transfer decisions. Furthermore, because of legal requirements, many clients expect a point estimate of value.

A point estimate should be rounded to reflect the degree of precision associated with the particular value estimate; however, even a rounded figure may imply greater precision than is warranted. Because an appraised value is an estimate, it implies a range in which the property value may fall. That value range usually reflects the range of conclusions derived from two or more approaches, but the final value opinion need not fall within this range. For example, an appraiser may report a value estimate of $9,400,000 to represent a result drawn from two approaches with preliminary conclusions of $9,390,000 and $9,380,000. In this case the conclusion of $9,400,000 is not statistically derived. It is outside the range indicated by the two approaches, but it reflects the market value of the property based on the two approaches. On the other hand, the value range might be $9,300,000 to $9,400,000, if that is the appraiser's judgment.

An appraisal is an opinion of value. Although it is an impartial, expert, and reasoned conclusion formed by a trained professional based on an analysis of all relevant evidence, it is still an opinion. It represents the appraiser's perception of the most likely, most probable price available in an arm's-length transaction for the appraised interest subject to the qualifying conditions imposed.

Sometimes an appraiser may deliberately avoid stating a single point estimate and report a range of value. By reporting a range, the appraiser indicates that the value lies somewhere within the range—i.e., that the value is no lower than the low end and no higher than the high end of the range. A wide range is of no use to a client; a narrow range may imply precision that is not warranted. When provided with a value range, a client is likely to see the extreme that suits his or her purpose as a virtual guarantee. Accordingly, most appraisers choose to report their final value conclusions as single figures.

Aside from a *range value*, an appraiser may report a *probability range* to suggest the confidence level or optimism or pessimism associated with the value estimate. The evidence considered in each approach should allow for such variation. For example, an appraiser may consider a more aggressive and a less aggressive market rent schedule for a proposed shopping center. Different capitalization rates may be applied to the two income streams as well as different discount rates and gross income multipliers. Any value differences resulting from the higher and lower projected rents in the income approach should also be related to different levels of risk-related entrepreneurial profit in the cost approach.

ROUNDING

Customarily appraisal conclusions are rounded to reflect the lack of precision associated with value opinions. The more confidence the appraiser has in the opinion, the less need there is for rounding. For example, a value opinion of $404,000 might be rounded to $400,000 if the appraiser has moderate confidence in the estimate. If, on the other hand, the appraiser has a great deal of confidence in the accuracy of the estimate, this opinion might be rounded to $405,000.

Rounding generally reflects market pricing. However, the listing prices of typical dwellings are often misleading. A price of $129,900 may be listed, but an appraiser would generally prefer a rounded conclusion of $130,000.

SUMMARY

Reconciliation is the analysis of alternative conclusions to arrive at a final value estimate. Reconciliation is required because different value indications result from the use of multiple approaches and within the application of a single approach.

To prepare for reconciliation an appraiser reviews the entire appraisal to ascertain that the data, techniques, and logic used are valid and consistent. Inconsistencies among the approaches should be reconciled. For example, the effective age of a property estimated in the cost approach should be consistent with the property's physical condition as stated in the sales comparison approach. All the approaches applied must be based on the same highest and best use determination.

The appraiser should make sure that the approaches and methods used relate to the real property interests being appraised, the definition of value under consideration, and the purpose and use of the appraisal. An independent check of all mathematical calculations is advisable.

Subtle differences in the appraisal objectives or the real property interests being appraised may account for differences in value indications. For example, a proposed investment property will have different values if appraised as though completed but empty and as completed and occupied. The definition of value should be reexamined during reconciliation, especially if the appraisal is required for litigation or financing.

The final value estimate is not derived simply by applying technical and quantitative procedures; rather, it involves the exercise of judgment. The value conclusion reached must be consistent with market thinking, and the quantity of data used should correspond to the amount of data the market considers relevant to the problem. Approaches that are not of primary importance in a specific case may be useful in reconciliation.

An appraiser produces a meaningful, defensible value estimate by considering three criteria: appropriateness, accuracy, and quantity of evidence. Appropriateness relates to the market's preference for certain approaches in specific circumstances and the degree of inclusiveness associated with the comparable data analyzed and reported. All data, calculations, estimates, and adjustments are examined for accuracy. The quantity of evidence is analyzed to determine if the conclusion reached is sufficiently supported in the market. Market data necessarily reflect past phenomena. An appraiser must rely on such data when estimating value, which is the present worth of the future benefits of ownership. Nevertheless, the data analyzed should not dictate the appraiser's opinion.

The final value estimate may be stated as a single figure, a range, or both— i.e., a single figure within a range.

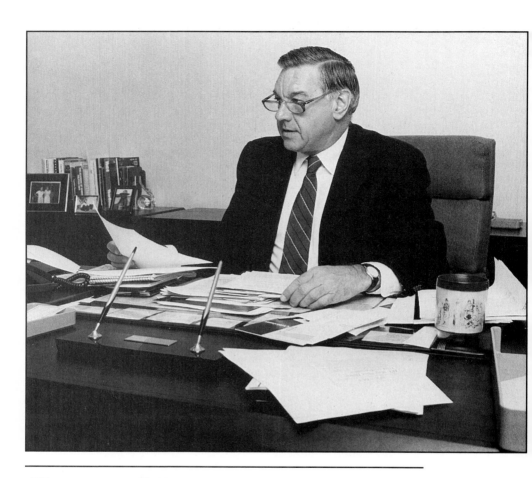

Chapter 24

THE APPRAISAL REPORT

*A*n appraisal report leads the reader from the definition of the appraisal problem through analysis and relevant descriptive data to a specific conclusion. The appraiser must present all facts, reasoning, and conclusions clearly and succinctly. The length, type, and content of appraisal reports are dictated by the client, regulatory requirements, the courts, the type of property being appraised, and the nature of the problem.

Every appraisal report is prepared to answer a particular question and provide specific information needed by a client. Some common appraisal questions are: What is the market value of the property? What is the highest and best use of the land as though vacant and the property as improved? What is the value of the part taken in condemnation? What is the damage or benefit to the remainder of the property as a result of the taking?

APPRAISAL INSTITUTE STANDARDS FOR WRITTEN REPORTS

Each analysis, opinion, or conclusion that results from an appraisal must be communicated in a manner that is meaningful to the client and will not be misleading to concerned parties or the public. To ensure the quality of appraisal reports, the Uniform Standards of Professional Appraisal Practice set minimum standards for the facts, descriptions, and statements of work and purpose to be included in all types of appraisal reports.

All members and affiliates of the Appraisal Institute are required to conduct their professional appraisal activities in compliance with the requirements of the Standards of Professional Appraisal Practice, which include both the Uniform Standards of Professional Appraisal Practice and three supplemental standards.

The Preamble to the Uniform Standards states "It is essential that a professional appraiser arrive at and communicate his or her analyses, opinions, and advice in a manner that will be meaningful to the client and will not be misleading in the marketplace." The 10 Uniform Standards are augmented by the supplemental standards, which are applicable only to members and affiliates of the Appraisal Institute. (See Appendix A.)

The Uniform Standards of Professional Appraisal Practice address the minimum requirements for all written and oral reports as well as the responsibility of the review appraiser. Standards Rule 2-1 states that each oral or written report or communication concerning the results of an appraisal must:

(a) clearly and accurately set forth the appraisal in a manner that will not be misleading;
(b) contain sufficient information to enable the person(s) who receive or rely on the report to understand it properly;
(c) clearly and accurately disclose any extraordinary assumption or limiting condition that directly affects the appraisal and indicate its impact on value.

Standards Rule 2-2 requires that each written appraisal report must:

(a) identify and describe the real estate being appraised;
(b) identify the real property interest being appraised;
(c) state the purpose of the appraisal;
(d) define the value to be estimated;
(e) set forth the effective date of the appraisal and the date of the report;

(f) describe the extent of the process of collecting, confirming, and reporting data;

(g) set forth all assumptions and limiting conditions that affect the analyses, opinions, and conclusions;

(h) set forth the information considered, the appraisal procedures followed, and the reasoning that supports the analyses, opinions, and conclusions;

(i) set forth the appraiser's opinion of the highest and best use of the real estate being appraised, when such an opinion is necessary and appropriate;

(j) explain and support the exclusion of any of the usual valuation approaches;

(k) set forth any additional information that may be appropriate to show compliance with, or clearly identify and explain permitted departures from, the requirements of Standard 1; and

(l) include a signed certification in accordance with Standards Rule 2-3. (For members and affiliates of the Appraisal Institute, the certification must also conform to the Supplemental Standards Rules.)

TYPES OF REPORTS

An appraisal report may be oral or written. Written communications include letter, form, and narrative reports. Usually a report is presented in the manner requested by the client. However, when a client asks for the appraiser's opinion only, without detailed documentation, the appraiser must still perform the analysis required for a complete appraisal. In this case all material, data, and working papers used to prepare the report are kept in the appraiser's permanent file. Although the appraiser may never need to provide written substantiation for the opinion submitted in abbreviated form, he or she may be asked to explain or defend the opinion at a later time.

Oral Reports

An appraiser may make an oral report when the circumstances or the needs of the client do not permit or warrant a written report. Expert testimony whether presented in deposition or in court is considered an oral report. Most oral reports are not made under oath; they are communicated to the client in person or by telephone. To the extent that it is possible and appropriate, oral reports must address the substantive matters set forth in Standards Rule 2-2. Each oral report should include a property description and the facts, assumptions, conditions, and reasoning on which the conclusion is based. After communicating an oral report, the appraiser should keep on file all notes and data relating to the assignment and a complete memorandum on the analysis, conclusion, and opinion.

Limited Reports

Sometimes, by prior agreement with the client, an appraiser submits the results of an appraisal in a limited report. Although these reports are abbreviated, they still must conform to the Uniform Standards. The Departure Provision of the standards specifies which elements of the appraisal report may be omitted under certain circumstances and which may not. Although the discussion of some topics may be less extensive in a limited report, the report must contain sufficient information to lead the reader to the appraiser's conclusions. The two types of limited reports most frequently requested are letter reports and form reports.

The term *letter report* is somewhat of a misnomer. In the past such reports may have consisted of only a page or two of conclusions, but given current standards, letter reports today must run several pages in length to ensure compliance with the reporting requirements. Such a report usually includes references to extensive material in the appraiser's file.

Although the usefulness of a letter report is limited, a client may specifically request that the appraiser communicate his or her opinion in a letter without detailed documentation. A typical letter report sets forth only the conclusions of the appraiser's investigations and analyses. Although much of the data and reasoning is omitted, the report must include certain items to be meaningful and to comply with the requirements of the Standards of Professional Appraisal Practice.

A letter report should indicate that all significant market data and other information that support the analyses, conclusions, and opinions in the report have been retained in the appraiser's files. The following guidelines apply to the preparation of letter reports.

- The property rights being appraised must be adequately identified.
- The purpose of the appraisal should be stated.
- The property and the purpose of the appraisal should be identified in the first paragraph of the report.
- The analysis or analyses performed should be described.
- The date of valuation, the date of the report, and all limiting conditions should be set forth.
- The definitions, premises, assumptions, and limiting conditions that apply to the appraisal should precede the discussion of the approaches to value applied and the value opinion reached.
- The required certification must be included.

A statement regarding the limited nature of the report and analysis must also be included.

As in the case of an oral report, the appraiser who prepares a letter report must keep all notes and data on file with a complete summary of the analysis, conclusion, and opinion. In addition, the client should be informed that many regulatory agencies and third-party users of appraisal reports do not accept letter reports or short narrative reports.

Form Reports

In many instances form reports meet the needs of financial institutions, insurance companies, and government agencies. Form reports are required for the purchase and sale of most existing mortgages on residential properties in the secondary mortgage market created by government agencies and private organizations. Because these clients review many appraisals, using a standard report form is more efficient and convenient. When such a form is used, those responsible for reviewing the appraisal know exactly where to find each category or item of data in the report. By completing the form, the appraiser ensures that no item required by the reviewer is overlooked. Figure 24.1 is a sample of a Uniform Residential Appraisal Report form.

Figure 24.1 Uniform Residential Appraisal Report Form

X | X

Property Description

UNIFORM RESIDENTIAL APPRAISAL REPORT File No.

SUBJECT

Property Address		City		State	Zip Code

Legal Description			County	

Assessor's Parcel No.		Tax Year	R.E. Taxes $	Special Assessments $

Borrower	Current Owner		Occupant	Owner	Tenant	Vacant

Property rights appraised ☐ Fee Simple ☐ Leasehold Project Type ☐ PUD ☐ Condominium (HUD/VA only) HOA$ ___ /Mo.

Neighborhood or Project Name		Map Reference	Census Tract

Sales Price $	Date of Sale	Description and $ amount of loan charges/concessions to be paid by seller

Lender/Client		Address	

Appraiser		Address	

NEIGHBORHOOD

Location	☐ Urban	☐ Suburban	☐ Rural	Predominant occupancy	Single family housing		Present land use %	Land use change

					PRICE $ (000)	AGE (yrs)		

Built up ☐ Over 75% ☐ 25-75% ☐ Under 25% | | | One family ___ | ☐ Not likely ☐ Likely

Growth rate ☐ Rapid ☐ Stable ☐ Slow | ☐ Owner Low ___ | 2-4 family ___ | ☐ In process

Property values ☐ Increasing ☐ Stable ☐ Declining | ☐ Tenant High ___ | Multi-family ___ | To: ___

Demand/supply ☐ Shortage ☐ In balance ☐ Over supply | ☐ Vacant (0-5%) ☐ Predominant ___ | Commercial ___

Marketing time ☐ Under 3 mos. ☐ 3-6 mos. ☐ Over 6 mos. | ☐ Vacant (over 5%) | (___)

Note: Race and the racial composition of the neighborhood are not appraisal factors.

Neighborhood boundaries and characteristics: ___

Factors that affect the marketability of the properties in the neighborhood (proximity to employment and amenities, employment stability, appeal to market, etc.): ___

Market conditions in the subject neighborhood (including support for the above conclusions related to the trend of property values, demand/supply, and marketing time - - such as data on competitive properties for sale in the neighborhood, description of the prevalence of sales and financing concessions, etc.): ___

PUD

Project Information for PUDs (If applicable) - - Is the developer/builder in control of the Home Owners' Association (HOA)? ☐ Yes ☐ No

Approximate total number of units in the subject project ___ . Approximate total number of units for sale in the subject project ___ .

Describe common elements and recreational facilities: ___

SITE

Dimensions ___	Topography ___

Site area ___ Corner Lot ☐ Yes ☐ No	Size ___

Specific zoning classification and description ___ | Shape ___

Zoning compliance ☐ Legal ☐ Legal nonconforming (Grandfathered use) ☐ Illegal ☐ No zoning | Drainage ___

Highest & best use as improved ☐ Present use ☐ Other use (explain) | View ___

Utilities	Public	Other	Off-site Improvements	Type	Public	Private	Landscaping ___

Electricity ☐ ☐ | Street ___ | ☐ ☐ | Driveway Surface ___

Gas ☐ ☐ | Curb/gutter ___ | ☐ ☐ | Apparent easements ___

Water ☐ ☐ | Sidewalk ___ | ☐ ☐ | FEMA Special Flood Hazard Area ☐ Yes ☐ No

Sanitary sewer ☐ ☐ | Street lights ___ | ☐ ☐ | FEMA Zone ___ Map Date ___

Storm sewer ☐ ☐ | Alley ___ | ☐ ☐ | FEMA Map No. ___

Comments (apparent adverse easements, encroachments, special assessments, slide areas, illegal or legal nonconforming zoning use, etc.): ___

DESCRIPTION OF IMPROVEMENTS

GENERAL DESCRIPTION	EXTERIOR DESCRIPTION	FOUNDATION	BASEMENT	INSULATION
No. of Units ___	Foundation ___	Slab ___	Area Sq. Ft. ___	Roof ☐
No. of Stories ___	Exterior Walls ___	Crawl Space ___	% Finished ___	Ceiling ☐
Type (Det./Att.) ___	Roof Surface ___	Basement ___	Ceiling ___	Walls ☐
Design (Style) ___	Gutters & Dwnspts. ___	Sump Pump ___	Walls ___	Floor ☐
Existing/Proposed ___	Window Type ___	Dampness ___	Floor ___	None ☐
Age (Yrs.) ___	Storm/Screens ___	Settlement ___	Outside Entry ___	Unknown ☐
Effective Age (Yrs.) ___	Manufactured House ___	Infestation ___		

ROOMS	Foyer	Living	Dining	Kitchen	Den	Family Rm.	Rec. Rm.	Bedrooms	# Baths	Laundry	Other	Area Sq. Ft.
Basement												
Level 1												
Level 2												

Finished area **above** grade contains: ___ Rooms; ___ Bedroom(s); ___ Bath(s); ___ Square Feet of Gross Living Area

INTERIOR	Materials/Condition	HEATING		KITCHEN EQUIP.		ATTIC		AMENITIES		CAR STORAGE:	
Floors	___	Type	___	Refrigerator	☐	None	☐	Fireplace(s) # ___		None	☐
Walls	___	Fuel	___	Range/Oven	☐	Stairs	☐	Patio ___		Garage	☐ # of cars
Trim/Finish	___	Condition	___	Disposal	☐	Drop Stair	☐	Deck ___		Attached	☐
Bath Floor	___	COOLING		Dishwasher	☐	Scuttle	☐	Porch ___		Detached	☐
Bath Wainscot	___	Central	___	Fan/Hood	☐	Floor	☐	Fence ___		Built-In	☐
Doors	___	Other	___	Microwave	☐	Heated	☐	Pool ___		Carport	☐
		Condition	___	Washer/Dryer	☐	Finished	☐			Driveway	☐

COMMENTS

Additional features (special energy efficient items, etc.): ___

Condition of the improvements, depreciation (physical, functional, and external), repairs needed, quality of construction, remodeling/additions, etc.: ___

Adverse environmental conditions (such as, but not limited to, hazardous wastes, toxic substances, etc.) present in the improvements, on the site, or in the immediate vicinity of the subject property: ___

Figure 24.1 Uniform Residential Appraisal Report Form (continued)

Valuation Section

UNIFORM RESIDENTIAL APPRAISAL REPORT   File No.

COST APPROACH

ESTIMATED SITE VALUE . . . . = $ _____	Comments on Cost Approach (such as, source of cost estimate, site value, square foot calculation and, for HUD, VA and FmHA, the estimated remaining economic life of the property): _____
ESTIMATED REPRODUCTION COST-NEW OF IMPROVEMENTS:	
Dwelling _____ Sq. Ft @ $ _____ = $ _____	
_____ Sq. Ft @ $ _____ = _____	
_____ = _____	
Garage/Carport _____ Sq. Ft @ $ _____ = _____	
Total Estimated Cost-New . . . . = $ _____	
Less Physical | Functional | External	
Depreciation _____	
Depreciated Value of Improvements . . . . = $ _____	
"As-is" Value of Site Improvements . . . . = $ _____	
INDICATED VALUE BY COST APPROACH . . . . = $ _____	

SALES COMPARISON ANALYSIS

ITEM	SUBJECT	COMPARABLE NO. 1	COMPARABLE NO. 2	COMPARABLE NO. 3
Address				
Proximity to Subject				
Sales Price	$	$	$	$
Price/Gross Liv. Area	$	$	$	$
Data and/or				
Verification Sources				

VALUE ADJUSTMENTS	DESCRIPTION	DESCRIPTION	+ (−) $ Adjustment	DESCRIPTION	+ (−) $ Adjustment	DESCRIPTION	+ (−) $ Adjustment
Sales or Financing Concessions							
Date of Sale/Time							
Location							
Leasehold/Fee Simple							
Site							
View							
Design and Appeal							
Quality of Construction							
Age							
Condition							
Above Grade	Total Bdrms Baths	Total Bdrms Baths		Total Bdrms Baths		Total Bdrms Baths	
Room Count							
Gross Living Area	Sq. Ft.	Sq. Ft.		Sq. Ft.		Sq. Ft.	
Basement & Finished							
Rooms Below Grade							
Functional Utility							
Heating/Cooling							
Energy Efficient Items							
Garage/Carport							
Porch, Patio, Deck, Fireplace(s), etc.							
Fence, Pool, etc.							
Net Adj. (total)		+ ☐ − ☐ $		+ ☐ − ☐ $		+ ☐ − ☐ $	
Adjusted Sales Price of Comparable		$		$		$	

Comments on Sales Comparison (including the subject property's compatibility to the neighborhood, etc.) _____

ITEM	SUBJECT	COMPARABLE NO. 1	COMPARABLE NO. 2	COMPARABLE NO. 3
Date, Price and Data Source for prior sales within year of appraisal				

Analysis of any current agreement of sale, option, or listing of the subject property and analysis of any prior sales of subject and comparables within one year of the date of appraisal

INDICATED VALUE BY SALES COMPARISON APPROACH . . . . $ _____

INDICATED VALUE BY INCOME APPROACH (If Applicable) Estimated Market Rent $_____ /Mo. x Gross Rent Multiplier _____ = $ _____

This appraisal is made ☐ "as is" ☐ subject to the repairs, alterations, inspections, or conditions listed below ☐ subject to completion per plans and specifications.

Conditions of Appraisal: _____

RECONCILIATION

Final Reconciliation: _____

The purpose of this appraisal is to estimate the market value of the real property that is the subject of this report, based on the above conditions and the certification, contingent and limiting conditions, and market value definition that are stated in the attached Freddie Mac Form 439/Fannie Mae Form 1004B (Revised _____).

I (WE) ESTIMATE THE MARKET VALUE, AS DEFINED, OF THE REAL PROPERTY THAT IS THE SUBJECT OF THIS REPORT, AS OF _____ (WHICH IS THE DATE OF INSPECTION AND THE EFFECTIVE DATE OF THIS REPORT) TO BE $ _____ .

APPRAISER:	SUPERVISORY APPRAISER (ONLY IF REQUIRED):	
Signature _____	Signature _____	☐ Did ☐ Did Not
Name _____	Name _____	Inspect Property
Date Report Signed _____	Date Report Signed _____	
State Certification # _____ State	State Certification # _____	State
Or State License # _____ State	Or State License # _____	State

Freddie Mac Form 70   6-93   10 CH   PAGE 2 OF 2   Fannie Mae Form 1004   6-93

Form reports prepared by Appraisal Institute members and affiliates must meet the reporting requirements of the Appraisal Institute or qualify as limited reports under the conditions set forth in the Standards of Professional Appraisal Practice. Certain forms do not contain a certification statement that complies with these standards. Therefore, Appraisal Institute members and affiliates must attach supplemental material when these forms are used. Guide Note 3 to the Standards of Professional Appraisal Practice addresses the use of form reports in the appraisal of residential property.

The methodology employed in a valuation is determined by the nature of the specific appraisal problem. If a report form seems too rigid and does not provide for the inclusion of all data that the appraiser believes to be pertinent, the relevant information and comments should be added as a supplement.

The appraiser should make sure that the completed form report is consistent in its description of the property being appraised and provides all the data indicated by the categories listed. If the highest and best use of the property does not conform to the use for which the form is appropriate, the form cannot be used. The properties and neighborhoods compared should be as similar as possible and all appropriate adjustments should be made. Data must be presented in a clear and comprehensible manner and all form reports should include a proper certification and statement of limiting conditions.

A form appraisal report is unacceptable if the appraiser fails to 1) consider the purpose of the report, the value definition, and the assumptions and conditions inherent in the report; 2) question the client about any underwriting criteria that conflict with proper appraisal practice; and 3) review the report before signing it.

Narrative Reports

A narrative appraisal report gives an appraiser the opportunity to support and explain his or her opinions and conclusions fully and to convince the reader of the soundness of the final value estimate. Narrative reports often provide the best means for appraisers to fulfill their obligations to their clients. Because this type of report is the most common and complete, this chapter focuses primarily on the narrative report.[1]

The objectives of a narrative appraisal report are to answer in writing the client's questions and to substantiate those answers with facts, reasoning, and conclusions. To achieve these objectives and be most useful to the client, an appraisal report must guide the reader to the appraiser's conclusions by presenting adequate, pertinent supporting data and logical analysis.

A narrative report summarizes the facts and appraisal methods and techniques that the appraiser has applied within the framework of the valuation process to arrive at a value estimate or another conclusion. This type of report reflects the appraiser's ability to interpret relevant data and select appropriate valuation methods and techniques to estimate a specifically defined value.

In preparing an appraisal report, the appraiser should keep descriptions separate from analysis and interpretation. Factual and descriptive data are usually

---

1. For a thorough discussion of appraisal reports, see William C. Himstreet, *Communicating the Appraisal: A Guide to Report Writing* (Chicago: American Institute of Real Estate Appraisers, 1988).

presented in early sections of the report, so subsequent analysis and interpretation may refer to these facts and indicate how they influence the final value estimate. Repetition and unnecessary duplication should be avoided, but the presentation of data may depend on the nature and length of the report.

Because the appraiser may not be present when a narrative report is reviewed or examined, the report is the appraiser's representative; a good report creates a favorable impression of the appraiser's professional competence. The following suggestions may help an appraiser improve the impression created by a report.

- The paper, cover, and binding used should be of good quality.
- The report may be typed or professionally printed. In either case the size and style of the type should be attractive and readable. Graphic illustrations such as photographs and charts should be carefully prepared. The style of headings and subheadings should be appropriate to the subject matter.
- Ideally, illustrations should be presented on pages that face the material being discussed. For example, a photograph of the subject property may be placed on the page facing the identification of the property. An area map could face the regional and area data to show the location of the neighborhood. A neighborhood map could be included on a page facing the neighborhood description to show the location of the subject property. Charts and graphs may be presented on facing pages when they relate to the narrative discussion. Photos of comparable sales can appear next to the narrative discussion of how the sales were adjusted to reflect the value of the subject property. Illustrations that are not directly related to the report should be placed in the addenda.
- The contents of a report should be presented in clearly labeled sections that are identified in the table of contents.

NARRATIVE REPORT FORMAT

A narrative appraisal report should be designed for maximum communication with the reader, who may be the client or another person to whom the report is submitted. Readers may scan rather than study a narrative report, so it is wise to organize the report in a manner that readily discloses the property description, the essential analysis of the problem, and the value conclusion.

A well-prepared report has more than thorough research, logical organization, and sound reasoning. These basic attributes are enhanced by good composition, a fluid writing style, and clear expression. The use of technical jargon and slang should be avoided. To communicate with the reader effectively, the contents of the report should be set forth as succinctly as possible.

General Outline

Narrative appraisal reports may vary in content and organization, but they all contain certain elements. Essentially, a narrative report follows the order of the valuation process.

Most narrative reports have four major parts. The contents of each section may be formally divided with subheadings or presented in a continuous narrative. In either case the major divisions of the report should be identified with individual headings and be separated from one another. The four basic parts of a report are the introduction, the premises of the appraisal, the presentation of data, and the analysis of data and conclusions. Many reports have a fifth section, the addenda, which includes supplemental information and illustrative material that would interrupt the text. The organization of narrative reports varies, but the following outline can be used as a general guide.

Part One—Introduction
Letter of transmittal
Title page
Table of contents
Certification of value
Summary of important conclusions

Part Two—Premises of the Appraisal
Assumptions and limiting conditions
Purpose and use of the appraisal
Definition of value and date of value estimate
Statement as to whether the value estimate is expressed in terms of cash, terms equivalent to cash, or other precisely defined terms
Property rights appraised
Scope of the appraisal

Part Three—Presentation of Data
Identification of the property, legal description
Identification of any personal property or other items that are not real property
Area, city, neighborhood, and location data
Site data
Description of improvements
Zoning
Taxes and assessment data
History, including prior sales and current offers or listings
Marketability study, if appropriate

Part Four—Analysis of Data and Conclusions
Highest and best use of the land as though vacant
Highest and best use of the property as improved
Land value
Sales comparison approach
Cost approach, including feasibility study, if appropriate
Income capitalization approach
Reconciliation of value indications into a final value estimate
Qualifications of the appraiser

Addenda
Detailed legal description, if not included in the presentation of data
Detailed statistical data
Leases or lease summaries
Other appropriate information

The arrangement of items in this outline is flexible and can be adapted to almost any appraisal assignment and any type of real property. In practice, an appraiser would adapt this outline to the particular requirements of the assignment and to suit his or her personal preference. Some types of property may require unique treatment within or in addition to the basic framework presented here.

Part One—Introduction

Letter of transmittal. The letter of transmittal formally presents the appraisal report to the person for whom the appraisal was prepared. It should be drafted in proper business style and be as brief as the character and nature of the assignment permit. A suitable letter of transmittal may include these elements:

- Date of letter and salutation
- Street address of the property and a brief description, if necessary
- Statement identifying the interest in the property being appraised
- Statement that the property inspection and all necessary investigation and analyses were made by the appraiser
- Reference that the letter is accompanied by a complete appraisal report
- Effective date of the appraisal
- Value estimate
- Any extraordinary assumptions or limiting conditions
- Appraiser's signature

Title page. The title page lists the property address, the date of valuation, and the name and address of the appraiser. The name of the client and the name and address of the person authorizing the report may also be included.

Table of contents. The various sections of the report are customarily listed in order in the table of contents. The major divisions of the report and any subheadings used in the report should be shown here.

Certification of value. The certification of value may follow the final value estimate or be combined with it. The signature of the appraiser, the date, and a seal, if appropriate, may then be added. The certification states that the appraiser has personally conducted the appraisal in an objective manner.

According to Standards Rule 2-3 and the Supplemental Standards Rules, the certification must be similar in content to the following:

I certify that, to the best of my knowledge and belief:
- the statements of fact contained in this report are true and correct.
- the reported analyses, opinions, and conclusions are limited only by the reported assumptions and limiting conditions, and are my personal, unbiased professional analyses, opinions, and conclusions.
- I have no (or the specified) present or prospective interest in the property that is the subject of this report, and I have no (or the specified) personal interest or bias with respect to the parties involved.
- my compensation is not contingent upon the reporting of a predetermined value or direction in value that favors the cause of the client, the amount of the value estimate, the attainment of a stipulated result, or the occurrence of a subsequent event.

- my analyses, opinions, and conclusions were developed, and this report has been prepared, in conformity with the Uniform Standards of Professional Appraisal Practice.
- I have (or have not) made a personal inspection of the property that is the subject of this report. (If more than one person signs the report, this certification must clearly specify which individuals did and which individuals did not make a personal inspection of the appraised property.)
- no one provided significant professional assistance to the person signing this report. (If there are exceptions, the name of each individual providing significant professional assistance must be stated.)
- the reported analyses, opinions, and conclusions were developed, and this report has been prepared, in conformity with the requirements of the Code of Professional Ethics and the Standards of Professional Appraisal Practice of the Appraisal Institute.
- the use of this report is subject to the requirements of the Appraisal Institute relating to review by its duly authorized representatives.

One of the following statements must be included, in any report prepared by a member of the Appraisal Institute:

Either
- As of the date of this report, I (or Member's name or Members' names) have/has completed the requirements of the continuing education program of the Appraisal Institute.

or
- As of the date of this report, I (or Member's name or Members' names) have not/has not completed the requirements of the continuing education program of the Appraisal Institute.

Whether the certificate is included in the transmittal letter or presented on a separate, signed page, certification is important because it establishes the appraiser's position, thereby protecting both the appraiser's integrity and the validity of the appraisal.

Summary of important conclusions. When an appraisal report is long and complicated, a summary of the major points and important conclusions in the report may be useful. Such a statement is convenient for readers of the report and allows the appraiser to stress the major points considered in reaching the final estimate. The following list indicates the type of material that is frequently included in a summary; however, all of the items do not apply to every appraisal assignment.

- Brief identification of the property
- Any special assumptions and conclusions
- Determinations of the highest and best use of the land as though vacant and the property as improved
- Age of improvements
- Estimate of land value
- Value indication from the cost approach

- Value indication from the sales comparison approach
- Value indication from the income capitalization approach
- Final estimate of defined value
- Allocation of value between the land and the improvements, between the leased fee and the leasehold estates, or between real and personal property

An appraiser may use a different type of summary for longer or more complex reports. In many appraisal reports a summary is omitted, particularly if the letter of transmittal briefly discusses the major conclusions set forth in the report.

Part Two—Premises of the Appraisal

Assumptions and limiting conditions. Assumptions and limiting conditions may be stated in the letter of transmittal, but they are usually included as separate pages in the report. These statements are used to protect the appraiser and to inform and protect the client and other users of the report. Appropriate standard conditions are an important part of a report and should be stated clearly. Some typical general assumptions and limiting conditions are listed below as they might appear in an appraisal report.

This appraisal report has been made with the following general assumptions:
1. No responsibility is assumed for the legal description provided or for matters pertaining to legal or title considerations. Title to the property is assumed to be good and marketable unless otherwise stated.
2. The property is appraised free and clear of any or all liens or encumbrances unless otherwise stated.
3. Responsible ownership and competent property management are assumed.
4. The information furnished by others is believed to be reliable, but no warranty is given for its accuracy.
5. All engineering studies are assumed to be correct. The plot plans and illustrative material in this report are included only to help the reader visualize the property.
6. It is assumed that there are no hidden or unapparent conditions of the property, subsoil, or structures that render it more or less valuable. No responsibility is assumed for such conditions or for obtaining the engineering studies that may be required to discover them.
7. It is assumed that the property is in full compliance with all applicable federal, state, and local environmental regulations and laws unless the lack of compliance is stated, described, and considered in the appraisal report.
8. It is assumed that the property conforms to all applicable zoning and use regulations and restrictions unless a nonconformity has been identified, described and considered in the appraisal report.
9. It is assumed that all required licenses, certificates of occupancy, consents, and other legislative or administrative authority from any local, state, or national government or private entity or organization have been or can be obtained or renewed for any use on which the value estimate contained in this report is based.
10. It is assumed that the use of the land and improvements is confined within the boundaries or property lines of the property described and that there is no encroachment or trespass unless noted in the report.

11. Unless otherwise stated in this report, the existence of hazardous materials, which may or may not be present on the property, was not observed by the appraiser. The appraiser has no knowledge of the existence of such materials on or in the property. The appraiser, however, is not qualified to detect such substances. The presence of substances such as asbestos, urea-formaldehyde foam insulation, and other potentially hazardous materials may affect the value of the property. The value estimated is predicated on the assumption that there is no such material on or in the property that would cause a loss in value. No responsibility is assumed for such conditions or for any expertise or engineering knowledge required to discover them. The client is urged to retain an expert in this field, if desired.

This appraisal report has been made with the following general limiting conditions:

1. Any allocation of the total value estimated in this report between the land and the improvements applies only under the stated program of utilization. The separate values allocated to the land and buildings must not be used in conjunction with any other appraisal and are invalid if so used.
2. Possession of this report, or a copy thereof, does not carry with it the right of publication.
3. The appraiser, by reason of this appraisal, is not required to give further consultation or testimony or to be in attendance in court with reference to the property in question unless arrangements have been previously made.
4. Neither all nor any part of the contents of this report (especially any conclusions as to value, the identity of the appraiser, or the firm with which the appraiser is connected) shall be disseminated to the public through advertising, public relations, news, sales, or other media without the prior written consent and approval of the appraiser.

An appraisal report might contain the following items as additional assumptions and limiting conditions.

1. Any value estimates provided in the report apply to the entire property, and any proration or division of the total into fractional interests will invalidate the value estimate, unless such proration or division of interests has been set forth in the report.
2. Only preliminary plans and specifications were available for use in the preparation of this appraisal; the analysis, therefore, is subject to a review of the final plans and specifications when available.
3. Any proposed improvements are assumed to have been completed unless otherwise stipulated; any construction is assumed to conform with the building plans referenced in the report.
4. The appraiser assumes that the reader or user of this report has been provided with copies of available building plans and all leases and amendments, if any, that encumber the property.
5. No legal description or survey was furnished, so the appraiser used the county tax plat to ascertain the physical dimensions and acreage of the property. Should a survey prove this information to be inaccurate, it may be necessary for this appraisal to be adjusted.

6. The forecasts, projections, or operating estimates contained herein are based on current market conditions, anticipated short-term supply and demand factors, and a continued stable economy. These forecasts are, therefore, subject to changes with future conditions.

7. This report should be considered a limited analysis in that the appraiser did not perform all of the requirements for an appraisal as set forth in the Uniform Standards of Professional Appraisal Practice.

Purpose of the appraisal. The purpose of an appraisal report is the question for which the client seeks an answer. This section can be combined with the property identification section of the report or the appraiser may simply state

The purpose of this report is to estimate market value on (specify date).

Definition of value and date of value estimate. An acceptable definition of the value being appraised is included in the report to eliminate any confusion in the mind of the client or another reader of the report. (Acceptable definitions of various types of value are cited in Chapter 2.)

An appraisal assignment may call for an estimate of current value or an estimate of value as of some point in the past. It is essential to report the date as of which the value conclusion is applicable. When an estimate of value as of a future date is requested by a client, special care and analysis are required. The report must clearly identify the future date of the value estimate and include a statement of qualifying assumptions and limiting conditions appropriate to the terms of the assignment.

Statement as to whether the value estimate is expressed in terms of cash, terms equivalent to cash, or other precisely defined terms. When market value is estimated, the report must clearly state whether the estimate reflects cash, terms or financial arrangements equivalent to cash, or other precisely defined terms.

Property rights appraised. In identifying the subject property, the appraiser must define the particular rights or interests being valued. This is particularly important in appraisals of a partial interest in a property, limited rights such as surface or mineral rights, a leased fee estate subject to a long-term lease, or a leasehold interest. Other encumbrances such as easements, mortgages, or special occupancy or use requirements should also be identified and explained in relation to the defined value to be estimated.

Scope of the appraisal. A clear and accurate description of the *scope of the appraisal* is desirable to protect third parties whose reliance on the appraisal may be affected. The term *scope of the appraisal* refers to the extent of the process of collecting, confirming, and reporting data. The standards clearly impose a responsibility on the appraiser to determine the extent of the work and the report required in relation to the significance of the appraisal problem. By describing the scope of the appraisal the appraiser signifies his or her acceptance of this responsibility.

Part Three—Presentation of Data

Identification of the property. The subject property is identified so that it cannot be confused with any other parcel of real estate. This can be achieved by including a full legal description of the property in the report. When a copy of the official plat or an assessment map is used, the appraiser may refer to it at this point and present it on a facing or following page. If the official plat is unavailable, the appraiser can describe the property by name, specifying the side of the street on which the property fronts, the street address, and the lot and block number. A photograph of the subject property on a facing page can enhance this section of the report. *Personal property and other items that are not real property should be identified.*

Area, city, neighborhood, and location data. All facts about a city and its surroundings that the appraiser considers pertinent to the appraisal problem should be included in the area data. (Different types of data, their appropriate uses in relation to various classifications of property and specific appraisal problems, and their degrees of influence are discussed in Chapters 7 and 8.) An appraiser weighs and considers all pertinent factors in data analysis, but the report should discuss only those data that are found to be significant to the problem at hand. Both positive and negative aspects of the area should be discussed; if the appraiser only provides data in support of either positive or negative factors the report will be misleading.

If a considerable amount of supporting statistical data—e.g., population figures, cost of living indexes, or family income figures—is needed, the appraiser may incorporate these data into the body of the report or present them in tabular form on facing pages and refer to them in the discussion. A separate section for area data is not needed in many reports; area data are often combined with neighborhood data.

Area data that may be significant to an appraisal report include

- Distance and direction from employment centers
- Public transportation
- Road patterns, road layout, and street widths
- Adequacy of utilities and street improvements
- Proximity to shopping
- Proximity to schools
- Proximity to parks and recreational areas
- Proximity to sources of nuisances
- Police and fire protection
- Rubbish collection
- Trends in the neighborhood or district
- Population trends
- Percentage of home ownership
- Types of employment and wage levels
- Conformity of development
- Vacancy and rent levels
- Restrictions and zoning
- New construction activity
- Percentage of vacant land

- Changing land use
- Level of taxes
- Adequacy of street parking and off-street parking
- Type and amount of street traffic
- Type and amount of pedestrian traffic
- Proximity to expressways, tollroads, and airports
- Rail connections and service for freight
- Concentration of advertising by retail merchants
- Other beneficial or detrimental influences

The amount of neighborhood and location data required depends on the appraisal assignment and the client. For example, when an appraisal is prepared for an out-of-town client who is unfamiliar with the property and the community, it may be wise to include more community and neighborhood data than would be needed by a local client. If the appraisal concerns an important business property that derives its income from the purchasing power of the surrounding area, the appraiser should provide a detailed description of the neighborhood and discuss how the population and its purchasing power affect the value of the subject property.

An appraiser should also note the presence of special amenities or detrimental conditions in the neighborhood and provide reasons or data to support any conclusions about these items. For example, if the appraiser states that the area is growing, actual growth figures or building projections should be included in the report. If a report states that a neighborhood is in decline due to abnormal deterioration or poor maintenance, the appraiser might refer to specific properties that exhibit these detrimental conditions or use photographs to illustrate this conclusion.

Area and neighborhood data form the background against which a property is considered. The data are significant to the extent that they affect property value. Therefore, this section of the appraisal is incomplete if the trends indicated by the data are not analyzed. The appraiser applies professional experience and judgment to interpret how relevant data affect the marketability of the subject property. Without interpretation, city and neighborhood data lose their significance; proper analysis of data is needed to establish the potential of the property being appraised.

In studying neighborhood trends, appraisers must avoid stereotyped or biased assumptions relating to race, age, color, religion, gender, or national origin and not presume that racial, ethnic, or religious homogeneity is necessary to maximize property value in a neighborhood. Moreover, appraisers must not make assumptions or use unsupported premises about neighborhood decline or a property's effective age or remaining economic life.

Site data. Pertinent facts about the subject site belong in the site data section. Site data may include descriptions of the property's frontage, depth, site area, and shape; soil and subsoil conditions; easements and restrictions; utilities; and any improvements that benefit or harm the site. The appraiser should offer a conclusion as to the utility or adaptability of the site for existing or proposed improvements.

Description of improvements. In the description of improvements section, all building and improvement data relevant to the appraisal problem are presented and discussed. Although an appraiser considers and processes much data in the course of an appraisal, only significant property characteristics that influence the value conclusion are presented in the report. These characteristics may include

- Actual and effective building age and building size
- Number and size of units
- Structural and construction details
- Mechanical equipment
- Physical condition
- Functional utility or inutility

Property information may be supported with drawings, photographs, floor plans, and elevations. If the description of structural details and mechanical equipment is long, an outline may be used in the body of the report with emphasis on the important items.

Zoning. Zoning data are either included in the land description section of the appraisal report or presented in a separate section. When they are significant, zoning and private restrictions should be discussed in detail. The actual text of the specific zoning ordinance may be incorporated into the body of the report or reproduced in the addenda. If the specific ordinance is not included, the appraiser should provide sufficient data to help the reader understand the limitations that zoning regulations place on the use or development of the site. If appropriate, the appraiser may explore the possibility of a zoning change. Other existing public and private restrictions such as floodplain regulations, scenic easements, and wetland restrictions should be discussed and their effect on the utility and value of the property described.

Taxes and assessment data. Current assessed values and ad valorem tax rates should be reported and a calculation of the current annual tax load of the subject property should be included. Existing assessment trends or prospective changes in tax rates should be analyzed. It may be appropriate to discuss the tax assessment or tax load on the subject in relation to the taxes on other properties, particularly if the difference is significant.

History. The most recent sale of the subject property should be discussed as well as any other sales transacted within the past three years. For properties other than single-family residences, existing or former leases should be analyzed along with any offers to sell or purchase. Historical property data may include information on original assemblage, acquisition, or construction costs; expenditures for capital additions or modernization; financial data or transfers of ownership; casualty loss experience; history and type of occupancy; reputation or prestige; and any other facts that may pertain to or affect the computations, estimates, or conclusions presented in the report. An appraiser should also investigate the previous history of ownership and use of the property for possible environmental problems.

Marketability study. In the appraisal of income-producing properties such as office buildings, shopping centers, and apartment buildings, a marketability study may be performed to find out how the subject property fits into the overall market in terms of rent levels and absorption rates. A marketability study is usually directly related to the conclusions presented in the appraisal report. Such a study may examine the specific real estate market or submarket, the supply of existing properties (e.g., inventory of space, construction trends, vacancy patterns, and absorption rates), the demand forecast (e.g., projected expansion or shrinkage), the current balance of supply and demand, and competitive rent levels.

Part Four—Analysis of Data and Conclusions

Highest and best use should be expressed in terms of the property's most probable and profitable use. Land use patterns in the area, zoning regulations, and the profitability of existing or proposed improvements should be discussed. (A complete discussion of how an appraiser determines highest and best use is provided in Chapter 12.)

Highest and best use of the land as though vacant. Land is generally appraised as though vacant and available for development to its highest and best use. The highest and best use upon which the appraiser's estimate of the value of the land as though vacant is based should be clearly stated in the report. The appraiser should specify that the value estimate does not apply unless the future property use is in accordance with the program proposed. If a short-term lease precludes immediate development and the property cannot be adapted to its highest and best use in the near future, the report should indicate this fact and identify the use that underlies the appraiser's value estimate. The character and amount of data presented and analyzed in this section are dictated by the purpose of the appraisal.

Highest and best use of the property as improved. To determine the highest and best use of a property as improved, an appraiser considers whether or not the removal and replacement of the existing improvements are economically warranted on the date of the appraisal. If the existing improvement is to be retained, the property's highest and best use is based on how the entire property should be used to maximize its benefits or the income it produces. An appraiser may suggest a possible course of action such as rehabilitation, improved maintenance, or better property management.

Land value. In the land value section of an appraisal report, market data and other information pertaining to land value are presented along with an analysis of the data and reasoning that lead to the land value estimate. The factors that affect land value should be presented in a clear and precise manner. The narrative should lead the reader to the land value estimate.

Approaches to value. An appraiser develops the approaches applicable to the assignment and derives indications of value. For each approach used, factual data and the analysis and reasoning leading to the value indication are presented.

Many clients are not familiar with the mechanics of the three approaches to value, so the appraiser may want to explain the procedures in the development of the data. The extent of the explanation depends on the circumstances of the appraisal. Simple statements that describe what is included in each of the three approaches can help the reader understand the report.

For example, the approaches could be described as follows.

In the cost approach, an estimated reproduction or replacement cost of the building and land improvements as of the date of appraisal is developed together with an estimate of the losses in value that have taken place due to wear and tear, design and plan, or neighborhood influences. To the depreciated building cost estimate, entrepreneurial profit and the estimated value of the land are added. The total represents the value indicated by the cost approach.

In the sales comparison approach, the subject property is compared to similar properties that have been sold recently or for which listing prices or offering figures are known. Data for generally comparable properties are used and comparisons are made to demonstrate a probable price at which the subject property would be sold if offered on the market.

In the income capitalization approach, the current rental income to the property is calculated with deductions for vacancy and collection loss and expenses. The prospective net operating income of the property is then estimated. To support this estimate, operating statements for the subject property in previous years and for comparable properties are reviewed along with available operating cost estimates. An applicable capitalization method and appropriate capitalization rates are developed and used in computations that lead to an indication of value.

The three approaches are seldom completely independent. An appraisal is composed of a number of integrated, interrelated, and inseparable procedures that have a common objective—a convincing, reliable estimate of value. At times the three approaches are so intertwined that some appraisers use a "one- approach" system and do not make separate presentations.

Reconciliation of value indications. The reconciliation of the value indications should lead the reader logically to the final estimate of value. The final estimate of defined value may be stated in many ways. The following is a simple example.

As a result of my investigation and analysis, it is my opinion that the market value of the identified interest in the property, on July 20, 19_____ is:

FOUR HUNDRED THOUSAND DOLLARS
($400,000)

Note that the date on which the value opinion is applicable may differ from the date of the letter of transmittal.

When the appraiser chooses to allocate the value estimate among property components, a breakdown may be added after the final value estimate.

. . . which may be allocated as follows:

Land	$ 80,000
Improvements	300,000
Personal property and other items	+ 20,000
Total	$400,000

Qualifications of the appraiser. The appraiser's qualifications are usually included in the appraisal report as evidence of his or her competence to make such an appraisal. These qualifications may include facts concerning

- Professional experience
- Educational background and training
- Business, professional, and academic affiliations and activities
- Clients for whom the appraiser has rendered professional services, the types of properties appraised, and the nature of the appraisal assignments

The use of qualifications is so widespread that many appraisers find it expedient to insert a printed statement of their qualifications in each appraisal report. Of course, the appraiser's qualifications must be presented accurately and in a manner that is not misleading.

Addenda

Depending on the size and complexity of the appraisal assignment, addenda may be included to present information that would interrupt the narrative portions of the report. The following items may be included in the addenda:

- Plot plan
- Plans and elevations of buildings
- Photographs of properties referred to in the report
- City, neighborhood, and other maps
- Charts and graphs
- Abstracts of leases
- Historical income and expense data
- Building specifications
- Detailed estimates of the reproduction or replacement costs of buildings
- Sales and listing data
- Tax and assessment data
- Marketability analysis data (e.g., construction trends, vacancy trends, and competitive rent levels)

SUMMARY

The function of an appraisal report is to lead a reader from the definition of an appraisal problem through the analysis of relevant data to a specific conclusion. An appraisal should be communicated in a meaningful and straightforward manner. The Appraisal Institute requires its members and affiliates to abide by the Uniform Standards of Professional Appraisal Practice of The Appraisal Foundation and the Supplemental Standards of the Appraisal Institute. Both sets of standards address reporting requirements.

Appraisal reports may be oral or written; written reports may be limited, form, or narrative reports. Regardless of how the report is conveyed, all data and notes as well as a summary of the analysis and conclusions should be kept in the appraiser's permanent file.

An *oral report* must include a property description and the facts, assumptions, conditions, and reasoning on which the value conclusion is based. A *limited report* identifies the property and the property rights appraised; states the purpose of the appraisal; describes the analysis performed; cites the date of the valuation and the date of the report; sets forth all definitions, premises, assumptions, and limiting conditions that apply to the appraisal; and includes the required certification. *Form reports*, which are often used by financial institutions, insurance companies, and government agencies, offer a standard, comprehensive format for recording data and may be supplemented with other relevant information.

A *narrative report* illustrates an appraiser's ability to interpret pertinent data and select appropriate methods to estimate a specifically defined value. Appraisers are advised to keep factual and descriptive data separate from analysis and interpretation, and not to repeat or unnecessarily duplicate material in their reports.

Narrative reports follow the steps in the valuation process. Most reports have four major divisions: the *introduction*, the *premises of the appraisal*, the *presentation of data*, and the *analysis of data and conclusions*. Addenda may include supplemental information and illustrative material.

The introduction to the report contains a *letter of transmittal, title page, table of contents, certification of value*, and *summary of important conclusions*. The letter of transmittal identifies the property and the real property interests appraised, states that an inspection and an investigation have been carried out by the appraiser, cites the effective date of the appraisal, sets forth the value estimate, and lists any extraordinary assumptions and limiting conditions. The title page lists the property address, the date of valuation, the name of the appraiser, and sometimes the name of the client. The table of contents outlines the four major divisions of the report, any subheadings, and the addenda if applicable.

In the certification of value, the appraiser *must* certify that the statements of fact are correct to the best of his or her knowledge; that the analysis and conclusions are limited only by the reported assumptions and conditions; that the appraiser has no (or the specified) interest in the subject property; that the appraiser's compensation is not contingent upon any aspect of the report; that the appraisal was performed in accordance with the Code of Professional Ethics and Standards of Professional Practice of the Appraisal Institute, which may review the report; that the appraiser has (has not) satisfied continuing education requirements; that the appraiser has (or has not) made a personal inspection of the property; and that no one, except those specified, has provided assistance in preparing the report.

The summary of important conclusions provides information on the highest and best use of the land as though vacant and the property as improved, the age of the improvements, land value, the property value indications derived from each approach, the final estimate of defined value, the allocation of value between the land and the improvements.

The premises of the appraisal section includes all *assumptions and limiting conditions*, the *purpose and use of the appraisal*, the *definition of value and the date of the value estimate*, a *statement as to how the value estimate is expressed*, the *property rights appraised*, and the *scope of the appraisal*.

Assumptions and limiting conditions are used to protect the appraiser and to inform the client and others using the report. Assumptions may concern the credibility of the legal description and title, the absence of liens or encumbrances, the nature of the ownership and management, engineering and structural conditions, compliance with zoning and environmental regulations, and the legality of the property use. Limiting conditions may restrict the appraisal to the stated program of property use or current market conditions, disavow any proration or division of value according to fractional interests, repudiate subsequent demands on the appraiser, or prohibit the dissemination or publication of the report. The scope of the appraisal refers to the extent of the process of collecting, confirming, and reporting data, and its relation to the significance of the appraisal problem.

The presentation of data section contains an *identification of the property and legal description; identification of any personal property; area, city, neighborhood, and location data; site data; a description of the improvements; zoning; taxes and assessment data; history*; and possibly a *marketability study* to examine rent levels, vacancy patterns, construction trends, and absorption rates for income-producing property.

The final section contains data analysis and conclusions and addresses *highest and best use of the land as though vacant*, with qualifications when the value conclusion is contingent on this determination, and *highest and best use of the property as improved*, with suggestions on how to maximize income through rehabilitation, better maintenance, or better management. Also covered are *land value*, with an analysis of market data and the reasoning behind the conclusion; the *approaches to value*, with explanations of the procedures applied in the three approaches; *reconciliation of value indications*, which is a logical transition to the appraiser's final value estimate; and the *appraiser's qualifications*, a printed statement on the training, experience, and professional affiliations of the appraiser and a record of his or her professional services.

The addenda to the report contain material that might interrupt the narrative if it were included in the body of the report. These items could include plans, photographs, maps, charts, abstracts of leases, building specifications, income and expense data, cost estimates, sale and listing figures, tax assessments, and marketability analysis data.

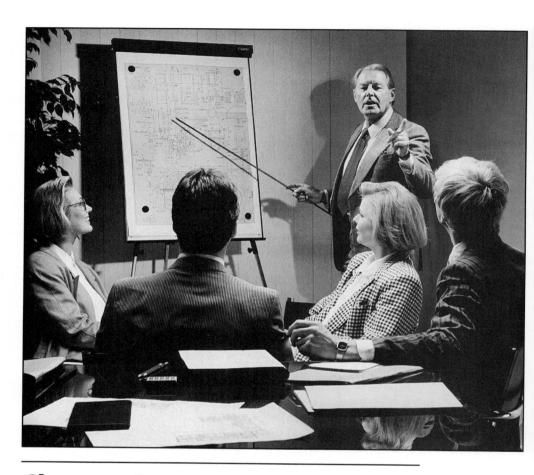

Chapter 25

CONSULTING

$\mathcal{R}$eal estate appraisals may involve valuation, consulting (analysis or evaluation), or both. In valuation assignments a specific type of value is sought; in consulting assignments values are estimated with valuation techniques or other methods and used in making real estate decisions. Consulting may be either general or specific in nature. Both valuation and consulting services are covered by the Appraisal Institute's Code of Professional Ethics and Standards of Professional Appraisal Practice.

Specific consulting assignments include highest and best use studies, market studies, marketability studies, rent studies, absorption analyses, feasibility studies, and other studies that have a specific analytical objective. In more general assignments, practitioners provide clients with unbiased advice regarding real estate decisions. This advice may help clients set goals, establish an analytical framework for real estate investment, or finalize real estate decisions.

Many real estate valuation assignments call for consulting services. In conducting a market value appraisal required for mortgage loan purposes, an appraiser may also provide data and advice that can be used to structure the specific terms of the mortgage.

Buyers and sellers who wish to establish market value for transaction purposes are usually interested in other market facts as well—e.g., high and low market price indicators, the frequency of offers and sales, and the average market exposure of properties before sale. This information can help investors finalize their decisions.

Although valuation and consulting are closely associated, consulting has long been considered as distinct from the appraisal function. Traditionally professional real estate organizations have conferred a special designation on members who demonstrate the training and experience required to perform analytical assignments.[1]

RELATIONSHIP OF CONSULTING TO VALUATION

Valuation studies are primarily microeconomic analyses because they focus on valuing identified interests in specified real estate as of a given date. Broad economic trends and forces are considered, but the analyst concentrates on a specific parcel or parcels of real estate.

Consulting, on the other hand, may include macroeconomic analyses, microeconomic analyses, or a combination of both. It may relate to broad market categories or to a given parcel or parcels of real estate. Valuation assignments always include the identification and definition of one or more types of value. In consulting assignments the nature and scope of the services being performed must be explained, but a particular type of value may not be specified because a value estimate may not be sought. Appraisers must clearly distinguish between valuation and consulting assignments to avoid confusion and possible misunderstanding.

---

1. Holders of the MAI and SREA designations are qualified to perform evaluative and analytical assignments. These designations were conferred by the American Institute of Real Estate Appraisers and the Society of Real Estate Appraisers, which merged in 1991 to form the Appraisal Institute. The American Society of Real Estate Counselors (ASREC), which was founded to enhance the quality of advice on real estate matters available to the public, confers the CRE (Counselor of Real Estate) designation.

Market Value and Investment Value

When the word *value* is applied to real estate, it must be qualified. The statement "The value of your property is $150,000" is not specific enough to be meaningful to real estate professionals. If, however, an appraiser says, "Your property is estimated to have a market value of $150,000" an explicit meaning is conveyed. Of necessity, appraisers refer to market value, insurable value, liquidation value, and other precisely identified and defined types of value. Consulting assignments frequently call for estimates of market value or investment value as well as associated analyses that will enable a client to make one or more real estate decisions. Just as appraisers must distinguish between valuation and consulting assignments, they must also distinguish between market value and investment value.

Market value can be called "the value in the marketplace"; *investment value is the specific value of goods or services to a particular investor (or class of investors) based on individual investment requirements.* Market value and investment value are different concepts; the values estimated for each may or may not be numerically equal depending on the circumstances. Moreover, market value estimates are commonly made without reference to investment value, but investment value estimates are frequently accompanied by a market value estimate to facilitate decision making.

Market value estimates assume no specific buyer or seller. Rather, the appraiser considers a hypothetical transaction in which both the buyer and the seller have the understanding, perceptions, and motivations that are typical of the market for the property or interests being valued. Appraisers must distinguish between their own knowledge, perceptions, and attitudes and those of the market or markets for the property in question. The special requirements of a given client are irrelevant to a market value estimate.

In contrast, the goals of a specific investor are directly related to investment value, as are the advantages or disadvantages of a particular property or real estate situation to that investor. An appraiser may be asked to analyze a series of investment opportunities or possible decisions and evaluate them in terms of their benefits to a given client. Even decisions involving a single parcel of real estate will normally require the evaluation of other possible decisions and an analysis of how each possibility may affect the decision being considered.

For example, an appraiser may be asked to consider whether a parcel of land that is adjacent to the client's industrial property is worth $500,000, the price being asked by its owner. Market analysis indicates that the property is overpriced in comparison with other properties and that its market value is $400,000. However, the client's successful business must be expanded and it will have to be relocated if the additional land is not acquired. If the existing operation is moved, disruption of business and other factors will create a loss of more than $100,000. Because this loss exceeds the difference between the property's market value and its asking price, it might be concluded that the property has an investment value of $500,000 or more to the client in question.

Each voluntary purchase or sale of real estate is based on an investment value decision made by the parties to the transaction. Thus, the market is made up of transactions in which willing participants make investment decisions.

The transaction price of a property varies with the bargaining strength and motivation of buyers and sellers and with the number of opportunities available to these market participants. Ultimately a property's market price reflects the interaction of those who create market supply and demand. Depending on the circumstances of the buyer and the seller in each case, the transaction price at a given moment can be expected to fluctuate above or below the property's value at perfect market equilibrium. Sellers are normally expected to accept a price that equals or exceeds investment value, while buyers will pay a price that does not exceed investment value. Market value estimates synthesize these transactions without considering any particular buyer or seller.

The field of real estate consulting is diverse, so the remainder of this chapter focuses on the techniques used by investors, developers, lenders, and real estate professionals to estimate investment value. Although these techniques can be applied in various types of valuation assignments, they are especially useful in providing clients with specific advice for real estate decision making.

COMMON MEASURES OF INVESTMENT PERFORMANCE

Great strides have been made in the field of real estate consulting since the 1950s. The analytical tools used in consulting now generally parallel the techniques used in other investment fields. However, some measures of investment performance are particularly applicable to real estate. These measures are not individually perfect, but as a collection of tools they have proven effectiveness. They reflect a common market understanding and are useful in typical real estate applications.

It is beyond the scope of this text to explore all analytical techniques, but a basic understanding of the most common measures of investment performance is considered essential to both valuation and consulting.

Simple Ratios

For many years investors have used simple ratio relationships to compare and evaluate the returns from investment properties. One of the most common relationships is the overall rate of return, which is the ratio between the net earnings of a given parcel of investment real estate and the price or value of that parcel. It is expressed as R in the formula

$$R = \frac{I}{V}$$

Other formulas employ simple gross income or net income multipliers. In these formulas the price or value of a property is expressed as a multiple of its potential gross or effective gross earnings, or as a multiple of its net earnings. This multiple is the reciprocal of the overall rate.

Each of these measures can be an effective tool of comparison when applied to very similar properties. Comparing the gross incomes of investments reflects differences among properties to a degree, but measures of investment performance that relate to net income produce better results.

Unfortunately, simple measures of investment performance incorporate many factors that may require specific analysis in a consulting assignment. For example, if an overall rate is used alone, future changes in net incomes, terminal investment values, financing structures, the effects of income taxes, and other elements that may be crucial to a particular property decision are not considered. The overall rate may reflect the combined effect of these and other factors but, in its simple form, it does not consider these factors individually. Therefore, the overall rate and related simple measures of comparison can be misunderstood or misapplied in some situations.

Payback Period

As a measure of investment return, the payback period is seldom used alone, but it is commonly employed in conjunction with other measures. *The payback period is defined as the length of time required for the stream of cash flows produced by an investment to equal the original cash outlay.* The breakeven point is reached when the investment's cumulative income is equal to its cumulative loss. The payback period can be calculated from either before- or after-tax cash flows, so the type of cash flow selected should be identified. The equation for payback period may be expressed as follows:

$$PB = \frac{\text{Equity capital outlay}}{\text{Annual net equity cash flows}}$$

This measure of performance is used by investors who simply want to know how long it will take them to recapture the dollars they have invested. In theory an investment with a payback period of three years would be preferable to one with a payback period of five years, all else being equal. Similarly, an investment that will return the investor's capital in six years would be unacceptable to an investor who seeks investment payback within four years.

For an equity investment that is expected to produce equal cash flows, the payback period is simply the reciprocal of the equity capitalization, or equity dividend, rate.

$$PB = \frac{1}{R_E}$$

If annual equity cash flows are not expected to be equal over the payback period, the equity cash flows for each year must be added until they equal or exceed the equity capital outlay; this point indicates the year in which payback occurs.

Although the payback period is simple and easily understood, it has a number of drawbacks. First, it measures the amount of time over which invested money will be returned to the investor, but it does not consider the time value of the money invested. A five-year investment payback for a $100,000 investment that pays $10,000 in Year 1 and $90,000 in Year 5 is not distinguished from the payback for a $100,000 investment that pays $90,000 in Year 1 and $10,000 in Year 5. The time value of money allows the first investment to use an additional $80,000 (i.e., the difference between the $90,000 paid in the second investment and the $10,000 paid in the first investment) from the second year through the fifth.[2] Another shortcoming of the payback period is that it does not consider the

---

2. A more sophisticated, but less popular, measure is the discounted payback period, which recognizes the time value of money at a stipulated rate of return. In this context the payback period is the amount of time required for the discounted benefits to equal the discounted costs.

effect of any gain or loss of invested capital beyond the breakeven point and does not specifically account for investment risks. An investment with a three-year payback may be far riskier than another investment with a five-year payback, but the shorter period generally appears preferable. Thus this measure of performance should only be used to compare investments with similar investment characteristics or in conjunction with other performance measures in carefully weighted applications.

Investment Proceeds per Dollar Invested

Investment proceeds per dollar invested is a simple relationship calculated as the anticipated total proceeds returned to the investment position divided by the amount invested. The resulting index or multiple provides a crude measure of investment performance that is not time-weighted. It is sometimes used to compare very similar investments over similar time periods.

Profitability Index

Although measuring the investment proceeds per dollar invested is too imprecise for general use, a refinement of this technique is commonly applied. *A profitability index (PI), or benefit/cost ratio, is defined as the present value of the anticipated investment returns (benefit) divided by the present value of the capital outlay (cost).* The formula is

$$PI = \frac{\text{Present value of anticipated investment returns}}{\text{Present value of capital outlay}}$$

This measure employs a desired minimum rate of return or a satisfactory yield rate. The present value of the anticipated investment returns and the present value of the capital outlay are calculated using the desired rate as the discount rate. If, for example, the present value of the capital outlay discounted at 10% is $12,300 and the present value of the benefits is $12,399, the profitability index, based on a satisfactory yield rate of 10%, is $12,399/$12,300 = 1.008.

A profitability index greater than 1.0 indicates that the investment is profitable and acceptable in light of the chosen discount rate. A profitability index of less than 1.0 indicates that the investment cannot generate the desired rate of return and is not acceptable. A profitability index of exactly 1.0 indicates that the opportunity is just satisfactory in terms of the desired rate of return and, coincidentally, the chosen discount rate is equal to the *IRR*. The discount rate used to compute the profitability index may represent a minimum desired rate, the cost of capital, or a rate that is considered acceptable in light of the risks involved.

This refined measure of investment performance considers the time value of money, which is not considered in calculating the proceeds per dollar invested. A profitability index is particularly useful in comparing investments that have different capital outlay requirements, different time frames for receiving income or other investment returns, and different risk characteristics.

A profitability index is commonly used in conjunction with other measures, particularly net present value. When combined, these measures provide special insights into the investments under consideration. Like all other measures of investment performance, a profitability index is *not* generally used alone in making investment decisions. A common rule of thumb for investors is that the profitability index of an investment should be at least 1.0—i.e., the present value of the benefits divided by the capital outlay should be equal to or greater than one.

Net Present Value

Net present value (dollar reward) is defined as the difference between the present value of all expected benefits, or positive cash flows, and the present value of capital outlays, or negative cash flows. Net present value (NPV) is simply the present value of anticipated investment returns *minus* the present value of the capital outlay. This measure, like a profitability index, is based on a desired rate of return. It is computed using the desired rate as a discount rate and the result is viewed as an absolute dollar reward. The reward (or penalty) is expressed in total dollars, not as a ratio. The formula is

$$NPV = CF_0 + \frac{CF_1}{(1+i)} + \frac{CF_2}{(1+i)^2} \ldots + \frac{CF_n}{(1+i)^n} - CO$$

where i is the applicable discount rate and n is the number of periods in the analysis. This formula calculates the difference between the present value of all investment returns and the amount of the original capital investment. The dollar reward is simply NPV at a stipulated discount rate. A positive NPV indicates a reward; a negative NPV indicates a penalty. An NPV of zero indicates that the chosen discount rate coincides with the IRR.

A number of decision rules can be established for applying the NPV. For example, assume that a property with an anticipated present value of $1,100,000 for all investment returns over a 10-year holding period can be purchased for $1,000,000. If one investor's NPV goal is zero, this investment exceeds that criterion. It also meets a second investor's goal for an NPV of $100,000, but it would not qualify if the goal were $150,000.

Net present value does consider the time value of money and different discount rates can be applied to different investments to account for general risk differences. However, this method cannot handle different required capital outlays. It cannot differentiate between an NPV of $100,000 on a $1,000,000 capital outlay and the same NPV on a $500,000 capital outlay. Therefore, this technique is best used in conjunction with other measures.

Time-Weighted Rate

A *time-weighted rate is technically an average of all actual, instantaneous rates over a period of time.* It is similar to the rate of growth for capital invested in a mutual fund in which all dividend income is automatically reinvested. The time-weighted rate, which is also known as the *unit-method rate* or the *share-accounting rate*, is used primarily to measure the performance of a portfolio manager, not the performance of the portfolio itself.

Discounted Cash Flow

Discounted cash flow (DCF) analysis provides appraisers and other investment analysts with the most detailed, precise means of considering the amounts and timing of investment cash inflows and outflows over the life of an investment. With this procedure any series of cash inflows and outflows over any specified time frame at any rate of return can be analyzed and the present value of the investment's anticipated performance can be measured.

In discounted cash flow analysis, compound interest measurements are used to convert future dollars into their present value equivalents. Because dollars to be received in the future are worth less than current dollars, successive cash inflows and outflows are discounted at a selected rate to their present value as of a given date. The sum of the present values of future positive and negative cash flows represents the DCF value indication at a given discount rate. Different rates may be used to reflect differences in investment risks.

Given similar data, DCF calculations may produce the same results as other income comparison methods. However, methods that are less precise may produce different results because they do not consider the explicit details considered in DCF analysis. Discounted cash flow techniques may be applied to cash flows before or after income taxes. The results of DCF analysis can then be used as the present value component (PV) in comparisons made with profitability indexes or net present value methods.

Discounted cash flow techniques can be applied on either a constant-dollar or nominal-dollar basis. If constant dollars are used, they are discounted with rates that do not include an allowance for inflation. Consequently, investment performance is measured without considering the effects of inflation. More often, nominal or actual dollars are measured for the cash inflows and outflows anticipated. In this case the discount rate applied contains a component that accounts for inflation. However, because the rate of inflation is an element of risk, a specific analysis of future inflation rates or components of inflation is not usually included in the discount rate, although this may be done in more detailed analyses.

For income streams that extend over many years, such as those stipulated in long-term leases, DCF is commonly performed for terms of five, 10, or 15 years. Although these terms may be shorter than the term of a given property lease, they offer two principal advantages. First, buyers and sellers in many markets develop their expectations of future price changes over short or medium-length terms. Therefore, the appraiser can establish market expectations regarding the terminal values of the investment and factor these expectations into income analysis time frames that are consistent with market thinking and behavior. Second, the mathematics of compound interest are data-specific and precise, but they sometimes lead to conclusions that are difficult to accept.

Consider, for example, the table on the following page, which shows the amounts to which $100,000 will grow at 10% interest compounded annually over various investment periods. Although these figures are accurate and a 10% rate of growth may well represent market thinking for a given property, many people cannot accept the implication that the property *must* have a value of more than $127 million in 75 years. Therefore, an appraiser may determine that the market is acting as though it considers a 10% growth rate appropriate over the income projection period, but conclude that the market is not actually considering the effect produced by that growth rate over an extremely long time frame.

Although DCF analysis can be applied to historical investment results, it is usually applied to future expectations. Therefore, DCF analysis frequently involves

Years	Future Value
10	$259,374
20	$672,750
30	$1,744,940
40	$4,525,926
50	$11,739,085
75	$127,189,537

forecasting cash inflows and outflows. In valuation assignments, the analyst applies the anticipations of the marketplace; in performing DCF analysis in evaluation assignments, different investment scenarios are presumed to test the subjective judgments of the appraiser or others.

Discounted cash flow techniques are precise, persuasive, and time-sensitive. They can be applied to different income patterns and risk situations. They reduce the number of assumptions required for a given analysis and explicitly consider both advantageous and disadvantageous investment expectations.

Discounted cash flow techniques have some disadvantages. They are based on forecast estimates and the analyst must consider and have access to historical data. The precision of DCF techniques can suggest greater accuracy than is warranted and the rates applied in discounting may be highly subjective.

Internal Rate of Return

The internal rate of return (*IRR*), which is discussed in Chapter 22 in the context of yield analysis, expands on present value calculations and techniques; it represents a special case among investment performance measures. *The IRR is simply defined as that rate of discount that produces a profitability index of one and a net present value of zero.* Measured separately, the *IRR* is the discount rate at which the present value of all net investment returns, including any return of capital from the disposal of the investment, exactly equals the capital outlay for the investment.

In other words, the *IRR* calculation is a DCF analysis solved backwards—i.e., all cash inflows and outflows are analyzed to find what discount rate can be applied to make them exactly equivalent to the original capital outlay. Thus the *IRR* considers all positive and negative cash flows from the inception of the investment to its termination and reflects the indicated return *on* investment in addition to the return *of* investment.

The *IRR* concept and method are also referred to as *yield analysis*. Although the term is imprecise and appears in different contexts, the *IRR* is considered a prominent example of yield analysis.

As mentioned in Chapter 22, the reinvestment presumption is a controversial aspect of *IRR* analysis. The presumption that money received from the investment before its termination is actually reinvested is not essential to the *IRR* concept. Nevertheless, mathematical consistency can be demonstrated between the results of such an analysis and the presumption that these funds are reinvested at the same rate of interest as the *IRR*. This controversy, and other weaknesses in the

IRR, have led to the development of alternative measures such as the financial management rate of return (*FMRR*), the adjusted internal rate of return, and the modified internal rate of return. These methods were created to address other factors or to compensate for the reinvestment consideration.

Calculating an *IRR* is an iterative process. A successive series of calculations is made to establish a range for the *IRR* and this range is refined to the required degree of precision. These calculations can be facilitated with financial calculators and computers, but they can also be done manually. Because many variables are usually involved, no formula can calculate the *IRR* in a single step.

The *IRR* is one of the most important performance measures for real estate investments. Real estate has historically produced higher returns than many other forms of capital investments, and *IRR* methods have the advantage of producing marginally higher results than other measures of investment. They can also provide a limited measure of the advantage or disadvantage of the real estate investment under consideration.

Despite its precision and persuasiveness, the *IRR* has many weaknesses, which are analyzed in Chapter 22. These weaknesses are reviewed below.

More than one IRR. In some situations it is possible that more than one number will mathematically satisfy the *IRR* definition. Although this is somewhat unusual, appraisers are cautioned against the unqualified use of *IRR* measures and concepts.

Discounting of negative cash flows. Standard *IRR* and *DCF* methods discount both positive and negative cash flows at the applicable discount rate. Some investors argue that different risks are attributable to these cash flows and that this methodology does not make financial sense.

Disparity with NPV. The *IRR* of an investment may vary considerably from the *NPV* for that investment. To illustrate, consider the following data for a one-year investment.

	Required Capital	Net Receipt at Year End
Investment A	$20,000	$24,000
Investment B	30,000	35,100

The *IRR* calculated for Investment A is 20% and the *IRR* for Investment B is 17%. For an investor who requires a 10% yield, the net present values for each investment are calculated as follows:

Investment A: $24,000 × 0.909091 − 20,000 = $1,818
Investment B: $35,100 × 0.909091 − 30,000 = $1,909

Both techniques are based on compound interest, but these calculations reveal that Investment B, the larger investment, produces a higher *NPV*, while Investment A, the smaller investment, has a higher *IRR*.

No recognition of differences in capital outlays. A primary weakness of the *IRR* is that it does not account for differences in the amount of capital outlay required for the various properties under consideration. It presumes that all capital amounts have both the opportunity *and the obligation* to earn a return at the same rate as the calculated *IRR*. Consequently, the *IRR* is less effective when it is applied to investments that have widely different capital requirements. In these cases the profitability index is used in conjunction with the *IRR*. In the example presented above, the *PI* for Investment A ($21,818/$20,000) is 1.09, while the *PI* for Investment B ($31,909/$30,000) is 1.06. Although the *PI* supports the *IRR* indication in this case, it is possible that the higher the *IRR* becomes, the lower the corresponding *PI*.

Despite its weaknesses the *IRR* is commonly given substantial weight in the analysis of investment properties. The *IRR* is particularly applicable in evaluating investment portfolios. Like other investment performance measures, it frequently must be used in conjunction with other techniques and considerations.

The "Correct" Investment Performance Measure

No single investment performance measure is the best or most appropriate in all situations; each has its advantages and disadvantages and all are more effective when used in conjunction with other measures. Under certain circumstances one or more of these measures should be given greater weight, but the analyst must always recognize the individual limitations of each measure.

Omitting one or more of these measures in making a given real estate decision does not indicate the likely failure of that investment; similarly, applying appropriate measures is no guarantee of success. All decisions are made under conditions of uncertainty, but the measures of investment performance discussed here represent valuable tools that allow appraisers and investors to weigh the facts, exercise sound judgment, and make reasoned decisions. They also provide a framework for implementing an investment program and monitoring investment decisions once they are made.

Judgment is the ability to draw on information and individual experience to make better decisions. As used in valuation and consulting assignments, investment performance measures are not panaceas, but aids that can be useful in developing, considering, and explaining investment decisions and judgments.

CONSULTING SERVICES

Appraisers are called upon to perform consulting services because they have the market knowledge and experience needed to help clients solve real estate problems. Just as the valuation process is a time-honored approach to conducting real estate valuations, an appropriate problem-solving process is needed to perform consulting assignments.

Most, if not all, of the techniques used in valuation studies are also applicable to the evaluation analyses performed in consulting. However, an evaluation may not require any valuation or it may use one or more valuations as part of a broader analysis. In addition, consulting frequently involves consideration of the specific needs and objectives of the client, not the generalized, composite market perspective that characterizes market value assignments.

Although the tools common to valuation and consulting may be used differently in each type of assignment, appraisers must at all times maintain their objectivity and support their findings with facts extracted from competent research. By their nature, consulting assignments are often more subjective than valuation assignments. Therefore, a practitioner who undertakes a consulting assignment must identify and evaluate both facts and judgments and then relate the findings to the financial decisions under consideration.

In the remainder of this chapter, essential consulting services and elements common to typical consulting assignments are reviewed. Risk analysis is a fundamental part of any type of decision making. The analytical tools employed include the investment performance measures previously discussed as well as other techniques. Consulting studies commonly focus on specific analyses of the income tax consequences of investments, but there are many other types of studies that appraisers may be asked to perform. Appraisers may be retained to provide real estate counseling services in conjunction with their valuations or consulting work. Each of these activities is briefly discussed.

Risk Analysis

The concepts of risk and uncertainty are fundamental to real estate consulting and any other form of investment analysis. Frequently valuation analyses and many of the investment performance measures used in consulting are viewed as point estimates—i.e., single parameter estimates. Real estate professionals typically regard point estimates as the *most probable* numbers, not the only possible numbers. Recognizing and dealing with other possibilities is a major function of risk analysis.

Risk is defined as the probability that foreseen events will not occur. An appraiser may identify the most probable amounts and timing of cash flows and then analyze both the probability that the cash flow forecasts are correct as stated and the risk that they are not. If the appraiser is absolutely certain that the exact amounts forecast will be realized, there is no risk.

Uncertainty is the probability that unforeseen events will occur. With the supplementary concept of uncertainty, an appraiser can analyze the range of probabilities that certain events will happen and also allow for the possibility that unforeseen events will occur. These two considerations form the basis for risk analysis.

Most analysts who consider the investment implications of future cash flow opportunities do not expect their forecasts to be realized exactly as they have anticipated. Appraisers avoid predictions, even in valuation assignments; instead they make forecasts. Thus when a single figure is used in an analysis, it is usually considered the point of central tendency or the most probable number within a range of possible numbers.

In some situations, however, appraisers deal with exact figures—e.g., contract rents, purchase prices, mortgage terms, calculated units of comparison, and other historical data. A distinction must be made between a number that represents a fact and a number that reflects a future estimate. If a practitioner does not understand an estimated or forecast number in terms of its range of possibilities and associated probabilities, he or she may seriously misjudge investment risks or fail to consider other uncertainties.

A number of methods have been developed to analyze the risk and uncertainty of real estate investments directly. None of these methods offers any special insight into the future, but each provides an opportunity to analyze the factors upon which the success or failure of an investment is contingent and to deal with the expected consequences.

Probability Analysis

Probability is the relative likelihood that a specified event will occur. Although the concept is usually associated with games of chance, the concept of probability is basic to life. As people grow and learn, they translate their experiences into intuitive probabilities. Thus people carry umbrellas on cloudy days, stop at red lights, avoid harmful foods, and generally act in accordance with the probability of possible future outcomes.

The same processes are applicable to real estate consulting. Based on past experience and other factors, judgments can be made about the foreseeable future. Various possibilities are identified and their relative probabilities are assessed. Probability, the relative frequency of an expected occurrence, is linked to risk, the identification of events that are unlikely to occur, in the framework of risk analysis.

Ranges of probability can be determined with at least four methods. First, observation and analysis of past events may indicate patterns or measures of relative frequency. Second, probability may be determined through controlled experiment and observation, which is the method applied in scientific experiments. In real estate applications survey research methods may be employed. Third, theoretical distributions may be used to establish probability. For example, an appraiser may infer that the rates of return on a particular type of real estate investment will fall within a given range because of a theoretical relationship between these rates and the rates of return obtainable in other capital markets. Fourth, probability ranges can be based on subjective judgment. When ranges of probability are determined in this way, they should be tested and all judgments should be evaluated.

Some analysts avoid identifying several possible outcomes (e.g., for cash flow amounts or resale prices) and the probabilities associated with each because the process seems too indefinite. However, when the process is conducted properly, the limitations of a single point estimate are overcome. In fact, risk analysis facilitates judgments and investment decision making.

Some prominent risk analysis methods are briefly described here. These methods may not be applied in every consulting assignment, but each is applicable in specific circumstances. Occasionally two or more of these methods are used together to confirm or contrast their conclusions and provide another basis for making investment decisions.

Utility Functions

Utility functions are subjective weights that are assigned to possible investment outcomes to reflect a particular investor's relative preference for each. According to this concept, an investor who believes in taking risks would give a higher ranking of personal utility to a riskier investment than would an investor with a more conservative investment outlook.

Although utility functions are very subjective, they do offer a quantitative means of analyzing differences between investment options. For example, assume that an investor has two real estate investment alternatives. The first is a relatively conservative investment that is judged to have a 60% chance of developing an NPV of $20,000 and a 40% chance of producing an NPV of $10,000. The second investment has an 80% chance of earning a $40,000 NPV for the same capital outlay, but a 20% chance of suffering a $10,000 loss.

Different investors may view these outcomes and probabilities in different ways. If an investor is particularly interested in the opportunity to earn a $40,000 NPV, he or she may be willing to accept the risk of loss associated with the second investment. In this case the investor may assign the utility functions shown below to calculate the total utility of each investment.

	Possible Outcomes	Utility Function	Probability	Utility × Probability
First investment	$20,000	125	0.60	75
	10,000	90	0.40	36
Total utility				111
Second investment	$40,000	200	0.80	160
	−10,000	−30	0.20	−6
Total utility				154

The second investment, with a total utility measure of 154, would be selected over the first investment, which has a total utility measure of 111. However, another investor may be unable or unwilling to deal with the possibility of loss. This investor would assign a different set of utility functions to the risks associated with each investment and would probably prefer the first investment.

Debt Coverage Ratio

The debt coverage ratio (DCR) is a risk measure that is commonly used in mortgage loan situations. It can be useful in structuring a mortgage or deed of trust and in testing the relative degree of safety associated with a given set of loan terms.

A debt coverage ratio is measured as the ratio of a property's net operating income to its annual debt service. The DCR for a property with debt service of $800,000 and a net operating income of $1,000,000 would be calculated as

$$DCR = \frac{\text{Net operating income}}{\text{Annual debt service}} = \frac{\$1,000,000}{\$800,000} = 1.25$$

If the lender's risk measurement criterion precluded any loan with a DCR of less than 1.25 as being too risky, the property in this example would be marginally acceptable.

The DCR is commonly used in simple feasibility analyses. If a builder or developer knows that a DCR of 1.25 would probably apply to the project being undertaken, he or she might develop an estimate of the most probable NOI that the property could produce and calculate the amount of debt service required to obtain a ratio of 1.25. Then the allowable mortgage could be determined on the basis of that debt service. If the amount were sufficient, the developer could proceed with the proposed project.

To illustrate another use of the DCR, assume that an 80% mortgage is available for a particular type of development and that the applicable mortgage constant is 0.12. If the required DCR is 1.3, the overall rate necessary to warrant the loan would be

$$R_O = M \times R_M \times DCR$$
$$= 0.80 \times 0.12 \times 1.3$$
$$= 0.1248$$

With further calculations, the pre-tax cash flow rate can be found.

Overall rate:	1.00	0.1248
Mortgage portion:	0.80 × 0.12 =	0.0960
Equity portion:	0.20	0.0288

The indicated pre-tax cash flow rate is $0.0288/0.20 = 0.1440$. Thus, given the details and requirements of the loan, the equity position must be capable of producing income at a pre-tax cash flow rate of 14.4% to make the investment's risk acceptable to the lender.

Debt service coverage requirements vary for different lenders at different times. To use the ratio effectively, a reasonably accurate estimate of net operating income must be presumed. Although the DCR is simple to use, it does not measure the amount of risk associated with the borrower. However, because DCRs establish a standard ratio of risk between property income and debt service, they are commonly used for mortgage underwriting purposes.

Payback Period

The payback period discussed previously can also be used as a simple risk measurement. Its use varies in different situations, but in any application the payback period indicates the amount of time that investment money will be exposed to the risks inherent in a given investment.

If the economy is moving from a recession into a period of anticipated continuous growth, investors may be more willing to expose their real estate investments to longer periods of risk because they anticipate that longer terms will allow them to take advantage of the growth cycle. Conversely, when economic problems are expected, investors may desire shorter payback periods to avoid the adverse conditions of a downward business cycle.

In managing investment portfolios that may include real estate, it is possible to commit funds for discrete time periods. Thus, the payback period may also be used to help determine exactly when to enter into and exit from a given investment.

Upside/Downside Potential

Considering the upside and downside potential of an investment is a general analytical tool for comparing investment risk. To apply this method to alternative properties or investment concepts, the analyst first quantifies the best and worst anticipations for the investments being analyzed and then forms general conclusions regarding the risks associated with each.

No single analytical procedure characterizes this method of risk analysis. Commonly a series of possible DCF outcomes under alternative hypotheses or situations are presumed; then the best outcomes are compared with one another and the worst outcomes are compared with one another. This method also identifies the factors that create downside situations and recommends possible steps to avoid these factors or mitigate their effect.

An analysis of upside/downside potential does not provide any absolute measure of risk, but it does avoid the pitfalls of single point estimates and can be especially useful in developing hypothetical outcomes for risk analysis and investment planning.

Expected Values

The use of expected values, which are determined with probabilities, was illustrated in the example of utility functions. The concept is simple. A series of possibilities is defined for each investment decision under consideration and the probability of each is assessed. *P* indicates the probability of various investment outcomes. Every investment outcome is multiplied by a weighted probability and the sum of these figures indicates the expected value of that investment. This procedure is shown below.

| | Investment A | | | Investment B | | |
	NPV	*P*	Expected Value	*NPV*	*P*	Expected Value
Best case	$600,000	0.30	$180,000	$500,000	0.40	$200,000
Most probable case	500,000	0.60	300,000	450,000	0.40	180,000
Worst case	200,000	0.10	20,000	400,000	0.20	80,000
		1.00	$500,000		1.00	$460,000

Given these data, Investment A has a higher expected value than Investment B. Note, however, that the method also allows the analyst to identify other important risk factors, such as the possibility that Investment A may realize an *NPV* of only $200,000. If the investor has established a target *NPV* of at least $350,000, the risk of Investment A would be considered higher than the risk of Investment B because there is no probability of a lower *NPV* in the latter investment.

Monte Carlo Simulation

To perform a Monte Carlo simulation, the practitioner constructs an analytical model in which all the elements of the investment are assigned probabilities. These various elements are then integrated into a larger theoretical population. By repeatedly sampling from this group, the range of possible outcomes and the "values" that each of the underlying assumptions produces can be determined.

For example, a simple DCF model can be used to identify high, low, and best case possibilities for each income and expense item and the associated probabilities. Monte Carlo simulation can then be applied to sample the possibilities repeatedly as though they existed in a very large population of occurrences. The expected values are totaled and a probability distribution for the outcomes is indicated.

This method enhances the utility of risk analysis because it lets the practitioner see the range of consequences associated with different combinations of possible outcomes and weigh their expected values. The method is particularly valuable because it can be used to identify extreme possible outcomes so that extremes of risk can be properly considered.

As its name suggests, Monte Carlo simulation is based on gaming studies. It is frequently used in development analysis and other large-scale real estate decision-making situations. It is especially effective in consulting work because the consequences of various alternatives can be tested against their expected outcomes and the associated probabilities.

Risk-Adjusted Discount Rates

Risk-adjusted discount rates are frequently used in financial analysis; they are also applicable in some real estate valuations and consulting work. Generally an analyst capitalizes income with a discount rate that reflects all the elements of risk associated with the income stream. However, in some situations the specific analysis of one or more risk factors may warrant a special adjustment to the discount rate used.

For example, consider a real estate developer who seeks a return of 18% on his development activities. This developer generally rejects projects that extend beyond five years to avoid the risk of a future downswing in the business cycle. Accordingly, if the developer were attracted to an opportunity that extended beyond five years, the additional term risk—i.e., the risk associated with the extra time—would be offset by adjusting the discount rate applied to the periods after the fifth year.

It is mathematically possible to develop a single discount rate to cover multiple-term, multiple-risk situations. However, when direct market evidence is available to support risk-adjusted rates in each individual situation, these rates are more representative of market behavior and their direct application is more appropriate than the use of an indirect, synthesized discount rate.

Risk-adjusted discount rates may be used in at least two ways. When market research indicates that they are supportable and produce reliable results, risk-adjusted discount rates are used in valuation applications to incorporate market information directly into risk analysis. In consulting work, these rates help adjust financial analyses for perceived risks by identifying outcomes that directly reflect the risk factors used in adjusting the discount rate.

Other Analytical Methods

So far this chapter has focused on measures of real estate investment performance and ancillary risk analysis methods. Like the broader field of financial analysis, real estate consulting abounds with analytical tools and methods. A survey of some important techniques follows.

Sampling

Appraisers rarely have access to all available information for use in their analyses. Even when an appraiser has conducted extensive research, sample information frequently must be used. Therefore, the principles and implications of sampling should be understood by all appraisers.

Appraisers frequently must deal with incomplete information due to time and cost limitations. Consequently, research involves the collection of both specific data and sample data for analytical purposes.

The use of sample data has both strengths and weaknesses. Samples are generally cheaper and more readily obtained than complete data; selected samples are sometimes more indicative than the results of a broader survey. They are easily tabulated, lend themselves to cross-referencing, and provide a foundation for statistical inference, including probability studies. Often, samples may be the only source of data available. However, sampling must be conducted carefully and the data must be properly interpreted. If not, the results can be inaccurate and misleading, more expensive than they are worth, or less reliable than they appear. Sampling requires special training and understanding; many people misunderstand or mistrust samples for a variety of reasons.

Whether or not the appraiser conducts formal sampling, the extent to which sample data have been used should be considered in the analytical process. The risks associated with identified sample data and the uncertainties associated with other potential data must be considered.

Data samples may be particularly important when other data are scarce or when the available data are less applicable due to market changes. Sampling may be the only way to obtain some types of data. Samples are particularly important in quantifying market demand; defining market characteristics; identifying market attitudes, perceptions, motivation, and understanding; analyzing market behavior; and interpreting market activities and intentions.

Sensitivity Analysis

Sensitivity analysis, which is applied in both valuations and consulting work, is performed by entering one or more variables at a time into an analytical model to determine the model's sensitivity to each change. Factors that cause greater changes in the results are considered more sensitive and, therefore, pose greater risk to the expected outcome.

For example, assume that a property has an estimated NOI expectancy of $200,000. It is possible that the NOI could be as much as 10% less, or only $180,000. A 75% mortgage is available for the property with a debt service constant of 13%. The equity capitalization, or equity dividend, rate is most probably 10%, but it may range up to 11%. The analyst wants to know which variable is more sensitive, a 10% change in the NOI or a 10% change in the equity capitalization rate. The calculations are shown below.

	$200,000 NOI	$180,000 NOI
0.75 mortgage × 0.13 constant	0.0975	0.0975
0.25 equity × 0.10 cap rate	0.0250	0.0250
Indicated overall rate	0.1225	0.1225
Indicated value (NOI/R_o)	$1,632,653	$1,469,388

	$200,000 NOI	$180,000 NO
0.75 mortgage × 0.13 constant	0.0975	0.0975
0.25 equity × 0.11 cap rate	0.0275	0.0275
Indicated overall rate	0.1250	0.1250
Indicated value (NOI/R_o)	$1,600,000	$1,440,000

This sensitivity test indicates that a 10% change in the *NOI* is substantially more significant than a 10% change in the equity capitalization rate. The largest resulting change for the discount rate was approximately $32,500 ($1,632,653–$1,600,000), compared with a maximum change of more than $163,000 ($1,632,653–$1,469,388) for the *NOI*.

Sensitivity tests can be applied to virtually any element in the analysis that is subject to change. The results of sensitivity analysis facilitate decisions regarding the need for further data, the ranges and consequences of risk factors, and the steps that should be taken to implement these decisions.

Network Analysis

Network analysis is commonly used as a management tool to schedule and conduct project activities. In real estate consulting, network analysis allows an appraiser to outline the steps to be followed in implementing real estate decisions, to identify critical variables and contingencies, and to deal with the risks and uncertainties associated with given decisions.

Project Evaluation and Review Technique (PERT) charts illustrate how network analyses are conducted. Simple flow charts can also be used to show the orderly processing of decisions and to indicate the critical timing aspects involved. Large-scale analyses may rely on computer programs, which are available even for small computers, but network analysis can also be applied with manual computations.

Rating Grids

Rating grids have many applications and can be used in many different ways. A "most appropriate" investment alternative is selected by assigning arbitrary weights to the factors considered in a given decision and then totaling the weights for each alternative.

For example, assume that three people are given the responsibility to select a site for a new building. They consult an appraiser who identifies seven factors that are important to the decision and locates three properties from which the choice must be made. Each factor is to be judged on a scale of one to 10; a rating of 10 is extremely good and a rating of one is unacceptable. The analysis is represented by the following grid.

Factor	Alternative 1 Joe	Sam	Ann	Alternative 2 Joe	Sam	Ann	Alternative 3 Joe	Sam	Ann
Lot size	8	7	7	5	4	6	6	5	4
Exposure	3	3	4	9	7	7	5	6	7
Quality of area	6	7	6	8	6	7	5	6	4
Traffic conditions	8	6	8	7	5	6	3	5	4
Price	4	7	5	7	6	6	9	9	8
Utilities	6	6	7	6	7	6	8	9	8
Distance to homes	3	8	8	9	6	3	6	5	4
Totals	38	44	45	51	41	41	42	45	39

A grid such as this can be very helpful to those who must reach a specific real estate decision. In an actual application, decision makers may center their discussion on individual preferences, the various weights assigned to individual factors, and the adequacy of the original list of factors. As the grid shows, each individual favors a different alternative, so it is unlikely that any choice can be made without further discussion.

Linear Programming

Linear programming is a complex type of mathematical analysis which is concerned with optimizing the allocation of resources. An equation in linear form is developed and the various resources are subjected to linear inequality constraints.

The optimization model designates certain values as constants and then tests for one or more investment-decision variables. For example, one application may identify dollar returns and capital outlay requirements at varying times as constants and test for the present value of the investment in dollars. Another model could be constructed to solve for the minimum cost of an annuity to produce a desired minimum result.

Linear programming provides an opportunity to deal with two or more projects simultaneously; thus, it is especially effective in making portfolio investment decisions. The optimization technique is a unique way to consider risk-return relationships and to analyze the diversification of opportunities. Due to the complexity of linear programming, however, a computer is required.

Regression Analysis

With the increased accessibility and capability of small computers, regression analysis has become an important tool for all types of financial analyses. It is particularly useful and applicable to real estate studies. Regression analysis may be used for explanatory purposes, to make predictions or forecasts, or for a combination of these activities. Regression identifies the possible relationships between or among variables to provide a better understanding of the underlying data.

Simple regression analysis measures the relationship between an independent variable and a dependent variable with the equation

$$Y_C = a + bX$$

where Y_c is the forecast value, a is a constant, b is a multiplier or coefficient, and X is the value of an independent variable. Thus the equation states that for the independent variable, X, the expected value of the Y variable to which it is being related is Y_c.

Regression analysis does not necessarily imply or attempt to quantify causative relationships. Rather, it reveals the apparent relationships between the values of different variables and their tendency to vary regularly with one another. When strong relationships are found, measuring these relationships can help explain one or more of the variables and forecast their values.

When more than one independent variable is involved in the analysis, multiple regression is used. For multiple regression analysis, the simple regression equation is expanded by adding terms for subsequent independent variables. The equation becomes

$$Y_C = a + b_1X_1 + b_2X_2 + \ldots + b_nX_n$$

This equation uses the same symbols as the basic equation, but each independent variable and its associated multiplier or coefficient are identified with an appropriate numerical subscript.

Regression analysis takes a number of mathematical forms, but it is relatively simple to perform even with a small computer. Care should be exercised in entering the data and interpreting the results; both require special consideration. Computer applications also allow practitioners to analyze situations in which the relationships among variables are best expressed graphically with some type of curved line.

Regression is an important tool in real estate valuation, particularly when a large number of properties or a large quantity of data is being considered. It is equally applicable to a broad range of market and property analyses in real estate consulting. Regression analysis is often used in forecasting, but its explanatory powers should not be overlooked. It may, for example, be used to identify the factors to be analyzed, explain their significance, and avoid duplication in weighting two variables that are closely associated.

Geographic Information Systems (GIS)

Geographic Information Systems (GIS) technology combines spatial information from a national database with computer mapping and modeling capabilities. While GIS real estate applications are still in an embryonic stage, GIS is expected to have a strong impact on traditional location analysis just as computerized discounted cash flow modeling has dramatically influenced financial analysis in the past two decades. GIS can create highly sophisticated digital maps with a process that represents a computer-age refinement of map overlay procedures which were once expensive and time-consuming.

GIS can integrate digital maps with point- or area-specific data to answer basic questions such as:

1. What is found in a specific location?
2. Where within a given area is a specific feature, activity, or event located?
3. What changes have occurred in an area over a given period of time?
4. What type of spatial patterns characterize a given area?
5. What impact will a specific change have upon the area?

The data used to generate such maps are typically found in a computer database that includes referents to a specific point on the earth's surface (i.e., latitude and longitude) and/or a specific area (e.g., city, zip code area, census tract).

Given sufficient information, the system can quickly pinpoint properties with very specific characteristics. For example, the system can identify the locations of all parcels of vacant land in a given county that have the following characteristics:

- Contain 40 or more acres
- Meet specific soil suitability standards
- Are equipped with municipal water and sewer lines
- Are zoned residentially
- Have an elementary school within a one-half mile radius and are adjacent to neighborhoods where median home value exceeds $150,000

The dramatic increase in the use of GIS equipment is the result of three factors: 1) the decline in the price of high-powered personal computers, 2) improvements in GIS software, and 3) expansion of commercially available geo-referenced data. In the 1990 census, data were gathered and reported with reference to a computer-based digital street map of the entire United States. Topologically Integrated Geographic Encoding and Referencing (TIGER) data files are commercially available to GIS users; the system will continue to provide a wealth of information as new data are released.

Highly accurate digital base maps for most areas of the United States are also available at reasonable prices from the United States Geological Survey (USGS). Many local governments sell geo-referenced digital data on individual parcels that are compiled from assessment data and public record information. Data vendors will continue to expand the amount of commerically available data compatible with GIS.

STUDIES UNDERTAKEN IN CONSULTING

Real estate appraisers are frequently asked to provide both valuation and consulting services for use in real estate decision making. The decisions being contemplated may involve the acquisition or disposition of real estate, the development or redevelopment potential of a property, or financial management and planning alternatives.

The specific services performed for a client must be tailored to the individual circumstances and meet established professional standards. The range of possible services is nearly infinite, but some typical studies undertaken in consulting work are discussed below. Each study may be conducted independently or it may be a component of a more detailed investment analysis.

Feasibility Studies

Feasibility studies are performed to test the ability of various investment scenarios to meet explicit investment objectives. Scenarios that meet the objectives are feasible, while those that do not are infeasible.

Feasibility studies are frequently confused with highest and best use studies. Highest and best use studies, which are also commonly undertaken in consulting work, seek to determine the optimum use or uses for a specified parcel of real estate. The use that produces the highest net return is considered the highest and best use. Feasibility studies focus on specific investment objectives and analyze all contributing and limiting factors to determine whether a given combination of factors meets the minimum objectives established by the decision makers.

Highest and best use studies center on a property and its use. Feasibility studies are concerned not only with a property and its selected use, but also with an investment alternative and the objectives of a given client. The business interests or motivations of a particular client may lead to real estate decisions that appear to defy highest and best use determinations, but meet the standards established by the feasibility criteria. Even when common uses are being considered, a given investment alternative may be feasible for one investor and infeasible for another.

These distinctions demonstrate that feasibility studies involve both objective analysis and the subjective interpretation of findings in light of a particular client's circumstances. In providing consulting services, appraisers must help clients distinguish among facts, estimates, and subjective factors and weigh the results of analyses and the anticipated consequences of the real estate decision. Virtually any analytical tool may be used in a feasibility study, but DCF analysis is the technique most commonly applied. A proper feasibility study provides for analysis at several points to test the internal consistency and findings of the study and to facilitate the application of the decision-making guidelines established to determine feasibility.

For example, an appraiser who is assessing the feasibility of a developer's plans for a subdivision could devise a test to monitor cumulative positive and negative cash flows. If the developer has established that the development must at no time have a negative cash flow of more than $200,000, the appraiser can determine the possibility and associated probability of the negative cash flow exceeding this limit and report that the plan is infeasible if an excess appears likely. Feasibility analysis may also identify crucial variables which by themselves indicate that a planned investment is impracticable.

Market Studies

Market studies relate to the general market conditions of supply, demand, and pricing or to the demographics of specific areas or property types. They are generally considered macroeconomic studies and often focus on housing conditions in a given sector of a community, a region, or the nation as a whole. Market studies may include analyses of construction and absorption trends, pricing and price changes, construction types and locations, or other factors relating to housing.

The studies may reveal or explain facts and behavior regarding property types, investor activities, or other matters of market concern. Market studies pertaining to the activities of mortgage lenders and borrowers, the construction of various types of buildings, and the preferences of investors are particularly common.

Marketability Studies

Marketability studies are microeconomic studies that focus on the marketability of a given property or class of properties. Usually the appraiser must identify one or more market segments in which the property would generate market demand and all the factors related to that demand.

Marketability studies are especially useful in determining highest and best use and testing specific development proposals. In either case a marketability study can provide a client with the information needed to judge the source or sources of likely demand, the timing of this demand, the amount of money that would probably be spent by each demand component, and the property's ability to capture the available demand.

Marketability studies are commonly undertaken to project the tenant composition of planned retail facilities or to improve the tenant mix in existing facilities. They are fundamental to an economic understanding of how potential demand is translated into effective demand and the risks involved in achieving cash flow objectives.

Marketability studies often provide the basis for development decisions on single-family subdivisions, multifamily projects, and residential condominiums. In fact, these studies are useful whenever time and money are available to conduct a detailed analysis of demand factors and to adapt the proposed plans to the findings.

Cost-Benefit Studies

Cost-benefit studies can be conducted on a macroeconomic or microeconomic basis. For example, a community may require a cost-benefit study to determine the economic benefits that would most likely result from a new public project such as an expressway or a sewage treatment plant. The cost-benefit study would focus on the relationship between the benefits created and the costs associated with the project to determine whether the benefits warrant the costs. Developers also use cost-benefit studies, particularly when they are called upon to install major items that properly belong to the infrastructure. Such work clearly goes beyond direct project requirements, so developers must look to the future to recapture the extra dollars invested. A cost-benefit study can establish the relative worth of such expenditures in relation to the benefits.

Pricing and Rent Projection Studies

Pricing and rent projection studies may be components of marketability studies or the subject of separate studies. These analyses are frequently conducted to establish sales and marketing strategies for real estate projects and to facilitate decisions involving property management and investment.

Other Real Estate Studies

Other types of real estate studies include economic base studies, consumer profile studies, absorption studies, land-use strategy studies, and studies of other economic characteristics. Many call for special skills and training on the part of the real estate appraiser and some require the services of other professionals. Most real estate appraisers possess a variety of skills and many are qualified by their experience and training to provide a range of real estate services.

INCOME TAXES AND REAL ESTATE CONSULTING

Federal and state income taxation affects all types of investments. Real estate has long been the subject of special provisions under various income tax codes and rulings and these provisions influence investors' decisions regarding different real estate types and locations, the prices they will pay, and the structuring of legal ownership to obtain every available advantage.

Income tax codes have historically provided real estate investors with the advantages of tax shelter, the deduction of expenses, income tax deferral, leverage, and the conversion of ordinary income into capital gains.

Tax shelter. To encourage investment in real estate, income tax laws have long allowed some investors to shelter all or part of the income produced by a real estate investment from income taxes. Surplus benefits that exceed the income produced by a given investment could also be credited toward the income produced by other investments, thereby multiplying the benefits produced by the tax-sheltered real estate.

The deduction of passive activity losses, yet another type of tax-sheltered investment, was disallowed by the Tax Reform Act of 1986. Passive activity is an arrangement in which the individual who receives the income has no material participation in the enterprise—i.e., no regular, continuous, or substantial involvement in the business operation. The Tax Reform Act of 1986 allows the deduction of losses only to the extent that the financial resources of the operation are at risk. In other words, the deduction cannot exceed the amount of the investment. Moreover, deductions are reduced and eventually eliminated as the investor's income increases. A ceiling on deductions is placed on taxable income of $150,000 or more.

Deduction of expenses. Specified operating expenses and depreciation allowances, which reduce the income tax liability of a given real estate investment, qualify as deductions from taxable income.

Income tax deferral. The tax laws provide a means to shift the time frames in which income taxes must be filed and paid. This provision allows investors to structure their investments to take advantage of special timing and reduce their total income tax liability. However, the Tax Reform Act of 1986 strongly recommends that investors adhere to the calendar year for income tax reporting purposes.

Leverage. Leverage is important to virtually all types of investors. In real estate investments leverage is considered both before and after income taxes. Under the old tax laws, some cash flow situations that looked particularly onerous before income taxes could be structured to provide attractive after-tax cash flows.

Conversion of ordinary income into capital gains. The treatment of capital gains as qualifying income items once permitted taxpayers in high income brackets to state the returns from profits on real estate investments at the time of sale and obtain lower marginal tax rates for these returns. Due to the differences among tax brackets, this provision was a major consideration in the income tax structuring of investments. The Tax Reform Act of 1986 eliminated this treatment of capital gains from real estate and other investments. Now capital gains are taxed like income, but filed under a separate classification.

In the 1980s federal income taxes were subject to frequent and sweeping changes. There was strong public support for income tax simplification and the revision of federal and state income taxes as a means to reduce the public debt.

In real estate consulting, the fundamental economics of a real estate investment must be distinguished from the marginal benefits that may accrue as a result of income tax advantages, investment structuring schemes, favored financing plans, or other programs that manipulate the specific circumstances of a given situation. Fundamental economic laws and relationships remain operative in all business cycles and investment situations. Although the marginal benefits associated with specific investment circumstances are important, the value of these benefits depends on the underlying economics of the real estate operation to which they pertain. The importance of marginal benefits to a real estate investment should not be overstated.

In consulting assignments appraisers must understand how federal and state income taxes influence real estate investments, especially when specific client needs are involved and general market data reflect the effects of income tax provisions.

COUNSELING AS AN EXTENSION OF CONSULTING

Real estate counseling is defined by the American Society of Real Estate Counselors of the National Association of Realtors® (ASREC) as

Providing competent, disinterested, and unbiased advice, professional guidance, and sound judgment on diversified problems in the broad field of real estate involving any or all segments of the business such as merchandising, leasing, management, planning, financing, appraising, court testimony, and other similar services. Counseling may involve the utilization of any or all of these functions.

Unlike appraisers, counselors may go beyond consulting or offering advice to a client and directly represent the client's interests. The Code of Professional Ethics and Standards of Professional Appraisal Practice of the Appraisal Institute distinguish between appraisal assignments and the ancillary services that go beyond appraising; these documents set forth the procedures to be followed by appraisers in such situations. Similarly, ASREC has ethical and performance standards to guide practitioners in the field of real estate counseling.

Counseling assignments cover a variety of real estate situations; counseling services can be provided in all real estate fields and the range of situations covered is unlimited. Counseling services may include appraising just as appraisers may counsel clients within the scope of consulting assignments. Appraisers may offer advice on real estate economics and the components and consequences of the economic decisions a client must make.

When counseling clients as part of real estate consulting, appraisers base their advice on supportable facts and conclusions. The typical result of a consulting assignment is a letter or report that summarizes the appraiser's facts, data, analyses, and conclusions and confirms any advice that has been rendered orally. A report for consulting work not only establishes the appraiser's services on a professional basis, but also provides direct communication that can prevent misunderstandings and give the client a framework within which to apply the appraiser's findings and advice.

SUMMARY

Real estate appraisals may involve valuation services, consulting services, or both. Consulting is usually performed to provide assistance in real estate decision making. Many valuation assignments include consulting services because market participants who need to know market value may also be interested in other data that characterize the market. Both consulting and valuation assignments are covered by the Code of Professional Ethics and Standards of Professional Appraisal Practice of the Appraisal Institute.

Consulting assignments may call for general market analysis or the analysis of a specific parcel of real estate. In valuation assignments real property interests are identified and particular categories of value are defined; by contrast, the nature and scope of consulting assignments must be specified in each individual case.

The distinction between market value and investment value is important. *Investment value* is the specific value of goods or services to a particular investor. Market value does not relate to a specific buyer or seller; rather, a hypothetical or typical market participant is assumed. The market is made up of a multitude of transactions that involve willing parties making individual investment decisions. The *transaction price* of a property varies with the strength of the participants' motivation and with the availability of investment opportunities. Depending on the specific circumstances, the transaction price of a property at any given moment may fluctuate above or below its exact value at *perfect market equilibrium.* Market value estimates are a synthesis of these transactions.

Certain measures of investment performance are particularly applicable to real estate. Simple ratios ($R = I/V$) may be used, but they do not reflect the effect of specific factors. The *payback period* or *breakeven point* (PB = equity capital outlay/annual net equity cash flows) does not consider the time value of money or specific investment risks. A *profitability index* or *benefit/cost ratio* (PI = PV of anticipated investment returns/PV of capital outlay) is commonly used in conjunction with *net present value* (NPV) or *dollar reward* which does consider the time value of money. The formula for calculating net present value is

$$NPV = CF_0 + \frac{CF_1}{(1+i)} + \frac{CF_2}{(1+i)^2} \cdots + \frac{CF_n}{(1+i)^n} - CO$$

Time-weighted rates, which may also be called *unit-method rates* or *share-accounting rates,* are used primarily in portfolio management.

Discounted cash flow (DCF) analysis is the most detailed and precise way to measure cash inflows and outflows over the life of an investment. The sum of the present values of all future positive and negative cash flows represents the DCF value indication at a given discount rate. Discounted cash flow analysis can be performed on a before- or after-tax basis. It can be used in conjunction with other measures and applied on a constant, noninflated or nominal, actual dollar basis. The techniques of DCF analysis can be used to account for varying risk situations and explicitly consider investment advantages and disadvantages. This type of analysis relies on forecast estimates and very subjective discount rates may be applied.

The *internal rate of return* (IRR), which is the rate of discount that produces a profitability index of one and a NPV of zero, may be regarded as a DCF analysis that is solved backwards. All cash inflows and outflows are analyzed to find the discount rate that renders them equivalent to the original capital outlay. Thus the IRR reflects the indicated return *on* and *of* the investment. The IRR has some disadvantages. Controversy over the reinvestment presumption and weaknesses such as the possibility of more than one *IRR*, the discounting of negative cash flows, conflict with the *NPV*, and a lack of recognition for differences in capital outlays have led to modifications of the *IRR*. Nevertheless, the *IRR* is a prominent example of yield analysis and a very important measure of investment performance.

No single measure of investment performance is always the best or most appropriate. Each has its limitations and all are more effective when used in conjunction with other measures. Measures of performance are tools that can help an appraiser inform or refine his or her professional judgment.

To complete a consulting assignment, an appropriate problem-solving process must be identified for the specific situation. Consulting usually focuses on the subjective goals of a specific client, rather than a general composite of the market. Because consulting relates the appraiser's findings to a specific decision-making situation, *risk analysis* is a fundamental component.

Probability is the relative likelihood that a specified event will occur. Recognizing the range of probability, appraisers regard point estimates as the most probable numbers, not the only possible numbers. *Risk* is the probability that unforeseen events will not occur, while *uncertainty* is the probability that unforeseen events will occur. When the future is involved, appraisers use forecasts but avoid predictions.

Within the framework of risk analysis, probabilities are linked with risks. Ranges of probability are determined in four different ways: analysis of past events, controlled experiment and observation, theoretical distribution, and individual judgment. By identifying several possible outcomes, the limitations of a single point estimate are overcome.

To analyze risk, appraisers may assign *utility functions*, which are subjective weights given to each possible investment outcome to reflect the investor's relative preferences. A *debt coverage ratio (DCR)* is calculated by dividing *NOI* by annual debt service; this measure is commonly used in structuring or underwriting mortgages and in feasibility analysis. Investors may consider an investment's *payback period* or its *upside/downside* potential. The latter is measured by analyzing best and worst case anticipations in conjunction with DCF analysis.

Expected values are weighted probabilities similar to utility functions. Using *Monte Carlo simulation*, specific investment elements are assigned probabilities and integrated into a larger theoretical population; sampling from this larger group provides a range of possible outcomes. *Risk-adjusted discount rates* reflect all the risk elements associated with an income stream for a specified period and are adjusted to offset additional term risk.

In addition to investment performance measures and risk analysis methods, real estate consulting may draw on other analytical tools. These techniques include *sampling*, the application of statistical inference to *sample* data for use in forecasting market demand; *sensitivity analysis*, which isolates how changes in variables such as the *NOI* or R_E affect risk; *network analysis*, which diagrams the flow of processes and the critical timing aspects involved; *rating grids*, which assign arbitrary weights to the different factors involved in a decision to be made by several individuals; and *linear programming*, which is used to optimize the allocation of resources and employs a linear equation that subjects variables to inequality constraints.

Regression analysis examines the relationship between one or more independent variables and a dependent variable by plotting lines on graphs. It is used to identify and weight analytical factors and to make forecasts. Simple linear regression is based on the equation $Y_c = a + bX$; multiple regression uses the equation

$$Y_c = a + b_1 X_1 + b_2 X_2 + \ldots + b_n X_n$$

Geographic Information Systems (GIS) represent a computer-age refinement of map overlay procedures. GIS integrates spatial information from a national database and computer mapping and modeling capabilities.

The range of consulting services available is extremely wide. *Feasibility studies* test the ability of given investment alternatives to meet explicit objectives (e.g., cash flow expectations) by analyzing all contributing and limiting factors and determining which combination or combinations meet the investor's criteria. Feasibility studies begin with a highest and best use determination and focus on a specific investment scenario. *Market studies* are macroeconomic studies that relate to supply and demand, demographics, pricing, and construction and absorption trends. *Marketability studies* are microeconomic studies that focus on the marketability of a given property or a class of properties to determine a specific highest and best use, test development proposals, or project an appropriate tenant mix. *Cost-benefit studies* examine the probable economic benefits that will result from proposed public projects, and *pricing and rent projection studies* are conducted to determine marketing strategies.

In the 1980s federal income tax laws underwent extensive changes. Tax reform redirected the attention of investors toward the fundamental economics of real estate investments and away from the marginal benefits that result from tax advantages. Many traditional tax advantages were curtailed by the Tax Reform Act of 1986. The tax shelter benefits of real estate were diminished by the "at risk" rule, which provides that passive losses deducted cannot exceed the amount of the investment. Deductions were also limited according to the taxable income of the investor. Income tax deferral is also threatened because adherence to the calendar year is recommended for income tax purposes. The conversion of ordinary income into capital gains is no longer advantageous because the special treatment of capital gains has been eliminated.

Real estate counseling is defined by the American Society of Real Estate Counselors of the National Association of Realtors® and recognized in the Appraisal Institute's Code of Professional Ethics and Standards of Professional Appraisal Practice. Counseling involves services that are often associated with consulting, but are beyond the scope of appraising. To prevent misunderstandings and establish counseling services on a professional basis, appraisers are advised to prepare a letter or report for the client summarizing the data, analyses, and conclusions applied and confirming any oral advice rendered.

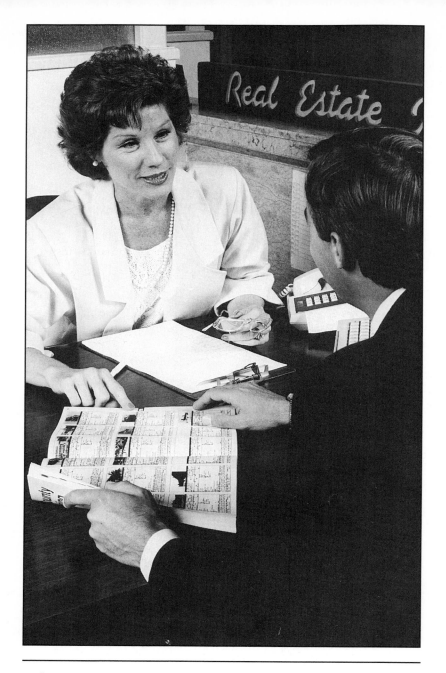

Chapter 26

APPRAISAL REVIEW

*I*n most fields of endeavor, the final product is subject to examination by inspectors or controllers. The appraisal review procedure may be likened to a quality control or auditing function. Usually the appraisers in an office review the work of one another before submitting it to their staff managers or clients. In an appraisal review, the logic and procedures employed in an appraisal report are investigated and verified to ensure that the value estimate derived is a reliable indication that the client can use in his or her decision making.

Appraisals may also be reviewed by clients. Typically a formal review process is conducted in offices that receive a large volume of appraisal reports. Government entities such as regulatory agencies, revenue offices, agencies that exercise the power of eminent domain, and quasi-governmental offices that insure mortgages perform appraisal reviews. Private lending organizations that employ review appraisers as staff members include thrift institutions, commercial banks, insurance companies, mortgage bankers, pension fund managers, and investment trusts.

Review appraisers serve the corporate and private sectors in several ways. They assist in making decisions pertaining to the buying, selling, and leasing of property as well as decisions involving properties managed as fixed assets. Often reviewers are hired on a fee basis to assess the validity of an appraisal.

A review appraiser is an appraiser who examines the reports of other appraisers to determine whether their conclusions are consistent with the data reported and other generally known information.[1] The review appraiser interprets and critiques the methods and procedures applied in a valuation.

Because appraisal is both an art and a science, a value conclusion is the product of an appraiser's reasoning and judgment. To understand the appraiser's thought process and the rationale underlying the value conclusion, the appraisal must be carefully read. Differences arising from the use of nonstandardized reporting formats also require interpretation and verification.

PURPOSE OF APPRAISAL REVIEW

One of the primary functions of an appraisal review is to provide a test of reasonableness for the user of a report, who may have doubts or apprehensions about the data, analyses, and conclusions the report contains. The reasonableness of the assumptions and limiting conditions is also considered.

Appraisal reviews are performed as tests of appropriateness. The methodology and techniques employed in the appraisal are considered in terms of their appropriateness to the appraisal problem. A reviewer checks for consistency and mathematical accuracy throughout the report. Because appraisals are not standardized products, reviewers must determine whether the data have been analyzed in a logical fashion and whether the conclusions are consistent with the data presented.

Appraisal reviews are often conducted to *enhance* the client's confidence in an appraisal. The reviewer determines whether the quantity and quality of the data analyzed are suitable. The reviewer ascertains whether the appraiser has examined

---

1. *The Dictionary of Real Estate Appraisal*, second edition (Chicago: American Institute of Real Estate Appraisers, 1989).

all relevant economic indicators, considered all elements of comparison, and applied all available techniques consistent with the appraisal problem.

Appraisal reviews play an important role in the risk management procedures of lending organizations. A reviewer may attempt to identify the trends referred to in an appraisal report or to assess the degree of risk involved in a business decision by performing sensitivity analyses.

Appraisal review can raise appraisers' level of professionalism, ensuring a more uniform and higher-quality product which may assist appraisers in career advancement. An appraisal review may be conducted as a compliance check to determine whether the appraiser has met the requirements of a client that is a lender, regulatory agency, or public agency. Appraisal reviews can help appraisers become accepted as qualified professionals and may sometimes be a part of the ongoing process by which a client's list of approved and recommended appraisers is maintained.

CLIENT REVIEW REQUIREMENTS

Appraisal review requirements vary depending on the client. The review requirements of lenders may be tailored to their specific policies and procedures, which include compliance with the requirements of federal agencies as well as statutory requirements relating to foreclosure. Mortgage insurers have unique appraisal requirements. Federal and quasi-federal agencies that conduct appraisal reviews as a normal part of their audit procedures have their own specifications for appraisals. State and local governmental agencies such as highway departments conduct reviews in conjunction with the acquisition of rights of way and have their own requirements for condemnation proceedings. Many corporations and private organizations such as relocation companies perform appraisal reviews in conjunction with the services they provide.

It may be necessary for an appraiser to brief the client on the different levels of appraisal reviews available and to recommend the level appropriate to the client's needs.

REVIEWING APPRAISALS

An appraisal review differs significantly from an appraisal report. The function of the review appraiser is not to appraise the subject property, but to analyze the contents of the appraisal report itself.

A review appraiser identifies and judges the reasoning and logic that underlies another appraiser's work, but does not substitute his or her own judgment for the judgment of that other appraiser. The reviewer's task is to analyze the total work product of the appraiser in an impartial and objective manner.

Although reviews are performed for a variety of reasons, many are routine assignments. Appraisal reviews are regularly conducted for government agencies involved in takings for public projects and for financial entities contemplating the use of property as collateral for mortgage loans. Review assignments can have serious consequences, and reviews based on investigative work may have civil, or even criminal, implications.

Reviews of appraisals of distressed properties or properties taken back by financial institutions or regulatory agencies can result in lawsuits against the original appraiser. Reviewers cannot dismiss the possibility that their reviews may be used against the original appraiser in court proceedings.

In the past 60 years, real estate appraisal has evolved from an occupation filled with seasoned generalists into a highly technical discipline practiced by computer-literate specialists. In the past only the direct client reviewed appraisal reports and, since many clients were nonprofessionals, many appraisal reports were inadequately reviewed. More and more governmental and quasi-governmental agencies now require appraisal reviews, especially in the acquisition of rights of way and condemnation proceedings. Similarly, state and federal agencies that collect estate taxes have adopted the practice of using appraisal reviews. Corporations and private relocation firms have also realized their need for appraisal reviews in conjunction with the real estate services they render.

Reviews are increasingly necessary because the complexity of the appraisal process has increased; the vocabulary of appraisal has become more technical and the methodology more sophisticated. Increased specialization and responsibility have resulted from the internationalization and globalization of capital markets in general, and investment-grade real estate in particular. Regulators are needed to scrutinize appraisals and carry out other audit functions designed to protect the public interest. These developments have created a need for trained and qualified review appraisers, formal appraisal review procedures, and formal appraisal management policies.

APPRAISAL MANAGEMENT

Establishing a sound appraisal management policy makes good business sense for any financial institution or government agency. The proper valuation and evaluation of real estate used as loan collateral is essential in transactions involving real estate. A solid value basis is needed both to secure the loan or asset and to provide a reliable source of repayment. Any sound appraisal management policy must specify appraisal review procedures and practices.

A good appraisal management policy can help standardize the criteria used to evaluate property performance and measure risk. By creating a solid basis for decision making in regard to both associated risk and the quality of an investment portfolio, an appraisal management policy reflects an institution's commitment to operate in a safe and sound manner.

Because appraisal services play such an important role in loan and investment decisions, these services must meet the lending policies and investment guidelines of the institutions and agencies served. It is critical that the objectives of the appraiser match those of the client. Mutual understanding will tend to encourage the client to have confidence in the appraiser.

The development of an appraisal management policy begins with the review of existing policies on loans and investments. The policy established should be structured to provide the information needed to implement lending and investment policies. This policy must direct managers to work closely with appraisers to ensure that appraisal problems are properly defined and that appropriate appraisal data, techniques, and methods are employed to provide solutions to these problems.

An appraisal management policy should reflect regulatory obligations, mandate due diligence, ensure conformance to professional standards, generate current and meaningful valuations, and establish criteria for a thorough review process. In addition, the policy should provide guidelines on why and when to require appraisals and how to implement appraisals once they are initiated.

Developing an Appraisal Policy

The responsibility for developing, implementing, and maintaining a valuation policy must be assigned to competent staff and committee members. This responsibility includes:

- Development of a set of written policies and procedures to be communicated to all employees affected
- Maintenance of independent control over the actual appraisal process
- Approval of all appraisals utilized
- Maintenance of files documenting the auditing of all appraisals governed by the policy
- Assurance that all appraisals are prepared according to accepted standards of professional appraisal practice and in compliance with regulatory requirements

Among the issues that must be addressed in the formulation of an appraisal policy are definitions of value, the qualifications of staff members, selection of outside fee appraisers, appraisal practices, appraisal review procedures, specific appraisal guideline criteria, appraisal update requirements, and procedures to ensure quality control and compliance with standards.

Specific considerations include:

- The type of appraisal reports the institution requires—i.e., form reports or narrative reports
- The standards of practice that appraisers must follow and the minimum requirements for content and documentation that appraisers must meet
- The types of value required in appraisal reports prepared for the institution
- The appraisers authorized to prepare appraisals on behalf of the institution—i.e., appraiser selection procedures
- The procedures for commissioning appraisals and the manager to whom this task will be delegated
- The type of information to be furnished to appraisers
- The managers who will monitor the process to ensure that the objectives of the assignment are understood, the work is submitted on time, and the product is of good quality
- Appraisal review policies and procedures
- The supervisor responsible for determining if the appraisals obtained are acceptable to the institution
- A policy on appraisals that may be too dated to be reliable
- The procedures to be followed when market conditions are rapidly changing, the plans or specifications of a projected property have been altered, or the appraised property no longer matches the original real estate interest

Appraiser Guidelines

Management is responsible for the selection of both staff appraisers and contractual fee appraisers. Whether the work is performed internally or externally, appraisal expertise is needed to provide a reliable foundation for decision making. The criteria for selecting apraisers depend on the size of the institution or agency, the location, and the institution's current and anticipated involvement in real estate transactions. The appraisal function must remain independent of the other functions of the agency. In banks and thrift institutions, the appraisal function must be totally separate from lending and collection functions. The institution can have no interest, financial or otherwise, in the collateral appraised.

The appraisers selected should demonstrate the competence required to perform appraisals according to accepted standards and regulations. They must be qualified to perform the assignments they are given, and their experience should be commensurate with the complexity of their assignments. The hiring guidelines established should apply to both staff appraisers and appraisers retained on a contractual fee basis.

To evaluate an appraiser's professional qualifications, management must consider the appraiser's education, training, type of experience, and membership in professional appraisal organizations. A review of recent appraisal reports completed by the appraiser and a check of client references are usually necessary to complete the selection process.

Hiring guidelines for appraisers must be tailored to the needs of the institution or agency and should be guided by the character of the targeted market, the type of property likely to be appraised, the complexity of the anticipated assignments, and the availability of appraisal services in the community.

It is extremely important that staff appraisers, both review appraisers and field appraisers, meet training and experience qualifications. All valuations ultimately fall under the authority of the internal valuation unit, which may decide not to accept the value conclusions of independent appraisers contracted from outside the institution.

Appraisal Report Content

The volume of an institution's business, the size and complexity of the typical property, and the degree of client involvement in the typical property determine whether the institution should use a form or narrative report format. Regardless of the format in which the report is presented, each appraisal should 1) contain sufficient information to enable management to determine reasonable loan amounts, 2) support classification of the specified assets as collateral for real estate loans, and 3) help determine other terms significant to credit arrangements.

The practices and procedures described below reflect accepted appraisal standards and are appropriate for most institutions:

- Appraisals should be prepared according to accepted standards and meet the reporting requirements set forth in the written appraisal guidelines of the institution. All appraisers approved by the institution should be provided with a copy of these guidelines.

- Each appraisal should be sufficiently current to ensure that any change in market conditions is unlikely to reduce the collateral value of the property.
- An appraisal should reflect the market value of the property rights in the realty involved in the transaction or being offered as security. All other values or interests appraised must be clearly labeled and separately valued—e.g., the value of personalty, the value of financing terms, the value of the business component in the property, or the value of furniture, fixtures, and equipment.
- Appraisals must contain adequate information on current and anticipated market conditions and their likely impact on value. With this information the institution can determine whether its financial position will be suitably secured during the term of the loan. The scope of the market information provided will depend on the property type, the credit or investment arrangement, and the financial considerations involved in the contemplated transaction.
- The appraiser must be aware of, understand, and correctly employ the recognized methods and techniques required to arrive at a creditable appraisal.

Appraisals that do not conform to standards can usually be identified in the appraisal review process. A reviewer who does not possess the requisite real estate experience, education, and training will not perform a satisfactory review. It is absolutely essential that reviewers have the appropriate qualifications to carry out the review function properly.

Customized Criteria

Each institution should develop its own appraisal specifications to ensure that the appraisal reports it uses contain adequate information to prudently evaluate all potential underwriting risks. Many short-term and interim-term lenders, in particular, require specific information which may not be included in standard appraisal reports. Such specific needs do not always represent extraordinary requirements. The institution may simply need to direct the emphasis of an appraisal to meaningful value issues such as appropriate market analysis or substantiation of key assumptions upon which the valuation is based. Most institutions need to develop customized criteria to guide appraisers in performing appraisals. Such criteria should address:

- The defined market area
- The effective date of the value estimate
- The approach appropriate to the specific property type (e.g., sales comparison for single-family residential property or the income approach for commercial real estate)
- Formal market studies required for specialized property types such as lodging facilities or congregate care centers
- Other estimates required to meet the special needs of the appraisal (e.g., an estimate of the costs incurred during lease-up and those required to carry a newly constructed project to stabilized occupancy). An alternative, downside estimate of a property's value for quick sale or liquidation is sometimes required. This worst case scenario might be investigated for purposes of internal risk management.

- An institution's criteria should also remind appraisers to comply with accepted requirements—e.g., state if the site is located in a flood hazard zone identified by the Federal Emergency Management Agency (FEMA); specify the known presence of hazardous materials, toxic waste, or seismic fault lines; stipulate that the appraisal meets accepted uniform standards.

Each appraisal report must:

- Be clearly written so as not to mislead a reader
- Contain sufficient information to enable a lender relying on the conclusion to understand the report properly
- Disclose any extraordinary assumptions or limiting conditions that directly affect the appraisal and indicate their impact on the value concluded.

The level of analysis in an appraisal generally reflects the complexity of the market for the property and the resources of the appraisal firm investigating this market. In the past decade it has become possible to segment real estate appraisal firms into three distinct tiers:

1. Local appraisal firms which typically appraise real estate such as residential or small commercial properties for which the scope of demand is local
2. Regional firms which focus on properties such as mid-rise, Class A office buildings, regional shopping centers, and industrial plants for which the scope of demand is regional
3. National and upper-echelon firms which almost exclusively analyze institutional-class properties such as superregional shopping centers, large planned unit developments, and trophy office towers

Appraiser Selection

An institution or agency should only retain appraisers who consistently provide a satisfactory work product, apply accepted appraisal methods and techniques, and, above all, demonstrate good judgment. Prospective appraisers should be asked to submit samples of completed reports on properties that are comparable to the client's targeted property in regard to type, size, value, and market.

Recommendations from other clients who have used the services of an appraiser or appraisal firm are a good source of contacts. Appraisers and appraisal firms should provide prospective employers with a summary of their professional qualifications, the resumes of their principal officers and staff members, and references from their major clients.

Sample reports should be carefully reviewed as they typically represent the appraiser's best efforts. The appraiser must demonstrate an ability to perform appraisals of good quality. Client references should be checked, preferably by means of written questionnaires. Many lenders and agencies send performance ratings to an appraiser's former clients. These contain inquiries about the overall expertise of the appraiser, the timeliness and quality of the report submitted, and the client's satisfaction with the services provided.

Appraisers will receive an "approved" or "qualified" rating based on their knowledge of a certain geographical market area, their expertise in valuing a particular type of realty, and the performance capability of their firm (e.g., the firm may be able to perform lease-by-lease analysis using computers). Once a list of appraisers has been compiled, the performance of those who are approved or qualified must be continually reviewed and the record updated. The work of newly qualified appraisers can be processed and their names added to the list. The performance of all approved appraisers must be periodically reviewed to ensure compliance with professional standards and reporting requirements. Firms that perform unsatisfactory work or work of uneven quality should not be retained.

Real estate lenders and other clients would be ill-advised to select an appraiser or an appraisal firm solely because it will perform the assignment for the lowest fee. An institution may eventually pay for such frugality with loan losses, greater sums expended on asset management, or additional reserves committed as loan collateral. Other clients who rely on poor appraisal reports may make bad investment decisions or risk monetary losses.

Problem appraisal reports typically result from

- Selection of the appraiser who charges the lowest fee
- Selection of the appraiser who can provide the quickest appraisal, even if the time frame is unrealistic
- Retention of an appraiser who lacks expertise in valuing the specific property type or an understanding of the market
- Use of appraisals that are not prepared in accordance with accepted standards
- Failure to provide specific guidelines to the appraiser retained
- Lack of communication resulting from the client's failure to communicate potential problems to the appraiser or the appraiser's failure to inform the client of critical problems in the assignment

Clients should demand well-reasoned appraisals based upon substantiated assumptions. They should also be willing to pay fees that are commensurate with the scope and quality of work performed.

To ensure quality control, independent valuation consultants may be called upon to do periodic spot checks of the appraisals on file. This procedure should include a field inspection of sample properties, especially high-priced, "market-sensitive" properties. A representative sample of more typical appraisals should also be reviewed. Spot checks serve to verify the sound judgment of the appraiser as well as that of the internal reviewer. Furthermore, they test whether an appraiser's value conclusions have been properly supported and documented.

Because it is the institution or agency that ultimately relies on the appraisal reports prepared, contracts with appraisers should be negotiated directly. Federally regulated lenders require appraisals prepared by appraisers who are selected by and directly under contract to the lender. Borrowers or loan brokers should not be assigned responsibility for procuring appraisals.

When clients retain an appraiser, it is recommended that they draw up an engagement letter. While this may not be required, an engagement letter generally makes sound business sense. The letter describes the nature and scope of the assignment, the client's specifications and guidelines, and the definition of market value to be used. The agreed-upon fee and delivery date for the report should also be stated.

Any extraordinary services should be fully described in the engagement letter. Use of an engagement letter helps formalize the contract and ensures that the nature of the assignment is clearly understood by all parties.

REVIEW PROCEDURES

Before an appraisal is submitted to a review appraiser, another staff member may conduct a compliance review to check the calculations and determine whether the appraisal report complies with basic content specifications. If any errors or omissions of items specified in the appraisal contract are found during the compliance review, the review appraiser determines how significant the errors are and whether the omissions are justified.

The review appraiser then undertakes a complete technical review of the appraisal report. Upon completion, he or she renders a written opinion as to whether to accept, reject, or modify the conclusions contained in the report. In drafting this written opinion, the review appraiser generally follows the process prescribed below.

The review appraiser first checks the appraisal file on the subject property or project. The file will reveal the purpose of the appraisal, the scope of the assignment, and the contractual obligations incumbent upon the appraiser. Many review appraisers then do a preliminary reading of the entire appraisal report to get an overall impression. This initial perusal may suggest several intermediate courses of action. For example, the reviewer may recommend that additional market data be obtained, that specific pages be corrected for the compliance review, that interviews be scheduled with people familiar with the property (including the appraiser), or that opinions be obtained from experts in other disciplines such as timber cruising, building demolition, property management, environmental hazards, or real estate law. If the reviewer has received more than one appraisal of the same property, he or she may compare the reports at this point to uncover any inconsistencies.

The review appraiser then analyzes the contents of the appraisal report. This analysis focuses on specific questions such as:

• Are the data compiled by the appraiser of adequate quality and quantity?

• Are the limiting conditions imposed by the appraiser both required and reasonable? Too many limiting conditions may diminish the usefulness of a report.

• If more than one appraiser has worked on an assignment, are their methodologies consistent?

• If the highest and best use of the property is rehabilitation, what level of rehabilitation has been suggested?

• If the purpose of the appraisal is to provide an estimate of value to determine the amount of a mortgage loan, does the report satisfy the requirements of the appropriate regulatory agency?

• If the report is subject to litigation, is the supporting evidence admissible in court?

When a field review is needed, the review appraiser conducts a thorough field inspection. In some offices to which appraisal reports are routinely submitted, most reports are subject to a desk review; field inspections are performed only for a representative sampling. A field inspection is a quality control procedure. A field review may be undertaken to augment the data reported by the appraiser or to resolve discrepancies between the facts or assumptions reported by two appraisers who have arrived at divergent market value estimates for the same property. Supplementary information can often be obtained or clarified by telephone and letter. Many offices do not routinely conduct field reviews; others do field reviews for every appraisal report submitted. The extent of the review required may be determined by the relative importance of the investment decision contemplated by the client.

A review appraiser must clearly distinguish between an individual difference of opinion with the appraiser who prepared the report and an objective review of the report containing that opinion. The review appraiser is usually not asked to write up an opinion of the reasonableness of the value estimate contained in an appraisal report. Rather, the review appraiser determines whether the data and analyses in the appraiser's report justify the opinion reached. Often the review appraiser does not have the means to find omissions by an appraiser, who may have neglected to uncover or report certain pertinent market transactions.

Review appraisers often have additional responsibilities. For example, they may have to clarify client guidelines for an appraisal, assess the qualifications of appraisers and decide which appraisers to retain, or serve as liaisons between clients and appraisers. Review appraisers also monitor the progress of appraisers on assignments to ensure that reports are timely and comply with regulations.

REVIEW REPORT FORMAT

Although there is no standard format for review reports, each review will contain certain items, including: identification of the appraiser; specification of the property rights appraised, the purpose and date of the appraisal, and the defined value; statement of the qualifying conditions and assumptions upon which the appraisal is based; the conclusion(s) of the appraiser; and the opinions, conclusions, and recommendations of the reviewer. The review must be dated, signed, and certified.

Review appraisers should be aware that their activities are subject to the Uniform Standards of Professional Appraisal Practice promulgated by The Appraisal Foundation.

APPRAISER-REVIEWER RELATIONSHIPS

Role of the Appraiser

The professional appraiser is accountable for his or her valuation and should be available to answer the client's question after the report has been submitted. Although it is not the appraiser's responsibility to educate the client about appraisal theory, the appraiser must be certain that the client understands the content of the appraisal report. An appraisal should be performed independently of all parties who have a vested interest in the proposed transaction—e.g., the buyers, sellers, borrowers, lenders, or brokers.

The appraiser is a neutral agent with the ethical responsibility to develop an objective value conclusion. A well-reasoned appraisal provides market data that will assist the client, whether he or she is a purchaser, a seller, a borrower, or a lender.

As mentioned earlier, lending institutions that commission appraisals should separate the appraisal function from the lending function. This separation creates a buffer between the lending officer who has a vested interest in making a loan, and the appraiser, who must conduct an impartial valuation. Such a separation also provides some assurance to the client that the appraisal conclusion has not been influenced by coercion.

Appraisers enhance their image and standing in the real estate community when they communicate well and promote good working relationships with clients. Clients should be encouraged to provide all information required by the appraiser. Full disclosure of pertinent data allows the appraiser to begin an assignment with assurance and not waste time puzzling through incomplete data.

The real estate appraiser is a trained professional who has the abilities to gather and analyze relevant data, to evaluate these data in light of current conditions and anticipated trends, and to determine whether the data provide an acceptable basis for the proposed transaction. Sound real estate appraisals promote stability and security in the marketplace. The review process is predicated on the assumption that expert appraisers are genuinely committed to providing the highest quality work to the user of appraisal services.

Role of the Reviewer

The qualifications of an appraisal reviewer include appropriate education, training, and experience. Appraisal reviewers should possess the same level of skill as the appraisers who carry out assignments for the institution. Review appraisers who do not have extensive experience should at least attend basic appraisal courses offered by professional appraisal associations and pursue their duties to appropriate levels of complexity. For example, a review appraiser who reviews reports on income-producing or investment properties should have successfully completed the income capitalization courses. A varied appraisal background will obviously increase the qualifications of the review appraiser.

Like appraisers, reviewers are accountable for their decisions. They must not violate the rules of fairness and objectivity. Each review assignment should be approached with an open, receptive attitude because each assignment represents an opportunity to learn something new. Reviewers need both analytical ability and mature judgment to perform their function effectively. They should refrain from adopting a superior attitude in their role as overseer.

Most professional review appraisers have appraisal experience and are as competent as the appraisers whose work they review. It is entirely appropriate for an appraiser to inquire into the professional credentials of the review appraiser before accepting an assignment—just as a client reviews the appraiser's credentials before retaining the appraiser for an assignment.

Training and Experience of Review Appraisers

The desired minimum educational qualifications for a review appraiser are

- Academic training in appraisal techniques

- Successful completion of appropriate appraisal courses
- Membership in one of the preeminent appraisal associations which have strict testing and standards requirements
- Active participation in a continuing education program

The desired minimum level of experience should include

- Several years of specialized appraisal experience in the reviewer's field of employment
- Court experience if the reviewer examines appraisals for condemnation purposes
- Administrative experience in the reviewer's field of employment to ensure that the reviewer fully understands the purpose and use of the appraisal

The desired minimum level of competence includes

- Adherence to professional ethics and standards of professional practice
- A good professional reputation and unquestionable integrity
- Analytical ability and mature judgment
- Objectivity and fairness

Not all reviewers are professional appraisers. The reviewer's qualifications should match the complexity of the appraisal problem and the level of responsibility associated with the assignment. For upper-echelon reviewers, the desired level of formal and continuing education has increased dramatically in the past decade.

Limitations of Appraisal Reviews

The role of the review appraiser is not universally understood. An appraiser is sometimes asked to act as a review appraiser without clearly understanding what services he or she is expected to provide.

The distinction between an appraisal review and a second opinion of value is critical. An appraisal review does not lead to an alternative value conclusion. The reviewer may disagree with the value estimate or the analytical process applied in the report, and may even recommend that another appraisal be commissioned. Nevertheless, the reviewer should not offer, nor be required to offer, a second opinion of value. The reviewer must distinguish between the review process and appraising or consulting. Once a reviewer suggests an alternative opinion of value, he or she has assumed the role of an appraiser and is no longer acting as a reviewer. To preclude any confusion concerning these different functions on the part of market participants, appraisers who review appraisal reports should not sign the report under review.

Reviewer Guidelines

Appraisal reviewers should follow the guidelines cited below:

1. Identify the report under review, the real estate and real property rights being appraised, the effective date of the opinion in the report, and the date of the review.
2. Explain the scope of the review process that was conducted and specify whether or not the reviewer inspected the subject property.

3. Form an opinion as to the adequacy and relevance of the data and the appropriateness of any adjustments applied to the data. The reviewer must determine whether the report contains all available data relevant to the problem and whether these data support the appraiser's judgment.

4. Form an opinion as to the appropriateness of the methods and techniques employed in the appraisal and if they are considered inappropriate, explain why.

5. Form an opinion as to the soundness and appropriateness of the analyses, opinions, and conclusions in the report under review and explain the reasons for any disagreement with these conclusions.

6. Determine whether the reasoning demonstrated in the appraisal leads to a logical conclusion.

Reviewers have an obligation to their clients or employers to be conscientious and exercise due diligence. Sound decision-making ultimately depends on the review function. The reviewer should assume that the appraisal under review was performed competently and is acceptable unless the review process proves otherwise.

The following practices constitute serious misrepresentations or deficiencies in a review appraisal:

1. Analyzing only parts of an appraisal report and identifying this analysis as an appraisal review without reporting on the total work product.

2. Refuting data in the original report without verifying that such data are inaccurate.

3. Criticizing the methodology applied in the appraisal without fully explaining why it is improper.

4. Using an appraisal prepared at a different time as a yardstick for judging the appraisal report.

5. Using hindsight in reviewing an appraisal. Reviews should be based on the market's activity and perspective at the time of the valuation. Subsequent events should not be used to refute the report unless at the time of the appraisal they seemed certain to occur.

6. Ignoring or altering the definition of the appraisal problem stated in the report.

7. Ignoring or altering any limiting conditions or special assumptions of the appraisal report without demonstrating why the assumptions are blatantly invalid.

8. Overemphasizing the significance of minor errors in data, calculations, or word processing that the report may contain.

9. Substituting the reviewer's own judgment for that of the appraiser when the appraiser's original conclusion was a reasonable one.

10. Submitting an unprofessional review, report, or other communication that contains subjective or pejorative comments.

Review appraisers violate rules of fairness and objectivity when they level undue criticism against an appraisal. If an appraisal review contains factual errors or substitutes a reviewer's judgment for that of the appraiser, it may result in a serious breach of ethics regardless of the significance of the assignment. Ethics violations cause harm to others.

At the outset of an assignment, the review appraiser must clearly understand the consequences of approving or rejecting an appraisal. Review appraisers are often required to examine the format of the appraisal as well as the valuation techniques and final conclusion in the report. The review appraisal statement should clearly identify what has been reviewed and comment on all significant aspects of the appraisal that affect the value conclusion.

Communication with the Appraiser

It is extremely important that the review appraiser communicate his or her conclusion to the appraiser who prepared the report. The appraiser should be prepared to defend the methodology applied, the comparables selected, and the key assumptions made. The appraiser must also be willing to discuss these items with the client or reviewer. Without feedback, appraisers cannot know how their performance measures up against that of their peers. For maximum effectiveness, the reviewer's critique must be communicated in a fair and objective manner. To ensure that their reviews are defensible, reviewers are advised to follow the guidelines listed below.

- The review should be written in a positive tone to serve as a constructive learning experience for the appraiser.
- The reviewer should distinguish between major deficiencies in the report and minor errors.
- The report should be evaluated to determine whether it is reasonable or unreasonable, not whether it is right or wrong.
- The critique should be grammatical, well-documented, and offer the appraiser meaningful suggestions.
- The reviewer should not be patronizing or condescending. The reviewer should present his or her comments in a tactful manner.

TYPES OF APPRAISAL REVIEWS

The type of appraisal review performed varies depending on factors such as the scope or nature of the assignment, the requirements of the client, and the complexity of the property under appraisal. There are two basic types of review procedures: desk reviews and field reviews. Both represent acceptable procedures for checking the thoroughness and consistency of appraisals. The desk review is the more common type of review.

Desk Review

A desk review is completed without a field inspection. Desk reviews are usually limited by the data presented in the report. The data in the appraisal report may or may not be independently confirmed and usually additional market data are not researched. The reviewer often uses a customized checklist. Mathematical calculations are checked; the appraiser's methodology is reviewed for appropriateness; and the appraisal is reviewed to ascertain that it was completed in accordance with the client's guidelines, appraisal policy requirements, regulatory requirements, and the Uniform Standards of Professional Appraisal Practice.

The thoroughness of desk reviews varies greatly. The levels of analysis described below reflect the performance range for desk reviews.

1. The report is merely scanned.
2. The mathematical calculations are checked and the data are examined for reasonableness.
3. Selected pertinent sections of the report are read.
4. The appraisal is checked to ascertain that the methodology is appropriate.
5. The entire report is read thoroughly.
6. Limited confirmation of market data is sought.
7. Full confirmation of market data is sought.

Field Review

As a minimum, a field review must include inspection of the exterior of the subject property. Special conditions often warrant an inspection of the interior as well. The reviewer may also inspect the comparable properties that provided the sales or rental data. Data cited in the report are confirmed in the field; additional market data may be researched independently. A review checklist tailored to the specifications of the subject property is used. Mathematical calculations are checked for accuracy and the appraiser's methodology is reviewed for appropriateness. Generally, this type of review does not uncover errors of omission such as the appraiser's failure to report or confirm other pertinent market transactions.

In addition to the tasks peformed in a desk review, a field review may also include:

- Inspection of the exteriors of comparable properties
- Limited verification of select market data
- Full verification of market data
- Independent research to gather additional market data
- Verification of electronic spreadsheet software, including the integrity of formulas and the accuracy of the data
- Verification of computer software used in lease-by-lease analysis and the data input

Many variations exist in desk reviews, field reviews, and combinations of the two. The client should keep the review policy flexible enough to allow reviewers to exercise due diligence in each case. The scope of the review process varies with the needs of the client and the level of confidence the client has in the skill and expertise of the appraiser. The extent of the review is a function of the complexity of the property and the transaction value involved.

Another type of appraisal review is a quality control check on the investment portfolio of a lending institution. This type of review may be undertaken to test the validity of previous appraisal reports. Usually the regulatory agency or an independent appraiser retained as a consultant conducts a compliance review on a sampling of the appraisals in the portfolio. Quality control checks may also be performed within a professional appraisal firm or by the staff of a lending institution. Reviewers monitor the quality of appraisals and the daily performance of appraisers to ensure quality control. An appraisal review may also be needed in value disputes when an appraiser is called upon to review appraisals as an independent, third-party arbitrator.

Preliminary and Formal Appraisal Reviews

A preliminary review addresses the thoroughness of the appraisal and the report's adherence to performance requirements pertaining to format, methodology, consistency, and reasonableness. The reviewer uses a checklist to determine whether the appraisal is complete and conforms to the criteria of the client.

A checklist is commonly used because it helps a reviewer systematize the review process. Its use ensures that no section is inadvertently overlooked and that the appraisal conforms to client requirements. The basic premises and facts that the reviewer notes on the checklist help him or her determine the report's internal consistency. The list also helps the reviewer relate the appraisal to market conditions and check its reasonableness in terms of externalities.

Strict adherence to a checklist, however, may be overdone and can result in the qualitative aspects of the report being shortchanged. The checklist does not determine the acceptability or unacceptability of the appraisal; it is merely a tool to help the reviewer systematize the review process. The soundness and reasonableness of the value conclusion determine the acceptability or unacceptability of the appraisal. Like appraisal formats, appraisal review checklists vary. At present, no single review checklist is universally accepted. Most need to be tailored to the specific criteria of the institution, agency, or corporation that will use them.

The extent of a formal appraisal review depends on the quality and thoroughness of the appraisal. A review appraiser need not duplicate work that was adequately performed in the appraisal. If the appraisal is well researched and well documented, little additional work may be required of the review appraiser. If additional data are required, however, the review appraiser may have to complete a process almost as involved as a complete appraisal. When the review appraiser believes additional data or a different valuation technique is required, the matter should be discussed with the appraiser prior to completion of the review appraisal assignment.

Reviewer's File

The reviewer's file on a completed appraisal review should contain:

- A copy of a summary of the review report
- A copy of the appraisal report
- The field notes and working papers of the appraiser and reviewer
- Copies of final computer runs used to check calculations
- The names and phone numbers of all persons interviewed during the course of the review process—e.g., appraisers, brokers, investors.

ITEMS TARGETED FOR REVIEW

An appraisal report should convey the appraiser's confidence in the solution being offered to the appraisal problem. A poorly written report will not be convincing to the reviewer. All the effort put into an appraisal assignment can be lost if the report lacks organization and is carelessly written. A clear and concise report does more than simply ensure comprehension; it creates a favorable impression of the appraiser as well. If boilerplate is used in the report, it must be relevant to the valuation problem and updated so that it is current.

It is in the interest of all parties to get to the point early in the report. A 150-page report that does not describe the property until page 85 or does not address the problem of real value until page 148 will only frustrate the reader. Critical issues should be highlighted, not evaded in the report.

It is unnerving for a reviewer to read a report that contains tantalizing hints about potential investment risk but that never really addresses the problem head on. The reviewer is forced to read between the lines, and therefore loses confidence in the value conclusion. The usual outcome is that the reviewer orders another appraisal to confirm or refute his or her suspicions about the original report. Because appraising is problem solving, it is reasonable for a reviewer to expect a clear-cut solution.

Reviewers should be alert for incongruities. Is a claim made too often, too emphatically, or in too facile a manner? Is an issue being avoided? Are there implicit rather than explicit references to a potential problem? Deception can take many forms. Inconsistencies within an appraisal—e.g., discrepancies between the data and analyses—detract from a report and erode confidence in its conclusions.

Some appraisers cloud otherwise straightforward appraisal issues by the overuse of technical jargon or "appraisalese." An appraiser may resort to jargon in an effort to disguise his or her lack of understanding of a situation. Overwhelming the reader with jargon helps deflect attention from what the appraiser does not understand. Excessive reliance on jargon may also create the impression that the value indication obtained in the appraisal process is both precise and scientific.

The use of pretentious jargon has increased since the advent of the computer. Computer output appears authoritative and many people are duly impressed. The reviewer, however, must not be taken in by the attractivenss of the latest desktop publishing printouts or graphics.

Valuation is both an art and a science. It should never abdicate to an overreliance upon technology. An appraiser's main task is to interpret the behavior of market participants—i.e., the buyers, sellers, investors, landlords, and tenants who make up the market. No scientific process has ever been devised to measure or predict market behavior with total accuracy.

Appropriate Emphasis

To provide a meaningful service, the appraiser must offer guidance in the decision making process. An appraiser should never ignore obvious problems. Too often the critical part of a report lacks essential analysis. For example, in valuing a property under an older, uneconomic use in a growth area, an appraiser may fail to consider that the land might be worth more if developed to an alternative use. In this case appropriate emphasis was obviously not given to the analysis of the highest and best use of the land as though vacant.

The rationale an appraiser uses in arriving at a solution to the appraisal problem should be straightforward, reasonable, and supportable. The analysis must lead to a logical conclusion and should be presented as simply as possible. The analysis employed should reflect the way active market participants would approach the problem. Appraisers should avoid the use of esoteric techniques that are not recognized by market participants.

Competency Issues

Risk Analysis

An appraiser must directly address risk factors. All real estate, particularly investment-grade property, involves potential risks. Appraisers must analyze the components of risk in a real estate investment and weigh these risks against those found in alternative investments.

Bases for Decision Making

Appraisers must thoroughly investigate the motivation of market participants. Whether valuing a single-family residence in suburbia or a trophy office building in the CBD, an appraiser must ultimately know who the market participants are, what motivates them, and why. Without this knowledge, the analysis that underlies the value conclusion is totally meaningless.

Often appraisers do not have complete information about a sale or a lease. They may not have asked the right questions or interviewed the right people. Some may proceed with an analysis based on partial data without alerting the client of the limitations imposed by incomplete data.

In an appraisal of a property that is being purchased, the appraiser should include the current transaction price. For a newly constructed property, the appraiser should include a cost analysis. In both cases the rationale for variances between the market data and the concluded value should be explained. When a transaction price differs from the concluded value the variance may be explained by the poor negotiating skills of one party, duress, or the inordinate market influence wielded by a limited number of suppliers (oligopoly). A cost analysis at odds with the concluded value may reflect an overimprovement or underimprovement.

Appraisal reports on existing, income-producing properties should clearly reconcile differences between the revenue and expense history of the subject property and the revenue and expense projections used in the appraisal analysis. The client should not have to surmise how the appraiser arrived at the revenue and expense projection for the subject or how it correlates with the past performance of the property. The report should present this information clearly, explaining where and why the projection differs from the property's recorded history. An appraiser may choose to synthesize much of the property's financial history in the text of the report, but it is good practice to include a complete copy of the historical data provided by the client in the report addenda.

Common Deficiencies

Most of the problems that reviewers find in appraisal reports may be attributed to deficiencies in one or more of the areas listed below.

Analysis and Reasoning

- Inadequate analysis and reasoning, reliance on old market data, and discrepancies between the data presented in the report and key assumptions deemed essential to the final value conclusion. An appraiser may fail to strike a balance between aggressive, upside assumptions and conservative, downside assumptions.

- Inadequate highest and best use analysis when the highest and best use determination is critical to the value conclusion.
- Failure to present both the negative and positive attributes of the subject property or to identify negative and positive influences on property value and marketability. If an appraiser soft pedals negative features and overstates positive features, the reviewer is forced to read between the lines looking for clues about the actual situation.
- Overreliance on historical trends and scant attention to current conditions which may significantly diverge from historical trends. For example, rental growth figures over the past 10 years may show an overall 10% increase per year while rates for the past three years show a decline of 2% per year, which is considered a more meaningful figure.
- Inadequate explanation of a wide discrepancy between current or recent transaction price and the value the appraiser concluded.
- Misinterpretation of data.

Appraisal Management and Quality Control

- Errors resulting from carelessness, lack of attention to detail, and poor quality control. Typographical errors, grammatical errors, mathematical errors, and inappropriate exhibits are detrimental to an appraisal report.
- Inconsistencies such as stating different value conclusions in the letter of transmittal at the front of the report and the reconciliation section at the end of the report.
- Overreliance on boilerplate to document the appraisal and the overuse of promotional reports published by a chamber of commerce.
- Problems resulting from the delegation of complex assignments to inexperienced staff.
- Submission of a form report for a complex valuation that warrants a narrative report.
- Confusion over the specified date of the value conclusion. An "as is" date of value falls before or on completion of a project; an "as of" date assumes that the proposed project is already completed and perhaps operating at stabilized occupancy.
- Ineffective quality control procedures.
- Submission of the appraisal report after the contracted date of delivery.

Appraiser-Client Communication

- Misunderstanding the scope of the assignment.
- Failure to complete the report in accordance with the client's guidelines, disregard for the client's specifications, or poor communication between the appraiser and client regarding guidelines. Many of these problems can be avoided by the use of an engagement letter, which ensures a meeting of the minds at the inception of the assignment. Of course, the client's instructions should not prevent an appraiser from exercising his or her professional judgment.

- Failure to comply with regulatory requirements such as those of the Financial Institutions Reform, Recovery and Enforcement Act (FIRREA) and other federal or state regulations.
- Failure to segregate the value of non-realty items when appropriate—e.g., business value, personalty, furniture, trade fixtures, equipment.
- Preparing an appraisal based on specific financing assumptions or after-tax considerations, which potentially limit the concluded value to a narrow range of circumstances that are extremely unlikely to occur.
- Failure to highlight critical problems in an appraisal. Open dialogue with the client should be encouraged.
- Failure to inform the client in advance that major, unforeseen problems in the assignment will require an extension of the due date or an adjustment to, or renegotiation of, the original fee.

Assumptions and Limiting Conditions

- Imposition of limiting conditions or disclaimers designed to remove virtually all responsibility from the appraiser, thereby rendering the value conclusion useless to the client.
- Failure to emphasize special, unusual, or unique value definitions, limiting conditions, and assumptions up front in the letter of transmittal and in the value summary section of the appraisal.
- Failure to disclose whether or not the appraiser personally conducted an inspection of the property.

Valuation Approaches and Reconciliation

- Confusion over or misunderstanding of entrepreneurial profit.
- Use of a "back-door" approach to developing a cost analysis. An appraiser should not arrive at an estimate of depreciation by deducting the indication of property value (less land value) obtained in the sales comparison or income approach from a replacement cost estimate. Rather, an independent cost analysis should be developed.
- Abuse of statistical techniques. Some appraisers overwhelm the client with technical jargon used to describe statistical distributions (e.g., linearity, nonlinearity, multicollinearity, heteroskedasticity) and variance (e.g., ordinary least squares fit, standard error, statistical coefficients). Deferring to statistics is often inappropriate. Only in extraordinary situations are the comparable data sufficient to provide a meaningful sampling for accurate statistical analysis.
- Confusion over the distinction between overall capitalization rates and yield or discount rates. A discount rate is used to convert a specified future income stream for a given period plus terminal or reversionary value into present value. It is equivalent to a yield rate or internal rate of return. An overall capitalization rate is

computed by dividing the net operating income of a recently sold comparable by its sale price. A definite relationship exists between the overall capitalization rate, the discount rate, and the compounded change in value over the holding period of the investment.

- Inadequate analysis of existing leases or overreliance on externally prepared abstracts. An appraiser may fail to read a representative sampling of primary leases or neglect to exercise due diligence in considering lease terms.
- Errors in the data input into computer software—i.e., electronic spreadsheets and programs for lease-by-lease analysis. Keystroke errors and incorrect formulas may affect value conclusions.
- Unrealistic cash flow projections on the operating statement. It is unrealistic to base cash flows on perfectly regular growth in rental income over the projection term, a declining expense ratio that runs contrary to actual experience, or an assumption that expenses can be fully recovered from the tenants with no operating costs payable by the owner. It is also improper to omit line items such as capital expense or replacement reserve and to fail to recognize regional variations in revenues and expenses.
- Lack of clarity as to whether gross rents or net rents were derived from the analysis of comparable rental properties.
- Failure to cross-check a value indication obtained through computer analysis with an indication obtained directly from the cost approach or the sales comparison approach. Tests of reasonableness must be applied to detect errors in the data input. Cross-check tests are also needed to detect errors lurking in the program.
- Inconsistencies in report data as well as inconsistencies between the analyses and conclusions. Appraisers must recognize the interdependency of the three approaches. An appraisal comprises a variety of interrelated and inseparable procedures directed at the common objective of producing a reliable and convincing value estimate.
- Failure to keep in touch with rapidly changing market conditions, transactional data, and market behavior.
- Inadequate analysis of the profile of potential tenants or buyers. Such an analysis is particularly important in the appraisal of complex projects and projects proposed for construction or rehabilitation.
- Failure to estimate the available supply— i.e., the total amount of unoccupied square footage in the specific property market—which provides a basis for forecasting market absorption.
- A meaningless boilerplate reconciliation of the value indications derived.
- The use of obsolete valuation techniques which are probably unknown to the investors whose actions they purportedly simulate.

Data Collection and Investigation

- Inadequate research or documentation.
- Overreliance on data provided by the owner or developer of the intended project without cross-checking the data against other viable data or undertaking an independent investigation.

- Failure to question an assumption about the likelihood of a zoning change or to provide appropriate verification of the reasonableness of such an assumption.
- Reliance on insufficient transactional data in a given market. If the market is characterized by little sales activity, the appraiser should describe market conditions and explain the reasons for the lack of viable data.
- Failure to confirm a sales transaction by at least one party to the transaction. Confirming a sale can verify transactional data, provide information on purchaser motivation, and offer additional information on the reuse or redevelopment of the purchased property.
- Failure to identify potential environmental problems or hazardous waste evident during the site inspection. Hazardous substances may be indicated by the presence of chemical drums, underground storage tanks, nearby transmission lines, deteriorating basement insulation, and evidence of sludge, paints, chemical residues, and oil spillage.

Vocabulary and Syntax

- Lack of clarity and conciseness. Reports may be adversely affected by the excessive use of legalese, appraisalese, or other jargon; hackneyed or arcane vocabulary; and the passive voice.
- Reports that are verbose or overwritten, contain redundancies, or rely on vague or general statements.
- Overuse of hedge words such as *appear, seem, likely, probably* which leave the reviewer in doubt about the true meaning of an otherwise decisive statement.

Standards Issues

- Reports that do not meet the minimum requirements of the Uniform Standards of Professional Appraisal Practice.
- Reports that are not entirely self-contained.
- Reports that do not clearly identify the property rights being appraised.
- Reports that fail to distinguish between the value of a property at sellout and its wholesale or bulk sale value, particularly in the appraisal of subdivision developments and condominium projects.
- Appraisals of the "as is" value of a project being built or rehabilitated that are intentionally vague regarding what work has been done and what work remains to be completed.
- Submission of an incompetent work product. Appraisers are sometimes reluctant to turn down an assignment on a complex or special-purpose property such as a lodging or health care facility which requires specialized knowledge or experience. They may unrealistically overestimate their own professional capabilites.

Unacceptable Practices in the Preparation of Form Reports

The following list specifies practices that are considered unacceptable by the Federal National Mortgage Association (Fannie Mae).

- Inclusion of inaccurate data on the subject site and improvements, comparable sales, or the neighborhood.

- Failure to consider negative factors in regard to the subject property, the neighborhood, or adverse influences in proximity to the property.
- Use of data from comparable properties which the appraiser has not personally inspected or at least seen.
- Selection and use of inappropriate comparables or use of comparables that are physically or locationally dissimilar to the subject property.
- Use of data that were provided by parties with a financial interest in the sale or financing of the subject property without independent verification through a disinterested source. For example, it would be inappropriate for an appraiser to use comparable sales data provided by the real estate broker who is handling the sale of the subject property unless the appraiser verifies the accuracy of the data. The appraiser must consult a disinterested source and independently investigate whether the comparables provided are the best ones available.
- Adjustments applied to comparable sales that do not reflect the market's perception of the effect on value produced by the differences between the subject and the comparables. Appraisers must make such adjustments when they are clearly indicated.
- A value conclusion developed on the basis of the race, ethnicity, or religion of the prospective owners or occupants of the subject property or the current owners or occupants of properties in the vicinity of the subject.
- A value conclusion that is not supported by available market data.

The most common errors found in form reports are described below.

1. Errors in mathematical calculations.
2. Inadequate explanation of atypical factors, adjustments, or analyses.
3. Incorrect identification of the type of property under appraisal—e.g., single-family detached or attached, condominium or planned unit development (de minimis PUD).
4. Blank line items on the completed form. Lines should be marked "n/a" to indicate that data are not available or that the entry does not apply to the subject property. An empty line creates the impression that the item was inadvertently overlooked.
5. Inconsistencies involving trend indicators, adjustments for market conditions, or estimates of marketing time.
6. Discrepancies between the photographs of the subject property and the physical description provided in the form.
7. Meaningless statements in the "Comments" sections of the form.
8. No explanation as to why large gross or net adjustments were made to the comparables; inconsistencies among the adjustments to the comparables.
9. No reasonable reconciliation of the wide range of adjusted values of the comparables or the values indicated by the other approaches employed.
0. Discrepancies between the factual data provided on the front of the form and the valuation analysis on the back.
1. Selection of dated or distant comparables or comparable sales that do not bracket the subject's value. Comparables should reflect a sampling of representative sales

that are priced both higher and lower than the subject. The rationale for the selection of the comparables must be explained.

12. Failure to recognize and adjust for functional problems evident on the floor plan sketch of the subject.

13. Inconsistencies between items reported by the appraiser (e.g., replacement costs, land values, sales data, and comparable adjustments) and the same items reported by other appraisers for similar properties in similar neighborhoods.

14. Failure to meet FIRREA requirements that additional data be furnished with form reports, such as:

- The sales history of the subject property
- A rationale for estimates of marketing time
- A statement regarding personal property
- The mandatory competency statement
- The mandatory certification statement
- A legal description

ADHERENCE TO STANDARDS RULES

Reviewers should be aware that their activities are subject to Standards Rule 3-1 of the Uniform Standards of Professional Appraisal Practice promulgated by the Appraisal Foundation.

After forming an opinion as to the adequacy and appropriateness of the report being reviewed, the reviewer must prepare a separate report or memorandum setting forth the results of the review process and disclosing the precise nature of the review process undertaken. This requirement can be met in three different ways:

- A separate report or letter.
- A checklist form prepared and signed by the reviewer and attached to the report under review.
- A stamped imprint on the appraisal, signed by the reviewer, briefly indicating the extent of the review and referencing the file memorandum in which the review process is outlined. (This procedure separates the review function from the actual signing).

Standards Rule 2-5 of the Uniform Standards of Professional Appraisal Practice states:

> An appraiser who signs a real property appraisal report prepared by another, even under the label of "review appraiser," must accept full responsibility for the contents of the report.

This rule is directed at the employer or supervisor who reviews and signs an appraisal prepared by an employee or contractor. The employer or supervisor is as liable for the content and conclusions in the report as the individual who prepared the appraisal. Furthermore, insertion of a conditional clause next to the signature of the employer or supervisor does not exempt that individual from adherence to the standards.

Assumptions and Limiting Conditions

The review should contain a statement of assumptions and limiting conditions similar in content to the following:

1. The review report attached hereto is based on data and information contained in the appraisal report that is the subject of this review as well as additional information from other sources that may be applicable.
2. It is assumed that the data and information are factual and accurate.
3. The reviewer reserves the right to consider any additional data or information that may subsequently become available to him or her and to revise his or her opinions and conclusions if such data and information indicate the need for such change.
4. All of the assumptions and limiting conditions contained in the appraisal report that is the subject of this review are also conditions of this review unless otherwise stated.

Certification

The reviewer's report must contain a statement of certification similar in content to the following:

I (we) certify that, to the best of my (our) knowledge and belief, the statements of fact contained in this appraisal review are true and correct.

I (we) further certify that the reported appraisal analyses and opinions are limited only by the reported qualifying conditions and are my (our) personal, unbiased, professional analyses and opinions. I (we) further certify that I (we) have no present or prospective interest in the appraised property.

My (our) appraisal analyses and opinions were developed, and this appraisal review has been prepared, in conformance with the requirements of the Uniform Standards of Professional Appraisal Practice of the Appraisal Foundation (to which the use of this review is also subject).

I (we) do not authorize anyone to quote this appraisal report out of context or partially reprint portions thereof. Further, neither all nor any part of this appraisal review shall be disseminated to the general public by the media without the prior written consent of the review appraiser(s) who has signed this appraisal review.

I (we) have (have not) made a personal inspection of the appraised property.

This review satisfies the requirements of Standard 3 of the Uniform Standards of Professional Appraisal Practice, and includes only those items listed on this form. The research upon which the appraisal is based has not been verified by the reviewer. I (we) have relied upon the appraiser to provide accurate, comprehensive information on the subject property and the other primary and secondary data presented in this report.

SUMMARY

Appraisal review may be likened to the quality control function of the appraisal profession. Reviewers test the reasonableness of the logic, assumptions and value conclusion contained in a report; they also evaluate the report for compliance with professional standards, the criteria of clients, and the regulatory requirements of governmental agencies. Appraisal reviews help organizations manage risk and investors make decisions to purchase or sell real estate assets. Appraiser accountability rests on the assumption that professional appraisers are sincerely committed to providing the highest quality service to users of appraisal services.

Lending institutions and governmental agencies often establish appraisal management policies which serve as guidelines on why and when appraisals are required, how to implement appraisals, and whom to assign the responsibility of selecting appraisers. Such policies also determine the procedures to follow in reviewing appraisals.

The qualifications of reviewers should include appropriate training, experience, and education. The skill level of reviewers should correspond to that of the appraisers whose work they will review. To perform the review function effectively, the reviewer should possess analytical ability and mature judgment. Like appraisers, reviewers are accountable for their decisions. They must never violate rules of fairness and objectivity and have an obligation to the client or employer to exercise due diligence.

The role of the review appraiser is often misunderstood. An appraisal review does not lead to an alternative value conclusion. Once a reviewer suggests an alternative opinion of value, he or she has assumed the role of an appraiser and is no longer acting in the capacity of a reviewer.

There are two basic types of review procedures: desk reviews and field reviews. Generally desk reviews are completed without the benefit of a field inspection and are limited by the data contained in the report. On the other hand, field reviews include an exterior inspection of the subject property and comparables and sometimes an interior inspection as well.

The scope of the review process varies with the needs of the client and the reviewer's level of confidence in the skill and expertise of the appraiser. Most of the problems that reviewers find in appraisals stem from competency issues (e.g., deficient economic forecasting, risk analysis, bases for decision making), inadequate research, faulty analysis and reasoning, report inconsistencies, poor quality control, misunderstandings as to the objective of the assignment, or failure to meet professional standards.

Reviewers should be aware that their activites are subject to standards rules of the Uniform Standards of Professional Appraisal Practice promulgated by the Appraisal Foundation. Like an appraisal report, a review should contain a statement of assumptions and limiting conditions as well as a certification statement.

Appraisal review is continually evolving as the techniques and methodology of appraisal change to reflect the activity of real estate markets. The objective of the reviewer, however, remains the same—i.e., to determine the acceptability or unacceptability of the appraisal report based on whether the report organizes the relevant data logically and presents a reasonable conclusion. A good report reflects the skill and judgment of its author, who has ultimate responsibility for communicating the valuation process in a clear, logical, and meaningful manner.

Appendix A

PROFESSIONAL PRACTICE

$\mathcal{T}$he body of knowledge that comprises the discipline of appraisal is the foundation of professional practice. In solving most appraisal problems, however, the final conclusions depend to a great extent on the ability, judgment, and integrity of individual appraisers. To form a sound conclusion, relevant data must be available and the appraiser must be committed to finding and analyzing the data; a valid analysis also depends on the skillful application of appraisal techniques. Because appraisal is an inexact science, appraisers must reach their conclusions in an impartial, objective manner, without bias or any desire to accommodate their own interests or the interests of their clients. Professional appraisers have the requisite knowledge and the ability to apply it capably and objectively.

A profession is distinguished from a trade or service industry by a combination of the following factors:

1. High standards of competence in a specialized field
2. A distinct body of knowledge that is continually augmented by the contributions of members and can be imparted to future generations
3. A code of ethics or standards of practice and members who are willing to be regulated by peer review

The Appraisal Institute was formed for three purposes.

1. To establish criteria for selecting and recognizing individuals with real estate valuation skills who were committed to competent and ethical practice
2. To develop a system of education to train new appraisers and sharpen the skills of practicing appraisers
3. To formulate a code of professional ethics and standards of professional conduct to guide real estate appraisers and serve as a model for other practitioners

The heart of the Appraisal Institute's commitment to professionalism is contained in the six canons of the Code of Professional Ethics and Standards of Professional Appraisal Practice, which include the Uniform Standards of Professional Appraisal Practice, the Supplemental Standards, and the Guide Notes.

Canon 1

A Member or an Affiliate of the Appraisal Institute must refrain from conduct that is detrimental to the Appraisal Institute, the real estate appraisal profession and the public.

Canon 2

A Member or an Affiliate must assist the Appraisal Institute in carrying out its responsibilities to the users of appraisal services and the public.

Canon 3

In the performance of an appraisal assignment, a Member or an Affiliate must develop and communicate each analysis and opinion without bias for the client's interest and without accommodation of his or her own interests.

Canon 4

A Member or an Affiliate must not violate the confidential nature of the appraiser-client relationship.

Canon 5

In promoting an appraisal practice and soliciting appraisal services, a Member or an Affiliate must use care to avoid advertising or solicitation that is misleading or otherwise contrary to the public interest.

Canon 6

A Member or an Affiliate must comply with the requirements of the Standards of Professional Practice.

Standard 1

In developing a real property appraisal, an appraiser must be aware of, understand, and correctly employ those recognized methods and techniques that are necessary to produce a credible appraisal.

Standard 2

In reporting the results of a real property appraisal, an appraiser must communicate each analysis, opinion, and conclusion in a manner that is not misleading.

Standard 3

In reviewing an appraisal and reporting the results of that review, an appraiser must form an opinion as to the adequacy and appropriateness of the report being reviewed and must clearly disclose the nature of the review process undertaken.

Standard 4

In performing real estate or real property consulting services, an appraiser must be aware of, understand, and correctly employ those recognized methods and techniques that are necessary to produce a credible result.

Standard 5

In reporting the results of a real estate or real property consulting service, an appraiser must communicate each analysis, opinion, and conclusion in a manner that is not misleading.

Standard 6

In developing and reporting a mass appraisal for ad valorem tax purposes, an appraiser must be aware of, understand, and correctly employ those recognized methods and techniques that are necessary to produce and communicate credible appraisals within the context of the property tax laws.

Standard 7

In developing a personal property appraisal, an appraiser must be aware of, understand, and correctly employ those recognized methods and techniques that are necessary to produce a credible appraisal.

Standard 8

In reporting the results of a personal property appraisal, an appraiser must communicate each analysis, opinion, and conclusion in a manner that is not misleading.

Standard 9

In developing a business appraisal, an appraiser must be aware of, understand, and correctly employ those recognized methods and techniques that are necessary to produce a credible appraisal.

Standard 10

In reporting the results of a business appraisal an appraiser must communicate each analysis, opinion, and conclusion in a manner that is not misleading.

Standards 7 through 10 will not be enforced by the Appraisal Institute. Three supplemental standards follow. These standards apply only to members and affiliates of the Appraisal Institute.

Supplemental Standard 1

The Uniform Standards of Professional Appraisal Practice shall apply to all activities of a Member or an Affiliate involving an analysis, opinion or conclusion relating to the nature, quality, value or utility of specified interests in, or aspects of, identified real estate.

Supplemental Standard 2

The form of certification used by a Member or Affiliate in a written report that contains an analysis, opinion or conclusion relating to the nature, quality, value or utility of specified interests in, or aspects of, identified real estate must include a statement indicating compliance with the Code of Professional Ethics and Standards of Professional Appraisal Practice and a statement advising the client and third parties of the Appraisal Institute's right to review the report. The form of certification used by a Member in a written report that contains an analysis, opinion or conclusion relating to the nature, quality, value or utility of specified interests in, or aspects of, identified real estate must include a statement indicating the current status of the Member under the Appraisal Institute's continuing education program.

Supplemental Standard 3

The Appraisal Standards Board of the Appraisal Foundation added an Ethics Provision to the Uniform Standards of Professional Appraisal Practice on December 4, 1989. The language in this Ethics Provision is very broad and the Appraisal Institute has interpreted this Ethics Provision to apply to appraisal conduct only. The Appraisal Institute has an existing Code of Professional Ethics that is adequate to carry out the intent of the Ethics Provision. Therefore, the Appraisal Institute will enforce its own Code of Professional Ethics under its existing enforcement procedures as the proper means of enforcing the Ethics Provision of the Uniform Standards of Professional Appraisal Practice.

FEDERAL LEGISLATION AFFECTING THE APPRAISAL PROFESSION*

Existing Legislation, Regulations, and Banking/Examining Circulars†	Areas of Appraisal Affected	Government Agencies Subject to Specific Legislation
Uniform Relocation Assistance and Real Properties Acquisition Act of 1970 (Public Law 91-646, Titles II & III) Amended in the Surface Transportation Bill (1987)‡	Just compensation for displaced owners and tenants affected by land acquisitions for federally funded projects	**Department of Agriculture; Department of the Interior— National Park Service; Department of Transportation (DOT)** (A total of 14 agencies are affected.)
R-41 Memoranda Series (1977-1987) The R-41 Memoranda Series was superseded by CEBA (see below)	Appraisals of properties under federally insured mortgages	**Federal Home Loan Bank Board** (independent agency)
12 CFR 7.3025 "Other Real Estate Owned" (8/28/79) Amended 3/28/84	Appraisals done for commercial banks	**Office of Comptroller of the Currency (OCC)** (Treasury Department)
Examining Circular 234 "Troubled Real Estate Loans" (10/30/ 85) and **Supplement No. 1 "Guidelines for Troubled Real Estate Loans Clarified"** (7/10/87)	Appraisals done for commercial banks	**Office of Comptroller of the Currency (OCC)** (Treasury Department)
Internal Revenue Service Regulation Section 1.170A-13 (1986)	Reporting requirements established for appraisals done for income tax purposes (specifically dealing with charitable contributions)	**Internal Revenue Service (Treasury Department)**

* The **Federal Interagency Real Property Appraisal Committee** (FIRPAC) is made up of various federal agencies with an interest in appraisal issues. FIRPAC, which is headed by OMB, was established to develop and revise Circular A-129. It includes many agencies not bound by FIRREA. FIRPAC is currently drawing up uniform standards for appraisals submitted to federal agencies.

† Appraisal policies and procedures may also be established by means other than regulatory legislation. Memoranda and banking or examining circulars and executive orders are noteworthy examples. Several federal agencies (OCC, FDIC, OTS) issue circulars that specify the definition of value they require, e.g., fair value, net realizable value. (See 12 CFR 7.3025 and the two other banking/examining circulars cited in this chart and note II on page 648.) Also note Executive Order 12630.

‡ Uniform appraisal standards for federal land acquisition, developed in the Yellow Book of 1973, have been revised and will be published in 1992.

FEDERAL LEGISLATION AFFECTING THE APPRAISAL PROFESSION* (continued)

Competitive Equality Banking Act of 1987 (CEBA) (Public Law 100-86) CEBA was the foundation for FIRREA.§	Appraisals done for the five Federal Financial Institutions Regulatory Agencies (FFIRAs) Brought appraisals for S&Ls under the same policies and procedures as those for commercial banks	**Office of Thrift Supervision (OTS)** (since 1989) and **Office of Comptroller of the Currency (OCC)**, both under the **Treasury Department;** the **Federal Reserve Board;** the **Federal Deposit Insurance Corporation (FDIC);** and the **National Credit Union Administration** (The last three are independent agencies.)
Banking Circular 225 "Guidelines for Real Estate Appraisal Policies and Review Procedures" (12/7/87) and **"Clarification of Guidelines for Real Estate Appraisal Policies and Review Procedures"** (9/8/88)	Appraisals done for commercial banks	**Federal Reserve Board, Federal Deposit Insurance Corporation (FDIC),** and the **Office of Comptroller of the Currency (OCC)**
Executive Order 12630 (1988) (Current legislation to codify this executive order is pending.)	Requires all agencies to determine whether an action will result in a taking	**All federal agencies**
Federal Land Exchange Facilitation Act of 1988 (Public Law 101-17)	Valuation of parcels involved in exchanges between federal agencies or federal and state agencies	**Department of Agriculture—U.S. Forestry Service; Department of the Interior—Bureaus of Land Management** (public land) and **Mines**
Circular A-129 of 1988	Appraisals done for any federal credit agency under the Office of Management and Budget (OMB) Does not apply to land acquisition agencies; mandates hiring of certified appraisers	**Office of Management and Budget (OMB)** (an executive agency)

§ In response to **CEBA**, the Federal Home Loan Bank Board (FHLBB) adopted **Regulation 563.17-1a** and **Statement of Policy 563-1b** (12/12/87).

FEDERAL LEGISLATION AFFECTING THE APPRAISAL PROFESSION* (continued)

Financial Institutions Reform, Recovery, and Enforcement Act of 1989 (FIRREA) (Public Law 101-73, Title XI) (8/8/89) Each of the five FFIRAs plus the RTC were directed to draft preliminary and final rules (within a year) to give substance to this legislation.ⁱⁱ
Title XI was amended 11/27/91; executive approval is pending.

Appraisals done for the five Federal Financial Institutions Regulatory Agencies (FFIRAs) Appraisals for all federal and state S&Ls and banking institutions

Office of Thrift Supervision (OTS) [superseding the **FHLBB**] and **Office of Comptroller of the Currency (OCC)** both under **Treasury;** the **Federal Reserve Board;** the **Federal Deposit Insurance Corporation (FDIC);** the **National Credit Union Administration** (The last three are independent agencies.); and the **Resolution Trust Corporation (RTC),** a quasi-independent agency set up to oversee the liquidation of insolvent S&Ls.

ⁱⁱ Pursuant to FIRREA, banking/examining circulars were issued in by the federal banking agencies. (The dates when these circulars were published appear below; all became effective between 8/9/90 and 9/21/90.)
Office of Comptroller of the Currency, 12 CFR Part 34, Subpart C "Real Estate Appraisals" (8/24/90)
Federal Reserve Board, 12 CFR Parts 208 and 225 (7/28/90)
Federal Deposit Insurance Corporation, 12 CFR Part 323 (8/20/90)
Resolution Trust Corporation, 12 CFR Part 1608 (8/22/90)
Office of Thrift Supervision, 12 CFR Parts 506, 545, 563, 564, 571 (8/23/90)
National Credit Union Administration, 12 CFR Parts 701, 722, 741 (7/25/90)

ENVIRONMENTAL LEGISLATION AFFECTING THE APPRAISAL INDUSTRY

Comprehensive Environmental Response, Compensation, and Liability Act (CERCLA) of 1980 provides for the establishment of a superfund to expedite the cleanup of contaminated sites; under CERCLA liability is adjudicated on a "strict, joint, several, and retroactive" basis. While the method(s) of determining the risk or environmental liability associated with a site are not defined by federal law, a procedure known as an **environmental property assessment (EPRA),** or transactional audit, is commonly conducted at commercial and industrial sites to identify potential environmental concerns prior to the transfer of a property.

Superfund Amendments and Reauthorization Act (SARA) of 1986 exempts third parties who acquired real property after the disposal or placement of hazardous materials, provided such defendants at the time of acquisition made "all appropriate inquiry into the previous ownership and uses of the property consistent with good commercial or customary practice in an effort to minimize liability."

In addition to **CERCLA** and **SARA,** legislation having an especially signifiant impact upon real estate appraisal includes:

- The Resource Conservation and Recovery Act (RCRA) of 1976, amended on various occasions over the subsequent decade, provided for the control of hazardous waste and the regulation of underground storage tanks.
- The Clean Water Act (CWA) of 1977, amended in 1987, expanded previous legislation aimed at regulating the discharge of pollutants and set goals for water quality improvement—Section 404 of CWA authorized the U.S. Corps of Army Engineers to issue dredge and fill permits for wetlands.
- The Endangered Species Act (ESA) of 1973, amended in 1988, prohibited development in habitats of endangered species, e.g., the snaildarter, furbish lousewort (Pedicularis furbishiae) or gopher turtle.
- The Toxic Substances Control Act (TSCA) of 1976, variously amended over the subsequent decade, provided for the regulation of polychlorinated biphenyls (PCBs) and the removal of asbestos.
- The Clean Air Act (CAA) of 1963, variously amended during the 1960s and 1970s and substantially expanded in 1990, provided for the establishment of air quality standards and the regulation of hazardous air pollutants.
- The Federal Insecticide, Fungicide, and Rodenticide Act (FIFRA) of 1972, amended in 1988, provided for the registration, storage, transport, and disposal of pesticides.
- The Safe Drinking Water Act (SDWA) of 1974, amended in 1988, set limits on the concentration of lead in drinking water (a result of lead piping commonly used in construction for many years) and regulated wells and water treatment plants.
- The National Flood Insurance Act (NFIA) of 1968, broadened by the Flood Disaster Protection Act (FDPA) of 1973, set up the National Flood Insurance Program (NFIP) and Federal Emergency Management Agency (FEMA). FEMA issues directives on where and where not to build in coastal and floodplain areas. Appraisers must report whether a property is located in a flood hazard area. They should also investigate the availability and cost of flood insurance, which is generally required for mortgagors of floodplain properties.

Appendix B

MATHEMATICS IN APPRAISING

*A*ppraisers use a wide variety of mathematical techniques ranging from simple arithmetic and algebraic formulas to the statistical techniques of multiple regression analysis. Addition, subtraction, multiplication, and division can be done manually or with a simple calculator, but more sophisticated calculators may be needed to solve algebraic formulas and to perform linear regression analyses. Computers are required for nearly all stepwise multiple regression analyses.

With the general availability of calculators and computers, the use of sophisticated techniques is increasing in appraisal practice. This section provides a review of the mathematical procedures and terminology used by appraisers. Familiar processes are illustrated and the rules that apply to each process are discussed.

BASIC ARITHMETIC FOR DATA PROCESSING

Data collected in the market are analyzed in the valuation process to derive an estimate of value. These data may include building dimensions, population figures, reproduction and replacement costs, rents, and sale prices. Processing these data ultimately leads to conclusions and final value estimates, which are expressed numerically. The mathematical relationships represented by rates and factors are usually stated as decimals rather than fractions.

Rates

Rates are percentages expressed in terms of a specific time period. For example,

$8 interest per year on $100 principal = 8% interest per year
$0.50 interest per month on $100 = 0.005 or 0.5% interest per month

A rate reflects the relationship between one quantity and another. In the first example, the 8% rate relates the $8 of interest returned to the $100 of principal invested. In appraising, an unknown capital amount can be determined when only the rate and the amount of annual return are known.

Reciprocals

The reciprocal of a number is 1 divided by that number. For example, the reciprocal of 4 is 1/4, which may be expressed as 0.25.

When two numbers have a reciprocal relationship, 1 divided by either number equals the other number. Reciprocal relationships exist between some financial factors. For example, the present value of $1 per period factor and the partial payment factor are reciprocals. These annual factors in the 10% tables for 10 periods are 6.144567 and 0.162745, respectively. Because they are reciprocals,

$$\frac{1}{6.144567} = 0.162745$$

and

$$\frac{1}{0.162745} = 6.144567$$

When a reciprocal relationship exists, multiplication by one of the numbers is equivalent to division by the other.

Factors

Factors are the reciprocals of rates and may be used to express relationships between income and capital value. Using *I, R,* and *V* to represent income, rate, and value, and *F* to represent a factor, the relationships may be expressed as

$$I = V \times R \qquad\qquad I = \frac{V}{F}$$

$$R = \frac{I}{V} \qquad\qquad F = \frac{V}{I}$$

$$V = \frac{I}{R} \qquad\qquad V = I \times F$$

These relationships, which are commonly referred to as *IRV* and *VIF,* may be shown as follows.

$$\frac{I}{R \mid V} \quad \text{and} \quad \frac{V}{I \mid F}$$

The formula for any single component is represented by the horizontal or vertical relationship of the remaining two components as one multiplied by, or divided by, the other.

The financial tables included in Appendix C reflect various rates that are applicable for specific numbers of compounding, or discounting, periods.

BASIC STATISTICS

Statistics can be applied to interpret available data and to support a value conclusion. In the language of statistics, a *population* is defined as all the items in a specific category. If, for example, the category is houses in Chicago, the population consists of all the houses in Chicago. However, data pertaining to an entire population are rarely available and conclusions often must be developed from incomplete data.

Using statistical concepts, conclusions about a population can be derived and evaluated from sample data. A *sample* is part of a population; the quality of conclusions based on a sample will vary with the quality and extent of the sample.

One item in a population is called a *variate*. In appraising, statistics can be used to identify the attributes of the typical variate in a population. When observations about a population can be measured, the analysis may be quantitative; when these observations cannot be measured, the analysis is qualitative—i.e., it reflects the attributes of the population.

A variate is *discrete* when it can assume a limited number of values on a measuring scale and *continuous* when it can assume an infinite number of values. A typical population of attributes for house types might include one-story, two-story, and split-level houses. It is usually impractical to display or identify a population of variates because there are many.

One common problem in statistics is how to describe a population in universally understandable terms. For example, how does one describe all the houses in a community that have sold in the past year without describing each sale individually? One possible solution is to use a single number called a *parameter* to describe the whole population. When one parameter is used to describe a population, it is called an *aggregate,* which is the sum of all the variates. For example, all the house sales in a community in a given year can be described by the total dollar amount of all the sales. In statistical language this is written as

$$\Sigma = \text{sigma or sum of}$$
$$X = \text{variate}$$
$$\Sigma X = \text{aggregate (summation of the variates)}$$

Measures of Central Tendency

Three common statistical measures are the mean, the median, and the mode. All three measure central tendency and are used to identify the typical variate in a population or sample. Measures that refer to a population are called *parameters*, while similar measures in a sample are called *statistics*.

The *mean*, which is commonly called the *average*, is by far the most commonly used parameter. It is obtained by dividing the sum of all the variates in a population by the number of variates. In real estate appraising, the mean may represent an average sale price, an average number of days for sale, an average apartment rent, or an average cost per square foot.

When the mean is used to describe a population, it can be distorted by extreme variates. Consider the following list of 36 house sales in a neighborhood. From these figures, the mean of the population can be calculated. (The list also indicates the median and the mode of the population, which are discussed next.)

$72,000
74,600
76,000
77,200
78,000
79,000
79,800
79,800
82,000
82,000
84,000
85,600
85,800
86,000
87,000
87,200

87,400
87,800 ← median (Md.) = $87,800
87,800
87,800
88,000
89,800
90,000 ⎫
90,000 ⎪ mode (Mo.) = $90,000
90,000 ⎪
90,000 ⎭
90,600
91,000
91,000
93,800
93,800
96,600
97,000
97,200
97,200
98,800
_____
$3,131,600

$$\text{Mean} = \overline{X} = \frac{\Sigma X}{N} = \frac{\$3,131,600}{36} = \$86,989$$

where ΣX = sum of the variates and N = number of variates.

The same procedure can be performed with grouped data. To group the data, the frequency (f) with which a given sale price occurs must be identified and its contribution must be effectively weighted. Given the same data, identical results are produced. (See table on next page.)

The average, or mean, price in this example might not accurately represent the population of houses that have been sold at prices outside the indicated range.

The *median* is another measure used to describe a population, a sample, or an average variate. The median divides the variates of a population or sample into equal halves. To find the median, the variates are arranged in numerical order like the list of sale prices in the example. If the total number of variates is odd, the median is the middle variate. If the total number of variates is even, as in the example, the median is the arithmetic mean of the two middle variates.

In the list of 36 house sales, the middle two variates are $87,800 and $87,800. The mean of these two variates is $87,800, which is the median of the 36 sales. The same number of sales occur above the median as below it.

Like the median and the mean, the *mode* is a parameter used to describe the typical variate of a population. The mode is the variate or attribute that appears most frequently in a population. Of the 36 house sales, four were sold at $90,000. No other sale price occurs with this frequency, so the mode in this

X	f	fX
$72,000	1	$72,000
74,600	1	74,600
76,000	1	76,000
77,200	1	77,200
78,000	1	78,000
79,000	1	79,000
79,800	2	159,600
82,000	2	164,000
84,000	1	84,000
85,600	1	85,600
85,800	1	85,800
86,000	1	86,000
87,000	1	87,000
87,200	1	87,200
87,400	1	87,400
87,800	3	263,400
88,000	1	88,000
89,800	1	89,800
90,000	4	360,000
90,600	1	90,600
91,000	2	182,000
93,800	2	187,600
96,600	1	96,600
97,000	1	97,000
97,200	2	194,400
98,800	1	98,800
	N = 36	fX = $3,131,600

$$\text{Mean} = \overline{X} = \frac{fX}{N} = \frac{\$3,131,600}{36} = \$86,989$$

sample is $90,000. If two variates occur with equal frequency, both are modes and the sample is bimodal.

To illustrate, consider the following population of the types of condominium apartments available in a nine-unit complex

efficiency
efficiency
efficiency
town house ⎫
town house ⎪
town house ⎬ mode (the most frequent attribute)
town house ⎪
town house ⎭
multibedroom

One of the problems in using statistics is selecting the appropriate measure of central tendency to describe a population. The following numbers could be used to describe the 36 variates in the group of house sales.

$$\overline{X} = \$86,989 \quad \text{(the mean of all the sales)}$$
$$\text{Md.} = \$87,800 \quad \text{(the median of the sales)}$$
$$\text{Mo.} = \$90,000 \quad \text{(the mode of the sales)}$$

The mean is often used to describe a sample or population because this measure is widely understood and amenable to further statistical analysis.

Measures of Variation

The parameters of mean, median, and mode are used to describe the central tendencies of a population. Other sets of parameters can provide more information about the population being described. *Measures of variation*, or *measures of dispersion*, describe the disparity among the values of the variates that make up the population. They indicate the degree of uniformity among the variates and reflect the quality of the data as a basis for a conclusion.

Range
One way to measure the disparity between the variates is with a *range (R)*. The range is the difference between the highest and the lowest variates.

$$R = \text{maximum variate minus minimum variate}$$

The range for the 36 house sales is calculated as

$$R = \$98,800 - \$72,000 = \$26,800$$

As a measure of variation, the range has limited usefulness because it considers only the variation between the highest and lowest values, not the variation in the remaining values. Furthermore, a range does not lend itself to further statistical analysis.

Average Deviation
Another parameter used to measure the variation in a population is the average deviation, which is also known as the *average absolute deviation* because positive and negative signs are ignored. The average deviation is a measure of how much the actual values of a population or sample deviate from the mean. It is the mean of the sum of the absolute differences of each of the variates from the mean of the variates.

The average deviation of the 36 sales can be calculated from ungrouped or grouped data.

Ungrouped Data

X Sale Price	$\|X-\overline{X}\|$ Absolute Deviation Between Each Variate and the Mean Sale Price of $86,989
$72,000	$14,989
74,600	12,389
76,000	10,989
77,200	9,789
78,000	8,989
79,000	7,989
79,800	7,189
79,800	7,189
82,000	4,989
82,000	4,989
84,000	2,989
85,600	1,389
85,800	1,189
86,000	989
87,000	11
87,200	211
87,400	411
87,800	811
87,800	811
87,800	811
88,000	1,011
89,800	2,811
90,000	3,011
90,000	3,011
90,000	3,011
90,000	3,011
90,600	3,611
91,000	4,011
91,000	4,011
93,800	6,811
93,800	6,811
96,600	9,611
97,000	10,011
97,200	10,211
97,200	10,211
98,800	11,811
$3,131,600 Total of sale prices	$192,088 Total deviation from mean $\Sigma\|X-\overline{X}\|$

Grouped Data

X	|X−X̄|	f	f|X−X̄|
$72,000	$14,989	1	$ 14,989
74,600	12,389	1	12,389
76,000	10,989	1	10,989
77,200	9,789	1	9,789
78,000	8,989	1	8,989
79,000	7,989	1	7,989
79,800	7,189	2	14,378
82,000	4,989	2	9,978
84,000	2,989	1	2,989
85,600	1,389	1	1,389
85,800	1,189	1	1,189
86,000	989	1	989
87,000	11	1	11
87,200	211	1	211
87,400	411	1	411
87,800	811	3	2,433
88,000	1,011	1	1,011
89,800	2,811	1	2,811
90,000	3,011	4	12,044
90,600	3,611	1	3,611
91,000	4,011	2	8,022
93,800	6,811	2	13,622
96,600	9,611	1	9,611
97,000	10,011	1	10,011
97,200	10,211	2	20,422
98,800	11,811	1	11,811
		36	$192,088

Total deviation from the mean $\Sigma f|X-\overline{X}|$

$$\text{A.D. (ungrouped data)} = \frac{\Sigma|X-\overline{X}|}{n} = \frac{\$192,088}{36} = \$5,336$$

$$\text{A.D. (grouped data)} = \frac{\Sigma f|X-\overline{X}|}{n} = \frac{\$192,088}{36} = \$5,336$$

A.D. = average deviation
Σ = sum of
f = frequency
X = observed value
$|\quad|$ = aggregation (ignore whether the difference is positive or negative)
n = number of observations in sample
$\overline{X}$ = mean of sample

These calculations indicate that the average deviation of the individual values in the population from the mean is $5,336, or about 6%. This relatively small variation suggests that the mean is an acceptable representation of the population.

Like the range, the average deviation does not lend itself to further statistical calculations.

Standard Deviation

The standard deviation is a way to describe a sample or a population that lends itself to further mathematical treatment. When this measure is used, the rules of probability can be applied to draw inferences from samples concerning the attributes of the population. The square of the difference between each observation and the mean of the observations is used in lieu of the absolute deviation. In this way the effects of extreme variance from the mean are magnified.

In the example the mean house sale price is $86,989; for an $82,000 sale, the standard deviation is $4,989 squared, or $24,890,121.

When the standard deviation of an entire population is being calculated, it is symbolized by the lowercase sigma (σ). The formula may be expressed verbally as follows: *The standard deviation of a population is the square root of the sum of the squared differences between each observation and the mean of all the observations in the population, divided by the number of observations in the population.*

When the standard deviation of a sample of a population is being calculated, it is symbolized by the lowercase letter s. Expressed verbally, the formula is: *The standard deviation of a sample is the square root of the sum of the squared differences between each observation and the mean of all the observations in the sample, divided by the number of observations in the sample minus one.*

One is subtracted from the number of observations in a sample to adjust for the one degree of freedom that is lost when the mean is calculated. (See the discussion of simple linear regression analysis that is presented later in this appendix.) A set of data starts with as many degrees of freedom as there are observations; each time a statistic is calculated directly from the data, one degree of freedom is lost.

Formulas for calculating the standard deviations follow.

For a population:

Ungrouped

$$\sigma = \sqrt{\frac{\Sigma(X-\overline{X})^2}{N}}$$

Grouped

$$\sigma = \sqrt{\frac{\Sigma f(X-\overline{X})^2}{N}}$$

For a sample:

Ungrouped

$$s = \sqrt{\frac{\Sigma(X-\overline{X})^2}{n-1}}$$

Grouped

$$s = \sqrt{\frac{\Sigma f(X-\overline{X})^2}{n-1}}$$

Samples are typically used in real estate appraising, so the second formula is usually applicable. The standard deviation for the 36 house sales as grouped data is calculated in Table B.1.

Table B.1 Standard Deviation for 36 House Sales

X	f	(X−X̄)	(X−X̄)²	f(X−X̄)²
$72,000	1	$14,989	$224,670,000	$224,670,000
74,600	1	12,389	153,487,000	153,487,000
76,000	1	10,989	120,758,000	120,758,000
77,200	1	9,789	95,824,500	95,824,500
78,000	1	8,989	80,802,100	80,802,100
79,000	1	7,989	63,824,100	63,824,100
79,800	2	7,189	51,681,700	103,363,000
82,000	2	4,989	24,890,100	49,780,200
84,000	1	2,989	8,934,120	8,934,120
85,600	1	1,389	1,929,320	1,929,320
85,800	1	1,189	1,413,720	1,413,720
86,000	1	989	978,121	978,121
87,000	1	11	121	121
87,200	1	211	44,521	44,521
87,400	1	411	168,921	168,921
87,800	3	811	657,721	1,973,160
88,000	1	1,011	1,022,120	1,022,120
89,800	1	2,811	7,901,720	7,901,720
90,000	4	3,011	9,066,120	36,264,500
90,600	1	3,611	13,039,300	13,039,300
91,000	2	4,011	16,088,100	32,176,200
93,800	2	6,811	46,389,700	92,779,400
96,600	1	9,611	92,371,300	92,371,300
97,000	1	10,011	100,220,000	100,220,000
97,200	2	10,211	104,265,000	208,530,000
98,800	1	11,811	139,500,000	139,500,000

| | | | | $1,631,755,444 |
| Rounded | | | | $1,631,760,000 |

The standard deviation is a useful way to describe the dispersion of a population or sample. It indicates how well the mean represents the whole sample or population by describing a standard measure of variation. The standard deviation is used and understood in many disciplines and it can be calculated easily with an electronic calculator. It will undoubtedly be more widely used by appraisers in the future.

The standard deviation can also indicate what percentage of the sample of a population may be expected to fall within selected ranges of *confidence intervals*. (Confidence levels are discussed later in this appendix.)

Approximately 68.26% of the sample or population will generally fall within plus or minus one standard deviation from the mean, provided the data meet the tests of normal distribution, which are explained later. Many types of real estate data conform to the pattern of a normal distribution when they are developed with appropriate sampling techniques.

Assuming this is a normal distribution, 68.26% of the house sales in the population will fall between $80,161 ($86,989−$6,828) and $93,817

($86,989 + $6,828). Approximately 95.44% of the sales should fall within two standard deviations from the mean and approximately 99.74% should fall within three standard deviations from the mean.

Because the standard deviation lends itself to further mathematical calculations, it can be used for analytical purposes as well as to describe a population.

$$s = \sqrt{\frac{\Sigma f(X - \overline{X})^2}{n-1}} \qquad \text{Mean: } \$86,989$$

$$s = \sqrt{\frac{\$1,631,760,000}{36-1}}$$

$$s = \sqrt{\$46,621,714}$$

$$s = \$6,828$$

Statistical Inference

Statistical inference is based on the assumption that past market actions provide a valid basis for forecasting present or future market actions. In the example, past sale prices are used to estimate current sale prices. The same technique can be used to forecast rents, costs, depreciation, and other amounts using the rules of probability.

A normal curve is produced when a normal distribution is plotted on a graph to illustrate a distribution of data. Although the original data may not be normally distributed, the results of repeated random samples may approximate a normal distribution. Sales are often treated as though they were normally distributed in competitive, open-market situations.

A normal curve often takes the form of a bell curve. One major characteristic of a bell curve is its symmetry. Both halves of the curve have the same shape and contain the same number of observations. The mean, median, and mode are the same value and fall at the midpoint, or apex, of the curve.

Figure B.1 is a bell curve that illustrates the 36 house sales. It shows that 68.26% of the observations will fall within the range of the mean, plus or minus one standard deviation; 95.44% will fall within plus or minus two standard deviations; and 99.74% will fall within plus or minus three standard deviations. The figure depicts an analysis of the probable population distribution for the 36 sales, assuming a normal distribution.

Under the bell curve, the ranges for one, two, and three standard deviations are shown. The percentage of the population that will fall within a given distance from the mean or within any specified range can be calculated. For example, the percentage of sales included within a range of $91,989 to $81,989 (i.e., the mean of $86,989 plus or minus $5,000) may be estimated by calculating the Z value

Figure B.1 Area Under the Normal Curve for 36 House Sales

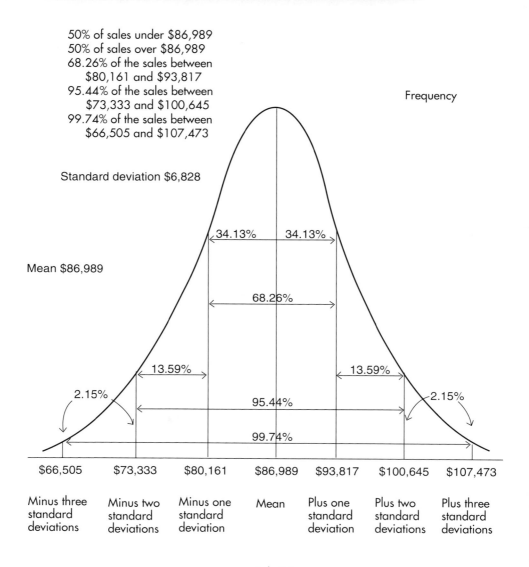

50% of sales under $86,989
50% of sales over $86,989
68.26% of the sales between
$80,161 and $93,817
95.44% of the sales between
$73,333 and $100,645
99.74% of the sales between
$66,505 and $107,473

Standard deviation $6,828

Mean $86,989

Frequency

34.13% 34.13%

68.26%

13.59% 13.59%

2.15% 95.44% 2.15%

99.74%

$66,505	$73,333	$80,161	$86,989	$93,817	$100,645	$107,473
Minus three standard deviations	Minus two standard deviations	Minus one standard deviation	Mean	Plus one standard deviation	Plus two standard deviations	Plus three standard deviations

Sale Price

Source: Joseph Lambert, PhD

for this range with the formula presented below and then consulting a table of areas under the normal curve for the calculated value of Z.

$$Z = \text{the deviation of } X \text{ from the mean measured in standard deviations}$$

$$Z = \frac{X - \text{mean}}{\text{standard deviation}}$$

$$Z = \frac{\$91,989 - \$86,989}{\$6,828} = 0.73$$

This formula shows that $91,989 and $81,989 each deviate from the mean of $86,989 by 0.73 standard deviations.

The percentage of sales within this Z range of plus or minus 0.73 standard deviations can be found by locating 0.7 in the Z column of Table B.2 and then looking across the top of the table for the next digit—i.e., 0.03. The table indicates that 26.73% of the sales fall between $86,989 and $91,989 or between $86,989 and $81,989; therefore, 53.46% of the sales will fall between $91,989 and $81,989.

The probability of a randomly selected sale falling within a given range can also be determined with the Z value. Using the sample of 36 house sales, which has a mean of $86,989 and a standard deviation of $6,828, the probability of a randomly selected sale falling between $86,989 and $88,989 is calculated as follows:

$$Z = \frac{X - \text{mean}}{\text{standard deviation}} = \frac{\$88,989 - \$86,989}{\$6,828} = 0.29$$

The table of areas under the normal curve, Table B.2, shows that a Z value of 0.29 corresponds to 0.1141. This indicates that there is an 11.41% chance that the sale will fall within $2,000 above the mean. Because the curve of normal distribution is symmetrical, there is the same probability that a sale will fall within $2,000 below the mean.

Probability a sale will fall between $88,989 and $86,989	11.41%
Probability a sale will fall between $84,989 and $86,989	11.41%
Probability a sale will fall between $84,989 and $88,989	22.82%

If the range in this example is expanded to $4,000 plus or minus the mean of $86,989—i.e., between $82,989 and $90,989—the probability of a randomly selected sale falling within this range is increased.

$$Z = \frac{X - \text{mean}}{\text{standard deviation}} = \frac{\$90,989 - \$86,989}{\$6,828} = 0.59$$

Table B.2 Areas Under the Normal Curve

z	.00	.01	.02	.03	.04	.05	.06	.07	.08	.09
0.0	0.0000	0.0040	0.0080	0.0120	0.0160	0.0199	0.0239	0.0279	0.0319	0.0359
0.1	0.0398	0.0438	0.0478	0.0517	0.0557	0.0596	0.0636	0.0675	0.0714	0.0753
0.2	0.0793	0.0832	0.0871	0.0910	0.0948	0.0987	0.1026	0.1064	0.1103	0.1141
0.3	0.1179	0.1217	0.1255	0.1293	0.1331	0.1368	0.1406	0.1443	0.1480	0.1517
0.4	0.1554	0.1591	0.1628	0.1664	0.1700	0.1736	0.1772	0.1808	0.1844	0.1879
0.5	0.1915	0.1950	0.1985	0.2019	0.2054	0.2088	0.2123	0.2157	0.2190	0.2224
0.6	0.2257	0.2291	0.2324	0.2357	0.2389	0.2422	0.2454	0.2486	0.2517	0.2549
0.7	0.2580	0.2611	0.2642	0.2673	0.2704	0.2734	0.2764	0.2794	0.2823	0.2852
0.8	0.2881	0.2910	0.2939	0.2967	0.2995	0.3023	0.3051	0.3078	0.3106	0.3133
0.9	0.3159	0.3186	0.3212	0.3238	0.3264	0.3289	0.3315	0.3340	0.3365	0.3389
1.0	0.3413	0.3438	0.3461	0.3485	0.3508	0.3531	0.3554	0.3577	0.3599	0.3621
1.1	0.3643	0.3665	0.3686	0.3708	0.3729	0.3749	0.3770	0.3790	0.3810	0.3830
1.2	0.3849	0.3869	0.3888	0.3907	0.3925	0.3944	0.3962	0.3980	0.3997	0.4015
1.3	0.4032	0.4049	0.4066	0.4082	0.4099	0.4115	0.4131	0.4147	0.4162	0.4177
1.4	0.4192	0.4207	0.4222	0.4236	0.4251	0.4265	0.4279	0.4292	0.4306	0.4319
1.5	0.4332	0.4345	0.4357	0.4370	0.4382	0.4394	0.4406	0.4418	0.4429	0.4441
1.6	0.4452	0.4463	0.4474	0.4484	0.4495	0.4505	0.4515	0.4525	0.4535	0.4545
1.7	0.4554	0.4564	0.4573	0.4582	0.4591	0.4599	0.4608	0.4616	0.4625	0.4633
1.8	0.4641	0.4649	0.4656	0.4664	0.4671	0.4678	0.4686	0.4693	0.4699	0.4706
1.9	0.4713	0.4719	0.4726	0.4732	0.4738	0.4744	0.4750	0.4756	0.4761	0.4767
2.0	0.4772	0.4778	0.4783	0.4788	0.4793	0.4798	0.4803	0.4808	0.4812	0.4817
2.1	0.4821	0.4826	0.4830	0.4834	0.4838	0.4842	0.4846	0.4850	0.4854	0.4857
2.2	0.4861	0.4864	0.4868	0.4871	0.4875	0.4878	0.4881	0.4884	0.4887	0.4890
2.3	0.4893	0.4896	0.4898	0.4901	0.4904	0.4906	0.4909	0.4911	0.4913	0.4916
2.4	0.4918	0.4920	0.4922	0.4925	0.4927	0.4929	0.4931	0.4932	0.4934	0.4936
2.5	0.4938	0.4940	0.4941	0.4943	0.4945	0.4946	0.4948	0.4949	0.4951	0.4952
2.6	0.4953	0.4955	0.4956	0.4957	0.4959	0.4960	0.4961	0.4962	0.4963	0.4964
2.7	0.4965	0.4966	0.4967	0.4968	0.4969	0.4970	0.4971	0.4972	0.4973	0.4974
2.8	0.4974	0.4975	0.4976	0.4977	0.4977	0.4978	0.4979	0.4979	0.4980	0.4981
2.9	0.4981	0.4982	0.4982	0.4983	0.4984	0.4984	0.4985	0.4985	0.4986	0.4986
3.0	0.4987	0.4987	0.4987	0.4988	0.4988	0.4989	0.4989	0.4989	0.4990	0.4990

According to Table B.2, $0.59 = 0.2224$.

Probability a sale will fall between $90,989 and $86,989	22.24%
Probability a sale will fall between $82,989 and $86,989	22.24%
Probability a sale will fall between $82,989 and $90,989	44.48%

In these examples the range being tested has been equally distributed above and below the mean sale price. However, the probability of a randomly selected sale falling within any selected range in the population can also be tested. For example, the probability of a sale falling between $80,000 and $100,000 can be calculated as follows.

$$Z \text{ area}^1 = \frac{X^1 - \text{mean}}{\text{standard deviation}} = \frac{\$80,000 - \$86,989}{\$6,828} = 1.02$$

$$Z \text{ area}^2 = \frac{X^2 - \text{mean}}{\text{standard deviation}} = \frac{\$100,000 - \$86,989}{\$6,828} = 1.91$$

A Z value of 1.02 in Table B.2 indicates a probability of	0.3461
A Z value of 1.91 in Table B.2 indicates a probability of	0.4719
Probability	0.8180

There is an 81.8% chance that a randomly selected sale in this sample will fall between $80,000 and $100,000.

Confidence Level

Using statistical inference and the laws of probability for a normal distribution, the previous examples have shown how confidence intervals can be constructed for a sample when normally distributed data have been assumed or approximated. These calculations may be valuable in loan administration, housing development, appraising, and other decision-making situations involving real estate.

The examples have illustrated that, with 36 sales as a sample, an appraiser can state with a 95% degree of confidence that any sale randomly selected from the population will fall between $73,333 and $100,645. Similarly, there is a 68% level of confidence that a given sale will fall between $80,161 and $93,817.

These measures may be meaningful when used in conjunction with other statistical conclusions. However, they depend on how accurately the estimated mean represents the true population mean, so some confidence in the reliability of the mean must be established. Regardless of the size of the population, there is a specific sample size that will permit a certain level of confidence in the estimated mean.

For the 36 house sales, the standard deviation for price has been calculated as $6,828. The arithmetic mean is $86,989, or approximately $87,000. If an appraiser wants to be 95% certain that the true mean is within $1,000 of the estimated mean of $86,989—i.e., between $86,000 and $88,000—the necessary sample size can be calculated with the following formula.

$$n = \frac{z^2 s^2}{e^2}$$

$$n = \frac{(1.96)^2 \, (\$6,828)^2}{(\$1,000)^2} = 179 \text{ sales}$$

where n = sample size required
z = Z statistic at 95% confidence level
s = standard deviation of the sample
e = required maximum difference in the mean

Thus, with a sample of 179 sales, the required level of confidence could be met. Similarly, for a confidence interval of not more than $1,500, the calculations would be

$$n = \frac{(1.96)^2 \, (\$6,828)^2}{(\$1,500)^2} = 80 \text{ sales}$$

Using the original sample of 36 sales, an appraiser may want to know the limits within which the true population mean may fall at a 95% confidence level. By substitution

$$e^2 = \frac{z^2 s^2}{n}$$

and

$$e^2 = \frac{(1.96)^2 \, (\$6,828)^2}{36} = \$4,975,041$$

$$e = \sqrt{\$4,975,041} = \$2,230$$

Thus, the appraiser can be 95% certain that the true population mean falls between $84,759 and $89,219.

Although calculations such as these may not seem to be directly related to day-to-day appraising, professional appraisers have a continuing interest in obtaining adequate data and understanding the markets in which they appraise. Statistical calculations can be useful in quantifying change and performing the neighborhood analyses that are essential to value estimation. Many appraisers routinely analyze the inferences that can be drawn from measures such as the standard deviations of raw and adjusted sale or rental data. These calculations are also applied in appraisal review, loan underwriting, and other analyses.

REGRESSION ANALYSIS

Regression analysis is another technique used by appraisers to analyze market data. It can be applied to estimate value and to isolate and test the significance of specific value determinants.

Simple Linear Regression Analysis

To estimate a probable sale price in the market, it is seldom sufficient to develop a sample of sales, calculate the standard deviation, and base an estimate on this evidence. In most cases the range of values at the confidence level required is too broad to be useful. However, the accuracy of an estimate can be substantially increased by considering one or more characteristics of the sale properties in addition to their sale prices.

In simple linear regression analysis, one independent variable, or property characteristic, is used to reflect a relationship that changes on a straight-line basis. In other words, a change in the independent variable is reflected in the same proportion in the dependent variable, which is unknown. The basic regression equation is

$$Y_c = a + bX$$

where Y_c is the predicted value of the dependent variable; a is the constant; b is the coefficient, or multiplier, for the independent variable; and X is the value of the variable. If, for example, the independent variable is the square foot area of a building and the dependent variable is its sale price, the simple linear regression equation $Y_c = 10,000 + 45X$ means that the sale price of the building is predicted to be $10,000 plus $45 times its square foot area.

To find the constant, a, the data for this regression must be graphed. Increasing square foot areas are indicated along the horizontal axis of the graph and increasing sale prices are indicated along the vertical axis. Then a number of sales are plotted on the graph and a line that evenly divides these points is drawn. This is the regression line, and its slope is the b coefficient. The point on the vertical axis of the graph at which the regression begins is the intercept, or the constant symbolized as a. In other words, this is a base value that represents all positive and negative factors that are not explained by the equation and to which the coefficients, or adjustment factors, are added.

Another important statistic that results from a simple linear regression is the coefficient of determination (r^2). This statistic represents the approximate percentage of variation in the dependent variable, which is explained by the equation and is one measure of the efficacy of the regression. When a regression is performed on an electronic, hand-held calculator, the coefficient of determination given is unadjusted for degrees of freedom (i.e., the number of observations minus the number of variables). This adjustment should be applied to the resulting coefficient of determination:

$$r^2_{adj} = 1-(1-r^2)\ (n-1/n-2)$$

The standard error of the estimate is another measure of how well the regression fits. It is expressed as S_{yx} and represents the remaining dispersion in the data after the regression equation is applied. The equation for arriving at the standard error of estimate is:

$$S_{yx} = S_y\ \sqrt{1-r^2}$$

The b coefficient also has a t value. The t value is the coefficient expressed as a ratio to its standard deviation; it is a measure of the significance of the coefficient. The precise degree of significance represented by a particular t value depends on several factors and must be calculated. As a general rule, however, coefficients with t values greater than 2 are usually significant at a reasonably high confidence level.

Simple regression analysis is particularly useful when one element is overwhelmingly important in determining a property's sale price. Furthermore, this technique allows appraisers to analyze the relationships between real estate values and the significance of their various components.

Example of Simple Linear Regression

Using the 36 house sales analyzed earlier, simple linear regression can be used to demonstrate the apparent relationship between the sale price of a property and its living area in square feet. The gross living area (GLA) of each of the 36 houses is shown in Table B.3. Most appraisers would only analyze properties with the

Table B.3 Comparable Sales Data Set for Simple Regression Analysis

Sale	GLA in Square Feet	Sale Price	Price per Square Foot GLA
1	1,321	$76,000	$57.53
2	1,372	88,000	64.14
3	1,394	78,000	55.95
4	1,403	74,600	53.17
5	1,457	85,800	58.89
6	1,472	87,400	59.38
7	1,475	84,000	56.95
8	1,479	85,600	57.88
9	1,503	72,000	47.90
10	1,512	77,200	51.06
11	1,515	82,000	54.13
12	1,535	79,000	51.47
13	1,535	87,800	57.20
14	1,577	91,000	57.70
15	1,613	90,000	55.80
16	1,640	79,800	48.66
17	1,666	91,000	54.62
18	1,681	79,800	47.47
19	1,697	87,200	51.38
20	1,703	87,000	51.09
21	1,706	89,800	52.64
22	1,709	90,600	53.01
23	1,709	93,800	54.89
24	1,720	93,800	54.53
25	1,732	82,000	47.34
26	1,749	97,200	55.57
27	1,771	97,200	54.88
28	1,777	86,000	48.40
29	1,939	87,800	45.28
30	1,939	90,000	46.42
31	1,939	90,000	46.42
32	1,939	90,000	46.42
33	1,939	96,600	49.82
34	1,940	87,800	45.26
35	2,014	98,800	49.06
36	2,065	97,000	46.97

same approximate square foot area as the subject property and disregard the other sales.

The appraiser is valuing a 1,375-sq.-ft. dwelling, so Sales 1, 2, and 3 are most similar in terms of size. Their prices are reported as $57.53, $64.14, and $55.95 per square foot, respectively. The other sales may provide a clue to the "right answer," but they do little to resolve the discrepancy between these figures. Adjustments could be made for other differences in the properties, but complications would develop if multiple adjustments produced overlapping effects.

Sales 1, 2, and 3 indicate a price range of $55.95 to $64.14 per square foot; when these figures are applied to the 1,375-sq.-ft. area of the subject property, a value range of $76,931 to $88,192 is indicated. (These figures would be rounded in the appraiser's report.) The remaining market information cannot be used effectively in traditional appraisal analysis except perhaps to reinforce the appraiser's judgment.

With simple linear regression, however, more of the market data can be analyzed. To apply the formula $Y_c = a + bX$, the 36 sales were analyzed with a calculator and produced the following figures.

$$a = \$49,261$$
$$b = \$22.59$$
$$r = 0.6599 \text{ (simple correlation coefficient)}$$
$$r^2 = 0.4354$$
$$r^2_{adj} = 1 - (1 - 0.4354)(36-1)/(36-2)$$
$$= 0.4188 \text{ (adjusted coefficient of determination)}$$

Thus, for the 1,375-sq.-ft. property being appraised,

$$Y_c = \$49,261 + \$22.59 \times 1,375$$
$$Y_c = \$80,322, \text{ or } \$58.42 \text{ per square foot}$$

The 36 sales are plotted on the graph shown in Figure B.2 and the calculated regression line is indicated. The graph also shows the standard error of the estimate, which allows the appraiser to construct confidence intervals around the regression line. The calculations in this example produce a standard error estimate of $5,205. When this figure is applied to the property being appraised, the appraiser can state that 36 sales in the market support an estimate of $80,300 for the appraised property, based only on a comparison of their square foot area. Moreover, at a 68% confidence level, the market price should fall between $80,300 ± $5,205—i.e., from $75,095 to $85,505. At a 95% confidence level, the price should fall between $80,300 ± 2 × $5,205, or from $69,890 to $90,710.

Although other statistical measures such as the standard error of the forecast (sf) may be used, most appraisers would consider this analysis to be sufficient and reasonably representative of most single-family market situations. Although a more refined analysis of these data could be performed, this example illustrates a simple application of a regression technique. The standard error of the forecast for the appraised property could be calculated as follows:

$$Sf = S_{yx} \sqrt{1 + \frac{1}{n} + \frac{(X_K - \overline{X})^2}{(X - \overline{X})^2}}$$

$$Sf = 5,205 \sqrt{1 + \frac{1}{36} + \frac{(1,720 - 1,670)^2}{1,469,045}}$$

$$Sf = 5,281$$

Applying this adjustment to the standard error makes only a small change because the measure of value (i.e., square footage) of the subject property is quite close to the mean square footage of the sample data. The greater the difference between the appraised property and the mean of the sample in regard to any property attribute, the more this distortion affects the standard error as a measure of variation in the regression prediction.

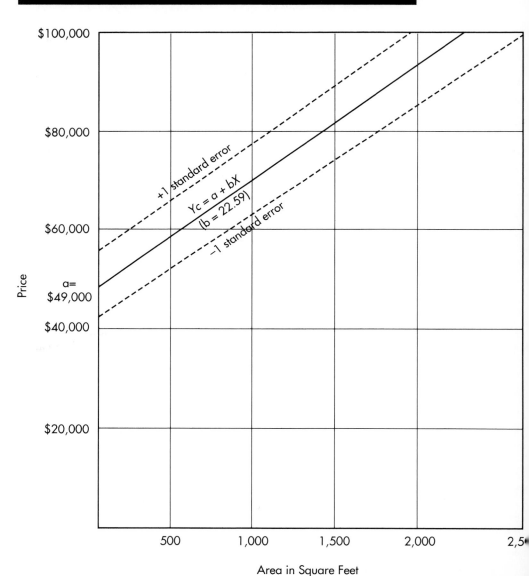

Figure B.2 Plot of Sales, Regression Line, and Standard Error for 36 Sales

Multiple Regression Analysis

Multiple regression analysis is performed with the same basic methods as simple linear regression, but the analysis is expanded to include more than one independent variable. Some hand-held calculators are preprogrammed or can be programmed to perform regressions using two or three independent variables, but multiple regressions are generally performed on a computer. Stepwise regression is an improvement on the standard regression procedure because variables can be added or removed from the regression equation depending on their degree of explanatory power. This type of regression produces an optimum combination of variables by retaining only the most significant.

Example of Stepwise Multiple Regression Analysis[1]

Assume that an appraiser is asked to appraise a 7,575-sq.-ft. lot improved with a recently constructed residence. The house contains 1,720 square feet of living area, and has three bedrooms and two full baths. This house has no porch or swimming pool, but some swimming pools are found in the neighborhood. The dwelling has central air-conditioning and its physical characteristics are similar to those of other properties in the neighborhood. There is an attached, two-car garage.

After inspection of the property and the collection and verification of comparable sales data, stepwise multiple regression analysis is selected for use in the sales comparison approach to value.

Figure B.3 shows a computer printout of the 36 sales selected for the initial analysis. These sales were randomly selected from the total data file after the appraiser identified the independent variables; the presence of a porch, number of bedrooms, lot size, garage size, living area, and any time parameters were considered to be the essential elements of the search. As indicated in the last column of the printout, sale price was selected as the dependent variable for multiple regression analysis.

Figure B.4 is a summary of the arithmetic means of each of the variables and their standard deviations. A simple correlation matrix of the calculated interaction among each of the variables is also shown.

Each step of the multiple regression analysis applied to the comparable sales data is summarized in Figure B.5. After the initial regression equation is calculated by computer, as shown in Step 5 of the figure, the equation is used to calculate the expected prices of the 36 comparable sale properties. Actual sale prices are compared with estimated sale prices for each comparable and the differences are shown in Figure B.6 as the "residuals." The calculated percentages of error in the estimate are indicated and the magnitude of the error is expressed in the number of standard deviations of the dependent variable. In this projection of actual comparable sales information, only two sales were found to have more than a 10% error and most have less than 5%.

The percentage of error in the residuals is shown in Figure B.7, which is a dynamic plot of residual error. The lowest amount of error is shown on the left side of the plot and the highest error is indicated on the right.

---

1. Figures B.3 through B.13 were adapted by Realty Researchers of Birmingham, Alabama from a model developed by Valuation Systems Company, Tulsa, Oklahoma. They are used with permission.

Next the regression equation is run again, deleting the sales that produced the highest amount of error and those that were not arm's-length transactions or involved unconventional financing terms. Appraisers should use extreme caution in discarding any observation in a regression. The basic objective of regression analysis is to account for price variations, and this objective can be thwarted if too many observations are discarded in an effort to retain only the most comparable sales. The results of the second run of the equation are shown in Figures B.8 through B.12. After the least comparable sales are deleted, the second run produces a maximum residual error of 3.44% of the actual price.

The appraiser recognizes and accepts the validity and statistical reliability of the analysis, so the computer can now be used to produce a final indication of value using the stepwise multiple regression analysis procedure. The final results of the projection for the property being appraised are shown in Figure B.13. The final projection indicates an estimated price that is essentially equal to the actual price of the property in a recent sale and establishes, at a 95% confidence interval, a range of approximately + $4,000 as a reasonable price for the property appraised.

Curvilinear Regression Analysis

Most appraisal data do not reflect straight-line relationships, but appraisers often deal with short segments of a curve so tools such as linear regression and correlation can be used. However, inferences can be distorted when linearity is assumed for data that are clearly curvilinear. Fortunately, many sets of curvilinear data can be transformed rather easily and processed as if they were linear.

Example of Curvilinear Regression Analysis

The following table is part of an analysis that compares a county's retail sales per capita with the per capita sales of the state and the entire country.

Retail Sales per Capita—Metropolitan County

Year	Sales
1979	$4,470
1978	4,784
1977	4,301
1976	3,912
1975	3,395
1974	3,059
1973	2,635
1972	2,254

Source: Calculated from population and retail sales data in various issues of *Sales and Marketing Management, Survey of Buying Power,* 1973 to 1980.

Figure B.3 Selected Sales—First Analysis

```
STEPWISE MULTIPLE REGRESSION ANALYSIS

OBSERVATIONS

                     INDEPENDENT VARIABLE                        DEP
OBS     PROPERTY     1       2        3       4       5         VAR.
NUM     I.D. #       PORCH   BDRMS    LT SZ   GAR A   LIV A     PRICE
***     *************  *****   *****    *****   *****   *****     *****
 1      6358500000230   1       3      8100     468    1666     91000
 2      6358500000290   1       3      8100     484    1457     85800
 3      6358500000110   1       3      7575     520    1720     93800
 4      6358500000270   3       3      9936     448    1749     97200
 5      6358500000120   1       3      7568     459    1709     93800
 6      6358500000150   3       4     10002     501    2014     98800
 7      6358500000100   1       3      7560     459    1709     90600
 8      6358500000070   1       3     10781     449    1771     97200
 9      6358500000140   4       2      9033     421    1479     85600
10      6594300000220   1       3      7861     444    1939     87800
11      6594300000150   1       3     13040     444    1939     90000
12      6594300000300   1       3      7700     444    1940     87800
13      6594300000250   3       3      9800     444    1939     90000
14      6594300000010   1       3      8400     459    1706     89800
15      6594300000100   1       3     11085     444    1939     90000
16      6594300000110   3       3     11022     444    1939     96600
17      6594300000080   1       3     19300     479    1681     79800
18      6268800040010   1       3      9191     441    1475     84000
19      6268800010070   1       3      8500     430    1515     82000
20      6268800010120   3       3      8800     441    1697     87200
21      6268800030090   1       3      7700     451    1732     82000
22      6268800030060   3       3      8580     524    1613     90000
23      6473900110150   0       3     11000     419    1777     86000
24      6473900600020   3       3      7125     422    1512     77200
25      6473900300060   3       3      7500     421    1403     74600
26      6473900700120   1       3      8040     454    1703     87000
27      6473900300160   1       3      7763     469    1503     72000
28      6473900500140   3       3      7125     458    1577     91000
29      6473900500080   3       3      7600     430    1394     78000
30      6473900050060   2       2      7410     455    1372     88000
31      6473900010570   3       3      8036     477    1472     87400
32      6473900010020   1       2      7500     460    1321     76000
33      6473900010250   1       3      7995     466    2065     97000
34      6473900010290   3       3      7500     471    1535     87800
35      6473900020060   3       3      8000     471    1535     79000
36      6473900110100   1       3     11000     427    1640     79800
```

Figure B.4 Means, Standard Deviations, and Simple Correlation Coefficients of Variables—First Analysis

```
MEANS

VARIABLE NO. 1 - PORCH =      1.8055
VARIABLE NO. 2 - BDRMS =      2.9444
VARIABLE NO. 3 - LT SZ = 8,978.5555
VARIABLE NO. 4 - GAR A =    455.5000
VARIABLE NO. 5 - LIV A = 1,670.4722
VARIABLE NO. 6 - PRICE = 86988.9000


STANDARD DEVIATIONS

VARIABLE NO. 1 - PORCH =      1.0642
VARIABLE NO. 2 - BDRMS =      0.3333
VARIABLE NO. 3 - LT SZ = 2,277.2125
VARIABLE NO. 4 - GAR A =     25.0855
VARIABLE NO. 5 - LIV A =    199.4894
VARIABLE NO. 6 - PRICE =   6828.0200


SIMPLE CORRELATION COEFFICIENTS

    1          2          3          4          5       DEP VAR
  PORCH      BDRMS      LT SZ      GAR A      LIV A      PRICE

 1.0000    -0.0313    -0.1746    -0.0069    -0.2225     0.0224
            0.9999     0.1511     0.2596     0.5082     0.2909
                       1.0000    -0.0168     0.3232     0.0686
                                  0.9999     0.0720     0.3210
                                             1.0000     0.6598
                                                        0.9999
```

Figure B.5 Summary of Comparable Sales—First Analysis

```
STEP NUMBER 1   ENTER VARIABLE 5

STANDARD ERROR OF ESTIMATE:    5205.38
ADJ COEFF DETERM:              .418814
DEGREES OF FREEDOM:            34
F RATIO:                       26.2216
CONSTANT TERM:                 49260.5

VARIABLE   COEFFICIENT    S.D. OF COEFF.      T VALUE
 5 LIV A     22.5855          4.41062          5.1207

STEP NUMBER 2   ENTER VARIABLE 4

STANDARD ERROR OF ESTIMATE:    4919.33
ADJ COEFF DETERM:              .480935
DEGREES OF FREEDOM:            33
F RATIO:                       17.2144
CONSTANT TERM:                 16311.5

VARIABLE   COEFFICIENT    S.D. OF COEFF.      T VALUE
 4 GAR A     74.8245         33.2339          2.25145
 5 LIV A     21.9069          4.17913         5.24197

STEP NUMBER 3   ENTER VARIABLE 1

STANDARD ERROR OF ESTIMATE:    4843.79
ADJ COEFF DETERM:              .496755
DEGREES OF FREEDOM:            32
F RATIO:                       12.5162
CONSTANT TERM:                 12236

VARIABLE   COEFFICIENT    S.D. OF COEFF.      T VALUE
 1 PORCH    1126.44         789.177           1.42737
 4 GAR A      74.3876        32.7249          2.27312
 5 LIV A      23.2482         4.22089         5.5079

STEP NUMBER 4   ENTER VARIABLE 2

STANDARD ERROR OF ESTIMATE:    4808.05
ADJ COEFF DETERM:              .504154
DEGREES OF FREEDOM:            31
F RATIO:                       9.89659
CONSTANT TERM:                 12661.4

VARIABLE   COEFFICIENT    S.D. OF COEFF.      T VALUE
 1 PORCH    1220.57         787.172           1.55058
 2 BDRMS   -3580.89        2945.92           -1.21554
 4 GAR A      85.0186        33.6402          2.52729
 5 LIV A      26.3048         4.88641         5.38325
```

Figure B.5 Summary of Comparable Sales—First Analysis (continued)

```
STEP NUMBER 5   ENTER VARIABLE 3

STANDARD ERROR OF ESTIMATE:     4803.71
ADJ COEFF DETERM:               .505047
DEGREES OF FREEDOM:             30
F RATIO:                        8.14275
CONSTANT TERM:                  14710.9

VARIABLE   COEFFICIENT     S.D. OF COEFF.      T VALUE
1 PORCH     1130.22         791.362            1.4282
2 BDRMS    -3563.51        2943.32            -1.21071
3 LT SZ     -.389959        .379485           -1.0276
4 GAR A     83.5747         33.6393            2.48444
5 LIV A     27.6346         5.05062            5.47153
```

Figure B.6 Comparison of Actual and Estimated Sale Prices of Comparables Showing Residuals and Percentages of Error—First Analysis

RESIDUAL ANALYSIS

OBSERVATION	PREDICTED Y	ACTUAL Y	RESIDUAL	% ERROR	# STD DEV
1	87144.10	91000.00	3855.87	4.24	0.56
2	82705.70	85800.00	3094.30	3.61	0.45
3	93187.00	93800.00	612.98	0.65	0.09
4	89310.80	97200.00	7889.22	8.12	1.16
5	87787.70	93800.00	6012.30	6.41	0.88
6	97474.20	98800.00	1325.84	1.34	0.19
7	87790.80	90600.00	2809.18	3.10	0.41
8	87412.40	97200.00	9787.64	10.07	1.43
9	84638.80	85600.00	961.21	1.12	0.14
10	92775.80	87800.00	-4975.78	-5.67	-0.73
11	90756.20	90000.00	-756.19	-0.84	-0.11
12	92866.20	87800.00	-5066.20	-5.77	-0.74
13	94280.10	90000.00	-4280.09	-4.76	-0.63
14	87380.40	89800.00	2419.65	2.69	0.35
15	91518.60	90000.00	-1518.55	-1.69	-0.22
16	93803.60	96600.00	2796.44	2.89	0.41
17	84110.40	79800.00	-4310.43	-5.40	-0.63
18	79184.00	84000.00	4816.04	5.73	0.71
19	79639.50	82000.00	2360.52	2.88	0.35
20	87731.80	87200.00	-531.75	-0.61	-0.08
21	87703.20	82000.00	-5703.23	-6.96	-0.84
22	92432.90	90000.00	-2432.95	-2.70	-0.36
23	83855.30	86000.00	2144.70	2.49	0.31
24	81684.60	77200.00	-4484.62	-5.81	-0.66
25	78442.60	74600.00	-3842.64	-5.15	-0.56
26	87020.00	87000.00	-19.96	-0.02	-0.00
27	82854.70	72000.00	-10854.70	-15.08	-1.59
28	86489.60	91000.00	4510.45	4.96	0.66
29	78907.10	78000.00	-907.10	-1.16	-0.13
30	82895.90	88000.00	5104.11	5.80	0.75
31	84820.60	87400.00	2579.41	2.95	0.38
32	80739.10	76000.00	-4739.09	-6.24	-0.69
33	98044.10	97000.00	-1044.13	-1.08	-0.15
34	86269.10	87800.00	1530.87	1.74	0.22
35	86074.20	79000.00	-7074.16	-8.95	-1.04
36	81868.20	79800.00	-2068.18	-2.59	-0.30

Figure B.7 Residuals Percentage of Error—First Analysis

RESIDUALS AS A PERCENT OF ACTUAL

Parcel	Residual	Index
6358500000230 *	4.23	* 1
6358500000290 *	3.60	* 2
6358500000110 *	0.65	* 3
6358500000270 *	8.11	* 4
6358500000120 *	6.40	* 5
6358500000150 *	1.34	* 6
6358500000100 *	3.10	* 7
6358500000070 *	10.06	* 8
6358500000140 *	1.12	* 9
6594300000220 *	-5.66	* 10
6594300000150 *	-0.84	* 11
6594300000300 *	-5.77	* 12
6594300000250 *	-4.75	* 13
6594300000010 *	2.69	* 14
6594300000100 *	-1.68	* 15
6594300000110 *	2.89	* 16
6594300000080 *	-5.40	* 17
6268800040010 *	5.73	* 18
6268800010070 *	2.87	* 19
6268800010120 *	-0.60	* 20
6268800030090 *	-6.95	* 21
6268800030060 *	-2.70	* 22
6473900110150 *	2.49	* 23
6473900600020 *	-5.80	* 24
6473900300060 *	-5.15	* 25
6473900700120 *	-0.02	* 26
6473900300160 *	-15.07	* 27
6473900500140 *	4.95	* 28
6473900500080 *	-1.16	* 29
6473900050060 *	5.80	* 30
6473900010570 *	2.95	* 31
6473900010020 *	-6.23	* 32
6473900010250 *	-1.07	* 33
6473900010290 *	1.74	* 34
6473900020060 *	-8.95	* 35
6473900110100 *	-2.59	* 36

Figure B.8 Selected Sales—Second Analysis

STEPWISE MULTIPLE REGRESSION ANALYSIS

OBSERVATIONS

OBS NUM	PROPERTY I.D. #	INDEPENDENT VARIABLE					DEP VAR.
		1 PORCH	2 BDRMS	3 LT SZ	4 GAR A	5 LIV A	PRICE
***	**************	*****	*****	*****	*****	*****	*****
2	6358500000290	1	3	8100	484	1457	85800
3	6358500000110	1	3	7575	520	1720	93800
6	6358500000150	3	4	10002	501	2014	98800
7	6358500000100	1	3	7560	459	1709	90600
9	6358500000140	4	2	9033	421	1479	85600
11	6594300000150	1	3	13040	444	1939	90000
14	6594300000010	1	3	8400	459	1706	89800
15	6594300000100	1	3	11085	444	1939	90000
16	6594300000110	3	3	11022	444	1939	96600
19	6268800010070	1	3	8500	430	1515	82000
20	6268800010120	3	3	8800	441	1697	87200
22	6268800030060	3	3	11000	419	1777	90000
23	6473900110150	0	3	8580	524	1613	86000
26	6473900700120	1	3	8040	454	1703	87000
29	6473900500080	3	3	7600	430	1394	78000
31	6473900010570	3	3	8036	477	1472	87400
33	6473900010250	1	3	7995	466	2065	97000
34	6473900010290	3	3	7500	471	1535	87800
36	6473900110100	1	3	11000	427	1640	79800

Figure B.9 Means, Standard Deviations, and Simple Correlation Coefficients of Variables— Second Analysis

```
MEANS

VARIABLE NO. 1 - PORCH =      1.8421
VARIABLE NO. 2 - BDRMS =      3.0000
VARIABLE NO. 3 - LT SZ = 9,098.3157
VARIABLE NO. 4 - GAR A =    458.6842
VARIABLE NO. 5 - LIV A = 1,700.6842
VARIABLE NO. 6 - PRICE = 88589.5000


STANDARD DEVIATIONS

VARIABLE NO. 1 - PORCH =      1.1672
VARIABLE NO. 2 - BDRMS =      0.3333
VARIABLE NO. 3 - LT SZ = 1,605.3780
VARIABLE NO. 4 - GAR A =     31.2908
VARIABLE NO. 5 - LIV A =    202.1781
VARIABLE NO. 6 - PRICE =   5479.8900


SIMPLE CORRELATION COEFFICIENTS
```

1 PORCH	2 BDRMS	3 LT SZ	4 GAR A	5 LIV A	DEP VAR PRICE
1.0000	-0.1427	-0.1895	0.1232	-0.2878	0.0431
	0.9999	0.1005	0.4261	0.4410	0.4014
		0.9999	-0.3764	0.5334	0.1066
			0.9999	0.0870	0.5390
				1.0000	0.7721
					1.0000

Figure B.10 Summary of Comparable Sales—Second Analysis

```
STEP NUMBER 1   ENTER VARIABLE 5

STANDARD ERROR OF ESTIMATE:    3583.14
ADJ COEFF DETERM:              .572451
DEGREES OF FREEDOM:            17
F RATIO:                       25.1005
CONSTANT TERM:                 52997

VARIABLE   COEFFICIENT    S.D. OF COEFF.      T VALUE
  5 LIV A    20.9283         4.17728          5.01004

STEP NUMBER 2   ENTER VARIABLE 4

STANDARD ERROR OF ESTIMATE:    2462.36
ADJ COEFF DETERM:              .798089
DEGREES OF FREEDOM:            16
F RATIO:                       36.5742
CONSTANT TERM:                 16714.5

VARIABLE   COEFFICIENT    S.D. OF COEFF.      T VALUE
  4 GAR A    83.2604        18.6186           4.47189
  5 LIV A    19.8066         2.88159          6.87348

STEP NUMBER 3   ENTER VARIABLE 1

STANDARD ERROR OF ESTIMATE:    2222.09
ADJ COEFF DETERM:              .835571
DEGREES OF FREEDOM:            15
F RATIO:                       31.4899
CONSTANT TERM:                 14425.3

VARIABLE   COEFFICIENT    S.D. OF COEFF.      T VALUE
  1 PORCH   1022.45        474.292           2.15573
  4 GAR A    77.5591        17.0087           4.55996
  5 LIV A    21.5828         2.72783          7.91208

STEP NUMBER 4   ENTER VARIABLE 3

STANDARD ERROR OF ESTIMATE:    2100.97
ADJ COEFF DETERM:              .853006
DEGREES OF FREEDOM:            14
F RATIO:                       27.1136
CONSTANT TERM:                 22393.8

VARIABLE   COEFFICIENT    S.D. OF COEFF.      T VALUE
  1 PORCH   1051.87        448.789           2.3438
  3 LOT SZ  -.703438        .421954          -1.6671
  4 GAR A    62.0166        18.5888           3.33624
  5 LIV A    24.8207         3.22866          7.68762
```

Figure B.10 Summary of Comparable Sales—Second Analysis (continued)

```
STEP NUMBER 5  ENTER VARIABLE 2

STANDARD ERROR OF ESTIMATE:      2025.46
ADJ COEFF DETERM:                .863383
DEGREES OF FREEDOM:              13
F RATIO:                         23.751
CONSTANT TERM:                   22030.7

VARIABLE   COEFFICIENT      S.D. OF COEFF.        T VALUE
 1 PORCH    990.254          434.779              2.2776
 2 BDRMS   -2559.79          1782.04             -1.43644
 3 LT SZ   -.670822          .407421             -1.64651
 4 GAR A    73.7264          19.6877              3.7448
 5 LIV A    26.2837          3.275                8.02554
```

Figure B.11 Comparison of Actual Correlated Sale Prices of Comparables Showing Residuals and Percentages of Error—Second Analysis

RESIDUAL ANALYSIS

OBSERVATION	PREDICTED Y	ACTUAL Y	RESIDUAL	% ERROR	# STD DEV
1	83886.90	85800.00	1913.15	2.23	0.35
2	93805.80	93800.00	-5.80	-0.01	0.00
3	97925.00	98800.00	874.97	0.89	0.16
4	89029.40	90600.00	1570.57	1.73	0.29
5	84725.00	85600.00	874.99	1.02	0.16
6	90292.70	90000.00	-292.68	-0.33	-0.05
7	88387.10	89300.00	1412.91	1.57	0.26
8	91604.10	90000.00	-1604.13	-1.78	-0.29
9	93626.90	96600.00	2973.09	3.08	0.54
10	81161.80	82000.00	838.25	1.02	0.15
11	88535.60	87200.00	-1335.63	-1.53	-0.24
12	92594.70	90000.00	-2594.67	-2.88	-0.47
13	84569.80	86000.00	1430.23	1.66	0.26
14	88181.10	87000.00	-1181.09	-1.36	-0.22
15	80565.70	78000.00	-2565.67	-3.29	-0.47
16	85788.50	87400.00	1611.54	1.84	0.29
17	98610.70	97000.00	-1610.70	-1.66	-0.29
18	87361.50	87800.00	438.46	0.50	0.08
19	82549.00	79800.00	-2748.98	-3.44	-0.50

Figure B.12 Residuals Percentage of Error—Second Analysis

RESIDUALS AS A PERCENT OF ACTUAL

ID	Value	
6358500000290	*	2
6358500000110	0.00 *	3
6358500000150	0.88 *	6
6358500000100	1.73 *	7
6358500000140	1.02 *	9
6594300000150	-0.32 *	11
6594300000010	1.57 *	14
6594300000100	-1.78 *	15
6594300000110	3.07 *	16
6268800010070	1.02 *	19
6268800010120	-1.53 *	20
6268800030060	-2.88 *	22
6473900110150	1.66 *	23
6473900700120	-1.35 *	26
6473900500080	-3.28 *	29
6473900010570	1.84 *	31
6473900010250	-1.66 *	33
6473900010290	0.49 *	34
6473900110100	-3.44 *	36

2.22

Figure B.13 Final Summary of Data Analyzed

```
                    HOME FEDERAL SAVINGS AND LOAN

                      MARKET DATA ANALYSIS

PROPERTY ADDRESS  9290   132 ST  NO

APPRAISER                                DATE

PARAMETERS FOR COMPARABLES SEARCH:

PORCHES        GENERAL   BEDROOMS      GENERAL   LOT SIZE   GENERAL
GARAGE AREA    GENERAL   LIVING AREA   GENERAL

COMPARISON GRID:

                                  COMPARABLE PROPERTIES
                       PROPERTY    ************************
       ITEM            APPRAISED    #1        #2        #3
*****************      *********   *******   *******   *******
DATE SOLD             10/82       9/82      10/82     10/82
LOT SIZE              7,575       8,400     11,000    11,000
CONSTRUCTION DATE     1976        1976      1972      1972
PORCHES               NONE        NONE      UNKWN     NONE
BEDROOMS              THREE       THREE     THREE     THREE
BATHS                 TWO         TWO       TWO       TWO
LIVING AREA           1,720       1,706     1,777     1,640
POOL                  NONE        NONE      NONE      NONE
PARKING               2 GR'GE     2 GR'GE   2 GR'GE   2 GR'GE
COOLING               CNTRL       CNTRL     CNTRL     CNTRL
FINANCING             CNTRL       CNTRL     CNTRL     CNTRL
EXTRAS                N           N         N         N
SALES PRICE           $93800      $89800    $86000    $79800

ADDRESSES             #1    9002 127LANE NO
                      #2    11455 131 AVE N
                      #3    11450 132 AVE N



                          (Continued)
```

Figure B.13 Final Summary of Data Analyzed (continued)

```
STEPWISE MULTIPLE REGRESSION VALUATION ANALYSIS

SUMMARY DATA FOR ALL COMPARABLE SALES ANALYZED:
     TOTAL NUMBER OF SALES ANALYZED.......................          19
     MEAN SALES PRICE FOR ALL SALES.......................     $88590
     STANDARD DEVIATION IN PRICE FOR ALL SALES............      $5480

SUMMARY DATA FOR THE MULTIPLE REGRESSION ANALYSIS:
     ADJ COEFF DETERM.....................................     0.8634
     STANDARD ERROR OF THE ESTIMATE.......................    2025.46
     NUMBER OF VRIABLES IN REGRESSION EQUATION............          5
     DEGREES OF FREEDOM...................................         13
     F RATIO..............................................    23.7492

APPLICATION OF REGRESSION RESULTS FOR PROPERTY VALUATION:

VARIABLE   SIGNIFICANCE    MULTIPLIER     DATA FOR        EXTENSION
  NAME      (T VALUE)      CALCULATED     SUBJECT        FOR SUBJECT
********   ************    **********     ********       ***********
PORCH        2.2775          990.254       1.0000        $  990
BDRMS       -1.4363        - 2559.79       3.0000        $- 7679
LT SZ       -1.6463         0.670822    7575.0000        $- 5081
GAR A        3.7445         73.7264      520.0000        $ 38338
LIV A        8.0251         26.2837     1720.0000        $ 45208

       CONSTANT TERM OF THE REGRESSION EQUATION..............    $22031
       INDICATED VALUE FOR THE PROPERTY APPRAISED...........     $93807

CONFIDENCE INTERVALS FOR THE VALUE ESTIMATE:

DEGREE OF       RANGE OF CONFIDENCE        REASONABLE VALUE INTERVAL
CONFIDENCE    IN PERCENT    IN DOLLARS       MINIMUM  TO  MAXIMUM
**********    **********    **********     *************************
68.26%        +/- 0.0228    +/- $2025      $91782        $95832
95.44%        +/- 0.0457    +/- $4050      $89757        $97857
```

The objective of the analysis was to predict the county's retail sales per capita for 1980 before the data were published. A basic calculation indicates a simple linear average growth rate of 14% per year. Projecting this average would indicate retail sales of $5,098 in 1980. However, this type of figure, like the Consumer Price Index, relates to the preceding value, not to the beginning value; therefore, the relationship is curvilinear.

Several types of curves can be fitted to this analysis using a hand-held calculator. First, the estimate can be improved somewhat by using linear regression to separate the slope and intercept figures. Moreover, this is not an extremely long-term trend. Simple linear regression produces these results: $a = -23,812.4$, $b = 363.095$, $r^2 = 0.942$, $S_{yx} = 219.07$, and predicted Y (retail sales per capita for 1980) = $5,235.

The exponential curve, expressed as

$$Y = ae^{bx}$$

reflects a positive or negative compounding over time. This equation is transformed into a linear format by substituting the natural logarithms of the Ys, the dependent variable, and entering the Xs in their original form. The equation becomes

$$ln\ Y = bX + ln\ a.$$

Fitting the data to this type of curve yields the following results: $a = 1.13776$, $b = 0.106353$, $r^2 = 0.939$, $S_{yx} = 0.07143$, and predicted $Y = $5,638.

Another curve that may be considered when exploring regressions on data is the logarithmic curve. The equation for this curve is

$$Y = a + b(ln\ X)$$

In this equation the Xs, or independent variables, are not transformed. The natural logarithms of the Xs, the independent variables for 1972 to 1979, are used. With this approach, the results are:

$a = -115,052.34$; $b = 27,442.8$; $r^2 = 0.9538$ unadjusted, 0.9472 adjusted; and predicted $Y = $5,203.

Next the power, or geometric, curve can be used. This curve is expressed as

$$Y = ax^b$$

which may be transformed to

$$ln\ Y = ln\ a + b(ln\ x)$$

To apply this equation the natural logarithms of both the independent and dependent variables are entered, and these data points are then regressed as if they were linear. The results of this curve are

$$Y = 2.63162E{-}12 \times X^{8.05383}$$

The b figure could easily be lost in a small calculator because 11 zeroes precede the first digit. The adjusted $r^2 = 0.968$, standard error $= 0.06823$, and predicted $Y = $5,590.

This relationship may be explored in a slightly more complex form with a polynomial regression. In addition to the original Xs, this type of regression employs the specified powers of the Xs. This results in the following equation.

$$Y = a + b_1X + b_2X^2 + b_3X^3 + \ldots + b_nX^n$$

The highest power used in the regression is called the *order*, or *degree*, of the equation. Using a second-order equation, the results are: constant $= 137089.9847499$, first-degree coefficient $= 3902.4547389$, second-degree coefficient $= 28.2440798$, coefficient of determination $= 0.929$, standard error $= 288.118$, and predicted $Y = \$5,656$.

Adding the cube of the Xs to the equation for a third-order polynomial regression produces these results: constant $= -37241.803694$, first-degree coefficient $= -376.947096$, second-degree coefficient $= 6.434948$, third-degree coefficient $= -0.056301$, $R^2 = 0.984$, standard error $= 160.889$, and predicted $Y = \$5,271$.

With fourth-order polynomial regression, the coefficient of determination declines to 0.979 and the standard error increases to 203.955. Although it is difficult to conceptualize exactly what the standard error measures in a fourth-order polynomial, it does indicate that the regression equation can be complicated past the point of diminishing returns.

One variation on polynomial regressions should be noted. Using the Cramer's Rule algorithm, a parabolic regression program seems to produce better results over the long term than the standard second-degree polynomial. In the present example, the results would be: constant $= -163746.7262$, first-degree coefficient $= 4073.3810$, second-degree coefficient $= -24.5714$, coefficient of determination $= 0.968$, standard error $= 163.227$, and predicted $Y = \$4,867$. It is interesting to note that the actual 1980 per capita retail sales figure was \$4,843; not all regression-based predictions will be this close. However, by testing the various techniques available, the validity of the work product can always be enhanced.

Appendix C
FINANCIAL TABLES

$\mathcal{T}$he formulas and financial tables presented in this appendix have been adapted from the Appraisal Institute's Capitalization Theory and Techniques course, Parts A and B, and from published financial tables.[1] Although the tables were developed for real estate appraisers, they should also prove useful to students of finance, lenders, investment consultants, and other financial analysts. Sample tables from the nine sets of financial factor tables are prefaced by the formulas, brief explanations, and practical examples. The tables illustrate continuous compounding and discounting factors; annuities changing in a constant amount; annuities changing in a constant ratio; sinking fund factors for annual payments with daily interest; the part paid off for monthly, direct-reduction loans; and straight-line J factors for income adjustment in mortgage-equity analysis.

BASIC FORMULAS

Where:

I	=	income
R	=	capitalization rate
V	=	value
M	=	mortgage ratio
DCR	=	debt coverage ratio
F	=	capitalization factor (multiplier)
GIM	=	gross income multiplier
EGIM	=	effective gross income multiplier
NIR	=	net income ratio

Subscript:
O	=	overall property
M	=	mortgage
E	=	equity
L	=	land
B	=	building

Basic Income/Cap Rate/Value Formulas

$I = R \times V$
$R = I/V$
$V = I/R$

Basic Value/Income/Factor Formulas

$V = I \times F$
$I = V/F$
$F = V/I$

Adaptations for Mortgage/Equity Components
Band of investment (using ratios)

$R_O = M \times R_M + [(1 - M) \times R_E]$
$R_E = (R_O - M \times R_M)/(I - M)$

Equity residual
$V_O = [(I_O - V_M \times R_M)/R_E] + V_M$
$R_E = (I_O - V_M \times R_M)/V_E$

Cap Rate/Factor
Relationships

$R = I/F$
$R_O = NIR/GIM$
$R_O = NIR/EGIM$

Note. NIR may relate to scheduled gross or effective gross income; care should be taken to ensure consistency.

---

1. James J. Mason, MAI, ed. and comp., *American Institute of Real Estate Appraisers Financial Tables*, rev. ed. (Chicago: American Institute of Real Estate Appraisers, with tables computed by Financial Publishing Company, 1982).

Mortgage residual

$$V_O = [(I_O - V_E \times R_E)/R_M] + V_E$$

Debt coverage ratio

$$R_O = DCR \times M \times R_M$$
$$DCR = R/(M \times R_M)$$
$$M = R/(DCR \times R_M)$$

Adaptations for Land/Building Components
Land residual

$$V_O = [(I_O - V_B \times R_B)/R_L] + V_B$$
$$R_L = (I_O - V_B \times R_B)/V_L$$
$$R_B = (I_O - V_L \times R_L)/V_B$$

Building residual

$$V_O = [(I_O - V_L \times R_L)/R_B] + V_L$$

Where:

PV = present value
CF = cash flow
Y = yield rate
R = capitalization rate
$\triangle$ = change
a = annualizer
$1/S_{\overline{n}|}$ = sinking fund factor
$1/n$ = 1/projection period
CR = compound rate of change
V = value

Subscript:

n = projection periods
O = overall property
I = income

Discounted Cash Flows/Present Value (DCF/PV)

$$PV = \frac{CF_1}{1 + Y} + \frac{CF_2}{(1 + Y)^2} + \frac{CF_3}{(1 + Y)^3} + \ldots + \frac{CF_n}{(1 + Y)^n}$$

Basic Cap Rate/Yield Rate/Value Change Formulas

$$R = Y - \triangle a$$
$$Y = R + \triangle a$$
$$\triangle a = Y - R$$
$$\triangle = (Y - R)/a$$

Adaptations for Common Income/Value Patterns

Pattern	Premise	Cap Rate (R)	Yield Rate (Y)	Value Change ($\triangle$)
Perpetuity	$\triangle = O$	$R = Y$	$Y = R$	
Level annuity*	$a = 1/S_{\overline{n}\|}$	$R = Y - \triangle 1/S_{\overline{n}\|}$	$Y = R + \triangle 1/S_{\overline{n}\|}$	$\triangle = (Y - R)/1/S_{\overline{n}\|}$
Straight-line change	$a = 1/n$	$R = Y - \triangle 1/n$	$Y = R + \triangle 1/n$	$\triangle = (Y - R)/1/n$
Exponential change	$\triangle_O a = CR$	$R_O = Y_O - CR$	$Y_O = R_O + CR$	$\triangle_O = (1 + CR)^n - 1$

*Inwood premise: $1/s_{\overline{n}\|}$ at Y rate; Hoskold premise: $1/S_{\overline{n}\|}$ at safe rate

Straight-Line Change* **in Income**	**Straight-Line Change*** **in Value**	**Compound Rate** **of Change**
$\$\triangle_1 = V \times \triangle 1/n \times Y$	$\$\triangle 1/n = \$\triangle_1/Y$	$CR = \sqrt[n]{FV/PV} - 1$
$\triangle_1 = (Y \times \triangle 1/n)/(Y - \triangle 1/n)$	$\triangle 1/n = (Y \times \triangle_1)/(Y + \triangle_1)$	$CR = Y_O - R_O$

*In these formulas $\triangle_1$ is the ratio of one year's change in income to the first year's income.

Table Relationships

The following formulas may be used to convert the annual constant (R_M) for a monthly payment loan to the corresponding monthly functions.

Function for Monthly Frequency	**Formula**
Amount of $1	$S^n = R_M/(R_M - 1)$
Amount of $1 per month	$S_{\overline{n}\|} = 12/(R_M - 1)$
Sinking fund factor	$1/S_{\overline{n}\|} = (R_M - 1)/12$
Present value of $1	$1/S_{\overline{n}\|} = (R_M - 1)/R_M$
Present value of $1 per month	$a_{\overline{n}\|} = 12/R_M$
Partial payment	$1/a_{\overline{n}\|} = R_M/12$

In these formulas, 1 = nominal interest rate.

Present Value of Increasing/Decreasing Annuities

Straight-line changes. To obtain the present value of an annuity that has a starting income of *d* at the end of the first period and *increases h dollars* per period for *n* periods:

$$PV = (d + hn) a_{\overline{n}\|} - \frac{h(n - a_{\overline{n}\|})}{i}$$

To obtain the present value of an annuity that has a starting income of *d* at the end of the first period and *decreases h* dollars per period for *n* periods, simply make *h* negative in the formula.

Exponential-curve (constant-ratio) changes. To obtain the present value of an annuity that starts at \$1 at the end of the first period and *increases each period* thereafter at the rate x for n periods:

$$PV = \frac{1 - (1 + x)^n/(1 + i)^n}{i - x}$$

Where i is the periodic discount rate and x is the ratio between the increase in income for any period and the income for the previous period.

To obtain the present value of an annuity that starts at \$1 at the end of the first period and *decreases each period* thereafter at rate x, simply make x negative in the formula.

Where:

r	=	basic capitalization rate
Y	=	yield rate
M	=	mortgage ratio
C	=	mortgage coefficient
P	=	ratio paid off—mortgage
$1/S_{\overline{n}}$	=	sinking fund factor
R	=	capitalization rate
$S_{\overline{n}}$	=	future value of \$1 per period
$\triangle$	=	change
J	=	J factor (changing income)
n	=	projection period
NOI	=	net operating income
B	=	mortgage balance
I	=	nominal interest rate

Subscript:

E	=	equity
M	=	mortgage
P	=	projection
O	=	overall property
I	=	income
1	=	1st mortgage
2	=	2nd mortgage

Mortgage/Equity Formulas

Basic capitalization rate (r)

$r = Y_E - MC$

$r = Y_E - (M_1 C_1 + M_2 C_2)$

$C = Y_E + P\,1/S_{\overline{n}} - R_M$

$P = (R_M - I)/(R_{MP} - I)$

$P = 1/S_{\overline{n}} \times S_{\overline{n}}\,P$

Capitalization rates (R)

Level income

$R = Y_E - MC - \triangle 1/S_{\overline{n}}$

$R = r - \triangle 1/S_{\overline{n}}$

J-factor changing income

$$R_O = \frac{Y_E - MC - \triangle_O 1/S_{\overline{n}}}{1 + \triangle_I J}$$

$$R_O = \frac{r - \triangle_O 1/S_{\overline{n}}}{1 + \triangle_I J}$$

Required change in value $(\triangle)$

Level income

$$\triangle = \frac{r - R}{1/S_{\overline{n}}}$$

$$\triangle = \frac{Y_E - MC - R}{1/S_{\overline{n}}}$$

Note. For multiple mortgage situations, insert M and C for each mortgage.

*This formula assumes value and income change at the same ratio.

J-factor changing income

$$\triangle_O = \frac{r - R_O(1 + \triangle_1 J)}{1/S_{\overline{n}}}$$

$$*\triangle_O = \frac{r - R_O}{R_O J + 1/S_{\overline{n}}}$$

Equity yield (Y_E)

Level income

$$Y_E = R_E + \triangle_E 1/S_{\overline{n}}$$

J-factor changing income

$$Y_E = R_E + \triangle_E 1/S_{\overline{n}} + \left[\frac{R_O \triangle_1}{1 - M}\right] J$$

Change in equity

$$\triangle_E = (\triangle_O + MP)/(1 - M) \text{ or}$$
$$\triangle_E = [V_O(1 + \triangle_O) - B - V_E]/V_E$$

Assumed mortgage situation

Level income

$$V_O = \frac{NOI + BC}{Y_E - \triangle_O 1/S_{\overline{n}}}$$

J-factor changing income

$$V_O = \frac{NOI(1 + \triangle_1 J) + BC}{Y_E - \triangle_O 1/S_{\overline{n}}}$$

Mortgage/Equity Without Algebra Format

Loan ratio × annual constant	=	_____
Equity ratio × equity yield rate	=	+ _____
Loan ratio × paid off loan ratio × SFF	=	− _____
Basic rate (r)	=	_____
+ Dep or − App × SFF	=	+ / − _____
Cap rate (R)	=	_____

Note. SFF is sinking fund factor at equity yield rate for projection period. Dep/App is the change in value from depreciation or appreciation during the projection period.

Where:

PV	=	present value
NPV	=	net present value
CF	=	cash flow
i	=	discount rate in NPV formula
n	=	projection period
IRR	=	internal rate of return
PI	=	profitability index
MIRR	=	modified internal rate of return
FVCFj	=	future value of a series of cash flows
i	=	reinvestment rate in MIRR formula

Subscript:

0	=	at time zero
1	=	end of 1st period
2	=	end of 2nd period
3	=	end of 3rd period
n	=	end period of series

Net Present Value (NPV)

$$NPV = CF_0 + \frac{CF_1}{1+i} + \frac{CF_2}{(1+i)^2} + \frac{CF_3}{(1+i)^3} + \cdots + \frac{CF_n}{(1+i)^n}$$

Internal Rate of Return (IRR)

$$\text{Where } NPV = 0;\ IRR = i$$

Profitability Index (PI)

$$PI = PV/CF_0$$

Modified Internal Rate of Return (MIRR)

$$MIRR = \sqrt[n]{\frac{FVCF_j}{CF_0}} - 1$$

$$MIRR = \sqrt[n]{\frac{CF_1(1+i)^{n-1} + CF_2(1+i)^{n-2} + CF_3(1+i)^{n-3} + \ldots + CF_n}{CF_0}} - 1$$

Note. In these formulas individual CFs may be positive or negative for *PV* and *NPV* solutions; however, CF_0 is treated as a positive value for *PI* and *MIRR* solutions.

COMPOUND INTEREST (Future Value of $1)

This factor reflects the amount to which an investment or deposit will grow in a given number of time periods including the accumulation of interest at the effective rate per period. It is also known as the *amount of one*.

$$S^n = (1+i)^n$$

Where: S^n = future value factor
   i = effective rate of interest
   n = number of compounding periods

and $S^n = (e)^{in}$ for continuous compounding

Where: S^n = future value factor
   i = nominal rate of interest
   n = number of years
   e = 2.718282

This factor is used to solve problems dealing with compound growth.

Example 1

What is the future value of $10,000 assuming interest at 6% compounded annually for 10 years?

$$\$10,000 \times 1.790848 = \$17,908.48$$

Example 2

What is the future value of $10,000 assuming interest at 6% compounded annually for 10 years and 7 months?

$$\$10,000 \times 1.790848 \times 1.035000 = \$18,535.28$$

This calculation assumes simple interest for any time that is less than one conversion period.

Example 3

A property is sold for \$135,000, but five years previously it was sold for \$100,000. What is the trend in its sale price expressed as a monthly compound rate of growth?

$$\$135,000 \div \$100,000 = 1.350000 \text{ (future value factor)}$$

Scan the table of future value factors, monthly frequency, for 1.350000 at five years. The closest match is found at a 6% nominal rate, so the monthly rate of growth is approximately 0.5%.

Example 4

How long would it take prices to double if a 6% rate of inflation is assumed?

$$2.00 \div 1.00 = 2.000000 \text{ (future value factor)}$$

Scan the table of future value factors at 6% nominal interest for 2.000000. Assuming annual frequency, the target is between the factors for 11 and 12 years. Visual interpolation indicates an answer of slightly less than 12 years. Mathematical straight-line interpolation produces an answer of 11.9 years.

$$(2.000000 - 1.898299)/(2.012196 - 1.898299) + 11 = 11.9 \text{ years}$$

When money is invested or deposited at the beginning of a period in an account that bears interest at a fixed rate, it grows according to the interest rate and the number of compounding (conversion) periods that it remains in the account. To illustrate how and why this growth occurs, consider an investment of \$1.00, a nominal interest rate of 10% with annual compounding, and an investment holding period of five years.

Original investment	\$1.00
Interest, first year at 10%	.10
Accumulation, end of 1 year	\$1.10
Interest, second year at 10%	.11
Accumulation, end of 2 years	\$1.21
Interest, third year at 10%	.121
Accumulation, end of 3 years	\$1.331
Interest, fourth year at 10%	.1331
Accumulation, end of 4 years	\$1.4641
Interest, fifth year at 10%	.14641
Accumulation, end of 5 years	\$1.61051

One dollar grows to \$1.61051 in five years with interest at 10%, so the future value of \$1 factor at 10% annually for five years is 1.610510; \$1,000 would grow 1,000 times this amount to \$1,610.51, over the same five years at the same 10% annual rate. When interest is not collected or withdrawn as it is earned, it is added to the capital amount and additional interest accumulates in subsequent periods. This process is called *compounding*.

The results of compounding can be calculated with the formula $(1 + i)^n$, where n is the number of compounding periods and i is the interest rate per period.

$$
\begin{array}{lll}
n & & \\
1 & 1.10 \times 1 = 1.10^1 & = 1.10 \\
2 & 1.10 \times 1.10 = 1.10^2 & = 1.21 \\
3 & 1.10 \times 1.10 \times 1.10 = 1.10^3 & = 1.331 \\
4 & 1.10 \times 1.10 \times 1.10 \times 1.10 = 1.10^4 & = 1.461 \\
5 & 1.10 \times 1.10 \times 1.10 \times 1.10 \times 1.10 = 1.10^5 & = 1.61051 \\
\end{array}
$$

Thus, the factors in this table, the amount of one or the future value of $1, reflect the growth of $1.00 accumulating at interest for the number of compounding periods shown at the left and right sides of each page of tables. For example, the 10% annual column reveals a factor of 2.593742 for 10 periods. This means that $1.00 deposited at 10% interest compounded annually for 10 years will grow to 1.00×2.593742, or just over $2.59. In other words, $1.10^{10} = 2.593742$. The factors for seven and eight years indicate that $1.00 (or any investment earning 10% per year) will double in value in approximately 7.5 years. Similarly, an investment of $10,000 made 10 years ago, earning no periodic income during the 10-year holding period, must be liquidated in the current market at $10,000 \times 2.593742$, or $25,937.42, to realize a 10% return on the original investment.

This factor reflects the growth of the original deposit measured from the *beginning deposit period*. Thus, at the end of the first period at a rate of 10% the original $1.00 has grown to $1.10 and the factor is 1.100000, as shown above.

6% COMPOUND INTEREST (Future Value of $1)

Base:	2.718 282	1.005 000	1.015 000	1.030 000	1.060 000	
			Frequency of Conversion			
Months	**Continuous**	**Monthly**	**Quarterly**	**Semiannual**	**Annual**	**Months**
0	1.000 000	1.000 000	1.000 000	1.000 000	1.000 000	0
1	1.005 013	1.005 000	1.005 000	1.005 000	1.005 000	1
2	1.010 050	1.010 025	1.010 000	1.010 000	1.010 000	2
3	1.015 113	1.015 075	1.015 000	1.015 000	1.015 000	3
4	1.020 201	1.020 151	1.020 075	1.020 000	1.020 000	4
5	1.025 315	1.025 251	1.025 150	1.025 000	1.025 000	5
6	1.030 455	1.030 378	1.030 225	1.030 000	1.030 000	6
7	1.035 620	1.035 529	1.035 376	1.035 150	1.035 000	7
8	1.040 811	1.040 707	1.040 527	1.040 300	1.040 000	8
9	1.046 028	1.045 911	1.045 678	1.045 450	1.045 000	9
10	1.051 271	1.051 140	1.050 907	1.050 600	1.050 000	10
11	1.056 541	1.056 396	1.056 135	1.055 750	1.055 000	11
Years						**Years**
1	1.061 837	1.061 678	1.061 364	1.060 900	1.060 000	1
2	1.127 497	1.127 160	1.126 493	1.125 509	1.123 600	2
3	1.197 217	1.196 681	1.195 618	1.194 052	1.191 016	3
4	1.271 249	1.270 489	1.268 986	1.266 770	1.262 477	4
5	1.349 859	1.348 850	1.346 855	1.343 916	1.338 226	5
6	1.433 329	1.432 044	1.429 503	1.425 761	1.418 519	6
7	1.521 962	1.520 370	1.517 222	1.512 590	1.503 630	7
8	1.616 074	1.614 143	1.610 324	1.604 706	1.593 848	8
9	1.716 007	1.713 699	1.709 140	1.702 433	1.689 479	9
10	1.822 119	1.819 397	1.814 018	1.806 111	1.790 848	10
11	1.934 792	1.931 613	1.925 333	1.916 103	1.898 299	11
12	2.054 433	2.050 751	2.043 478	2.032 794	2.012 196	12
13	2.181 472	2.177 237	2.168 873	2.156 591	2.132 928	13
14	2.316 367	2.311 524	2.301 963	2.287 928	2.260 904	14
15	2.459 603	2.454 094	2.443 220	2.427 262	2.396 558	15
16	2.611 696	2.605 457	2.593 144	2.575 083	2.540 352	16
17	2.773 195	2.766 156	2.752 269	2.731 905	2.692 773	17
18	2.944 680	2.936 766	2.921 158	2.898 278	2.854 339	18
19	3.126 768	3.117 899	3.100 411	3.074 783	3.025 600	19
20	3.320 117	3.310 204	3.290 663	3.262 038	3.207 135	20
21	3.525 421	3.514 371	3.492 590	3.460 696	3.399 564	21
22	3.743 421	3.731 129	3.706 907	3.671 452	3.603 537	22
23	3.974 902	3.961 257	3.934 376	3.895 044	3.819 750	23
24	4.220 696	4.205 579	4.175 804	4.132 252	4.048 935	24
25	4.481 689	4.464 970	4.432 046	4.383 906	4.291 871	25
26	4.758 821	4.740 359	4.704 012	4.650 886	4.549 383	26
27	5.053 090	5.032 734	4.992 667	4.934 125	4.822 346	27
28	5.365 556	5.343 142	5.299 034	5.234 613	5.111 687	28
29	5.697 343	5.672 696	5.624 202	5.553 401	5.418 388	29
30	6.049 647	6.022 575	5.969 323	5.891 603	5.743 491	30
31	6.423 737	6.394 034	6.335 622	6.250 402	6.088 101	31
32	6.820 958	6.788 405	6.724 398	6.631 051	6.453 387	32
33	7.242 743	7.207 098	7.137 031	7.034 882	6.840 590	33
34	7.690 609	7.651 617	7.574 984	7.463 307	7.251 025	34
35	8.166 170	8.123 551	8.039 812	7.917 822	7.686 087	35
36	8.671 138	8.624 594	8.533 164	8.400 017	8.147 252	36
37	9.207 331	9.156 540	9.056 789	8.911 578	8.636 087	37
38	9.776 680	9.721 296	9.612 546	9.454 293	9.154 252	38
39	10.381 237	10.320 884	10.202 406	10.030 060	9.703 507	39
40	11.023 176	10.957 454	10.828 462	10.640 891	10.285 718	40

10% COMPOUND INTEREST (Future Value of $1)

Base:	2.718 282	1.008 333	1.025 000	1.050 000	1.000 000	
			Frequency of Conversion			
Months	**Continuous**	**Monthly**	**Quarterly**	**Semiannual**	**Annual**	**Months**
0	1.000 000	1.000 000	1.000 000	1.000 000	1.000 000	0
1	1.008 368	1.008 333	1.008 333	1.008 333	1.008 333	1
2	1.016 806	1.016 736	1.016 667	1.016 667	1.016 667	2
3	1.025 315	1.025 209	1.025 000	1.025 000	1.025 000	3
4	1.033 895	1.033 752	1.033 542	1.033 333	1.033 333	4
5	1.042 547	1.042 367	1.042 083	1.041 667	1.041 667	5
6	1.051 271	1.051 053	1.050 625	1.050 000	1.050 000	6
7	1.060 068	1.059 812	1.059 380	1.058 750	1.058 333	7
8	1.068 939	1.068 644	1.068 135	1.067 500	1.066 667	8
9	1.077 884	1.077 549	1.076 891	1.076 250	1.075 000	9
10	1.086 904	1.086 529	1.085 865	1.085 000	1.083 333	10
11	1.095 999	1.095 583	1.094 839	1.093 750	1.091 667	11
Years						**Years**
1	1.105 171	1.104 713	1.103 813	1.102 500	1.000 000	1
2	1.221 403	1.220 391	1.218 403	1.215 506	1.210 000	2
3	1.349 859	1.348 182	1.344 889	1.340 096	1.331 000	3
4	1.491 825	1.489 354	1.484 506	1.477 455	1.464 100	4
5	1.648 721	1.645 309	1.638 616	1.628 895	1.610 510	5
6	1.822 119	1.817 594	1.808 726	1.795 856	1.771 561	6
7	2.013 753	2.007 920	1.996 495	1.979 932	1.948 717	7
8	2.225 541	2.218 176	2.203 757	2.182 875	2.143 589	8
9	2.459 603	2.450 448	2.432 535	2.406 619	2.357 948	9
10	2.718 282	2.707 041	2.685 064	2.653 298	2.593 742	10
11	3.004 166	2.990 504	2.963 808	2.925 261	2.853 117	11
12	3.320 117	3.303 649	3.271 490	3.225 100	3.138 428	12
13	3.669 297	3.649 584	3.611 112	3.555 673	3.452 271	13
14	4.055 200	4.031 743	3.985 992	3.920 129	3.797 498	14
15	4.481 689	4.453 920	4.399 790	4.321 942	4.177 248	15
16	4.953 032	4.920 303	4.856 545	4.764 941	4.594 973	16
17	5.473 947	5.435 523	5.360 717	5.253 348	5.054 470	17
18	6.049 647	6.004 693	5.917 228	5.791 816	5.559 917	18
19	6.685 894	6.633 463	6.531 513	6.385 477	6.115 909	19
20	7.389 056	7.328 074	7.209 568	7.039 989	6.727 500	20
21	8.166 170	8.095 419	7.958 014	7.761 588	7.400 250	21
22	9.025 013	8.943 115	8.784 158	8.557 150	8.140 275	22
23	9.974 182	9.879 576	9.696 067	9.434 258	8.954 302	23
24	11.023 176	10.914 097	10.702 644	10.401 270	9.849 733	24
25	12.182 494	12.056 945	11.813 716	11.467 400	10.834 706	25
26	13.463 738	13.319 465	13.040 132	12.642 808	11.918 177	26
27	14.879 732	14.714 187	14.393 866	13.938 696	13.109 994	27
28	16.444 647	16.254 954	15.888 135	15.367 412	14.420 994	28
29	18.174 145	17.957 060	17.537 528	16.942 572	15.863 093	29
30	20.085 537	19.837 399	19.358 150	18.679 186	17.449 402	30
31	22.197 951	21.914 634	21.367 775	20.593 802	19.194 342	31
32	24.532 530	24.209 383	23.586 026	22.704 667	21.113 777	32
33	27.112 639	26.744 422	26.034 559	25.031 896	23.225 154	33
34	29.964 100	29.544 912	28.737 282	27.597 665	25.547 670	34
35	33.115 452	32.638 650	31.720 583	30.426 426	28.102 437	35
36	36.598 234	36.056 344	35.013 588	33.545 134	30.912 681	36
37	40.447 304	39.831 914	38.648 450	36.983 510	34.003 949	37
38	44.701 184	44.002 836	42.660 657	40.774 320	37.404 343	38
39	49.402 449	48.610 508	47.089 383	44.953 688	41.144 778	39
40	54.598 150	53.700 663	51.977 868	49.561 441	45.259 256	40

REVERSION FACTORS (Present Value of $1)

This factor is the present value of $1 to be collected at a given future time discounted at the effective interest rate for the number of periods between now and the date of collection. It is the reciprocal of the corresponding compound interest factor.

$$1/S^n = \frac{1}{(1+i)^n}$$

Where: $1/S^n$ = present value factor
  i = effective rate of interest
  n = number of compounding periods

and $1/S^n = \frac{1}{(e)^{in}}$ for continuous compounding

Where: $1/S^n$ = present value factor
  i = nominal rate of interest
  n = number of years
  e = 2.718282

This table is used to solve problems that involve compound discounting.

Example 1

What is the present value of $10,000 to be received in 10 years, assuming an interest rate of 6% and annual compounding?

$$\$10,000 \times .558395 = \$5,583.95$$

Example 2

What is the present value of $10,000 to be received in 10 years and 7 months, assuming an interest rate of 6% and annual compounding?

$$\$10,000 \times .558395 \times .966184 = \$5,395.12$$

This calculation assumes simple interest for any time that is less than one conversion period.

Example 3

Assuming a 6% rate and annual compounding, what is the present value of the following cash flows: $1,000 in one year, $2,000 in two years, and $3,000 in three years?

Cash Flows		Present Value Factor		Present Value
$1,000	×	.943396	=	$ 943.40
2,000	×	.889996	=	1,779.99
3,000	×	.839619	=	2,518.86
Present value				$5,242.25

Example 4

A property is sold for $100,000, but five years previously it was sold for $135,000. What is the depreciation in its sale price expressed as a monthly compound rate?

$$\$100,000 / \$135,000 = .740741 \text{ (present value factor)}$$

Scan the tables of present value factors, monthly frequency, for .740741 at five years. The closest match is found at 6% nominal rate, so the monthly rate is approximately 0.5%.

Example 5

How long will it take $1.00 to be worth $0.50 assuming a 6% rate of inflation?

$$.50 / 1.00 = .500000 \text{ (present value factor)}$$

Scan the tables of present value factors at 6% nominal interest for .500000. Assuming annual frequency, the target is between the factors for 11 and 12 years. Visual interpolation indicates an answer of slightly less than 12 years. Mathematical straight-line interpolation produces an answer of 11.9 years.

$$(.526788 - .500000) / (.526788 - .496969) + 11 = 11.9 \text{ years}$$

As demonstrated in the discussion of future value, $1.00 compounded annually at 10% will grow to $1.610151 in five years. Accordingly, the amount that will grow to $1.00 in five years is $1.00 divided by 1.61051, or $0.62092. In the 10% table, the present value of $1 factor for five years is .620921. In other words, $1.00 to be collected five years from today has a present value of $0.620921 when discounted at 10% per year. And $10,000 to be collected five years from today, discounted at the same 10% annual rate, has a present value of $10,000 × .620921, or $6,209.21. The $10,000 sum to be received in five years is a *reversion*.

6% REVERSION FACTORS (Present Value of $1)

Base:	2.718 282	1.005 000	1.015 000	1.030 000	1.060 000	
			Frequency of Conversion			
Months	**Continuous**	**Monthly**	**Quarterly**	**Semiannual**	**Annual**	**Months**
0	1.000 000	1.000 000	1.000 000	1.000 000	1.000 000	0
1	.995 012	.995 025	.995 025	.995 025	.995 025	1
2	.990 050	.990 075	.990 099	.990 099	.990 099	2
3	.985 112	.985 149	.985 222	.985 222	.985 222	3
4	.980 199	.980 248	.980 320	.980 392	.980 392	4
5	.975 310	.975 371	.972 467	.975 610	.975 610	5
6	.970 446	.970 518	.970 662	.970 874	.970 874	6
7	.965 605	.965 690	.965 833	.966 044	.966 184	7
8	.960 789	.960 885	.961 051	.961 261	.961 538	8
9	.955 997	.956 105	.956 317	.956 526	.956 938	9
10	.951 229	.951 348	.951 559	.951 837	.952 381	10
11	.946 485	.946 615	.946 849	.947 194	.947 867	11

Years						**Years**
1	.941 765	.941 905	.942 184	.942 596	.943 396	1
2	.886 920	.887 186	.887 711	.888 487	.889 996	2
3	.835 270	.835 645	.836 387	.837 484	.839 619	3
4	.786 628	.787 098	.788 031	.789 409	.792 094	4
5	.740 818	.741 372	.742 470	.744 094	.747 258	5
6	.697 676	.698 302	.699 544	.701 380	.704 961	6
7	.657 047	.657 735	.659 099	.661 118	.665 057	7
8	.618 783	.619 524	.620 993	.623 167	.627 412	8
9	.582 748	.583 533	.585 090	.587 395	.591 898	9
10	.548 812	.549 633	.551 262	.553 676	.558 395	10
11	.516 851	.517 702	.519 391	.521 893	.526 788	11
12	.486 752	.487 626	.489 362	.491 934	.496 969	12
13	.458 406	.459 298	.461 069	.463 695	.468 339	13
14	.431 711	.432 615	.434 412	.437 077	.442 301	14
15	.406 570	.407 482	.409 296	.411 987	.417 265	15
16	.382 893	.383 810	.385 632	.388 337	.393 646	16
17	.360 595	.361 513	.363 337	.366 045	.371 364	17
18	.339 596	.340 511	.342 330	.345 032	.350 344	18
19	.319 819	.320 729	.322 538	.325 226	.330 513	19
20	.301 194	.302 096	.303 890	.306 557	.311 805	20
21	.283 654	.284 546	.286 321	.228 959	.294 155	21
22	.267 135	.268 015	.269 767	.272 372	.277 505	22
23	.251 579	.252 445	.254 170	.256 737	.261 797	23
24	.236 928	.237 779	.239 475	.241 999	.246 979	24
25	.223 130	.223 966	.225 629	.228 107	.232 999	25
26	.210 136	.210 954	.212 585	.215 013	.219 810	26
27	.197 899	.198 699	.200 294	.202 670	.207 368	27
28	.186 374	.187 156	.188 714	.191 036	.195 630	28
29	.175 520	.176 283	.177 803	.180 070	.184 557	29
30	.165 299	.166 042	.167 523	.169 733	.174 110	30
31	.155 673	.156 396	.157 838	.159 990	.164 255	31
32	.146 607	.147 310	.148 712	.150 806	.154 957	32
33	.138 069	.138 752	.140 114	.142 149	.146 186	33
34	.130 029	.130 691	.132 013	.133 989	.137 912	34
35	.122 456	.123 099	.124 381	.126 297	.130 105	35
36	.115 325	.115 947	.117 190	.119 047	.122 741	36
37	.108 609	.109 212	.110 414	.112 214	.115 793	37
38	.102 284	.102 867	.104 031	.105 772	.109 239	38
39	.096 328	.096 891	.098 016	.099 700	.103 056	39
40	.090 718	.091 262	.092 349	.093 977	.097 222	40

10% REVERSION FACTORS (Present Value of $1)

Base:	2.718 282	1.008 333	1.025 000	1.050 000	1.100 000	
			Frequency of Conversion			
Months	**Continuous**	**Monthly**	**Quarterly**	**Semiannual**	**Annual**	**Months**
0	1.000 000	1.000 000	1.000 000	1.000 000	1.000 000	0
1	.991 701	.991 736	.991 736	.991 736	.991 736	1
2	.983 471	.983 539	.983 607	.983 607	.983 607	2
3	.975 310	.975 411	.975 610	.975 610	.975 610	3
4	.967 216	.967 350	.967 547	.967 742	.967 742	4
5	.959 189	.959 355	.959 616	.960 000	.960 000	5
6	.951 229	.951 427	.951 814	.952 381	.952 381	6
7	.943 335	.943 563	.943 948	.944 510	.944 882	7
8	.935 507	.935 765	.936 211	.936 768	.937 500	8
9	.927 743	.928 032	.928 599	.929 152	.930 233	9
10	.920 044	.920 362	.920 925	.921 659	.923 077	10
11	.912 409	.912 756	.913 376	.914 286	.916 031	11

Years						**Years**
1	.904 837	.905 212	.905 951	.907 029	.909 091	1
2	.818 731	.819 410	.820 747	.822 702	.826 446	2
3	.740 818	.741 740	.743 556	.746 215	.751 315	3
4	.670 320	.671 432	.673 625	.676 839	.683 013	4
5	.606 531	.607 789	.610 271	.613 913	.620 921	5
6	.548 812	.550 178	.552 875	.556 837	.564 474	6
7	.496 585	.498 028	.500 878	.505 068	.513 158	7
8	.449 329	.450 821	.453 771	.458 112	.466 507	8
9	.406 570	.408 089	.411 094	.415 521	.424 098	9
10	.367 879	.369 407	.372 431	.376 889	.385 543	10
11	.332 871	.334 392	.337 404	.341 850	.350 494	11
12	.301 194	.302 696	.305 671	.310 068	.318 631	12
13	.272 532	.274 004	.276 923	.281 241	.289 664	13
14	.246 597	.248 032	.250 879	.255 094	.263 331	14
15	.223 130	.224 521	.227 284	.231 377	.239 392	15
16	.201 897	.203 240	.205 908	.209 866	.217 629	16
17	.182 684	.183 975	.186 542	.190 355	.197 845	17
18	.165 299	.166 536	.168 998	.172 657	.179 859	18
19	.149 569	.150 751	.153 104	.156 605	.163 508	19
20	.135 335	.136 462	.138 705	.142 046	.148 644	20
21	.122 456	.123 527	.125 659	.128 840	.135 131	21
22	.110 803	.111 818	.113 841	.116 861	.122 846	22
23	.100 259	.101 219	.103 135	.105 997	.111 678	23
24	.090 718	.091 625	.093 435	.096 142	.101 526	24
25	.082 085	.082 940	.084 647	.087 204	.092 296	25
26	.074 274	.075 078	.076 686	.079 096	.083 905	26
27	.067 206	.067 962	.069 474	.071 743	.076 278	27
28	.060 810	.061 520	.062 940	.065 073	.069 343	28
29	.055 023	.055 688	.057 021	.059 023	.063 039	29
30	.049 787	.050 410	.051 658	.053 536	.057 309	30
31	.045 049	.045 632	.046 799	.048 558	.052 099	31
32	.040 762	.041 306	.042 398	.044 044	.047 362	32
33	.036 883	.037 391	.038 410	.039 949	.043 057	33
34	.033 373	.033 847	.034 798	.036 235	.039 143	34
35	.030 197	.030 639	.031 525	.032 866	.035 584	35
36	.027 324	.027 734	.028 560	.029 811	.032 349	36
37	.024 724	.025 105	.025 874	.027 039	.029 408	37
38	.022 371	.022 726	.023 441	.024 525	.026 735	38
39	.020 242	.020 572	.021 236	.022 245	.024 304	39
40	.018 316	.018 622	.019 239	.020 177	.022 095	40

ORDINARY LEVEL ANNUITY (Present Value of $1 per Period)

This factor represents the present value of a series of future installments or payments of $1 per period for a given number of periods discounted at an effective interest rate. It is commonly referred to as the *Inwood coefficient*.

$$a_{\overline{n}|} = \frac{1 - 1/S^n}{i}$$

Where: $a_{\overline{n}|}$ = level annuity factor
$1/S^n$ = present value factor
i = rate of interest yield

This table is used in solving problems that deal with the compound discounting of cash flows that are level or effectively level.

Example 1

What is the present value of an ordinary annuity of $1,000 per month for 10 years, assuming an interest rate of 6%?

$$\$1,000 \times 90.073453 = \$90,073.45$$

Assuming payments are made in advance, the PV of this annuity would be

$$\$1,000 \times 90.073453 \times 1.005000 = \$90,523.82$$

or

$$\$1,000 \times 90.073453 / .995025 = \$90,523.81$$

Example 2

What is the present value of an ordinary annuity of $1,000 per month for 10 years and 7 months, assuming an interest rate of 6%?

$$\$1,000 \times 90.073453 \qquad = \$90,073.45$$
$$\$1,000 \times 6.862074 \times .549633^* = \underline{\quad 3,771.62}$$
$$\$93,845.07$$

*Reversion factor for 120 months

Assuming payments in advance, the PV of this annuity would be

$$\$93,845.07 \times 1.005000 = \$94,314.30$$

or

$$\$93,845.07 / .995025 = \$94,314.28$$

Example 3

Assuming a 6% annual discount rate, what is the present value of an ordinary annuity consisting of the following cash flows: $1,000 per year for five years, then $2,000 per year for five years, and then $3,000 per year for five years?

$$\begin{array}{lll} \$1{,}000 \times 4.212364 & = & \$\ \ 4{,}212.36 \\ 2{,}000 \times (7.360087 - 4.212364) & = & 6{,}295.45 \\ 3{,}000 \times (9.712249 - 7.360087) & = & \underline{7{,}056.49} \\ & & \$17{,}564.30 \end{array}$$

Assuming payments are made in advance, the PV of this annuity would be

$$\$17{,}564.30 \times 1.060000 = \$18{,}618.16$$

or

$$\$17{,}564.30 / .943396 = \$18{,}618.16$$

Example 4

If a 10-year ordinary level annuity of $1,000 per month has a present value of $90,000, what is the indicated interest or yield rate?

$$\$90{,}000 / \$1{,}000 = 90.000000 \text{ (present value factor)}$$

Scan the ordinary level annuity tables at 10 years, monthly frequency, for 90.000000. The closest match is a 6% nominal rate.

Finding the present value of a future income stream is a discounting procedure in which future payments are treated as a series of reversions. The present value of a series of future receipts may be quickly ascertained using the precomputed present value of $1 per period factors for the selected discount rate provided the receipts are all equal in amount, equally spaced over time, and receivable at the end of each period.

If, for example, 10% per year is a fair rate of interest or discount, it would be justifiable to pay $0.909091 (i.e., the annual present value of $1 at 10%) for the right to receive $1.00 one year from today. Assuming that the cost of this right is $0.909091, the $1.00 received at the end of the year could be divided between principal and interest as follows.

Return of principal	$0.90909
Interest on principal for one year @ 10%	.09091
Total received	$1.00000

If approximately $.091 is the present value of the right to receive $1.00 of income one year from today at 10% interest, the present value of the right to receive $1.00 two years from today is less. According to the present value formula, the present value of $1.00 to be received two years from today is $0.826446. The present value of $1.00 payable at the end of two years can be confirmed with these calculations.

Return on principal	$0.82645*
Interest for first year at 10% on $0.82645	.08264
	$0.90909
Interest for second year at 10% on $0.90909	.09091
Total principal repayment + interest received	$1.00000

*Present value factor, $0.826446 \times \$1.00 = \$0.82645$ (rounded).

Similarly, the present value of the right to receive $1.00 at the end of three years is $0.751315, at the end of four years it is $0.683013, and at the end of the fifth year it is $0.620921. The present value of these rights to receive income at one-year intervals for five years is accumulated as the present value of $1.00 per year. This is known as the *compound interest valuation premise,* also referred to as the *ordinary annuity factor.* Therefore, the sum of the five individual rights to receive $1.00 each year, payable at the end of the year, for five years is $3.790787 (i.e., the 10% annual present value of $1 per period factor for five years).

Sum of Individual Present Values of $1.00

Payable at the End of the Period

Present value of $1.00 due in 1 year	$0.909091*
Present value of $1.00 due in 2 years	.826446*
Present value of $1.00 due in 3 years	.751315*
Present value of $1.00 due in 4 years	.683013*
Present value of $1.00 due in 5 years	.620921*
Total present value of $1.00 per year for 5 years	$3.790786**

*10% present value of $1 factor.
**10% present value of $1 per period factor is 3.790787; the difference is due to rounding.

The present value of $1 per period table for five annual discounting periods ($n = 5$) gives a factor that represents the total of the present values of a series of periodic amounts of $1.00, payable at the end of each period. The calculation presented above is unnecessary because multiplying $1.00 by the factor for the present value of $1 per year for five years produces the same present value ($1.00 × 3.790787 = $3.790787).

For appraisal purposes, the present value of $1 per period factor may be multiplied by a periodic income with the characteristics of an ordinary annuity to derive the present value of the right to receive that income stream. The future payments of income provide for recapture of, and interest on, this present value. Present value factors are multipliers and perform the same function as capitalization rates.

The 10% ordinary annuity factor for five years, 3.790787, represents the present value of each $1.00 of annual end-of-year collection based on a nominal annual discount rate of 10%. Tables and formulas for semiannual, quarterly, and monthly payments are also available. The ordinary annuity factor for semiannual payments in the 10% nominal annual rate table is 7.721735. If payment continues for five years, each $1.00 of semiannual payment represents $10.00 received, but reflects only $7.72 of the discounted present value of monthly payments for five years. In the table for a 10% nominal rate, the monthly factor is 47.065369, indicating that the present value of an ordinary annuity income stream of 60 monthly payments of $1.00 each discounted at a nominal rate of 10% is 47.065369 × $1.00, or about $47.065.

Based on a 10% nominal rate, semiannual payments would involve an effective rate of 5%. In the 5% annuity table, the factor for 10 periods is 7.721735; this is the same factor shown in the 10% semiannual table for a five-year period. Thus, when tables are not available at the effective rate, annuity factors for more frequent payment periods can be derived using nominal annual rate tables. Pre-programmed financial calculators can be used to facilitate these calculations.

In computing the present value of an annuity income stream, it may be desirable to assume that periodic payments are made at the beginning rather than the end of each payment period. The present value of an annuity payable in advance is equal to the present value of an ordinary annuity in arrears multiplied by the base (i.e., 1 plus the effective interest rate for the discounting period: $1 + i$). Thus, the present value of semiannual payments in advance over a five-year period discounted at a nominal rate of 10% becomes $\$1.00 \times 7.721735 \times 1.05 =$ $\$8.107822$, or $\$8.11$, compared to $\$7.72$ as computed for payments received at the end of each payment period.

6% ORDINARY LEVEL ANNUITY
(Present Value of $1 per Period)

Base:	1.005 000	1.015 000	1.030 000	1.060 000	
			Frequency of Payments		
Months	**Monthly**	**Quarterly**	**Semiannual**	**Annual**	**Months**
1	.995 025	—	—	—	1
2	1.985 099	—	—	—	2
3	2.970 248	.985 222	—	—	3
4	3.950 496	—	—	—	4
5	4.925 866	—	—	—	5
6	5.896 384	1.955 883	.970 874	—	6
7	6.862 074	—	—	—	7
8	7.822 959	—	—	—	8
9	8.779 064	2.912 200	—	—	9
10	9.730 412	—	—	—	10
11	10.677 027	—	—	—	11
Years					**Years**
1	11.618 932	3.854 385	1.913 470	.943 396	1
2	22.562 866	7.485 925	3.717 098	1.833 393	2
3	32.871 016	10.907 505	5.417 191	2.673 012	3
4	42.580 318	14.131 264	7.019 692	3.465 106	4
5	51.725 561	17.168 639	8.530 203	4.212 364	5
6	60.339 514	20.030 405	9.954 004	4.917 324	6
7	68.453 042	22.726 717	11.296 073	5.582 381	7
8	76.095 218	25.267 139	12.561 102	6.209 794	8
9	83.293 424	27.660 684	13.753 513	6.801 692	9
10	90.073 453	29.915 845	14.877 475	7.360 087	10
11	96.459 599	32.040 622	15.936 917	7.886 875	11
12	102.474 743	34.042 554	16.935 542	8.383 844	12
13	108.140 440	35.928 742	17.876 842	8.852 683	13
14	113.476 990	37.705 879	18.764 108	9.294 984	14
15	118.503 515	39.380 269	19.600 441	9.712 249	15
16	123.238 025	40.957 853	20.388 766	10.105 895	16
17	127.697 486	42.444 228	21.131 837	10.477 260	17
18	131.897 876	43.844 667	21.832 252	10.827 603	18
19	135.854 246	45.164 138	22.492 462	11.158 116	19
20	139.580 772	46.407 323	23.114 772	11.469 921	20
21	143.090 806	47.578 633	23.701 359	11.764 077	21
22	146.396 927	48.682 222	24.254 274	12.041 582	22
23	149.510 979	49.722 007	24.775 449	12.303 379	23
24	152.444 121	50.701 675	25.266 707	12.550 358	24
25	155.206 864	51.624 704	25.729 764	12.783 356	25
26	157.809 106	52.494 366	26.166 240	13.003 166	26
27	160.260 172	53.313 749	26.577 660	13.210 534	27
28	162.568 844	54.085 758	26.965 464	13.406 164	28
29	164.743 394	54.813 133	27.331 005	13.590 721	29
30	166.791 614	55.498 454	27.675 564	13.764 831	30
31	168.720 844	56.144 153	28.000 343	13.929 086	31
32	170.537 996	56.752 520	28.306 478	14.084 043	32
33	172.249 581	57.325 714	28.595 040	14.230 230	33
34	173.861 732	57.865 769	28.867 038	14.368 141	34
35	175.380 226	58.374 599	29.123 421	14.498 246	35
36	176.810 504	58.854 011	29.365 088	14.620 987	36
37	178.157 690	59.305 706	29.592 881	14.736 780	37
38	179.426 611	59.731 286	29.807 598	14.846 019	38
39	180.621 815	60.132 260	30.009 990	14.949 075	39
40	181.747 584	60.510 052	30.200 763	15.046 297	40

10% ORDINARY LEVEL ANNUITY
(Present Value of $1 per Period)

Base:	1.008 333	1.025 000	1.050 000	1.100 000	
		Frequency of Payments			
Months	**Monthly**	**Quarterly**	**Semiannual**	**Annual**	**Months**
1	.991 736	—	—	—	1
2	1.975 275	—	—	—	2
3	2.950 686	.975 610	—	—	3
4	3.918 036	—	—	—	4
5	4.877 391	—	—	—	5
6	5.828 817	1.927 424	.952 381	—	6
7	6.772 381	—	—	—	7
7					
8	7.708 146	—	—	—	8
9	8.636 178	2.856 024	—	—	9
10	9.556 540	—	—	—	10
11	10.469 296	—	—	—	11

Years					**Years**
1	11.374 508	3.761 974	1.859 410	.909 091	1
2	21.670 855	7.170 137	3.545 951	1.735 537	2
3	30.991 236	10.257 765	5.075 692	2.486 852	3
4	39.428 160	13.055 003	6.463 213	3.169 865	4
5	47.065 369	15.589 162	7.721 735	3.790 787	5
6	53.978 665	17.884 986	8.863 252	4.355 261	6
7	60.236 667	19.964 889	9.898 641	4.868 419	7
8	65.901 488	21.849 178	10.837 770	5.334 926	8
9	71.029 355	23.556 251	11.689 587	5.759 024	9
10	75.671 163	25.102 775	12.462 210	6.144 567	10
11	79.872 986	26.503 849	13.163 003	6.495 061	11
12	83.676 528	27.773 154	13.798 642	6.813 692	12
13	87.119 542	28.923 081	14.375 185	7.103 356	13
14	90.236 201	29.964 858	14.898 127	7.366 687	14
15	93.057 439	30.908 656	15.372 451	7.606 080	15
16	95.611 259	31.763 691	15.802 677	7.823 709	16
17	97.923 008	32.538 311	16.192 904	8.021 553	17
18	100.015 633	33.240 078	16.546 852	8.201 412	18
19	101.909 902	33.875 844	16.867 893	8.364 920	19
20	103.624 619	34.451 817	17.159 086	8.513 564	20
21	105.176 801	34.973 620	17.423 208	8.648 694	21
22	106.581 856	35.446 348	17.662 773	8.771 540	22
23	107.853 730	35.874 616	17.880 066	8.883 218	23
24	109.005 045	36.262 606	18.077 158	8.984 744	24
25	110.047 230	36.614 105	18.255 925	9.077 040	25
26	110.990 629	36.932 546	18.418 073	9.160 945	26
27	111.844 605	37.221 039	18.565 146	9.237 223	27
28	112.617 635	37.482 398	18.698 545	9.306 567	28
29	113.317 392	37.719 177	18.819 542	9.369 606	29
30	113.950 820	37.933 687	18.929 290	9.426 914	30
31	114.524 207	38.128 022	19.028 834	9.479 013	31
32	115.043 244	38.304 081	19.119 124	9.526 376	32
33	115.513 083	38.463 581	19.201 019	9.569 432	33
34	115.938 387	38.608 080	19.275 301	9.608 575	34
35	116.323 377	38.738 989	19.342 677	9.644 159	35
36	116.671 876	38.857 586	19.403 788	9.676 508	36
37	116.987 340	38.965 030	19.459 218	9.705 917	37
38	117.272 903	39.062 368	19.509 495	9.732 651	38
39	117.531 398	39.150 552	19.555 098	9.756 956	39
40	117.765 391	39.230 442	19.596 460	9.779 051	40

ORDINARY ANNUITIES CHANGING IN CONSTANT AMOUNT

(Present Value of Annual Payments Starting at $1 and Changing in Constant Amounts)

$$PVF = (1 + hn)a_{\overline{n}|} - \frac{h(n - a_{\overline{n}|})}{i}$$

Where: PVF = present value factor
       h^* = annual increase or de-
            crease after 1st year
        n = number of years
       $a_{\overline{n}|}$ = PVF for ordinary level
            annuity
        i = rate of interest yield

*h is positive for an increase and negative for a decrease

This table is used to solve problems dealing with the compound discounting of cash flows that are best represented by a straight-line pattern of change.

Example 1

Assuming a 15% interest or yield rate, what is the present value of an ordinary annuity consisting of 10 annual cash flows that start at $10,000 and increase $1,000 per year?

$$\$10,000 \times 6.7167 = \$67,167$$

Assuming payments are made in advance, the PV of this annuity would be

$$\$67,167 \times 1.150000 = \$77,242$$

or

$$\$67,167 / .869565 = \$77,242$$

Example 2

Assuming a 15% interest or yield rate, what is the present value of an ordinary annuity consisting of 10 annual cash flows that start at $10,000 and increase $300 per year?

$$\$10,000 \times (5.3584 + 5.6979)/2 = \$55,282$$

or

$$\$10,000 \times (5.018769 + 16.979477 \times .03) = \$55,281.53$$

Example 3

There are five years remaining on a lease that provides a level income of $1,000 per year. During this period inflation will cause purchasing power to decline an average of 10% per year (on a straight-line basis). What is the value of the income expressed in constant dollars and discounted at 6%?

$$\$1,000 \times (.90 \times 4.212364 - 7.934549 \times .10) = \$2,997.67$$

Proof:

Year	Income	×	Inflation Factor	×	PVF @ 6%	=	Value
1	$1,000	×	.90	×	.943396	=	$ 849.06
2	1,000	×	.80	×	.889996	=	712.00
3	1,000	×	.70	×	.839619	=	587.73
4	1,000	×	.60	×	.792094	=	475.26
5	1,000	×	.50	×	.747258	=	373.63
							$2,997.68

This table is similar to the ordinary level annuity table, but the annual receipts are converted into constant dollar amounts. For instance, assume that the amount to be received one year from today is $10,000, additional future receipts are expected to increase $1,000 per year for the next nine years, and 15% per year is a fair rate of interest. According to the 15% annual present value of $1 factor, it would be justifiable to pay $67,167 for the right to receive $10,000 one year from today and nine additional payments growing at $1,000 per year for nine additional years. The table indicates that the factor to be applied to the initial receipt is 6.7167.

Proof:

Year	Income	×	Present Value Factor	=	Present Value
1	$10,000	×	.869565	=	$ 8,695.65
1	11,000	×	.756144	=	8,317.58
2	12,000	×	.657516	=	7,890.19
4	13,000	×	.571753	=	7,432.79
5	14,000	×	.497177	=	6,960.48
6	15,000	×	.432328	=	6,484.92
7	16,000	×	.375937	=	6,014.99
8	17,000	×	.326902	=	5,557.33
9	18,000	×	.284262	=	5,116.72
10	19,000	×	.247185	=	4,696.52
Present value					$67,167.17

$$\frac{\text{Present value}}{\text{Initial receipt}} = \text{Factor}$$

$$\frac{\$67,167.17}{\$10,000.00} = 6.7167$$

10% ORDINARY ANNUITIES CHANGING IN CONSTANT AMOUNT (Present Value of Annual Payments Starting at $1 and Changing in Constant Amounts)

Base: 1.100 000

Years	Slope		Annual INCREASE of: .00	.02	.04	.05	.10	Years
1	.000	000	.909 091	.9091	.9091	.9091	.9091	1
2	.826	446	1.735 537	1.7521	1.7686	1.7769	1.8182	2
3	2.329	076	2.486 852	2.5334	2.5800	2.6033	2.7198	3
4	4.378	116	3.169 865	3.2574	3.3450	3.3888	3.6077	4
5	6.861	802	3.790 787	3.9280	4.0653	4.1339	4.4770	5
6	9.684	171	4.355 261	4.5489	4.7426	4.8395	5.3237	6
7	12.763	120	4.868 419	5.1237	5.3789	5.5066	6.1447	7
8	16.028	672	5.334 926	5.6555	5.9761	6.1364	6.9378	8
9	19.421	453	5.759 024	6.1475	6.5359	6.7301	7.7012	9
10	22.891	342	6.144 567	6.6024	7.0602	7.2891	8.4337	10
11	26.396	281	6.495 061	7.0230	7.5509	7.8149	9.1347	11
12	29.901	220	6.813 692	7.4117	8.0097	8.3088	9.8038	12
13	33.377	193	7.103 356	7.7709	8.4384	8.7722	10.4411	13
14	36.800	499	7.366 687	8.1027	8.8387	9.2067	11.0467	14
15	40.151	988	7.606 080	8.4091	9.2122	9.6137	11.6213	15
16	43.416	425	7.823 709	8.6920	9.5604	9.9945	12.1654	16
17	46.581	939	8.021 553	8.9532	9.8848	10.3507	12.6797	17
18	49.639	539	8.201 412	9.1942	10.1870	10.6834	13.1654	18
19	52.582	683	8.364 920	9.4166	10.4682	10.9941	13.6232	19
20	55.406	912	8.513 564	9.6217	10.7298	11.2839	14.0543	20

Years	Slope		Annual DECREASE of: .00	.02	.04	.05	.10	Years
1	.000	000	.909 091	.9091	.9091	.9091	.9091	1
2	− .826	446	1.735 537	1.7190	1.7025	1.6942	1.6529	2
3	− 2.329	076	2.486 852	2.4403	2.3937	2.3704	2.2539	3
4	− 4.378	116	3.169 865	3.0823	2.9947	2.9510	2.7321	4
5	− 6.861	802	3.790 787	3.6536	3.5163	3.4477	3.1046	5
6	− 9.684	171	4.355 261	4.1616	3.9679	3.8711	3.3868	6
7	−12.763	120	4.868 419	4.6132	4.3579	4.2303	3.5921	7
8	−16.028	672	5.334 926	5.0144	4.6938	4.5335	3.7321	8
9	−19.421	453	5.759 024	5.3706	4.9822	4.7880	3.8169	9
10	−22.891	342	6.144 567	5.6867	5.2289	5.0000	3.8554	10
11	−26.396	281	6.495 061	5.9671	5.4392	5.1752	—	11
12	−29.901	220	6.813 692	6.2157	5.6176	5.3186	—	12
13	−33.377	193	7.103 356	6.4358	5.7683	5.4345	—	13
14	−36.800	499	7.366 687	6.6307	5.8947	5.5267	—	14
15	−40.151	988	7.606 080	6.8030	6.0000	5.5985	—	15
16	−43.416	425	7.823 709	6.9554	6.0871	5.6529	—	16
17	−46.581	939	8.021 553	7.0899	6.1583	5.6925	—	17
18	−49.639	539	8.201 412	7.2086	6.2158	5.7194	—	18
19	−52.582	683	8.364 920	7.3133	6.2616	5.7358	—	19
20	−55.406	912	8.513 564	7.4054	6.2973	5.7432	—	20

15% ORDINARY ANNUITIES CHANGING IN CONSTANT AMOUNT (Present Value of Annual Payments Starting at $1 and Changing in Constant Amounts)

Base: 1.150 000

Years	Slope	Annual INCREASE of: .00	.02	.04	.05	.10	Years
1	.000 000	.869 565	.8696	.8696	.8696	.8696	1
2	.756 144	1.625 709	1.6408	1.6560	1.6635	1.7013	2
3	2.071 176	2.283 225	2.3246	2.3661	2.3868	2.4903	3
4	3.786 436	2.854 978	2.9307	3.0064	3.0443	3.2336	4
5	5.775 143	3.352 155	3.4677	3.5832	3.6409	3.9297	5
6	7.936 781	3.784 783	3.9432	4.1020	4.1813	4.5782	6
7	10.192 403	4.160 420	4.3643	4.5681	4.6700	5.1797	7
8	12.480 715	4.487 322	4.7369	4.9866	5.1114	5.7354	8
9	14.754 815	4.771 584	5.0667	5.3618	5.5093	6.2471	9
10	16.979 477	5.018 769	5.3584	5.6979	5.8677	6.7167	10
11	19.128 909	5.233 712	5.6163	5.9989	6.1902	7.1466	11
12	21.184 888	5.420 619	5.8443	6.2680	6.4799	7.5391	12
13	23.135 223	5.583 147	6.0459	6.5086	6.7399	7.8967	13
14	24.972 496	5.724 476	6.2239	6.7234	6.9731	8.2217	14
15	26.693 019	5.847 370	6.3812	6.9151	7.1820	8.5167	15
16	28.295 990	5.954 235	6.5202	7.0861	7.3690	8.7838	16
17	29.782 805	6.047 161	6.6428	7.2385	7.5363	9.0254	17
18	31.156 492	6.127 966	6.7511	7.3742	7.6858	9.2436	18
19	32.421 267	6.198 231	6.8467	7.4951	7.8193	9.4404	19
20	33.582 173	6.259 331	6.9310	7.6026	7.9384	9.6175	20

Years	Slope	Annual DECREASE of: .00	.02	.04	.05	.10	Years
1	− .000 000	.869 565	.8696	.8696	.8696	.8696	1
2	− .756 144	1.625 709	1.6106	1.5955	1.5879	1.5501	2
3	− 2.071 176	2.283 225	2.2418	2.2004	2.1797	2.0761	3
4	− 3.786 436	2.854 978	2.7792	2.7035	2.6657	2.4763	4
5	− 5.775 143	3.352 155	3.2367	3.1211	3.0634	2.7746	5
6	− 7.936 781	3.784 483	3.6257	3.4670	3.3876	2.9908	6
7	−10.192 403	4.160 420	3.9566	3.7527	3.6508	3.1412	7
8	−12.480 715	4.487 322	4.2377	3.9881	3.8633	3.2392	8
9	−14.754 815	4.771 584	4.4765	4.1814	4.0338	3.2961	9
10	−16.979 477	5.018 769	4.6792	4.3396	4.1698	3.3208	10
11	−19.128 909	5.233 712	4.8511	4.4686	4.2773	—	11
12	−21.184 888	5.420 619	4.9969	4.5732	4.3614	—	12
13	−23.135 223	5.583 147	5.1204	4.6577	4.4264	—	13
14	−24.972 496	5.724 476	5.2250	4.7256	4.4759	—	14
15	−26.693 019	5.847 370	5.3135	4.7796	4.5127	—	15
16	−28.295 990	5.954 235	5.3883	4.8224	4.5394	—	16
17	−29.782 805	6.047 161	5.4515	4.8558	4.5580	—	17
18	−31.156 492	6.127 966	5.5048	4.8817	4.5701	—	18
19	−32.421 267	6.198 231	5.5498	4.9014	4.5772	—	19
20	−33.582 173	6.259 331	5.5877	4.9160	4.5802	—	20

ORDINARY ANNUITIES CHANGING IN CONSTANT RATIO

(Present Value of Annual Payments Starting at $1 and Changing in Constant Ratio)

$$PVF = \frac{1 - (1+x)^n/(1+i)^n}{i - x}$$

Where: PVF = present value factor
      x^* = constant ratio change in income
       n = number of years
       i = rate of interest or yield

*x is positive for an increase and negative for a decrease

This table is used to solve problems dealing with the compound discounting of cash flows that are best represented by an exponential-curve pattern of change.

Example 1

Assuming a 15% interest or yield rate, what is the present value of an ordinary annuity consisting of 10 annual cash flows that start at $10,000 and increase 10% per year compounded?

$$\$10,000 \times 7.1773 = \$71,773$$

Assuming payments are made in advance, the PV of this annuity would be

$$\$71,773 \times 1.150000 = \$82,539$$

or

$$\$71,773 / .869565 = \$82,539$$

Example 2

Assuming a 15% interest or yield rate, what is the present value of an ordinary annuity consisting of 10 annual cash flows that start at $10,000 and decrease 3% per year compounded?

$$\$10,000 \times 4.5429 = \$45,429$$

Example 3

There are five years remaining on a lease that provides a level income of $1,000 per year. During this period inflation will cause purchasing power to decline 10% per year on a compound basis. What is the value of the income expressed in constant dollars and discounted at 6%?

$$\$1,000 \times .90 \times 3.4922 = \$3,142.98$$

Proof:

Year	Income	×	Inflation Factor	×	PVF @ 6%	=	Value
1	$1,000	×	.900000	×	.943396	=	$ 849.06
2	1,000	×	.810000	×	.889996	=	720.90
3	1,000	×	.729000	×	.839619	=	612.08
4	1,000	×	.656100	×	.792094	=	519.69
5	1,000	×	.590490	×	.747258	=	441.25
							$3,142.98

6% ORDINARY ANNUITIES CHANGING IN CONSTANT RATIO (Present Value of Annual Payments Starting at $1 and Changing in Constant Ratio)

Base: 1.060 000

Annual Percentage INCREASE of:

Years	7%	8%	9%	10%	11%	12%	Years
1	.9434	.9434	.9434	.9434	.9434	.9434	1
2	1.8957	1.9046	1.9135	1.9224	1.9313	1.9402	2
3	2.8570	2.8839	2.9110	2.9383	2.9658	2.9934	3
4	3.8273	3.8817	3.9368	3.9926	4.0491	4.1062	4
5	4.8068	4.8984	4.9916	5.0867	5.1835	5.2821	5
6	5.7956	5.9342	6.0763	6.2220	6.3714	6.5245	6
7	6.7936	6.9896	7.1917	7.4002	7.6153	7.8372	7
8	7.8011	8.0648	8.3386	8.6229	8.9179	9.2242	8
9	8.8181	9.1604	9.5180	8.8916	10.2820	10.6897	9
10	9.8447	10.2766	10.7308	11.2083	11.7104	12.2382	10
11	10.8810	11.4139	11.9779	12.5747	13.2061	13.8743	11
12	11.9270	12.5727	13.2603	13.9926	14.7725	15.6030	12
13	12.9829	13.7533	14.5790	15.4640	16.4127	17.4296	13
14	14.0488	14.9562	15.9350	16.9909	18.1302	19.3596	14
15	15.1247	16.1818	17.3294	18.5755	19.9288	21.3988	15
16	16.2108	17.4305	18.7632	20.2199	21.8123	23.5534	16
17	17.3072	18.7028	20.2376	21.9263	23.7846	25.8301	17
18	18.4138	19.9990	21.7538	23.6971	25.8499	28.2355	18
19	19.5309	21.3198	23.3129	25.5347	28.0126	30.7772	19
20	20.6586	22.6654	24.9161	27.4417	30.2773	33.4627	20

Annual Percentage DECREASE of:

Years	7%	8%	9%	10%	11%	12%	Years
1	.9434	.9434	.9434	.9434	.9434	.9434	1
2	1.7711	1.7622	1.7533	1.7444	1.7355	1.7266	2
3	2.4973	2.4728	2.4486	2.4245	2.4006	2.3768	3
4	3.1344	3.0896	3.0455	3.0019	2.9590	2.9166	4
5	3.6934	3.6250	3.5579	3.4922	3.4278	3.3647	5
6	4.1838	4.0896	3.9978	3.9085	3.8215	3.7367	6
7	4.6141	4.4929	4.3755	4.2619	4.1520	4.0456	7
8	4.9916	4.8429	4.6997	4.5620	4.4295	4.3020	8
9	5.3228	5.1466	4.9781	4.8168	4.6625	4.5149	9
10	5.6134	5.4103	5.2170	5.0331	4.8581	4.6916	10
11	5.8684	5.6391	5.4222	5.2168	5.0224	4.8383	11
12	6.0921	5.8377	5.5983	5.3728	5.1603	4.9601	12
13	6.2883	6.0101	5.7495	5.5052	5.2761	5.0612	13
14	6.4605	6.1597	5.8792	5.6176	5.3733	5.1452	14
15	6.6116	6.2896	5.9907	5.7131	5.4550	5.2148	15
16	6.7441	6.4023	6.0863	5.7941	5.5235	5.2727	16
17	6.8604	6.5001	6.1685	5.8629	5.5811	5.3207	17
18	6.9624	6.5850	6.2390	5.9213	5.6294	5.3606	18
19	7.0520	6.6587	6.2995	5.9710	5.6700	5.3937	19
20	7.1305	6.7226	6.3514	6.0131	5.7040	5.4212	20

10% ORDINARY ANNUITIES CHANGING IN CONSTANT RATIO (Present Value of Annual Payments Starting at $1 and Changing in Constant Ratio)

Base: 1.100 000

Annual Percentage INCREASE of:

Years	1%	2%	3%	4%	5%	6%	Years
1	.9091	.9091	.9091	.9091	.9091	.9091	1
2	1.7438	1.7521	1.7603	1.7686	1.7769	1.7851	2
3	2.5102	2.5337	2.5574	2.5812	2.6052	2.6293	3
4	3.2139	3.2586	3.3037	3.3495	3.3959	3.4428	4
5	3.8601	3.9307	4.0026	4.0759	4.1506	4.2267	5
6	4.4533	4.5539	4.6570	4.7627	4.8710	4.9821	6
7	4.9981	5.1318	5.2697	5.4120	5.5587	5.7100	7
8	5.4982	5.6677	5.8435	6.0259	6.2151	6.4115	8
9	5.9575	6.1646	6.3807	6.6063	6.8417	7.0874	9
10	6.3791	6.6253	6.8837	7.1550	7.4398	7.7388	10
11	6.7663	7.0526	7.3548	7.6738	8.0107	8.3664	11
12	7.1218	7.4487	7.7958	8.1644	8.5557	8.9713	12
13	7.4482	7.8161	8.2088	8.6281	9.0759	9.5542	13
14	7.7479	8.1568	8.5955	9.0666	9.5724	10.1158	14
15	8.0230	8.4726	8.9576	9.4811	10.0464	10.6571	15
16	8.2757	8.7655	9.2967	9.8731	10.4989	11.1786	16
17	8.5077	9.0371	9.6142	10.2436	10.9307	11.6812	17
18	8.7207	9.2890	9.9115	10.5940	11.3430	12.1656	18
19	8.9163	9.5225	10.1898	10.9252	11.7365	12.6323	19
20	9.0959	9.7390	10.4505	11.2384	12.1121	13.0820	20

Annual Percentage DECREASE of:

Years	1%	2%	3%	4%	5%	6%	Years
1	.9091	.9091	.9091	.9091	.9091	.9091	1
2	1.7273	1.7190	1.7107	1.7025	1.6942	1.6860	2
3	2.4636	2.4406	2.4177	2.3949	2.3723	2.3498	3
4	3.1264	3.0834	3.0410	2.9992	2.9579	2.9171	4
5	3.7228	3.6561	3.5907	3.5266	3.4636	3.4019	5
6	4.2596	4.1664	4.0755	3.9868	3.9004	3.8162	6
7	4.7428	4.6210	4.5029	4.3885	4.2776	4.1702	7
8	5.1776	5.0259	4.8798	4.7390	4.6034	4.4727	8
9	5.5689	5.3867	5.2122	5.0450	4.8848	4.7312	9
10	5.9211	5.7082	5.5053	5.3120	5.1277	4.9521	10
11	6.2381	5.9946	5.7638	5.5450	5.3376	5.1409	11
12	6.5234	6.2497	5.9917	5.7484	5.5188	5.3022	12
13	6.7801	6.4770	6.1927	5.9259	5.6754	5.4401	13
14	7.0112	6.6795	6.3699	6.0807	5.8105	5.5579	14
15	7.2192	6.8599	6.5262	6.2159	5.9273	5.6586	15
16	7.4063	7.0207	6.6640	6.3339	6.0281	5.7446	16
17	7.5748	7.1639	6.7855	6.4369	6.1152	5.8181	17
18	7.7264	7.2914	6.8927	6.5267	6.1904	5.8809	18
19	7.8629	7.4051	6.9872	6.6051	6.2553	5.9346	19
20	7.9857	7.5064	7.0705	6.6736	6.3114	5.9805	20

15% ORDINARY ANNUITIES CHANGING IN CONSTANT RATIO (Present Value of Annual Payments Starting at $1 and Changing in Constant Ratio)

Base: 1.150 000

Annual Percentage INCREASE of:

Years	7%	8%	9%	10%	11%	12%	Years
1	.8696	.8696	.8696	.8696	.8696	.8696	1
2	1.6786	1.6862	1.6938	1.7013	1.7089	1.7164	2
3	2.4314	2.4531	2.4750	2.4969	2.5190	2.5412	3
4	3.1319	3.1734	3.2154	3.2579	3.3010	3.3445	4
5	3.7835	3.8498	3.9172	3.9858	4.0557	4.1268	5
6	4.3899	4.4850	4.5824	4.6821	4.7842	4.8887	6
7	4.9541	5.0816	5.2129	5.3481	5.4874	5.6308	7
8	5.4790	5.6418	5.8105	5.9851	6.1661	6.3534	8
9	5.9674	6.1680	6.3769	6.5945	6.8212	7.0573	9
10	6.4219	6.6621	6.9137	7.1773	7.4535	7.7427	10
11	6.8447	7.1261	7.4226	7.7348	8.0638	8.4103	11
12	7.2381	7.5619	7.9049	8.2681	8.6529	9.0605	12
13	7.6042	7.9712	8.3620	8.7782	9.2215	9.6937	13
14	7.9447	8.3556	8.7953	9.2661	9.7703	10.3104	14
15	8.2616	8.7165	9.2060	9.7328	10.3000	10.9110	15
16	8.5565	9.0555	9.5952	10.1792	10.8113	11.4959	16
17	8.8308	9.3739	9.9642	10.6062	11.3048	12.0656	17
18	9.0861	9.6729	10.3139	11.0146	11.7812	12.6204	18
19	9.3235	9.9537	10.6453	11.4053	12.2410	13.1607	19
20	9.5445	10.2173	10.9595	11.7790	12.6848	13.6870	20

Annual Percentage DECREASE of:

Years	7%	8%	9%	10%	11%	12%	Years
1	.8696	.8696	.8696	.8696	.8696	.8696	1
2	1.5728	1.5652	1.5577	1.5501	1.5425	1.5350	2
3	2.1415	2.1217	2.1021	2.0827	2.0634	2.0442	3
4	2.6014	2.5670	2.5330	2.4995	2.4664	2.4338	4
5	2.9733	2.9231	2.8739	2.8257	2.7784	2.7319	5
6	3.2740	3.2081	3.1437	3.0810	3.0198	2.9601	6
7	3.5173	3.4360	3.3572	3.2808	3.2066	3.1347	7
8	3.7140	3.6184	3.5261	3.4371	3.3512	3.2683	8
9	3.8730	3.7643	3.6598	3.5595	3.4631	3.3705	9
10	4.0017	3.8810	3.7656	3.6552	3.5497	3.4487	10
11	4.1057	3.9744	3.8493	3.7302	3.6167	3.5086	11
12	4.1898	4.0490	3.9155	3.7888	3.6686	3.5544	12
13	4.2579	4.1088	3.9679	3.8348	3.7087	3.5895	13
14	4.3129	4.1566	4.0094	3.8707	3.7398	3.6163	14
15	4.3574	4.1949	4.0422	3.8988	3.7639	3.6368	15
16	4.3934	4.2254	4.0682	3.9208	3.7825	3.6525	16
17	4.4224	4.2499	4.0888	3.9380	3.7969	3.6645	17
18	4.4460	4.2695	4.1050	3.9515	3.8080	3.6737	18
19	4.4650	4.2852	4.1179	3.9620	3.8166	3.6808	19
20	4.4804	4.2977	4.1281	3.9703	3.8233	3.6862	20

SINKING FUND FACTORS
(Periodic Payment to Grow to $1)

This factor represents the level periodic investment or deposit required to accumulate to $1 in a given number of periods including interest at the effective rate. It is commonly known as the *amortization rate* and is the reciprocal of the corresponding sinking fund accumulation factor.

$$1/S_{\overline{n}} = \frac{i}{S^n - 1}$$

Where: $1/S_{\overline{n}}$ = sinking fund factor
  i = effective rate of interest
  n = number of compounding periods
  S^n = future value factor

This table is used to solve problems that involve calculating required sinking fund deposits or providing for the change in capital value in investment situations where the income or payments are level.

Example 1

Assuming a 6% interest rate, what monthly, end-of-period deposit would be required to yield $10,000 in 10 years?

$$\$10,000 \times .006102 = \$61.02$$

Assuming deposits are made at the beginning of the period, what amount would be required?

$$\$10,000 \times .006102/1.005 = \$60.72$$

Example 2

Assuming a 6% interest rate, what monthly, end-of-period deposit would be required to yield $10,000 in 10 years and 7 months?

$$\$10,000/(1/.006102 + 1.819397*/.140729) = \$56.56$$

*future value factor for 120 months

Assuming deposits are made at the beginning of the period, what amount would be required?

$$\$56.56/1.005 = \$56.28$$

Example 3

What is the annual constant for a direct reduction loan at 12% interest with monthly payments for 25 years?

$$.12 + 12 \times .000532 = .126384$$

In actual practice, loan payments are rounded up to the nearest penny. Published tables of annual constants reflect this practice. In a typical table of annual constants, factors are calculated for each $1,000 of loan, so the sinking fund factor is rounded up to the fifth decimal place. On this basis, the constant for a 12%, 25-year loan would be

$$.12 + 12 \times .000540 = .126480$$

Example 4

Assuming a 12% interest or yield rate, what monthly payment would provide for interest and 40% amortization of a $100,000 loan in 10 years?

$$\$100,000 \times (.12/12 + .4 \times .004347) = \$1,173.88$$

Example 5

A property has an anticipated net operating income of $10,000 per year for the next five years. The trend in prices indicates a 15% increase in value over this period of time. What is the calculated value of the property assuming a 12% yield rate?

$$\$10,000 / (.12 - .15 \times .157410) = \$103,747$$

When deposits are made at the end of each compounding period, sinking fund factors reflect the fractional portion of $1.00 that must be deposited periodically at a specified interest rate to accumulate to $1.00 by the end of the series of deposits.

If $10,000 is to be accumulated over a 10-year period and annual deposits are compounded at 10% interest, the factor shown on the 10-year line of the annual column in the 10% sinking fund table indicates that each annual deposit must amount to $10,000 × .062745, or $627.45.

6% SINKING FUND FACTORS
(Period Payment to Grow to $1)

Base: 1.005 000 1.015 000 1.030 000 1.060 000 1.061 831

Frequency of Payments and of Conversions

Months	Monthly	Quarterly	Semiannual	Annual	Annual Payment Daily Conversion	Months
1	1.000 000	—	—	—	—	1
2	.498 753	—	—	—	—	2
3	.331 672	1.000 000	—	—	—	3
4	.248 133	—	—	—	—	4
5	.198 010	—	—	—	—	5
6	.164 595	.496 278	1.000 000	—	—	6
7	.140 729	—	—	—	—	7
8	.122 829	—	—	—	—	8
9	.108 907	.328 383	—	—	—	9
10	.097 771	—	—	—	—	10
11	.088 659	—	—	—	—	11

Years						Years
1	.081 066	.244 445	.492 611	1.000 000	1.000 000	1
2	.039 321	.118 584	.239 027	.485 437	.485 006	2
3	.025 422	.076 680	.154 598	.314 110	.313 547	3
4	.018 485	.055 765	.112 456	.228 591	.227 971	4
5	.014 333	.043 246	.087 231	.177 396	.176 749	5
6	.011 573	.034 924	.070 462	.143 363	.142 703	6
7	.009 609	.029 001	.058 526	.119 135	.188 471	7
8	.008 141	.024 577	.049 611	.101 036	.100 374	8
9	.007 006	.021 152	.042 709	.087 022	.086 365	9
10	.006 102	.018 427	.037 216	.075 868	.075 218	10
11	.005 367	.016 210	.032 747	.066 793	.066 152	11
12	.004 759	.014 375	.029 047	.059 277	.058 646	12
13	.004 247	.012 833	.025 938	.052 960	.052 340	13
14	.003 812	.011 521	.023 293	.047 585	.046 977	14
15	.003 439	.010 393	.021 019	.042 963	.042 367	15
16	.003 114	.009 415	.019 047	.038 952	.038 369	16
17	.002 831	.008 560	.017 322	.035 445	.034 875	17
18	.002 582	.007 808	.015 804	.032 357	.031 799	18
19	.002 361	.007 141	.014 459	.029 621	.029 077	19
20	.002 164	.006 548	.013 262	.027 185	.026 654	20
21	.001 989	.006 018	.012 192	.025 005	.024 487	21
22	.001 831	.005 541	.011 230	.023 046	.022 541	22
23	.001 688	.005 112	.010 363	.021 278	.020 787	23
24	.001 560	.004 723	.009 578	.019 679	.019 201	24
25	.001 443	.004 371	.008 865	.018 227	.017 762	25
26	.001 337	.004 050	.008 217	.016 904	.016 452	26
27	.001 240	.003 757	.007 626	.015 697	.015 258	27
28	.001 151	.003 489	.007 084	.014 593	.014 166	28
29	.001 070	.003 244	.006 588	.013 580	.013 165	29
30	.000 996	.003 019	.006 133	.012 649	.012 247	30
31	.000 927	.002 811	.005 714	.011 792	.011 402	31
32	.000 864	.002 620	.005 328	.011 002	.010 624	32
33	.000 806	.002 444	.004 971	.010 273	.009 906	33
34	.000 752	.002 281	.004 642	.009 598	.009 243	34
35	.000 702	.002 131	.004 337	.008 974	.008 630	35
36	.000 656	.001 991	.004 054	.008 395	.008 062	36
37	.000 613	.001 862	.003 792	.007 857	.007 535	37
38	.000 573	.001 742	.003 548	.007 358	.007 046	38
39	.000 536	.001 630	.003 322	.006 894	.006 592	39
40	.000 502	.001 526	.003 112	.006 462	.006 170	40

10% SINKING FUND FACTORS
(Period Payment to Grow to $1)

Base: 1.008 333   1.025 000   1.050 000   1.100 000   1.105 156

Frequency of Payments and of Conversions

Months	Monthly	Quarterly	Semiannual	Annual	Annual Payment Daily Conversion	Months
1	1.000 000	—	—	—	—	1
2	.497 925	—	—	—	—	2
3	.330 571	1.000 000	—	—	—	3
4	.246 897	—	—	—	—	4
5	.196 694	—	—	—	—	5
6	.163 228	.496 827	1.000 000	—	—	6
7	.139 325	—	—	—	—	7
8	.121 400	—	—	—	—	8
9	.107 459	.325 137	—	—	—	9
10	.096 307	—	—	—	—	10
11	.087 184	—	—	—	—	11

Years						Years
1	.079 583	.240 818	.487 805	1.000 000	1.000 000	1
2	.037 812	.114 467	.232 012	.476 190	.475 024	2
3	.023 934	.072 487	.147 017	.302 115	.300 614	3
4	.017 029	.051 599	.104 722	.215 471	.213 843	4
5	.012 914	.039 147	.079 505	.163 797	.162 125	5
6	.010 193	.030 913	.062 825	.129 607	.127 932	6
7	.008 268	.025 088	.051 024	.105 405	.103 749	7
8	.006 841	.020 768	.042 270	.087 444	.085 821	8
9	.005 745	.017 452	.035 546	.073 641	.072 059	9
10	.004 882	.014 836	.030 243	.062 745	.061 212	10
11	.004 187	.012 730	.025 971	.053 963	.052 481	11
12	.003 617	.011 006	.022 471	.046 763	.045 334	12
13	.003 145	.009 574	.019 564	.040 779	.039 404	13
14	.002 749	.008 372	.017 123	.035 746	.034 427	14
15	.002 413	.007 353	.015 051	.031 474	.030 211	15
16	.002 126	.006 482	.013 280	.027 817	.026 609	16
17	.001 879	.005 733	.011 755	.024 664	.023 511	17
18	.001 665	.005 084	.010 434	.021 930	.020 831	18
19	.001 479	.004 520	.009 284	.019 547	.018 500	19
20	.001 317	.004 026	.008 278	.017 460	.016 464	20
21	.001 174	.003 593	.007 395	.015 624	.014 679	21
22	.001 049	.003 212	.006 616	.014 005	.013 108	22
23	.000 938	.002 875	.005 928	.012 572	.011 722	23
24	.000 841	.002 577	.005 318	.011 300	.010 495	24
25	.000 754	.002 312	.004 777	.010 168	.009 407	25
26	.000 676	.002 076	.004 294	.009 159	.008 440	26
27	.000 608	.001 867	.003 864	.008 258	.007 579	27
28	.000 546	.001 679	.003 480	.007 451	.006 811	28
29	.000 491	.001 512	.003 136	.006 728	.006 126	29
30	.000 442	.001 362	.002 828	.006 079	.005 512	30
31	.000 398	.001 227	.002 552	.005 496	.004 963	31
32	.000 359	.001 107	.002 304	.004 972	.004 471	32
33	.000 324	.000 999	.002 081	.004 499	.004 029	33
34	.000 292	.000 901	.001 880	.004 074	.003 632	34
35	.000 263	.000 814	.001 699	.003 690	.003 276	35
36	.000 238	.000 735	.001 536	.003 343	.002 955	36
37	.000 215	.000 664	.001 390	.003 030	.002 667	37
38	.000 194	.000 600	.001 257	.002 747	.002 408	38
39	.000 175	.000 542	.001 138	.002 491	.002 174	39
40	.000 158	.000 490	.001 030	.002 259	.001 963	40

12% SINKING FUND FACTORS
(Periodic Payment to Grow to $1)

Base: 1.010 000   1.030 000   1.060 000   1.120 000   1.127 474

Frequency of Payments and of Conversions

Months	Monthly	Quarterly	Semiannual	Annual	Annual Payment Daily Conversion	Months
1	1.000 000	—	—	—	—	1
2	.497 512	—	—	—	—	2
3	.330 022	1.000 000	—	—	—	3
4	.246 281	—	—	—	—	4
5	.196 040	—	—	—	—	5
6	.162 548	.492 611	1.000 000	—	—	6
7	.138 628	—	—	—	—	7
8	.120 690	—	—	—	—	8
9	.106 740	.323 530	—	—	—	9
10	.095 582	—	—	—	—	10
11	.086 454	—	—	—	—	11

Years	Monthly	Quarterly	Semiannual	Annual	Annual Payment Daily Conversion	Years
1	.078 849	.239 027	.485 437	1.000 000	1.000 000	1
2	.037 073	.112 456	.228 591	.471 698	.470 041	2
3	.023 214	.070 462	.143 363	.296 349	.294 233	3
4	.016 334	.049 611	.101 036	.209 234	.206 957	4
5	.012 244	.037 216	.075 868	.157 410	.155 090	5
6	.009 550	.029 047	.059 277	.123 226	.120 922	6
7	.007 653	.023 293	.047 585	.099 118	.096 862	7
8	.006 253	.019 047	.038 952	.081 303	.079 114	8
9	.005 184	.015 804	.032 357	.067 679	.065 568	9
10	.004 347	.013 262	.027 185	.056 984	.054 959	10
11	.003 678	.011 230	.023 046	.048 415	.046 479	11
12	.003 134	.009 578	.019 679	.041 437	.039 592	12
13	.002 687	.008 217	.016 904	.035 677	.033 925	13
14	.002 314	.007 084	.014 593	.030 871	.029 210	14
15	.002 002	.006 133	.012 649	.026 824	.025 253	15
16	.001 737	.005 328	.011 002	.023 390	.021 907	16
17	.001 512	.004 642	.009 598	.020 457	.019 060	17
18	.001 320	.004 054	.008 395	.017 937	.016 624	18
19	.001 154	.003 548	.007 358	.015 763	.014 530	19
20	.001 011	.003 112	.006 462	.013 879	.012 724	20
21	.000 887	.002 733	.005 683	.012 240	.011 159	21
22	.000 779	.002 404	.005 006	.010 811	.009 800	22
23	.000 686	.002 117	.004 415	.009 560	.008 617	23
24	.000 604	.001 866	.003 898	.008 463	.007 585	24
25	.000 532	.001 647	.003 444	.007 500	.006 683	25
26	.000 470	.001 454	.003 046	.006 652	.005 892	26
27	.000 414	.001 285	.002 696	.005 904	.005 199	27
28	.000 366	.001 136	.002 388	.005 244	.004 590	28
29	.000 324	.001 005	.002 116	.004 660	.004 054	29
30	.000 286	.000 890	.001 876	.004 144	.003 583	30
31	.000 253	.000 788	.001 664	.003 686	.003 168	31
32	.000 224	.000 698	.001 476	.003 280	.002 802	32
33	.000 198	.000 619	.001 310	.002 920	.002 479	33
34	.000 176	.000 548	.001 163	.002 601	.002 194	34
35	.000 155	.000 486	.001 033	.002 317	.001 942	35
36	.000 138	.000 431	.000 918	.002 064	.001 719	36
37	.000 122	.000 383	.000 815	.001 840	.001 523	37
38	.000 108	.000 339	.000 725	.001 640	.001 349	38
39	.000 096	.000 301	.000 644	.001 462	.001 195	39
40	.000 085	.000 267	.000 573	.001 304	.001 059	40

SINKING FUND ACCUMULATION FACTORS
(Future Value of Periodic Payments of $1)

This factor represents the total accumulation of principal and interest on a series of deposits or installments of $1 per period for a given number of periods with interest at the effective rate per period. It is also known as the *amount of one per period*. It is the reciprocal of the corresponding sinking factor.

$$S_{\overline{n}|} = \frac{S^n - 1}{i}$$

Where: $S_{\overline{n}|}$ = sinking fund accumulation factor
i = effective rate of interest
S^n = future value factor

This table is used to solve problems that involve the growth of sinking funds or the calculation of capital recovery in investment situations where the income or payments are level.

Example 1

Assuming a 6% nominal interest rate, how much money would be accumulated if deposits of $100 were made at the end of each month for a period of 10 years?

$$\$100 \times 163.879347 = \$16,387.93$$

Assuming the deposits were at the beginning of each month, how much money would be accumulated?

$$\$16,387.93 \times 1.005 = \$16,469.87$$

Example 2

Assuming a 6% nominal interest rate, how much money would be accumulated if deposits of $100 were made at the end of each month for a period of 10 years and 7 months?

$$\$100 \times (163.879347 + 7.105879 \times 1.819397^*) = \$17,680.78$$

*Future value factor for 120 months

or

$$\$100 \times (7.105879 + 163.879347 \times 1.035529^*) = \$17,680.77$$

*Future value factor for 7 months

Example 3

Assuming a 6% nominal interest rate and daily compounding, how much money would be accumulated in a Keogh Retirement Plan if deposits of $1,200 were made at the end of each year for 10 years?

$$\$1,200 \times 13.294699 = \$15,953.64$$

Assuming the deposits were made at the beginning of each year, how much money would be accumulated?

$$\$15,953.64 \times 1.061831 = \$16,940.07$$

Example 4

Given a $100,000 loan with monthly payments of $908.71 including nominal interest at 10%, how much will be paid off in 10 years?

$$[\$908.71 - (\$100{,}000 \times .10/12)] \times 204.844979 = \$15{,}440.53$$

Sinking fund accumulation factors are similar to the future value of $1 (amount of one) factors except that deposits are periodic (in a series) and are assumed to be made at the *end* of the first compounding period and at the *end* of each period thereafter. Thus, the initial deposit, which is made at the end of the first period, has earned no interest and the factor for this period is 1.000000.

If compounding at 10% per year for 10 years is assumed, a factor of 15.937425 reveals that a series of 10 deposits of $1.00 each made at the end of each year for 10 years will accumulate to $1.00 × 15.937425, or almost $15.94.

6% SINKING FUND ACCUMULATION FACTORS
(Future Value of Periodic Payments of $1)

Base:　1.005 000　　1.015 000　　1.030 000　　1.060 000　　1.061 831

Frequency of Payments and of Conversions

Months	Monthly	Quarterly	Semiannual	Annual	Annual Payment Daily Conversion	Months
1	1.000 000	—	—	—	—	1
2	2.005 000	—	—	—	—	2
3	3.015 025	1.000 000	—	—	—	3
4	4.030 100	—	—	—	—	4
5	5.050 251	—	—	—	—	5
6	6.075 502	2.015 000	1.000 000	—	—	6
7	7.105 879	—	—	—	—	7
8	8.141 409	—	—	—	—	8
9	9.182 116	3.045 225	—	—	—	9
10	10.228 026	—	—	—	—	10
11	11.279 167	—	—	—	—	11

Years						Years
1	12.335 562	4.090 903	2.030 000	1.000 000	1.000 000	1
2	25.431 955	8.432 839	4.183 627	2.060 000	2.061 831	2
3	39.336 105	13.041 211	6.468 410	3.183 600	3.189 137	3
4	54.097 832	17.932 370	8.892 336	4.374 616	4.386 516	4
5	69.770 031	23.123 667	11.463 879	5.637 093	5.657 740	5
6	86.408 856	28.633 521	14.192 030	6.975 319	7.007 565	6
7	104.073 927	34.481 479	17.086 324	8.393 838	8.440 851	7
8	122.828 542	40.688 288	20.156 881	9.897 468	9.962 760	8
9	142.739 900	47.275 969	23.414 435	11.491 316	11.578 769	9
10	163.879 347	54.267 894	26.870 374	13.180 795	13.294 699	10
11	186.322 629	61.688 868	30.536 780	14.971 643	15.116 727	11
12	210.150 163	69.565 219	34.426 470	16.869 941	17.051 413	12
13	235.447 328	77.924 892	38.553 042	18.882 138	19.105 723	13
14	262.304 766	86.797 543	42.930 923	21.015 066	21.287 053	14
15	290.818 712	96.214 652	47.575 416	23.275 970	23.603 258	15
16	321.091 337	106.209 628	52.502 759	25.672 528	26.062 677	16
17	353.231 110	116.817 931	57.730 177	28.212 880	28.674 164	17
18	387.353 194	128.077 197	63.275 944	30.905 653	31.447 123	18
19	423.579 854	140.027 372	69.159 449	33.759 992	34.391 538	19
20	462.040 895	152.710 852	75.401 260	36.785 591	37.518 009	20
21	502.874 129	166.172 636	82.023 196	39.992 727	40.837 794	21
22	546.225 867	180.460 482	89.048 409	43.392 290	44.362 846	22
23	592.251 446	195.625 082	96.501 457	46.995 828	48.105 855	23
24	641.115 782	211.720 235	104.408 396	50.815 577	52.080 300	24
25	692.993 962	228.803 043	112.796 867	54.864 512	56.300 489	25
26	748.071 876	246.934 114	121.696 197	59.156 383	60.781 618	26
27	806.546 875	266.177 771	131.137 495	63.705 766	65.539 821	27
28	868.628 484	286.602 288	141.153 768	68.528 112	70.592 229	28
29	934.539 150	308.280 125	151.780 033	73.639 798	75.957 034	29
30	1004.515 042	331.288 191	163.053 437	79.058 186	81.653 552	30
31	1078.806 895	355.708 115	175.013 391	84.801 677	87.702 292	31
32	1157.680 906	381.626 531	187.701 707	90.889 778	94.125 033	32
33	1241.419 693	409.135 393	201.162 741	97.343 165	100.944 900	33
34	1330.323 306	438.332 297	215.443 551	104.183 755	108.186 449	34
35	1424.710 299	469.320 826	230.594 064	111.434 780	115.875 751	35
36	1524.918 875	502.210 922	246.667 242	119.120 867	124.040 492	36
37	1631.308 097	537.119 271	263.719 277	127.268 119	132.710 069	37
38	1744.259 173	574.169 720	281.809 781	135.904 206	141.915 697	38
39	1864.176 824	613.493 716	301.001 997	145.058 458	151.690 520	39
40	1991.490 734	655.230 772	321.363 019	154.761 966	162.069 733	40

10% SINKING FUND ACCUMULATION FACTORS
(Future Value of Periodic Payments of $1)

Base: 1.008 333   1.025 000   1.050 000   1.000 000   1.105 156

Frequency of Payments and of Conversions

Months	Monthly	Quarterly	Semiannual	Annual	Annual Payment Daily Conversion	Months
1	1.000 000	—	—	—	—	1
2	2.008 333	—	—	—	—	2
3	3.025 069	1.000 000	—	—	—	3
4	4.050 278	—	—	—	—	4
5	5.084 031	—	—	—	—	5
6	6.126 398	2.025 000	1.000 000	—	—	6
7	7.177 451	—	—	—	—	7
8	8.237 263	—	—	—	—	8
9	9.305 907	3.075 625	—	—	—	9
10	10.383 456	—	—	—	—	10
11	11.469 985	—	—	—	—	11

Years	Monthly	Quarterly	Semiannual	Annual	Annual Payment Daily Conversion	Years
1	12.565 568	4.152 516	2.050 000	1.000 000	1.000 000	1
2	26.446 915	8.736 116	4.310 125	2.100 000	2.105 156	2
3	41.781 821	13.795 553	6.801 913	3.310 000	3.326 524	3
4	58.722 492	19.380 225	9.549 109	4.641 000	4.676 327	4
5	77.437 072	25.544 658	12.577 893	6.105 100	6.168 069	5
6	98.111 314	32.349 038	15.917 127	7.715 610	7.816 676	6
7	120.950 418	39.859 801	19.598 632	9.487 171	9.638 643	7
8	146.181 076	48.150 278	23.657 492	11.435 888	11.652 200	8
9	174.053 713	57.301 413	28.132 385	13.579 477	13.877 493	9
10	204.844 979	67.402 554	33 065 954	15.937 425	16.336 789	10
11	238.860 493	78.552 323	38.505 214	18.531 167	19.054 693	11
12	276.437 876	90.859 582	44.501 999	21.384 284	22.058 401	12
13	317.950 102	104.444 494	51.113 454	24.522 712	25.377 964	13
14	363.809 201	119.439 694	58.402 583	27.974 983	29.046 599	14
15	414.470 346	135.991 590	66.438 848	31.772 482	33.101 010	15
16	470.436 376	154.261 786	75.298 829	35.949 730	37.581 766	16
17	532.262 780	174.428 663	85.066 959	40.544 703	42.533 698	17
18	600.536 216	196.689 122	95.836 323	45.599 173	48.006 353	18
19	676.015 601	221.260 504	107.709 546	51.159 090	54.054 489	19
20	759.368 836	248.382 713	120.799 774	57.274 999	60.738 620	20
21	851.450 244	278.320 556	135.231 751	64.002 499	68.125 624	21
22	953.173 779	311.366 333	151.143 006	71.402 749	76.289 413	22
23	1065.549 097	347.842 687	168.685 164	79.543 024	85.311 670	23
24	1189.691 580	388.105 758	188.025 393	88.497 327	95.282 667	24
25	1326.833 403	432.548 654	209.347 996	98.347 059	106.302 170	25
26	1478.335 767	481.605 296	232.856 165	109.181 765	118.480 436	26
27	1645.702 407	535.754 649	258.773 922	121.099 942	131.939 313	27
28	1830.594 523	595.525 404	287.348 249	134.209 936	146.813 467	28
29	2034.847 258	661.501 133	318.851 445	148.630 930	163.251 721	29
30	2260.487 925	734.325 993	353.583 718	164.494 023	181.418 550	30
31	2509.756 117	814.711 013	391.876 049	181.943 425	201.495 721	31
32	2785.125 947	903.441 034	434.093 344	201.137 767	223.684 118	32
33	3089.330 596	1001.382 375	480.637 912	222.251 544	248.205 750	33
34	3425.489 447	1109.491 289	531.953 298	245.476 699	275.305 967	34
35	3796.638 052	1228.823 303	588.528 511	271.024 368	305.255 923	35
36	4206.761 236	1360.543 518	650.902 683	299.126 805	338.355 284	36
37	4659.829 677	1505.937 989	719.670 208	330.039 486	374.935 228	37
38	5160.340 305	1666.426 280	795.486 404	364.043 434	415.361 756	38
39	5713.260 935	1843.575 325	879.073 761	401.447 778	460.039 359	39
40	6324.079 581	2039.114 724	971.228 821	442.592 556	509.415 060	40

DIRECT REDUCTION LOAN FACTORS
(Monthly Payment and Annual Constant per $1 of Loan)

Payment: $\qquad 1/a_{\overline{n}|} = \dfrac{i}{1 - 1/S^n}$

Annual constant: $\qquad R_M = 12/a_{\overline{n}|}$

Where: $\qquad\quad 1/a_{\overline{n}|} =$ direct reduction loan factor

$\qquad\qquad\qquad 1/S^n =$ present value factor

$\qquad\qquad\qquad\quad i =$ effective rate of interest

$\qquad\qquad\qquad R_M =$ annual constant

Part paid off: $\qquad P = \dfrac{R_M - 12i}{R_{MP} - 12i}$

Where: $\qquad\qquad R_M =$ actual annual constant

$\qquad\qquad\qquad R_{Mp} =$ annual constant for projection period

$\qquad\qquad\qquad\quad i =$ effective rate of interest

This table is used to solve problems dealing with monthly payment, direct reduction loans. Payments and constants for quarterly, semiannual, and annual payment loans can be obtained by calculating the reciprocals of the present value of $1 per period factors.

Example 1

What is the level monthly payment and annual debt service for a direct reduction loan of $100,000, assuming nominal interest at 10% and full amortization over 25 years?

$$\$100,000 \times .0090870 = \$\quad 908.70^*$$
$$\$100,000 \times .1090441 = \$10,904.41^*$$

*In actual practice, the payment would be rounded up to $908.71 and the debt service would be $908.71 × 12 = $10,904.52.

Example 2

How much of the loan in Example 1 would be paid off in 10 years?

$$\$100,000 \times .1544 = \$15,440$$

or

$$\$100,000 \times [(\$10,904.52/\$100,000 - .10)/(.1585809 - .10)] = \$15,440.52$$

Example 3

What discounted price would achieve a 14% yield for this loan?
Assuming full term:

$$\$10,904.41/.1444513 = \$75,488.49$$

Assuming a 10-year call:

$$\begin{array}{lll} \$10{,}904.52/.1863197 & = & \$58{,}525.86 \\ (\$100{,}000 - \$15{,}440.53) \times .248603^* & = & \underline{21{,}021.74} \\ & & \$79{,}547.60 \end{array}$$

*Present value for 120 months

Example 4

What is the level monthly payment and annual debt service for a direct reduction loan of $100,000, assuming nominal interest at 10% and full amortization over 25 years and 7 months?

$$\$100{,}000/(1/.0090870 + .082940^*/.1476586) = \$904.09$$

$$\$904.09 \times 12 = \$10{,}849.08$$

*Present value factor for 300 months

Example 5

How much of the loan in Example 4 would be paid off in 10 years?

$$\$100{,}000 \times [(\$10{,}849.08/\$100{,}000 - .10)/(.1585809 - .10)] = \$14{,}494.14$$

These factors, which are known as *mortgage constants for loan amortization,* reflect the amount of ordinary annuity payment that $1.00 will purchase. They indicate the periodic payment that will extinguish the debt and pay interest on the declining balance of the debt over the life of the payments. The mortgage constant may be expressed in terms of the periodic payments. A mortgage constant related to a monthly payment is the ratio of the monthly payment amount to the original amount of the loan. Whether payments are monthly, semiannual, or annual, the mortgage constant is usually expressed in terms of the total payments in one year as a percentage of the original loan amount. This is called the *annual constant* and is represented by the symbol R_M. As the loan is paid off and the outstanding balance is reduced, a new annual mortgage constant can be calculated as the ratio of total annual payments to the unpaid balance of the loan at that time.

A loan of $10,000 to be amortized in 10 annual end-of-year payments at a mortgage interest rate of 10% would require level annual payments of $10,000 × .162745, the 10% direct reduction annual factor for 10 years. If monthly payments were made at 10% over 10 years, the amount of each payment would be $132.15 (i.e., $10,000 × .013215). The annual mortgage constant in this case would be .158580, or 12 × .013215.

Direct reduction factors consist of the interest rate plus the sinking fund factor at the specific point in time. They are reciprocals of the corresponding ordinary level-annuity factors.

10% DIRECT REDUCTION LOAN FACTORS
(Monthly Payment and Annual Constant per $1 of Loan)

Base: 1.008 333

Months	Payment	Annual Constant	Part Paid Off Projection 1 Year	5 Years	10 Years	15 Years	Months
1	1.008 3333	—	—	—	—	—	1
2	.506 2586	—	—	—	—	—	2
3	.338 9043	—	—	—	—	—	3
4	.255 2299	—	—	—	—	—	4
5	.205 0277	—	—	—	—	—	5
6	.171 5614	—	—	—	—	—	6
7	.147 6586	—	—	—	—	—	7
8	.129 7329	—	—	—	—	—	8
9	.115 7920	—	—	—	—	—	9
10	.104 6404	—	—	—	—	—	10
11	.095 5174	—	—	—	—	—	11

Years	Payment	Annual Constant	1 Year	5 Years	10 Years	15 Years	Years
1	.087 9159	1.054 9906	1.0000	—	—	—	1
2	.046 1449	.553 7391	.4751	—	—	—	2
3	.032 2672	.387 2062	.3007	—	—	—	3
4	.025 3626	.304 3510	.2140	—	—	—	4
5	.021 2470	.254 9645	.1623	1.0000	—	—	5
6	.018 5258	.222 3101	.1281	.7893	—	—	6
7	.016 6012	.199 2142	.1039	.6402	—	—	7
8	.015 1742	.182 0900	.0860	.5297	—	—	8
9	.014 0787	.168 9442	.0722	.4449	—	—	9
10	.013 2151	.158 5809	.0613	.3780	1.0000	—	10
11	.012 5199	.150 2385	.0526	.3242	.8576	—	11
12	.011 9508	.143 4094	.0455	.2801	.7410	—	12
13	.011 4785	.137 7418	.0395	.2436	.6443	—	13
14	.011 0820	.132 9843	.0345	.2129	.5631	—	14
15	.010 7461	.128 9526	.0303	.1868	.4942	1.0000	15
16	.010 4590	.125 5082	.0267	.1646	.4354	.8810	16
17	.010 2121	.122 5453	.0236	.1455	.3849	.7787	17
18	.009 9984	.119 9812	.0209	.1289	.3411	.6901	18
19	.009 8126	.117 7511	.0186	.1145	.3030	.6131	19
20	.009 6502	.115 8026	.0165	.1020	.2698	.5458	20
21	.009 5078	.114 0936	.0148	.0909	.2406	.4868	21
22	.009 3825	.112 5895	.0132	.0812	.2149	.4348	22
23	.009 2718	.111 2618	.0118	.0727	.1922	.3890	23
24	.009 1739	.110 0866	.0106	.0651	.1722	.3484	24
25	.009 0870	.109 0441	.0095	.0584	.1544	.3124	25
26	.009 0098	.108 1172	.0085	.0524	.1386	.2804	26
27	.008 9410	.107 2917	.0076	.0471	.1245	.2519	27
28	.008 8796	.106 5552	.0069	.0423	.1119	.2264	28
29	.008 8248	.105 8972	.0062	.0381	.1007	.2037	29
30	.008 7757	.105 3086	.0056	.0343	.0906	.1834	30
31	.008 7318	.104 7813	.0050	.0309	.0816	.1651	31
32	.008 6924	.104 3086	.0045	.0278	.0735	.1488	32
33	.008 6570	.103 8843	.0041	.0251	.0663	.1342	33
34	.008 6253	.103 5033	.0037	.0226	.0598	.1210	34
35	.008 5967	.103 1607	.0033	.0204	.0540	.1092	35
36	.008 5710	.102 8526	.0030	.0184	.0487	.0985	36
37	.008 5479	.102 5752	.0027	.0166	.0440	.0889	37
38	.008 5271	.102 3254	.0024	.0150	.0397	.0803	38
39	.008 5084	.102 1004	.0022	.0136	.0359	.0725	39
40	.008 4915	.101 8975	.0020	.0122	.0324	.0655	40

14% DIRECT REDUCTION LOAN FACTORS
Monthly Payment and Annual Constant per $1 of Loan)

Base: 1.011 667

Months	Payment	Annual Constant	Part Paid Off Projection 1 Year	5 Years	10 Years	15 Years	Months
1	1.011 6667	—	—	—	—	—	1
2	.508 7669	—	—	—	—	—	2
3	.341 1412	—	—	—	—	—	3
4	.257 3340	—	—	—	—	—	4
5	.207 0541	—	—	—	—	—	5
6	.173 5380	—	—	—	—	—	6
7	.149 6011	—	—	—	—	—	7
8	.131 6513	—	—	—	—	—	8
9	.117 6928	—	—	—	—	—	9
10	.106 5283	—	—	—	—	—	10
11	.097 3957	—	—	—	—	—	11

Years	Payment	Annual Constant	1 Year	5 Years	10 Years	15 Years	Years
1	.089 7871	1.077 4454	1.0000	—	—	—	1
2	.048 0129	.576 1546	.4653	—	—	—	2
3	.034 1776	.410 1316	.2882	—	—	—	3
4	.027 3265	.327 9177	.2005	—	—	—	4
5	.023 2683	.279 2190	.1485	1.0000	—	—	5
6	.020 6057	.247 2689	.1144	.7705	—	—	6
7	.018 7400	.224 8801	.0905	.6097	—	—	7
8	.017 3715	.208 4580	.0730	.4917	—	—	8
9	.016 3337	.196 0044	.0597	.4023	—	—	9
10	.015 5266	.186 3197	.0494	.3327	1.0000	—	10
11	.014 8867	.178 6399	.0412	.2775	.8342	—	11
12	.014 3713	.172 4553	.0346	.2331	.7007	—	12
13	.013 9510	.167 4124	.0292	.1969	.5918	—	13
14	.013 6049	.163 2588	.0248	.1671	.5021	—	14
15	.013 3174	.159 8090	.0211	.1423	.4277	1.0000	15
16	.013 0770	.156 9239	.0181	.1216	.3654	.8544	16
17	.012 8748	.154 4971	.0155	.1041	.3130	.7318	17
18	.012 7038	.152 4460	.0133	.0894	.2687	.6283	18
19	.012 5588	.150 7051	.0114	.0769	.2311	.5404	19
20	.012 4352	.149 2225	.0098	.0662	.1991	.4656	20
21	.012 3297	.147 9561	.0085	.0571	.1718	.4016	21
22	.012 2393	.146 8715	.0073	.0494	.1483	.3469	22
23	.012 1617	.145 9408	.0063	.0427	.1283	.2999	23
24	.012 0950	.145 1405	.0055	.0369	.1110	.2595	24
25	.012 0376	.144 4513	.0047	.0320	.0961	.2247	25
26	.011 9881	.143 8570	.0041	.0277	.0833	.1947	26
27	.011 9453	.143 3439	.0036	.0240	.0722	.1688	27
28	.011 9084	.142 9004	.0031	.0208	.0626	.1464	28
29	.011 8764	.142 5167	.0027	.0181	.0543	.1270	29
30	.011 8487	.142 1846	.0023	.0157	.0472	.1103	30
31	.011 8247	.141 8969	.0020	.0136	.0410	.0958	31
32	.011 8040	.141 6475	.0018	.0118	.0356	.0832	32
33	.011 7859	.141 4313	.0015	.0103	.0309	.0723	33
34	.011 7703	.141 2436	.0013	.0089	.0268	.0628	34
35	.011 7567	.141 0808	.0012	.0078	.0233	.0546	35
36	.011 7450	.140 9394	.0010	.0067	.0203	.0474	36
37	.011 7347	.140 8166	.0009	.0059	.0176	.0412	37
38	.011 7258	.140 7100	.0008	.0051	.0153	.0358	38
39	.011 7181	.140 6173	.0007	.0044	.0133	.0312	39
40	.011 7114	.140 5368	.0006	.0039	.0116	.0271	40

J FACTORS
(Adjustment Factors for Changes in Income)

Ellwood: $\quad J = 1/S_{\overline{n}}[n/(1 - 1/S^n) - (1/Y_E)]$

Straight-line: $\quad J = (1/n - 1/S_{\overline{n}})/Y_E$

Where: $\quad J = $ factor

$\quad 1/S_{\overline{n}} = $ SFF at equity yield rate for projection period

$\quad n = $ projection period

$\quad 1/S^n = $ reversion factor at Y_E for projection period

$\quad Y_E = $ equity yield rate

This table is used to solve mortgage/equity problems that involve changing income. The factors can be substituted in any of the J-factor changing income formulas that solve for overall rates, change in property values, or equity yield rates.

The Ellwood-premise J factors reflect curvilinear income that changes from time zero in relation to a sinking fund accumulation curve; the straight-line premise J factors describe income changing in equal annual amounts after the first year.

In the following examples, the change in both income and value is +25% in five years and the mortgage terms are 70% ratio at 12% nominal interest with a 25-year term. The desired equity yield rate is 18%.

$$C = Y_E + P\ 1/S_{\overline{n}} - R_M$$
$$C = .18 + .0435 \times .139778 - .1263869$$
$$C = .0596934, \textit{ or } .0597$$

Example 1

Assuming the income of a property at time zero is $10,000, what is its calculated value using the Ellwood premise?

$$R_O = (Y_E - MC - \triangle_O\ 1/S_{\overline{n}})/(1 + \triangle_1 J)$$
$$R_O = (.18 - .70 \times .0597 - .25 \times .139778)/(1 + .25 \times .4651)$$
$$R_O = .092509$$
$$V_O = I_O/R_O$$
$$V_O = \$10,000/.092509$$
$$V_O = \$108,098$$

Proof:

Debt service $\quad = \$108,098 \times .70 = \$75,668$

$\quad\quad\quad\quad\quad\quad\$75,668 \times .1263869 = \$9,563$

Reversion $\quad = \$108,098 \times 1.25 - \$75,668 \times (1 - .0435) = \$62,746$

Equity $\quad = \$108,098 \times .30 = \$32,429$

Time	Income	−	Debt Service	=	Cash to Equity	×	PVF @ 18%	=	Value
1	$10,349	−	$9,563	=	$ 786	×	.847458	=	$ 666
2	10,762	−	9,563	=	1,199	×	.718184	=	861
3	11,248	−	9,563	=	1,685	×	.608631	=	1,026
4	11,823	−	9,563	=	2,260	×	.515789	=	1,166
5	12,500	−	9,563	=	2,937	×	.437109	=	1,284
Reversion					62,746	×	.437109	=	27,427
Total equity									$32,430

Example 2

Assuming the income of the property at the end of Year One is $10,000, what is its calculated value using the straight-line premise:

$$R_O = (Y_E - MC - \triangle_O\, 1/S_n)/(1 + \triangle_1 J)$$
$$R_O = (.18 - .70 \times .0597 - .25 \times .139778)/(1 + .25 \times .3346)$$
$$R_O = .095294$$
$$V_O = I_O/R_O$$
$$V_O = \$10,000/.095294$$
$$V_O = \$104,938$$

Proof:

$$\text{Debt service} = \$104,938 \times .70 = \$73,457$$
$$\$73,457 \times .1263869 = \$9,284$$
$$\text{Reversion} = \$104,938 \times 1.25 - \$73,457 \times (1 - .0435)$$
$$= \$60,911$$
$$\text{Equity} = \$104,938 \times .30 = \$31,481$$

Time	Income	−	Debt Service	=	Cash to Equity	×	PVF @ 18%	=	Value
1	$10,000	−	$9,284	=	$ 716	×	.847458	=	$ 607
2	10,500	−	9,284	=	1,216	×	.718184	=	873
3	11,000	−	9,284	=	1,716	×	.608631	=	1,044
4	11,500	−	9,284	=	2,216	×	.515789	=	1,143
5	12,000	−	9,284	=	2,716	×	.437109	=	1,187
Reversion					60,911	×	.437109	=	26,625
Total equity									$31,479

If the income were expected to change by +25% in five years and the yield rate were 16%, the J factor would be .4790 under the Ellwood (sinking fund) premise and .3412 on a straight-line basis. The appropriate factor would be inserted into the mortgage-equity formula.

J FACTORS
(Adjustment Factors for Changes in Income)

	16.0%		16.5%		17.0%		17.5%		
Years	Ellwood	Straight Line	Ellwood	Straight Line	Ellwood	Straight Line	Ellwood	Straight Line	Years
1	1.0000	.0000	1.0000	.0000	1.0000	.0000	1.0000	.0000	1
2	.7116	.2315	.7104	.2309	.7093	.2304	.7082	.2299	2
3	.5986	.3005	.5966	.2995	.5946	.2986	.5926	.2977	3
4	.5298	.3289	.5270	.3276	.5242	.3263	.5215	.3250	4
5	.4790	.3412	.4755	.3395	.4720	.3379	.4685	.3362	5
6	.4374	.3455	.4333	.3435	.4291	.3415	.4250	.3395	6
7	.4015	.3453	.3968	.3430	.3921	.3406	.3874	.3384	7
8	.3695	.3423	.3642	.3397	.3590	.3371	.3538	.3345	8
9	.3403	.3377	.3345	.3348	.3289	.3319	.3233	.3290	9
10	.3134	.3319	.3072	.3287	.3012	.3255	.2952	.3224	10
11	.2884	.3253	.2820	.3219	.2756	.3185	.2694	.3152	11
12	.2652	.3182	.2585	.3146	.2519	.3110	.2454	.3074	12
13	.2435	.3109	.2366	.3070	.2299	.3032	.2233	.2995	13
14	.2233	.3033	.2163	.2993	.2095	.2953	.2028	.2914	14
15	.2045	.2957	.1974	.2915	.1905	.2873	.1838	.2832	15
16	.1870	.2880	.1799	.2837	.1730	.2794	.1663	.2752	16
17	.1707	.2804	.1636	.2759	.1568	.2715	.1502	.2672	17
18	.1555	.2729	.1486	.2683	.1419	.2638	.1354	.2594	18
19	.1415	.2656	.1347	.2609	.1281	.2563	.1219	.2518	19
20	.1286	.2583	.1219	.2535	.1155	.2489	.1095	.2443	20
21	.1166	.2513	.1101	.2464	.1040	.2417	.0981	.2371	21
22	.1056	.2444	.0994	.2395	.0934	.2347	.0879	.2301	22
23	.0955	.2377	.0895	.2328	.0838	.2280	.0785	.2233	23
24	.0862	.2312	.0805	.2263	.0751	.2215	.0700	.2168	24
25	.0778	.2249	.0723	.2200	.0672	.2152	.0624	.2105	25
26	.0700	.2188	.0648	.2139	.0600	.2091	.0555	.2044	26
27	.0630	.2130	.0581	.2080	.0535	.2032	.0493	.1986	27
28	.0565	.2073	.0519	.2024	.0477	.1976	.0437	.1930	28
29	.0507	.2018	.0464	.1969	.0424	.1922	.0387	.1876	29
30	.0455	.1965	.0414	.1917	.0377	.1870	.0343	.1825	30
31	.0407	.1915	.0369	.1866	.0334	.1820	.0303	.1775	31
32	.0364	.1866	.0328	.1818	.0296	.1772	.0267	.1728	32
33	.0325	.1819	.0292	.1771	.0262	.1726	.0236	.1683	33
34	.0290	.1773	.0259	.1727	.0232	.1682	.0208	.1639	34
35	.0258	.1730	.0230	.1684	.0205	.1639	.0183	.1597	35
36	.0230	.1688	.0204	.1642	.0181	.1599	.0161	.1557	36
37	.0205	.1648	.0181	.1603	.0160	.1560	.0141	.1519	37
38	.0182	.1609	.0160	.0565	.0141	.1522	.0124	.1482	38
39	.0162	.1572	.0142	.1528	.0124	.1486	.0109	.1447	39
40	.0143	.1536	.0125	.1493	.0109	.1452	.0095	.1413	40

J FACTORS
(Adjustment Factors for Changes in Income)

	18.0%		19.0%		20.0%		21.0%		
Years	Ellwood	Straight Line	Ellwood	Straight Line	Ellwood	Straight Line	Ellwood	Straight Line	Years
1	1.0000	.0000	1.0000	.0000	1.0000	.0000	1.0000	.0000	1
2	.7070	.2294	.7047	.2283	.7025	.2273	.7002	.2262	2
3	.5906	.2967	.5866	.2949	.5827	.2930	.5787	.2912	3
4	.5187	.3237	.5132	.3211	.5078	.3186	.5024	.3160	4
5	.4651	.3346	.4582	.3313	.4514	.3281	.4448	.3249	5
6	.4210	.3375	.4129	.3336	.4050	.3298	.3971	.3260	6
7	.3828	.3361	.3736	.3316	.3647	.3272	.3558	.3228	7
8	.3487	.3320	.3386	.3269	.3288	.3220	.3191	.3171	8
9	.3177	.3262	.3069	.3206	.2963	.3152	.2861	.3098	9
10	.2894	.3194	.2779	.3133	.2668	.3074	.2561	.3016	10
11	.2632	.3118	.2513	.3054	.2398	.2990	.2288	.2928	11
12	.2391	.3039	.2269	.2970	.2152	.2903	.2039	.2838	12
13	.2168	.2958	.2044	.2885	.1926	.2815	.1814	.2747	13
14	.1963	.2875	.1838	.2800	.1720	.2727	.1609	.2656	14
15	.1773	.2792	.1649	.2714	.1533	.2639	.1423	.2567	15
16	.1599	.2711	.1477	.2630	.1363	.2553	.1256	.2479	16
17	.1439	.2630	.1319	.2548	.1209	.2469	.1106	.2394	17
18	.1292	.2551	.1176	.2467	.1070	.2388	.0972	.2311	18
19	.1159	.2474	.1047	.2389	.0944	.2308	.0851	.2232	19
20	.1037	.2399	.0929	.2313	.0832	.2232	.0744	.2155	20
21	.0926	.2326	.0824	.2240	.0732	.2159	.0650	.2082	21
22	.0826	.2256	.0729	.2170	.0642	.2088	.0566	.2011	22
23	.0735	.2188	.0643	.2102	.0563	.2021	.0491	.1944	23
24	.0653	.2123	.0567	.2037	.0492	.1956	.0426	.1880	24
25	.0579	.2060	.0499	.1974	.0429	.1894	.0369	.1819	25
26	.0513	.2000	.0438	.1915	.0374	.1835	.0319	.1761	26
27	.0454	.1942	.0385	.1857	.0326	.1779	.0275	.1705	27
28	.0401	.1886	.0337	.1802	.0283	.1725	.0237	.1652	28
29	.0354	.1833	.0295	.1750	.0245	.1673	.0204	.1602	29
30	.0312	.1782	.0258	.1700	.0213	.1624	.0175	.1554	30
31	.0274	.1733	.0225	.1652	.0184	.1578	.0150	.1509	31
32	.0241	.1686	.0196	.1606	.0159	.1533	.0129	.1466	32
33	.0212	.1641	.0171	.1563	.0137	.1491	.0110	.1424	33
34	.0186	.1598	.0148	.1521	.0118	.1450	.0094	.1385	34
35	.0163	.1557	.0129	.1481	.0102	.1412	.0081	.1348	35
36	.0142	.1517	.0112	.1443	.0088	.1375	.0069	.1312	36
37	.0125	.1480	.0097	.1406	.0075	.1340	.0059	.1278	37
38	.0109	.1443	.0084	.1372	.0065	.1306	.0050	.1246	38
39	.0095	.1409	.0073	.1338	.0056	.1274	.0043	.1215	39
40	.0083	.1376	.0063	.1306	.0048	.1243	.0036	.1186	40

INTERRELATIONSHIPS AMONG THE TABLES

Note that mathematical relationships exist among the formulas for the various tables. These relationships can be useful in understanding the tables and solving appraisal problems. For example, appraisers should know that the factors in the ordinary level annuity and direct reduction loan tables are reciprocals; the factors in the ordinary level annuity table can be used as multipliers instead of using the direct-reduction loan factors as divisors.

Reciprocals

Reciprocals are numbers divided into 1. Thus, the reciprocal of 10 is $1/10$ and the reciprocal of .5 is $1/.5$. The factors in some of the tables are reciprocals of those in other tables. This is indicated by their formulas.

Future value of $1 and reversion factors

$$S^n \text{ and } \frac{1}{S^n}$$

The reversion factor at 12% for 10 years with annual compounding is .321973, which is the reciprocal of the future value of $1 factor.

$$.321973 = \frac{1}{3.105848}$$

Sinking fund accumulations and sinking fund factors

$$S_{\overline{n}|} \text{ and } \frac{1}{S_{\overline{n}|}}$$

The sinking factor at 12% for 10 years with annual compounding is .056984, which is the reciprocal of the sinking fund accumulation factor.

$$.056984 = \frac{1}{17.548735}$$

Ordinary level annuity and direct reduction loan factors

$$a_{\overline{n}|} \text{ and } \frac{1}{a_{\overline{n}|}}$$

The direct-reduction loan factor at 12% for 10 years with annual compounding is .176984, which is the reciprocal of the ordinary level annuity factor.

$$.056984 = \frac{1}{17.548735}$$

$$.176984 = \frac{1}{5.650223}$$

Summations

Ordinary level annuity factors

An ordinary level annuity factor represents the sum of the reversion factors for all periods up to and including the period being considered. For example, the ordinary level annuity factor for five years at 12% with annual compounding is 3.604776, which is the sum of all the reversion factors for Years One through Five.

$$
\begin{array}{r}
.892857 \\
.797194 \\
.711780 \\
.635518 \\
\underline{.567427} \\
3.604776
\end{array}
$$

Direct reduction loan factors

A direct reduction loan factor represents the sum of the interest, yield, or discount rate stated at the top of the table and the sinking fund factor. For example, the direct reduction loan factor at 12% for 10 years with monthly compounding is .1721651, which is the sum of .12 plus the monthly sinking fund factor of .0043471 times 12 (.12 + .0521651 = .1721651).

Conversely, the sinking fund factor can be obtained by subtracting the interest rate from the direct reduction loan factor. The sinking fund factor at 12% for 10 years with monthly compounding is .1721651 − .12 = .0521651. In addition, the interest rate can be obtained by subtracting the sinking fund factor from the direct reduction loan factor. Given a mortgage constant of .1721651 with monthly compounding for 10 years, the interest rate is .1721651 − .0521651 = .12000, or 12.0%.

Bibliography

SELECTED READINGS AND INFORMATION SOURCES

SELECTED READINGS AND INFORMATION SOURCES

Books

Akerson, Charles B. *The Appraiser's Workbook*. Chicago: Appraisal Institute, 1992.

_____. *Capitalization Theory and Techniques: Study Guide*. rev. ed. Chicago: American Institute of Real Estate Appraisers, 1984.

Albritton, Harold D. *Controversies in Real Property Valuation: A Commentary*. Chicago: American Institute of Real Estate Appraisers, 1982.

Alexander, Ian. *Office Location and Public Policy*. New York: Chancer Press, 1979.

American Association of State Highway Officials. *Acquisitions for Right of Way*. Washington, D.C., 1962.

American Institute of Real Estate Appraisers. *The Appraisal of Rural Property*. Chicago, 1983.

_____. *Appraisal Thought: A 50-Year Beginning*. Chicago, 1982.

_____. *The Dictionary of Real Estate Appraisal*. 2nd ed. Chicago, 1989.

_____. *Forecasting: Market Determinants Affecting Cash Flows and Reversions*, AIREA Research Series, Research Report 4. Chicago, 1989

_____. *Readings in Highest and Best Use*. Chicago, 1981.

_____. *Readings in Market Research for Real Estate*. Chicago, 1985.

_____. *Readings in Real Property Valuation Principles*, vol. II. Chicago, 1985.

_____. *Readings in the Income Capitalization Approach to Real Property Valuation*, vol. II. Chicago, 1985.

_____. *Real Estate Market Analysis and Appraisal*. AIREA Research Series, Research Report 3. Chicago, 1988.

Andrews, Richard B. *Urban Land Economics and Public Policy*. New York: Free Press, 1971.

Andrews, Richard N. L. *Land in America*. Lexington, Mass.: D. C. Heath, 1979.

Appraisal Institute. *Appraising Residential Properties*. rev. ed. Chicago, 1992.

Babcock, Frederick M. *The Valuation of Real Estate*. New York: McGraw-Hill, 1932.

Barlowe, Raleigh. *Land Resource Economics*. 4th ed. Englewood Cliffs, N.J.: Prentice-Hall, 1986.

Bierman, Harold, Jr., and Seymour Smidt. *The Capital Budgeting Decision*. 6th ed. New York: Macmillan, 1984.

Bish, Robert L., and Hugh O. Nourse. *Urban Economics and Policy Analysis*. New York: McGraw-Hill, 1975.

Bloom, George F., Arthur M. Weimer, and Jeffrey Fisher. *Real Estate*. 8th ed. New York: Wiley, 1982.

Bonright, James C. *The Valuation of Property*, vol. 1. New York: McGraw-Hill, 1937.

Burton, James H. *Evolution of the Income Approach*. Chicago: American Institute of Real Estate Appraisers, 1982.

Carn, Neil, Joseph Rabianski, Maury Seldin, and Ron Racster. *Real Estate Market Analysis: Applications and Techniques*. Englewood Cliffs, N.J.: Prentice-Hall, 1988.

Clapp, John M., *Handbook for Real Estate Market Analysis*. Englewood Cliffs, N.J.: Prentice-Hall, 1987.

Clark, Louis E., Jr., and F. M. Treadway, Jr. *Impact of Electric Power Transmission Line Easements on Real Estate Value*. Chicago: American Institute of Real Estate Appraisers, 1972.

Conroy, Kathleen. *Valuing the Timeshare Property*. Chicago: American Institute of Real Estate Appraisers, 1981.

Davies, Pearl Janet. *Real Estate in American History*. Washington, D.C.: Public Affairs Press, 1958.

Desmond, Glenn M., and Richard E. Kelley. *Business Valuation Handbook*. Llano, Calif: Valuation Press, 1988.

Dilmore, Gene. *Quantitative Techniques in Real Estate Counseling*. Lexington, Mass.: D. C. Heath, 1981.

Dombal, Robert W. *Appraising Condominiums: Suggested Data Analysis Techniques*. Chicago: American Institute of Real Estate Appraisers, 1981.

Eaton, James D. *Real Estate Valuation in Litigation*. Chicago: American Institute of Real Estate Appraisers, 1982.

Friedman, Edith J., ed. *Encyclopedia of Real Estate Appraising*. 3rd ed. Englewood Cliffs, N.J.: Prentice-Hall, 1978.

Gibbons, James E. *Appraising in a Changing Economy: Collected Writings of James E. Gibbons*. Chicago: American Institute of Real Estate Appraisers, 1982.

Gimmy, Arthur E., and Michael G. Boehm. *Elderly Housing: A Guide to Appraisal, Market Analysis, Development and Financing*. Chicago: American Institute of Real Estate Appraisers, 1988.

Gimmy, Arthur E., and Brian B. Woodworth. *Fitness, Racquet Sports, and Spa Projects: A Guide to Appraisal, Development, and Financing*. Chicago: American Institute of Real Estate Appraisers, 1989.

Gimmy, Arthur E., and Martin E. Benson. *Golf Courses and Country Clubs: A Guide to Appraisal, Market Analysis, Development, and Financing*. Chicago: Appraisal Institute, 1992.

Graaskamp, James A. *Graaskamp on Real Estate*. Stephen P. Jarchot, ed. Washington, D.C.: Urban Land Institute, 1991.

Graaskamp, James A. *A Guide to Feasibility Analysis*. Chicago: Society of Real Estate Appraisers, 1970.

Greer, Gaylon E. *The Real-Estate Investment Decision*. Lexington, Mass.: D. C. Heath, 1979.

Haggett, Peter. *Locational Analysis in Human Geography*. New York: St. Martin's, 1965.

Harrison, Henry S. *Houses—The Illustrated Guide to Construction, Design and Systems*. rev. ed. Chicago: Realtors® National Marketing Institute, 1990.

Heilbroner, Robert L. *The Worldly Philosophers*. rev. ed. New York: Simon and Schuster, 1964.

Himstreet, William C., *Communicating the Appraisal: The Narrative Report*. Chicago: Appraisal Institute, 1991.

Hoover, Edgar M. *The Location of Economic Activity*. New York: McGraw-Hill, 1963.

Institute on Planning, Zoning, and Eminent Domain. *Proceedings.* Albany, N.Y.: Matthew Bender. Series began in 1959.

International Association of Assessing Officers. *Property Appraisal and Assessment Administration.* Chicago, 1990.

_____. *Property Assessment Valuation.* Chicago, 1977.

Jevons, W. Stanley. *The Theory of Political Economy.* 5th ed. New York: Augustus M. Kelley, 1965.

Kahn, Sanders A., and Frederick E. Case. *Real Estate Appraisal and Investment.* 2nd ed. New York: Ronald Press, 1977.

Keune, Russell V., ed. *The Historic Preservation Yearbook.* Bethesda, Md.: Adler and Adler, 1984.

Kinnard, William N., Jr., *Income Property Valuation: Principles and Techniques of Appraising Income-Producing Real Estate.* Lexington, Mass.: D. C. Heath, 1971.

Kinnard, William N., Jr., ed. *1984 Real Estate Valuation Colloquium: A Redefinition of Real Estate Appraisal Precepts and Practices.* Boston, Mass.: Oelgeschlager, Gunn & Hain in association with the Lincoln Institute of Land Policy, 1986.

Kinnard, William N., Jr., and Byrl N. Boyce. *Appraising Real Property.* Lexington, Mass: D. C. Heath, 1984.

Kratovil, Robert, and Raymond J. Werner. *Real Estate Law.* 8th ed. Englewood Cliffs, N.J.: Prentice-Hall, 1983.

Levine, Mark Lee. *Real Estate Appraisers' Liability.* New York: Clark Boardman Callaghan, 1991.

Love, Terrence L., *The Guide to Appraisal Office Policies and Procedures.* Chicago: Appraisal Institute, 1991.

Mason, James J., ed. and comp. *American Institute of Real Estate Appraisers Financial Tables.* Chicago: American Institute of Real Estate Appraisers, 1981.

Mills, Arlen C. *Communicating the Appraisal: The Uniform Residential Appraisal Report.* Chicago: American Institute of Real Estate Appraisers, 1988.

National Cooperative Highway Research Program. *Reports.* Washington, D.C.: National Academy of Sciences Highway Research Board, 1966-1979.

North, Lincoln W. *The Concept of Highest and Best Use.* Winnipeg, Manitoba: Appraisal Institute of Canada, 1981.

Noyes, C. Reinold. *The Institution of Property.* London: Longmans, Green and Company, 1936.

Olin, Harold B., John L. Schmidt, and Walter H.Lewis. *Construction—Principles, Materials & Methods.* 4th ed. Chicago: Institute of Financial Education and Interstate Printers and Publishers, 1980.

Perin, Constance. *Everything in Its Place: Social Order and Land Use in America.* Princeton, N.J.: Princeton University Press, 1977.

Ratcliff, Richard U. *Modern Real Estate Valuation: Theory and Application.* Madison, Wis.: Democrat Press, 1965.

_____. *Urban Land Economics.* New York: Greenwood, 1972.

Reynolds, Judith. *Historic Properties: Preservation and the Valuation Process*. Chicago: American Institute of Real Estate Appraisers, 1982.

Ring, Alfred A., and James H. Boykin. *The Valuation of Real Estate*. 3rd ed. Englewood Cliffs, N.J.: Prentice-Hall, 1986.

Ring, Alfred A., and Jerome Dasso. *Real Estate Principles and Practices*. 10th ed. Englewood Cliffs, N.J.: Prentice-Hall, 1985.

Rohan, Patrick J., and Melvin A. Reskin. *Condemnation Procedures and Techniques; Forms*. Albany, N.Y.: Matthew Bender, 1968 (looseleaf service).

Roll, Eric. *A History of Economic Thought*. 3rd. ed. Englewood Cliffs, N.J.: Prentice-Hall, 1964.

Rushmore, Stephen. *Hotels and Motels: A Guide to Market Analysis and Valuations*. Chicago: Appraisal Institute, 1992.

Sackman, Julius L., and Patrick J. Rohan. *Nichols' Law of Eminent Domain*. 3rd rev. ed. Albany, N.Y.: Matthew Bender, 1973 (looseleaf service).

Sahling, Leonard. *Real Estate Economics Special Report*. "Rent or Buy: A Market Analysis." New York: Merrill Lynch, June, 1990.

Samuelson, Paul A., and William D. Nordhaus. *Economics*, 13th ed. New York: McGraw-Hill, 1989.

Schmutz, George L. *The Appraisal Process*. North Hollywood, Calif.: the author, 1941.

_____. *Condemnation Appraisal Handbook*, rev. and enl. by Edwin M. Rams. Englewood Cliffs, N.J.: Prentice-Hall, 1963.

Schwanke, Dean. *Smart Buildings and Technology-Enhanced Real Estate,* vol. I. Washington, D.C.: Urban Land Institute, 1976.

Seldin, Maury, and James H. Boykin. *Real Estate Analyses*. Homewood, Ill.: American Society of Real Estate Counselors and Dow Jones-Irwin, 1990.

Shenkel, William M. *Modern Real Estate Appraisal*. New York: McGraw-Hill, 1978.

Sirmans, C.F., and Austin J. Jaffe. *The Complete Real Estate Investment Handbook: A Professional Investment Strategy*, 4th ed. New York: Prentice Hall, 1988.

Smith, Halbert C. and Jerry D. Beloit. *Real Estate Appraisal*, 2nd ed. Columbus, Ohio: Century VII Publishing Company, 1987.

Smith, Halbert C., Carl J. Tschappat, and Ronald L. Racster, *Real Estate and Urban Development*. 3rd ed. Homewood, Ill.: Richard D. Irwin, 1981.

Society of Industrial Realtors®, *Industrial Real Estate,* 4th ed. Washington, D.C., 1984.

Sutte, Donald T., Jr. *The Appraisal of Roadside Advertising Signs*. Chicago: Appraisal Institute, 1992.

United States Department of Commerce, Bureau of the Census. *Statistical Abstract of the United States, 1990*. Washington, D.C.: U.S. Government Printing Office, 1990.

Vane, Howard R., and John L. Thompson. *Monetarism-Theory, Evidency and Policy*. New York: Halsted, 1979.

Vernor, James D., ed. *Readings in Market Research for Real Estate*. Chicago: American Institute of Real Estate Appraisers, 1985.

Vernor, James D., and Joseph Rabianski. *Shopping Center Appraisal and Analysis*. Chicago: Appraisal Institute, 1992.

Wendt, Paul F. *Real Estate Appraisal Review and Outlook*. Athens: University of Georgia Press, 1974.

White, John Robert. *Real Estate Valuing, Counseling, Forecasting: Selected Writings of John Robert White*. Chicago: American Institute of Real Estate Appraisers, 1984.

Witherspoon, Robert E., Jon P. Abbett, and Robert M. Gladstone. *Mixed-Use Developments: New Ways of Land Use*. Washington, D.C.: Urban Land Institute, 1976.

Wolf, Peter. *Land in America: Its Value, Use, and Control*. New York: Pantheon, 1981.

Building Cost Manuals

Boeckh Building Valuation Manual. Milwaukee: American Appraisal Co., 1967. 3 vols.

> Vol. 1—*Residential and Agricultural*; Vol. 2–Commercial; Vol. 3–*Industrial and Institutional*. Uses 1967 cost database and includes wide variety of building models. Built up from unit-in-place costs converted to cost per square foot of floor or ground area. *Boeckh Building Cost Modifier* is published bimonthly for updating with current modifiers.

Building Construction Cost Data. Duxbury, Mass.: Robert Snow Means Co., annual.

> Lists average unit prices on many building construction items for use in engineering estimates. Components arranged according to uniform system adopted by the American Institute of Architects, Associated General Contractors, and Construction Specifications Institute.

Dodge Building Cost Calculator & Valuation Guide. New York: McGraw-Hill Information Systems Co. (looseleaf service, quarterly supplements).

> Lists building costs for common types and sizes of buildings. Local cost modifiers and historical local cost index tables included. Formerly *Dow Building Cost Calculator*.

Marshall Valuation Service. Los Angeles: Marshall and Swift Publication Co. (looseleaf service, monthly supplements).

> Cost data for determining replacement costs of buildings and other improvements in the United States and Canada. Includes current cost multipliers and local modifiers.

Residential Cost Handbook. Los Angeles: Marshall and Swift Publication Co. (looseleaf service, quarterly supplements).

> Presents square-foot method and segregated-cost method. Local modifiers and cost-trend modifiers included.

Sources of Operating Costs and Ratios

Only a few published sources are cited below. Attention is directed to the first item listed.

Robert Morris Associates. *Sources of Composite Financial Data—A Bibliography*. 3rd ed. Philadelphia, 1971.

An annotated list of 98 nongovernment sources, arranged in manufacturing, wholesaling, retail, and service categories. Subject index to specific businesses. Publishers' names and addresses included for each citation.

Building Owners and Managers Association International. *Downtown and Suburban Office Building Experience Exchange Report*. Washington, D.C.
Published annually since 1920. Includes analysis of expenses and income quoted in cents per square foot as well as national, regional, and selected city averages.

Dun & Bradstreet, Inc. *Key Business Ratios in 125 Lines*. New York.
Published annually. Contains balance sheet and profit-and-loss ratios.

Pannell Kerr Forster. *Clubs in Town & Country*. Houston.
Published annually since 1953. Lists income-expense data and operating ratios for city and country clubs. Geographical data broken down into four U.S. regions.

_____. *Trends in the Hotel Industry*. Houston. Published annually since 1937.
Lists income-expense data and operating ratios for transient and resort hotels and motels. Geographical data broken down into five U.S. regions.

Institute of Real Estate Management. *Income/Expense Analysis: Apartments, Condominiums & Cooperatives*. Chicago.
Published annually since 1954. Data arranged by building type, then by national, regional, metropolitan, and selected city groupings. Operating costs listed per room, per square foot, etc. Formerly *Apartment Building Experience Exchange*.

_____. *Income/Expense Analysis: Suburban Office Buildings*. Chicago.
Published annually since 1976. Data analyzed on the basis of gross area and gross and net rentable office areas. Includes dollar-per-square-foot calculations; national, regional, and metropolitan comparisons; and detailed analyses for selected cities.

Laventhol & Horwath. *U.S. Lodging Industry*. Philadelphia.
Published annually since 1932. Includes income, expense, and profit data as well as historical trend tables.
Laventhol & Horowitz and National Restaurant Association. Table-Service Restaurant Operations. Philadelphia. Published annually since 1976. Lists income-expense data and operating ratios. Supercedes Laventhol & Horwath's *Restaurant Operations* report.

National Retail Merchants Association, Controllers' Congress. *Department Store and Specialty Store Merchandising and Operating Results*. New York.
Published annually since 1925. Merchandise classification base used since 1969 edition (1968 data). Includes geographical analysis by Federal Reserve districts. Known as the "MOR" report.

_____. *Financial and Operating Results of Department and Specialty Stores*. New York.
Published annually since 1963. Data arranged by sales volume category. Known as the "FOR" report.

National Institute of Real Estate Brokers. *Percentage Leases*. 13th ed. Chicago: 1973.
Based on reports of 3,100 leases for 97 retail and service categories in seven U.S. regions. Data broken down by type of operation, area, center, and build-

ing. Regional and store averages given for average minimum rent, rent per square foot, average gross leasable areas, and sales per square foot.

Urban Land Institute. *Dollars and Cents of Shopping Centers.* Washington, D.C., 1990.

First issued in 1961 and revised every three years. Includes income and expense data for neighborhood, community, and regional centers as well as statistics for specific tenant types.

Periodicals

American Right of Way Proceedings. American Right of Way Association, Los Angeles. Annual. Papers presented at national seminars.

Appraisal Institute Magazine. Appraisal Institute of Canada, Winnipeg, Manitoba.

Quarterly. General and technical articles on appraisal and expropriation in Canada. Includes information on institute programs, news, etc.

The Appraisal Journal. Appraisal Institute, Chicago.

Quarterly. Oldest periodical in the appraisal field, published since 1932. Includes technical articles on all phases of real property appraisal and regular feature on legal decisions. Bibliographies for 1932-1969, 1970-1980, and 1980-1987 are available.

Appraiser News. Appraisal Institute, Chicago.

Published twice each month. News bulletin covering current events and trends in appraisal practice. Previously published as *The Appraiser.*

Buildings. Stamats Communications, Inc., Cedar Rapids, Iowa.

Monthly. Journal of building construction and management.

Editor and Publisher Market Guide. Editor and Publisher, New York.

Annual. Standardized market data for more than 1,500 areas in the United States and Canada, including population estimates for trading areas. List of principal industries, transportation, climate, chain store outlets, etc.

Environmental Watch. Appraisal Institute, Chicago. Quarterly. Published since 1988. Up-to-date information on environmental issues affecting real estate appraisal.

Income Property Rates. Crittenden Publishing, Inc., Novato, California.

Weekly. Rates and terms on fundings for income properties.

Journal of the American Real Estate and Urban Economics Association. Bloomington, Indiana.

Quarterly. Focuses on research and scholarly studies of current and emerging real estate issues.

Journal of the American Society of Farm Managers and Rural Appraisers. Denver. Semiannual. Includes appraisal articles.

Journal of Property Management. Institute of Real Estate Management, Chicago.

Bimonthly. Covers a broad range of property investment and management issues.

Just Compensation. Sherman Oaks, California. Monthly. Reports on condemnation cases.

Land Economics. University of Wisconsin, Madison. Quarterly. Journal devoted to the study of economics and social institutes. Includes reports on university research and trends in land utilization. Frequently publishes articles on developments in other countries.

Market Source. Appraisal Institute, Chicago. Quarterly. Published since 1991. Data on key rates, economic trends, and real estate financing and market conditions.

The following periodicals on debenture and equity investment are published by Moody's Investors Service, Inc., New York.

Moody's Bank and Finance News Reports. Twice weekly.

Moody's Bond Record. Monthly.

Moody's Bond Survey. Weekly.

Moody's Commercial Paper Record. Monthly.

Moody's Dividend Record. Twice weekly.

Moody's Handbook of Common Stocks. Quarterly.

Moody's Handbook of Over-the-Counter Stocks. Quarterly.

Moody's Industrials. Twice weekly.

Moody's Investors Fact Sheets. Irregular.

Moody's Municipals and Governments. Twice weekly.

Moody's Over-the-Counter Industrials. Weekly.

Moody's Public Utilities. Twice weekly.

Moody's Transportation. Twice weekly.

Property Tax Journal. International Association of Assessing Officers, Chicago. Quarterly. Includes articles on property taxation and assessment administration.

The Quarterly Byte. Appraisal Institute, Chicago. Quarterly. Addresses use of computers in appraising.

The Real Estate Appraiser. Appraisal Institute, Chicago. Published three times a year. Technical articles, Appraisal Institute news, and regular feature on legal cases. Previously published as *The Review, The Residential Appraiser*, and *The Real Estate Appraiser and Analyst.*

Real Estate Finance. Crittenden Publishing, Inc., Novato, California. Weekly. Real estate finance information.

Real Estate Issues. American Society of Real Estate Counselors, Chicago. Semiannual.

Real Estate Law Journal. Warren, Gorham and Lamont, Inc., Boston. Quarterly. Publishes articles on legal issues and reviews current litigation of concern to real estate professionals.

Right of Way. American Right of Way Association, Los Angeles, California. Bimonthly. Articles on all phases of right-of-way activity—e.g., condemnation, negotiation, pipelines, electric power transmission lines, and highways. Includes association news.

Small Business Reporter. Bank of America, San Francisco. Irregular. Each issue devoted to a specific type of small business—e.g, coin-operated laundries, greeting card shops, restaurants.

The following periodicals on debenture and equity investment are published by Standard and Poor's Corporation, New York.

Standard and Poor's Bond Guide. Monthly.

Standard and Poor's Bond Record. Twice weekly.

Standard and Poor's Commercial Paper Ratings Guide. Monthly.

Standard and Poor's Daily Stock Price Record: American Exchange. Quarterly.

Standard and Poor's Daily Stock Price Record: N.Y. Stock Exchange. Quarterly.

Standard and Poor's Daily Stock Price Record: Over-the-Counter Exchange. Quarterly.

Standard and Poor's Dividend Record. Daily and quarterly.

Standard and Poor's Earnings Forecaster. Weekly.

Standard and Poor's Outlook. Weekly.

Standard and Poor's Registered Bond Interest Record. Weekly.

Standard and Poor's Stock Guide. Monthly.

Standard and Poor's Stock Summary. Monthly.

Survey of Buying Power. Sales Management, New York. Annual. Includes population totals and characteristics and income and consumption data presented in national, regional, metropolitan area, county, and city categories. Separate section for Canadian information. Population estimates between decennial censuses.

Survey of Current Business. U.S. Bureau of Economic Analysis, U.S. Department of Commerce, Washington, D.C.

Monthly. Includes statistical and price data. Biennial supplement, *Business Statistics.*

Valuation. American Society of Appraisers, Washington, D.C.

Three issues per year. Articles on real property valuation and the appraisal of personal and intangible property. Includes society news. Previously published as *Technical Valuation.*

Index

INDEX